"Combining rigorous scholarship with an intuitive understanding of contemplative practice, this impressive book makes a compelling case for mindfulness as an embodied bridge linking the broad domains of education and self-growth. It is a wonderful resource for educators, mindfulness teachers, and professionals interested in fostering curiosity, sensory processing, and awareness as platforms for lifelong learning and well-being."

**Zindel Segal, PhD**, *Distinguished Professor, University of Toronto, Scarborough*

"Seonaigh MacPherson and Patricia Rockman have integrated material from a wealth of disciplines, distilling the teaching and learning of secular-scientific mindfulness to cultivate personal and societal wellbeing. In so doing, they bring divergent views of western mindfulness together, emphasizing a common and critical goal in a western world that is in dire need of working toward well-being on all levels."

**Ellen Katz, PhD,** *associate professor, Factor-Inwentash Faculty of Social Work, University of Toronto*

"This book is a deep dive into the mindfulness field, exploring many of its significant questions, themes, and controversies: its history, how mindfulness emerged in multiple sectors, and scientific and clinical issues. A standout is the useful rubric for evaluating and training mindfulness teachers. Thoroughly researched, meticulous, and comprehensive, this book will be a landmark text for the mindfulness field for years to come."

**Diana Winston**, *director of mindfulness education, UCLA Mindful Awareness Research Center, and author of* The Little Book of Being

# MINDFULNESS-BASED TEACHING AND LEARNING

*Mindfulness-Based Teaching and Learning* is the first comprehensive survey text exploring the history, research, theory, and best practices of secular-scientific mindfulness. With a focus on how mindfulness is taught and learned, this book is an invaluable resource for aspiring or expert mindfulness specialists. Integrating and defining the emerging field of MBTL within a common purpose, evidence base, and set of transprofessional – and *transformational* – practices, the book provides both a visionary agenda and highly practical techniques and tools. Chapters provide curriculum design and teaching tips, explore the expert-validated MBTL-TCF competency framework, and reveal insights into the ways self-awareness can evolve into ecological awareness through intensive retreats.

**Seonaigh MacPherson, PhD,** is a professor in the Faculty of Education and Community Development at the University of the Fraser Valley, where she is the founder and coordinator of the MBTL graduate certificate programme. A certified MBSR and MBCT teacher, she lives in British Columbia, Canada.

**Patricia Rockman, MD,** is an associate professor at the University of Toronto Department of Family Medicine, where she is cross-appointed to psychiatry. She is co-founder of the Centre for Mindfulness Studies in Toronto where she teaches MBSR, MBCT, and mindfulness-certification programmes.

# MINDFULNESS-BASED TEACHING AND LEARNING

## Preparing Mindfulness Specialists in Education and Clinical Care

Seonaigh MacPherson and Patricia Rockman

Routledge
Taylor & Francis Group
NEW YORK AND LONDON

Cover image: © Getty Images

First published 2023
by Routledge
605 Third Avenue, New York, NY 10158

and by Routledge
4 Park Square, Milton Park, Abingdon, Oxon, OX14 4RN

Routledge is an imprint of the Taylor & Francis Group, an informa business



ISBN: 978-1-032-01894-2 (hbk)
ISBN: 978-1-032-01892-8 (pbk)
ISBN: 978-1-003-18246-7 (ebk)

DOI: 10.4324/9781003182467

Typeset in Baskerville
by Deanta Global Publishing Services, Chennai, India

**Seonaigh** would like to dedicate this book to her sisters – Morag, by blood, and Zeporah, by choice: For leading the way, for loyalty, and for never giving up.

**Patricia** would like to dedicate this book to her teachers, Molly Swan, Norman Feldman, Zindel Segal, Susan Woods, and Pascal Auclair.

# CONTENTS

# ACKNOWLEDGMENTS

We would like first to acknowledge those people who directly contributed to this book. The members of the expert review panel for the MBTL-TCF contributed well beyond what we expected or could have hoped for. Much of the credit for the depth and flexibility of the final version of that framework lies with them: Andrea Grabovac, Evan Collins, Diana Winston, and Tom Heah. Also, Rosemina Munjee swooped in at the final hour to provide feedback and suggestions to make the framework more inclusive and responsive to the needs of diverse teachers and learners alike. Our process was greatly eased with the help of our publisher at Routledge, Anna Moore, and our project manager, Bryan Moloney: Thanks are insufficient! We are indebted to you all for your service and support.

Faye Martin and Grace Kelly of UFV's MBTL graduate certificate programme generously offered the curriculum they designed for a local First Nation, showing us all how best to weave together Indigenous mindfulness traditions with those we are more familiar with in the secular-scientific context. Although we adapted it to guide readers in using effective curriculum design strategies, the model is the fruit of their imagination and their years of efforts in this area. Also, we would acknowledge Dr. Jackie Seidel of the University of Calgary for her help in reviewing Chapter 7 on preK-12.

On a more personal note, we acknowledge all the visible and invisible contributions of our many students, mentees, and colleagues at the University of the Fraser Valley and the Centre for Mindfulness Studies, who have enabled us to witness the rich contributions MBTL can make to our diverse professions and to the world. We would also like to acknowledge and thank those who made our own learning possible: for Seonaigh, first and foremost, the Dalai Lama, but also the late Namgyal Rinpoche and Cecilie Kwiat and Patricia Rockman; for Patricia, Zindel Segal, and, for both of us, Susan Woods, who led the MBSR Teacher Training Intensive at the Centre for Mindfulness Studies where we first met!

May you all thrive and continue to flourish and benefit the world!

# ABOUT THE AUTHORS

**Seonaigh MacPherson** is a Professor in the Faculty of Education and Community Development at the University of the Fraser Valley, where she founded the first graduate programme for mindfulness specialists in Canada. A practitioner of meditation since 1978, she has studied with leading teachers in Buddhist and secular-scientific mindfulness alike, including HH Dalai Lama, the late Namgyal Rinpoche and Cecile Kwiat, Pat Rockman, and Susan Woods. In the 1990s, she lived, studied, and worked with Tibetan refugees in the Indian Himalayas, ultimately completing a PhD in 2000 at the University of British Columbia for a dissertation entitled *A Path of Learning: Indo-Tibetan Buddhism as Education.* She is a certified MBSR and MBCT teacher and an MBSR mentor. She has published widely in intercultural studies and curriculum, including a book focused on her work with Tibetans: *Education and Sustainability: Learning Across the Diaspora, Indigenous, and Minority Divide.* She lives in British Columbia with her two faithful companions – Tashi and Karma – near many other fine friends.

**Patricia Rockman** is a family physician with a focused practice in mental health. She is the co-founder of and senior director of education and clinical services for the Centre for Mindfulness Studies in Toronto. She is responsible for curriculum development, service delivery, and professional training. She is an Associate Professor in the Department of Family and Community Medicine, cross-appointed to Psychiatry. Patricia Rockman has extensive experience teaching healthcare providers in the areas of Cognitive Behaviour Therapy, Change Management and Stress Reduction, Mindfulness-Based Programmes, and, most recently, psychedelic-assisted psychotherapy. She has a strong interest in continuing education in mental health and addictions, yoga, and meditative practice. She has co-authored a number of books and articles, including *Managing Uncertainty in Mental Healthcare* published by Oxford University Press.

# INTRODUCTION

Among Yuval Noah Harari's (2018) 21 key 'lessons' for humanity for the 21st century, the 21st and final was: 'Meditation: *Just Observe*.' Unlike the other 20, this last lesson was based on his personal experience – as a (Vipassana) mindfulness practitioner. Arguing the critical need for meditative tools of self-examination, he concludes the chapter and book with the following cautionary note:

> Self-observation has never been easy, but it might get harder with time. As history unfolded, humans created more and more complex stories about themselves, which made it increasingly difficult to know who we really are. ...In the near future, algorithms might bring this process to completion, making it well-nigh impossible for people to observe the reality about themselves. ...For a few more years or decades, we still have a choice. If we make the effort, we can still investigate who we really are. But if we want to make use of this opportunity, we had better do it now.
>
> *(p. 323)*

We have undertaken this book with just such a motive in mind: To shape a mindfulness-based teaching and learning approach to help us find our way, not just as individuals but as a species. In this sense, it is a response to an urgency that is at once personal and collective, simple yet profound: A way to improve access and programming in mindfulness-based self-observational techniques and approaches. Although we may lack Harari's insights across broad swathes of time and events, we share his sense that there is something deeply transformative and healing in the practice of mindfulness. For the authors, this confidence comes from decades of mindfulness practice, but also from our experiences as researchers and scholars within two of the dominant professional and disciplinary fields of secular-scientific mindfulness: education (SM) and clinical practice (PR). We believe that this book, summarizing the state of the research-to-date and applying it to a fulsome educational and clinical professional agenda, is a key piece of the cultural puzzle required at this particular historical juncture.

Mindfulness is the heart of this book – what is it and why it matters. At its core, mindfulness is the practice of paying attention to present-moment experience, including tracking such experiences across time, and doing so intentionally and with curiosity, interest, and openness. Although its precise meaning is contested across cultural, historical, popular, and scholarly contexts, mindfulness is emerging as a distinctive practice with potential universal applications in secular institutional and educational contexts. This secularization, in turn, is intertwined with its increasing adoption as a subject of scientific interest across disciplines. These contexts share a rapidly growing confidence in the potential of mindfulness as a way to empower people; to foster and conserve wellbeing; and to adapt to accelerating change. In a very real sense, mindfulness is becoming an applied science, whereby the insights of mind sciences and biological sciences are being applied to guide how mindfulness is interpreted, taught, learned, and used. That it can be learned, and learned so as to empower personal agency, suggests that the wellbeing it fosters is more democratically available than many other pathways to wellbeing.

As important as the construct of mindfulness is to this book, it is NOT a book about mindfulness per se. Just as the body of knowledge on mathematics *education* is different from the discipline and practice of maths, so too is the study of mindfulness-based

DOI: 10.4324/9781003182467-1

teaching and learning (MBTL) distinct from the study of mindfulness itself, however much their interests may intersect. Furthermore, although grounded in mindfulness as a pivotal quality and practice, MBTL includes a range of meditative, contemplative, and inquiry practices that take it beyond the narrow domain of mindfulness per se. In this respect, while mindfulness is the beginning, it is not the end. That end may best be labelled wellbeing, but how such wellbeing is operationalized varies across individuals, programmes, and contexts.

The book is premised on a distinctive interpretation of mindfulness that underpins its transprofessional practice in education and clinical care: What we refer to as *secular-scientific mindfulness.* While acknowledging the 2500+year history of mindfulness in Buddhism and, to a less extent, in Hindu yoga, the authors clearly distinguish MBTL as a body of teaching and learning associated with the emerging secular-scientific school of mindfulness. The term 'secular' is debated in the field. Some believe it is used to oppose 'spiritual,' thereby implying that it serves an overly narrow health-promotion agenda. Some prefer the adjective 'contemporary' instead; however, there are many fine examples of 'traditional' Buddhist or other sources of mindfulness also being translated into a contemporary modern context with innovations in practice and theory. So, the term 'contemporary' would not delineate the field of mindfulness we are attempting to describe.

Therefore, we use the hyphenated *secular-scientific* to describe how mindfulness adapted as it entered mainstream institutional and organizational contexts. The term 'secular' isn't an expectation that we are imposing but rather a necessary condition as mindfulness goes mainstream, where the appearance of a particular religious motive or technique becomes an obstacle and liability. In turn, within such secular contexts, standards of professional practice are expected to derive from scientific evidence. So, this pairing of secularization with scientific evidence, already in place, has become the defining feature of mindfulness as it adapts to these contexts as *secular-scientific mindfulness.*

To a great extent, the term *secular* signifies differences in *where* mindfulness is taught, but also *how.* There is no doubt that the more religious and belief-based aspects of traditional Buddhist approaches to mindfulness have been excised, at least for the time being. These would include doctrines of karma and reincarnation, for example, or the existence of realms not readily discernible by the senses. The term *scientific* signifies *why* mindfulness is taught, in particular to demonstrate efficacy in an ever-increasing array of disorders or benefits. At the same time, scientific evidence is being applied to shape what is taught and how it is taught, including the implications of the discovery of direct mechanisms, like decentering, that are then fed back into MBTL practice to improve teaching and learning.

## A New Mandate for MBTL as a Transprofessional Practice

MBTL defines an emerging field of transprofessional specialists who are applying mindfulness across a range of professional practices and contexts to address very different needs. When developing MBTL skills and abilities, these specialists find themselves moving beyond traditional professional identities, skills, and zones of comfort. Just as educators find themselves navigating and adopting clinical research and techniques associated with trauma, for example, clinicians find themselves becoming educators overnight as they reorient to teaching patients or clients as learners and students. Likewise, organizational leaders and trainers are broadening their view of their ethical relations and responsibilities to employees as they shift practices to include more clinical and educational activities. These professional border-crossings make MBTL an intriguing space for practitioners to navigate, demanding more complexity while freeing them from the narrower singular lens of their foundational profession. What they share as a transprofessional field of specialization is not merely intersecting professional identities, but an active and ethical commitment to wellbeing as an overarching interest, holistically defined.

Secular-scientific mindfulness was first molded and mainstreamed in clinical contexts, which came to define many features of its adaptations. In the process, research and practice became disproportionately focused on addressing whether mindfulness or related practices are efficacious in the treatment of conditions, whether experienced by specific populations or as a general health-promotion strategy (AMRA, 2010–2019; Brown et al, 2015). This led to mindfulness being defined more as an *intervention* than as a holistic form of learning and values-formation. This is evident in the popular use of the term mindfulness-based intervention (MBI) to describe standardized mindfulness programs. Therefore, we use the term MBTL to replace the term MBI to draw attention to our shared investments as an emerging field of transprofessional practice in teaching and learning.

Although the entire book is dedicated to outlining a more complex agenda for MBTL, we might begin by reflecting that mindfulness teaches three things rarely explicitly taught otherwise in education or clinical care: attention, intention, and attitudes. We will take time to consider each of these.

## ATTENTION

William James, a decisive figure in the emergence of American psychology, provided an early blueprint for the rationale and value of MBTL in his definitive text, *The Principle of Psychology* (1918):

> ...[T]he faculty of voluntarily bringing back a wandering attention, over and over again, is the very root of judgment, character, and will. No one is *compos sui* if he have it not. An education which should improve this faculty would be *the* education *par excellence.* But it is easier to define this ideal than to give practical directions for bringing it about. The only general pedagogic maxim bearing on attention is that the more interest the child has in advance in the subject, the better he will attend. Induct him therefore in such a way as to knit each new thing on to some acquisition already there; and if possible awaken curiosity, so that the new thing shall seem to come as an answer, or part of an answer, to a question pre-existing in his mind.
>
> *(p. 424)*

Self-regulating attention is the crux of what mindfulness *does.* Such attention training includes *selecting* processes (alerting, orienting, and filtering); *holding* or sustaining attention (with curiosity and interest); and *shifting* or changing attention. Such training doesn't just reduce distraction, it broadens attention to invite more objects of interest within the attentional field. In scientific inquiry, this has led to inquiries into how attention regulation can have such a profound impact on wellbeing, such as positive emotion or reduced depressive symptoms, to name a few. This has led to important scientific theories of mindfulness, like the Mindfulness-to-Meaning Theory (MMT), which attempts to explain how attentional training enacts downstream effects on mood and, ultimately, wellbeing (Garland et al., 2015a; 2015b).

## INTENTION

Intentions are the second distinctive area educated in MBTL. As a self-regulation method, mindfulness enables us to track experiences so as to sustain wellbeing. This is not wellbeing as an abstract or merely objective condition so much as an experience, and one beyond a narrow hedonic state of subjective happiness. This intention might best be described as *eudaimonic* wellbeing or human flourishing: a kind of natural motivation. Mindfulness appears to foster such wellbeing, according to fairly robust findings outlined in the book. As self-determination theory suggests, such wellbeing is associated with the intrinsic motivation for autonomy, competence, and relationships. Although mindfulness is associated with all three, it is particularly relevant to autonomy, where it has been found to have a significant impact (Ryan & Deci, 2017). Autonomy should not be confused with independence but rather with an increasing sense of empowerment, responsibility, self-efficacy, and agency in the face of suffering, both personal and collective. This may explain the seeming connections between mindfulness and empathy, kindness, compassion, and prosocial behaviour.

## ATTITUDES

Finally, mindfulness-based approaches are unique in directly targeting the development of key attitudes associated with wellbeing. When mindfulness is taught, the emphasis is on the cultivation of an attitude of curiosity, interest, and openness – sometimes stated in the negative as a non-judgmental attitude – towards whatever arises. Curiosity, or interest, is like a magic key that opens the doors for mindfulness to be more than a mere technique for calm but a full-fledged path of inquiry. Such interest can lead to the self-transcendence associated with mindfulness, moving from the automaticity of habitual experience to the capacity to savour life and find meaning. Last but not least, although mindfulness is associated with equanimity, this should not be confused with neutrality. Mindfulness invites a kind of enhanced feeling tone we refer to as *engaged appreciation* – learning to appreciate the world and all experience.

# The Book

This book can be read in a number of ways. First, it tells a story, offering a narrative journey through history, across cultures and times, to consider concepts and theories and their iteration and evolution within the changing landscapes of MBTL practice. We are confident that reading the text in this chronological way will enrichen yourself, not only as a practitioner, but as a citizen of this world in troubled times. Yet, another way to read the text is as discrete chapters with specified topics and bodies of knowledge that may be more or less relevant to you as a reader. MBTL specialists, for example, may want to pull out Section V to use the validated MBTL-TCF competency table of Chapter 15; the curriculum design methods of Chapter 16; or the trauma-informed practice approaches of Chapter 17. Others may be more interested in theories, practice, history. Mindfulness practitioners of all backgrounds may be interested in Chapter 19, describing the auto-ethnographic journey of one meditator's mindful encounters with wildlife during silent retreats over four decades. In this way, the book can be read in any order. Recognizing this flexibility in how the book is read and used, we do not provide a detailed outline here in the introduction of individual chapters nor do we provide a conclusion to the book itself. Instead, we offer Chapter 19 as an open-ended conclusion to a topic that has no conclusion. So rapidly is the evidentiary basis and scope of MBTL practice changing that any book like this can only serve as a snapshot in time. All we say is that here we are at this juncture – this is where we've come, this is where we are, and this is where we appear to be heading. It will be for the coming decades and centuries to write the conclusions.

## REFERENCES

AMRA (American Mindfulness Research Association). (2010–2019). *Archived issues of mindfulness research monthly, (vols. 1–10)*. Retrieved at: https://goamra.org/publications/archives/.

Brown, K. W., Creswell, J. D., & Ryan, R. M. (Eds.). (2015). *Handbook of mindfulness: Theory, research, and practice*. The Guilford Press.

Garland, E., Farb, N., Goldin, P., & Fredrickson, B. (2015a). Mindfulness broadens awareness and builds eudaimonic meaning: A process model of mindful positive emotion regulation. *Psychological Inquiry, 26*(4), 293–314. https://doi.org/10.1080/1047840X.2015.1064294.

Garland, E., Farb, N., Goldin, P., & Fredrickson, B. (2015b). The mindfulness-to-meaning theory: Extension, applications, and challenges at the attention-appraisal-emotion interface. *Psychological Inquiry, 26*(4), 377–387. https://doi.org/10.1080/1047840X.2015.1092493.

James, W. (1918). *The principles of psychology*. Henry Holt and Co. Retrieved at: https://www.gutenberg.org/files/57628/57628-h/57628-h.htm.

Ryan, R., & Deci, E. (2017). *Self-determination theory: Basic psychological needs in motivation, development, and wellness*. The Guilford Press.

# SECTION I

# Histories

## Why MBTL? From Mindfulness to Mindfulness-Based Teaching and Learning

In this section, we introduce readers to changes in how mindfulness is being redefined and practised as it moves from traditional to contemporary to secular-scientific contexts. Although the book focuses on secular-scientific mindfulness, we recognize the ongoing dialogue across these iterations and contexts as important to the vitality and continued growth of the secular-scientific mindfulness project. The key story we present in this section is how and why mindfulness moved across these three contexts. Finally, we consider why we are now moving into a phase necessarily focused on mindfulness-based teaching and learning (MBTL) as a new and emerging field of transprofessional practice.

In Chapter 1, we examine how secular-scientific mindfulness emerged out of its traditional trajectory. To do so, we focus on conceptual and definitional changes in mindfulness as it moved from traditional and contemporary Buddhist psychological contexts to modern secular-scientific contexts. Chapter 2 considers secular-scientific mindfulness as a key modern and post-modern enterprise. Using these terms very specifically, we demonstrate how, on the one hand, mindfulness has shifted to accommodate the three key features of modernity outlined by Charles Taylor – individualism, instrumental reason, and a certain loss of freedom – while paradoxically subverting the associated malaise or negative effects of these cultural features. As part of this discussion, we consider and address three major critiques of secular-scientific mindfulness: Stealth Buddhism; McMindfulness; and cultural misappropriation. In Chapter 3, we conclude this first section by examining the key historical and cultural trends that led to the mainstreaming of secular-scientific mindfulness.

DOI: 10.4324/9781003182467-2

# CHAPTER 1

# HOW WE GOT HERE

## From Traditional to Secular-Scientific Mindfulness

We live in the aftermath of modernity, in an epoch that has yet to be named consistently by history but is clearly marked by both the failures and triumphs of the modern era, leading some to label our times 'post-modern.' What is clear is that we share both continuities and discontinuities with the modern: continuities in the ascendency of science, technology, and globalization, albeit with resistance, and discontinuities in the turn towards sustainability, wellbeing, and Indigenous and other non-modern knowledge sources, including from religious and contemplative traditions. Mindfulness shares many of these paradoxical features and qualities, making it emblematic of our times. Characterized by 2500-year-old practices developed in traditional, largely Buddhist contexts, mindfulness is being reinvigorated and reinterpreted within modern secular institutions and subjected to often rigorous scientific scrutiny. Although traditional and contemporary variations in mindfulness overlap – as practices and theories of the mind and of learning – their contexts differ enough to treat them as distinct. Indeed, to avoid simple traditional/modern binaries, it is more accurate to refer to at least *three* extant versions of mindfulness: traditional (Buddhist), contemporary (Buddhist or other), and secular-scientific.

## TRADITIONAL (BUDDHIST) MINDFULNESS

> Monks, this is the ultimate path for the purification of beings; for the overcoming of sorrow and lamentation; for the disappearance of *dukkha* (sorrow) and discontent; for the attainment of the true method; for the realization of *Nibbāna;* namely, the four *satipatthana* (paths or foundations of mindfulness).
>
> *(Kusala, trans., 2015, p. 9)*

So begins the Satipatthana Sutta, a key early text on mindfulness attributed to the historical Buddha. The word *sati* means remembrance but is translated as *mindfulness,* while *patthana* conveys the sense of path, way, or establishing: hence, *the path (or way) to establish mindfulness.* These opening lines outline important features of traditional Buddhist mindfulness. First, it establishes the intended audience: monks. This suggests that mindfulness was conceived as a practice for monastics who lived free of productive and reproductive responsibilities, and that it was less relevant for lay people or more secular audiences. More ambiguous is the apparent exclusion of female monastics, which Collett and Analayo (2014) argue is a mistranslation insofar as the Pali term *bhikkhave*, translated here as *monks,* is an inclusive plural term referring to both monks and nuns. The second feature worth noting is the explicit purposes assigned to mindfulness, including a practical purpose to alleviate suffering and a more elevated and abstract soteriological purpose to provide a *true* method to *purify* the mind in pursuit of freedom or *Nibbāna.* Finally, the text presents four key paths for establishing mindfulness: Mindfulness of the body, feelings, mind, and phenomena.

In some translations, the English term *unbinding* is used as *Nibbāna* (e.g., Bikkhu, 2018), pointing to *Nibbāna* as a form of liberation. Later texts translate *Nibbāna* as enlightenment, another problematic term given its modern European associations. Analayo (2006) suggests that *Nibbāna* is more accurately translated as *awakening.* Regardless of which translation is

DOI: 10.4324/9781003182467-3

used, what is being communicated is that mindfulness is an effective path to the ultimate end of a human life - as a state of eudaimonic flourishing or wellbeing (Segall, 2020). What it is clearly not signifying is the alleviation of temporary maladies and discomforts sometimes associated with secular-scientific mindfulness.

## CONTEMPORARY (BUDDHIST) MINDFULNESS

> But what is the purpose of the [*Satipatthana*] Sutra's instruction? Where are we to find the time to practice such mindfulness? If you spend all day practicing mindfulness, how will there ever be enough time to do all the work that needs to be done to change and to build an alternative society? How does Allen manage to work, study Joey's (his son's) lesson, take Ana's (his daughter's) diapers to the laundromat, and practice mindfulness at the same time?
>
> *(p. 8)*

This passage concludes the first chapter of Thich Nhat Hahn's (1975/1999) The Miracle of Mindfulness, a key text introducing mindfulness to a secular, contemporary audience. Hahn's reframing of mindfulness as a lay activity suitable for householders with families and jobs made the reinvention of mindfulness as a secular-scientific enterprise possible. Although there were precedents in Zen and other Mahayana schools of practice, the contemporary distinction was to see mindfulness as something to be integrated within regular working and domestic life:

> [I]f one really wants to keep one's consciousness alive (from now on I'll use the term "mindfulness" to refer to keeping one's consciousness alive to the present reality), then one must practice right now in one's daily life, not only during meditation sessions. …You might well ask: Then how are we to practice mindfulness? My answer is: keep your attention focused on the work, be alert and ready to handle ably and intelligently any situation which may arise – this is mindfulness.
>
> *(p. 13–14)*

Although Hanh is a monk, the text is written to Allen, a French lay student with a young family. This reflected the original Vietnamese text, written as a letter to a lay activist and social worker in Vietnam - Brother Quang. The English translation signifies a cross-cultural shift in which Hahn addressed a broader, a more global, modern, and secular lay audience in English. One of the authors (SM) first purchased a copy of the English translation of this book in 1981 from the Buddhist Publication Society in Kandy, Sri Lanka, an indication of how widely the text was distributed and accepted by a wider English-speaking audience at the time. As this passage suggests, mindfulness was shifting from being viewed as the means to *Nibbāna* to refer instead to a re-invigorated and engaged awareness and attention: i.e., 'keeping one's consciousness alive to the present reality.' Also evident in this text is the shift from an emphasis on mindfulness as formal practices, such as sitting meditation, to informal mindfulness practices that bring attention to any and all experience.

Significantly, these contemporary reinterpretations began from within Buddhism itself, including by Thich Nhat Hahn but also by the Thai monk Buddhadasa (Ngưam, 1990); HH Dalai Lama (1999, 2011); and Stephen Batchelor (1999, 2010, 2017). These authors continued to represent mindfulness practices and perspectives as Buddhist but in ways that were free of supernatural references or beliefs like karma, reincarnation, or deities. Some, like HH Dalai Lama, continued to believe or teach supernatural aspects with more orthodox Buddhist audiences but limited their more public or popular writing and teaching to secular ideas and practices. In this way, secular-scientific mindfulness can be seen as developing out of nascent movements from within contemporary Buddhism itself, not as the product of a process of cultural misappropriation as some critics suggest.

## SECULAR-SCIENTIFIC MINDFULNESS

> In the emerging science of consciousness and the investigation of the mind and its various modalities, Buddhism and cognitive science take different approaches. Cognitive science addresses this study primarily on the basis of neurobiological structures and the biochemical functions of the brain, while Buddhist investigation of consciousness operates primarily from what could be called a first-person perspective. A dialogue between the two could open up a new way of investigating consciousness. The core approach of Buddhist psychology involves a combination of meditative contemplation, which can be described as a phenomenological inquiry; empirical observation of motivation, as manifested through emotions, thought patterns and behaviour; and critical philosophical analysis.
>
> *(p 165)*

This quote by the Dalai Lama (2005) was made after engaging in a decade of active dialogue with scientists that contributed to the emergence and acceptance of secular-scientific mindfulness. The late Francisco Varela, a cognitive scientist from the University of Paris and a Buddhist himself, originally from Chile, helped initiate these Mind and Life dialogues in the late 1980s, arguing persuasively from within cognitive science for the need to recognize first-person data in science from sources like introspection, phenomenology, and contemplative traditions like Buddhism. Varela's intention included the transformation of science itself, to provide a scientific – i.e., an instrumental and operationalized – approach to investigating *the gesture(s) of awareness* in the mind and experience (Kabat-Zinn, 2011; Varela et al., 1992). That said, there are other scientific disciplines in addition to cognitive science equally involved in this enterprise that contributed significantly to the validation of mindfulness, notably psychology and medicine – both in experimental and clinical contexts.

Two key developments in the 1980s had a significant role in the re-interpretation of mindfulness as a combined secular and scientific enterprise. One was the development of Mindfulness-Based Interventions (MBIs) in clinical and medical contexts in North America and Europe, beginning with the Mindfulness-Based Stress Reduction (MBSR) programme. The other was the establishment of research and scholarly networks arising from early initiatives of the Mind and Life Institute established by Francisco Varela and HH the Dalai Lama, among others, that began annual intercultural dialogues between leading scientists and Buddhism. Beginning as dialogues between elite scientists and the Dalai Lama, they later expanded into a broad community of practice in contemplative studies. Together, these developments provided increased institutional legitimization, global research networks, and forms of recognition to support the introduction of mindfulness in secular institutions on the bases of evidence-based practices.

The prototype for all MBIs is the eight-week MBSR programme, which was established in 1979 at the University of Massachusetts Medical School by Jon Kabat-Zinn (1990/2013), a Ph.D. molecular biologist. This programme began in a complementary medicine clinic to address stress and pain management, as a "safety net in the hospital to catch people who were falling through... cracks and challenge them to do something for themselves as a complement to whatever their doctors and their health care team were doing for them" (p. xxvii).

As a student of Zen Buddhism, Kabat-Zinn (2011) translated what he learned through more traditional meditation practices and retreats for use in secular medical contexts. MBSR programmes soon spread across North America and Europe with a standardized curriculum and a credentialing system for facilitators. At the same time, the programmes' standardized format and common sites in or near universities and hospitals resulted in a steady, soon-exponential increase in pre-/post-research studies in which MBSR was the intervention. These programmes expanded to medical schools themselves, to the extent that now approximately 80% of medical schools in the USA (Barnes et al., 2017) and UK (Harrison, 2019) offer mindfulness activities for medical students. In the US, the most common of these medical school programmes was the eight-week MBSR, followed by Mindful Movement or Mindfulness-Based Cognitive Therapy (MBCT) programs.

The MBSR template became reproduced in new programmes designed to support a widening range of disorders and therapeutic needs. This template included an eight-week programme structure with 2.5-hour weekly sessions; home practices; a mid-course full- or half-day silent retreat; training in key formal mindfulness practices like body scans, yoga, walking meditation, and sitting meditation and in informal mindfulness practices; as well as investigative inquiry into key topics using scientific concepts. One such programme was MBCT, inspired by growing empirical evidence in the 1990s suggesting that MBSR reduced depression relapse and anxiety. Developed by professors from the University of Toronto and Oxford University, MBCT began explicitly as a complementary intervention to reduce depressive relapse but has expanded to address mild to moderate anxiety and depression, addictions, and other cognitive and mood disorders (Segal et al., 2002). As these medical researchers recounted: "We soon discovered that the combination of Western cognitive science and Eastern practices was just what was needed to break the cycle of recurrent depression" (Williams et al., 2007, p. 5).

With time, mindfulness research expanded, replicating earlier studies, provide meta-analyses of clusters of previous studies, and adding active controls to enhance the validity of results. With mounting evidence of its efficacy in the treatment of depression, mindfulness became a candidate considered for a range of other mental health or health disorders and to enhance wellbeing and flourishing in non-medical contexts such as the workplace or education (Brown, Creswell, & Ryan, 2015). The net effect was to trigger an exponential increase in published, peer-reviewed scientific studies of mindfulness, from only one in 1981, by Jon Kabat-Zinn, to 21 in 2005 to 1203 in 2019 (AMRA, 2020). This rapidly expanding scientific interest in the efficacy of mindfulness legitimized its further expansion and adoption in secular institutions, beginning with healthcare and extending to the workplace and education. While the uptake of mindfulness into work and education outstrips the evidence, this integration is indicative of the appetite for this work. In addition, while there are many clinical studies of mindfulness, there remains the need for evidence from community effectiveness trials (Dimidjian & Segal, 2015). As this evidence has accumulated, the relationship between secular programmes and scientific research has created a genuinely distinctive form of mindfulness: *secular-scientific mindfulness*.

Universities played, and continue to play, a key role in defining and disseminating secular-scientific mindfulness by providing interconnecting research and practice hubs and networks. MBSR, for example, began at the University of Massachusetts Medical School, which supported early research on MBSR. MBCT was developed by Segal, a faculty member at the University of Toronto, and Teasdale and Williams and Teasdale from Oxford University. These researchers collaborated closely with university-based and affiliated centres of mindfulness education and teacher training in developing and designing the programme and protocols. Another example is UCLA's Mindful Awareness Research Centre (MARC) with its associated Mindful Awareness Practice (MAP) classes and programmes (MARC, n.d.). These programmes serve both the university community of UCLA students, faculty, and staff as well as the broader local community of Los Angeles and its environs. MARC now offers the Training in Mindfulness Facilitation (TMF) programme as well, which is accredited by the International Mindfulness Teachers Association. In this way, MARC reflects two important recent trends in MBTL: a) the emergence of community-specific programming, and b) initiatives to harmonize standards internationally.

The other development underpinning the emergence of secular-scientific mindfulness was the Mind and Life Institute and related research networks (Mind & Life Institute, 2020). Their initial annual meetings brought together elite scientists, the Dalai Lama, and observers, including, on one occasion, one of the authors (SM – 1997). Although the first meetings were small and intimate week-long dialogues, hosted alternatively in India and the USA, they have since expanded in participants and locations to a more global context. Focused on a broad range of topics that intersect with mindfulness, the meetings provide a context for sustained knowledge exchanges and peer feedback on overlapping topics of interest to both science and Buddhism. The elite scientists have since expanded to include expert practitioners, teachers, artists, and other scholars in the broader area of contemplative studies. This reflects the institute's stated mandate to 'bring science and contemplative wisdom together to better understand the mind and to create positive change in the world,' which mindfulness would exemplify.

The secular-scientific mindfulness movement, then, remains deeply invested in the dialogue with Buddhist theories of mind and learning. Yet, as a scientific project, it is established within an evidentiary system that precludes accountability to Buddhist epistemologies or historical or religious texts and traditions. As a form of scientific inquiry, it is accountable ultimately to a narrow scientific empirical system and community of practice in which knowledge and practice advance through the systematic observation of reality and critical reasoning. Although Buddhism uses a comparable epistemic approach that could even be labelled empirical, combining first-person phenomenological accounts and reason, the historical and cultural situatedness of the tradition imbues it with a range of unscientific and non-secular beliefs and norms, including the doctrine of karma and reincarnation, a plethora of god/goddess like Bodhisattvas, and a range of social norms established within male-dominated monastic institutions and their associated education systems. Although mindfulness research is restricted to scientific frames in principle, this strict orientation does not necessarily reflect what happens in communities where looser views of evidence and legitimate practices may apply (Dimidjian & Segal, 2015).

## The Meanings of Mindfulness

### From *Sati* to Mindfulness

The following passage offers one of the earliest definitions of *sati*, the original Pali term commonly translated as *mindfulness* in English from the 2nd or 3rd century BCE, the *Visuddhimagga* or *Path of Purification*:

> *Sati* is that by means of which [the qualities that constitute the mind] remember, or it itself is what remembers, or it is simply remembering. Its characteristic is not floating, its property absence of forgetting, its manifestation guarding or being face to face with an object of awareness; its basis is steady perception or the establishing of mindfulness of the body, and so on. Because of its being firmly set in the object of awareness, it should be seen as like a post and, because it guards the gates of the eye and other senses, as like a gatekeeper.
>
> *(Vism XIV, 141)*

Accordingly, *sati* involves memory, attention, *holding* attention or concentrating, and a form of combined recognition, vigilance, and discernment with respect to sensory experience (i.e., as guard and gatekeeper). Two key sutras associated with *sati* are the Satipatthana Sutta, on the path or cultivation of mindfulness, and the Anapanasati Sutta on mindfulness of breathing. These texts establish the practice of *sati* as central to the Buddhist path and its conception of liberation or enlightenment. Contemporary Buddhists like Thich Nhat Hanh (1976) have helped shift the meaning of the term *sati* from memory to present-focus. For example, Nyanaponika (1962), a German-born Sri Lankan ordained monk redefined mindfulness as 'bare attention,' a quality of perception that preceded object identification or self-referencing and a process that he likened to paying attention: "In its elementary manifestation, known under the term 'attention,' it is one of the cardinal functions of consciousness without which there cannot be the perception of any object at all" (p. 24). Analayo (2019b) demonstrates how precedents for practising mindfulness as 'bare awareness' date back to early Buddhism.

Rhys-Davids was the Welsh English–Pali translator who, in the 1880s, translated *sati* using the English term *mindfulness*. He took some time to decide on this translation of *sati*: "I have sometimes rendered it 'self-possession.' It means that activity of mind, the constant presence of mind, wakefulness of heart which is the foe of carelessness, inadvertence, self-forgetfulness" (Rhys-Davids in Levman, 2017, p. 126). Many translators, then and now, felt the most direct translation was *recollection* or *remembrance*, but Rhys-Davids and Rhys-Davids (1910) selected *mindfulness* instead because they believed *memory* distorted its quality of a sustained attention, presence of mind, and ethics.

> Etymologically Sati is Memory. But as happened at the rise of Buddhism to so many other expressions in common use, a new connotation was then attached to the word, a connotation that gave a new meaning to it, and renders 'memory' a most inadequate and misleading translation. It became the memory, recollection, calling-to-mind, being-aware-of, certain specified facts. Of these the most important was the impermanence (the coming to be as the result of a cause, and the passing away again) of all phenomena, bodily and mental. And it included the repeated application of this awareness to each experience of life, from the ethical point of view.
>
> *(p. 322)*

Interestingly, according to the *OED*, etymologically, mindfulness shared this original meaning of memory via a now-obsolete Old English term meaning 'to have a good memory.' This association was slowly lost but lingers in the relatively rare English verb *to mind*, meaning to remember, as in 'mind your manners.' By the time the word was used to translate *sati* in English, mindfulness had assumed the current vernacular meaning of 'the quality or state of being conscious or aware of something' (from Oxford Online Dictionary, in Grossman, 2014).

Secular-scientific mindfulness placed increased attention on the operationalized definitions of mindfulness, consistent with scientific inquiry. The most commonly referenced operationalized definition came from Jon Kabat-Zinn (1990/2013), who defined it as, 'Paying attention in a particular way: on purpose, in the present moment, and non-judgementally' (p. xxvii). A closely aligned operationalized definition was proposed later by Bishop et al. (2004), as a 'kind of nonelaborative, nonjudgmental, present-centered awareness in which each thought, feeling, or sensation that arises in the attention field is acknowledged and accepted as it is' (p. 232). In theorizing their Five Facets of Mindfulness Questionnaire (FFMQ), Baer, Smith, and Allen (2004) proposed five operationalized indicators of mindfulness: Observing; describing; acting with awareness; non-judging of internal experience; and non-reacting to inner experience. These five factors were later found to be valid only for experienced meditators, whereas for non-meditators, rather ironically, only four (minus *observing*) proved relevant and valid (Williams et al., 2014). These operationalized elements of how secular-scientific mindfulness is defined reflect and guide how it is taught and developed, providing insight into differences and orientations. At the same time, to identify these differences is not to imply that they are gaps to be remedied, but rather distinctions to be noted.

## DIFFERENCES IN SCOPE

Traditional and secular-scientific mindfulness also differ in how they interpret the scope of awareness. Modern secular-scientific interpretations of mindfulness are consistent with a cultural view that privileges the individual as separate and more important than connectedness to a collective or to the Earth. Many more traditional or contemporary Buddhist commentators critique secular-scientific mindfulness for its narrow preoccupation with internal objects related to self-awareness rather than how to cultivate mindfulness of external phenomena such as other sentient beings and the environment (Analayo, 2020a; Chapter 19 this text). This harkens back to early traditional texts like the Satipatthana, in which mindfulness is described as attending to internal, external, and internal and external manifestations, as in the first foundation of mindfulness, mindfulness of the body: 'In this way, in regard to the body he abides contemplating the body, internally, or he abides contemplating the body externally, or he abides contemplating the body both internally and externally' (Analayo, 2006, p. 4), wording that is repeated for the other three foundations of mindfulness: Mindfulness of feelings, the mind, and phenomena.

Analayo (2020a) presents the sequence of traditional texts from the earliest period of Buddhism to propose that the principal external objects referred to are others, notably human beings. He suggests further that the texts come to suggest the blurring of internal and external objects like self and others such that mindfulness becomes an observation of the nature of bodies, for example, in the case of mindfulness of the body, not merely of one's own body. Later texts extend the sense of internal and external to sense experience – internal senses and external sense objects – to suggest a widening context for mindfulness to all external objects of the environment or world. Because secular-scientific practices of mindfulness, at least in the MBIs, have tended to focus on health, they have emphasized internal objects and neglected external objects of mindfulness, variously conceived. One explanation for this neglect of emphasis on external objects like other sentient beings or the environment may be the conspicuous absence of the fourth foundation of mindfulness in secular-scientific approaches.

Related to the question of the scope of awareness is the scope of cognition. The secular-scientific approach to mindfulness has received some critique for being too narrowly focused on non-conceptual cognition in the process of paying attention and cultivating calm-abiding rather than on the dynamic between conceptual and non-conceptual thought in insight. Dreyfus (2011), for example, critiques secular-scientific mindfulness for treating mindfulness as exclusively about the retention of the object in attention rather than about its ripening as insight and wisdom. In contrast, he points to Buddhist psychology's presentation of a more systematic process in which conceptual engagement is developed in tandem with non-conceptual awareness. Wisdom is ripened ultimately by moving from non-conceptual attention through conceptual inquiry to non-conceptual realization or insight. To illustrate, he refers to the insight into impermanence (anicca), one of the so-called three characteristics or three marks of existence alongside suffering (dukkha) and no-self (anatta):

> But to be really effective, this insight [into impermanence] needs to take place at the non-conceptual level. This is where mindfulness plays a decisive role. When we are able to remain carefully in touch with our experiences and to comprehend them as being impermanent, we are able to change their meaningfulness so as to see them in a different light. We then gain a direct insight into their impermanent nature, insight that is brought about by close attention and clear comprehension but goes beyond this conceptual understanding.
>
> *(p. 51)*

This critique points to a valid shortcoming that we are beginning to address in this book and in MBTL as a field of inquiry: The unique and distinctive learning process and epistemology of mindfulness. Yet, the systematic dialectic between non-conceptual and conceptual cognition is already in place within secular-scientific mindfulness training. When properly done, participants are scaffolded to engage in sequences of direct meditation, experiential inquiry, and conceptual inquiry in a very deliberate manner to ripen non-conceptual experience as conceptual insights that are then extended to broader life experiences and continued practice, presumably to ripen into the kinds of transformative realizations and change described by Dreyfus. Furthermore, the three characteristics that define target insights for mindfulness in traditional Buddhism have now emerged empirically as salient mechanisms in scientific studies of mindfulness, operationalized as *change* (i.e., impermanence), *distress tolerance* (i.e., suffering), and *decentering* (i.e., no-self).

## DIFFERENCES IN ETHICAL ORIENTATION

Some commentators in the recent past have identified the seeming lack of *explicit* ethics in secular-scientific mindfulness as a shortcoming (e.g., Monteiro et al., 2015). The *explicit* focus of most mindfulness-based programmes (MBPs), such as MBSR and MBCT, is on the implicit or applied ethics associated with the intention for self-care; group participation guidelines and boundaries; and personal health and wellbeing. These are complemented by teachers modelling and teaching attitudinal foundations such as trust, patience, non-striving, kindness, and compassion as *implicit* ethics. Baer (2015) responded to this critique by elaborating on the full range of *explicit* ethical approaches available in the psychological sciences and suitable for secular MBIs. More recently, more empirical studies, notably a meta-analysis by Berry et al. (2020), have found small to moderate effects on prosocial behavioural outcomes of mindfulness programmes in the absence of explicit ethics, which suggests that it may not be as significant that ethics be taught explicitly as once supposed, at least if prosocial behaviour is the desired outcome. Although there is nascent scholarship suggesting a relationship between mindfulness and empathy or compassion, this work is new and emerging. The Mindful Self-Compassion (MSC) and Cultivating Compassion Training (CCT) programmes are supporting the extension of secular-scientific mindfulness in these directions.

Although different traditional Buddhist schools vary in how they present motivation and intention with respect to mindfulness, it is universally presented as essential as an explicit component of the practice. Furthermore, all schools follow the eightfold path as fundamental, in which right mindfulness is identified as one of the eight key activities leading to liberation or *Nibbana*, presented in the following order: Right understanding, right thought, right speech, right action, right livelihood, right effort, right mindfulness, and right concentration. The very fact that there is a *right* form of mindfulness suggests that there is a wrong form, which is not really part of the conception of mindfulness in the secular-scientific variant. In traditional mindfulness, ethics are framed as universal and inclusive of more forms of life beyond human beings than are commonly represented in other ethical frameworks; furthermore, as stated, such training is explicit. Yet, both traditional Buddhist and secular-scientific mindfulness begins with the awareness of motivation rather than the cultivation of one or another motives. HH the Dalai Lama's (2005, p. 165) suggests this as well when he states, as cited earlier in the chapter, that Buddhist psychology involves meditative contemplation as the 'empirical observation of motivation, as manifested through emotions, thought patterns and behaviour' alongside phenomenological and critical inquiry.

In another line of critique, Gethin (2011) argues that the modern reconceptualization of *sati* contributed to reductions and losses in the ethical impact of mindfulness, through reductions in both meaning and activities. The particular problem he identifies is the emphasis on a present-moment, non-judgemental awareness, whereby the secular-scientific definition lost a connotation of, or connection to, remembrance or to an intention beyond being present without judgement. In contrast, the traditional interpretation of mindfulness as remembrance is predicated on a form of judgement capable of discerning the causes and conditions of wholesome and unwholesome states of mind. To illustrate, Gethin refers to an early Buddhist text, the Milindapanha (Mil 27–28) or Questions to King Milinda, in which *sati* is defined with the qualities of calling to mind and taking possession:

> Thus sati is explained as calling to mind wholesome and unwholesome qualities such that the meditator is in a position to know which qualities are the ones he should pursue and which are the ones he should not... Secondly, sati is said to follow the outcome of qualities and so to know which qualities are beneficial and which are not with the result that the meditator can remove those which are not helpful and take possession of those which are helpful.
> *(pp. 269–270)*

This type of discerning judgement may not be formalized in the explicit definition and stated purposes of secular-scientific mindfulness, but it is arguably an implicit component. Programmes like MBSR include systematic analyses of stressors, such as communication difficulties or technology, aimed at identifying sources of distress and reducing or removing their negative impacts. Furthermore, Analayo (2020b) established precedents in early Buddhist texts for interpreting mindfulness as non-judgemental in the requirement to remain free of greedy desires and discontent: 'This would indeed require avoiding judgemental reactivity to whatever arises' (p. 476). Previously, Analayo (2019a) outlined early Buddhist precedents as well for considering mindfulness as a present-centred awareness, which is reflected as well in Nyanaponika's (1962) definition of mindfulness as bare attention.

## Conclusion

In this chapter, we introduced the historical trajectory of mindfulness from traditional to contemporary to secular-scientific manifestations, considering how they variously define, interpret, and apply mindfulness in practice. Although we distinguish them, it would be incorrect to interpret these differences as indicative of conflict. They are adaptations that allow people over time and within very specific cultural and lived experiences to participate in, and benefit from, mindfulness. Also, they are not subtractive of one another but rather offer promise to contribute and enrich the significance of one another. Indeed, overall, there is a great deal of mutual respect and continuing collaborations across all three contexts of mindfulness in both theory and practice (Analayo, 2019b; Farb, 2014).

## REFERENCES

AMRA. (2020). *Database: Mindfulness journal publications by year, 1980–2018.* American Mindfulness Research Association. Accessed from: https://goamra.org/resources/.

Anālayo, B. (2006). *Satipatthana: The direct path to realization.* Buddhist Wisdom Centre.

Anālayo, B. (2019a). The emphasis on the present moment in the cultivation of mindfulness. *Mindfulness, 10*, 571–581. https://doi.org/10.1007/s12671-018-1074-1.

Anālayo, B. (2019b). Adding historical depth to definitions of mindfulness. *Current Opinion in Psychology, 28*, 11–14. https://doi.org/10.1016/j.copsyc.2018.09.013.

Anālayo, B. (2020a). External mindfulness. *Mindfulness, 11*, 1632–1646. https://doi.org/10.1007/s12671-020-01377-8.

Anālayo, B. (2020b). The myth of McMindfulness. *Mindfulness, 11*, 472–479. https://doi.org/10.1007/s12671-019-01264-x.

Baer, R. (2015). Ethics, values, virtues, and character strengths in mindfulness-based interventions: A psychological science perspective. *Mindfulness, 6*, 956–969. https://doi.org/10.1007/s12671-015-0419-2.

Baer, R. A., Smith, G. T., & Allen, K. B. (2004). Assessment of mindfulness by self-report: The Kentucky inventory of mindfulness skills. *Assessment, 11*(3), 191–206. https://doi.org/10.1177/1073191104268029.

Barnes, N., Hattan, P., Black, D., & Schuman-Olivier, Z. (2017). An examination of mindfulness-based programs in US medical schools. *Mindfulness, 8*, 489–494. https://doi.org/10.1007/s12671-016-0623-8.

Batchelor, S. (1999) *Buddhism without belief: A contemporary guide to awakening.* Riverhead Books.

Batchelor, S. (2010). *Confession of a Buddhist atheist.* Random House.

Batchelor, S. (2017). *Secular buddhism: Imagining the dharma in an uncertain world.* Yale University Press.

Berry, D., Hoerr, J., Cesko, S., Alayoubi, A., Carpio, K., Zirzow, H., Walters, W., Scram, G., Rodriguez, K., & Beaver, V. (2020). Does mindfulness training without explicit ethics-based instruction promote prosocial behaviors? A meta-analysis. *Personality and Social Psychology Bulletin, 46*(8), 1247–1269. https://doi.org/10.1177/0146167219900418.

Bikkhu, T. (2018). The Buddha's original teachings on mindfulness. *Tricycle*, March 5. Accessed at: https://tricycle.org/trikedaily/satipatthana-sutta-mindfulness/.

Bishop, S., Lau, M., Shapiro, S., Carlson, L., Anderson, N., Carmody, J., Segal, Z., Abbey, S., Speca, M. Velting, D., & Devins, G. (2004). Mindfulness: A proposed operational definition. *Clinical Psychology: Science and Practice*, *11*(3), 230–241. https://doi.org/10.1093/clipsy.bph077.

Brown, K. W., Creswell, D., & Ryan, R. (Eds.). (2015). *Handbook of mindfulness: Theory, research, and practice*. Guilford Press.

Collett, A., & Analayo, B. (2014). Bhikkhave and bhikkhu as gender-inclusive terminology in early Buddhist texts. *Journal of Buddhist Ethics*, *21*, 760–797.

Dalai Lama, H. H. (1999). *Ethics for the new millennium*. Riverhead Books.

Dalai Lama, H. H. (2005). *The universe in a single atom: The convergence of science and spirituality*. Morgan Road Books.

Dalai Lama, H. H. (2011). *Beyond religion: Ethics for a whole world*. Houghton Mifflin Harcourt.

Dimidjian, S., & Segal, Z. (2015). Prospects for a clinical science of mindfulness intervention. *American Psychologist*, *70*(7), 593–620. https://doi.org/10.1037/a0039589.

Dreyfus, G. (2011). Is mindfulness present-centred and non-judgmental? A discussion of the cognitive dimensions of mindfulness. *Contemporary Buddhism*, *12*(1), 41–54. https://doi.org/10.1080/14639947.2011.564815.

Farb, N. (2014). From retreat center to clinic to boardroom? Perils and promises of the modern mindfulness movement. *Religions*, *5*, 1062–0186. http://doi:10.3390/rel5041062.

Gethin, R. (2011). On some definitions of mindfulness. *Contemporary Buddhism*, *12*(1), 263–279. https://doi.org/10.1080/14639947.2011.564843.

Hahn, T. (1975). *The miracle of mindfulness: An introduction to the practice of meditation*. Beacon Press.

Hanh, T. (1975/1999). *The miracle of mindfulness: An introduction to the practice of meditation*. Beacon Press.

Harrison, L. (2019). Is there a movement towards acceptance of mindfulness in medical education? An audit of mindfulness activity in UK medical schools. *MedEdPublish*, *8*(2), 84. https://doi.org/10.15694/mep.2019.000084.1.

Kabat-Zinn, J. (1990/2013). *Full catastrophe living: Using the wisdom of your body and mind to face stress, pain, and illness*. Bantam.

Kabat-Zinn, J. (2011). Some reflections on the origins of MBSR, skillful means, the trouble with maps. *Contemporary Buddhism*, 12(1), 281–306. https://doi.org/10.1080/14639947.2011.564844.

Kusala, B. (2015). *The Satipatthana Sutta*. Dhamma Sukha Publications.

Levman, B. (2017). Putting *smrti* back into *sati* (putting remembrance back into mindfulness). *Journal of the Oxford Centre for Buddhist Studies*, *13*, 121–149.

MARC. (n.d.). *UCLA mindful awareness research centre*. Accessed at: https://www.uclahealth.org/marc/.

Mind & Life Institute. (2020). *About mind & life*. Accessed at: https://www.mindandlife.org/about/.

Monteiro, L., Musten, R., & Compson, J. (2015). Traditional and contemporary mindfulness: Finding the middle path in the tangle of concerns. *Mindfulness*, *6*, 1–13. https://doi.org/10.1007/s12671-014-0301-7.

Ngū̃am. (1990). *Radical conservatism: Buddhism in the contemporary world: Articles in honour of Bikkhu Buddhadasa's 84th birthday anniversary*. Thai Interreligious Commission for Development.

Nyanaponika. (1962). *The heart of Buddhist meditation: A handbook of mental training based on the Buddha's way of mindfulness*. Rider & Company.

Rhys Davids, T. W., & Rhys Davids, C. A. F. (1910). *Dialogues of the Buddha*. Henry Frowde/Oxford University Press.

Segal, Z., Teasdale, J., Williams, M., & Gemar, M. (2002). The mindfulness-based cognitive therapy adherence scale: Interrater-reliability, adherence to protocol, and treatment distinctiveness. *Clinical Psychology & Psychotherapy*, *9*(2), 131–138. https://doi.org/10.1002/cpp.320.

Segall, S. (2020). *Buddhism and human flourishing: A modern Western perspective*. Palgrave MacMillan.

Varela, F., Thompson, E., & Rosch, E. (1992). *The embodied mind: Cognitive science and human experience*. MIT Press.

Williams, M., Dalgleish, T., Karl, A., & Kuyken, W. (2014). Examining the factor structures of the five-facet mindfulness questionnaire and the self-compassion scale. *Psychological Assessment*, *26*(2), 407–418. https://doi.org/10.1037/a0035566.

Williams, M., Teasdale, J., Kabat-Zinn, J., & Segal, Z. (2007). *The mindful way through depression: Freeing yourself from chronic unhappiness*. The Guilford Press.

# CHAPTER 2

# WHERE WE ARE NOW

## Secular-Scientific Mindfulness and the *Malaise of Modernity*

Secular-scientific mindfulness emerged from an encounter between scientific research and secular practice that fundamentally recontextualized mindfulness within modern cultural contexts and institutions. Yet, seldom are these two critical components of science and secularism in mindfulness adequately and explicitly discussed or explained. Instead, criticisms tend to focus on one or the other, obscuring their mutual co-dependent bases. Just as most secular institutions require scientific evidence as a standard to guide practice, most scientific inquiry is organized to inform disciplines and professions associated with secular institutions and activities.

So, to better understand these intertwined pillars of mindfulness, it is worthwhile taking time to review some dominant critiques of either the secularism or scientific orientation of mindfulness. According to the *stealth Buddhism* critique, for example, secular mindfulness is the result of teachers code-switching from Buddhist to modern secular or scientific terminology to mask or sanitize the prior religious language and context (Goodman, 2014, cited in Brown, 2014). For different reasons, the *McMindfulness* critique accused the mindfulness movement of misappropriating traditional Buddhist cultural knowledge and repackaging it into undigested, bite-sized pieces to serve neoliberal corporate interests (Purser & Loy, 2013). Both critiques implied that secular-scientific mindfulness was equivalent to traditional mindfulness but somehow masked the equivalency. Critics of the impact of science on mindfulness, on the other hand, fault its reliance on scientific empirical and utilitarian procedures for reducing it scope of effects and purposes. All of these critiques fail to account adequately for the incremental way science proceeds to generate and apply insights within established institutional systems and educational practices (Farb, 2014). Consistent with the implicit conservativism and slow unpacking of scientific knowledge, mindfulness is by definition an unfinished project.

What secularism and science have in common is a shared cultural basis in modernity. Indeed, secularism and science go so far as to define modernity as a social practice (secularism) and as an epistemology (science). With this in mind, this chapter considers the cultural roots of modernity and its malaise to understand the distinctive role that mindfulness plays in both reinforcing and correcting modernity and its aftermath.

## CRITIQUING MINDFULNESS AS MODERN

Here we will consider three critiques of mindfulness as a secular practice: a) stealth Buddhism; b) McMindfulness; and c) cultural (mis)appropriation. We address each of these critiques, followed by our own perspective that identified mindfulness mindfulness instead as an example of cultural recontextualization. Although the first two critiques gained momentum in the popular media, they were taken up, albeit to a less extent, in peer-reviewed responses. The final cultural (mis)appropriation critique was addressed in the peer-reviewed literature. Accordingly, the first two seem weak to us in both argumentation and evidence, though they do raise valid questions. We take them up briefly here for the sole purpose, like Analayo (2020), to eliminate them as popular "'myths'" to enable us to proceed.

DOI: 10.4324/9781003182467-4

## STEALTH BUDDHISM

This critique claims that secular-scientific mindfulness is disingenuous in its attempt to eliminate religious contents by code-switching from Buddhist to secular-scientific terms and intentions. Referred to as *stealth Buddhism*, this critique suggests that the motive of this modern variant of mindfulness is to teach Buddhism, even to convert people to Buddhism, through a skilful and strategic, even manipulative, use of language and deception. Gaining prominence in the popular press (Goodman in Brown, 2014), the critique was free to make the specious claim, unchallenged by experts, that the alterations in language and content of secular-scientific mindfulness were used to obscure the traditional Buddhist origins of concepts or practices introduced to students. The term *stealth* has negative connotations of transgressing: The etymology derives from the Old English "'to steal,'" while the contemporary meaning of *secret or hidden* is commonly used to describe military technologies that can elude radar detection, thereby associating the term violence and deception.

What is more likely is that the code-switching is being done to render concepts more culturally accessible or to operationalize them for the purposes of analysis and scientific study. Ultimately, these networks of concepts are becoming the backbone constructs of a consistent scientific theory about mindfulness, which is expressed through language and the relationship between the concepts. For example, the Buddhist concept of *dukkha* suggesting life is imperfect and consists of suffering and struggle becomes *stress* and distress tolerance in MBSR, culturally accessible and specified terms. For research and analysis, stress is further reduced to a series of operationalized indicators of distress or suffering, including hormonal indicators like cortisol levels and adrenaline; psychological indicators like subjective distress; and behavioural indicators like reactivity.

Paradoxically, some critics claim secular-scientific mindfulness exploits Buddhism to attract participants because Buddhism is popular, while others suggest secular-scientific mindfulness is disassociating from Buddhism because the religious association might deter participants and make it less popular. Others have defended secular-scientific mindfulness from accusations of intentional deception by referring to its adaptations as *skilful means* (Brown, 2014). This Buddhist idea of skilful means refers to the ability to teach different students in culturally and psychologically appropriate ways, which would imply that secular-scientific mindfulness is still Buddhist but presented in a culturally appropriate form. Yet, this defense still presumes that secular-scientific mindfulness *is* Buddhist and that stealth Buddhism is therefore a valid critique, which we dispute. From its inception, secular-scientific mindfulness was conceived of as a clinical rather than a religious project. Also, given that many, if not most, teachers of mindfulness have limited knowledge of Buddhism, they are ill-equipped to translate or code-switch directly across the religious and secular-scientific divides as they teach. Although there is a process of skilful means at work in the development of MBTL and in the teaching of mindfulness, it is not intended to represent Buddhism.

## McMINDFULNESS

Neale (2011), an American-Buddhist teacher and psychotherapist, first introduced this critique in an unpublished essay entitled "'McMindfulness and Frozen Yoga.'" The critique problematizes the removal of ethics from the popular approach to teaching yoga in North

America, which he rather obliquely extends to mindfulness meditation. He argued that both yoga and mindfulness are examples of the American tendency to engage in "'plucking the desirable from foreign cultures and simply disregarding the rest'" (p. 1). He believed that by connecting yoga and mindfulness back to their traditional cultural and psychological contexts, they promise "a spiritual revolution unlike any in our young country" (p. 1). He is, therefore, taking an optimistic view of the potential of dialogue across traditional and modern or secular-scientific contexts while at the same time faulting mainstream mindfulness and yoga for what he sees as the misappropriation of the traditions. Using the analogy of fast food, he was implying that they suffer from too much emphasis on quick fixes with inadequate attention to providing food of sustaining nutritional value. He implied that a narrow and stricter adherence to traditional Buddhism offered such sustaining nutriment, despite the fact that, in his own professional practice, he offered hybrid secularized contemplative practices as therapeutic interventions.

This unpublished paper might have gone unnoticed were it not for a spate of subsequent opinion pieces in the popular press – from *Huffington Post* to *The Guardian* – that exploited the catchy notion of McMindfulness. Notably, Purser and Loy (2013), two academics who also self-identify as Zen monks, mounted often vitriolic, unsubstantiated attacks on both mindfulness and on Jon Kabat-Zinn, the founder of MBSR. There are two key claims made in this critique of secular-scientific mindfulness: (a) it dilutes and exploits traditional Buddhism for neoliberal, for-profit capitalist purposes; and b) by focusing on health, well-being, and the present-moment, it functions to pacify and de-politicize practitioners, making them more subject to oppressive capitalist structures while reducing their inclination to engage in organizational or social change (Purser, 2018). It is worth emphasizing that Purser and other proponents of this critique provide little empirical evidence to substantiate their claims, beyond isolated anecdotes.

With respect to the critique that secular-scientific mindfulness is a diluted form of Buddhism, it is worth repeating that secular-scientific mindfulness doesn't claim to be Buddhist and is not diluted so much as recontextualized to accommodate evidence-based practices. Problematic as well is the claim that it is somehow linked to neoliberalism. Although neoliberalism may well pose persistent challenges to the integrity of secular-scientific mindfulness, it doesn't make mindfulness a neoliberal enterprise. Any popular and in-demand trend is equally susceptible to neo-liberal corruption: Think of education, healthcare, and pharmaceuticals. While the critique of neoliberalism is deserved, the suggestion that secular-scientific mindfulness is complicit in neo-liberalism is not. In fact, secular-scientific mindfulness programmes rarely, if ever, mention capitalist interests or market needs as a motive, but repeatedly refer instead to the intention to reduce suffering, which closely mirrors the explicit intention of Buddhist mindfulness. For example, a public health information page in Canada describes MBSR as follows: "MBSR is a program that helps you learn to calm your mind and body to help you cope with illness, pain, and stress. MBSR teaches 'mindfulness,' which is a focus only on things happening in the present moment" (Healthlink BC, 2020). Here, as is commonly the case, mindfulness is being promoted in the context of public healthcare rather than neoliberal corporate interests.

When mindfulness *is* promoted within organizational contexts, it is commonly framed as a way to help employees cope with stress and other workplace challenges or as a way to enhance leadership skills and productivity. When organizations use mindfulness to deflect attention from problematic organizational cultures and work environments, the McMindfulness critique presents a valid concern that mindfulness may be inappropriately used to download systemic workplace problems onto individual employees. Still, mindfulness can be effective as part of a broader package of interventions that encourage collaborative communication, action, and change, as in the example of the mindful team, organizational, or community approaches. With respect to leaders, they benefit as anyone can from improved executive functioning, stress management, and self-determination. On the other hand, using mindfulness to improve productivity is not well supported by evidence. (See chapter 8 for more on these topics.)

With respect to the claim that mindfulness somehow depoliticizes practitioners in ways that traditional Buddhism did not, Anālayo (2020b) points out that early Buddhist texts offer evidence that mindfulness was *not* intended to politicize practitioners from its earliest iteration. For example, clear distinctions were made between a Buddha and temporal leader in prophesies about the life of the historical Buddha. Also, early Buddhism also included clinical applications for mindfulness, as when the Buddha agreed to teach mindfulness to a king who wished to lose weight. Indeed, the Buddha is sometimes likened to a physician, and his teachings to medicines, reinforcing the pragmatic orientation on what heals rather than merely on what is true. Equally ungrounded is the suggestion that secular-scientific mindfulness doesn't address oppression. Berila (2015) presents a programme to integrate mindfulness in anti-oppressive pedagogies in higher education, while mindfulness is being researched as a possible method to decolonize body-minds in the aftermath of colonialism and its intergenerational impacts on Indigenous people (Yellow Bird, 2013); to recover from race-based trauma (Munjee & MacPherson, unpublished); and to protect vulnerable populations against the effects of chronic exposure to violence (Pillay & Eagle, 2019).

While educated, privileged Whites disproportionately have access to mindfulness and participate in its benefits, this critique can be made of Buddhism, too, at least in the modern context. The solution to this disproportionate uptake by those with privilege is surely to expand access rather than rejecting it altogether, given its evidence of both health promotion and improved agency and self-determination. Furthermore, Anālayo (2020a) points out the potential of mindfulness for cultivating environmental awareness and climate change activism, a topic taken up in Chapter 19. Consequently, we join Anālayo in concluding that "the term 'McMindfulness' fails to offer a convincing assessment of MBSR and similar mindfulness-based practices in healthcare and therefore can be considered to have by now become a 'myth'" (p. 476).

## CULTURAL (MIS)APPROPRIATION

A related critique is that secular-scientific mindfulness resulted from the inappropriate cultural (mis)appropriation of traditional Buddhist mindfulness. The concept of *appropriation* does not necessarily suggest inappropriateness, so we qualify appropriations specifically to mean those that are inappropriate or misappropriated. Appropriation is the use of one culture's assets by another, including but not limited to symbols, artifacts, knowledge, genres, rituals, or technologies. Although it has assumed a pejorative sense these days, as Farb (2014) argues, in the context of mindfulness, the term *appropriation* is not necessarily derogatory:

> [T]his paper uses the term appropriation to describe the transfer of knowledge from Buddhists to clinician/scientists to popular secular culture, [but] it is not meant in a derogatory light. Rather, each stage of appropriation represents an important synthesis of perspectives, one that may ultimately benefit both scientific and Buddhist traditions.
>
> *(pp. 1063–1064)*

Rogers (2006) theorized four types of appropriation that vary according to the exchange and power dynamics between two cultures: a) *cultural exchange*, that is, reciprocal exchanges between cultures of equal power; b) *cultural dominance*, as the imposition of cultural elements from a dominant to a subordinate culture; c) *cultural exploitation*, when elements of a subordinated culture are used by a dominant culture without reciprocity, permission, and/or compensation; and d) *transculturation*, which he defines as "cultural elements created from and/or by multiple cultures, such that identification of a single originating culture is problematic, for example, multiple cultural appropriations structured in the dynamics of globalization and transnational capitalism creating hybrid forms" (p. 477).

Historically, colonialism created conditions of unequal power that could well be viewed as subordinating traditional Buddhist cultures to dominant modern Western states, and this power dynamic no doubt impacted how mindfulness became appropriated; however, according to Rogers (2006), to be exploitative, such appropriation would need to lack reciprocity, permission, and/or compensation, none of which is the case. Yet, quite aside from this, the historical appropriations giving rise to secular-scientific mindfulness are best described as *transculturation* rather than mere cultural exchanges. It is impossible even to identify an originating culture for mindfulness that is empowered to negotiate such an exchange given that the originating cultures were northern India and Nepal from about 500 BCE through to about 900 CE; by the 11th century, Buddhism was all but wiped out from India. It survived instead in satellite cultures across Asia that had adopted and adapted mindfulness: Sri Lanka, Myanmar, Indonesia, Tibet, China, Viet Nam, Cambodia, Japan, and Korea.

By the time contemporary and secular-scientific variants of mindfulness began appearing, these countries were themselves being transformed through colonialism, modernism, and globalization. Consequently, secular-scientific mindfulness manifested from multiple and complex cultural contact sites and forms of interactions leading to diverse instances of appropriation in multiple directions. In Textbox 2.1, we provide an example of one such global contact zone emerging from within a so-called traditional Buddhist context, Dolma Ling Institute, researched over years by one of the authors (MacPherson, 2005, 2011, 2019). Not only did their early curriculum include modern subjects alongside the more traditional monastic curriculum, but the curriculum itself was an innovation for nuns and women, who had been historically excluded from such studies. Also, the institution's funding derived in large part from donations from more developed countries through the US-based Tibetan Nuns Project.

## TEXTBOX 2.1 EXEMPLAR OR CASE:

### Dolma Ling as a Global Contact Zone

Perhaps due to its proximity to Dharamsala, about 30 km away along the Kangra River Valley in India, Dolma Ling emerged in its earliest days as a key site of global contacts and exchanges. Although this claim may sound reasonable in the abstract, the relative remoteness and privacy of the institution make the actual experience *in situ* ironic and even dissonant. This irony was most pronounced during an incident in the fall of 1997, shortly after I returned to Dolma Ling to teach and do doctoral research. The principal, Gen. Pema Shastri, had forwarded an email link to an article by Pico Iyer in the Asian edition of *Time Magazine*. Writing about the Dalai Lama, Iyer, himself a noted commentator on globalization, recounted a recent trip he'd taken to Dharamsala. While staying with friends in a small house behind Dolma Ling, he walked through the nunnery's courtyard and found an article posted on a bulletin board. The article, from an Australian newspaper, included a critique of the popular fervour raised during a recent trip by HH the Dalai Lama to Australia. Iyer argued that the posting of this rather critical article reflected the Tibetans' capacity for self-criticism.

Curious about the content of the Australian article, I decided to see for myself. So, walking 50 metres from my front door to the courtyard, I found and read the same article posted on the bulletin board. At the time, most of the nuns and institute staff were in Dharamsala, so the nunnery was empty. Alone in the courtyard, with only a few dogs, rice paddies, grazing cattle, water buffalo, and goats on the horizon, I was struck by the strangeness and irony of the moment: verifying and re-living a global story from *Time Magazine* in this remote and seemingly un-cosmopolitan milieu. In this respect, the nature of the global contacts at Dolma Ling was not just actual and palpable but remote and virtual, reflecting a range of relations and networks between elites, organizations, communities and individuals around the globe. We were a unique local experience becoming a global contact hub.

(MacPherson, 2019, p. 152 – adapted with permission from Cambridge Scholars Press)

As mentioned previously, many leaders associated with traditional mindfulness were some of the first to clear pathways for both contemporary and secular-scientific mindfulness, people like the Thai monk Buddhadasa, HH the Dalai Lama, and Thich Nhat Hanh. This reminds us of the error of misconstruing such appropriation as misappropriation or exploitation when supported and endorsed by key "traditional" leaders and insiders. The process is much more of a partnership than a struggle, navigating what is, more accurately, a mutual appropriation process. Farb (2014), a leading neuro-psychologist researching mindfulness, argued that the story of the nature of such appropriation is unfinished:

> In this way, [mindfulness] research and teaching may contribute to Western science [and] Buddhist theories of mindfulness alike, potentially generating a deeper understanding of well-being promotion. To romanticize the project somewhat, through these efforts we may witness the rise of a novel culture within secular society, one fueled by a unique blend of faith, skepticism, and willingness to experiment with one's own human experience.
>
> *(p. 1081)*

## APPROPRIATION AS RECONTEXTUALIZATION

In these critiques, we revisit a familiar struggle between premodern traditional knowledge and the modern cultural landscape, dominated as it has become by secular-scientific practices and institutions. The problem has been that, historically, unequal power relations arising from colonial and racist policies and practices have made these dynamics potentially oppressive and exploitative. In this respect, the project of establishing a decolonizing agenda and practice of MBTL is critical, a topic taken up later in the book. The key is to navigate a more mutually beneficial appropriation process while continuing to engage traditional sources. This is not that difficult insofar as the appropriations are happening equally within many Asian and non-Western cultures and countries, as attested to by a perusal of the origins or recent published scientific research in the field (AMRA, 2020). Furthermore, the driving force for the recontextualization process has been to adapt mindfulness for clinical and educational uses, which is consistent with the values and interests of traditional Buddhism but not necessarily with its perceived purposes, which are more concerned with liberation. Indeed, of all secular activities, it is the clinical and therapeutic potentials of mindfulness that have distinguished and redefined secular-scientific mindfulness most directly. So, while we refer to such mindfulness as secular-scientific, it might be more accurate to refer to it as secular-*clinical*-scientific.

## Modern Malaise

What is it about modernity that created the need, even hunger, for mindfulness and its reconceptualization as a secularized clinical practice? Charles Taylor (1991), a leading philosopher of modernity and its aftermath, pointed to three key cultural features that define the modern period: i) individualism, which gave rise to a diminished sense of purpose and meaning; ii) instrumental reasoning, which gave rise to a broader disenchantment of the world through the ascendancy of economic and utilitarian efficiencies, such as bureaucracies; and, iii) the loss of freedoms through the reduction of choices. According to Taylor, these produced a disenchantment with the world that he called *malaise*. We consider each of these, as well as *secularism* itself, to position secular-scientific mindfulness in relationship to modernity.

### INDIVIDUALISM

Chronicling the history behind the emergence of modern individualism, Taylor (1989) described its key feature as *radical reflexivity*: 'The turn to oneself is now also inescapably a turn to oneself in the first-person perspective – a turn to the self as a self. That is what I mean by radical reflexivity' (p. 176).

The self-reflexive inwardness, initially attributed as beginning with the fourth-century autobiographical writings of Augustine of Hippo, became more radical and extreme in the modern period. Taylor identified three activities associated with this internalized radical self-reflexivity: self-exploration, self-control, and personal commitment. Socially, these manifested in modern individualism, whereby individuals became atomized and detached from their embeddedness in communities and societies and, therefore, from others. According to Taylor, this detachment contributed to a malaise with modernity. As a modernist or postmodernist project, secular-scientific mindfulness does accommodate many of these features of modern individualism. Evidence of this can be noted in changes in practice, with diminished emphasis on relationships with teachers or fellow students as members of communities of practice (i.e. *the Sangha*). Another indicator is the easy access to mindfulness training and support through digitally automated forms of new technologies, such as Web-based asynchronous programmes or apps, thereby eliminating the need to depend on, or interact with, others.

Although this implies that secular-scientific mindfulness accommodates and reproduces modernity, there are subtle ways in which it also subverts it. Much like a vaccine inoculates the immune system against a virus by mimicking the virus itself, mindfulness training uses aspects of individualism while inoculating practitioners against its more deleterious effects. So, rather than reinforcing the independence and social disengagement of modern individualism, empirical studies suggest that mindfulness cultivates a more flexible and open sense of self or personhood. Using neurological imaging data, Farb et al. (2007) found evidence of changes in practitioners' sense of self following an eight-week mindfulness programme. Previous areas of the brain associated with narrative self-referencing became reduced and uncoupled from areas associated with the experiencing self. So too, Ryan and Deci (2017) found mindfulness to be associated with *autonomy*, a basic intrinsic motivation associated with self-determination that is characterized by self-regulation and choice, but not independence as such. Critically, rather than malaise, these changes in the sense of self were associated with enhanced wellbeing (Brown & Ryan, 2003; Farb & Segal, 2014). Finally, in Chapter 21, we offer a longitudinal qualitative study suggesting that sustained intensive mindfulness practice can develop and transform self-awareness into ecological awareness through identification with non-human or greater-than-human life.

Although mindfulness could be described using Taylor's (1989) three radical reflexivity nouns – self-exploration, self-control, and personal commitment – on closer examination, each of these activities could be described as being targeted to be subverted. So, for example, the above neural imaging studies by Farb et al. (2007) and Farb and Segal (2014) suggest that mindfulness practices lead to a loosening of identification with a fixed sense of self, whereby through decentering, the self becomes more removed from over-identification and storytelling about experiences, including stories about the self; furthermore, this was associated with improved executive control. In mindfulness programmes, this shift is actively encouraged, for example, through the intentional removal of the first-person perspective – i.e. the 'I' – in the guidance of mindfulness practices. In this respect, although self-exploration is an intention, in practice such exploration serves to subvert over-reified views about the self and what it is being explored as 'the self', i.e., experience. Similarly, with respect to self-control, while mindfulness increases autonomous self-regulation (Deci et al., 2015; Ryan & Deci, 2017), this should not be confused with self-control. As Lynch et al. (2015) point out, mindfulness corrects excesses in self-control associated with a range of pathologies like OCD and anorexia nervosa, yet it is impossible to suffer from excesses in self-regulation, which is significantly associated with enhanced wellbeing.

Similarly, while mindfulness training relies initially on personal commitments to encourage participants to practice, rather than on social obligations or cultural expectations, these become intrinsically motivating rather than extrinsically committed actions (Deci & Ryan, 2017). By explicitly teaching non-striving and a more open, flexible, and responsive relationship to the changing nature of circumstances, secular-scientific mindfulness actually discourages and counters the control-orientation of personal commitment. Indeed, MBTL emphasizes invitational language and stances to deepen informed and voluntary consent, not only in teaching practices but also in learning orientations – i.e., in approaches to internalizing expectations, setting and realizing goals, and altering behaviour. This is accomplished by encouraging a willingness to be with experience, investigating it, and then deciding what, if anything, needs to be done. Experience itself becomes the guide. So, while executive control *is* enhanced through mindfulness, with demonstrable neural evidence of this effect (Farb et al., 2007), it is realized not through self-control and personal commitment so much as through attention regulation and its impact on functional integration.

Accordingly, secular-scientific mindfulness appeals to people socialized and acculturated within modern institutional life while mitigating what Taylor (1991) described as its sources of malaise or disenchantment. The capacity of mindfulness to reduce malaise is supported by empirical studies associating mindfulness with enhanced wellbeing, both directly and indirectly through a range of mental health and wellbeing indicators (Dawson et al., 2020; Gu et al., 2015; Vonderlin et al., 2020). This relationship between mindfulness and wellbeing has become so established as to lead researchers to search for explanatory mechanisms to account for the effect. Klussman et al. (2020), for example, found evidence that self-connection mediated the effects of mindfulness on wellbeing, that is, 'being aware of your values, goals, beliefs, and attitudes, and acting in a way that is consistent with those internal states' (p. 3). In this respect, the self of individualism is not so much diminished as altered, integrated, or transformed through mindfulness.

Clinical studies of mindfulness have focused significantly on its impact on depression, a clinical manifestation of malaise. In this respect, it is not just a generalized malaise that is reduced but biological preconditions and relapse susceptibilities to the far more pernicious condition of clinical depression. For example, in their meta-analysis of MBSR and MBCT, Gu et al. (2015) found largescale reported improvements in psychological functioning and wellbeing that were mediated by reduced rumination and worry, key symptoms of depression and anxiety. Farb et al. (2012) used neuroimaging data to identify underlying neural mechanisms, notably those related to present-moment awareness as a being mode, in lieu of cognitive evaluative processes associated with the prefrontal cortices of the doing mode. Collins and Segal (2020) concluded from these studies that: 'Favouring non-conceptual sensory pathways over habitual cognitive reappraisal responses to negative stimuli seems to lead to an emotional regulation characterized by lessened negative self-evaluation, increased distress tolerance and greater self-compassion and empathy' (p.15). In this respect, mindfulness seems to be more effective than cognitive reappraisal strategies, that is, thinking through the malaise.

## INSTRUMENTAL REASON

The second of Taylor's (1991) three sources of modernity's malaise is the *instrumental reason*. Instrumental reason refers to the use of reason as a means to realize unspecified, including unethical, ends, leading to what Taylor refers to as 'the eclipse of ends.' Maura (2013) contrasts instrumental with other forms of practical reason: '[I]instrumental reason ...focuses on effective means to an end and not ...on improving living conditions, promoting reasonable agreement, or human understanding. It has traditionally meant domination, manipulation of nature and social relations.' Instrumental reason has three features that are distinctively modern: First, the narrowing and restrictive identification of reason as the superior function and expression of the human intellect, mind, or character; second, the logical rationalization of all structures and organizations within social institutions, bureaucracies, and civic relationships; and, third, instrumentalism, that is, using reason to assess value on the bases of utility and efficiency, often through positivistic scientific inquiry.

Reason came to define modernity through the European Enlightenment period. Kant (1784/1996) famously reflected this in his essay, What is Enlightenment? 'Enlightenment is mankind's exit from self-incurred immaturity. *Immaturity* is the inability to make use of one's own understanding without the guidance of another' (p.58). Kant articulated here a significant shift in values from traditional authoritarian collectives to individuals and their ability to reason autonomously. A few months earlier, Mendelssohn (1784/1996) argued in the same journal that enlightenment, culture, and education must 'go forward in step' to avoid what he called corruption (p. 56). For Mendelssohn, Enlightenment was a theoretical and rational project associated with Enlightenment epistemologies, which became identified with the scientific inquiry over time. Culture was the practices arising from the collective habits of the people. Education brought the two together. In this way, education became interpreted as a critical public institution involved in the enlightenment of the people.

Secular-scientific mindfulness has adapted to accommodate the modern, rational, bureaucratized institutions of the European Enlightenment and the professions that serve them: doctors, nurses, and other clinicians in healthcare; teachers and college professors; and scientists investigating human cognition and behaviour. Indeed, secular-scientific mindfulness manifests some features of modern instrumental reasoning: a strong emphasis on specifying and demonstrating utility with scientific evidence; applying mindfulness to clinical or educational problems; and excising all but the most rational elements of traditional Buddhist perspectives. Meanwhile, controlled scientific studies continue to generate evidence of its utility in the treatment of evermore pathologies and health outcomes. In the process, the strong instrumental rational orientation of secular-scientific mindfulness has rendered it culturally congruent with modern cultural life, giving mindfulness cultural currency, legitimacy, and recognition within institutions that took shape during the modern period: education, health care, social services, for example, and workplace education.

Yet, on deeper analysis, mindfulness explicitly trains practitioners to regulate attention away from discursive thought, including reasoning, towards more non-conceptual sensory and decentred experiential awareness. This self-regulation of attention away from thought towards sensation is associated with enhanced wellbeing. Accordingly, through attention regulation, mindfulness practice or training shifts our reliance on thought as a mediator for experience to focus instead on the direct perceptual experience itself. Indeed, it is this feature of attention regulation through mindfulness that is used, at least in part, to explain its efficacy in reducing depression symptoms (Watkins, 2015). Likewise, in their review of studies of the use of mindfulness in the treatment of depression, Collins and Segal (2020) found two other non-cognitively oriented abilities cultivated through mindfulness that helped to explain its efficacy: Decentering, through reduced identification with, and storytelling about, experience, and compassion (Collins & Segal, 2020).

Participants learn these skills as part of the standardized delivery of mindfulness programmes, whereby participants are systematically guided to restrict reporting to concrete, observed experiences during post-meditative inquiry and only subsequently to use reason to reflect and generalize rationally about those experiences and their implications for wellbeing. In the process, teachers and participants alike learn to discern by observing, describing, and reasoning and to engage each faculty more intentionally. This standardized inquiry process that progresses stage-wise from experiential practices to concrete descriptions to more abstract, conceptual inquiry is designed to scaffold practitioners to learn to engage faculties of mind more intentionally in the service of wellbeing. Indeed, in its secular-scientific variant, mindfulness is explicitly defined as being in the present, free of judgement, which can be interpreted as both evaluative and instrumental reasoning. Many mindfulness practitioners, in turn, report feeling re-enchanted with the world through this more direct awareness of internal and external experience. As Williams (2021), co-founder of the clinical MBCT programme, suggests, in 'contrast to intellectual assent,' mindfulness offers 'a focus on a different sort of knowing, *a direct, embodied knowing.*'

## SECULARISM

Much is made of the use of the term 'secular' to describe this emerging form of mindfulness, so it is important to understand the term. For Taylor (2007), secularism contributed to the malaise of modernity. In defining it, he emphasized the sense of time buried etymologically in the word *secular*:

> 'Secular', as we all know, comes from 'saeculum', a century or age. ....People who are in the saeculum are embedded in ordinary time, they are living the life of ordinary time; as against those who have turned away from this in order to live closer to eternity. The word is thus used for ordinary as against higher time. A parallel distinction is temporal/spiritual. One is concerned with things in ordinary time, the other with the affairs of eternity.
>
> *(p. 54–55)*

Using a more empirical v. philosophical lens, Norris and Inglehart (2004) proposed an alternative thesis of secularization as changes in existential security rather than as changes in the experience of time. Supported by largescale international survey data, they concluded that the degree of secularism of a country correlated positively with the degree of human development and security and varied with its dominant historical religion. The relationship between development and secularism appeared to be reciprocal, with each supporting the other. Through this lens, secularism was framed differently, as a kind of natural change accompanying increased existential security. This theory included suppositions that less developed states depended on more authoritarian and patriarchal institutions like the family and church to provide social and existential securities. With development, these provisions shifted to the state, thereby allowing more autonomy and less dependence on authoritarian institutions. In the following subsections, we consider each perspective of secularism in the question of the relationship of mindfulness to spirituality and to social development.

### *Mindfulness and Spirituality*

Conventionally, secularism is imputed in opposition to the sacred or religious. So, with respect to Taylor's (2007) definition, while proximity to eternity may explain the appeal of religion and the sacred, the secular seems cast as parochial, mundane, and concrete. Yet, theologically, the opposite of the sacred as eternity and transcendence is not the mundane but *immanence*, that is, the sense of presence or meaning derived from sensory experience and the present-time of the world. Immanence in religion, for example, is about seeking God in nature, in the eyes of others, and in the sensed practical engagement with the world. In the case of secular-scientific mindfulness, the removal of the more religious, supernatural, and seemingly remote transcendental spiritual claims of Buddhism may seem to have severed the transcendent promise of mindfulness. Yet, it would be wrong to claim that mindfulness is not *spiritual* insofar as it trains people instead to find meaning through the encounter with the immanence of life. So, while secular-scientific mindfulness is secular as it is intended for delivery in secular institutions and contexts, it is also spiritual insofar as it offers a valid pathway for people to fulfill spiritual desires for meaning, to savour sensory experience, and to enhance their sense of belonging in the community of life.

Intentionally altering the experience of time is deeply embedded in the practice of mindfulness. Participants are explicitly trained to move from the past or future to attend to the present. In this sense, the shift to ordinary time is explicit, reminding us again how much mindfulness is a prototypical modern practice. We attend to the present in the experience of the body scanned while at rest; in the inbreath and outbreath; in the experience of eating a single raisin, slowly and with attention; or simply in the most ordinary and habitual activities of everyday life. The reports of participants after these experiences often include surprise at the ability of ordinary objects to generate so much interest and, in some cases, even extraordinary experiences and insights. Also common are reports of changes in the experience of time, which studies have found can involve expansions or contractions in perceived durations during mindfulness (Droit-Volet et al., 2019; Kramer et al., 2013; Tonnes & Wittmann, 2016). In this respect, the experience of time in secular mindfulness may not be as ordinary as the theory of secularism suggests.

As a construct, *spirituality* is differentiated from religion in mental health research and literature, often as faith in 'something' in contrast to religion as a more organized social phenomenon involving orthodox or shared beliefs, rituals, and observances (Forrester-Jones et al., 2018). Many scholars define spirituality as a sense of existential connectedness to something religious or non-religious beyond the personal (Koslander et al., 2020; McClintock et al., 2019; Naor & Mayseless, 2019). In their empirical study of inpatient mental health patients, Koslander et al. linked spiritual experiences to the *existential*, that is, to experiences concerning life and death. They found evidence of spirituality in three types of phenomena: a) perceptual: perceiving an extra-mundane presence; b) interpretive: making sense of reality; and c) social or normative: struggling for acceptance. They describe these as 'near life experiences' to emphasize their existential quality rather than feeling tone, which were both positive (hope, connection, meaning, coherence) and negative (doubt, anxiety, loneliness, or hopelessness.)

Research into secular-scientific mindfulness offers evidence that many participants do experience enhanced spirituality through mindfulness training. For example, Carmody et al. (2008) found changes in both state and trait mindfulness associated with increases in spirituality in a pre-/post- study of MBSR participants, with associated improvements in psychological and medical symptoms. Shapiro et al. (1998) found medical students who participated in an eight-week programme modelled after the MBSR programme experienced enhanced spirituality and empathy alongside reductions in anxiety and depression. Greeson et al. (2015) researched 322 adult participants of community MBSR and found significant reductions in depressive symptoms that were uniquely explained by changes in both spirituality (daily spiritual experiences) and mindfulness. This finding is relevant additionally insofar as spirituality itself is linked to improved stress resilience and mental health, as evidenced in a review with preliminary neuroimaging proof-of-concept conducted by McClintock et al. (2019).

A contradictory finding appeared recently in Lima et al. (2020) in a study of 128 Portuguese patients with mild Alzheimer's disease. The researchers hypothesized positive relationships between mindfulness, spirituality, and quality of life; however, what they found instead was that spirituality was negatively associated with both mindfulness and quality of life. In other words, higher levels of 'spirituality' were associated with lower levels of trait mindfulness and quality of life. The problem with this study was it conflated spirituality with religiosity, insofar as participants were from an elderly Portuguese population that included many Roman Catholics with beliefs in the afterlife. The authors speculated that it could have been the future orientation of spirituality [*sic*] that interfered with the present-moment orientation of mindfulness, and that this loss of present-moment orientation interfered with quality of life. Yet, it is not spirituality so much as religiosity that fosters a future-orientation through doctrines associated with death, after-life, and the existence of other realms such as heaven, etc. What is helpful about this study is that it demonstrated the value of secularization in diminishing such future-oriented views.

Although mindfulness is more associated spiritual immanence, it does include elements of transcendence. For example, through the seemingly mundane act of following the breath we can encounter the primordial will supporting our own existence, whether named as the autonomic nervous system or God. They share the experience of a volition beyond our conscious effort and will that acts to sustain our life. This can be experienced as compassionate as well. Through such a close encounter with the breath, we can connect to a vastness beyond our individual will and existence, to experience or deepen the sense of connection with nature, existence, even God, while experiencing the awe and wonder that naturally ensue from such connections. In this way, as one of the most immanent – and intimate – of experiences that is readily accessible in each and any moment – the breath – invites us to experience transcendence. Echoing a similar view, Williams (2021), co-architect of MBCT (Segal, Williams, & Teasdale, 2002), reflected on how mindfulness can enhance the sense of the presence of God for those who seek it:

> It is striking that a mainstream form of an ancient spiritual practice may liberate us from the habits of mind that make us strangers to ourselves and can create deep emotional distress. Many are now seeing that mindfulness practice may also be an important part of what is needed to dissolve some of the barriers that get in the way of sensing the presence of God.
>
> *(p. 84)*

### *Mindfulness, Secularism, and Social Development*

Harkening back to Inglehart and Norris' (2005) reinterpretation of secularism as enhanced existential security, we might ask what this implies for mindfulness. What was critical in the findings of this global values survey was that wellbeing increased with development and secularism. The findings helped to elevate wellbeing as an economic and social indicator of progress to replace the prior, rather crude, use of GDP. For example, the 38-member OECD (Organization for Economic Co-operation and Development) (2009) developed a framework with 11 criteria to measure the wellbeing of a people, including subjective wellbeing. This linked practices to improve subjective wellbeing like mindfulness to collective goals to augment the wellbeing of people globally. In this respect, the secularization of mindfulness has made it available for this important global project to improve access to wellbeing. As a process to enhance wellbeing through agency and autonomy, mindfulness should be considered to complement rather than replace structural changes aimed at improving wellbeing through social and economic development.

## FREEDOM AND CHOICE

Taylor's (1991) final factor giving rise to the malaise of modernity was the loss of freedom that accompanied modern transformations. The cause of this loss of freedom, according to Taylor, was increased conformity and the narrowing of choice. This narrowing of choice can be seen in the shift to secular-scientific mindfulness, including the use of standardized programmes like MBSR and MBCT, which vary little with one another in curriculum or delivery. At the same time, the standardized structure has also enabled a more reliable base of evidence to amass based on the consistency of the format. Still, the very fact that there is a standardized programme is a modern feature, as are the narrow focus on mindfulness and evidence-based practices that eliminate or marginalize a range of possible meditative alternatives and choices: Visualizations, mind training, analytical meditations, ethics, and some aspects of the cultivation and practices of compassion are examples.

Yet, paradoxically, this apparent loss of freedom and choice in curriculum and teaching also enhances freedom and choice in what is actually taught and learned. The explicit purposes of mindfulness training is to support practitioners to learn to recover more quickly from reactivity; to distance more readily from difficult or challenging situations; and to respond to challenges with more agency and choice. In this respect, mindfulness could accurately be called a practice of freedom. Furthermore, the programmes are largely successful in realizing these purposes, with participants demonstrating enhanced executive control and reduced emotional reactivity in controlled studies (Casedas et al., 2020; Gu et al., 2015). So, too, mindfulness teachers are trained to use invitational language and behaviours when teaching to foster participants' sense of freedom, choice, and agency. Finally, empirical studies of motivation confirm that mindfulness significantly expands autonomy, a trait associated with enhanced freedom and choice in self-determination theory (SDT). In their systematic review and meta-analysis of 89 studies of mindfulness and its relationships to SDT motivational orientations, Donald et al. (2020) found strong evidence in both intervention and correlation studies that mindfulness predicts more autonomous forms of motivation, and in correlation studies, evidence of less controlled motivation and amotivation.

In conclusion, we would suggest that secular-scientific mindfulness has emerged by accommodating modernity while simultaneously subverting it so as to reduce or correct its deadening, disempowering effects, which Taylor described as malaise. In this respect, secular-scientific mindfulness and MBTL are more *post*modern than modern. Like the postmodern, it embeds important correctives or critiques of modernity while still using them to resist or subvert its debilitating restrictions and impacts. In this respect, secular-scientific mindfulness may well prove to enact in time the 'uncovering of buried goods through re-articulation' as Taylor (1989) himself hoped for on concluding Sources of the Self. And so we conclude with the same passage he used to finish his critical work on modernity.

> The kind of study I have embarked on here can be a work, we might say, of liberation. The intuition which inspired it, which I have recurred to, is simply that we tend in our culture to stifle the spirit.... The intention of this work, [therefore], was one of retrieval, an attempt to uncover buried goods through re-articulation – and thereby to make these sources again empower, to bring the air back again into the half-collapsed lungs of the spirit.
>
> *(p. 520)*

## REFERENCES

Anālayo, B. (2020). The myth of McMindfulness. *Mindfulness, 11*, 472–479. https://doi.org/10.1007/s12671-019-01264-x.

Berila, B. (2015). *Integrating mindfulness in anti-oppressive pedagogy: Social justice in higher education.* Routledge.

Brown, C. G. (2014). Mindfulness: Stealth Buddhism strategy for mainstreaming Buddhism? The Blog. *Huffington Post*, December 2. https://www.huffpost.com/entry/mindfulness-stealth-buddh_b_6243036.

Brown, K. W., & Ryan, R., (2003). The benefits of being present: Mindfulness and its role in psychological well-being. *Journal of Personality and Social Psychology, 84*(4), 822–848.

Carmody, J., Reed, G., Kristeller, J., & Merriam, P. (2008). Mindfulness, spirituality, and health-related symptoms. *Journal of Psychosomatic Research, 64*, 393–403.

Casedas, L., Pirruccio, V., Vadilla, M., & Lupianez, J. (2020). Does mindfulness meditation training enhance executive control? A systematic review and meta-analysis of randomized controlled trials in adults. *Mindfulness, 11*, 411–424. https://doi.org/10.1007/s12671-019-01279-4.

Collins, E., & Segal, Z. (2020). Therapeutic mindfulness and depression. In M. Trivedi (Ed.), *Depression* (pp. 357–371). Oxford University Press.

Dawson, A., Brown, W., Anderson, J., Datta, B., Donald, J., Hong, K., Allan, S., Mole, T., Jones, P., & Galante, J. (2020). Mindfulness-based interventions for university students; A systematic review and meta-analysis of randomised controlled trials. *Health and Wellbeing, 12*(2), 384–410. https://doi.org/10.1111/aphw.12188.

Deci, E., Ryan, R., Schultz, P., & Niemiec, C. (2015). Being aware and functioning fully: Mindfulness and interest taking within self-determination theory. In K. Brown, D. Creswell, & R. Ryan (Eds.), *Handbook of mindfulness: Theory, research, and practice* (pp. 112–129). The Guilford Press.

Donald, J., Bradshaw, E., Ryan, R., Basarkod, G., Ciarrochi, J., Duineveld, J., Guo, J., & Sahdra, B. (2020). Mindfulness and its association with varied types of motivation: A systematic review of meta-analysis using self-determination theory. *Personality and Social Psychology Bulletin, 46*(7), 1121–1138. https://doi.org/10.1177/0146167219896136.

Droit-Volet, S., Chaulet, M., Dutheil, F., & Dambrun, M. (2019). Mindfulness meditation, time judgment and time experience: Importance of the time scale considered (seconds or minutes). *PLoS ONE, 14*(10), e0223567. https://doi.org/10.1371/journal.pone.0223567.

Farb, N. (2014). From retreat center to clinic to boardroom? Perils and promises of the modern mindfulness movement. *Religions, 5*, 1062–0186. http://doi:10.3390/rel5041062.

Farb, N., Anderson, A., & Segal, Z. (2012). The mindful brain and emotion regulation. *Canadian Journal of Psychiatry, 57*(2), 70–77. https://doi.org/10.1177/070674371205700203.

Farb, N., Segal, Z. V., Mayberg, H., Bean, J., McKeon, D., Fatima, Z., & Anderson, A. (2007). Attending to the present: Mindfulness meditation reveals distinct neural modes of self-reference. *Social Cognitive and Affective Neuroscience, 2*, 313–322. https://doi.org/10.1093/scan/nsm030.

Forrester-Jones, R., Dietzfelbinger, L., Stedman, D., & Richmond, P. (2018). Including the 'spiritual' within mental health care in the UK, from the experiences of people with mental health problems. *Journal of Religion and Health, 57*, 384–407. https://doi.org/10.1007/s10943-017-0502-1.

Greeson, J., Smoski, M., Suarez, E., Brantley, J. Ekblad, A., Lynch, T., & Wolever, R. Q. (2015). Decreased symptoms of depression after mindfulness-based stress reduction: Potential effects of religiosity, spirituality, trait mindfulness, sex and age. *The Journal of Alternative and Complementary Medicine, 21*(3), 166–174. https://doi.org/10.1089/acm.2014.0285.

Gu, J., Strauss, C., Bond, R., & Cavanagh, K. (2015). How do mindfulness-based cognitive therapy and mindfulness-based stress reduction improve mental health and wellbeing? A systematic review and meta-analysis of meditation studies. *Clinical Psychology Review, 37*, 1–12. https://doi.org/10.1016/j.cpr.2015.01.006..

Healthlink BC. (2020). *Mindfulness-based stress reduction.* https://www.healthlinkbc.ca/health-topics/abl0293.

Kant, I. (1784/1996). An answer to the question: What is enlightenment? In J. Schmidt (Ed.), *What is enlightenment? Eighteenth-century answers and twentieth-century questions* (pp. 58–64). University of California Press.

Klussman, K., Curtin, N., Langer, J., & Nichols, A. L. (2020). Examining the effect of mindfulness on well-being: Self-connection as a mediator. *Journal of Pacific Rim Psychology, 14*(e5), 1–7. https://doi.org/10.1017/prp.2019.29.

Koslander, T., Ronning, S., Magnusson, S., & Gustin, L. W. (2020). A 'near-life experience:' Lived experiences of spirituality from the perspective of people who have been subject to inpatient psychiatric care. *Scandinavian Journal of Caring Sciences.* Advance online publication. https://doi.org/10.1111/scs.12863.

Kramer, R., Weger, U., & Sharma, D. (2013). The effect of mindfulness meditation on time perception. *Consciousness and Cognition, 22*, 846–852. https://doi.org/10.1016/j.concog.2013.05.008.

Lima, S., Garrett, C., Machado, J., Vilaca, M., & Pereira, G. (2020). Quality of life in patients with mild Alzheimer disease: The mediator role of mindfulness and spirituality. *Aging and Mental Health, 24*(12), 2103–2110. https://doi.org/10.1080/13607863.2019.1650891.

Lynch, T., Lazarus, S., & Cheavens, J. (2015). Mindfulness interventions for undercontrolled and overcontrolled disorders: From self-control to self-regulation. In K. Brown, D. Creswell, & R. Ryan. (Eds.), *Handbook of mindfulness: Theory, research, and practice* (pp. 329–347). The Guilford Press.

MacPherson, S. (2005). Negotiating language contact and identity change in a bilingual Tibetan/English program. *TESOL Quarterly, 39*(4), 585–607. https://doi.org/10.2307/3588523.

MacPherson, S. (2011). *Education and sustainability: Learning across the diapora, Indigenous, and minority divide.* Routledge.

MacPherson, S. (2019). "A nun is not a woman:" Contesting gender in a Himalayan global contact zone. In M. Saudelli, J. Kusch, & S. Carroll (Eds.), *Voices from faraway lands: From divergent to convergent* (pp. 143–164). Cambridge Scholars Press.

Maura E. (2013). Instrumental reason. In A. L. C. Runehov & L. Oviedo (Eds.), *Encyclopedia of sciences and religions.* Springer. https://doi.org/10.1007/978-1-4020-8265-8_200937.

McClintock, C., Worhunsky, P., Balodis, I., Sinha, R., Miller, L., & Potenza, M. (2019). How spirituality may mitigate against stress and related mental disorders: A review and preliminary neurobiological evidence. *Current Behavioral Neuroscience Report, 6*, 253–262. https://doi.org/10.1007/s40473-019-00195-0.

Mendelssohn, M. (1784/1996). On the questions: What is enlightenment? In J. Schmidt (Ed.), *What is enlightenment? Eighteenth-century answers and twentieth-century questions* (pp. 53–57). University of California Press.

Munjee, R., & MacPherson, S. (unpublished). Mindfulness and compassion approaches for race-based trauma: A trauma-informed, anti-oppressive framework.

Naor, L., & Mayseless, O. (2019). The therapeutic value of experiencing spirituality in nature. *Spirituality in Clinical Practice, 7*(2), 114–133.

Neale, M. (2011). *McMindfulness and frozen yoga: Rediscovering the essential teachings of ethics and wisdom.* https://static1.squarespace.com/static/5a8e29ffcd39c3de866b5e14/t/5b5303d91ae6cf630b641909/1532167130908/McMindfulness.pdf.

Norris, P., & Inglehart, R. (2004). *Sacred and secular: Religion and politics worldwide.* Cambridge University Press.

OECD (Organization for Economic Cooperation and Development). (2009). *Measuring well-being and progress: Well-being research.* https://www.oecd.org/wise/measuring-well-being-and-progress.htm.

Pillay, K., & Eagle, G. (2019). The case for mindfulness interventions for traumatic stress in high violence, low resource settings. *Current Psychology, 40*, 2400–2414. https://doi.org/10.1007/s12144-019-00177-1

Purser, R. (2018). Critical perspectiveson corporate mindfulness. *Journal of Management, Spirituality, and Religion, 15*(2), 105–102. https://doi.org/10.1080/14766086.2018.1438038.

Purser, R., & Loy, D. (2013). Beyond *McMindfulness. Huffington Post,* July 1. https://www.huffpost.com/entry/beyond-mcmindfulness_b_3519289.

Rogers, R. (2006). From cultural exchange to transculturation: A review and reconceptualization of cultural appropriation. *Communication Theory, 16*, 474–503. https://doi.org/10.1111/j.1468-2885.2006.00277.x.

Ryan, D., & Deci, E. (2017). *Self-determination theory: Basic psychological needs in motivation, development, and wellness.* The Guilford Press.

Segal, Z., Williams, M., & Teasdale, J. (2002). *Mindfulness-based cognitive therapy for depression: A new approach to preventing relapse.* Guilford Press.

Shapiro, S., Schwartz, G., & Bonner, G. (1998). Effects of mindfulness-based stress reduction on medical and premedical students. *Journal of Behavioral Medicine, 21*(6), 581–599. https://doi.org/10.1023/A:1018700829825.

Taylor, C. (1989). *Sources of the self: The making of the modern identity.* Harvard University Press.

Taylor, C. (1991). *The malaise of modernity.* House of Anansi Press Ltd.

Taylor, C. (2007). *A secular age.* Belknap Press of Harvard University Press.

Vonderlin, R., Biermann, M., Bohus, M., & Lyssenko, L. (2020). Mindfulness-based programs in the workplace: A meta-analysis of randomized controlled trials. *Mindfulness, 11*, 1579–1598. https://doi.org/10.1007/s12671-020-01328-3.

Watkins, E. (2015). Mindfulness in the context of processing mode theory. In K. W. Brown, J. D. Creswell, & R. M. Ryan (Eds.), *Handbook of mindfulness: Theory, research, and practice* (pp. 90–111). The Guilford Press.

Williams, M. (2021). Mindfulness, secular spirituality, and the psychology of religious knowing. In R. R. Manning (Ed.), *Mutual enrichment between psychology and theology* (pp. 73–84). Routledge.

Yellow Bird, M. (2013). Chapter 15: Neurodecolonization: Applying mindfulness research to decolonizing social work. In J. Coates, T Hetherington, & M. Gray (Eds.), *Decolonizing social work* (p. 18). Routledge.

# CHAPTER 3

# WHAT HAPPENED

## The Mainstreaming of Mindfulness

Mainstreaming is the process whereby the marginal, special, or different becomes normalized and integrated within the ordinary activities, practices, or discourse of an institution or society. Initially exoticized as an ancient hermetic Asian practice and, later, as a symbol of the counter-culture movement of the 1960s and 1970s, mindfulness has made its way since into the heart of the modern mainstream. In this chapter, we consider the concrete historical events and trends that marked milestones in this mainstreaming of mindfulness, ultimately leading to its acceptance within key secular institutions and professions.

## THE 1960s AND 1970s: COUNTER-CULTURE AND TRANSCENDENTAL MEDITATION

The mainstreaming of mindfulness was seeded in the youth counter-culture(s) of the 1960s. This may seem ironic given that counter-cultures are defined as reactions against mainstream values and norms. Yet, perhaps the pattern reflects a natural historical dialectic given the 1960s counter-culture became normative for a generation. Reacting against the post-war consumer culture of their upbringing, youth in North America, Europe, and beyond found their discontent intensified by serious social justice crises in civil rights, sexual and gender equality rights, and the Viet Nam war, notably after the US draft. As an unprecedented proportion of the population, this youthful post-war generation came of age together in the midst of these crises, learning to collaborate in resistance and dissent, whether on college campuses, at rock concerts, in protests, or in the ravages of war, and all in a time of prosperity.

Yet, such social challenges were unlikely to have fuelled a radical counter-culture on their own were it not for the expanding use of psychedelic medicines, which enacted in individual experience and consciousness what soon became manifest in society: Conflicts in values and perception, radical change, and rebellion. Pollan (2018) described psychedelics as a transformative correction to modernity, as we argued about mindfulness itself last chapter:

> One of the gifts of psychedelics is the way they reanimate the world, as if they were distributing the blessings of consciousness more widely and evenly over the landscape, in the process breaking the human monopoly on subjectivity that we moderns take as a given.
>
> *(p. 413)*

Pollan chronicled the troubling history of psychedelics from their legitimate mainstream clinical and experimental use in the 1950s and early 1960s to their popularization and eventual criminalization as illicit substances. At the same time, they created a distinctive generational response, as columnist Herb Caen famously summarized: "Turn on, tune out, drop out" (p. 204).

With the curiosity triggered by psychedelics and other counter-culture phenomena, a keen interest developed in this generation for alternative ways of knowing and being in the world. For example, after being fired from Harvard, LSD researcher and professor Richard Alpert transformed into yoga practitioner Ram Dass to author the 1971 counter-culture classic, *Be Here Now*. This interest in cultural alternatives to modernity drove many young people

DOI: 10.4324/9781003182467-5

to travel to places like India or Nepal in search of encounters with masters and oral teachings in yoga or Buddhism. Many of these pilgrims were celebrities like The Beatles or Mia Farrow, while others became leaders of the high-tech hyper-modern aftermath of the counter-culture, like Apple co-founder Steve Jobs. In 1974, having heeded the dictum to "drop out" of university, Jobs travelled to northern India to roam around barefoot in search of enlightenment while experimenting with psychedelics. Indeed, although he found enlightenment elusive, he reread the *Autobiography of a Yogi* every year for the remainder of his life (Isaacson, 2011).

Given their scepticism of conspicuous consumption, members of the counterculture flaunted signs and symbols of poverty, like Steve Jobs' shoeless feet, his communal lifestyle, and sustenance-level living during his pilgrimage period and even his modest lifestyle after amassing considerable wealth at Apple. Yet, this appearance of modesty or non-material values belied the fact that the counter-culture was enabled by the very prosperity and affluence of America during that time. In Steve Jobs' case, for example, his India trip was financed by a lucrative job at Atari, to which he returned. Jon Kabat-Zinn, like many cultural icons that emerged from the 1960s, had attended graduate studies at MIT, a leading Ivy League university. During his time at MIT, he founded the Cambridge Zen Centre that catered to prosperous local elites attending or employed with the many universities in that small New England city. Accordingly, even during these early years, the upper middle-class and White bias of mindfulness was emerging through the class and race divisions of the counter-culture movement itself. Freed from the narrow focus on survival by generous parents with excess money and by a surplus in well-paid jobs, this generation of middle- and upper-middle-class, largely White, youth could afford to "drop out" without bearing the scars that others of different classes, races, or times may have had to endure.

Transcendental Meditation (TM) was one of the pivotal transitional phenomena during this counter-culture period and a precursor of the mindfulness movement. Established by Maharishi Mahesh Yogi, TM was made famous by The Beatles and other celebrities who went to Rishikesh India to do TM retreats in 1968. Unlike other movements exploring traditional knowledge, TM intentionally migrated into the modern mainstream to foreshadow what would happen later with mindfulness, using scientific studies to corroborate its claims of enhancing creative forms of intelligence. What distinguished the two was that TM maintained a very traditional, non-modern mode of training and leadership (see Textbox 3.1 below).

## TEXTBOX 3.1 EXEMPLAR OR CASE:

### On Learning TM in 1978

While still in high school, I (SM) decided to write a paper on creativity, using my younger 15-year-old sister as a case study. She had started to meditate (TM) and seemed noticeably more creative. Beyond TM's promotional materials, suggesting a link between TM and creative intelligence (e.g., Haynes et al., 1976), I found little corroborating evidence. Nonetheless, convinced by the effect it seemed to be having on my sister, I resolved do the training myself. After waiting a year to act, as my first year of university drew to a close, I gifted myself the $80 for the training.

Arriving at a low-rise apartment building in the suburbs, I was met by a middle-aged woman who ushered me up the stairs to her apartment to a bedroom with a shrine under a picture of Maharishi Mahesh Yogi, the founder of TM. I took a seat on a cushion by an open window as the guide lit a candle and a stick of pungent sandalwood incense, rang a bell, and began to chant. At some point she threw rice on me, instructing me to repeat a mantra, first together and then in silence. She left the room, inviting me to continue for the next 20 minutes.

As the practice subsided, a bird began to sing outside a nearby window. The sound surprised me, so clear and real, as if I were hearing a bird sing for the very first time. The sound seemed to be more inside than outside of me, with a timbre and clarity that made me feel like I had just woken up from a dream, but the dream had been my entire life up to that moment. It left me wondering how it could be that I had lived on the Earth for this long and never heard a bird sing, properly, *really*, in this way. So motivated, I continued TM as a daily practice for the following few years before shifting over to Buddhist and other meditative practices. Yet, even today, 44 years later, the recollection of that bird's song has never left me – a clear reminder of why I keep meditating.

Scientific articles on TM began appearing in the 1970s with results both supporting and countering claims of its physical and psychological benefits. At the same time, scientific studies of Buddhist meditation and mindfulness began to appear, introducing themes that continue to this day. As the decade drew to a close, Walsh (1979) reviewed research on the topic, identifying the following four themes: psychological benefits like wellbeing to psychosomatic support; physiological variables including metabolic effects, autonomic responses, and changes in brain physiology; phenomenological experiences; and interactions between mindfulness and psychotherapy. Articles on the potential role of meditation in psychotherapy were particularly apparent in this early period (Deatherage, 1975; Goleman, 1971, 1976; Smith, 1975). At the same time, the fact that these articles were all published in the *Journal of Transpersonal Psychology* suggests that mindfulness was still viewed as a distinctively esoteric Buddhist practice (Goleman, 1972a, 1972b). By the end of the decade, the first study linking mindfulness to empathy appeared, auguring the emerging interest in emotions (Schuster, 1979).

## THE 1980s AND 1990s: MBSR AND THE MEDICALIZATION OF MINDFULNESS

When Jon Kabat-Zinn established the first mindfulness-based stress reduction (MBSR) programme in 1979 at the University of Massachusetts Medical School, he had one decisive foot in the American counter-culture and one in the mainstream. He was an MIT graduate with a Ph.D. in molecular biology who'd also taught yoga, directed a Zen Centre, and participated in American anti-war activism and Buddhism on campus. Equipped with a research post at the new medical school of the University of Massachusetts and a strong desire to find his "'karmic assignment' on the planet," Kabat-Zinn (1990/2013) first conceived of the MBSR programme during a brief vision on the tenth day of a two-week Insight Meditation Society (IMS) Buddhist silent retreat in the late 1970s. This vision clarified his purpose, as he described it:

> A flood of thoughts following the extended moment filled in the picture. Why not try to make meditation so commonsensical that anyone would be drawn to it? Why not develop

> an American vocabulary that spoke to the heart of the matter, and didn't focus on the cultural aspects of the traditions out of which the dharma emerged...What better place than a hospital to make the dharma available to people in ways that they might understand it and be inspired...to elucidate the nature of suffering and its root causes, as well as provide a practice path to liberation from suffering? All this to be undertaken, of course, without ever mentioning the word 'dharma.'
>
> *(pp. 287–288)*

Physicians at his hospital said they were unable to help a significant number of chronic patients, so he garnered their support for a complementary programme to which they could refer patients who were dissatisfied with current treatments and results. So, during the autumn of 1979, they launched the Stress Reduction and Relaxation Program, the precursor of MBSR, to train people in mindfulness and yoga as a strategy to manage stress and pain, free of the Buddhist or Hindu components from which they derived. At the time, their cause was bolstered by nascent scientific studies suggesting a link between meditation and stress reduction (Goleman & Schwartz, 1976; Carrington et al., 1980). Kabat-Zinn (1982) expanded these findings through his research into mindfulness and pain management, thereby forging the close collaboration between scientific research and secular mindfulness-based interventions (MBIs), as they would come to be known. In this way, he kick-started a movement.

Eventually, MBSR and other MBIs became increasingly accepted in healthcare environments as part of alternative and complementary care, palliative care, psychiatry and psychotherapy, and pain and cancer care. Meanwhile, there was a growing interest and uptake of programmes for physicians. As Epstein (1999) concludes at the time, "As a link between relationship-centred care and evidence-based medicine, mindfulness should be considered a characteristic of good clinical practice" (p. 833). In this respect, there are clear indications that secular-scientific mindfulness had become sufficiently normalized to be mainstreamed within medical contexts by the advent of the millennium.

The same cannot be said of educational contexts, where mindfulness remained a marginal religious or pejoratively "spiritual" or "contemplative" activity. A small breakthrough came with the publication of Langer's (1989, 1997) work on a watered-down concept of mindfulness as openness and choice. She would later describe it as "the simple act of noticing new things" while also advising people not to "worry about meditating" (Radio Boston, 2014). With the 1997 incorporation of the US Center for Contemplative Mind in Society (Bush, 2011), seeds were sown for a network of scholars interested in the integration of mindfulness in higher education; however, these networks remained dominated by Buddhist and religious studies scholars, a few clinical researchers, and practitioners who tended to theorize and speculate on possible futures with only limited inroads into actual practice. Although there were some early studies on workplace education with Carrington et al.'s (1980) study of stress and mindfulness in the workplace and in K-12 education with Kratter and Hogan (1982) study for the US Department of Education on meditation and ADHD, these studies were isolated and did not trickle down to affect practice.

## THE 2000s: MBCT, MENTAL HEALTH, AND THE SCIENTIFIC SNOWBALL

By the advent of the new millennium, secular-scientific mindfulness was poised to enter the mainstream. What led to its acceptance and emerging research base was the mounting evidence of its efficacy in the treatment of depression, especially when combined with cognitive

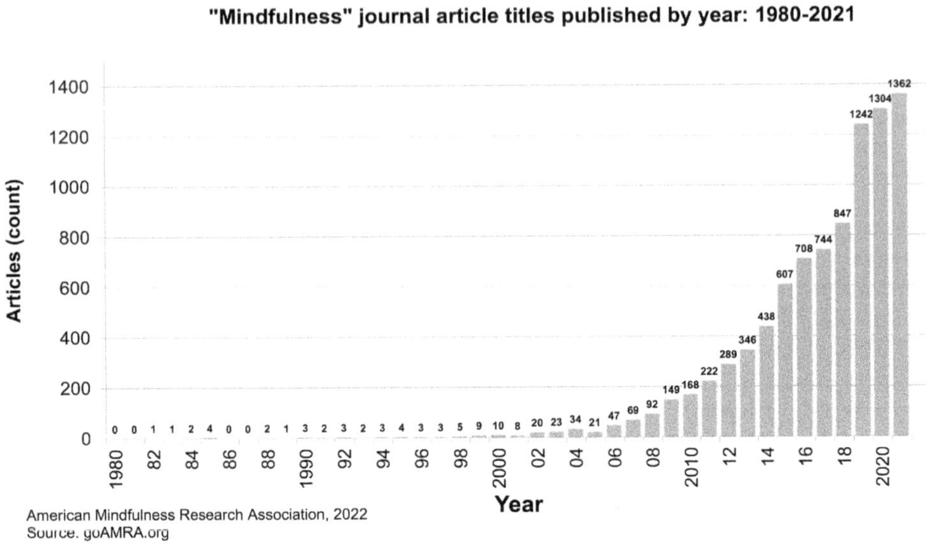


**Figure 3.1** Mindfulness Journal Articles by Year, 1980–2021 (AMRA, 2021)

behavioural therapy. The theory was that people with a history of depression were highly vulnerable to relapse because of their susceptibility to negative rumination, even in the face of only mildly depressed moods (Teasdale et al., 2000). On this premise, Segal, Williams, & Teasdale (2002) developed Mindfulness-Based Cognitive Therapy (MBCT) to integrate aspects of cognitive behavioural therapy (CBT) and mindfulness using the MBSR programme template.

Because the three MBCT developers were career university professors and researchers, the training programme and practice of this MBI were validated extensively early on in their development through scientific theories and research to support the methods and claims of efficacy (Segal et al., 2002). Situated powerfully between practice and research communities at the Universities of Toronto and Oxford, evidence emerged rapidly to establish efficacy and effectiveness and to refine specific mechanisms. They then began to extend systematic research to specific clinical applications (Dimidjian & Segal, 2015). Indeed, for MBCT, this close connection between research and practice was stronger than it had been for MBSR, despite the rich and extensive studies eventually done on MBSR globally. Figure 3.1 depicts the rapid, at times exponential, increase in mindfulness research, rising dramatically after 2005 as MBCT programming began expanding (AMRA, 2021). In this respect, it was its use in preventing depression relapse that drove the scientific investigation of mindfulness. Thereafter, the number of publications began to double every two to four years, moving from 21 in 2005 to 147 by 2010 and accelerating in this pattern to 1362 by 2021. During this same period, MBSR and MBCT programmes were moving from university and college campuses to community-based settings.

## THE 2010s: MINDFULNESS GOES MAINSTREAM IN THE USA, UK, AND CANADA

As more active controls have been added to studies of mindfulness, thereby strengthening the validity of claims of causal relationships between mindfulness and the reduction of depression and improved mental health, researchers have progressed from questions of efficacy to questions of mechanisms and effectiveness within complex natural, rather than clinical, settings. For example, Brown et al. (2015) explored decentering as a meta-mechanism. Also known as "reperceiving," decentering refers to a state of reduced attachment or identification with thoughts and emotions. These researchers hypothesized four mechanisms associated, in turn, with decentering: Cognitive flexibility, values clarification, self-regulation, and exposure, all associated with positive health outcomes. They found all these mechanisms were associated with improved outcomes in the hypothesized positive direction.

Farb et al. (2018) and Segal et al. (2019) found a direct link between decentering and reduced depressive relapse and an indirect link between self-regulation and increased decentering. Furthermore, the decentering continued to strengthen relapse prevention over a two-year period following the MBCT programme for those who continued to practise; however, these effects were equally identified for the mindfulness and cognitive therapy components of the programme, with decentering the key explanatory mechanism, with weaker results for distress tolerance. These are topics that we will revisit, but they are presented to demonstrate how science is directly working with secular programming to investigate mindfulness and to improve or inform mindfulness-based teaching and learning.

Distinctive national trends emerged in the mainstreaming of secular-scientific mindfulness within various countries during this second decade of the new millennium. Replicating the original MBSR model in a range of newly designed MBIs, the field remained straddled across the margins and mainstream. In the US, unlike the UK, mindfulness teacher training programmes were established outside of the formal, for-credit programming of higher education. The differences between the for-credit and non-credit branches of higher education are numerous and vast, not the least of which is that continuing studies or extension programmes work on for-profit models. The uptake in healthcare, education, and the workplace or corporate sector was significant enough to refer to it as mainstreaming, but it resisted full institutional uptake in many contexts like higher education. In the US, most major mindfulness teacher training programmes remain in non-credit branches of institutions.

US Congressman Tim Ryan (2012), a Democrat from Ohio, did succeed in mapping out a political and public agenda for mindfulness in a book entitled *A Mindful Nation*. This model proposes the use of mindfulness in a number of key public sectors, including with children and teachers in schools, in healthcare, with the military and first responders, and in the economy. He formed an NGO in 2013 to launch this agenda called the Mindful Nation Foundation (2015). Though promising, it fell short of mainstreaming mindfulness within the political or public sector. One indication of this was that the book was published and promoted in New Age circles and remained associated with just one politician rather than with his party or with an all-party committee as happened in the UK. This pattern of uptake may well be reflective of the underlying political culture of the USA, which has a weaker public sector, tends to favour private sector initiatives, and has some public scepticism of science and secularism.

In the United Kingdom, the trajectory of mindfulness began to diverge increasingly from that of the US during this period. MBCT was closely associated with Oxford University and the University of Toronto in Canada, so this programme began to grow quickly alongside the associated MBCT teacher education programming in these places. Also, graduate for-credit programmes began to appear in the UK, where professional certifications and credentialed degrees are now offered at four leading universities.[1] In contrast, in the USA, only two, small for-credit credentialed programmes[2] were operating by the end of the decade, all of the rest were in Extension or Continuing Studies. Furthermore, the UK had a much more formal uptake of mindfulness in the public sector, particularly in education and healthcare, bolstered in part by the fact that these responsibilities are administered centrally in London rather than in a federal system with mixed responsibilities as in the USA. Also, in the UK, there is more public tolerance and expectations for government involvement in such enterprises.

This public uptake of mindfulness was given a significant boost in the UK by the *Mindful Nation, UK* initiative, which appears to have drawn inspiration from US Congressman Tim Ryan. The difference was that in the UK, a UK Mindfulness All-Party Parliamentary Group took the lead rather than an individual politician, with members who comprised some or all of the 100 or more parliamentarians who actually completed mindfulness training. The Mindfulness Initiative (2015), as it was called, collected data and heard testimonies across the country for a year, including at eight hearings in the British Parliament, before tabling their report in October 2015. The evidence-based report recommends the uptake of mindfulness in three public sectors in the UK – education, healthcare, and corrections – and in the workplace. It recognizes as well that most of the research is new and emerging and some are only weak as yet, so it recommends significantly more research on the topic. Given the centralization of key government responsibilities in the UK, including both healthcare and prescription drugs, there is a strong interest in policy and research of economic analyses of the cost-effectiveness of mindfulness-related interventions, for example, which have begun to generate promising data (Duarte et al., 2019). Likewise, in K-12 education, the Government of the UK (2019) initiated a pilot programme in mindfulness in 370 schools with associated research, reflecting the immense boost to access and equity that mainstreaming within public institutions can garner (more on this study in Chapter 7).

Canada lands somewhere between the US and UK developmental trajectories for the mainstreaming and uptake of mindfulness. The first MBCT teacher training was developed and offered in the early 2000s in Toronto by Zindel Segal, co-founder of MBCT. The city continued to be a hub for MBCT training through Social Work and Continuing Studies at the University of Toronto and now, more commonly, through the Centre for Mindfulness Studies. Until recently, most Canadian MBSR teachers trained in the USA at the now-disbanded non-credit teacher training programme at UMass, where MBSR was first established by Jon Kabat-Zinn. This reinforced the US pattern being replicated in Canada, whereby private mindfulness teachers hung out shingles to offer classes in the community, university extension programmes, or in clinical-related businesses. Yet, because Canada has more in common with the UK than the US with respect to public sector institutional supports, Canada has the potential to expand mainstreamed secular-scientific mindfulness into education, healthcare, and other public institutions to improve equity in, and access to, mindfulness programmes. Indeed, already for many years in Canada there has been growing uptake of MBSR/MBCT/MBCP/MBRP in hospital outpatient programmes, now paid for under the public healthcare insurance system in Ontario. Also, there is an emerging pan-national Canadian mindfulness teachers' network emerging through the increasing numbers of multi-disciplinary mindfulness teachers certifying as trainers through the Centre for Mindfulness Studies in Toronto and the associated for-credit graduate MBTL programme at the University of the Fraser Valley in BC, where, in both cases, the authors met and collaborated.

## THE 2020s: MINDFULNESS-BASED TEACHING AND LEARNING

In this way, the mainstreaming of mindfulness in modern developed states like the US, Canada, and the UK is now well underway. The trends supporting this mainstreaming process include: a) expanding research and improved research standards; b) the adoption of mindfulness programming in the public sector; and, c) the development of mindfulness teacher networks within and across major professions and institutions. The critical next step for this coming decade is to generate a body of evidence-based practices to effectively deliver mindfulness in a range of high-stakes institutions. This is the mandate of the emerging field of Mindfulness-Based Teaching and Learning (MBTL).

## NOTES

1 Bangor University, Aberdeen University, Coventry University, and the University of Oxford (though offered through Continuing Studies, it leads to what is called a Master of Studies from Oxford.)
2 The private Lesley University offers graduate certificate and degree and Antioch in New England a graduate certificate.

## REFERENCES

AMRA (American Mindfulness Research Association). (2021). *"Mindfulness" journal articles published by year (1980–2021).* https://goamra.org/Library.

Brown, D. B., Bravo, A., Roos, C., & Pearson, M. (2015). Five facets of mindfulness and psychological health: Evaluation a psychological model of the mechanisms of mindfulness. *Mindfulness*, *6*(5), 1021–1032. https://doi.org/10.1007/s12671-014-0349-4.

Bush, M. (2011). Mindfulness in higher education. *Contemporary Buddhism*, *12*(1), 183–197. https://doi.org/10.1080/14639947.2011.564838.

Carrington, P., Collings, G., Benson, H., Robinson, H., Wood, L., Lehrer, P., Woolfolk, R., & Cole, J. (1980). The use of meditation–relaxation techniques for the management of stress in a working population. *Journal of Occupational Medicine*, *22*(4), 221–231.

Deatherage, G. (1975). The clinical use of 'mindfulness' meditation techniques in short-term psychotherapy. *Journal of Transpersonal Psychology*, *7*(2), 133–143.

Dimidjian, S., & Segal, Z. (2015). Prospects for a clinical science of mindfulness intervention. *American Psychologist*, *70*(7), 593–620. https://doi.org/10.1037/a0039589.

Duarte, R., Lloyd, A., Kotas, E., Andronis, L., & White, R. (2019) Are acceptance and mindfulness-based interventions "value for money"? Evidence from a systematic literature review. *British Journal of Clinical Psychology*, *58*, 187–210. https://doi.org/10.1111/bjc.12208.

Epstein, R. (1999). Mindful practice. *JAMA*, *282*(9), 833–839. https://doi.org/10.1001/jama.282.9.833.

Farb, N., Anderson, A. Ravindran, A., Hawling, L., Irving, J., Mancuso, E., Gulamani, T., Williams, G., Ferguson, A., & Segal, Z. (2018). Prevention of relapse/recurrence in major depressive disorder with either mindfulness-based cognitive therapy or cognitive therapy. *Journal of Consulting and Clinical Psychology*, *86*(2), 200–204. https://doi.org/10.1037/ccp0000266.

Goleman, D. (1971). Meditation as meta-therapy: Hypotheses toward a proposed fifth state of consciousness. *Journal of Transpersonal Psychology*, *3*(1), 1–26.

Goleman, D. (1972a). The Buddha on meditation and states of consciousness. Part I: The teachings. *Journal of Transpersonal Psychology*, *4*(1), 1–44.
Goleman, D. (1972b). The Buddha on meditation and states of consciousness. Part II: A typology of meditation techniques. *Journal of Transpersonal Psychology*, *4*(2), 151–210.
Goleman, D. (1976). Meditation and consciousness: An Asian approach to mental health. *American Journal of Psychotherapy*, *30*(1), 41–54.
Goleman, D. J., & Schwartz, G. E. (1976). Meditation as an intervention in stress reactivity. *Journal of Consulting and Clinical Psychology*, *44*(3), 456–466.
Government of the UK. (2019). *One of the largest mental health trials launches in schools.* https://www.themindfulnessinitiative.org/mindful-nation-report.
Haynes, C., Hebert, R., Reber, W., & Orme-Johnson, D. (1976). The psychophysiology of advanced participants in the transcendental meditation program: Correlations of EEG coherence, creativity, H-reflect recover, and experience of transcendental consciousness. *Scientific Research on the Transcendental Meditation Program: Collected Papers, Vol. 1, Paper 21*, pp. 208–212.
Isaacson, W. (2011). *Steve Jobs.* Simon & Schuster.
Kabat-Zinn, J. (1982). An outpatient program in behavioral medicine for chronic pain patients based on the practice of mindfulness meditation: Theoretical considerations and preliminary results. *General Hospital Psychiatry*, *4*(1), 33–47. https://doi.org/10.1016/0163-8343(82)90026-3.
Kabat-Zinn, J. (1990/2013). *Full catastrophe living: Using the wisdom of your body and mind to face stress, pain, and illness.* Bantam.
Kabat-Zinn, J. (2011). Some reflections on the origins of MBSR, skillful means, the trouble with maps. *Contemporary Buddhism*, *12*(1), 281–306. https://doi.org/10.1080/14639947.2011.564844.
Kabat-Zinn, J., Lipworth, L., & Burney, R. (1985). The clinical use of mindfulness meditation for the self-regulation of chronic pain. *Journal of Behavioral Medicine*, *8*(2), 163–190. https://doi.org/10.1007/BF00845519.
Kratter, J., & Hogan, J. D. (1982). *The use of meditation in the treatment of attention deficit disorder with hyperactivity.* U.S. Department of Education, National Institute of Education, pp. 1–30.
Langer, E. (1989). *Mindfulness.* Addison Wesley.
Langer, E. (1997). *The power of mindful learning.* Addison-Wesley.
Mindful Nation Foundation. (2015). https://mindfulnationnetwork.com/about/.
Mindfulness Initiative. (2015). *Mindful nation, UK report.* https://www.themindfulnessinitiative.org/mindful-nation-report.
Pollan, M. (2018). *How to change your mind: What the new science of psychedelics teaches us about consciousness, dying, addiction, depression, and transcendence.* Penguin.
Radio Boston. (2014). 9 ways to be more mindful from the 'Mother of Mindfulness,' Ellen Langer. WBUR. Accessed on Nov. 21, 2022 at: https://www.wbur.org/radioboston/2014/10/15/mindfulness-langer
Ryan, T. (2012). *A mindful nation: How a simple practice can help us reduce stress, improve performance, and recapture the American spirit.* Hay House.
Schuster, R. (1979). Empathy and mindfulness. *Journal of Humanistic Psychology*, *19*(1), 71–77.
Segal, Z., Anderson, A., Gulamani, T., Williams, L. D., Desormeau, P., Ferguson, A., Walsh, K., & Farb, N. (2019). Practice of therapy acquired regulatory skills and depressive relapse/recurrence prophylaxis following cognitive therapy or mindfulness-based cognitive therapy. *Journal of Consulting and Clinical Psychology*, *87*(2), 161–170. https://doi.org/10.1037/ccp0000351.
Segal, Z., Teasdale, J., Williams, J., & Gemar, M. (2002). The mindfulness-based cognitive therapy adherence scale: Interrater reliability, adherence to protocol and treatment

distinctiveness. *Clinical Psychology and Psychotherapy*, *9*, 131–138. https://doi.org/10.1002/cpp.320.
Smith, J. C. (1975). Meditation as psychotherapy: A review of the literature. *Psychological Bulletin*, *82*(4), 558–564. https://doi.org/10.1037/h0076888.
Teasdale, J., Segal, Z., Williams, J. M., Ridgeway, V., Soulsby, J., & Lau, M. (2000). Prevention of relapse/recurrence in major depression by mindfulness-based cognitive therapy. *Journal of Consulting and Clinical Psychology*, *68*, 615–623. https://doi.org/10.1037/0022-006X.68.4.615.
Walsh, R. N. (1979). Meditation research: An introduction and review. *Journal of Transpersonal Psychology*, *11*(2), 161–174.

# SECTION II

# Contexts

## Where We Teach: MBTL in Institutional Contexts

This section outlines histories and issues as mindfulness and MBTL became mainstreamed, adopted, and/or integrated within key secular institutions and professions. The sequence reflects the order in which various institutions took up formal mindfulness and MBTL programming. In Chapter 4, we consider where it all began, that is, community-based and continuing education programs. Then, in Chapter 5, we consider clinical and medical contexts and the significant impact these have had in legitimizing mindfulness as a method to promote health and wellbeing. Chapter 6 considers the trajectory of mindfulness as it became adopted in higher education as an instance of contemplative practice or on its own. From there, in Chapter 7, we consider the topic of mindfulness in pre-K-12 education, where mindfulness arrived as part of the broader social-emotional learning agenda in schools. From that topic, in Chapter 8, we consider the use of mindfulness in the workplace.

Each chapter covers four topics: Defining the context; outlining research within that context; presenting critiques and critical issues; and identifying emerging trends, promising or concerning. Throughout, we try to present the distinctive characteristics of each context or sector while identifying ways in which it overlaps with other delivery models or sectors covered in other chapters. These porous borders are important to defining the integrated field of MBTL in the midst of its diversity and complexity.

DOI: 10.4324/9781003182467-6

# CHAPTER 4

# COMMUNITY AND CONTINUING EDUCATION

## Beyond Institutional Constraints

We begin this section on Where We Teach with the original context where it all began: The community. The Buddha's first discourse on suffering and the path, that included the notion of right mindfulness, was not delivered in a temple, monastery, or university, nor during a formal meditative retreat, but rather in a community in Deer Park, Sarnath, around 500 BCE. The students, furthermore, were community members, five former companions of the Buddha.

In contemporary research contexts, MacQueen et al. (2001) defined "community" in participatory public health partnerships as "a group of people with diverse characteristics who are linked by social ties, share common perspectives, and engage in joint action in geographical locations or settings" (p. 1929). They found that the five most commonly agreed features were shared physical location, shared perspective, joint action, social ties, and diversity, in descending order of frequency. While it is common to try to cultivate a community of practice within a mindfulness class, this chapter considers the situatedness of the course itself within a broader community from which students are drawn. Worth emphasizing is the notable absence of an external, often hierarchical and administrative, institution or organization mediating access to participation.

## DEFINING THE CONTEXT

Like its origins in India, mindfulness education began as community education in Europe and North America in the 20th century. Indeed, the initial template for these community-based programmes came from traditional Buddhist teachers who taught mindfulness and other forms of meditation in these new contexts quite independently of centralized religious or educational institutions and hierarchies. Local students interested in meditation would self-organize in the community and invite a teacher to visit or serve as a resident teacher or, alternatively, just teach and support one another. Some of these initiatives were tied to specific schools of Buddhism and others, like the UK Buddhist Society founded in 1924, were non-sectarian and open to many schools and teachers. As mindfulness shifted to secular-scientific practices, this prior community-based model continued to evolve, with autonomous and largely informal local, rather than formal religious or institutional, accountability structures.

### Informal and Non-Formal Community Education

The concept of formality is critical to understand the dynamics of the mainstreaming and eventual professionalization and institutionalization of mindfulness and MBTL in the West. There are three common terms used to differentiate educational formality: Informal, non-formal, and formal. These distinctions are based on the degree of structure of the learning; teaching and learning requirements; the systematicity of assessment; and the level of institutional recognition, principally in the form of credits but also credentials. Community education is usually either informal, learning without any specific, structured

DOI: 10.4324/9781003182467-7

programme, or non-formal, learning in a structured course without systematic assessments or earned credits.

For example, informal community-based mindfulness opportunity with education could be a weekly drop-in guided mindfulness session, whereby those who attend learn implicitly by doing or participating without many expectations or outcomes beyond that. Non-formal community education refers to more structured non-credit programmes that can be characterized as having a fixed beginning and end; a curriculum or sequence of sessions or tasks expected of participants; and often involving an active role for a teacher or facilitator in structuring learning. That said, unlike formal learning, the assessment and outcomes are often ill- or un-defined, less explicit, and inconsistently implemented, which prevent them from providing recognized and transferable credits or even credentials in most cases. Mindfulness-based programmes (MBPs) like MBSR, MBCT, MSC, or CCT are all examples of programmes often conducted as non-formal community education. Other examples can be found in agencies specializing in community-based education, like a seven-week online non-formal mindfulness programme developed and delivered by the YMCA in British Columbia, Canada: *Teen Y Mind.*

## Continuing Education

Although housed in higher education or K-12 institutional contexts, continuing education programmes are designed to interface with the community, thereby offering a facsimile to community-based education. Also referred to as continuing studies or extension programmes, they function outside of the usual credit granting and exchange structures of higher education. The entrance requirements are more open or unspecified and the final credentials are less recognized than in the for-credit system, though this is changing with new trends in credit recognition and transfer. Continuing education programmes tend not to receive public funds, even when located in public institutions, and rely instead on for-profit or cost-recovery models. Also, they exercise more flexibility in hiring and in setting tuition fees and the terms for instructor contracts. Only rarely are their instructors unionized or included as members of faculty associations. Administrators also have more discretion in programming and in the quality assurance and accountability systems these programmes are subjected to. However, in the case of continuing education for regulated professions, the guidelines and standards of professional organizations that recognize the courses can indirectly exert considerable pressure or influence. Therefore, continuing education programmes can enjoy enhanced autonomy and flexibility from their home institutions' controls but with less recognition and status.

These features made continuing education a key site early on for the delivery of mindfulness education. Being free to respond to community and professional needs and demands rather than to the sometimes rigid standards and inherited contents of academic disciplines, mindfulness courses in continuing education sites benefitted from some degree of intellectual legitimation and networks within educational institutions while remaining free of some of their constraints. The founding programme of MBSR was technically a clinic at the UMass Memorial Medical Centre, which makes it more of a medical than a continuing education programme, though in fact its status was ambiguous and not clearly clinical, given that it was created by a non-clinician. In addition, at this time, there was no formal training programme, and those interested in learning MBSR came to the clinic to apprentice with those teaching in it. Yet, in many other cases, universities that engaged in significant research and development in the field of mindfulness established associated teaching programmes through their continuing studies branches. This is particularly notable in the development of MBCT, where the University of Toronto and the University of Oxford both developed significant MBCT programming with teacher training initiatives associated with Continuing Education branches, though in the case of the University of Toronto, this specific program was created by the non-profit Centre for Mindfulness Studies and was originally located within the Factor-Inwentash School of Social Work, alongside numerous other mindfulness courses and workshops. Other examples of higher educational institutions that situated mindfulness programmes and teacher training in non-formal or less formal continuing education contexts in the US are at Brown University, UCLA, and UC-San Diego. Indeed, this is a prevalent model and location still for the delivery of MBTL professional training and credentials in the USA.

## Instructor Qualifications

Within both community and continuing education contexts, instructors and faculty can vary widely as these programmes are freer of hiring constraints found in more institutionalized settings. Therefore, the background of instructors can be diverse. One common type of community mindfulness teacher, for example, is a yoga teacher who extends their certification and credentials to include non-clinical (usually) mindfulness teaching and learning. At the other end of the spectrum are physicians, nurse practitioners, and other medical professionals not usually engaged in teaching except within their disciplines. In continuing education programmes, professors or faculty from the institution may teach a mindfulness course outside of their usual departments and areas, so their disciplines can vary widely. In some instances, traditional Buddhists or Buddhist scholars are hired to teach mindfulness. In the case of adult MBPs like MBSR or MBCT or other standardized mindfulness programmes, specific credentials are expected of teachers by convention in the field rather than by regulation. In the case of MBCT, however, it is regulated in some jurisdictions like Ontario, Canada, as a controlled clinical act.

## Continuing Professional Development

A special case of community and continuing education is professional development education, sometimes referred to as continuing professional development (CPD). This form of education derives from the expectation that professionals participate actively in ongoing training and lifelong professional learning to keep apprised of changes in research, practices, and the field. The location of such learning varies widely from highly formal education in higher education to informal, self-directed, self-organized learning. In many instances, given the strong role of professional associations, CPD is often community-based in that it often transpires outside the workplace or formal education at conferences or in communities of practice that are not workplace-specific.

Furthermore, CPD is often initiated and organized by the professionals themselves, even if paid for or accounted for as part of a professional expense or activity. One common pathway, for example, would be the case of someone attending a plenary or workshop session on mindfulness at a conference or training event, perhaps with a focus on applications within a particular profession or professional practice. Following this, participants might opt to pursue more in-depth training, such as MBSR courses in the community, individually as self-direct learning, or with others through professional networks, for example. What follows is one example of a community-based centre for mindfulness-based teaching and learning in Toronto – the Centre for Mindfulness Studies – which offers the full range of non-formal, community and continuing education and continuing professional development (see Textbox 4.1).

## TEXTBOX 4.1 EXEMPLAR OR CASE:

### The Centre for Mindfulness Studies: a community organization

Tita Angangco, a retired public servant and volunteer activist for those experiencing homelessness, and Patricia Rockman, one of the authors, and a physician with a focused practice in mental health and mindfulness, launched The Centre for Mindfulness Studies, in Toronto, in 2011. They both have an interest in mental health and recognized the challenges endemic to the marginalized. They were also aware of a lack of professional mindfulness training programmes in Canada.

They created an organization that would directly serve both the public and professionals and it had a number of aims. One was to provide mindfulness to the community, particularly those with affordability and access issues, suffering from mental health problems, insecure housing, and other concerns that increase marginalization. The second was to offer group MBPs to the public as a social enterprise. The third was to develop continuing education and professional development programmes, and certification in MBCT, MBSR, and other workshops on related topics. This undertaking has had its challenges due to a lack of resources, but also benefits, consisting of the ability to create programmes free from much of the bureaucracy of healthcare facilities and universities.

The professional development programmes have received accreditation from the College of Family Physicians of Canada. To date, the Centre has served approximately 17,000 people and 250 social service organizations. Approximately 1500 people have attended training workshops. This year (2021) marks its tenth anniversary.

## RESEARCH

Research reveals key demographics and communities that continue to benefit from access to community-based and continuing education mindfulness programmes. We review some of these groups, including: The elderly; non-clinical populations; professionals; parents; and BIPOC communities. Each case points to benefits and opportunities when mindfulness and MBTL are located in communities.

### Geriatric Populations and Programmes

Hazlett-Stevens et al. (2019) conducted a qualitative review of seven randomized controlled studies of elderly participants over 65 exposed to eight-week MBSR or MBCT programmes. Three of the studies were from a large community sample investigation and three others from community-based elderly participants recruited through clinical referrals. The remaining MBCT study was the only one from a group care facility. The results across the studies found that MBSR enhanced participants' mindfulness, executive functioning, and positive emotions, with significant improvements in affect and sleep quality and in reducing symptoms associated with chronic insomnia and chronic lower back pain. For clinically diagnosed participating elders, facing depression and cognitive decline, benefits extended to significant reductions in worry, anxiety, and depression and improved cognitive functioning, while MBCT was found to reduce geriatric anxiety and improved mindfulness and quality of life. Although one study was conducted with Chinese elders, all others used disproportionately White participants, from 70% to as high as 98% in one of the largest studies. Also, some of the controls were passive waitlist controls rather than active controls who received an alternative treatment. Nonetheless, these findings suggest that community-dwelling elders, who are less likely to access mindfulness through formal medical or institutional pathways, can benefit from mindfulness in improved quality of life, health, and wellbeing through community access.

## Non-Clinical Populations and Programmes

Likewise, the general non-clinical – healthy, undiagnosed, or anti-psychiatry – populations who do not pursue or meet the criteria for medical or psychiatric diagnoses or treatment stand to benefit from enhanced access to mindfulness through community programmes. Such "non-medicalized" community programmes that have a focus on wellbeing may be more acceptable to these groups. Querstret et al. (2020) conducted a systematic review and meta-analysis of the impact of mindfulness, via eight-week MBSR and MBCT programmes, on psychological health and wellbeing for non-clinical populations. By restricting the studies to non-clinical samples, the researchers offered indirect evidence as well of the effectiveness of community-based or continuing education on health and wellbeing. The review included controlled and uncontrolled studies with a range of control conditions, with 4733 participants across 49 studies, 25 of which were based on randomized controlled trials. There were 28 MBSR studies and 11 MBCT studies. Furthermore, the studies included a wide geographical and cultural range by including research in North America, Europe, and Asia.

The results indicated that both of these MBPs – MBSR and MBCT – promoted health and wellbeing for general populations through reductions in symptoms of anxiety, depression, rumination/worry, and stress/psychological distress. They also improved quality of life/wellbeing, mindfulness, and facets of mindfulness (i.e., observing, describing, acting with awareness, non-judging, non-reacting). Furthermore, reductions in anxiety and depressive symptoms and improvements in overall mindfulness measures were greater for MBCT than for MBSR, with possible effects from the cognitive behavioural components of MBCT. The researchers also found that adapted programmes of shorter duration or lower intensity reduced effect sizes, suggesting that programme fidelity and/or teacher training in curricular decision-making may impact programme outcomes. The results of this meta-analysis demonstrated that non-clinical populations experienced significant mental health benefits from mindfulness when delivered through MBPs, in this case, MBSR and MBCT, and that *as* non-clinical populations, their access to MBPs would most likely come through community or continuing education. As Querstret et al. (2020) concluded:

> MBPs are associated with benefits to health and well-being as well as increased levels of mindfulness. These findings add to the growing evidence-base suggesting that MBSR and MBCT may be effective approaches for sub-clinical levels of mental ill-health and could form part of the public mental health agenda.
>
> *(p. 408)*

## Professional Populations and Programmes

Professionals are another key group served by community-based and continuing education mindfulness training programmes, given their training can impact the health and wellbeing of clients and, hence, the general public. For example, Klatt et al. (2017) studied a range of 286 healthcare professionals (HCPs) who participated in a brief one-hour mindfulness session during various conferences. In the on-site survey, over 75% indicated that they had been asked about mindfulness practices by clients, while over 90% expressed a need for additional mindfulness education. In a follow-up survey three months later with 62 respondents and a 21% response rate, 58% indicated that they had used mindfulness personally, 48% indicated that they had pursued more information about mindfulness, and 28% indicated that they had used mindfulness techniques professionally. This study points to professionals' demand for mindfulness, the potential impacts such exposures have on their personal and professional practices, and the pathways they commonly follow in learning and applying mindfulness. Community or continuing education sites serve their pathways in various ways beyond formal studies in higher education or as part of workplace education. They can channel information and interest when offered as part of formal CPE conferences, as in this case, and provide access to further studies in MBPs through community-based and continuing education offerings.

## Parenting and BIPOC Populations

Community education in mindfulness can have impacts beyond health that affect familial and community wellbeing. For marginalized communities, such as Black, Indigenous, and People of Colour (BIPOC) communities that may not have access otherwise to mindfulness training, community-based programmes can provide MBTL education to entire communities to address outcomes beyond mere personal wellbeing. For example, Burns et al. (2019) used a mindfulness-based, trauma-informed parenting intervention to nurture parenting skills in adults and resilience in children in a Latino community in the US. Sustained over five years, this university research and community partnership resulted in a sustainable community-led parenting programme supported by an experienced local community workforce. This form of participatory research was designed to support key community members to develop mindfulness skills that they in turn transmitted as teachers or facilitators to the community. Other non-profit organizations such as Mindfulness Without Borders (Canada), The Centre for Mindfulness Studies (Canada), Yoga4Change (United States), and Friendly Care (Philippines) to name a few, are engaged in community-based programmes targeted at diverse populations with affordability and access issues. Some of these organizations are increasing the representation of mindfulness teachers from diverse communities but many barriers persist, including socio-economic, educational, and lack of cultural relevancy.

Parental mindfulness training is another area of interest both from a research and implementation perspective. In a meta-analysis of 25 studies of the impact of such training on families, Burgdorf et al. (2019) found significant evidence of reductions in parental stress *alongside* improved youth outcomes. In this way, community-based mindfulness provides opportunities for mindfulness education to address nested levels of impacts on individual, familial, and community wellbeing.

## CRITICAL ISSUES AND CRITIQUES

There are a few challenges and issues presented by the teaching and learning of mindfulness in the community and continuing education contexts.

### Lack of Continuing Networks of Care

Perhaps ironically given the reference to community, one of the shortcomings is the individual orientation of most of these programmes and their lack of follow-up support or communities of practice following training. While there are special pilot programmes directed at community development like the Latino community project studied by Burns et al. (2019) described above, in most cases the community programmes just mean that they are autonomous from institutions. That autonomy is itself a strength or opportunity but also a challenge in that it distances the programme from having a direct impact on the quality of institutional life in a community, and instead reinterprets mindfulness as something aimed at personal development. Furthermore, the selection of communities and community sites such as yoga studios or even community centres within those communities have tended to privilege and encourage the participation of White females, as indicated in the Hazlett-Stevens et al. (2019) study of elders in the community. The fees, being for-profit or cost-recovery, are often set too high for people of lower socio-economic backgrounds to participate, so this can discourage teachers from offering classes in lower socio-economic communities or in accommodating these participants.

Edwards et al. (2014) analyzed some key challenges facing the implementation of MBSR in the community and identified five key areas of concern: Managing participants' expectations; supporting participants' daily practice; accommodating participants with physical limitations; accommodating participants with psychiatric conditions; and managing group dynamics. In groups where participants have high needs and serious mental health conditions, developing group guidelines on an ongoing basis may become central. In fact, these issues are common to all programmes wherever they are delivered; however, what aggravates these challenges in community delivery contexts is the relative isolation of the programme from institutional resources like medical or counselling referral processes as found in both clinical and higher educational delivery. Likewise, these teachers can be quite isolated from networks of support from other teachers or communities of practice to assist in collaborative problem-solving and reflective practice. This can be problematic when there is no oversight either from an institution or governing body in terms of quality assurance and maintaining competency.

### Quality and Recognition of MBTL-Based CPD/CPE

While continuing studies contexts in higher education offer enhanced flexibility, access, and ease of delivery, the overreliance on such sites exerts a certain toll on the quality and development of mindfulness and MBTL education. Some of these challenges include the reduced priority, prestige, and legitimacy they have as non-credit or extra-curricular programmes or credentials, which can impact both their professional recognition, scope of practice, ability to deliver what they have learned, and their transferability within higher stakes professional academic programmes. Whether for continuing professional development/education (CPD/CPE) or to train mindfulness teachers and professionals, there is a persistent overreliance in North America on non-credit education without transfer pathways to formal academic credentials.

A related issue is the separation between research and practice that ensues when the academic branch where research is conducted is separated from a non-academic teaching and practice branch in the same university. Such separation of research and practice across academic and non-academic boundaries tends to reinforce the message that the practice is less important or involves less skill. Serious as well are the reduced compensation and incentives for instructors in continuing education as compared to those in academic programmes; the absence of many of the accountability or standardization structures and practices that formal academic programmes are subjected to, which are developed and applied to improve quality; and the less formal or rigorous use of key teaching and learning tools like formal assessments and constructive alignment (between outcomes, activities, and assessments).

## TRENDS: PROMISING AND CONCERNING

### Serving Oppressed and Traumatized Communities

One promising trend in the community-based delivery of mindfulness is its potential role in community and social development with underserved, under-resourced, and traumatized populations. For example, Pillay and Eagle (2019) propose the use of mindfulness training with traumatized communities in South Africa, including both clinical and non-clinical populations, as a way to address the "individually intensive and socially extensive impact" of psychological trauma associated with high levels of violence and limited professional resources (p. 1). They postulate that such trauma is continuous rather than *post* given the ongoing and realistic assessments of threat and restricted mobility arising in impoverished and refugee communities. The authors conclude that mindfulness offers a promising way for communities and individuals suffering from continuous trauma exposure to recover from trauma and mitigate its ongoing effects. They point to three sources of evidence in making this claim: a) its evidence-based effectiveness as an intervention for trauma-related responses, including those arising from violence; b) its role in neuroplasticity; and c) the building of resilience in community members unable to remove themselves from exposures to chronic violence and threat. Finally, and significantly, they point to the low-resource demand required to learn and apply mindfulness, which can be done without technologies or expensive professional staffing and resources.

## Access to, and Recognition of, MBTL

In the USA, many of the continuing education programmes are associated with elite universities like Brown, UCLA, or UC-San Diego that charge premium rates in their extension branches with few if any tuition release rates in recognition of need or merit. This has served to reinforce mindfulness and mindfulness teaching as a White, middle-class, or even upper middle-class enterprise. Furthermore, some of these programmes promote less professionally rigorous standards, disregarding or only weakly applying competency frameworks, assessments, accountability structures, and standards for the delivery of mindfulness training and teacher training than might be the case within for-credit academic contexts. These tendencies can serve to reinforce mistaken impressions that mindfulness is a para-professional rather than a professional evidence-based practice.

## Prior Learning Assessment and Recognition (PLAR) of Informal and Non-Formal MBTL

One way to enhance recognition of these community programmes is through PLAR, another trend in higher education that offers promise to the community-based or continuing education delivery of mindfulness programming and teacher training (MacPherson et al., 2019). The spectrum of PLAR ranges from recognizing various informal or non-formal learning through prior learning assessments (PLA) for credits within formal institutions through to establishing formal transfer agreements between community-based programmes and programmes in higher education. An example of this kind of arrangement is a transfer agreement the authors negotiated between the community-based Centre for Mindfulness Studies teacher-training intensives and practicums in MBSR and MBCT and the academic graduate certificate in MBTL at the University of the Fraser Valley. This enabled students in UFV's graduate programme to pursue MBSR- or MBCT-specific certification as part of their academic programme. To ensure reasonable alignment across the institutions to legitimate the transfer recognition, the Centre's courses have come to include more research and assessment, while UFV has become more practice-oriented.

## Digital "Communities"

MacQueen et al. (2001) reported that 77% of respondents to their public health survey identified "geographical locatedness" as a central feature of community in public health collaborations. With the recent increase in the creation of digital "communities" for the delivery of mindfulness during the pandemic, this aspect of "geographical locatedness" in what defines a community has been eroded. Yet, as challenging as the shift to online formats may have been, usually using synchronous platforms like Zoom, unexpected benefits and opportunities also became apparent. For example, the potential pool of participants expanded dramatically with the loss of previous geographic constraints. People living in more remote locations found they had access. And some people found the ability to practise and learn in the safety and comfort of home helpful. In this way, digital communities are becoming the norm.

## REFERENCES

Burgdorf, V., Szabo, M., & Abbott, M. (2019). The effect of mindfulness interventions for parents on parenting stress and youth psychological outcomes: A systematic review and meta-analysis. *Frontiers in Psychology, 10*, Article 1336 [27 Pages]. https://doi.org/10.3389/fpsyg.2019.01336.

Burns, B., Merritt, J., Chyu, L., & Gil, R. (2019). The implementation of mindfulness-based, trauma-informed parent education in an underserved Latino community: The emergence of a community workforce. *American Journal of Community Psychology, 63*(3–4), 338–354. https://doi.org/10.1002/ajcp.12342.

Edwards, A., Evans, S., Aldao, A., Haglin, D., & Ferrando, S. (2014). Implementing a mindfulness-based stress reduction program in the community: Lessons learned and suggestions for the future. *The Behavior Therapist, 37*(1), 13–17.

Hazlett-Stevens, H., Singer, J., & Chong, A. (2019). Mindfulness-based stress reduction and mindfulness-based cognitive therapy with older adults: A qualitative review of randomized controlled outcome research. *Clinical Gerontologist, 42*(4), 347–358. https://doi.org/10.1080/07317115.2018.1518282.

Klatt, M., Weinhold, K., Taylor, C., Zuber, K., & Sieck, C. (2017). A pragmatic introduction of mindfulness in a continuing education setting: Exploring personal experience, bridging to professional practice. *EXPLORE, 13*(5), 327–332. https://doi.org/10.1016/j.explore.2017.06.003.

MacPherson, S., Abram, K., Brophey, A., & Mauger, D. (2019). Aligning, recognizing, and transferring undergraduate-level adult education competencies. *Canadian Association for the Study of Adult Education (CASAE) Annual Conference Proceedings* (pp. 229–237). Congress of Social Sciences and Humanities, UBC, Vancouver, BC. https://www.dropbox.com/s/04lcxsvmvek8kkh/2019_CASAE_Proceedings.pdf?dl=0.

MacQueen, K., McLellan, E., Metzger, D., Kegeles, S., Strauss, R., Scotti, R., Blanchard, L., & Trotter, R. (2001). What is community? An evidence-based definition for participatory public health. *American Journal of Public Health, 91*(12), 1929–1938.

Pillay, K., & Eagle, G. (2019). The case for mindfulness interventions for traumatic stress in high violence, low resource settings. *Current Psychology, 40*, 2400–2414. https://doi.org/10.1007/s12144-019-00177-1.

Querstret, D., Morison, L., Dickinson, S., Cropley, M., & John, M. (2020). Mindfulness-based stress reduction and mindfulness-based cognitive therapy for psychological health and well-being in non-clinical samples: A systematic review and meta-analysis. *International Journal of Stress Management, 27*(4), 394–411. https://doi.org/10.1037/str0000165.

# CHAPTER 5

# HEALTHCARE

## The Medicalization of Mindfulness

In this chapter, we examine the medicalization of mindfulness and the evidence to support its use in clinical contexts, including critiques of the limitations of medicalizing both mental health and mindfulness. The medicalization of mindfulness is apparent in the explosive expansion of its use in treating a variety of medical and mental health and addiction disorders. There are adaptations of mindfulness for new and evermore discrete conditions, and it has been accepted into a number of national mental health guidelines (e.g. NICE and CANMAT for MBCT). At the same time, synchronous and asynchronous forms of digital delivery have further expanded its accessibility. Mindfulness programmes are provided in or through hospitals, clinics, and community settings; healthcare provider professional training; and continuing professional development. This is happening in many countries, including the United States, Canada, England, most European countries, Mexico, Australia, China, and the Philippines, to name a few. Mindfulness concepts and practices have been introduced to healthcare providers to increase self-compassion, subjective awareness, and reflective capacity; enhance competency; reduce error as well as anxiety and depression; and maintain mental health to cope with work stressors (Epstein, 2003; Kriakous et al., 2021). As Epstein (2020) concluded, mindfulness offers healthcare professionals a way to address "the need for moment-to moment clarity, tolerance of ambiguity, emotional intelligence and ethical awareness – framed by an ability to hold contradictions and inconstancies in information and guidance" (p.197).

The medicalization of mindfulness is integral to its mainstreaming. Therefore, how it has been approached within healthcare contexts is essential to understanding the mainstreaming process. We define medicalization as "the process by which some aspects of human life come to be considered as medical problems, whereas before they were not considered pathological" (Maturo, 2012, p. 123). In the case of mindfulness, medicalization is used to describe how it came to be recontextualized as a treatment for a range of pathologies of the body, mind, moods, and dispositions. Although there are some precedents in early Buddhism of mindfulness being applied to health, such as when the Buddha taught King Pasenadi mindfulness "to know the measure of food" as an antidote to overeating (Analayo, 2020, p. 474), these were the exception rather than the rule. Instead, the dominant motivation for mindfulness was more soteriological: To foster liberation from abject aspects of the human existential condition. These abject conditions were explicitly identified as sickness, old age, and death, which Prince Siddhartha is said to have encountered only in adulthood. This encounter led him to renounce his domestic life, to become a wandering ascetic, and, ultimately, to discover the path of awakening that made him a Buddha. In this chapter, we examine how mindfulness and mindfulness meditation, originally framed as part of a path to liberation within a Buddhist context, moved into modern contexts to become embedded increasingly in medicine and mental healthcare. In the process, mindfulness has been shaped into a treatment modality.

## CONTEXTS

A key driver of the adoption of mindfulness in healthcare settings has been its alignment with new cognitive models of mind and brain:body:mind relations. This alignment gave

DOI: 10.4324/9781003182467-8

healthcare providers a scientifically compatible view to evaluate mindfulness interventions using measurable clinical outcomes such as awareness, intention, attentional control, decentering, and self-regulation, applying these same criteria to their own judgment and decision-making in clinical practice. In this way, mindfulness is promoted in clinical contexts both as a complementary medicine for patients and as a way to improve healthcare and healthcare providers' wellbeing. Healthcare organizations, for example, use mindfulness to assist with the mental health, performance, and productivity of employees. This adoption by healthcare professionals and systems have increased its accessibility and acceptability. Meanwhile, clients and patients learn how to manage their medical conditions and/or mental disorders through a mindfulness lens. As Wilson (2014) concluded, this "recontextualization of mindfulness as a psychological technique intended to provide physical and mental benefits" led to the medicalization of mindfulness as "properly part of the purview of the medical and psychological establishments in the United States, especially as embodied in its most significant representation: Mindfulness-Based Stress Reduction (MBSR)" (p. 76–77).

## Stress and Mindfulness-Based Stress Reduction (MBSR)

With the advent of MBSR in 1979, Jon Kabat-Zinn (1991/2013) helped set the stage for the *medicalization* of mindfulness by introducing it into the healthcare context. This process was further supported by its explicit purpose to assist in managing *stress* (a euphemism for *suffering*) for those chronically ill patients not responding to traditional medical therapies. MBSR was viewed as a transdiagnostic intervention targeting those with chronic pain and other persistent conditions not well addressed by a medical model focused on a cure. MBSR also came to deal increasingly with mental health concerns, and in particular the depression and anxiety associated with these conditions (Kabat-Zinn, 2003). Soon after its development, Kabat-Zinn et al. (1985) attempted to evaluate MBSR formally for mental health symptoms secondary to chronic pain and for primary anxiety disorders (Miller et al., 1995).

Within healthcare, mindfulness was stripped of references to its Buddhist and religious origins, making it a secular and therapeutic group-based modality. This made it palatable and acceptable to the medical and scientific community. At this time, *stress* was also being studied in the then-early field of behavioural medicine, formally recognized in 1977 and now well established (Jiménez & Mills, 2012; Bialkowska et al., 2020). Kabat-Zinn (2003), a molecular biologist, Zen Buddhist, and Vipassana and yoga practitioner with an interest in research, chose to deliver the MBSR programme in a hospital setting. He was, it could be argued, in effect delivering aspects of Buddhist psychology and yoga covertly through the vehicle of the MBSR programme. Delivering mindfulness in this setting lent credibility to the programme, and colleagues began to refer patients. This significant step in the medicalization of mindfulness through MBSR involved three associated trends: The increase of mindfulness in medical research; the formalization of protocols to standardize curricula and associated teacher training; and the limited adoption of mindfulness as a viable medical or healthcare expense. We will take up each of these significant historical developments in more depth.

### *MBSR Research*

One key feature of medicalization is the reliance on evidence-based practice informed by peer-reviewed scientific research. According to the American Mindfulness Research

Association (AMRA) library, one of the earliest peer-reviewed scientific papers on the clinical applications of mindfulness was by Deatherage (1975) on mindfulness in psychotherapy, published in the *Journal of Transpersonal Psychology*, the same journal in which other articles on the topic appeared through the 1970s and 1980s. More mainstream medical research began to appear in the 1980s, beginning with Kabat-Zinn's (1982) paper on the use of MBSR for chronic pain and extending to other studies of its effects on chronic disease and anxiety (Kabat-Zinn et al., 1985, 1986, 1992). By 2021, there were almost 20,000 citations on mindfulness and 1294 specific citations on MBSR in the US National Institute of Health's (NIH) PubMed index. This is one indication of how the scientific enterprise helped to medicalize mindfulness through MBSR, thereby propelling a broader social and institutional acceptance. As a standardized programme, MBSR offered the standardization and control required for experimental medical research. Therefore, it is not surprising that it became a common programme used to research the impact of mindfulness on a range of health issues or needs.

## *MBSR Protocols and Curriculum*

Although ostensibly a standardized programme, in fact MBSR had no published protocol for teachers to rely on during the first decades of its use. Kabat-Zinn's (1990/2013) first published book on the topic, *Full Catastrophe Living*, was neither a research protocol nor a training manual for teachers. Therefore, because the programme was both standardized and copyrighted, those who wished to teach MBSR had to register for an apprenticeship-based MBSR clinic at the University of Massachusetts Memorial Medical Center. This clinic was overseen by non-clinicians, while MBSR was and continues to be delivered by clinicians and non-clinicians alike.

Ultimately, a continuing education certification programme was developed and offered through the Center for Mindfulness in Medicine, Health Care, and Society at the University of Massachusetts Medical School (Woods & Rockman, 2021). Expectations for applicants included having a "deep [personal mindfulness] practice" to become a teacher. The MBSR programme template includes an eight-week format with 2.5-hour weekly sessions in which participants engage in a range of meditation and reflection practices, Hatha yoga, and a silent retreat (McCown, Reibel, & Micozzi, 2010). Explicit protocols and curriculum were not available until 2017, with the *Mindfulness-Based Stress Reduction, Authorized Curriculum Guide* by Santorelli, Meleo-Meyer, & Koerbel, 2017 which stresses the need for both an instrumental (formal curriculum) and a non-instrumental (lived curriculum) guide. MBSR teacher training sites soon expanded beyond these beginnings at the University of Massachusetts.

Today, MBSR is widely accessible and available, perceived to be helpful to anyone, anywhere, well beyond the narrow stress and chronic pain rationales of its origins. In addition to being offered in healthcare settings, it can be found in schools, healthcare organizations, and corporate settings. On the other hand, the longstanding lack of an explicit protocol and broad variety of authorized teachers has led to enormous confusion concerning what MBSR actually is – a protocol, a curriculum, a set of skills, or a way of life. This has also contributed to inconsistent research outcomes and to issues related to who can or should teach and in what context (Woods & Rockman, 2021).

### *Legitimizing MBSR as a Healthcare Expense*

In addition to research and the formalization of the curriculum, the introduction of mindfulness into the healthcare system was bolstered by health insurance companies beginning to reimburse patients for attending the programmes as a viable healthcare *treatment*. Such reimbursement is indicative of its acceptance and an important aspect of the medicalization of mindfulness. In addition, the delivery of programmes in hospitals and the use of MBSR for an increasing scope of health- and mental health-related conditions has supported its further uptake as a viable expense, given it is a secular and scientifically studied modality.

### *Recontextualizing Suffering as Stress*

**Stress**. That Kabat-Zinn identified mindfulness as a corrective to *stress* in particular requires some unpacking. "Stress" is a broad term with many definitions and is not a specifically identified disorder in the *Medical Subject Headings (MeSH)* (National Library of Medicine, 2021). The term stress, however, is associated with other medical conditions, such as a stress fracture or stress incontinence. Nor is it to be found in medical or mental health nosology as a discrete condition, except as stress reaction not elsewhere classified in *The International Classification of Diseases (ICD-10)* or stress reaction not otherwise classified in the *Diagnostic and Statistical Manual (DSM-5)*. The *ICD-10* refers to Acute Stress Reactions as "transient emotional, somatic, cognitive or behavioural symptoms as a result of exposure to an event or situation (either short or long-lasting) of an extremely threatening or horrific nature" (ICD, 2020). The *DSM-5* has a category for Acute Stress Disorder under Trauma- and Stressor-Related Disorders, but both are linked to the potential development of Post-Traumatic Stress Disorder (PTSD) dependent upon the severity and duration of the reaction.

As a health-related concept and theory, stress originated with endocrinologist Hans Seyle's (1956) book, *The Stress of Life*, in which he introduced the term into the medical lexicon to describe the "nonspecific response of the body to any demand" (Tan and Yip, 2018). He described stress as a phenomenological response to illness, for example, resulting in symptoms such as fatigue, anorexia, or weakness. Stress became categorized as either acute or chronic and could be perceived as positive or negative; it was a normal reaction to an internal or external *stressor* to which we attempt to adapt.

**Mindfulness and Coping**. Lazarus and Folkman (1984) developed stress and coping theory. They viewed stress as an interaction between a person and the environment that exceeds their ability to cope. Extreme and/or chronic, stress was and continues to be associated with many diseases (Bialkowska, Juranek, & Wojtkiewicz, 2020). While correlated with many physical and mental disorders, there is no direct causal link between stress and specific illnesses (Salleh, 2008). How stress is defined and utilized in the medical and mental health lexicon and in society is important when considering its relationship to mindfulness. We can see that definitions of stress are myriad and reflect the interaction between humans as complex adaptive systems and the life events they face. MBSR and other MBIs are not concerned with curing a disease but rather with helping people to manage their relationship to, or their distressing encounter with, a particular disorder or life problem. Thus, we can see how stress served as a bridge for mindfulness to cross into medicine as it linked its use from dealing with the suffering of life, through healthy and adaptive coping, to the sick and maladaptive reactions to environmental or internal stressors associated with illness.

While Selye's theories and research initially received support, ultimately stress was viewed as vague and not easily operationalized or measurable. The complexity of stress makes it extremely difficult to establish causation between stress and disease outcomes. Furthermore, because the term is ubiquitous and applied broadly by the lay public, mindfulness, and MBSR in particular, can be interpreted as a panacea, which of course, they are not. Mindfulness is, however, being used in a variety of contexts for many issues beyond what we consider illness. We would suggest that the current interest in the scientific study of mindfulness in healthcare and elsewhere elevate its status as a modality, give it credibility, and provide support for its use in many aspects of society. These areas of use include, but are not limited to, day-to-day concerns or the stress of living associated with work pressures, financial concerns, aging, relationship problems, eating, parenting, and childbirth. We can all relate to the phrase, "I'm so stressed out!" Kabat-Zinn was really interested in applying mindfulness in this way, as a corrective for *distress* arising from any source.

**Stress as Threat**. Recently, the US National Institute of Mental Health (NIMH, n.d.) developed six research domain criteria (RDoC) to assist in correcting previous definitional vagueness associated with stress: "The goal is to understand the nature of mental health and illness in terms of varying degrees of dysfunction in general psychological/biological systems" rather than focusing on diagnostics. The RDoC frameworks align neurodevelopmental with environmental research on both the neural systems and behavioural dimensions of mental disorders associated with a particular construct. The first of the six RDoC domains is *Negative Valence Systems*, in which stress, or more accurately *distress*, is operationalized as *threat*: Acute threat (fear), potential threat (anxiety), and sustained threat associated with exposure to chronic stress. Research is beginning to align research on MBSR and mindfulness in stress reduction to develop models and theories of chronic stress using these constructs. For example, Garland et al. (2017) used the RDoC construct of *sustained threat* to develop an evidence-based model demonstrating how mindfulness appears to correct the negative impacts of chronic stress.

## Depression and Mindfulness-Based Cognitive Therapy (MBCT)

While MBSR initiated the medicalization of mindfulness, the advent of Mindfulness-Based Cognitive Therapy (MBCT) entrenched it, especially within healthcare systems. The rigour of research on MBCT established mindfulness as a viable treatment for mental disorders, beginning with its application for discrete conditions, in particular, depression and the prevention of depressive relapse. In 1991, Zindel Segal, John Teasdale, and Mark Williams, clinician scientists in psychology, began collaborating to develop a maintenance version of Cognitive Behaviour Therapy (CBT). Throughout the decade, they collaborated, first examining the role of decentering in Dialectical Behaviour Therapy (DBT) and then the reduction of depression symptoms in MBSR, in consultation with Kabat-Zinn. Identifying rumination and self-perpetuating modes of mind as key culprits in the vulnerability to relapse, they theorized how attentional training and decentering might help.

Proposing mindfulness-based Attentional Control Training (ACT) (1995) to increase awareness of potential negative moods, they proposed decentering to reduce rumination and CBT to instil problem-solving strategies to deal with negative thoughts and sad moods to prevent depressive relapse. However, they discovered that this approach to combining mindfulness and CBT for prevention was inadequate.

Although ACT combined mindfulness and CBT, they concluded that a different model was required to fully integrate the two methods. This required moving away from a strategy of problem-solving or fixing and toward the development of a different relationship to difficult mind and mood states, one that involved allowing, turning toward, and accepting such difficulties. It also meant that those who delivered the training needed to have a meditation practice. Teasdale et al. (2000) then published the first RCT of MBCT, providing concrete evidence of the efficacy of MBCT in preventing relapse/recurrence in depression as compared to treatment as usual. Segal, Williams, and Teasdale (2002) released the first edition of *Mindfulness-Based Cognitive Therapy for Depression: A New Approach to Preventing Relapse*, explicitly describing the MBCT protocol in a step-by-step manner. Complete with agendas, handouts, and recorded meditations, it provided a comprehensive and standardized means for delivery of the modality. Because it was specifically designed to work with those with depression, its mandate was clear, narrow, and explicit. The publishing of its protocol made it accessible as a treatment regime for clinicians and as a protocol for researchers globally. The clear and measurable outcomes and narrow focus invited a plethora of research studies on its applications in depression and a multitude of adaptations for related purposes and populations.

The impact of depression worldwide is devastating, from its distressing symptoms and association with medical diseases, to years lived with disability and lives lost to suicide. It is estimated that 264 million people worldwide suffer from this condition, with up to 85% of those with middle to low incomes unable to obtain treatment (WHO, 2021). As a leading cause of disability, depression needed a new non-pharmacologic group-based and more accessible intervention to prevent relapse. To date, Segal, Williams, and Teasdale's (2002, 2013) initial book on MBCT has sold approximately 40,000 copies and has been translated into 12 languages (Segal, 2021). The prodigious research and evidence of the outcomes of MBCT and its promise in relieving a disease with suca h high global burden firmly embedded mindfulness in healthcare. Furthermore, MBCT has continued to expand its applications to many other medical, mental health, and addiction conditions. This expansion can be traced through the story of research into MBCT.

In the original randomized controlled trial (RCT) of MBCT, Segal et al. (2000) compared MBCT to treatment as usual (TAU) in the prevention of depressive relapse or recurrence in 145 patients. The study took place over 60 weeks, after which those in the TAU group who had experienced three or more bouts of depression relapsed at a rate of 66%. In contrast, in the MBCT group, the relapse rate was 37%. Other studies confirmed these results. Bondolfi et al. (2010) who found similar outcomes when subjects were allowed to continue anti-depressants (Ma &Teasdale, 2004; Godfrin & van Heeringen, 2010). Kuyken et al. (2015) published a subsequent RCT showing that MBCT used in conjunction with tapering and/or discontinuing anti-depressants was equivalent to anti-depressant maintenance over a 24-month period. This study provided evidence that MBCT could be used as a maintenance treatment to prevent relapse, offering a viable alternative to medication for those who decline or wish to limit psychopharmacological treatment. Since the introduction of MBCT, a multitude of studies with varying degrees of rigour, alongside many reviews and meta-analyses, have investigated the efficacy of MBCT and other MBPs. Some studies have adapted MBSR or MBCT for use in other mental health and health disorders, including bipolar disorder, ADHD, pain, addictions, smoking, schizophrenia, weight/eating, and PTSD. Adaptations have included the setting in which the modality is offered as well as cultural adaptations (Goldberg et al., 2018; Cairncross & Miller, 2016, Michalak, Mander, & Heidenreich, 2020).

## RESEARCH AND RESEARCH PERSPECTIVES

Tables 5.1 and 5.2 demonstrate the diversity, sectors, and countries involved in the scientific study of mindfulness from a single recent monthly sample, reported in the February 2021 issue of the *Mindfulness Research Monthly*, a well-regarded monthly digest of published articles on mindfulness (AMRA, 2021). This publication presents studies of a vast range of populations and problems to which mindfulness is being applied, from healthcare to the formal education system to the workplace.

Many have criticized the clinical research on mindfulness in ways that have and will impact its absorption into healthcare and science. Yet, such critiques are ultimately beneficial to the project of secular-scientific mindfulness. The very fact that the area is being studied inside and outside of healthcare reflects the broad societal acceptance of MBIs as worthy of investigation in the treatment and training of individuals with a variety of

**Table 5.1** Mindfulness Research by Type and Population Reported for a Single Month (AMRA, Feb. 2021)

| *General Category* | *Specific Topic(s)* | *Number of Studies* |
|---|---|---|
| **By Study Type** | | |
| All studies reported (N=46) | intervention studies (9=RCTS) | 13 |
| | associational studies (correlation) | 16 |
| | methodological studies | 9 |
| | reviews and meta-analyses | 7 |
| | trial (announcing new funding) | 1 |
| **By Populations Studied** | | |
| Mental health studies (N=14) | affective disorders (depression, bipolar, anxiety) | 6 |
| | children's mental health | 3 |
| | substance use | 2 |
| | cognitive impairment (elderly) | 2 |
| | autism | 1 |
| | pregnant women | 1 |
| Physical health studies (N=9) | kidney disease (haemodialysis) | 2 |
| | cancer | 2 |
| | cardiovascular disease | 2 |
| | Parkinson's disease | 1 |
| | osteoarthritis | 1 |
| | sleep disorders | 1 |
| Education | | 9 |
| Workplace | | 4 |
| Bereaved parents | | 1 |
| Long-term meditators | | 1 |
| General or non-specific | | 8 |

**Table 5.2** Mindfulness Research by Other Parameters for a Single Month (AMRA, Feb 2021)

| *General Category* | *Specific Topic(s)* | *Number of Studies* |
|---|---|---|
| Programme variation | MBCT | 4 |
| All studies (N=46) | modified MBPs – one-hour to nine-months | 40 |
| | mindful eating | 1 |
| | walking | 1 |
| Digital format (N-8) | smartphone apps | 4 |
| | virtual reality | 3 |
| | online learning tool | 2 |
| Sample size variation (examples) | single case study | |
| | N=283 | |
| | meta-analysis of 18 students, N=1223 | |
| Geographical variation | USA | 19 |
| All studies (N=46) | UK & Europe | 9 |
| | Asia | 7 |
| | Canada | 6 |
| | Australia/New Zealand | 5 |
| | Brazil | 1 |
| | Israel | 1 |
| Controlled (i.e., intervention) studies (N=13) | active control group | 4 studies (all interventions) |
| | passive control – e.g., waitlist | 9 |

problems, mental health or otherwise. This kind of broad interdisciplinary and cross-cultural interest is unique and reflects the degree of interest and viability of mindfulness. Also, these critiques of the research are intended to improve it, to establish its effectiveness or lack thereof, and to specify domains in which it may or may not be effective. Firmly establishing both the effectiveness and efficacy of mindfulness interventions through more rigorous research will support their development and status as evidence-based, mainstream treatments.

As Goldberg et al. (2021) point out, in evaluating the evidence on mindfulness to date, "the sheer number of RCTs and meta-analyses makes it difficult to draw firm conclusions" (p.2). This challenge compelled them to set out to provide more clarity by using specifications outlined by the Cochrane Collaboration, an international organization that guides evidence-based decision-making in health and social services. In particular, the specification called for the use of predetermined eligibility criteria to delineate the scope of the review or meta-analysis. In this case, the criteria were the five PICOS criteria (Populations or problems; Interventions used; Comparisons or controls; Outcomes; and Study design, if not using RCTs (Higgins et al., 2021; Methley et al., 2014). Using these criteria, the researchers systematically reviewed all previously published meta-analyses of RCTs up to September 2019, which included 44 meta-analyses consisting of 336 RCTs with a total number of 30,483 participants.

The resulting meta-analysis identified 160 effect sizes in a range of MBIs that were predominantly applied to address psychiatric problems and symptom outcomes. MBIs, for the most part, outperformed passive controls, such as treatment as usual or waitlist control. When measured against active and specific active controls, like relaxation or psychoeducation, effect sizes were smaller but significant in psychiatric disorders, substance use, smoking cessation, and depression. MBIs for smoking cessation produced greater results than evidence-based treatments like medications or CBT post-treatment, and MBCT was the only modality with better outcomes than evidence-based treatments for the prevention of depressive relapse at follow-up. Goldberg et al. (2021) concluded that, despite multiple sources of bias, there was a "pattern of efficacy observed for MBIs across numerous, but not all, PICOS" (p. 17) and that "interventions based on mindfulness meditation indeed hold substantial transdiagnostic potential, albeit with stronger evidence for some...than others. Therefore, the utilization of MBIs as a family of interventions is at least partially supported by scientific evidence" (p. 19).

## Methodological Rigour

Despite the abundance of research publications available on mindfulness in 2021, there is significant variability in methodological rigour, including the lack of adequate follow-up and use of active controls. Dimidjian and Segal (2015) raised and addressed other issues, such as the need to specify the population targets of interventions and to examine potential mediators and moderators of an intervention's effects in order to know why they work and for what specific purpose. The authors also speak to the fact that much of the mindfulness research is located within the early stages of the National Institute of Health model of research with few community efficacies or effectiveness trials and a lack of dissemination and implementation studies. Related to this is the dearth of reporting on failed trials and adverse events resulting from MBIs. Research findings are mixed, and "few active controls have been truly matched to MBSR or MBCT on all components except mindfulness meditation" (p. 606). There has also been little work done in addressing the quality of instructor training or in the development of standards (see also Shonin et al., 2013). While mindfulness interventions are promising as a means to reduce suffering, the field continues to be limited in terms of how much it can claim to be strongly evidence-based.

We must also remember that what constitutes evidence in one moment may change in the next. Prasad et al. (2013), for example, examined 363 articles that looked at a range of existing medical practices and found that 146 of these practices were found to be ineffective when subjected to more rigorous evidence-based standards (most commonly, RCTs). This medical reversal is important because it speaks to the fact that an evidence base is nuanced and constitutes a developing foundation that changes over time, thereby requiring a critical approach to the literature.

Mindfulness and its applications are being investigated both in clinical trials and through neuroscience. Mapping the effects of mindfulness on the brain or within neural networks provides further evidence of its ability to invoke objective physiological changes. Such neurological mapping of the effects of mindfulness is critical to its becoming embedded in healthcare as a treatment modality, particularly in mental health where we have few, if any, objective measures or tests. But we must remember that the scientific method is but one way of knowing, though often upheld as "a superior form of knowledge" (Smith, 2002). Science has its limitations, not the least of which – as in the case of mindfulness – is the difficulty in generalizing from laboratory efficacy to real-world effectiveness, where there are often uncontrolled variables and inconsistencies with respect to delivery and to the competence of the teacher, all of which affect outcomes. We can always say that mindfulness works because of the existence of supportive studies, but this is a simplistic approach to evidence. As discussed, some research is better than others, and it is essential that those delivering MBIs understand the literature, learning how to appraise it critically in order to be able to determine both the strength of the evidence and its relevance to practice and outcomes.

## The Study of Adverse Effects

An important area of study that has only recently been receiving attention concerns adverse events in mindfulness practice, which has a paucity of good research. Britton (2019) attributed this oversight to "assuming an ubiquitous, positive and linear relationship between mindfulness and wellbeing." (p. 6). The current underreporting of mixed, null, or harmful results regarding MBIs makes it impossible to determine ideal dosing; individuated instruction using specified techniques or practices; and who is best suited for different practices in particular contexts. Concerned by this lack of publication of meditation adverse events (MAEs), Farias et al. (2020) undertook the first meta-analysis of meditation using the aforementioned strategy proposed by the Cochrane Collaboration for interventions when such events are unknown. Prior to this review, two publications examining RCTs of MBIs found no difference in reported MAEs between the intervention and waitlist controls, but it was noted that there was little monitoring for such events (Wong et al., 2018; Hirschberg et al., 2020). Therefore, in their study, Farias and colleagues examined any study that reported, "a harmful event or deterioration of current physical or mental condition that occurred during or after meditation practice" (p.377–378). Eight-three studies consisting of 6464 participants were evaluated: 54 experimental, 14 observational, and 15 case studies. The prevalence of MAEs was 8.3%, though much less for the experimental studies at 3.7%. Predominant adverse event symptoms consisted of depression, anxiety, cognitive anomalies, and hallucinations. Delusions, dissociation, depersonalization, trauma symptoms, and fear or terror were reported less frequently. While finding equivalent reporting of adverse events in their study with other psychological treatment modalities, they speculated underreporting as a significant research concern. They identified a range of reasons why mindfulness studies might underreport MAEs, including passive monitoring versus active assessment of MAEs; inconsistent appraisal of MAEs (as either positive or negative); and the difficulty in attributing causation in observational studies.

Attending to the reporting and examination of adverse events in MBIs is relevant for protecting participants; determining suitability and contraindications; determining its acceptance as a treatment; as well as for the professionalization of MBTL. While the term "professionalization" may have many definitions, in this case we refer to it as an occupation's mandate to self-regulate or control its own work. This self-regulation tends to be done by a governing body. Interestingly, such regulations and mandates are directly tied to the ability of an occupation to cause harm, thereby involving member training in recognizing when one is outside one's scope of practice and when a client would be served better by another modality. Even those who are educated to attend to these issues have high rates of error with respect to such judgment and decision-making. Such a lack of recognition of these limitations can result in treatment delays and other opportunity costs for the person seeking help through mindfulness. These errors of omission may also be viewed as adverse events for participants. The turning of attention to MAEs is a further indication of their medicalization as a treatment modality.

For many delivering MBSR and other MBIs, there is no regulation in place unless the teacher is a clinician with a professional designation, registration, or licence. MBSR and other MBIs are not themselves regulated, though in certain jurisdictions (e.g. Ontario, Canada), MBCT is now a controlled act. In fact, some who deliver mindfulness or seek to learn it may believe that it is completely benign and preferable to medical interventions. This positivity bias is in part a result of the publication bias cited above and reflective of common anti-medical views of the public and those who engage in complementary alternative medicine practices. Implicit is the view that mindfulness is not only benign but always helpful. As Kesavadev et al. (2017) remind us, "The popularity of these practices among the general public is in no way a testimony to their safety and efficacy" (p. 60).

In healthcare or medicalized environments, mindfulness is being utilized as a treatment, and treatments are known to have side effects or adverse effects, that is, effects not associated with therapy or a target outcome that may be unwanted. If mindfulness is shown to cause harm by evidence of adverse effects, paradoxically this further advances its medicalization as a treatment modality. Consequently, this may also increase the professionalization of mindfulness as an occupation, further delineating who delivers it since practitioners will require regulation.

Accordingly, the recognition of MAEs leads to discussions of teacher training, the contexts of delivery, the intentions of the programmes being offered, and the competency of teachers from a variety of perspectives. When competency is understood as effectiveness in achieving desired target outcomes, there is little literature to date on MBTL teacher competency. Teacher training in mindfulness is offered in a variety of settings, including as professional training for healthcare providers. It is also found in continuing professional development and graduate-level training for those who come from many disciplines and sectors interested in mindfulness, not as a treatment, but as education or a skill to enhance leadership, productivity, and wellbeing. Thus, competency and teacher training with respect to MBIs, from a medical treatment lens, or MBPs, from an educational or workplace perspective, may be offered in a variety of ways using specific protocols or curricula, depending on the aim of the training or context. What these formal MBTL training programmes have in common is a commitment to experiential learning, underpinned by specific concepts relevant to the teaching of mindfulness, as well as assessment that includes mentoring or supervision. Competency and teacher training are discussed elsewhere and in greater detail in this book.

## TRENDS

The evolution of MBSR and MBCT inside and outside of healthcare has produced a plethora of mindfulness modalities with varying levels of evidence. MBSR, MBCT, mindfulness-based eating awareness training (MB-EAT), and mindfulness-based relapse prevention for substance misuse (MBRP) are formal programmes for which meditation is central, whereas DBT and acceptance and commitment therapy (ACT) are considered programmes for which meditation practices are not central. DBT and ACT may be offered to individual clients or in groups, whereas the other MB-ESTs are most commonly provided as group-based modalities. These six mindfulness-based therapeutic interventions are the ones with the most rigorous research at present. While there are many other programmes, not cited here, they are not yet as empirically supported (Fielding, 2009; Kochamba, 2017; Woods & Rockman, 2021).

## Mindfulness as a Transdiagnostic Mental Health Intervention

Consistent with a diagnostic frame of reference, mental disorders are primarily viewed as discrete entities like other medical conditions. Therefore, many mindfulness modalities proposed as treatments for these mental conditions, and ostensibly specific to these conditions, are currently under development and/or investigation. Mental health conditions, however, are not actually discrete entities; they are collections of phenomena that have been categorized by consensus in the DSM and ICD to signify conditions. In fact, these diagnoses overlap considerably, with a wide range of symptoms identified for each disorder. Also, such conditions exist along continua, with most mental disorders co-existing with comorbidities and non-specific treatments, whether pharmacological or psychotherapeutic. In addition, there are no known aetiologies or identified pathophysiology for them, despite the fact that it is evident that mental disorders exist and have a significant global impact (Silveira & Rockman, 2021). Hence for these and other reasons, there is increasing interest in transdiagnostic approaches to mental health and addictions (Dalgleish et al., 2020).

Mindfulness-based programmes are also transdiagnostic. This is more evident in the case of MBSR and less evident with MBCT; yet, MBCT has also been adapted for use in many conditions. MBIs cut across diagnoses because they consist of common elements that are applicable to aspects of any condition that includes dysregulation and the fusion of thinking and emotions. Therefore, they appear to be using similar mechanisms, mediators, and moderators; however, there is a need for more dismantling studies and studies to identify both mediators and moderators with respect to MBIs. At present it would appear that awareness, decentering, and mindfulness meditation paired with acceptance are at least part of the recipe for positive outcomes (Stein & Witkiewitz, 2020). While these mindfulness-based adaptations are varied in certain respects, they consist of similar interventions, assumptions, principles, and constructs, working with thoughts, emotions, body sensations/senses, and impulses and associated acts and behaviours as sources of insight in both individual and group learning contexts.

## Towards a Common Elements Mindfulness Approach

Therefore, a common elements mindfulness approach that cuts across conditions could be a more cost-effective way of delivering mindfulness to those who might benefit. It is unreasonable to expect individual clinicians to learn multiple mindfulness modalities to treat various conditions when these modalities consist of the same elements and may be applicable to a variety of problems. It is simply not scalable with respect to the time and financial means it takes to learn them. The work of Fielding (2009) and Kochamba (2017) point toward a solution to this problem through their early work in identifying these common elements. Given the increasing focus on transdiagnostic approaches to mental disorders; the use of unified protocols such as *The Unified Protocol for Transdiagnostic Treatment of Emotional Disorders* or modular approaches to treatment; and interest in identifying the specific mechanisms and ingredients of mindfulness, it is conceivable that we may begin to see the development of unified protocols applied to the delivery of mindfulness (Barlow et al., 2017).

## CONCLUSION

In conclusion, the medicalization of mindfulness was critical to its uptake into the mainstream of modern life. While issues related to its evidence base and concerns about its adverse effects and relative contraindications have limited its uptake as a recognized medical treatment, these issues can be seen as further evidence of its ultimate professionalization and medicalization within healthcare contexts. The common elements of mindfulness modalities in the treatment of transdiagnostic mental disorders hold great promise in developing more unified mindfulness protocols to make them more available and accessible. Furthermore, medicalization helped make mindfulness a transprofessional enterprise, drawing educators, for example, into clinical studies they might not otherwise have undertaken.

## REFERENCES

American Mindfulness Research Association (AMRA). (2021). *Mindfulness Research Monthly, 12*(134), February 2021. https://goamra.org/2021-Monthly-Bulletins.

Analayo, B. (2020). The myth of McMindfulness. *Mindfulness, 11*, 472–479. https://doi.org/10.1007/s12671-019-01264-x.

Barlow, D., Farchione, T., Bullis, J., Gallagher, M., Murray-Latin, H., Sauer-Zavala, S., Bentley, K., Thompson-Hollands, J., Conklin, L., Boswell, J., Ametaj, A., Carl, J., Boettcher, H., & Cassiello-Robbins, C. (2017). The unified protocol for transdiagnostic treatment of emotional disorders compared with diagnosis-specific protocols for anxiety disorders: A randomized clinical trial. *JAMA Psychiatry, 74*(9), 875–884. https://doi.org/10.1001/jamapsychiatry.2017.2164.

Bialkowska, J., Juranek, J., & Wojkiewicz, J. (2020). Behavioral medicine methods in treatment of somatic conditions. *BioMed Research International.* Advance online publication. https://doi.org/10.1155/2020/5076516.

Bondolfi, G., Jermann, F., der Linden, M., Gex-Fabry, M., Bizzini, L., Rouget, B. W., Myers-Arrazola, L., Gonzalez, C., Segal, Z., Aubry, J., & Bertschy, G. (2010). Depression relapse prophylaxis with mindfulness-based cognitive therapy: Replication and extension in the Swiss health care system. *Journal of Affective Disorders, 122*(3), 224–231. https://doi.org/10.1016/j.jad.2009.07.007.

Britton, W. (2019). Can mindfulness be too much of a good thing? The value of a middle way. *Current Opinion in Psychology, 28*, 159–165. https://doi.org/10.1016/j.copsyc.2018.12.011.

Brosschot, J., Verkuil, B., & Thayer, J. (2018). Generalized unsafety theory of stress: Unsafe environments and conditions, and the default stress response. *International Journal of Environmental Research and Public Health, 15*(3), 464. https://doi.org/10.3390/ijerph15030464.

Cairncross, M., & Miller, C. (2016). The effectiveness of mindfulness-based therapies for ADHD: A meta-analytic review. *Journal of Attention Disorders.* Advance online publication. https://doi.org/10.1177/1087054715625301.

Dalgleish, T., Black, M., Johnston, D., & Bevan, A. (2020). Transdiagnostic approaches to mental health problems: Current status and future directions. *Journal of Consulting and Clinical Psychology, 88*(3), 179–195. https://doi.org/10.1037/ccp0000482.

Deatherage, G. (1975). The clinical use of 'mindfulness meditation techniques in short-term psychotherapy. *Journal of Transpersonal Psychology, 7*(2), 133–143.

Dimidjian, S. & Segal, Z. (2015). Prospects for a clinical science of mindfulness-based intervention. *American Psychologist (70*(7), 593–620. https://doi.org/10.1037/a0039589

Epstein, R. (2003). Mindful practice in action (II): Cultivating habits of mind. *Families, Systems & Health, 21*(1), 11. https://doi.org/10.1037/h0089495.

Epstein, R. (2020). Mindfulness in medical education: Coming of age. *Perspectives on Medical Education, 9*, 197–198. https://doi.org/10.1007/s40037-020-00598-w.

Farias, M., Maraldi, E., Wallenkampf, K., & Lucchetti, G. (2020). Adverse events in meditation practices and meditation-based therapies: A systematic review. *Acta Psychiatrica Scandinavica, 142*(5), 374–393. https://doi.org/10.1111/acps.13225.

Fielding, L. (2009). *A clinicians' guide to integrating mindfulness into evidence-based practice: A common elements approach.* Pepperdine Digital Commons, Pepperdine University. https://core.ac.uk/download/pdf/288853441.pdf.

Garland, E., Hanley, A., Baker, A., & Howard, M. (2017). Biobehavioral mechanisms of mindfulness as a treatment for chronic stress: An RDoC perspective. *Chronic Stress, 1*, 1–14. https://doi.org/10.1177/2470547017711912.

Godfrin, K., & van Heeringen, C. (2010). The effects of mindfulness-based cognitive therapy on recurrence of depressive episodes, mental health and quality of life: A randomized controlled study. *Behaviour Research and Therapy, 48*(8), 738–746. https://doi.org/10.1016/j.brat.2010.04.006.

Goldberg, S., Riordan, K., Sun, S., & Davidson, R. (2021). The empirical status of mindfulness-based interventions: A systematic review of 44 meta-analyses of randomized controlled trials. *Perspectives on Psychological Science, 17*(1), 108–130. https://doi.org/10.1177/1745691620968771.

Goldberg, S., Tucker, P., Greene, P., Davidson, R., Wampold, B., Kearney, D., & Simpson, T. (2018). Mindfulness-based interventions for psychiatric disorders: A systematic review and meta-analysis. *Clinical Psychology Review, 59*, 52–60. https://doi.org/10.1016/j.cpr.2017.10.011.

Higgins, J., Thomas, J., Chandler, J., Cumpston, M., Li, T., Page, M., & Welch, V. (Eds.). (2021). *Cochrane handbook for systematic reviews of interventions, version 6.2 (updated February 2021).* Cochrane. www.training.cochrane.org/handbook.

Hirshberg, M.J., Goldberg, S. B., Rosenkranz, M., & Davidson, R.J. (2020). Prevalence of harm in mindfulness-based stress reduction. *Psychological Medicine.* Advance online publication. https://doi.org/10.1017/s0033291720002834.

ICD. (2020). *ICD-11 for mortality and morbidity statistics. QE84 acute stress reaction.* https://icd.who.int/browse11/l-m/en#/http://id.who.int/icd/entity/505909942.

Jiménez, J., & Mills, P., (2012). Behavioral medicine. In V. Ramachandran (Ed.), *Encyclopedia of human behavior* (2nd ed., pp. 311–318). Academic Press.

Kabat-Zinn, J. (1982). An outpatient program in behavioral medicine for chronic pain patients based on the practice of mindfulness meditation: Theoretical considerations and preliminary results. *General Hospital Psychiatry, 4*(1), 33–47.

Kabat-Zinn, J. (1990/2013). *Full catastrophe living: Using the wisdom of your body and mind to face stress, pain, and illness.* Bantam Books.

Kabat-Zinn, J. (2003). Mindfulness-based interventions in context: Past, present, and future. *Clinical Psychology: Science and Practice, 10*(2), 144. https://doi.org/10.1093/clipsy.bpg016.

Kabat-Zinn, J., Lipworth, L., & Burney, R. (1985) The clinical use of mindfulness meditation for the self-regulation of chronic pain. *Journal of Behavioral Medicine, 8*(2), 163–190. https://doi.org/10.1007/BF00845519.

Kabat-Zinn, J., Lipworth, L., & Burney, R. (1986). Four-year follow-up of a meditation-based program for self regulation of chronic pain: Treatment outcomes and compliance. *The Clinical Journal of Pain, 2*(3), 159–173.

Kabat-Zinn, J., Massion, A., Kristeller, J., Peterson, L., Fletcher, K., Pbert, L., Lenderking, W., & Santorelli, S. (1992). Effectiveness of a meditation-based stress reduction program in the treatment of anxiety disorders. *American Journal of Psychiatry, 149*(7), 936–943.

Kesavadev, J., Saboo, B., Sadikot, S., Das, A., Joshi, S., Chawla, R., Thacker, H., Shankar, A., Ramachandran, L., & Kalra, S. (2017). Unproven therapies for diabetes and their implications. *Advances in Therapy*, *34*(1), 60–77. https://doi.org/10.1007/s12325-016-0439-x.

Kochamba, K. (2017). *Integrating mindfulness-based empirically supported treatments (MB-ESTs) into evidence-based practice (EBP): A replication and extension study*. Doctoral Dissertation, Azusa Pacific University.

Kriakous, S., Elliot, K., Lamers, C., & Owen, R. (2021). The effectiveness of mindfulness-based stress reduction on the psychological functioning of healthcare professionals: A systematic review. *Mindfulenss*, *12*, 1–28. https://doi.org/10.1007/s12671-020-01500-9.

Kuyken, W., Hayes, R., Barrett, B., Byng, R., Dalgleish, T., Kessler, D., Lewis, G., Watkins, E., Brejcha, C., Cardy, J., Causley, A., Cowderoy, S., Evans, A., Gradinger, F., Kaur, S., Lanham, P., Morant, N., Richards, J., Shah, P., … Byford, S. (2015). Effectiveness and cost-effectiveness of mindfulness-based cognitive therapy compared with maintenance antidepressant treatment in the prevention of depressive relapse or recurrence (PREVENT): A randomised controlled trial. *Lancet*, *386*(9988), 63–73. https://doi.org/10.1016/S0140-6736(14)62222-4.

Kuyken, W., Hayes, R., Barrett, B., Byng, R., Dalgleish, T., Kessler, D., Lewis, G., Watkins, E., Morant, N., Taylor, R., & Byford, S. (2015). The effectiveness and cost-effectiveness of mindfulness-based cognitive therapy compared with maintenance antidepressant treatment in the prevention of depressive relapse/recurrence: Results of a randomised controlled trial (the PREVENT study). *Health Technology Assessment*, *19*(73), 1–124. https://doi.org/10.1016/S0140-6736(14)62222-4.

Lazarus, R., & Folkman, S. (1984). *Stress, appraisal, and coping*. Springer.

Ma, S. H., & Teasdale, J. D. (2004). Mindfulness-based cognitive therapy for depression: Replication and exploration of differential relapse prevention effects. *Journal of Consulting and Clinical Psychology*, *72*(1), 31–40. https://doi.org/10.1037/0022-006X.72.1.31.

Maturo, A. (2012) Medicalization: Current concept and future directions in a bionic society. *Mens Sana Monographs*, *10*(1), 122–133. https://doi.org/10.4103/0973-1229.91587.

McCown, D., Reibel, D., & Micozzi, M. S. (2010). *Teaching mindfulness: A practical guide for clinicians and educators*. Springer.

Methley, A., Campbell, S., Chew-Graham, C., McNally, R., & Cheraghi-Sohi, S. (2014). PICO, PICOS and SPIDER: A comparison of specificity and sensitivity in three search tools for qualitative systematic reviews. *BMC Health Services Research*, *14*, 579. https://doi.org/10.1186/s12913-014-0579-0.

Michalak, J., Mander, J., & Heidenreich, T. (2020) Implementation and dissemination of mindfulness-based interventions. *Mindfulness*, *11*, 275–278. https://doi.org/10.1007/s12671-019-01250-3.

Miller, J., Fletcher, K., & Kabat-Zinn, J. (1995). Three-year follow-up and clinical implications of a mindfulness meditation-based stress reduction intervention in the treatment of anxiety disorders. *General Hospital Psychiatry*, *17*(3), 192–200.

National Library of Medicine. (2021). Medical subject headings. Retrieved on Nov. 22, 2022 at: https://www.nlm.nih.gov/mesh/meshhome.html

NIMH. (n.d.). *About RDoC. Research domain criteria initiative*. https://www.nimh.nih.gov/research/research-funded-by-nimh/rdoc/about-rdoc.

Prasad, V., Vandross, A., Toomey, C., Cheung, M., Rho, J., Quinn, S., Chacko, S., Borkar, D., Gall, V., Selvaraj, S., Ho, N., & Cifu, A. (2013). A decade of reversal: An analysis of 146 contradicted medical practices. *Mayo Clinic Proceedings*, *88*(8), 790–798. https://doi.org/10.1016/j.mayocp.2013.05.012.

Salleh, M. (2008). Live event, stress and illness. *Malaysian Journal of Medical Science*, *15*(4), 9–18.

Santorelli, S., Meleo-Meyer, F., & Koerbel, L. (2017). *Mindfulness-based stress reduction: Authorized curriculum guide.* https://mindfulness.nhsggc.org.uk/media/2105/mbsr-curriculum-guide-2017.pdf.

Segal, Z. V., Williams, J. M. G., & Teasdale, J. D. (2002). *Mindfulness-based cognitive therapy for depression: A new approach to preventing relapse.* Guilford.

Seyle, H. (1956). *The stress of life.* McGraw-Hill.

Shonin, E., Van Gordon, W., & Griffiths, M. (2013). Mindfulness-based interventions: Towards mindful clinical integration. *Frontiers in Psychology, 4,* 194. https://doi.org/10.3389/fpsyg.2013.00194.

Silveira, J., & Rockman, P. (2021). *Managing uncertainty in mental health care.* Oxford University Press.

Smith, R. (Ed.). (2002). The discomfort of patient power: Medical authorities will have to learn to live with "irrational" decisions by the public. *BMJ, 324,* 497–498. https://doi.org/10.1136/bmj.324.7336.497.

Stein, E., & Witkiewitz, K. (2020) Dismantling mindfulness-based programs: A systematic review to identify active components of treatment. *Mindfulness, 11,* 2470–2485. https://doi.org/10.1007/s12671-020-01444-0.

Tan, S., & Yip, A. (2018). Hans Selye (1907–1982): Founder of the stress theory. *Singapore Medical Journal, 59*(4), 170–171. https://doi.org/10.11622/smedj.2018043.

Teasdale, J., Segal, Z., Williams, J. Ridgeway, V., Soulsby, J. & Lau, M. (2000) Prevention of relapse/recurrence in major depression by mindfulness-based cognitive therapy. *Journal of Consulting and Clinical Psychology, 68*(4), 615–623. https://doi.org/10.1037/0022-006X.68.4.615

Wilson, J. (2014) *Mindful America: The mutual transformation of Buddhist meditation and American culture.* Oxford University Press.

Wong, S, Chan, J., Zhang, D., Lee, E., & Tsoi, K. (2018) The safety of mindfulness-based interventions: A systematic review of randomized controlled trials. *Mindfulness, 9,* 1344–1357.

Woods, S., & Rockman, P. (2021). *Mindfulness-based stress reduction: Protocol, practice, and teaching skills.* New Harbinger.

World Health Organization. (2021). https://www.who.int/health-topics/depression#tab=tab_1.

Zinn, J.K., (1991/2013). *Full catastrophe living: Using the wisdom of your body and mind to face stress, pain, and illness.* Bantam.

# CHAPTER 6

# HIGHER EDUCATION

## From Contemplative Studies to "Student Success"

Nothing symbolizes the mainstreaming of mindfulness more than its acceptance in the formal curriculum of higher education. Although that milestone only began in the last few years, it is the culmination of incremental steps taken over many years. Higher education and post-secondary education are interchangeable terms (here) to refer to the spectrum of informal, non-formal, and formal education recognized and supported by institutions of higher learning, be they colleges, polytechnic institutes, or universities. Not included are continuing studies or extension divisions as they were covered as instances of community education in Chapter 4.

Mapping the development of mindfulness in higher education as informal, non-formal, and/or formal learning helps to elucidate some of its challenges and opportunities. Informal learning is the broad spectrum of learning that occurs, intentionally or unintentionally, outside of recognized and assessed outcomes in classes or in ad hoc, less institutionalized "spaces" in higher education. "Non-formal learning" refers to intentional learning within structured programmes that lie outside of for-credit or academic structures or systems. In the case of mindfulness, non-formal programmes are often sponsored by extracurricular institutional bodies like student services, counselling, and physical education. Formal learning and education refer to activities that are recognized for credit as part of explicit curricular or learning outcomes, usually as part of for-credit degree, diploma, or certificate programs. The informal-nonformal-formal spectrum overlaps with parallel distinctions in implicit-explicit and unrecognized-recognized learning spectra.

Until recently, MBTL programming and associated research in higher education have tended to focus on non-formal extracurricular initiatives aimed at student mental health, stress management, and wellbeing. These programmes have tended to be sponsored and taught by non-academic student service divisions, often drawing on MBSR or related stress management programmes. Alternatively, where mindfulness has entered academic programming, it has tended to be informally conducted as short "small-dose" meditations to improve student attention, stress management, or self-care. This has begun to change of late, however, as interest and research continue to grow in integrating mindfulness into formal disciplinary and professional education (e.g., Gockel & Deng, 2016). This growing interest with its associated theoretical and case study research is often conducted under the banner of contemplative studies, the topic to which we now turn.

## MINDFULNESS AS A CONTEMPLATIVE PRACTICE

Mindfulness has steadily migrated over the past few decades across informal and non-formal programming to enter the formal curriculum of higher education. Its mandate has expanded as it did so from serving as a temporary mental health and stress-management "intervention" to becoming a distinctive epistemology or way of knowing and a strategy for self-regulating learning in relation to wellbeing. The dominant interdisciplinary umbrella for researching and navigating these changes has been Contemplative Studies. Although mindfulness is distinctive from many other contemplative methods, it is commonly taught

DOI: 10.4324/9781003182467-9

alongside a range of meditative or cross-cultural practices. Dorjee (2016) defined contemplative science as the "interdisciplinary study of the metacognitive self-regulatory capacity (MSRC) of the mind and associated modes of existential awareness (MEA) modulated by motivational/intentional and contextual factors of contemplative practices" (p. 1). Unpacking this definition, contemplative practices can be said to have in common the following characteristics: developing and using meta-awareness, self-regulation, and motivation.

Jarvis (1992) was one of the first adult and higher education scholars to begin to redefine contemplation as a form of secular learning. He linked contemplation to both experiential learning (Kolb, 1983) and reflective practice (Schon, 1984). Using qualitative data on student learning, Jarvis identified four types of learning from experience: non-learning; incidental learning; non-reflective learning (preconscious learning; skills learning; and memorization); and reflective learning (contemplation; reflective cognitive learning; and action learning). As a form of reflective learning, contemplation involved a combined perceptual and conceptual process of interiority: Awareness of direct experience followed by thinking or reasoning about that experience. As he concluded: "Contemplation is the process of thinking about an experience and reaching a conclusion about it without necessarily referring to a wider social reality" (Jarvis, Holford, & Griffin, 2003, p. 64). This final step of arriving at a conclusion differentiated contemplation from ordinary thinking, according to Jarvis. Unlike contemplation, the other two types of reflective practice – reflective cognitive and action learning – were about theorizing and experimenting and linking theory and concepts to practice. In this way, Jarvis located contemplation in the continuum of reflective practice that Schon had ascribed to professional learning. This shift from a religious to a secular connotation for the process of contemplation was key to its development and legitimization in higher education.

As contemplative studies became reintroduced in higher education, the religious connotation of contemplation become steadily secularized as reflective practice, albeit in a rather confused, pell-mell manner. A key figure in the contemplative mind movement was the American physicist Arthur Zajonc (2013), who described contemplative pedagogy as a quiet revolution in higher education. Despite his claims of a "wide range of methods," he specified only four exemplars: Mindfulness; concentration training; open awareness; and sustaining contradictions. These practices, in turn, were imputed to support a range of desirable learning outcomes:

> [Contemplative pedagogy] offers to it practitioners a wide range of educational methods that support the development of student attention, emotional balance, empathetic connection, compassion, and altruistic behaviour, while also providing new pedagogical techniques that support creativity and the learning of course content.
>
> *(p. 83)*

According to Zajonc (2014), the scope of practices labelled as contemplative in higher education goes beyond any previous traditional definitions. As represented in the so-called "Tree of Contemplative Practices" (Centre of Contemplative Mind, 2020), contemplative practices includes activities as diverse journalling and storytelling; work, vigils, and pilgrimages; art, chanting, and singing; and a range of meditative practices. What these varied contemplative practices have in common, according to Zajonc, are that they contribute to an integrative, holistic, and multidisciplinary education that includes learning to attend but also to create and live ethically with compassion. The dominant contemplative practices advocated in contemplative studies is mindfulness, leading Beer et al. (2015) to go so far as to argue that contemplation and mindfulness are interchangeable terms. We disagree. The scope of practices and scholarship termed "contemplative" can be so wide and diffuse as to dilute the intent and potential benefits of mindfulness. For example, the Tree of Contemplative Practices includes methods like journalling that have long been recognized as educational activities and are highly cognitive and discursive. Therefore, we prefer to call the use of mindfulness in higher education as mindfulness-based teaching and learning (MBTL).

## Contemplative Studies in Higher Education

The history of the marginalization of Europe's indigenous contemplative traditions during the Inquisition, the Renaissance, and later Enlightenment periods (MacPherson, 1997, 2011) is beyond the purview of this book. Suffice to say that the traditional contemplative traditions persisted, albeit often in relative secrecy or obscurity, mainly within monastic education. Given this history, contemporary struggles to reintegrate mindfulness in higher education are evidence of challenges associated with reclaiming forgotten and lost pieces of Western educational traditions. Therefore, it should not be considered principally about cross-cultural or cross-civilizational dialogues involving something originating in South Asia exclusively. The same can be said of Indigenous contemplative practices in North America, which were even more intentionally and aggressively excluded than monastic contemplative traditions from the recognized curricula of higher education. So, it is not surprising to find that today, the path for mindfulness in higher education is part of a broader agenda to (re)introduce contemplation in higher education, variously referred to as contemplative studies (Roth, 2006); contemplative pedagogy (Zajonc, 2013, 2014); contemplative practices (Barbezat & Bush, 2013); contemplative education (Heredia et al., 2020); and contemplative mind (Hart, 2004).

Contemplative practices include mindfulness but extend beyond it, so it is worth defining it for clarification. In traditional Buddhist contexts, mindfulness would be called a type of meditation, whereas contemplation, a less common term, would refer to discursive or reflective techniques more commonly referred to as analytical meditation. Yet, these terms were reversed in traditional European contexts, where meditation was often used to refer to discursive analysis mediated by thought and reason, like Descartes' *Meditations on First Philosophy, in which the existence of God and the immortality of the soul are demonstrated.* Contemplation, on the other hand, tended to be used to refer to direct experiences unmediated by thought or words, often used in reference to the direct experience of God, such as the practice of *contemplative prayer* described by the American Trappist monk Thomas Merton and modernized by fellow American priest Fr. Thomas Keating as Centering Prayer (Bourgeault, 2004).

Heredia et al. (2020) classified mindfulness as a method associated with the development of what they referred to as *spiritual competence* in contemplative education, which, in turn, was defined as meaning-making through social-emotional learning. Social-emotional learning posits that all learning is relational, thereby linking social-emotional learning to improved student learning and academic performance (Lawlor, 2016). Although it is inclusive of the social-emotional learning agenda, contemplative education goes further by contributing interiority, meta-awareness, and transcendence to this socializing agenda.

## THE RESEARCH

### Extra-Curricular, Non-Formal Courses

Student mental health concerns are leading to increased access to mindfulness in higher education. Nowhere is this motivation more explicit than in extracurricular non-credit classes offered through student, health, or athletic services. To get a sense of the extent of this mental health crisis, Auerbach et al. (2018) conducted a widescale college mental health study through the World Health Organization (WHO) of 13,984 first-year students from 19 colleges in eight countries (Australia, Belgium, Germany, Mexico, Northern Ireland, South Africa, Spain, and United States). They reported that 35% of respondents tested positive for at least one lifetime mental health disorder and 31% for at least one 12-month disorder, the most common being anxiety.

Furthermore, there is evidence to suggest that these mental health challenges interrupt students' academic performance or success. In national surveys of college students in the USA and Canada, the American College Health Association (ACHA) (2019) reported that the top four of the 32 major causes of major academic interruptions were stress, anxiety, sleep disturbances, and depression (affecting 20%–42% of student respondents). Each of these four challenges have strong to moderate evidence of being helped by mindfulness (Bamber & Morpeth, 2019; Dawson et al., 2020; Galante et al., 2018). Furthermore, outside of higher education in studies of clinical populations, the finding that mindfulness builds resilience to stress and depression relapse has proved robust (Segal et al., 2019; Collins & Segal, 2020). The question remains, however, as to which type of mindfulness programme and approach is best to address student mental health challenges *and* to optimize its promise as a contemplative practice in higher education.

To provide a snapshot of the state of the field, Grunwald and LaMontagne (2021) conducted an online environmental scan of mindfulness programming for students and employees in the 25 top-ranked US public universities. All of the 25 institutions offered extracurricular mindfulness programmes in face-to-face formats, including courses, workshops, events, and regularly scheduled sessions, with some supplementary online resources. All these extracurricular initiatives were organized by non-academic components of the universities, mostly student services or student health and recreation, but also HR or faculty development centres. Among the 25 universities, 13 had explicit mindfulness centres associated with academic units like medicine, education, and child, youth and family studies but also student services, university counselling, or in the form of interdisciplinary programming. Most of these centres appeared to be research-focused but offered programming as well for students, employees, and/or the broader community.

In the UK, Galante et al. (2018) conducted a randomized-controlled study on the impact of mindfulness on students' psychological distress at the University of Cambridge, one of the largest mindfulness studies of its kind in higher education. Of the 616 students to enrol, 309 were offered an extra-curricular mindfulness course while the remaining received support as usual. Students in the mindfulness intervention group experienced reduced psychological distress as compared to the treatment as usual group to a moderate effect size, leading the researchers to conclude that mindfulness increased resilience to stress in university students. One important confounding issue was the high attrition rate, which is a ubiquitous issue in extra-curricular mindfulness programmes in higher education. In this case, only 59% (n=182) of the total (n=309) experimental group completed 50% or more of the programme. High attrition rates are common in such extracurricular programmes, in marked contrast to MBSR courses in the general population, for example, that average about 15% (deVibe et al., 2017). Attrition is variously defined, but in MBSR it is generally considered to be missing three or more of the eight sessions (Marjani, 2017), which means completion is defined as attending over 75% of the programme, a much higher bar than the 50% attrition bar for this study.

Anxiety is the most prevalent mental health challenge facing college students, beyond general stress, which is not a diagnosable condition (Auerbach et al., 2018: ACHA, 2019). Research suggests that mindfulness has a moderate-to-strong impact on reducing anxiety for this population. For example, in their meta-analysis of 25 primary studies, including 1492 college students, Bamber and Morpeth (2019) found that mindfulness had a large, significant impact on relieving anxiety symptoms. Interestingly, home practice and expectations for home practice decreased the positive effect, which the researchers speculated could be explained by increasing pressure and therefore, indirectly, anxiety. In most of the studies they examined, anxiety was assessed through self-report data rather than formal clinical diagnoses, so many students were not in treatment when tested. In contrast, studies of depression in clinical contexts with non-college populations found continued mindfulness practised over a two-year period following an MBCT course lowered relapse rates (Segal et al., 2019). Accordingly, we would be reluctant to conclude that home practice didn't matter; instead, the resistance to homework could have arisen from the extra-curricular nature of these programmes and the demand they placed on students' limited time. For-credit programming may have made students more willing to engage in home practice as they expect homework. Another finding was that the number of sessions increased the positive effect, which adds to the problem of high-attrition rates in these non-credit programmes. Finally, there were no differences in the efficacy of established programmes like MBSR and MBCT as compared to researcher-designed programmes.

## Mindfulness in the Formal Curriculum

As Bamber and Morpeth (2019) reported, one problem with mindfulness programmes in extra-curricular contexts in higher education is that student anxiety can increase if merely added to existing workloads. Consequently, introducing mindfulness in the formal, for-credit, and/or compulsory curriculum is an important milestone for mindfulness in higher educational contexts.

### *Small-Dose Mindfulness in Social Work*

Thomas (2017) introduced small dose mindfulness practices to undergraduate social work students - informally in required courses of their formal professional curriculum. Students participated in ten minutes of mindfulness in ten classes of a professional practice course, but showed no significant changes in mental health when compared to controls; however, they did report a range of other qualitative benefits, including increased appreciation of learning from videotaped practice tasks; calming anxiety; staying present-focused with clients; reducing premature judgement; and feeling safe in the classroom. Although the general health-promotion effects of mindfulness were not realized, the small doses were easy to provide without requiring students to be assessed for mindfulness learning components, thereby eliminating the need to introduce additional units or courses to the curriculum,.

In a comparable study, Gockel et al. (2013) used small doses of mindfulness with social work students in a clinical interviewing course, with ten minutes' practice and five minutes' discussion for each of the 28 classes. They found students in the intervention group reported significant changes in counselling self-efficacy but not in wellbeing as compared to a non-randomized control. Other benefits included students valuing the training, seeing it as relevant to their work as clinicians, and continuing to draw on the training once they transitioned to clinical work in the field. Critical to consider is the finding that students with long-term engagement with mindfulness on entry to the programme reported higher levels of improvement in counselling self-efficacy. In other words, this finding suggests that mindfulness is of considerable value to this population in higher doses, but that lower doses can plant seeds for future pursuits by increasing students' awareness and appreciation of the practices as they move into the field.

### *Diversity and Anti-Oppressive Studies*

The teaching and learning of diversity and anti-oppressive practices offer another application of mindfulness in higher education. Berila (2014, 2016) developed an approach to use mindfulness to deepen learning about systemic discrimination and internalized oppression. Mindfulness supports the introspective focus on students' own experiences of oppression, which are used to cultivate empathic concern for others suffering from oppression. Berila defined mindfulness as a set of "critical first-person inquiry" skills, all aimed at observing:

> ...how gendered or racialized power dynamics affect [students]. They can become more mindful of their reactions to intense discussions and learn to process them rather than to merely react to them. They can then more effectively learn the tools to cultivate oppositional, more empowered narratives.
>
> *(p. 58)*

Berila (2014, 2016) uses mindfulness to help students to reflect on personal experiences more honestly and directly, without judgment, including the nuanced responses to oppression in their lives, past and present. This process of encountering the experience of oppression without judgment is done to stay narrowly focused on the experience itself, including the impact on the body, emotions, and thoughts. This direct knowledge is then used to extend empathic or compassionate concern for others subjected to oppression. In this way, the direct exploration of oppression in personal experience is designed to foster insights into social experience, social awareness, and social justice. The focus on oppression is used with all students – potential or actual victims, bystanders, and perpetrators of discrimination alike. It recognizes that these positions often overlap. This use of mindfulness to teach diversity awareness in higher education has been extended to anti-racist (Fleming et al., 2022; Gaard & Erguner-Tekinalp, 2022); multicultural (McIntosh, 2023); and feminist (Berila, 2021; Burrows, 2021) topics and to specific inclusive and trauma-informed approaches (Burrows, 2018).

Reducing implicit bias is another promising purpose for mindfulness in diversity, anti-oppressive, and discrimination studies in higher education. Implicit bias refers to conditioned biases beneath the threshold of conscious awareness that distort a person's

views of the social world and can adversely impact their behaviour towards members of that biased group. Empirical research suggests that implicit biases operate independently of our identities or conscious views. Implicit bias is commonly measured using the implicit association test (to view or do the IAT, go to https://implicit.harvard.edu/implicit/takeatest.html), which is used, alternatively and sometimes problematically, to measure bias, to raise awareness, or to trigger reflection (Sukhera et al., 2019). Preliminary studies suggest that mindfulness weakens the conditioned automatic associations of implicit biases or, alternatively, extends the threshold of awareness of implicit biases. For example, Lueke and Gibson (2014) found that a short mindfulness audio session increased state mindfulness and reduced both race and age implicit biases in an experimental vs. control group. Also promising was Edwards et al.'s (2017) finding that negative implicit associations towards the elderly decreased when mindfulness was used in conjunction with a perspective-taking task. Hunsinger et al. (2019), investigating mindfulness as a way to improve weapons identification among law enforcement officers, found that mindfulness did not reduce stereotype reliance in decisions to draw weapons, but it did increase effort and control by officers when responding to Black versus While male targets.

A specific type of social-cognitive bias is the correspondence bias (CB), whereby there is a tendency for people to rely on dispositional, including stereotypical, rather than situational factors to explain behaviour. In a controlled study of mindfulness and CB, Hopthrow et al. (2017) found that mindfulness significantly reduced CB but did not eliminate it. Likewise, for minority or discriminated groups, mindfulness has been shown to reduce some of the accumulated harms of racism. For example, Weger et al. (2012) found evidence that mindfulness reduced stereotype threat in undergraduate women when told they would be asked to do a second maths test for gender comparison. One group received a brief, five-minute mindfulness session and the control group did not. The mindfulness group improved significantly from test 1 to test 2, whereas the control group's performance actually declined across the two tests, thereby suggesting that mindfulness reduces the stereotype threat. Other evidence of mindfulness being applied to reduce bias has been found in clinical education in relation to patient care (Burgess et al., 2017) and in law enforcement officer training to reduce reactive aggression to implicit biases (Ribeiro et al., 2020). Meanwhile, Owen (2020) combined mindfulness with self-compassion and loving-kindness meditation practices to reduce implicit bias and reinforce empathy and perspective-taking.

### *Physics and Sciences*

Science education is a promising but under-explored and under-researched application of mindfulness in higher education. Mindfulness is part of a broader call for first-person reflection in scientific inquiry. This is reflected, for example, in Gaston et al.'s (2017) call for a *personalized ecology* in scientific ecology studies (see Chapter 21) and Buttarazzi's (2020) call for an *embodied curriculum*. In one clear example of how first-person inquiry might be used in science, Coalson et al. (2020) report applying somatic mindfulness in teaching electrodynamics in undergraduate physics. Students completed a somatic meditation followed by a contemplative reflection aimed at connecting formal physical principles to students' immediate, direct personal experiences of electromagnetic phenomena. The practice enhanced students' curiosity and intrinsic motivation to study this topic and their appreciation of the somatic, affective, and cognitive benefits of mindfulness and other contemplative practices.

## Discrete For-Credit Mindfulness Courses

Another class of mindfulness programming in higher education is for-credit courses in which mindfulness is an explicit learning outcome of the course. These can be stand-alone elective courses or required courses in mindfulness, in what Sarath (2003) described two decades ago as "the next wave" in contemplative studies in higher education. The shift to discrete courses in mindfulness offers a number of advantages and opportunities. In contrast to small-dose mindfulness, these courses approximate or surpass the eight-week duration for training found in standardized MBPs like MBSR and MBCT, thereby making them capable of generating comparable positive mental health outcomes. Also, compared to extra-curricular courses, these for-credit courses seem to correct the high attrition rates and home practice issues, such as Bamber and Morpeth's (2019) finding of increased anxiety being correlated with home practice in extra-curricular courses. In for-credit courses, students expect homework, such that mindfulness practice may well reduce pressures associated with regular assignments or exams.

### *First-Year Orientation or MBP Stand-Alone For-Credit Courses*

There are several models for introducing mindfulness through discrete for-credit courses. One model involves stand-alone courses, introduced as a required first-year university preparation class or as an elective undergraduate course. For example, Tang et al. (2020) compared two groups of students enrolled in either a for-credit course on the science and practice of mindfulness or a positive psychology course with a range of psychological and cognitive outcomes. Results indicated that students in the mindfulness course improved significantly in most of the indicators of psychological wellbeing as compared to controls, including self-compassion, life satisfaction, trait mindfulness, and general anxiety.

In a comparable study, Danitz et al. (2016) compared mental health outcomes for first-year students enrolled in a for-credit mindfulness workshop with a control group enrolled in a regular for-credit first-year orientation course of similar duration. Depression rates decreased significantly for the mindfulness condition vs. controls, but only for the subset of those with higher levels of depression at baseline. The authors speculated that depression levels did not decrease for the entire mindfulness group because the participants were drawn from the general university population, where many students would not have depression symptoms at baseline.

Another form of discrete for-credit mindfulness courses are those teaching an academic version of standardized mindfulness programmes like MBSR or MBCT. They can be developed as lower- or upper-level undergraduate courses depending on whether or not additional upper-level outcomes are added (such as reviewing research or learning to facilitate practices). One of the authors (SM), for example, introduced three upper-level mindfulness courses at the fourth-year level as advanced studies MBSR, MBCT, and well-being. The "advanced" designation was based on book-ending the eight-week programme with assignments to read and present relevant research and to lead small groups in practice. At the same institution, there was a second-year course in MBSR that was justified at the lower level for not including these added outcomes. These are practice-focused courses that use an explicit or adapted MBSR, MBCT, or related eight-week curriculum. These courses could be, alternatively, required of all majors in a programme; elective courses in a program; or elective courses open to all students.

## *Integrating Mindfulness in Degree Programmes*

Mindfulness can be integrated into degree programmes, where the focal topic of the degree is a specific disciplinary or professional content area, but mindfulness is used to deepen the learning of the other content.

**Fine Arts**. For example, the Jazz and Contemplative Studies programme at the University of Michigan includes required and explicit mindfulness or contemplation courses that are staggered in challenge and depth across the four-year undergraduate programme (Sarath, 2003). It is unclear if the intention is to support students to engage in the mindfulness or contemplative practice on the presumption of its intrinsic value, or if it is to apply mindfulness to enhance content or performance outcomes in the associated artistic or professional practice. It cannot be assumed that merely practising mindfulness will lead to applying mindfulness in an art or profession as such bridges to practice would need to be explicitly supported.

**Medicine**. Professional programmes frequently provide mindfulness training to students as part of the established curriculum. For example, Dobkin and Huchinson (2013) identified 14 medical schools in Canada, the USA, and Australia that offered mindfulness as part of the formal curriculum of their programmes. Two programmes with fully-integrated mindfulness components across the curriculum exist at Monash Medical School (Australia) and the University of Rochester School of Medicine and Dentistry (USA). These included the use of discrete for-credit required courses. Many of the other schools offered elective courses using the eight-week MBSR or MBCT template. These varied programmes identified a range of benefits to medical students from these courses, including reducing negative emotions and stress and enhancing mindfulness, empathy, and self-compassion. Later studies of both US (Barnes et al., 2017) and UK (Harrison, 2019) medical schools found that approximately 80% had some form of mindfulness education or activities available to students, including as part of the curriculum.

**Interdisciplinary Electives**. DeBruin (2018) chronicled the development of a for-credit mindfulness programme as part of undergraduate and professional education in two institutions in Munich, Germany. This Munich Model programme offered for-credit mindfulness courses in every term to students in nine fields of study from four faculties. The courses included training in meditative practices; neuro-scientific research; and applying mindfulness in disciplines or professional work as psychologists, social workers, and teachers. What is of note is that the programmes were rationalized and framed to foster students' creativity and cognitive development (both neurological and intellectual). The research outcomes focused on improved concentration, compassion, stress management, emotional regulation, and overall mental and physical wellbeing, but the overall value of the programme was described in terms of its intrinsic value to students and its impact on academic performance and creativity.

## *MBTL as Professional Education in Higher Education*

One final model of for-credit mindfulness programmes in higher education is specialist transprofessional mindfulness teaching training and MBTL graduate certificate or degree programmes for aspiring mindfulness teachers from across professions. As outlined in Chapter 3, these programmes have been long-established in the UK for over a decade but are just beginning to appear in North America, where the dominant model until recently has been non-credit, often for-profit continuing studies programming. All professions rely on higher education for initial and some continuing professional development, certification, and education. So, the inclusion of mindfulness professional training in the curriculum of higher education is an important indicator of its mainstream acceptance. Also, these programmes are fairly unique in teaching trans-professional skills to practitioners from a range of professions who learn together.

## Mindfulness in Faculty Development

Brendel and Cornett-Murtada's (2019) two-year action research study of 33 university professors who participated in a four-day seminar on "Mindful Meditation in Teaching" found a wide range of responses and methods used by professors to integrate mindfulness in their teaching. Many of these outcomes resembled longstanding reflective practices in teaching in higher education, such as "orienting on students' minds when grading" or "paying fuller attention to students and listening more deeply" in class. The greatest reported improvements were in vague and less measurable categories like "paying fuller attention to students," while the lowest reported scores were for more objective and concrete indicators like "ending class with a breath." In the end, the researchers lacked sufficient evidence, in our view, to justify their claim that the programme and its aftermath constituted transformative learning experiences for either the professors or their students, which is not to say it was not of value. This points to a recurring problem in both mindfulness and contemplative studies in higher education: The reliance on loose methods of inquiry and training while continuing to make inflated claims about benefits.

That said, faculty development *is* a critical component needed to introduce mindfulness in the formal curriculum of higher education. For some, the preliminary step of practising mindfulness on its own may also be highly motivating and even sufficient as it is likely to prove intrinsically beneficial to students given evidence that mindfulness training improves teachers' stress levels, mindfulness, reflective practice, and life satisfaction (Becker et al., 2020; Beer et al., 2015; Brendel & Cornett-Murtada, 2019; Lomas et al., 2017). Yet, the more difficult challenge is to design, deepen, and extend faculty professional development in mindfulness to realize impacts for students as well through significant, if not transformative, changes in teaching, learning, and/or curriculum. Also, while personal practice is an expectation of mindfulness teachers so they can model or *embody* mindfulness in teaching, this requirement can be challenging in higher education where such demands can be viewed as inappropriate incursions on private or personal matters.

## From Transformative Learning to Wellbeing

In this respect, it is helpful for faculty and faculty development programmes to be clear concerning purposes, methods, and scope. A faculty member could fall anywhere on a spectrum in their purposes from the personal through to the professional to the most transformative. These goals may well shift, expand, or retract over time based on experience. The methods used to realize these goals could develop from learning to practice through to learning to apply, communicate, and teach mindfulness. Faculty may learn to practise mindfulness by participating in an eight-week MBSR or in an extended silent retreat. They may learn to apply mindfulness by joining a communities of practice in higher education or by reading about or viewing examples of MBTL. They may learn to communicate about mindfulness through scholarship and writing or by engaging in-class discussions or lectures. Finally, they may learn to teach mindfulness through completing certification as facilitators of established programmes like MBSR or MBCT and/or by engaging in the systematic introduction of mindfulness in their institutions. The scope of their commitment to integrating mindfulness into their personal and professional lives can vary accordingly. All points on this spectrum of possible impacts are valuable and reasonable goals and should not be viewed as superior or inferior.

Too often, "mindfulness light" initiatives are represented as transformative when they don't meet that high bar. Overall, the transformative label is overused in adult and higher education to describe initiatives that enhance reflective practice or awareness but fall short of transforming learners in the true sense of that term. As Beer et al. (2015) argue, connections between contemplative practices, which they use interchangeably with mindfulness, and transformative education need to be clarified or risk losing meaning. Transformative learning is routinely defined as a process of critical self-reflection in which critical thinking is used to evaluate the self and, ultimately, society (Dirkx, 1997; Mezirow, 1997). What is transformed is the individual, via self-reflection and consciousness of society, as well as "frames of reference" in the mind associated with contested beliefs as they are altered by critical reflection. Although Beer et al. claim these processes of transformative learning mirror those of contemplative practices, in fact the emphasis on discursive reasoning and judgement is inconsistent with mindfulness. Not only are they at odds with mindfulness as a process of inquiry, which is defined as paying attention in the present *without judgement*, the outcomes are also at odds. While existing approaches to transformative learning are designed to cultivate critical self-awareness, mindfulness-based learning would be more accurately described as compassionate self-awareness or merely awareness.

In fact, transformation is usually gradual and intentional but can be cataclysmic and unexpected. What seems clear is that such transformation is rare and exceptional and not to be confused with mere reflection or cognitive complexity, both of which have their own merits and are correlated with higher levels of mindfulness (Goonetilleke, 2016). Although MBTL is not oriented narrowly on transformative learning, it does aim to foster experiences and insights of interdependence and decentering that are associated in research with mindfulness as well as increased levels of empathy, compassion, identification with nature, voluntary simplicity, justice orientations, wellbeing, and activism, all considered to be aspects or outcomes of transformative learning (Albrecht, 2020). See the Exemplar/Case of transformation in the experience of an experimental quantum physicist through contemplating light in the next chapter.

In contrast, traditional Buddhist mindfulness training *does* aim explicitly for transformation – individual transformation and, in some cases, universal transformation as described in Mahayana texts – even if students display incremental intentions that fall short of that high bar (Analayo, 2020). This is not the case in higher education, where transformative learning is a possible outcome of mindfulness but not the dominant intention. The key motivation for mindfulness in higher education appears to be student success, health, and wellbeing. Accordingly, goal clarification matters because it informs what faculty teach, how students are assessed, and the criteria used to evaluate courses. These goals should be different from other mindfulness contexts and well-considered.

## CRITICAL ISSUES AND CRITIQUES

There are a range of challenges and critiques of mindfulness in higher education across the research and practice community. Salient issues are discussed below:

### Programme Motivation

As discussed, there are a range of constructive reasons to introduce mindfulness in higher education, including to enhance: Wellbeing, student performance or success, self-awareness, experiential learning, and mental health. Yet, in many cases, these motivations and programmes can be viewed as decontextualizing mindfulness as it moves from the noble enterprise of enlightenment, awakening, and liberation to these narrower and more restrictive purposes.

### Extra-Curricular or Curricular

As discussed, the extracurricular model of mindfulness in higher education poses a challenge. These extracurricular programmes often have 30–50% attrition rates, well above the average 15% attrition rates in MBSR classes in the general population (deVibe et al., 2017). What is wrong with high attrition? It is not just that it creates a bias in research or even that it suggests that students abandoned a practice that might have benefited them. There is also an opportunity cost in having people agree to participate in mindfulness training and then stop, which may make them less prone to pursue it in the future because it didn't seem to work. Also, most of those dropping out are unlikely to continue to engage in the practices immediately following their premature departures. Meanwhile, studies point to the significant benefits of sustained practice, studies like Segal et al. (2019) that have found that continued practice, in this case over a two-year period following an MBCT class, significantly lowered participants' likelihood of depression relapse.

Meanwhile, as mental health challenges rise in the higher education student population, there are emerging pressures to deliver mindfulness in virtual extra-curricular formats. El Morr et al. (2020) argued that these digital programmes are "for a scalable and economically sound innovation to address these challenges" (p. 1560). Yet, students have reported concerns over the loss of direct contact with other students and the fear of cyberbullying.

On the other hand, there are also challenges in the curricular offering of mindfulness. For example, such courses would be taught by faculty, who are rarely compelled to train or certify to teach any content or topic. This poses a challenge to ensure that those faculty or instructors who teach mindfulness are adequately qualified and competent to do so. Yet, these teachers have advanced research degrees as well, usually PhDs or EdDs, which put them in a unique position to link skills and abilities like mindfulness to the wider outcomes of courses, disciplines, and programmes. In extra-curricular programmes, in contrast, mindfulness teachers are often counsellors or clinicians, most of whom would have clinical and mindfulness teaching credentials; however, they are less likely to have advanced research degrees. The advantage for these instructors is that they tend to be more trained, qualified (with explicit certificates), and skilled in trauma-informed practices, for example, which are important even for general populations in higher education (Burrows, 2018).

## Student Motivation

What motivates students to do mindfulness in higher education is another potentially challenging issue. Extracurricular courses are invariably voluntary and so depend on students' intrinsic motivation (Donald et al., 2020). Because mindfulness is linked to enhanced self-determination and intrinsic motivation, it is important to maintain, where possible, voluntary participation, invitation practices, and informed consent. In the case of curricular courses or programmes, voluntary participation can prove challenging to safeguard. When courses are part of the required curriculum of a programme, they are not voluntary; however, attempts can be made to secure informed choice as students enter the programme, ensuring that they understand and agree to the mindfulness or contemplative orientation of the programme. Making mindfulness courses elective and ungraded (credit/non-credit or pass/fail) is one way to support more intrinsic motivation in students, yet it is imperfect since their motivation could well be for an *easy credit,* that is, credit courses without a heavy burden of assignments or examinations.

## Credit Load and Level

Another consideration in designing for-credit mindfulness courses is to determine the number of credits assigned and at what level. Conventions in higher education would say that the scope of the course, as determined by its duration and level of demand, would determine the number of credits awarded on completion. The level would be determined by the degree of challenge implied by the outcomes and assessments. With respect to duration, the established template of the eight-week course with an orientation and half-day silent retreat would constitute ten classes, which is approximating the requirements for a one-semester three-credit course. The practice orientation of mindfulness courses is not unlike that of labs or performance courses as found in science and music, respectively, for example. In this respect, the practice focus of mindfulness courses does have precedents in the academic curriculum.

With respect to assigning levels for mindfulness courses, this is trickier. In higher education, the level of an undergraduate course – lower (100 or 200) or upper (300 or 400) – is usually determined by its level of cognitive challenge or difficulty; however, contemplative practices like mindfulness challenge modern assumptions about cognitive challenge as represented, for example, by Bloom's Taxonomy. As a case in point, consider the five facets used to measure and operationalize mindfulness in the FFMQ. The first two, *observing* and *describing* experience, are represented in Bloom's model as low-demand learning outcomes. The third facet, *applying* mindfulness, is associated with higher cognitive demand, but the remaining two facets of *non-judging* and *non-reacting to* experiences are barely conceived of in the paradigm.

As anyone who practices mindfulness can attest, observing and describing meditational experiences is not a low-demand task. In the case of *observing,* as awareness deepens, experiences become subtler and so more challenging to discern. Regulating attention during mindfulness practice so as to return to and hold an object of observation is also an advanced skill. With respect to *describing,* for those unaccustomed to using language to describe internal experiences, it can be a struggle to find even simple descriptors. Similarly, recognizing and labelling emotions requires skill, experience, and an adequate lexicon. Yet, as we grow accustomed to using language for this purpose, there is an indirect effect on our capacity to recognize similar features of experience as they arise in the future. In this respect, even practice-oriented mindfulness courses may be labelled at various levels from lower to upper levels in the undergraduate or even graduate curriculum, much like labs, practice, or performance courses in other disciplines or fields. Likewise, like ethnographic studies in anthropology, education, or other social sciences, when observation is turned to observing and describing an unfamiliar context beyond our habitual experience, then how we observe and describe become subject to high standards that can be applied to earn even the highest degree: i.e., a Ph.D.

Furthermore, when outcomes involving interpreting or applying research or engaging in applied professional outcomes like teaching mindfulness, a predominantly practical course is certainly qualified to be situated at higher levels of the credit hierarchy.

## Assessment

More than anything else, assessment distinguishes formal for-credit curricular and informal non-credit extra-curricular mindfulness courses in higher education. Therefore, it is critical to develop and apply competency-based assessment to support the adaptation and acceptance of MBTL in higher education. Yet, this need for assessment practices can prove to be a stumbling block to the full integration of mindfulness into the academic curriculum. Its introspective orientation on experience means there are few directly observable or measurable features beyond participation and the self-reporting of experiences. Furthermore, because *non-judgmental* awareness is a defining feature of mindfulness, anything that encourages judging or critique of experiences could have a serious washback effect in encouraging participants to internalize a critical attitude to experience and to censor experiences that they report.

In assessing mindfulness practice, for example, the focus is often placed on participation and on trust in participants' claims about their engagement in home practice. Participation measures can use a range of indicators like attendance, contributing to class discussions and in groups, and home practice logs. Regular oral reports in groups or in class on weekly home practice can help make this element more accountable for instructors. Furthermore, when the assessment is focused on feedback rather than grades, it offers a way for participants to gradually learn to recognize and respond to their own experiences without relying on harsh judgements. Yet, to surveil students with too much vigour will shift them into their often-conditioned extrinsic motivation to practise to appease instructors for credits and grades rather than for the intrinsic value of learning. In addition, there are more conventional assessment methods that can be used like meditative journals; reports and presentations (e.g., for research components); and peer observations during teaching or facilitating mindfulness. Sarath (2003) reported using the following types of assessments in their contemplative coursework: Regular meditation practice; meditation journals; reading and writing assignments; participation in classroom discussions.

It is important to point out that assessment is not merely a challenge but also an opportunity and advantage of for-credit mindfulness. In non-credit or community courses, the absence of assessment can be a shortcoming. Formative assessment is about feedback rather than evaluation as grades. Without assessments, it is easy for an instructor to lose track of individual students and to neglect to provide individualized support. With formal assessment, there are more feedback and communication channels between students and instructors such that students can become more motivated in ways that are not necessarily extrinsic e.g., for being competent and assessed as such.

### Mindfulness or Contemplation

A lingering critique concerns the tendency in the scholarship of teaching and learning to refer to mindfulness and contemplation interchangeably. Most scholars would recognize that contemplative studies are an umbrella term and mindfulness a particular instance; however, to generalize what is true of mindfulness to other contemplative practices is not appropriate given the wide scope and purposes of such practices. For example, to equate and generalize reflective journalling with mindfulness disregards the predominant non-discursive effects of mindfulness. Furthermore, this confusion of terms may function to obscure the particularity of the traditions, practices, and effects of mindfulness and MBTL, implying that it is equivalent to a full range of contemplative practices, including prayer, journal writing, or arts-based practices.

### Mindfulness as Transformative Learning

Another critical issue concerns the focus in higher education and contemplative studies on representing mindfulness as a form of transformative learning (à la Mezirow, 1997). Such transformative outcomes are presented as if they are ideal and so used to legitimate mindfulness beyond its more seemingly mundane outcomes in health and wellbeing. In fact, the transformation of our brains, minds, sense of self, or worldview is a disorienting and disturbing experience in many cases, which may well come with accompanying mental instabilities, even if they lead to long-term outcomes like post-traumatic growth. In fact, the tendency to use small-dose or limited exposure practices with students in higher education makes transformative outcomes highly improbable. These are more associated with intense practices such as in retreats (see Chapter 19 for an example). Yet, the less-intensive form of exposure makes such programmes more trauma-sensitive and less likely to generate the mental instability that can accompany intensive training (Lindahl, 2017).

## TRENDS: PROMISING AND CONCERNING

### Linking Mindfulness to Student Success

"Student success" is an ambiguous construct used ubiquitously to describe the goal of higher education. Therefore, it is not surprising that scholarship has begun to appear on the relationship between mindfulness and student success in higher education (Leland, 2015; Mafouz et al., 2018). Of course, in doing so, there is the ever-present danger that the more holistic purposes of mindfulness will be narrowed and skewed to serve whatever definition of student success prevails in an institution or jurisdiction. Alternatively, mindfulness can challenge and support the expansion of our interpretations of student success, in particular to include wellbeing and lifelong learning.

To date, the interpretation of student success has been narrowly focused on measurable performance indicators related to access, retention, academic success, completion rates, employment, and, at best, an economic interpretation of wellbeing based on income and job satisfaction (e.g., Wiggers and Arnold, 2011). Several studies have rationalized mindfulness in higher education as serving these outcomes directly or indirectly. For example, in his review of mindfulness in higher education, Leland (2015) postulated four areas that mindfulness may improve with implications for student success: a) learning skills and academic performance (e.g., through executive control and reduced test anxiety); b) critical thinking (e.g., through introspection); c) behaviour and self-control (through self-regulation); and d) job-specific skills development, such as withholding judgment and listening; managing stress and avoiding burnout, and cultivating empathy, compassion, and positive social skills. Similarly, Malfouz et al. (2018) focused on the application of mindfulness to improve first-year retention rates by implementing an eight-session mindfulness programme for first-year students called *Just Breathe*. Students reported improvements in organization and time management; commitment to a healthy lifestyle; improved emotional awareness and relationships; and self-compassion. These are described as effective stress management skills to promote in higher education.

More recently, initiatives to expand the interpretation of student success to include indicators of student wellbeing, engagement, lifelong learning, and health are paving the way for better recognition of how mindfulness may contribute to the lifelong "success" of students in these other dimensions. For example, the US Higher Learning Commission (HLC) (2018) issued a report aimed at altering the definition of student success from a narrow focus on graduation rates to a more "flexible framework of success from a student view" (p. 05). The report recommended four contexts to measure this expanded definition of success: a) learning environment and supports; b) exit point outcomes and measures; c) external measures; and d) systems measures.

In Australia, Picton et al. (2018) challenged the transition metaphor of most student success rhetoric, with its focus on the first year, and instead advocated an educational interface model. This model represented student success as the effect of a dynamic and complex interaction between institutions, students' structural backgrounds, and their educational engagement. This interface metaphor describes a psychosocial rather than a temporal space, one based on a sense of self that is dynamic and fluctuating. Rather than a set of performance indicators, this interface is understood to be based on four psychosocial factors that determine student success and engagement: a) self-efficacy, that is, students' sense of their capabilities and engagement; b) emotional responses, such as interest and enthusiasm and the impacts of anxiety arising from money, deadlines, performance issues; c) belonging, and in particular the sense of belonging to the institution, faculty and staff, and other students; and d) wellbeing, and its opposite, stress. This reimagined view of student success as students navigate the interface between institutions, students' structural backgrounds, and their academic outcomes are designed to accommodate more culturally diverse and non-traditional students. Yet, it also helps represent better the value of mindfulness and other contemplative practices on student success. Mindfulness is demonstrably linked to all of the psychosocial factors impacting engagement: Self-efficacy, emotions, belonging, and wellbeing.

## Faculty and Staff Training

A promising trend is that faculty are beginning to opt voluntarily for formal MBTL certification or training. As a rule, faculty are hired based on disciplinary expertise, educational credentials (usually terminal degrees), and tenure and promotion processes that establish peer-reviewed performance assessment in disciplinary-based teaching, research, and service. Thereafter, they are protected following hiring and promotion to teach without unreasonable restrictions within their areas of expertise. Because mindfulness is unregulated, it can be taught without certification or training, despite the fact that such training has been shown to be beneficial and impact student outcomes. For example, Ruijgrok-Lupton et al. (2017) reported that an added year of training in MBTL significantly improved the outcomes of these teachers' MBSR participants, whereas the extent of teachers' personal meditational experience did not. Yet, too often there is a misconception among some faculty that their qualification to teach mindfulness is based on their personal practice and, perhaps, background reading. Personal practice matters, for embodiment and more, but teacher training *does* matter.

Therefore, it is helpful if faculty themselves take initiatives to train and receive certification in any one of many programs to support MBTL. This has the added advantage of increasing the institutional capacity in MBTL insofar as these trained faculty can support the professional development of other staff and faculty at the institution. At the same time, it is suitable for higher education institutions to cover the training costs for these instructors as a valid professional development expense, including their participation in annual silent retreats, which is a professional expectation for secular-scientific mindfulness teachers and trainers. Faculty members bring a value-added aspect to MBTL that may be absent in non-credit certified instructors in the community or student services. Skills in assessing students, in curricular adaptation and design, and in applied research are all examples of specialist skills of faculty in higher education that can be missing in community, counselling, or other clinical instructors. For this reason, we added several competencies associated with these skills in our MBTL-TLC (see Chapter 15).

## Contemplation and Epistemology

A promising trend in the scholarship on mindfulness as contemplation is that it has enabled a deeper analysis and critique of epistemological biases in Western secular education, which is too often dehistoricized and presented as if its organization and contents are objective and complete. That this assumption is being exported globally alongside the modern template of secular education is a cause for significant concern. Mindfulness, with its extensive empirical evidence of efficacy, offers a clear case backed by evidence of the problems of excluding alternative forms of knowing from the curriculum of higher education. Furthermore, it offers an example for how alternative forms of knowledge and practice can navigate their way to inclusion or acceptance within the secularized environment of higher education.

## Experience vs. Analysis

A related trend arising from the introduction of mindfulness in higher education is its valuable contribution to our understanding of the variation and value of experiential learning. Dominant approaches to experiential learning through practice, work experience, service learning, or study abroad, for example, are very different from the kinds of outcomes and methods of experiential learning associated with mindfulness. Narrowly defined, mindfulness is about paying attention to experience intentionally and without judgment and involves regulating attention in the process, often away from thinking and towards sensory or somatic experiences; however, as a path of learning and insight, mindfulness does involve thinking, reasoning, and reflection. For one, in memory and through language, describing and inquiry into mindfulness helps transform passive observation into active recognition. For another, the process of identifying and applying what those experiences imply for suffering and wellbeing is a process of insight navigated with the help of cognitive investigation. In this respect, the oversimplification of mindfulness as merely experiential is also of concern. This is a topic taken up in the next chapter as well as in Chapter 14, for example, on mindfulness as inquiry-based learning.

## REFERENCES

Albrecht, N. (2020). Nature-based mindfulness and the development of the ecological self when teaching in higher education. In O. Ergas & J. Ritter (Eds.), *Exploring self toward expanding teaching, teacher education and practitioner research: Advances in research on teaching* (Vol. 34, pp. 157–177). Emerald Publishing Limited. https://doi.org/10.1108/S1479-368720200000034010.

American College Health Association (ACHA). (2019). *(US) Reference group executive summary and Canadian reference group executive summary. Summary reports of the ACHA on National College Health Assessment.* https://www.acha.org/NCHA/ACHA-NCHA_Data/Publications_and_Reports/NCHA/Data/Reports_ACHA-NCHAIIc.aspx.

Anālayo, B. (2020). The myth of McMindfulness. *Mindfulness, 11*, 472–479. https://doi.org/10.1007/s12671-019-01264-x.

Auerbach, R., Mortier, P., Bruffaerts, R., Alonso, J., Benjet, C., Cuijpers, P., Demyttenaere, K., Ebert, D., Green, J., Hasking, P., Murray, E., Nock, M., Pinder-Amaker, S., Sampson, N., Stein, D., Vilagut, G., Zaslavsky, A., & Kessler, R. (2018) The WHO world mental health surveys international college student project: Prevalence and distribution of mental disorders. *Journal of Abnormal Psychology, 127*(7), 623–638. https://doi.org/10.1037/abn0000362.

Bamber, M., & Morpeth, E. (2019). Effects of mindfulness meditation on college student anxiety: A meta-analysis. *Mindfulness, 10*, 203–214. https://doi.org/10.1007/s12671-018-0965-5.

Barbezat, D., & Bush, M. (2013). *Contemplative practices in higher education: Powerful methods to transform teaching and learning.* Wiley.

Barnes, N., Hattan, P., Black, D., & Schuman-Olivier, Z. (2017). An examination of mindfulness-based programs in US medical schools. *Mindfulness, 8*, 489–494. https://doi.org/10.1007/s12671-016-0623-8.

Becker, M., Bartalotta, A., Morton, M., Helminen, E., Clawson, A., & Felver, J. (2020). The effects of mindfulness-based stress reduction in the higher education workplace: A pilot study. *Journal of Integrated Social Sciences, 10*(1), 136–154.

Beer, L., Rodriquez, K., Taylor, C., Martinez-Jones, N., Griffin, J., Smith, T., Lamar, M., & Anaya, R. (2015). Awareness, integration and interconnectedness: Contemplative practices of higher education professionals. *Journal of Transformative Education, 13*(2), 161–185. https://doi.org/10.1177/1541344615572850.

Berila, B. (2014). Contemplating the effects of oppression: Integrating mindfulness into diversity classroom. *The Journal of Contemplative Inquiry, 1*, 55–68.

Berila, B. (2016). *Integrating mindfulness into anti-oppression pedagogy: Social justice in higher education.* Routledge.

Berila, B. (2021). *Radiating feminism: Resilience practices to transform our inner and outer lives*. Routledge.
Bourgeault, C. (2004). *Centering prayer and inner awakening*. Cowley Press.
Brendel, W., & Cornett-Murtada, V. (2019). Professors practicing mindfulness: An action research study on transformed teaching, research, and service. *Journal of Transformative Education, 17*(1), 4–23. https://doi.org/10.1177/1541344618762535.
Burgess, D., Beach, M., & Saha, S. (2017). Mindfulness: A promising approach to reducing the effects of clinician implicit bias on patients. *Patient Education and Counselling, 100*, 372–376. https://doi.org/10.1016/j.pec.2016.09.005.
Burrows, L. (2018). *Safeguarding mindfulness in schools and higher education: A holistic and inclusive approach*. Routledge.
Burrows, L. (2021). *Empowering mindfulness for women*. Routledge.
Buttarazzi, G. (2020). *The integration of self-inquiry meditation into higher education: Between philosophy and practice, beyond mindfulness, towards and embodied curriculum*. Ed.D. Thesis, University of Nottingham.
Centre of Contemplative Mind. (2020). *The tree of contemplative practices*. http://www.contemplativemind.org/practices/tree.
Coalson, E., Feldman, A., & Krusberg, Z. (2020). *Contemplative practice and classical electrodynamics: Discovering electromagnetic phenomena in lived experience through somatic meditation*. arXiv:2001.08661v1 [physics.ed-ph].
Collins, E., & Segal, Z. (2020). Therapeutic mindfulness and depression. In M. Trivedi (Ed.), *Depression* (pp. 357–371). Oxford University Press.
Danitz, S., Suvak, M., & Orsillo, S. (2016) The mindful way through the semester: Evaluating the impact of integrating an acceptance-based behavioral program into a first-year experience course for undergraduates. *Behavior Therapy, 47*, 487–499. https://doi.org/10.1016/j.beth.2016.03.002.
Dawson, A., Brown, W., Anderson, J., Datta, B., Donald, J., Hong, K., Allan, S., Mole, T., Jones, P., & Galante, J. (2020). Mindfulness-based interventions for university students: A systematic review and meta-analysis of randomised controlled trials. *Applied Psychology: Health and Well-Being, 12*(2), 384–410. https://doi.org/10.1111/aphw.12188.
deBruin, A. (2018). The Munich model brings mindfulness and meditation to university students. In Pixel (Ed.), *Conference proceedings: The future of education* (pp. 37–41), Webster srl.
deVibe, M., Bjorndal, A., Fattah, S., Dyrdal, G., Halland, E., & Tanner-Smith, E. (2017). Mindfulness-based stress reduction (MBSR) for improving health, quality of life and social functioning in adults: A systematic review and meta-analysis. *Campbell Systematic Reviews, 11*. https://doi.org/10.4073/csr.2017.11.
Dirkx, J. M. (1997). Nurturing soul in adult learning. In P. Cranton (Ed.), *Transformative learning in action: Insights from practice. New directions for adult and continuing education* (Vol. 74, pp. 79–88). Jossey-Bass.
Dobkin, P., & Huchinson, T. (2013). Teaching mindfulness in medical school: Where are we now and where are we going? *Medical Education, 47*(8), 768–779. https://onlinelibrary.wiley.com/doi/full/10.1111/medu.12200.
Donald, J., Bradshaw, E., Ryan, R., Basarkod, G., Ciarrochi, J., Duineveld, J., Guo, J., & Sahdra, B. (2020). Mindfulness and its association with varied types of motivation: A systematic review of meta-analysis using self-determination theory. *Personality and Social Psychology Bulletin, 46*(7), 1121–1138. https://doi.org/10.1177/0146167219896136.
Dorjee, D. (2016). Defining contemplative science: The metacognitive self-regulatory capacity of the mind, context of meditation practice and modes of existential awareness. *Frontiers in Psychology, 7*, Article 1788. https://doi.org/10.3389/fpsyg.2016.01788.
Edwards, D., McEnteggart, C., Barnes-Holmes, Y., Lowe, R., Evans, N., & Vilardaga, R. (2017). The impact of mindfulness and perspective-taking on implicit associations toward

the elderly: A relational frame theory account. *Mindfulness*, *8*, 1615–1622. https://doi.org/10.1007/s12671-017-0734-x.

El Morr, C., Ritvo, P., Ahmad, F., Moineddin, R., & MVC Team. (2020). Effectiveness of an 8-week web-based mindfulness virtual community intervention for university students on symptoms of stress, anxiety, and depression: Randomized controlled trial. *JMIR Mental Health*, *7*(7). https://doi.org/10.2196/24131.

Farb, N., Segal, Z. V., Mayberg, H., Bean, J., McKeon, D., Fatima, Z., & Anderson, A. (2007). Attending to the present: Mindfulness meditation reveals distinct neural modes of self-reference. *Social Cognitive and Affective Neuroscience*, *2*, 313–322. https://doi.org/10.1093/scan/nsm030.

Fleming, C., Womack, V., & Proulx, J. (Eds.) (2022). *Beyond White mindfulness: Critical perspectives on racism, well-being, and liberation*. Routledge.

Gaard, G., & Erguner-Tekinalp, B.(Eds.) (2022). *Contemplative practices and anti-oppressive pedagogies for higher education: Bridging the disciplines*. Routledge.

Galante, J., Dufour, G., Vainre, M., Wagner, A., Stochl, J., Benton, A., Lathia, N., Howarth, E., & Jones, P. (2018). A mindfulness-based intervention to increase resilience to stress in university students (the Mindful Student Study): A pragmatic randomised controlled trial. *Lancet Public Health*, *3*, e72–e81. http://dx.doi.org/10.1016/S2468-2667(17)30231-1.

Gaston, K., Soga, M., Duffy, J., Garrett, J., Gaston, S., & Cox, D. (2017). Personalized ecology. *Trends in Ecology & Evolution*, *33*(12), 916–925. https://doi.org/10.1016/j.tree.2018.09.012.

Gockel, A., Burton, D., James, S., & Bryer, E. (2013). Introducing mindfulness as a self-care and clinical training strategy for beginning social work students. *Mindfulness*, *4*, 343–353. https://doi.org/10.1007/s12671-012-0134-1.

Gockel, A., & Deng, X. (2016). Mindfulness training as social work pedagogy: Exploring benefits, challenges, and issues for consideration in integrating mindfulness into social work education. *Journal of Religion & Spirituality in Social Work: Social Thought*, *35*(3), 222–244. https://doi-org.proxy.ufv.ca:2443/10.1080/15426432.2016.1187106.

Goonetilleke, D. (2016). *Cognitive complexity, mindfulness, and reflection in mental health professionals*. Doctoral Dissertation, Minnesota State University. Cornerstone. https://cornerstone.lib.mnsu.edu/cgi/viewcontent.cgi?article=1637&context=etds.

Grunwald, S., & LaMontagne, L. (2021). The state of mindfulness at top US public universities: A brief review and lessons learned. In *The Routledge companion to mindfulness at work*. Routledge.

Harrison, L. (2019). Is there a movement towards acceptance of mindfulness in medical education? An audit of mindfulness activity in UK medical schools. *MedEdPublish*, *8*(2), 14. https://doi.org/10.15694/mep.2019.000084.1.

Hart, T. (2004). Opening the contemplative mind in the classroom. *Journal of Transformative Education*, *2*(1), 28–46. https://doi.org/10.1177/1541344603259311.

Heredia, L., Torrente, M., & Vicens, P. (2020). Spiritual competence, contemplatic education, and mindfulness in schools (Competencia espiritual, educación contemplativa y atención plena en la escuela). *Studies in Psychology/Estudios de Psicologia*, *41*(3), 467–489. https://doi-org.proxy.ufv.ca:2443/10.1080/02109395.2020.1794716.

Higher Learning Commission (HLC). (2018). *Defining student success data: Recommendations for changing the conversation*. https://download.hlcommission.org/initiatives/StudentSuccessConversation.pdf.

Hopthrow, T., Hooper, N. Mahmood, L., Meier, B., & Weger, U. (2017). Mindfulness reduces the correspondence bias. *The Quarterly Journal of Experimental Psychology*, *30*(3), 351–360. https://doi.org/10.1080/17470218.2016.1149498.

Hunsinger, M., Christopher, M., & Schmidt, A. (2019). Mindfulness training, implicit bias, and force response decision-making. *Mindfulness*, *11*, 2555–2566. https://doi-org.proxy.ufv.ca:2443/10.1007/s12671-019-01213-8.

Jarvis, P. (1992). *Paradoxes of learning: On becoming an individual in society.* Jossey-Bass.
Jarvis, P., Holford, J., & Griffin, C. (2003). *The theory and practice of learning.* Kogan Page.
Kolb, D. (1983). *Experiential learning: Experience as the source of learning and development.* FT Press/ Pearson Education.
Lawlor, M. (2016). Mindfulness and social emotional learning (SEL): A conceptual framework. In K. Schonert-Reichl & R. Roeser (Eds.), *Handbook of mindfulness in education: Integrating theory and research into practice* (pp. 65–80). Springer.
Leland, M. (2015). Mindfulness and student success. *Journal of Adult Education, 44*(1), 19–24.
Lindahl, J. (2017). The varieties of contemplative experience: A mixed-methods study of meditation-related challenges in Western Buddhists. *PLoS One, 12*(5), e0176239. https://doi .org/10.1371/journal.pone.0176239.
Lomas, T., Medina, J., Ivtzan, I., Rupprecht, S., & Eiroa-Orosa, F., (2017). The impact of mindfulness on the wellbeing and performance of educators: A systematic review of the empirical literature. *Teaching and Teacher Education, 61,* 132–141. https://doi.org/10.1016/j .tate.2016.10.008.
Lueke, A., & Gibson, B. (2014). Mindfulness meditation reduces implicit age and race bias: The role of reduced automaticity of responding. *Social Psychological and Personality Science, 6*(3), 284–291. https://doi.org/10.1177/1948550614559651.
MacPherson, S. (1997). Desire in the margins: A medieval love story and the hidden curriculum of *desire. Journal of Curriculum Theorizing, 13*(2), 19–26.
MacPherson, S. (2011). *Education and sustainability: Learning across the Diaspora, Indigenous, and minority education divide.* Routledge.
Malfouz, J., Levitan, J., Schussler, D., Broderick, T., Dvorakova, K., Argusti, M., & Greenberg, M. (2018). Ensuring college student success through mindfulness-based classes: Just breathe. *College Student Affairs Journal, 36*(1), 17. https://doi.org/10.1353/csj.2018.0000.
Marjani, M. (2017). *Factors predictive of participant attrition in mindfulness-based stress reduction (Publication #10281688).* Doctoral Dissertation, Alliant International University. ProQuest Doctoral Publishing.
McIntosh, K. (2023). *Mindfulness in multicultural education: Critical race feminist perspective.* Routledge.
Mezirow, J. (1997). Transformative learning: Theory to practice. In P. Cranton (Ed.), *Transformative learning in action: Insights from practice. New directions for adult and continuing education* (Vol. 74, pp. 5–12). Jossey-Bass.
Owen, R. (2020). Using mindfulness to promote transformative learning in implicit racial bias training. *Adult Learning.* Advance online publication. https://doi.org/10.1177 /1045159520981165.
Picton, C., Kahu, E., & Nelson, K. (2018). 'Hardworking, determined and happy': First-year students' understanding and experience of success. *Higher Education Research & Development, 37*(6), 1260–1273. https://doi.org/10.1080/07294360.2018.1478803.
Ribeiro, L., Colgan, D., Hoke, C., Hunsinger, M., Bowen, S., Okey, B., & Christopher, M. (2020). Differential impact of mindfulness practices on aggression among law enforcement officers. *Mindfulness, 11,* 734–745. https://doi.org/10.1007/s12671-019-01289-2.
Roth, H. (2006). Contemplative studies: Prospects for a new field. *Teachers College Record, 108*(9), 1787–1815.
Ruijgrok-Lupton, P., Crane, R., & Dorjee, D. (2017). Impact of mindfulness-based teacher training on MBSR participant well-being outcomes and course satisfaction. *Mindfulness, 9,* 117–128. https://doi.org/10.1007/s12671-017-0750-x.
Sarath, E. (2003). Meditation in higher education: The next wave? *Innovative Higher Education, 27*(4), 215–233. https://doi.org/10.1023/A:1024072313202.
Schon, D. (1984). *The reflective practitioner: How professionals think in action.* Basic Books.

Segal, Z., Anderson, A., Gulamani, T., Williams, L.D., Desormeau, P., Ferguson, A., Walsh, K., & Farb, N. (2019). Practice of therapy acquired regulatory skills and depressive relapse/recurrence prophylaxis following cognitive therapy or mindfulness based cognitive therapy. *Journal of Consulting and Clinical Psychology, 87*(2), 161–170. https://doi.org/10.1037/ccp0000351.

Sukhera, J., Wodzinski, M., Rehman, M., & Gonzalez, C. (2019). The implicit association test in health professions education: A meta-narrative review. *Perspectives on Medical Education, 8*, 267–275. https://doi.org/10.1007/s40037-019-00533-8.

Tang, R., Broderick, P., Bono, T., Dvorakova, K., & Braver, T. (2020). A college first-year mindfulness seminar to enhance psychological well-being and cognitive function. *Journal of Student Affairs Research and Practice.* Advance online publication. https://www.tandfonline.com/doi/full/10.1080/19496591.2020.1740719.

Thomas, J. (2017). Mindfulness training in the social work practice classroom. *Social Work Education, 36*(1), 102–118. http://doi.org/10.1080/02615479.2016.1250878.

Weger, U., Hooper, N., Meier, B., & Hopthrow, T. (2012). Mindful maths: Reducing the impacts of stereotype threat through a mindfulness exercise. *Consciousness and Cognition, 21*, 471–475. http://doi.org/10.1016/j.concog.2011.10.011.

Wiggers, R., & Arnold, C. (2011). *Defining, measuring and achieving "student success" in Ontario colleges and universities.* Higher Education Quality Council of Ontario. https://heqco.ca/wp-content/uploads/2020/03/AtIssueStudent-Success-ENG.pdf.

Zajonc, A. (2013). Contemplative pedagogy: A quiet revolution in higher education. *New Directions for Teaching and Learning, 134*, 83–94.

Zajonc, A. (2014). Contemplative pedagogy in higher education: Toward a more reflective academy. In O. Gunnlaugson, E. Sarath, C. Scott, & H. Bai (Eds.), *Contemplative learning and inquiry across disciplines* (pp. 15–29). SUNY Press.

# CHAPTER 7

# PREK-12 EDUCATION

## Where Social-Emotional and Inquiry-Based Learning Intersect

The systematic introduction of mindfulness to children and youth is a significant innovation of secular-scientific mindfulness. Traditional Buddhism held ambivalent or even negative views of children and of childhood overall, which meant they had few precedents for distinctive approaches for teaching mindfulness to this population (von Gontard, 2017). One rare mention of a child in the early Buddhist community was of the Buddha's son, Rahula, who became a novice monk when still a child. After his mother is purported to have objected, children and youth had to wait until they were 20 years of age to take final vows. Today, monasteries don't offer a clear educational pathway for children or novices leading up to final vows. All the moreso for children outside of monasteries, for whom there is little access or exposure to mindfulness education or mentors. Within the Tibetan exile community in India, for example, many children were subjected to the antithesis of monastic or MBTL education in traditional, colonial-legacy teacher-centred secular schools, with little if any inquiry or mindfulness training. This began to change with the 2005 curricular innovations and the Basic Tibetan Education movement to integrate more traditional Buddhist-inspired inquiry-based learning practices (MacPherson, 2011, 2018). This chapter examines the rich and emerging field of research and practice in applying MBTL with children and youth, principally in pre-K-12 but with implications for community education serving this demographic.

## THE CONTEXT

PreK-12 education was slower and more resistant to the uptake of mindfulness than medical systems and higher education. The reasons for this are manifold, but probably include two explanations. First, education systems are not as stringently evidence-based as medical systems. Regardless of how strong the evidence may be, cultural, parental, or public perceptions and preferences may override it. An example is that, despite longstanding evidence of the benefits of dual-language bilingual education for improved academic achievement for minority language students in North America, relatively few minority language students have access to dual-language bilingual education in North America or the UK. These benefits extend to wide-ranging cognitive benefits including improved attentional control, working memory, metalinguistic awareness, and abstract and symbolic representation (Adesope et al., 2010;). Furthermore, when they have had access, it has often been because of parental or political pressure rather than the persuasion of evidence. Added to this is the fact that the gold standard of experimental evidence – the randomized controlled trial (RCT) – is rare and difficult to implement. Given challenges in designing RCTs in school-based research and, alongside children's vulnerability, research is limited to, at best, quasi-experimental designs.

The second explanation for the delayed uptake of mindfulness in preK-12 education is the relative absence of traditional precedents for this age group. While the emergence of adult mindfulness programmes, notably MBSR, involves the direct translation and

DOI: 10.4324/9781003182467-10

adaptation of practices from traditional to modern contexts, there were few if any traditional templates or norms for the teaching of mindfulness to children and youths. That said, there were notable attempts to correct gap this by reimagining preK-12 education as contemplative spaces. For example, Seidel (2006) provided a window into what such contemplative practice might look like in schools, describing contemplative teaching in preK-12 as follows:

> In this way, meditation becomes a source of focus, energy, and awareness. We stop being distracted. We can be here, in schools, with children, in life... Contemplative teaching moves with time and in space, to the rhythms of life, to what is happening now. It is willing to doubt. To be uncertain. To not know what to do. It is responsive and responsible. Obligated to this time and not an unknowable future.

## THE RESEARCH

Black (2015) reviewed 41 studies of mindfulness studies with children and youth, including 13 randomized controlled trials (half of which used active controls) across an 11-year publishing history. The majority (*n*=32; 78%) of these programmes were administered to youth at risk of specified conditions, with only nine studies involving "healthy" youth. The majority of the studies occurred in schools (*n*=19), followed by clinics (*n*=15), homes (*n*=4), corrections facilities (*n*=2), and in the community (*n*=1). The review found that executive functioning (EF) improved significantly through mindfulness, as did prosocial outcomes linked to positive emotions and SEL skills. There was evidence of reduced depressive symptoms, rumination, anxiety, and externalizing problems, with effects lasting up to three months post-intervention, and improved psychobiological effects like blood pressure, heart rate, and stress physiology. Therefore, the author concluded that mindfulness was "probably efficacious" in the neurocognitive (EF), psychosocial (SEL), and psychobiological (stress-related) outcomes identified in the studies.

Significantly and more recently, Kuyken et al. (2022) reported on a large-scale UK study using a 10-week mindfulness intervention delivered by classroom teachers in 41 schools (n=3572) to 11-14 year-olds found no effect on adolescent mental health when compared to treatment-as-usual (TAU). Boyce (2022) followed-up with the researchers and noted that students did not engage in home practice and the teachers were not trained mindfulness teachers (though they had received some mindfulness training). In fact, it was the teachers who were found to benefit most, including in reduced burnout, and school climate.

### Liaisons and Entryways for Mindfulness into Schools

Below we consider three dominant entry pathways for mindfulness in the preK-12 context: a) individual teachers; b) whole-school and district-wide; and c) curriculum.

#### *Individual Teachers*

Most K-12 teachers have some autonomy over what they teach within the broad parameters of required curricular outcomes. With respect to mindfulness, this autonomy has enabled teachers who are self-motivated to use mindfulness techniques in their teaching. As the Kuyken et al. (2022) study demonstrated, this pathway through teachers themselves practicing and introducing mindfulness in classrooms and schools through their own embodiment, much as Seidel (2006) described, may be the most significant contribution of mindfulness through its impact on classroom climates and indirectly on students. In-service teacher training and teacher practice is one of Willard's (2015) early stages for integrating mindfulness in schools.

In their review, Hwang et al. (2017), found all 16 studies showed positive effects from mindfulness training on teacher wellbeing and performance, including in reductions in self-perceived stress and burnout, sleep quality, anxiety, and overall psychological distress, as well as increases in mindfulness and self-compassion. Teacher performance outcomes included increased organization, self-efficacy, forgiveness, and use of positive affect words, as well as decreased psychological and physiological reactivity. Some data showed changes in student outcomes as well, including reductions in maladaptive behaviours and increased compliance. In their study of dispositional mindfulness and teaching, Brophey-Herb et al. (2019) surveyed 618 pre-service teachers enrolled in child development/early education courses in nine US universities. Those with higher levels of mindfulness reported stronger commitments to reflective practices and more mindful relations with others including kindness, greater child development knowledge, and more developmentally appropriate responses to young children's needs during common challenging situations.

When teachers do become more committed mindfulness practitioners, they may introduce mindfulness on their own initiative. For example, Albrecht (2018) studied a sample of eight individual teachers who introduced mindfulness to children in schools in Australia and the US: Four primary teachers, one middle-school teacher, a special needs teacher, and two after-school programme developers. Four overlapping themes emerged in their experiences and understanding of those experiences: a) the spiritual nature of a teacher's mindfulness practice; b) redefining modern conceptions of creativity; c) responsibility for nurturing a child's wellbeing; and d) being a mindful role model. With respect to the latter, also known as *embodiment*, the author found three sub-themes: i) incorporating formal and informal practices throughout the day (i.e., *personal* practice rather than with children, though they all did teach mindfulness to children); ii) cultivating a mindful school (i.e., cultivating organizational and parental support so as to recognize mindfulness in an ecosystem of relations); and iii) mindfulness as a personal journey (i.e., teachers' own mindfulness practice matters).

This idea that a teacher's personal practice and embodiment of mindfulness are more important than teaching mindfulness to children is a finding reiterated in Grant's (2017), who investigated two teachers who independently introduced mindfulness to children. Yet, as Albrecht (2018) pointed out, the research does not fully support the conclusion that a teacher needs to practise mindfulness in order to teach it to children. Bakosh et al. (2016), for example, reported on a mindfulness-based social-emotional learning programme using audiotapes and guides for teachers, which didn't require specialized training or that teachers practise mindfulness themselves. The results found high levels of participation by teachers with significant improvement in students' grades and reduced behavioural disruptions as compared to a control group. Ruijgrok-Lupton et al. (2017) likewise found that the duration of MBSR teachers' training affected outcomes more than the duration of their personal practice. Yet, this critical issue of teacher expertise and background tends to be under-emphasized or overlooked in research, as Hwang et al. (2017) noted in their review.

The Kuyken et al. (2022) study also raised question about the kinds of training teachers need to teach mindfulness effectively to children and youth in school-based contexts (Boyce, 2022).

## *Whole School and District-Wide Initiatives*

Ergas (2019) distinguishes mindfulness *in*, *as*, or *of* education in preK-12. Mindfulness *in* education refers to the use of mindfulness as an economic-therapeutic tool to address distinctive problems or issues, such as mental health or conduct issues. Mindfulness *as* education involves mindfulness as an educational activity with inherent value, whereby an education system seeks *to embody* the virtues and capacities of mindfulness. As he argues, this *as-education* approach emphasizes implementation rather than method and shifts the focus from individuals to the whole school. As the Kuyken (2022) study suggests, the whole school effect is impacted when mindfulness is taught to teachers and, indirectly, directed at impacting school climate. Such a whole-school approach is about "liberating education for economic imperialism" by shifting outcomes from future economic workforces to wellbeing. Finally, he suggests a third approach, mindfulness *of* education, whereby mindfulness is used to critique education itself. He associates this "radical form of critique" with contemplative inquiry and its critical first-person perspective, which uses curiosity and inquiry to examine the experience of education.

**Whole-School Models**. Many mindfulness-based whole-school approaches (M-WSA) emanate from the UK, where studies like the MYRIAD project reported by Kuyken et al. (2020) are beginning to demonstrate that the most important contribution of mindfulness may be for school and classroom cultures rather than for individual mental health. This study and others have begun to untangle what is required for an M-WSA. For example, Wilde et al. (2019) examined the implementation of mindfulness across seven secondary/high schools in the UK, in which four cornerstones emerged for the successful implementation of M-WSA: a) *people* (committed teachers and senior leadership); b) *resources* (time and financial); c) *journey* (allowing time for implementation; and d) *perceptions* (language and communication). Furthermore, they found that context (setting, culture, resources) was the salient factor affecting successful implementation, which the researchers concluded was most dependent on key people, including the involvement of one key school leader. Similarly, Hudson et al.'s (2020) UK study of 15 schools using an M-WSA to address mental health identified school leadership as a key factor determining high or low implementation schools.

Sheinman et al. (2018) compared three schools in Israel that reflected, respectively, an established M-WSA programme; a newly-established M-WSA programme (one year); and no coordinated school-based mindfulness. Results indicated that student mindfulness-based coping was strongest in the established M-WBA programme, weaker in the one-year programme, and weakest with no school-based programme. The coping situations measured and compared were specified as exams, concentration, sleep, facing anger, and disappointment. The study findings reinforced that long-term, whole-school mindfulness programming is worth the investment of time and effort to support student learning and coping skills. In a US study, Penna-Wilkos (2018) investigated ten teachers, all involved in school-wide mindfulness initiatives, who reported improved student attention skills, self-regulation, and social-emotional abilities; however, they also pointed to time and student interruptions as challenges, which might be addressed through district-wide, ministry-wide, or broader curricular supports.

**District-Wide Strategies**. One key rationale for fostering a whole-school approach to MBTL are the benefits it offers as a universal prevention strategy for managing stress and promoting wellbeing for all members of the school community (Stuart et al., 2017). This approach is often referred to as a Tier 1 strategy, as opposed to the progressively more classroom-based and individualized supports of Tier 2 and 3 (see also Berkowitz, 2019). Therefore, it is reasonable to extend this approach to an entire school district not just a whole school, so the benefits to the community might be more fulsomely impacted as well as all members and agents within a school system. Rani (2018) identified three key motives for district-wide approaches: Cultivating meaningful growth opportunities; valuing the importance of positive relations with others; and acknowledging the impact of top-down leadership on environmental mastery. Berkowitz identifies mindfulness as one of only a few strategies to improve school climate and to foster more inclusive schools for diverse and minority learners, which reinforces the value of district-wide approaches.

### *Curriculum*

Another pathway for mindfulness into preK-12 education is through curricular interventions or programmes that may or may not involve teacher training components. Unlike the adult sector that is dominated by standardized programmes like MBSR, MBCT, and MSC (Mindful Self-Compassion), the child and youth curricula and programmes are more varied and less standardized. In preK-12 education, local communities and many teachers enjoy considerable autonomy and flexibility in how curricular outcomes are taught, learned, and assessed. In Tables 7.1, 7.2, and 7.3, we provide overviews and research on 17 of these varied MBTL curricula used in K-12 education in North America (and one in Israel). Some of these were collated in a related paper by Semple et al. (2017).

It is important to emphasize that all of these K-12 mindfulness curricula are designed to address SEL and behavioural outcomes for generic or universal K-12 programming. Yet, SEL outcomes reflect only a small component of the required curriculum of schools. This compartmentalization of mindfulness as SEL limits the time and opportunities allotted to mindfulness to periods assigned to SEL-based outcomes. This SEL focus is a limited interpretation of the potential of mindfulness as a form of inquiry across the K-12 curriculum. Although some of the research included academic performance measures, these benefits were presented as the indirect effects of SEL outcomes rather than a direct effect of mindfulness on learning.

A related area of concern is that many of these MBTL curricula represented in Table 7.1 require externally trained personnel to lead the mindfulness sessions with students or school personnel. On the one hand, this reliance on external agents may be an efficient and effective way to ensure properly trained facilitators in mindfulness to optimize the impact and fidelity to the curriculum. This was a proposed weakness in the MYRIAD program, for example (Boyce, 2022). On the other hand, this reliance on outsiders limits the sustainable and transformative potential of mindfulness, both as a source of improved school and classroom climate and as an inquiry technique across the curriculum. To integrate mindfulness across the curriculum so as to impact learning and classroom climate,

**Table 7.1** Sample Evidence-based MBTL Programmes for PreK-8

| *Programme Type* | *Programme Name* | *Purpose* | *Target Learners* | *Curricular Focus* | *Research* |
|---|---|---|---|---|---|
| **pre-K-8** | **MindUP** (Hawn Foundation, 2011a,2011b,2011c; Maloney et al., 2016) | SEL: mindfulness; self-regulation; empathy; perspective-taking | preK-2<br>gr. 3–5<br>gr. 6–8 | Each w/ 15 lessons in 4 units:<br>i) brain-based mindfulness<br>ii) the senses<br>iii) attitudes<br>iv) taking action | Schonert-Reichl and Lawlor (2010) RCT (246 x 4–7th graders) – improved attention, behavioural regulation, social skills & decreased aggression<br>Schonert-Reichl (2015) (2 x 4/5th grade classes + 2x controls) – improved executive functioning, empathy, perspective-taking, optimism; emotional control; school self-concept, and social responsibility. Rated higher by peers for pro-social behaviours and likability and for fewer negative social traits. Higher year-end math scores. |
| | **Inner Explorer (IE)** | Adapted MBSR format for children. | In 2017 – in 250 schools across 50 US states | Partially audio-recorded | Bakosh (2013) – 18 classrooms (383 Ss) across two schools – some passive controls. Teachers reported improved stress and students improved grades in maths, science, and social studies.<br>Bakosh et al. (2016) – In eight third-grade classes with half assigned to control condition with treatment group showing improved quarterly grades and reduced behavioural incidents, whereas controls' behavioural incidents increased. |
| | **MMBS (Israel)** | Mindfulness and Mind-Body Skills for Children | 6–13 year olds | Whole-school approach: two-yr programme | Semple et al. (2017) – After six years, school high in violence/below nat'l average in academics developed supportive and cohesive climate with above average performance in math and English.<br>Sheinman et al. (2018) – Compared three schools using MMBS and found higher levels of coping in students. |

**Table 7.2** Sample Evidence-based MBTL Programmes for Youth, or Children and Youth

| *Programme Type* | *Programme Name* | *Purpose* | *Target Learners* | *Curricular Focus* | *Research* |
|---|---|---|---|---|---|
| **Youth** | **Learning to BREATHE** (Broderick, 2013) | emotion regulation using mindfulness | adolescents | body<br>thoughts<br>emotions<br>attention<br>tenderness (self & other)<br>habits | Broderick and Metz (2008) – decreased neg. affect and tiredness; increased pos. affect and emotion regulation.<br>Metz et al. (2013) – controlled - lower levels of stress, psycho-somatic complaints, and higher levels of emotion regulation skills |
| | **MARS-A** | relieve distress (anxiety or depression) | adolescents – clinical @ BC Children's Hospital | combines aspects of MBSR and MBCT | Vo et al. (2015) – Significant declines in perceived stress, distress, and depression. |
| | **SRMC / MM** | stress-reduction & mindfulness /mindful moment | at-risk youth in Baltimore, MD | after-school / in-school – mindfulness, yoga, Tai Chi, discussion | Semple et al. (2017) – Programme evaluations found improved attendance, academic performance, stress management and reduced behaviour problems, rumination, intrusive thoughts, and emotional arousal. |
| **Children & Youth** | **Master Mind (MM)/**<br>**Moment Programme (MP)** | **MM** –prevent substance abuse<br>**MP** –improve relationships and academic performance | children and youth | 15-min daily per four weeks – breathing, eating, body scan, movement | Semple et al. (2017) – **MM** improved EF but not likelihood to use substances; **MP** improved behavioural regulation, metacognition, reduced aggression, improved academic performance (girls) – not EF |
| | **MBSR** | childhood stress, trauma | children and youth | MBSR-adapted | Dunning et al. (2019)Ortiz and Sibinga (2017) |

*(Continued)*

**Table 7.2** (Continued)

| *Programme Type* | *Programme Name* | *Purpose* | *Target Learners* | *Curricular Focus* | *Research* |
|---|---|---|---|---|---|
| | **MBCT-C** | MBCT-based to reduce anxiety and depression | children and youth | MBCT-adapt. Novak & Mihic, (2018) – later adapted for schools | Abedini et al. (2020) – cancer<br>Pinhas-Hamiel et al. (2020) –type-2 diabetes<br>Bruns et al. (2021); Cotton et al., (2020) – anxiety and genetic risks for bipolar disorder<br>LaGue et al. (2019) – reduced math anxiety |
| | **Resilient Kids (RK)** | attention, transitioning, emotional balance | kids and youth | movement, breath meditation, discussion, min. 50% experiential 30-min sessions twice a week for a year (delivered by a specialist with teacher present) | |
| | **Still Quiet Place (SQP)** | MBSR adapted for children | children and youth | trained facilitators each week for 30-60 mins/ eight weeks | Semple et al. (2017) – several non-RCT for a similar programme for families – found improved cognitive control and depression symptom reduction |

**Table 7.3** Sample Evidence-based MBTL Programmes for (Students via) Teachers and School Personnel

| *Programme Type* | *Programme Name* | *Purpose* | *Target Learners* | *Curriculum* | *Research* |
|---|---|---|---|---|---|
| **Teachers or School Personnel** | **CARE** | help students indirectly | school personnel | mindfulness; emotion skills; caring & listening; | Sharp et al. (2016) – Interview data – improved present-centred emotion awareness; emotional reappraisal of situations. |
| | **IRP** | mindfulness-based SEL | teachers, parents, students | retreats; PD workshops; stress reduction days; monthly teacher workshops; parent workshop; K-8 curriculum; 10-hr teacher training | Lantieri et al. (2016) – 2 year pilot of 33 NYC schools, 55 teachers, 855 gr. 3–5 (471 in treatment & 384 controls) – treatment group teachers – improved stress reduction, attention, and relational trust. 3rd–4th gr. reduced frustration levels – though stronger pos. effects *within* treatment for high-risk students. |
| | **Mindful Schools (MS)** | train-the-trainer (i.e., teacher) model | teachers (directly) / students (indirectly) | manualized, three-course teacher training with 30-/25-modular programmes for elem./ second students | Semple et al. (2017) – initial programme evaluations identified improvements for teachers in mindfulness and for students in a range of attentional, physical, and social metrics |
| | **SMART/ MBEB** (Cullen & Pons, 2015) | mindfulness-based emotional balance | teachers | 50% MBSR plus emotional regulation practices | Roeser (2016) – 13 teachers (uncontrolled) – improved awareness; mindfulness; verbalizing experience; non-judgment; non-reactivity; self-compassion; and transfer of skills to classroom. |
| | **Wellness and Resilience Programme (WRP)** | derives from MBSR and IRP (above) | Vermont school personnel | teachers use the same curriculum with students | Semple et al. (2017) – one study showed improved stress levels, but pre-test at beginning of year when stress levels known to be higher |

both teachers and some senior leadership need to be involved. Teachers in particular are the key curriculum experts able to recognize where and how mindfulness can be integrated within specific disciplines and contents. They also have the strong network and relational leverage to support others in the school community to learn mindfulness or to use it in their teaching or parenting.

In Text Box 7.1, we provide an example of how a cross-curricular mindfulness programme might be adapted for use in a Grade 4 science curriculum in the Province of British Columbia, Canada. This process requires classroom teachers skilled in both mindfulness and curriculum design to ensure fidelity to established practices in mindfulness training while accommodating local curricular outcomes. With this in mind, we added curriculum design skills as an MBTL competency, as presented in Chapter 15. Optimally, the kind of curriculum model we present in Text Box 8.1 would be reinforced across the curriculum with mindfulness woven to support learning and inquiry directly, not only indirectly through social-emotional outcomes. Without this shift in the perceived purposes of mindfulness, the time challenge will persist if mindfulness is only legitimated as an activity used to address wellness and behaviour. Well-trained teachers in preK-12 are pivotal for this deep learning approach.

## TEXTBOX 7.1 INTEGRATING MINDFULNESS INTO A GRADE 4 SCIENCE CURRICULUM

Mindfulness can be integrated across the curriculum as an overarching metacognitive inquiry into the mind, observing experiences, and thinking. For example, in science, it can ground children's inquiry in their own direct somatic or perceptual experiences. Here we provide an example using the BC Ministry of Education (2021) Science 4 course curriculum, where the overarching theme – "mind, life, and matter" – is woven throughout the year. Below is an example of how two of the four "big ideas" (outcomes) of the curriculum can be connected and deepened through mindfulness.

**Life Science**: *All living things sense and respond to their environment.*

Mindfulness is an inductive form of inquiry, moving from direct experiences to reasoning, generalizations, and inferences based on those experiences. By using mindfulness as part of a "mind, life, and matter" inquiry, students are invited to explore their own senses and the experiences they generate, before comparing these with the senses and inferred experiences of other people and animals, to draw inferences about animal life and to develop empathy as well. From here, students might consider plant life and how plants interact and respond to their environments without the same kinds of senses or mind and then on to matter, all the while asking the question: How do mind, life, and matter relate?

**Physical Science**: *Matter has mass, takes up space, and can change phase.*

Mindfulness can be used to train observational skills while bridging from the life science inquiry to the phases of matter – solid, liquid, gas – as they manifest in students' own bodies and in the bodies of humans and animals write large. One interesting line of inquiry could be to examine how matter in the body changes phases – e.g., homeostasis whereby rising body temperatures lead to the release of water (sweat) which, when it evaporates, cools the skin. A possible related line of inquiry could be the relationship between matter and mind, with the mind as an emergent phenomenon but non-reducible to matter. This offers a way to reflect on living and non-living systems, which comes up in the final earth science component.

### *Exposure Beyond Classrooms*

At the same time, there are alternative access routes to schools for children and youth to access mindfulness education. There is a range of extra-curricular access points in which children and youth learn about mindfulness outside of the formal curriculum of schools. Examples are through clubs and sports teams and through before- or after-care programmes. These varied access points outside of the preK-12 curriculum or outside the institution of schools altogether may help some children and youth to feel more comfortable learning and using the associated skills.

**Parent and Family Education**. The home is a source for mindfulness training for children and youth, arguably more important than schools given the pivotal role the home has in the socialization of children. The value of parent and family mindfulness education approaches are suggested by Parent et al.'s (2016) study of 615 parents, wherein higher levels of parental dispositional mindfulness were indirectly related to children and youth having a lower level of internalizing and externalizing problems. The direct relationship was between disposition mindfulness and decreased negative parenting practices, which directly reduced internalizing and externalizing problems in youth. These findings held for each three developmental ages of the children: Young childhood (3 to 7 years; $n$=210); middle childhood (8-12 years; $n$=200); and adolescence (13-17 years; $n$=205). Bogels (2015) offers a detailed model of a parenting mindfulness programme for parents in mental health treatment. Of course, one key benefit of school access is that it is universal and doesn't discriminate by parental dispositions or willingness to participate.

**Clinical and Community Access**. Children can learn mindfulness in the community or in clinics, as discussed in other chapters and below under mental health and behavioural management. As mentioned at the beginning of this segment, Black (2015) found clinical contacts ($n$=15 of 41) to be the most common source after school contact, with community contacts far less common ($n$=1).

## Rationales and Purposes for Mindfulness in preK-12

Given the relative newness of MBTL in preK-12 and with children and youth overall, the ways mindfulness has been rationalized for use with this demographic are distinctive. As mentioned, the research, discourse, and programmes for mindfulness in preK-12 are overwhelmingly dominated by assumptions about its role in social-emotional learning and development. Other rationales are closely connected to SEL, such as mental health promotion or behavioural management, in particular behaviours associated with violence. Far fewer are studies representing programmes using mindfulness as a form of inquiry-based experiential learning. We will consider relevant research on these topics below.

## *Social-Emotional Learning (SEL)*

Social-emotional learning (SEL) is an approach to promote positive identity development, socialization, and behavioural outcomes through education. The movement with scholarship on emotional intelligence, popularized by Goleman (1995), and by mounting concerns with school bullying and violence in the 1990s. Today, SEL outcomes are integrated across the preK-12 curriculum and are aimed at promoting students' intrapersonal, interpersonal, and social development beyond academic achievement. Weissbeg et al. (2015) argued that SEL programmes have been justified and rationalized as an indirect benefit to academic performance given their direct promotion of coping skills and prevention of negative behavioural, health-related, and social outcomes. According to these authors, the strong evidence-base of mindfulness secured its place in SEL and SEL curricula. Invariably, these curricula are based on CASEL's widely accepted framework of five interrelated cognitive-affective-behavioural SEL competencies: self-awareness, self-management, social awareness, relationships skills, and responsible decision-making (www.casel.org). Lawlor (2016), for example, showed how mindfulness practices align with each of CASEL's five SEL competencies. Her table is adapted in the following summary showing how SEL and mindfulness align.

**Self-awareness**. Mindfulness improves *self-awareness,* the ability to understand the nature of the mind and to recognize emotions, strengths and limitations, and values using practices like focused breathing or through more common academic tasks like reflective journal writing.

**Self-management**. Mindfulness helps *self-management* through emotion regulation, inhibitory control, deployment of attention, and executive functioning, which are developed through focused mindfulness practices like breathing and movement practices like yoga or Tai Chi.

**Social awareness**. Mindfulness enhances *social awareness,* that is, showing empathy and compassion for others, through a range of arts-based mindfulness practices such as literature, drama, and art or through compassion and loving-kindness meditations using visualization or analytical meditation.

**Relationship skills**. Mindfulness impacts *relationship skills* through a range of interpersonal awareness skills such as mindful listening, thoughtful dialogue, and managing conflict. Practices like mindful listening and cooperative activities, including pair and group work, can further these skills.

**Responsible decision-making**. Mindfulness is used to support *responsible decision-making* and ethical action by helping students to learn to state facts without biased judgements; to make ethical choices based on awareness and caring; and to take multiple perspectives. Applying mindfulness in community service learning and through active witnessing are examples of how it can be used.

## *Mental Health and Behavioural Management*

Another rationale for child and youth mindfulness programming is to improve mental health and to reduce disruptive, destructive, or problematic behaviours. Although this rationale is more associated with clinical programmes (Black, 2015), schools also introduce mindfulness as preventative mental health and behavioural management. The aforementioned MYRIAD study in the UK was designed as a preventative mental health programs for adolescents, for example, whose negative findings suggest that these intervention approaches may not be the most effective strategy (Kuyken et al., 2022). Other studies have generated more promising results. For example, in a meta-analysis of 33 controlled studies of MBIs with children and youth (*n*=3,666) in school-based, clinical, and community programmes, Dunning et al. (2019) reported significant improvements in mindfulness, depression, anxiety/stress, executive function, negative behaviours, and attention; however, when limited to 17 studies using active controls (*n*=1762), only mindfulness, depression, and anxiety/stress findings were significant. In a clinical study, Cotton et al. (2016) found mindfulness reduced the clinical severity of anxiety disorders for youth at risk of bipolar disorder. These ambiguous findings require more research and analysis on where and how mindfulness is best introduced to youth to support their mental health.

### *Classroom or School Climate*

Borrowing from organizational and workplace climate studies, schools began to adopt the metaphor and construct of *school climate.* The term came to include the following aggregate factors: a) social, indicated by the relations between agents; b) physical, indicated by the school environment; c) individual, indicated by student attitudes to learning and belonging; and d) cultural, indicated by expectations, rules, and norms. School climate, so defined, was found to be associated with a range of student achievement and performance outcomes (Chirkina & Khavenson, 2018).

Recently, the lens has narrowed further to consider *classroom climate*, where the impacts are more direct and observable. Operationalized in the *Brief Classroom Climate Scale*, classroom climate is represented by two dimensions: Group cohesion (satisfaction; cohesion among members) and classroom management (organization; relationships between teacher and students). Lopez-Gonzales et al. (2018) offered evidence that classroom climate may be the key mediating link between mindfulness and academic performance, building on an earlier finding that personal and familial relaxation/mindfulness impacted student performance and mediated classroom climate (Lopez-Gonzales et al., 2016). Yet, there are ambivalent findings on this relationship (Meyer & Eklund, 2020). The Kuyken et al. (2022) study, on the other hand, given it's large scope and use of active controls, found significant improvements to classroom climate when teachers underwent training as well.

Willard (2015) provides a model for how mindfulness can impact school climate positively so as to improve or transform school culture. He presents five stages in the teaching and learning of mindfulness, developing from self to system to awareness to integration through to life. *Self* refers to the decision of teachers and other personnel to learn, practise, and embody mindfulness so as to be more authentically present with children. The *system* stage refers to efforts to educate the entire school community through sharing of research with, or teaching mindfulness to, leaders, personnel, and parents. The next *awareness* stage refers to actually leading mindfulness or awareness practices and exercises with students. The *integration* stage refers to the integration of a full spectrum of informal mindfulness practices and approaches in classrooms and schools. And the final *life* stage involves the full integration of mindfulness in the lives of students and school personnel, such that they are fully committed to both formal and informal mindfulness practices throughout their lives, not just at school.

### *Academic Performance*

Another important rationale for introducing mindfulness in schools concerns its effects on academic performance. Findings linking mindfulness indirectly to academic performance improvements are fairly robust. For example, in their systematic review of 24 studies (19 controlled) with 1348 students learning mindfulness and 876 in controlled conditions, Zenner et al. (2014) found cognitive performance had the greatest between-group differences ($g$=0.80) as compared to established SEL and psychological outcomes like stress (0.39), resilience (0.36), and emotional problems (0.19). Cognitive performance was most commonly measured using attention tests, but also a creativity test, a mind wandering test, and grades as dependent variables, with improved attention being proposed as the key mediator of these improvements. Critical questions remain, such as how mindfulness impacts cognitive-academic performance and the mediators that best explain these effects. Some proposed mediators are SEL factors (Bakosh et al., 2016; Lawlor, 2016; Maloney et al., 2016; Schonert-Reichl et al., 2015); school climate (Lopez-Gonzalez et al. (2018); and reductions in inattention and hyperactivity and improved emotional regulation and executive functioning for students with ADHD (Pozneanscaia, 2019). What is less reported are motivation-related mediators from mindfulness' effects on autonomy and intrinsic motivation, an issue raised by Maloney et al. (2016).

### *Inquiry-Based Experiential Learning*

The preoccupation with mindfulness as SEL and mental health promotion has eclipsed the potential role of mindfulness in inquiry in preK-12 contexts. Inquiry-based learning (IBL) is a form of student-centred constructivist education that leverages students' intrinsic motivation by grounding learning activities in authentic, relevant studies (Buchanan et al., 2016). Often collaborative, self-directed, and minimally guided, IBL nonetheless requires a keen and active role for teachers as facilitators and guides. It is associated with the use of more authentic learning tasks as found in project-based learning, problem-based learning, collaborative learning, and challenge learning (Barron & Darling-Hammond, 2008; Freisen & Scott, 2013). In his meta-analyses, Hattie (2009) describes inquiry-based *teaching* as follows:

> Inquiry-based teaching is the art of developing challenging situations in which students question phenomena…Such learning situations are meant to be open-ended in that they do not aim to achieve a single "right" answer for a particular question being addressed, but rather involve students more in the process of observing, posing questions, engaging in experimentation or exploration, and learning to analyze and reason.
>
> *(pp. 208–209)*

IBL methods are most associated with science education, where they are used to shift learning from teacher-talk to lab work (Hattie, 2009); however, because lab work is often highly prescriptive and procedural with a correct answer and pathway to a solution, particularly in K-12, it is not always a good example of inquiry-based learning. Across disciplines, inquiry-based learning approaches have been found effective in teaching critical thinking skills. For example, Tali et al. (2019) researched IBL with teachers in ecology, sociology, and archeology field studies in the "outdoor environment." Seixis (1993) describes its adapted use in history teaching when experts, teachers, and students form communities of inquiry translating expert knowledge into classroom learning. Wale and Bishaw (2020) researched English language students in an academic writing course using inquiry-based instruction to teach argumentative writing as a strategy to improve their critical thinking abilities, a vital skill for academic success. The authors attributed the inquiry-based approach with improved student capacities to interpret, analyze, infer, evaluate, explain and self-regulate, core critical thinking skills.

As an inductive method, mindfulness offers an inquiry orientation to investigating phenomena. Beginning with regulating attention and enhancing executive control, mindfulness improves the capacity to notice, observe, and sustain attention on the sensed and phenomenal world of experience. At the same time, by fostering a non-judgmental open awareness, mindfulness can enhance cognitive openness and flexibility. Indeed, properly instructed, it is not that judgement is suppressed so much as replaced with curiosity and interest. According to the *Satipatthana sutta*, for example, mindfulness is only the first of seven factors of what might be termed *existential* learning (see Chapter 11). What follows mindfulness to kick-start its capacity to give rise to such learning is translated as *investigation*, the second factor of *awakening*. Such investigation manifests operationally as a question and leads in succession to, among other factors, energy, joy, tranquility, concentration, and equanimity. In this respect, mindfulness offers a distinctive approach to inquiry learning, whereby its investigative capacity is linked to emotional regulation and wellbeing (Opelt & Schwinger, 2020).

## Mindfulness with Children with Special Abilities and Needs

Here we consider learner-specific applications with specific child and youth populations.

### *Very Young Children*

Practising mindfulness with very young children is both innovative and new and, at the same time, well-established. For example, there are precedents for using mindfulness with young children in the long-standing global network of Montessori preschools, which rely on methods developed by Italian educator Maria Montessori over a century ago. Lillard (2011) identified three key approaches in the Montessori method that align with – and, indeed, *constitute* – mindfulness practices with very young children: Privileging concentrated attention; attending to sensory experience; and engaging in practical work. She speculates that these mindfulness approaches may be responsible for the social-emotional and executive function benefits of Montessori schools and their popularity internationally. Baynham (2018) shares an intriguing representation of this connection between Montessori and mindfulness in an account in the *Montessori International* newsletter. She visited a small school in rural Tibet and profiled their US teacher from San Francisco, Andrew Taylor, who was using daily guided mindfulness practices to start each school day. There was a certain irony that Taylor was reintroducing Tibetan children to mindfulness when their local Chinese-Tibetan school did not. The school not only had a reputation for poor quality education but, on completing the three-year primary programme, the children were required to leave their homes to attend residential boarding schools to finish their education. Observing their eight-minute silence practice in the morning, Baynham was reminded, in her words: "of Montessori's silence game. Montessori recognized the importance of developing the skill of silence" (p. 28).

### *Adolescents and Gender Differences*

Many of the adolescent mindfulness programmes adapted from adult programmes, including MBSR, MBCT, and MARS-A, are modified to include more emotion regulation components. Yet, one challenge in delivering universal SEL-focused mindfulness programmes to adolescents is how to address gender and sex differences, which can be salient in that developmental period. For example, Rose and Rudoph (2006) found significant sex differences in the quality of girls' and boys' same-sex friendships and responses to stress, with girls demonstrating more self-disclosure, support-seeking, prosocial behaviours, emotional expression, rumination, and interpersonal sensitivity while receiving more provisions from friendships, including affection, closeness, validation, trust, security, and acceptance. Meanwhile, boys experience more peer stress through overt verbal or physical victimization. All these sex differences were found to increase with age through adolescence. At the same time, girls are at higher risk of depression (Breslau et al., 2017) and post-traumatic stress disorder (Hamblen & Barnett, 2018) during adolescence. Kreager and Staff (2009) also found differences in opposite-sex relations, with permissive sexual behaviour associated with increased stigma for girls and increased popularity for boys. Orenstein's recent popular studies of adolescent girls' and boys' self-reported experiences of sexuality suggested that these trends are continuing, with widespread accounts of non-consensual sexual pressures or harassment of girls by boys (Orenstein, 2016, 2020). Worth noting is the fact that mindfulness workbooks for teens or for their teachers (Broderick, 2019; Cullen & Pons, 2015; Vo, 2015) don't address these critical areas.

## Traumatized Children and Youth.

Youth in mainstream preK-12 classes are known to suffer from undiagnosed childhood traumas and their deleterious aftermath (Hamblen & Barnett, 2018). Mindfulness in K-12 school contexts offers a preventative approach to reducing trauma-related challenges in children, including offsetting long-term effects on health, mental health, and behaviour (Ortiz & Sibinga, 2017).

**Trauma as Adverse Childhood Experiences (ACEs)**. As with adults, child and youth traumas arise from various sources. When adverse impacts are sustained, it is usually either from observing or being subjected to violent or life-threatening incidents or from repeated exposure to lesser traumas over a sustained period. Hamblen and Barnett (2018) offer a snapshot of the incidence of childhood trauma in the US, extrapolating from the 19% of substantiated child protection referrals of which more than 75% arise from neglect, 17.6% from physical abuse, and 9.1% from sexual abuse. In another study, they found that nearly half (47%) of adolescents reported experiencing or witnessing major assault or violence. In the case of chronic, repetitive childhood traumas or abuse, commonly referred to as *adverse childhood experiences* (ACEs), measured through two clusters of issues: Childhood maltreatment (e.g., abuse, neglect) and household challenges (parental mental health, divorce, violence, absence, or low socio-economic status, though there are mounting concerns about how these are measured and interpreted (McLennan et al., 2020). Part of the assessment is exposure to peer and community violence (Turner et al., 2020). These ACEs are associated with a range of lifelong negative health and mental health effects (Karatekin, 2018). Whether as major acute or less severe repetitive traumas, ACEs can accumulate over time and progress from coping challenges in children to become health or mental health morbidities with increased risky behaviour in adults (Ortiz & Sibinga, 2017).

**Responses to Trauma in Children and Adolescents**. Hamblen and Barnett (2018) outline how PTSD in children and youth present common and uncommon features with adult PTSD. For example, like adults, children with PTSD present re-experiencing, avoidance and numbing, and arousal symptoms. Yet, they also display symptoms not found in adults. In very young children, for example, up to four years old, PTSD can present as bedwetting, numbing, post-traumatic play, avoidance, and hyperarousal manifesting in such behaviour as temper tantrums, developmental delays, or regressions (Haag et al., 2019; Saleem et al., 2020). Elementary-aged children can experience "time skew" (mis-sequencing traumatic events) and "omen formation": believing there was a warning sign that predicted the trauma, so if they are sufficiently alert, they can avoid future traumas. Like their younger counterparts, these school-age children often engage in post-traumatic play involving reliving some aspect of the trauma through play, drawing, or verbalizations. Adolescents display symptoms more like adults, and, unlike the post-traumatic play behaviour of children, they can engage in traumatic re-enactment, where they incorporate certain features of the trauma in their daily behaviour.

**Race-Based Trauma**. Race-based trauma is an emerging and specific type of trauma affecting children and youth of colour and of oppressed ethnicities (Jernigan & Daniel, 2011). Although not formally identified as a diagnostic category in DSM-5, it is recognized as a viable source of PTSD and ACEs. This form of trauma can originate through the direct experience or threat of racially motivated violence to oneself or to a caretaker or loved one. Alternatively, it can arise through recurring exposures to mildly traumatic experiences or racism that accumulate over time to result in PTSD, which is common with racial trauma. The ensuing vulnerabilities from race-based traumas increase susceptibilities to being triggered by new racist encounters, whereby covert or overt threats are amplified by past emotions and experiences resurfacing. Furthermore, as Saleem et al. (2020) illustrate, racial trauma can be direct, but it can also be vicarious through racial violence encountered in social media or on the news. It can also be historical, as when it is passed down generationally from slavery, occupation, genocide, oppression-related drug addiction or alcoholism, or mass incarceration. These authors present a combined developmental and ecological model for youth racial trauma (DEMYth-RT), which identifies how familial and community contexts of historical and vicarious trauma interact with an individual youth's immediate traumatic reactions to generate four of the five classic trauma symptoms: Re-experiencing intrusion; avoidance; negative mood and cognition; and/or psychological arousal. Missing is dissociative symptoms (Boyd et al., 2018).

**Mindfulness in the Treatment of Trauma**. Marchand et al. (2021) completed their systematic review of 27 (of 88 identified) studies on mindfulness and PTSD by recommending mindfulness as an adjunctive complementary intervention for the reduction of PTSD for military veterans. In Boyd et al.'s (2018) earlier review, the authors concluded that the strongest evidence for the use of standardized mindfulness programmes in the treatment of PTSD was for MBSR, MBCT, and metta meditation (i.e., loving-kindness), all of which had low attrition levels and moderate to large effect sizes. MBSR results were the strongest with one MBCT study also reporting a significant reduction in self-blame, numbing, and avoidance. Theorizing on how mindfulness addresses each of the five symptoms associated with trauma, the authors posited that by shifting attention to the present, mindfulness regulates *intrusion symptoms* associated with PTSD; by increasing openness, it counters the *avoidance symptoms*; through non-judgmental acceptance of trauma-related cognitions, it helps to regulate *moods and cognition*; by reducing attentional bias to trauma stimuli and enhancing present-centred awareness, it reduces the *arousal and reactivity*; and, finally, by connecting to, and becoming aware of, somatic sensations and by enduring aversive internal experiences, mindfulness corrects the *dissociative symptoms* of PTSD.

**Neurobiological Evidence**. Extrapolating from neurobiological studies of mindfulness and PTSD, Boyd et al. (2018) chart the neurobiology of mindfulness to explain how it may assist in regulating PTSD symptoms. In PTSD, both the over- and under-modulation of emotional responses arise from the impaired ability of the cortical midline structure to regulate the responses of the limbic system. Cumulative studies suggest an apparent loss of top-down inhibition through hypoactivation of the cortical midline and hyperactivation of the limbic system (e.g., amygdala, cingulate cortex). This neurocognitive pattern is linked to classic PTSD symptoms like hypervigilance, startle responses, and emotional reactivity. On the other hand, there is a dissociative subtype of PTSD (PTSD+DS) identified in DSM-5 as presenting with symptoms of depersonalization and derealization, which has a distinctive and opposite neurobiology. In this PTSD+DS subtype, both under- and over-modulation can occur simultaneously or, more commonly, over-modulation occurs alone with a hyperactive cortical midline corresponding to a hypoactive limbic system (e.g., amygdala) associated with such symptoms of numbing and dissociation. As this research team concludes, mindfulness enhances functional connectivity between the ventrolateral prefrontal cortex and the amygdala – that is, between the cortical midline and the limbic system – and this neurobiology is associated with reduced anxiety. This improved functional connectivity is associated with improved self-regulation, rather than the increased inhibition associated with self-control.

In a retrospective study analyzing amygdala reactivity in 60 women (34 diagnosed with PTSD and 26 healthy), which analyzed their ACEs across the ages of one to 17 years, Sicorello et al. (2020) found two sensitive periods in which trauma appeared to affect the right amygdala as a neurobiological marker: one in early childhood, between three and four years of age and the other in post-puberty, between 16 and 17 years of age. A finding of interest was that *attenuated* or *hypoactive* right amygdala activity was found with ACEs during these sensitive periods, whereas *hyperactive* right amygdala reactivity was found in PTSD-diagnosed participants with trauma-associated pathologies. This finding of both hyper- and hypo-activity in response to trauma in the reactivity of the (right) amygdala, an emotion centre of the limbic system, was replicated in controlled studies (Boyd et al., 2018). Hyperactivity is associated with PTSD-associated hyperarousal, whereas hypoactivity with withdrawal, numbness, and dissociation.

A consistent neurobiological effect of mindfulness is its capacity to regulate amygdala reactivity, correcting both hyper- and hypo-arousal (e.g., Boyd et al., 2018). Furthermore, this effect appears to become enhanced with mindfulness experience over time. For example, in Kral et al.'s (2018) study of adult participants completing an MBSR course, the amygdala was found to be less reactive for participants compared to controls in response to positive pictures but not negative pictures. Yet, with expert practitioners with over 9000 hours of lifetime practice on average, decreased amygdala reactivity was found for both negative and positive pictures. Furthermore, within the group of expert practitioners, lifetime retreat practice time was associated with lower amygdala reactivity to negative pictures. This suggests that with increased experience and intensity, mindfulness may cultivate the ability to downregulate and mitigate the effects of trauma in the face of adverse experiences that might otherwise result in PTSD-related pathologies associated with hyperactive or hypoactive amygdala responses. It is worth pointing out as well, however, that these effects or capacities may take time to develop.

MBSR trainees also experienced increased functional connectivity between the amygdala and ventromedial prefrontal cortex, a region of the brain associated with emotion regulation, in contrast to controls. These same effects have been found in children, as in Bauer et al.'s (2019) study, which found reduced amygdala reactivity and increased functional connectivity between the amygdala and pre-frontal cortex in middle-school students shown fear-inducing pictures after receiving mindfulness training. The strength of the finding is reflected in mindfulness being recommended as an adjunctive therapy for PTSD even by fairly conservative bodies like the Canadian Agency for Drugs and Technologies (2015).

### *Other Vulnerable and At-Risk Children*

As Ortiz and Sibinga (2017) argue, high-quality structured mindfulness training programmes offer an evidence-based approach to mitigate the negative effects of stress and trauma, adverse childhood experiences, and their associated increased allostatic load on short- and long-term health and wellbeing. In this respect, well-integrated mindfulness programming in preK-12 contexts, targeting the sensitive periods of preschool and post-puberty, offers a way to lower the risk of all children to trauma. Yet, for children deemed *at-risk*, mindfulness may offer disproportionate benefit. For example, Lantieri et al. (2016) found high-risk students appeared to benefit more than healthy or less challenged students from mindfulness. In their study of youth with anxiety and at-risk for bipolar disorder, Cotton et al. (2020) found mindfulness reduced clinical severity significantly in the mindfulness condition. In a meta-analysis of 33 studies of 3,666 children, 17 of which were random controlled trials (RCTs) ($n$=1762), Dunning et al. (2019) found significant evidence across all RCTs of improved mental health and cognition following mindfulness, and in those using an active control, the scope of evidence narrowed but demonstrated significant improvements in mindfulness, depression, and anxiety. Finally, in their study of the effects of a school-based mindfulness programme for children with autism spectrum disorder, Juliano et al. (2020) found improved inhibition (medium effect) and attention (large effect). Finally, Burrows (2018) provides some practical ways that teachers in preK-12 or instructors in higher education can provide more universal support using mindfulness-based, trauma-informed practices.

## CRITICAL ISSUES AND CRITIQUES

There are a few critical issues worth discussing at more length concerning the introduction of mindfulness with children and youth in preK-12 schools or elsewhere.

### Mindfulness Teacher Qualifications and Training

One challenge in preK-12, not unlike that in higher education, is how to train teachers adequately in mindfulness to give them the capacity to integrate it effectively across the curriculum. While small-dose uses or limited-time programmes may offer band-aid relief, the promise of significant impacts on both wellbeing and academic achievement appears to come with more sustained and integrated programming. This requires skillful teachers, curricula, and teacher resources capable of enacting these transformations. The formidable contents and pressures of the pre-service teacher training curriculum make it an unlikely stage in teacher education to introduce these skills in anything but a cursory way. So, it would require in-service professional development and continuing education commitments from teachers, schools, and district-level bodies to be taught and implemented well.

## Informed Consent, Voluntary Participation, and Opting Out

The same critiques of organizations adopting mindfulness are applicable to schools. Indeed, as a rule, children have even less autonomy as employees in a workplace. Given that voluntary, informed, and invitational practices in mindfulness are a key principle of MBTL and its ethical practice, a key challenge becomes how to respect this requirement with children in schools while still providing targeted and effective programmes for all children. Not only are they captive to the classroom curriculum, they may be challenged in understanding the purposes and benefits of mindfulness when informed consent is solicited. One safeguard is the inductive manner in which mindfulness is taught. Rather than compelling students to adopt a teacher's perspectives, optimally participants engage in structured forms of inquiry designed to help them to arrive at their own inferences and insights about their experiences, either alone, with peers, and/or with teachers. Such inquiry is conducted to conserve participant autonomy over the meaning and significance of their experiences. Still, children's informed consent to participate is important and needs to be secured in a distinctive and unique manner. Parental consent is also often required, which may mean they opt out, leaving the added challenge of how to accommodate these children, while alternative methods may be required to accommodate children with special needs.

## Wellbeing or Behavioural Control

The SEL focus of schooling in mindfulness is grounds for another important critique on the ethics of mindfulness in preK-12 contexts. SEL is understood to have key behavioural and emotional regulation goals or outcomes. Although a highly-skilled and trained MBTL teacher should know how to safeguard student autonomy and conserve mindfulness as a self-regulatory process, less skilled teachers or leaders may misconstrue mindfulness as a behavioural management or control strategy using extrinsic motivators, external regulation, and/or self-control strategies. In fact, self-regulation is not synonymous with effortful self-control as it can be *effortless*, arising from what Milyavskya et al. (2015) and Werner and Milyavskaya (2019) call *want-to* motivation (vs. *have-to*). Such motivation is intrinsic and reduces temptation without effortful self-control while improving goal attainment. *Effortless* self-regulation is closer to describing the self-regulatory processes of mindfulness. In contrast, self-control strategies use inhibition, often motivated by introjected forms of externalized control imposed on the self rather than effortless self-regulation naturally arising through executive functioning and awareness (Ryan & Deci, 2000). (See Chapter 13 for more on this topic).

Therefore, teachers need to be supported to understand key ethical elements of the practice of MBTL, not the least of which is moving away from more authoritarian, teacher-centred tendencies towards the intentional fostering of students' autonomy and self-determination. In this respect, mindfulness is a practice of freedom, something not entirely lost from its traditional origins. This ethic involves recognizing people as ends-in-themselves, as human beings with agency, motivated to learn, to cultivate autonomy, and to establish wellbeing and self-regulate to conserve such wellbeing across the lifespan. This ethic needs to be understood as critical to achieving the ends of wellbeing. Mindfulness is not an end-in-itself either, for that matter; wellbeing is the end. Schools and schooling have problematic institutional legacies of social control, with ample historical and contemporary evidence. Sometimes these social control elements are systemic and implicit, part of what is sometimes referred to as the hidden curriculum of schooling. Accordingly, they have not always fully respected or fostered the wellbeing and self-determination of children and youth as persons who are ends-in-themselves rather than the ends of families or societies. So, when mindfulness is introduced, in particular when it is introduced to address classroom management or classroom climate issues, this intention needs to be jealously guarded against slippage into control models, rhetoric, or assumptions.

## TRENDS: PROMISING AND CHALLENGING

Below we consider a few significant trends in the application of MBTL in schools:

### Mindfulness as SEL or Inquiry-Based Learning

The dominance of SEL in the teaching of mindfulness in preK-12 education is so embedded that it is difficult to see a pathway for an expansion to support broader purposes like inquiry and learning. Promising is the gradual recognition of self-determination theory in education. Ryan & Deci (2000, 2017) have long-researched and theorized how mindfulness, alongside what they call *interest-taking*, support the critical shift from externalized loci of control and motivators to internal loci of control, intrinsic motivation, and autonomy. This points to a deepened understanding of the role of curiosity, interest, and investigation in learning, something described as well in traditional Buddhist theories, most notably in the Seven Factors of Awakening discussed earlier in this chapter and again in Chapter 11. The first three factors – mindfulness, investigation, and energy – are also often referred to in oral teachings in contemporary Buddhism as generating a state of *interest.* This theory, like self-determination theory itself, links such a state of ongoing interest to wellbeing, as indicated by the final four factors of joy, calm, concentration, and equanimity.

### From Intervention to Eudaimonic Education

A related promising trend is to shift from referring to mindfulness in preK-12 or other educational contexts as "interventions" and instead to consider it a form of teaching and learning, a trend reflected in our use of MBTL rather than MBIs, for example. This marks a shift in perspective from viewing mindfulness as a temporary, medicalized treatment for pathologies to one capable of enacting the kinds of transformations implied by mindfulness as inquiry, community development, or self-determination. Interventions treat specific pathologies and are not part of normal experience, behaviour, or conduct, which conveys a very limited role for mindfulness *in* education. The etymology of the word *education* is "to draw out," which suggests fulfillment and realization of potential, which implies the flourishing associated with *eudaimonic* wellbeing. For mindfulness to be an educational activity, therefore, requires that it address more holistic and integrative qualities than specified pathologies needing treatment. That said, blurring health and education outcomes is not a bad thing and is consistent with shifting the ends of education from a narrow academic agenda to wellbeing.

## Arts-Based Inquiry in MBTL

Given that the teaching of mindfulness to children has had few precedents prior to the last few decades, it is important to consider alternative, more age-appropriate methods to teach them besides the standard approaches used with adults. One key trend is the increasing use of arts-based rather than verbal inquiry to represent, describe, and interpret mindfulness experiences or even to engage children or youth in mindfulness practices in the first place. In their scoping review of research on the use of arts-based mindfulness interventions with children and youth, Coholic et al. (2020) found a range of arts-based approaches to teach mindfulness to this demographic, including drawing, painting, sculpting, drama, music, and poetry. Outcomes included increased wellbeing, motivation and interest, and reductions in stress, depressive symptoms, and oppositional defiant and conduct problems (in children with ADHD). Many other studies focused on special populations such as children or youths with eating disorders, chronic illnesses, or in residential treatment, leading the authors to conclude that arts-based methods may be particularly useful with at-risk or special populations.

## Outdoor Nature-Based Inquiry in MBTL

The impact of mindfulness on children's felt connection to nature and the environment has become a keen topic of inquiry. Djernis et al. (2019) reviewed 25 quantitative studies of youth and adults (aged 12 and up) participating in mindfulness training in outdoor natural settings. The authors found significant medium effects in the combined psychological, physiological, and interpersonal outcomes and that environments classified as forests/wild had a greater effect than those characterized as gardens/parks. So too, informal mindfulness practices had a bigger effect than formal practices, which the authors speculated may have been because informal practices can be done while still moving around in the natural milieu, a known health benefit. Likewise, in their study of children 7–11 years old from four different classes and schools visiting nature reserves to practise mindful approaches, Adams and Beauchamp (2020) reported that children experienced increased calm, time-sense changes, and feelings of transcendence. They concluded the approach was consistent with Indigenous approaches to pedagogy.

In their study of adults ($n$=467), Hanley et al. (2017) found that dispositional mindfulness was associated with increased nature connectedness and that two facets of mindfulness accounted for most of this relationship: observing and non-reacting. The solid evidence that mindfulness training increases dispositional mindfulness implies that explicitly teaching mindfulness as observing and non-reacting in nature would enhance nature connectedness in children and youth. In addition, these researchers found that decentering mediated the relationship between mindfulness and nature connectedness, the same mechanism found critical in MBCT's prevention of depression relapse (Segal et al., 2019). Nature too can have a SEL effect, as Capaldi et al. (2014) found in identifying a significant positive relationship between nature-connectedness and happiness. In this respect, outdoors or nature education and mindfulness can work closely together to enact common ends.

### Community-Based Alternatives for At-Risk Children

Finally, another trend worth mentioning is community-based learning in which entire communities, including children and youth and their neighbourhood schools, become participants in MBTL initiatives. This was described in the scoping study of Pillay and Eagle (2019) in Chapter 4, who proposed using mindfulness training with traumatized communities in South Africa, involving both clinical and non-clinical populations, as a way to address the "individually intensive and socially extensive impact" of psychological trauma associated with high levels of violence and limited professional resources (p. 1). The strengths of such an approach is to recognize that the deleterious effects of trauma on children and youth – from violence, adverse childhood experiences, and/or race-based discrimination – cannot be countered effectively by individual programmes or even transformed schools. Ultimately, it requires the transformation of the entire community.

## REFERENCES


Abedini, A., Habibi, M., Abedini, N., Achenbach, T., & Semple, R. (2020). A randomized clinical trial of a modified mindfulness-based cognitive therapy for children hospitalized with cancer. *Mindfulness, 12*, 141–151. https://doi.org/10.1007/s12671-020-01506-3.

Adams, D., & Beauchamp, G. (2020). A study of the experiences of cildren aged 7–11 taking part in mindful approaches in local nature reserves. *Journal of Adventure Education and Outdoor Learning*. Advance online publication. https://doi.org/10.1080/14729679.2020.1736110.

Adesope, O., Lavin, T., Thompson, T., & Ungerleider, C. (2010). A systematic review and meta-analysis of the cognitive correlates of bilingualism. *Review of Educational Research, 80*(2), 207–245.

Albrecht, N. (2018). Teaching mindfulness with children: Being a mindful role model. *Australian Journal of Teacher Education, 43*(10), 1–23. http://dx.doi.org/10.14221/ajte.2018v43.n10.1.

Bakosh, L., Snow, R., Tobias, J., Houlihan, J., & Barbosa-Leiker, C. (2016). Maximizing mindful learning: Mindful awareness intervention improves elementary school students quarterly grades. *Mindfulness, 7*, 59–67. https://doi-org.proxy.ufv.ca:2443/10.1007/s12671-015-0387-6.

Bakosh, L. S. (2013). *Investigating the effects of a daily audio-guided mindfulness intervention for elementary school students and teachers* (Dissertation, Institute of Transpersonal Psychology).

Barron, B., & Darling-Hammond, L. (2008). *Teaching for meaningful learning: A review of research on inquiry-based and cooperative learning.* The George Lucas Educational Foundation.

Bauer, C., Caballero, C., Scherer, E., West, M., Mrazek, M., Phillips, D., Whitfield-Gabrieli, S., & Gabrielli, J., (2019). Mindfulness training reduces stress and amygdala reactivity to fearful faces in middle-school children. *Behavioral Neuroscience, 133*(6), 569–585. https://doi.org/10.1037/bne0000337.

Baynham, H. (2018). Mindful teaching on the Tibetan Plateau. *Montessori International, Autumn/Winter* (pp. 26–28). https://www.montessori.org.uk/wp-content/uploads/2019/02/MI126_Winter-2018.pdf#page=28.

BC Ministry of Education. (2021). *BC's course curriculum: Science 4*. Province of British Columbia. https://curriculum.gov.bc.ca/curriculum/science/4/core.

Berkowitz, K. (2019). The art of integrating school climate initiatives. In M. Thorsborne, N. Riestenberg, & G. McCluskey (Eds.), *Getting more out of restorative practice in schools: Practical approaches to improve school wellbeing and strengthen community engagement* (pp. 59–79). Jessica Kingsley Publishers.

Black, D. (2015). Mindfulness training for children and adolescents: A state-of-the-science review. In K. Brown, D. Creswell, & R. Ryan (Eds.), *Handbook of mindfulness in theory, research, and practice* (pp. 283–310). The Guilford Press.

Bogels, S. (2015). Mindfulness course for parents in mental health treatment. In C. Willard & A. Saltzman (Eds.), *Teaching mindfulness skills to kids and teens* (pp. 155–175). The Guilford Press.

Boyce, B. (2022). Researchers and key figures reflect on the results and implications of one of the largest studies on mindfulness in schools ever conducted. *Mindful*, Nov.22, 2022. Retrieved at: https://www.mindful.org/a-recent-study-found-a-school-based-mindfulness-program-doesnt-work-lets-unpack-that/

Boyd, J., Lanius, R., & McKinnon, M. (2018). Mindfulness-based treatments for posttraumatic stress disorder: A review of the treatment literature and neurobiological evidence. *Journal of Psychiatry & Neuroscience*, *43*(1), 7–25. https://doi.org/10.1503/jpn.170021.

Breslau, J., Gilman, S., Stein, B., Ruder, T., Gmelin, T., & Miller, E. (2017). Sex differences in recent first-onset depression in an *epidemiological* sample of adolescents. *Translational Psychiatry*, *7*, e1139. https://doi.org/10.1038/tp.2017.105.

Broderick, P. (2013). *Learning to breathe: A mindfulness curriculum for adolescents to cultivate emotion regulation, attention, and performance*. New Harbinger.

Broderick, P. (2019). *Mindfulness in the secondary classroom: A guide for teaching adolescents*. W.W. Norton & Co.

Broderick, P., & Metz, S. (2008). Learning to BREATHE: A pilot trial of a mindfulness curriculum for adolescents. *Advanced in School Mental Health Promotion*, *291*, 35–46. https://doi.org/10.1080/1754730X.2009.9715696.

Brophy-Herb, H., Williamson, A., Cook, G., Torquati, J., Decker, K., Vu, J., Vallotton, C., Duncan, L., & The Collaborative for Understanding the Pedagogy of Infant/Toddler Development. (2019). Preservice students' dispositional mindfulness and developmentally supportive practices with infants and toddlers. *Mindfulness*, *10*, 759–768. https://doi.org/10.1007/s12671-018-1036-7.

Buchanan, S, Harlan, M., Bruce, C., & Edwards, S. (2016). Inquiry based learning models, information literacy, and student engagement: A literature review. *School Libraries Worldwide*, *22*(2), 23–39. https://eprints.qut.edu.au/102823/.

Burrows, L. (2018). *Safeguarding mindfulness in schools and higher education: A holistic and inclusive approach*. Routledge.

Canadian Agency for Drugs and Technologies in Health. (2015). *Mindfulness interventions for the treatment of post-traumatic stress disorder, generalized anxiety disorder, depression, and substance use disorders: A review of the clinical effectiveness and guidelines: Rapid response report with critical appraisal*. https://www.ncbi.nlm.nih.gov/books/NBK304574/.

Capaldi, C., Dopko, R., & Zelenski, J. (2014). The relationship between nature connectedness and happiness: A meta-analysis. *Frontiers in Psychology*. Advance online publication. https://doi.org/10.3389/fpsyg.2014.00976.

Chirkina, T., & Khavenson, T. (2018). School climate: A history of the concept and approaches to defining and measuring it on PISA questionnaires. *Russian Education and Society*, *60*(2), 133–160. https://doi.org/10.1080/10609393.2018.1451189.

Coholic, D., Schwabe, N., & Lander, K. (2020). A scoping review of arts-based mindfulness interventions for children and youth. *Child and Adolescent Social Work Journal, 37*, 511–526. https://doi.org/10.1007/s10560-020-00657-5.

Cotton, S., Kraemer, K., Sears, R., Strawn, J.,, Wasson, R., McCune, N., Welge, J., Blom, T., Durling, M., & Delbello, M. (2020). Mindfulness-based cognitive therapy for children and adolescents with anxiety disorders at-risk for bipolar disorder: A pyschoeducation waitlist controlled pilot trial. *Early Intervention in Psychiatry, 14*, 211–219. https://doi.org/10.1111/eip.12848.

Cotton, S., Luberto, C. M., Sears, R. W., Strawn, J. R., Stahl, L., Wasson, R. S., Blom, T. J., & Delbello, M. P. (2016). Mindfulness-based cognitive therapy for youth with anxiety disorders at risk for bipolar disorder: A pilot trial. *Early Intervention in Psychiatry, 10*(5), 426–434. https://doi.org/10.1111/eip.12216

Cullen, M., & Pon, G. (2015). *The mindfulness-based emotional balance workbook: An eight-week program for improved emotion regulation and resilience.* New Harbinger Publications.

Djernis, D., Lerstrup, I., Poulsen, D., Stigsdotter, U., Dahlgaard, J., & O'Toole, M. (2019). A systematic review and meta-analysis of nature-based mindfulness: Effects of moving mindfulness training into an outdoor natural setting. *International Journal of Environmental Research and Public Health, 16*, 3202. https://doi.org/10.3390/ijerph16173202.

Dunning, D., Griffiths, K., Kuyken, W., Crane, C., Foulkes, L., Parker, J., & Dagliesh, T. (2019). Research review: The effects of mindfulness-based interventions on cognition and mental health in children and adolescents - A meta-analysis of randomized controlled trials. *The Journal of Child Psychology and Psychiatry, 60*(3), 244–258. https://doi.org/10.1111/jcpp.12980.

Ergas, O. (2019). Mindfulness *in, as* and *of* education: Three roles of mindfulness in education. *Journal of Philosophy of Education, 53*(2), 340–358.

Friesen, S., & Scott, D. (2013). *Inquiry-based learning: A review of the research literature.* Prepared for the Alberta Ministry of Education.

Goleman, D. (1995). *Emotional intelligence: Why it can matter more than IQ.* Bantam Books.

Gontard, A. (2017). *Buddhist understanding of childhood spirituality: The Buddha's children.* Jessica Kingsley Publishers.

Grant, K. (2017). From teaching to being: The qualities of a mindful teacher. *Childhood Education, 93*(2), 147–152. https://doi.org/10.1080/00094056.2017.1300493

Haag, A., Celi, S., & Landolt, M. (2019). Chapter 8: Trauma and PTSD in preschool-aged children. In B. Fisak & P. Barrett (Eds.), *Anxiety in preschool children: Assessment, treatment, and prevention.* Routledge.

Hamblen, J., & Barnett, E. (2018). *PTSD in children and adolescents. PTSD: National centre for PTSD.* U.S. Department of Veterans Affairs. https://www.ptsd.va.gov/professional/treat/specific/ptsd_child_teens.asp.

Hanley, A., Derringer, A., & Hanley, R. (2017). Dispositional mindfulness may be associated with deeper connections with nature. *Ecopsychology, 9*(4), 225–231. http://doi.org/10.1089/eco.2017.0018.

Hattie, J. (2009). *Visible learning: A synthesis of over 800 meta-analyses relating to achievement.* Routledge.

Hawn Foundation. (2011a). *The MindUP curriculum grades preK-2: Brain-focused strategies for learning and living.* Scholastic. https://mindup.org.

Hawn Foundation. (2011b). *The MindUP curriculum grades 6–8: Brain-focused strategies for learning and living.* Scholastic. https://mindup.org.

Hawn Foundation. (2011c). *The MindUP curriculum grades preK-2: Brain-focused strategies for learning and living.* Scholastic. https://mindup.org.

Hudson, K., Lawton, R., & Hugh-Jones, S. (2020). Factors affecting the implementation of a whole school mindfulness program: A qualitative study using the consolidated framework for implementation research. *BMC Health Services Research*, *20*, 13. https://doi.org/10.1186/s12913-020-4942-z.

Hwang, Y., Barlett, B., Greben, M., & Hand, K. (2017). A systematic review of mindfulness interventions for in-service teachers: A tool to enhance teacher wellbeing and performance. *Teaching and Teacher Education*, *64*, 26–42. http://dx.doi.org/10.1016/j.tate.2017.01.015.

Jernigan, M., & Daniel, J. (2011). Racial trauma in the lives of Black children and adolescents: Challenges and clinical implications. *Journal of Child & Adolescent Trauma*, *4*, 123–141. https://doi.org/10.1080/19361521.2011.574678.

Juliano, A., Alexander, A., DeLuca, J., & Genova, H. (2020). Feasibility of a school-based mindfulness program for improving inhibitory skills in children with autism spectrum disorder. *Research in Developmental Disabilities*, *101*, 103641. https://doi.org/10.1016/j.ridd.2020.103641.

Karatekin, C. (2018). Adverse childhood experiences (ACEs), stress and mental health in college students. *Stress and Health*, *34*(1), 36–45. https://doi.org/10.1002/smi.2761.

Kral, T., Schuyler, B., Mumford, J., Rosenkranz, M., Lutz, A., & Davidson, R. (2018). Impact of short- and long-term mindfulness meditation training on amygdala reactivity to emotional stimuli. *NeuroImage*, *181*(1), 301–313. https://doi.org/10.1016/j.neuroimage.2018.07.013.

Kreager, D., & Staff, J. (2009). The sexual double-standard and adolescent peer acceptance. *Social Psychology Quarterly*, *72*(2), 143–164. https://doi.org/10.1177/019027250907200205.

Kuyken, W.,Ball, S., Crane, C., Ganguli, P.,Jones, B., Montero-Marin,J., Nuhall, E., Raja, A., Taylor, L., Tudor, K., Viner, R., Allwood, M., Aukland, L., Dunning, D., Casey, T., Dalrymple, N., DeWilde, K., Farley, E., Harper,J., .Williams,J.M. (2022). Effectiveness and cost-effectiveness of universal school-based mindfulness training compared with normal school provision in reducing risk of mental health problems and promoting well-being in adolescence: The MYRIAD cluster randomised control trial. *Evidence-Based Mental Health*, *25*, 99–109. http://dx.doi.org/10.1136/ebmental-2021-300396.

La Gue, A., Eakin, G., & Dykeman, C. (2019). The impact of mindfulness-based cognitive therapy on math anxiety in adolescents. *Preventing School Failure: Alternative Education for Children and Youth*, *63*(2), 142–148. https://doi.org/10.1080/1045988X.2018.1528966.

Lantieri, L. Nambiar, M., Harnett, S., & Nagler-Kyse, E. (2016). Cultivating inner resilience in educators and students: The inner resilience program. In K. Schonert-Reichl & R. Roeser (Eds.), *Handbook of mindfulness in education: Integrating theory and research into practice* (pp. 119–132). Springer.

Lawlor, M. (2016). Mindfulness and social emotional learning (SEL): A conceptual framework. In K. Schonert-Reichl & R. Roeser (Eds.), *Handbook of mindfulness in education: Integrating theory and research into practice* (pp. 65–80). Springer.

Lillard, A. (2011). Mindfulness practices in education: Montessori's approach. *Mindfulness*, *2*, 78–85. https://doi.org/10.1007/s12671-011-0045-6.

Lopez-Gonzalez, L., Amutio, A., & Herrero-Fernandez, D. (2018). The relaxation-mindfulness competence of secondary and high school students and its influence on classroom climate and academic performance. *European Journal of Education and Psychology*, *11*(1), 5–17.

Lopez-Gonzalez, L., Amutio, A., Oriol, X., & Bisquerra, R. (2016). Habits related to relaxation and mindfulness of high school students: Influence on classroom climate and academic performance. *Revista de Psicodidactica*, *21*(1), 121–138. https://doi.org/10.1387/RevPsicodidact.13866.

MacPherson, S. (2011). *Education and sustainability: Learning across the diaspora, Indigenous, and minority education divide*. Routledge. https://www.taylorfrancis.com/books/education-sustainability-seonaigh-macpherson/10.4324/9780203825723.

MacPherson, S. (2018). Ethno-cultural diversity education in Canada, the USA and India: The experience of the Tibetan diaspora. *Compare: A Journal of Comparative and International Education*, *48*(6), 844–860. https://doi.org/10.1080/03057925.2017.1362547.

Maloney, J., Lawlor, M., Schonert-Reichl, K., & Whitehead, J. (2016). A mindfulness-based social and emotional learning curriculum for school-aged children: The MindUP program. In K. Schonert-Reichl & R. Roeser (Eds.), *Handbook of mindfulness in education: Integrating theory and research into practice* (pp. 313–334). Springer.

Marchand, W., Sandoval, K., Lackner, R., Parker, S., Herrmann, T., Yabko, B., Velasquez, T., Lewis, L., & Butler, J. (2021). *Complementary therapies in clinical practice* (Vol. 42). https://doi.org/10.1016/j.ctcp.2020.101274.

McLennan, J., MacMillan, H., & Afifi, T. (2020). Questioning the use of adverse childhood experiences (ACEs) questionnaires. *Child Abuse & Neglect, 101*, 104331. https://doi.org/10.1016/j.chiabu.2019.104331.

Metz, S., Frank, J., Reibel, D., Cantrell, T., Sanders, R., & Broderick, P. (2013). The effectiveness of the learning to BREATH program on adolescent emotion regulation. *Research in Human Development, 10*(3), 252–272. https://doi.org/10.1080/15427609.2013.818488.

Meyer, L., & Eklund, K. (2020). The impact of a mindfulness intervention on an elementary classroom climate and student mindfulness: A pilot study. *Mindfulness, 11*, 991–1005. https://doi.org/10.1007/s12671-020-01317-6.

Milyavskaya, M. Inzlicht, M., Hope, N., & Koestner, R. (2015). Saying "no" to temptation: Want-to motivation improves self-regulation by reducing temptation rather than by increasing self-control. *Journal of Personality and Social Psychology, 109*(4), 677–693. https://doi.org/10.1037/pspp0000045.

Novak, M., & Mihic, J. (2018). Prevention of internalized problems of children and youth in academic setting. In B. Bernal-Morales (Ed.), *Health and academic achievement* (pp. 123–141). IntechOpen. http://dx.doi.org/10.5772/intechopen.68719.

Opelt, F., & Schwinger, M. (2020). Relationships between narrow personality traits and self-regulated learning strategies: Exploring the role of mindfulness, contingent self-esteem, and self-control. *AERA Open, 6*(3), 2332858420949499. https://doi.org/10.1177/2332858420949499.

Orenstein, P. (2016). *Girls and sex: Navigating the complicated new landscape*. HarperCollins.

Orenstein, P. (2020). *Boys and sex: Young men on hookups, love, porn, consent, and navigating the new masculinity*. HarperCollins.

Ortiz, R., & Sibinga, E. (2017). The role of mindfulness in reducing the adverse effects of childhood stress and trauma. *Children, 4*, 19. https://doi.org/10.3390/children4030016.

Parent, J., McKee, L., Rough, J., & Forehand, R. (2016). The association of parent mindfulness with parenting and youth psychopathology across three developmental stages. *Journal of Abnormal Child Psychology, 44*, 191–202. https://doi.org/10.1007/s10802-015-9978-x

Penna-Wilkos, A. (2018). *Exploring the influence of mindfulness on elementary-aged students through the lens of the classroom teacher: A case study*. Dissertation, Seton Hall University.

Pillay, K., & Eagle, G. (2019). The case for mindfulness interventions for traumatic stress in high violence, low resource settings. *Current Psychology*. Advance online publication. https://doi.org/10.1007/s12144-019-00177-1.

Pozneanscaia, C. (2019). *The effects of mindfulness-based interventions on functioning of children and youth with ADHD: A systematic literature review*. Thesis, Jonkoping University.

Rani, A. (2018). *The convergence of mindfulness and well-being: An exploration of a district-wide mindfulness initiative for educators*. Dissertation, Fielding Graduate University.

Roeser, R. (2016). Processes of teaching, learning, and transfer in mindfulness-based interventions (MBIs) for teachers: A contemplative education perspective. In K. Schonert-Reichl & R. Roeser (Eds.), *Handbook of mindfulness in education: Integrating theory and research into practice* (pp. 149–170). Springer.

Rose, A., & Rudoph, K. (2006). A review of sex differences in peer relationship processed: Potential trade-offs for the emotional and behavioral development of girls and boys. *Psychological Bulletin, 132*(1), 98–131. https://doi.org/10.1037/0033-2909.132.1.98

Ruijgrok-Lupton, P., Crane, R., & Dorjee, D. (2017). Impact of mindfulness-based teacher training on MBSR participant well-being outcomes and course satisfaction. *Mindfulness, 9*, 117–128. https://doi.org/10.1007/s12671-017-0750-x.

Ryan, R., & Deci, E. (2000). Self-determination theory and the facilitation of intrinsic motivation, social development, and well-being. *American Psychologist, 55*(4), 68–78.

Ryan, R., & Deci, E. (2017). *Self-determination theory: Basic psychological needs in motivation, development, and wellness.* The Guilford Press.

Saleem, F., Anderson, R., & Williams, M. (2020). Addressing the "myth" of racial trauma: Developmental and ecological considerations for youth of color. *Clinical Child and Family Psychology Review, 23*, 1–14. https://doi.org/10.1007/s10567-019-00304-1.

Schonert-Reichl, K., & Lawlor, M. (2010). The effects of a mindfulness-based education program on pre-and early adolescents' well-being and social and emotional competency. *Mindfulness, 1*, 137–151. https://doi.org/10.1007/s12671-010-0011-8.

Schonert-Reichl, K., Oberle, E., Lawlor, M., Abbott, D., Thomson, K., Oberlander, T., & Diamond, A. (2015). Enhancing cognitive and social-emotional development through a simple-to-administer mindfulness-based school program for elementary school children: A randomized controlled trial. *Developmental Psychology, 51*(1), 52–66. https://doi.org/10.1037/a0038454.

Segal, Z., Anderson, A., Gulamani, T., Williams, L.D., Desormeau, P., Ferguson, A., Walsh, K., & Farb, N. (2019). Practice of therapy acquired regulatory skills and depressive relapse/recurrence prophylaxis following cognitive therapy or mindfulness based cognitive therapy. *Journal of Consulting and Clinical Psychology, 87*(2), 161–170. https://doi.org/10.1037/ccp0000351.

Seidel, J. (2006). Some thoughts on teaching as contemplative practice. *Teachers College Record, 108*(9), 1901–1914. https://www.tcrecord.org/Content.asp?ContentId=12687.

Seixis, P. (1993). The community of inquiry as a basis for knowledge and learning. The case of history. *American Educational Research Journal, 30*(2), 305–324. https://doi.org/10.3102/00028312030002305.

Semple, R., Droutman, V., & Reid, B. (2017). Mindfulness goes to school: Things learned (so far) from research and real-world experiences. *Psychology in the Schools, 54*(1), 29–52. https://doi.org/10.1002/pits.21981.

Sharp, J., & Jennings, P. (2016). Strengthening teacher presence through mindfulness: What educators say about the Cultivating Awareness and Resilient in Education (CARE) program. *Mindfulness, 7*, 209–218. https://doi.org/10.1007/s12671-015-0474-8.

Sheinman, N., Hadar, L., Gafni, D., & Milman, M. (2018). Preliminary investigation of whole-school mindfulness in education program and children's mindfulness-based coping strategies. *Journal of Child and Family Studies, 27*, 3316–3328.

Sicorello, M., Thome, J., Herzog, J., & Schmahl, C. (2020). Differential effects of early adversity and posttraumatic stress disorder on amygdala reactivity: The role of developmental timing. *Biological Psychiatry: Cognitive Neuroscience and Neuroimaging.* Advance online publication. https://doi.org/10.1016/j.bpsc.2020.10.009.

Stuart, S., Collins, J., Toms, O., & Gwalla-Ogisis, N. (2017). Mindfulness and an argument for Tier 1, whole school support. *International Journal of Whole Schooling, 13*(3), 14–27.

Tali, T., Levin-Peled, R., & Levy, K. (2019). Teacher views on inquiry-based learning: The contribution of diverse experiences in the outdoor environment. *Innovation and Education, 1*(2), 1–17. https://doi.org/10.1186/s42862-019-0004-y.

Turner, H., Finkelhor, D., Mitchell, K., Jones, L., & Henly, M. (2020). Strengthening the predictive power of screening for adverse childhood experiences (ACEs) in younger and older children. *Child Abuse & Neglect, 171*, 104522. https://doi.org/10.1016/j.chiabu.2020.104522.

Vo, D. (2015). *The mindful teen: Powerful skills to help you handle stress one moment at a time*. New Harbinger (Instant Help Books).

Vo, D., Locke, J., Johnson, A., & Marshall, S. (2015). The effectiveness of the Mindful Awareness and Resilience Skills for Adolescents (MARS-A) intervention on adolescent mental health: A pilot clinical trial, Poster 50. *Journal of Adolescent Health*, *56*(2), S27. https://doi.org/10.1016/j.jadohealth.2014.10.054.

Wale, B., & Bishaw, K. (2020). Effect of using inquiry-based learning on EFL students' critical thinking skills. *Asian-Pacific Journal of Second and Foreign Language Education*, *5*(9), 1–14. https://doi.org/10.1186/s40862-020-00090-2.

Weissberg, R., Durlak, J., Domitrovich, C., & Gullotta, T. (2015). Social and emotional learning: Past, present, and future. In J. Durlak, C. Domitrovich, R. Weissberg, & T. Gullotta (Eds.), *Handbook of social and emotional learning: Research and practice* (pp. 3–19). Guilford Press.

Werner, K., & Milyavskaya, M. (2019). Motivation and self-regulation: The role of want-to motivation in the processes of underlying self-regulation and self-control. *Social and Personality Psychology Compass*, *13*(1), e12425. https://doi.org/10.1111/spc3.12425.

Wilde, S., Sonley, A., Crane, C., Ford, T., Raja, A., Robson, J., Taylor, L., & Kukyen, W. (2019). Mindfulness training in UK secondary schools: A multiple case study approach to identification of the cornerstones of implementation. *Mindfulness*, *10*, 376–389. https://doi.org/10.1007/s12671-018-0982-4.

Willard, C. (2015). Introduction: Toward a model of teaching and learning mindfulness. In C. Willard & A. Saltzman (Eds.), *Teaching mindfulness skills to kids and teens* (pp. 1–15). The Guilford Press.

Zenner, C., Herrnleben-Kurz, S., & Walach, H. (2014). Mindfulness-based interventions in schools – A systematic review and meta-analysis. *Frontiers in Psychology*, *5*, 1–20. https://doi.org/10.3389/fpsyg.2014.00603.

# CHAPTER 8

# WORKPLACE AND ORGANIZATIONAL CONTEXTS

In this chapter, we consider mindfulness in workplaces and organizations. Organizations extend mindfulness as a practice of individuals to a practice of collectives on the assumption that such collectives may manifest that same self-regulating and wellbeing benefits as individuals. Therefore, these contexts call for the nesting of mindfulness programmes to impact individual employees; teams or units; leaders; and the broader organizational culture (Lhl et al., 2020).

## CONTEXT

The ground for the interest in mindfulness in organizations was laid in the late 20th century by the widespread shift to systems thinking and the idealized promise of designing what Senge (1990) popularized as learning organizations: "Organizations where people continually expand their capacity to create the results they truly desire, where new and expansive patterns of thinking are nurtured, where collective aspiration is set free, and where people are continually learning how to learn together" (p. 3). Yet, the more direct catalyst for the interest of mindfulness in organizations was a very different objective, that of providing individual employees and leadership work-related stress reduction, health promotion, and resilience training. Bolstered by the mounting clinical evidence of the efficacy of mindfulness in the first decade of the 21st century, research and programmes soon expanded rapidly to include programmes located at the source of so many people's stress and anxiety: work and workplaces.

Organizational mindfulness programmes come in a variety of forms, involving voluntary or less voluntary programmes that may be scheduled during or after work hours. These programmes may be targeted to employees, high-risk personnel, managers, or leadership. Although the sponsors of the programmes tend to be human resource departments, they can be individual teams or units, employees, or leaders. The teachers or facilitators may be internal HR personnel, employees, or external specialists. Programmes may be delivered in face-to-face intensives; as discrete face-to-face or online (synchronous) courses; or as asynchronous online programs or apps. Programmes vary significantly with respect to rationale and objectives; who they target; and/or in how they are measured or assessed, including whether or not they provide indicators of transfer of learning from training to job performance.

There is a wide spectrum of organizations using mindfulness, from corporate to nonprofit to governmental. Certain high-stress workplaces with employees at risk of trauma and re-traumatization may have multiple and complex needs and motives for such programmes. These include first responders (police, fire fighters, paramedics), the military, hospitals, schools with high-risk and vulnerable populations, and corrections facilities. In other instances, organizations are motivated to explore mindfulness as a strategy to enhance creativity and innovation, as in the high-tech sector, while others anticipate that mindfulness might assist with organizational culture or structural change. Such organizational mindfulness involves more than individuals in a workplace or organization doing mindfulness. Organizational mindfulness is premised on the idea that mindfulness can

DOI: 10.4324/9781003182467-11

benefit collectives, not just individuals. Such collective mindfulness was defined by Weick & Sutcliffe (2001/2007) as a way to grow organizations through the "ongoing scrutiny of existing expectations, continuous refinement and differentiation of expectations based on newer experiences." This implies a kind of executive functioning with self-regulating features functioning at the collective level.

# RESEARCH

Research on the work-related applications of mindfulness investigates the effectiveness of mindfulness using a wide range of criteria, such as employee health and wellbeing; employee performance; leadership skills; work team functioning; and organizational cultures. Research methods include correlation studies that rely on measures of trait or dispositional mindfulness via tests like the Five Facets of Mindfulness Questionnaire (FFMQ); they also include Randomized Controlled Trials (RCT) where findings impute causality between mindfulness as a "treatment" and a range of effects. Although many of these RCT studies use passive and waitlist control conditions, more are using active control conditions to increase validity. Workplace mindfulness programmes are now commonplace, and the expectation for measurable outcomes has helped to increase the collecting and reporting of data. In their *Mindful Nation, UK* study, the Mindfulness All-Party Parliamentary Group (2015) identified work-related mindfulness as one of four significant and promising areas to develop mindfulness programming, alongside education, health care, and the criminal justice system. As they describe in the report: "This is the sector where there has been the most intense interest, widespread experimentation and enthusiastic media coverage of the subject of mindfulness" (p. 39).

## Employee Health and Wellbeing

One key motive for introducing mindfulness in the workplace is to support employee health and wellbeing. The health promotion potential of mindfulness offers both intrinsic benefits for workers and instrumental benefits for the business or organization in reducing absenteeism and benefit claims, work-related conflicts or interruptions, and burnout. This motive is borne out in research as well. In their meta-analysis, Mesmer-Magnus et al. (2017) found trait mindfulness was positively correlated with confidence, mental health, emotion regulation and negatively correlated with perceived life stress, negative emotions, anxiety, and depression. Such trait mindfulness, in turn, improves with state mindfulness, that is, through training and practice. Below, we consider a range of health-related effects in more detail, including stress reduction, improved mental health and wellbeing, and enhanced work-life balance.

### *Stress Reduction*

Work-related stress is a significant source of chronic and persistent stress in the population. To explain the persistence of stress responses in the absence of identifiable stressors, Brosschot et al. (2018) proposed the Generalized Unsafety Theory of Stress (GUTS). This theory attempts to explain prolonged and generalized stress-related physiological activity, even in the absence of direct stressors. They argue that the stress response is almost entirely unconscious and is the default physiological response in the absence of explicit triggers of safety. Therefore, the stress response can persist indefinitely, even in the absence of any immediate stressors. Meanwhile, generalized unsafety is used to explain the perseverative worrying and rumination associated with these states of prolonged generalized stress.

Chronic stress leads to many negative health effects, especially if the stressor is unclear or difficult to remove. For example, Brosschot et al. (2018) offered evidence that high levels of work stress quadruple the likelihood of developing cardiovascular disease. Although these authors focus on the implications of exposure to nature, there is a multiplying effect when mindfulness is combined with immersion in nature (Djernis et al., 2019). Indeed, meditation has been theorized to impact stress levels precisely because it enhances the perception of safety, even at an autonomic level where it has been found to alter DNA through telomere biology (Conklin et al., 2019). In this way, mindfulness is speculated to dampen the threat-detection system, making possible the learning or relearning of safety cues until they are accepted and habitual.

Evidence of the impact of mindfulness on workplace stress corroborates this relationship. Eby et al. (2019), for example, conducted a qualitative review of 67 published studies of mindfulness-based training with employees and found that the most common intended motive was to reduce stress/strain (80.6%). They also found that Mindfulness-Based Stress Reduction (MBSR) or some adaptation of this stress reduction programme was the most common type of programme (41.8%). So too, in their meta-analysis of RCTs of workplace mindfulness programmes, Bartlett et al. (2019) found significant benefits for reducing stress and psychological distress and for increasing trait mindfulness, wellbeing, and sleep. Likewise, using measured physiological effects, Heckenberry et al. (2018) found evidence of improvements in key physiological stress responses, with lower daily cortisol levels, improved autonomic balance (via heart-rate variability coherence measures), and improvement in the immune response to a viral vaccine and reduced C-reactive protein concentrations.

### *Mental Health and Wellbeing*

The most significant financial incentives for organizations to adopt mindfulness programmes concern costs related to mental illness. The UK Mindfulness All-Party Parliamentary Group (MAPPG, 2015) reported that in the six-year period leading up to the publication of the report, the total sick days claimed in the US from stress, depression, and anxiety increased 24% while the number of days from serious mental illness doubled. Mindfulness offers a relatively inexpensive and effective approach to reducing such costs and the associated distress they signify. For example, in their meta-analysis of RCTs of workplace mindfulness programmes, Vonderlin et al. (2020) found evidence of small to large effect sizes for reducing stress, burnout, mental distress, and somatic complaints and improving (trait) mindfulness, wellbeing, compassion, and job satisfaction. It is worth noting that among the 53 studies, the most common employees studied were healthcare workers ($k$=19, 36%), followed by teachers, and industrial and financial sector employees.

The general population bears the burden of mental health challenges, with many sufferers remaining untreated when they opt to suffer beyond clinical surveillance. To ascertain the impact of mindfulness on the psychological health and wellbeing of such non-clinical, untreated populations, Querstret et al. (2020) reviewed 49 studies of mindfulness-based conflicts. Likewise, Michel et al.'s (2014) found improved work-life segmentation and boundary-setting following a mindfulness training for employees (*n*=246), with significantly less strain-related work-family conflict and more psychological detachment and satisfaction with work-life balance.

### *Job Satisfaction, Burnout, and Resilience*

Related to work-life balance is the construct of job satisfaction. Mesmer-Magnus et al.'s (2017) meta-analysis of 270 studies (*N*=58,592) found evidence of significant links between trait mindfulness and higher levels of job satisfaction, performance, interpersonal relations, and reduced burnout and work withdrawal. Burnout, in turn, is associated with job-related emotional exhaustion, depersonalization, and the loss of a sense of personal accomplishment. In their meta-analysis and review, Suleiman-Martos et al. (2020) found mindfulness training significantly lowered burnout syndrome among high-risk nurses through its effects on these three variables. Kaplan et al. (2017) examined the disaggregated effects of mindfulness delivered to first responders via a Mindfulness-Based Resilience Training (MBRT) training programme. They found that increased mindfulness was related to increased resilience, which in turn was related to decreased burnout. Finally, Surguladze et al. (2020) studied 37 female professionals working with traumatized populations in a range of caring professions. They tested them for empathy, trait mindfulness, and professional quality of life, which includes subscales of burnout, compassion satisfaction, and compassion fatigue/ secondary trauma. The results demonstrated that not only did trait mindfulness reduce burnout directly, but it mediated the effects of empathy to make it strongly negatively related to burnout. In other words, the higher the trait of mindfulness, the more that empathy or caring became a protective, rather than vulnerability, factor in burnout.

## Individual Performance and Productivity

The general effects of mindfulness on employee performance and productivity are second only to the effects on health and wellbeing, both to the organization and, presumably, to an employee. Below, we present research on five key performance indicators in which mindfulness has been shown to be impactful: Attention, multitasking, relationships, decision-making, and creativity.

### *Attention Regulation*

Echoing Garland et al.'s (2015a, 2015b) Mindfulness-to-Meaning Theory (MMT), discussed later in Chapter 9, Good et al. (2016) proposed an evidence-based integrative model of mindfulness, theorizing how to explain the efficacy of mindfulness in work-related contexts. The most direct, immediate impact of mindfulness was on attention – its stability, control, and efficiency. They theorized that mindfulness-based attention regulation exerted downstream effects on four functional domains: Cognition (capacity and flexibility); emotion (life cycle, reactivity, valence); behaviour (self-regulation and reduced automaticity); and physiology (stress response, neuroplasticity, aging). These downstream functional effects were then used to explain the effects of mindfulness on common workplace outcomes programmes (MBPs) – MBSR and MBCT – and pooled their data from non-clinical samples (*n*=4,733). They found these MBPs significantly reduced symptoms of rumination/worry, stress/psychological distress, depression, and anxiety, while significantly improving quality of life/wellbeing. Furthermore, MBCT had a larger effect size than MBSR for these outcomes. These findings are important as most of the research on MBCT has focused on clinical contexts and patients in or emerging from treatment. Likewise, in their review of 35 studies of more varied MBPs, Lomas et al. (2019) found a range of moderate effects on reducing stress, distress, depression, anxiety, and burnout and improving health, job performance, compassion, empathy, mindfulness, and wellbeing.

As an example of this, the UK Mindfulness Initiative's (2016) *Building the Case for Mindfulness in the Workplace* reported on a case study of a mindfulness initiative by CVS, one of the largest providers of veterinary care in the UK. Veterinarians have a much higher likelihood of committing suicide than other medical professionals, more than double the rate of the next highest group, dentists. So, the mindfulness programme was introduced for mental health promotion purposes. A recent hire, who came with a history of clinical mental health issues, participated in the program and reported afterwards:

> I was sceptical; after all, if tablets and psychiatry hadn't helped, why would concentrating on the here and now help?...I was so wrong; this course has helped me more than I could have imagined...Another unexpected positive outcome of the course is the confidence it has given me. I am now happy to participate in meetings and actually have the confidence to put my ideas across.
>
> *(p. 10)*

## *Work-Life Balance*

Brough et al. (2020) present the broad range of work-life balance indicators, such as time spent in work and non-work activities, satisfaction with the performance and time spent on each domain, and the relative salience of the respective roles. Although commonly associated with work-family balance, the better term is "work-life balance" to reflect the range of non-work activities highly valued by working people that contribute to their wellbeing and quality of life, such as study, travel, friendships, in addition to family. In one study of physicians and advance practice clinicians, Thimmapuram et al. (2019) found a significant decrease in emotional exhaustion with positive implications for work-life balance following a mindfulness intervention (as compared to a control). Allen and Kiburz (2012) found trait mindfulness to be related to work-family balance as mediated by sleep quality and vitality, a finding they attributed to mindfulness' effects on improved self-regulation and enhanced segmentation through present-moment awareness. Allen and Paddock (2015) further explained this apparent link to work-life balance via four key effects of mindfulness on: i) attention and the minimization of distractions; ii) emotion regulation; iii) executive control (resource allocation); and iv) time perception.

Kiburz et al. (2017) reported on a related study of the effects of short mindfulness training on work-family conflicts. Building on previous findings of a positive correlation between trait mindfulness and reduced conflicts, they designed a mindfulness-based intervention to determine its impact on reduced work-to-family or family-to-work conflict. They found significantly reduced reported instances of work interfering with family following the intervention, especially among those who maintained a behavioural self-monitoring journal, but found no effects in the reverse direction, that is, on family-to-work even in the absence of direct stressors. They argue that the stress response is almost entirely unconscious and is the default physiological response in the absence of explicit triggers of safety. Therefore, the stress response can persist indefinitely, even in the absence of any immediate stressors. Meanwhile, generalized unsafety is used to explain the perseverative worrying and rumination associated with these states of prolonged generalized stress.

Chronic stress leads to many negative health effects, especially if the stressor is unclear or difficult to remove. For example, Brosschot et al. (2018) offered evidence that high levels of work stress quadruple the likelihood of developing cardiovascular disease. Although these authors focus on the implications of exposure to nature, there is a multiplying effect when mindfulness is combined with immersion in nature (Djernis et al., 2019). Indeed, meditation has been theorized to impact stress levels precisely because it enhances the perception of safety, even at an autonomic level where it has been found to alter DNA through telomere biology (Conklin et al., 2019). In this way, mindfulness is speculated to dampen the threat-detection system, making possible the learning or relearning of safety cues until they are accepted and habitual.

Evidence of the impact of mindfulness on workplace stress corroborates this relationship. Eby et al. (2019), for example, conducted a qualitative review of 67 published studies of mindfulness-based training with employees and found that the most common intended motive was to reduce stress/strain (80.6%). They also found that Mindfulness-Based Stress Reduction (MBSR) or some adaptation of this stress reduction programme was the most common type of programme (41.8%). So too, in their meta-analysis of RCTs of workplace mindfulness programmes, Bartlett et al. (2019) found significant benefits for reducing stress and psychological distress and for increasing trait mindfulness, wellbeing, and sleep. Likewise, using measured physiological effects, Heckenberry et al. (2018) found evidence of improvements in key physiological stress responses, with lower daily cortisol levels, improved autonomic balance (via heart-rate variability coherence measures), and improvement in the immune response to a viral vaccine and reduced C-reactive protein concentrations.

## *Mental Health and Wellbeing*

The most significant financial incentives for organizations to adopt mindfulness programmes concern costs related to mental illness. The UK Mindfulness All-Party Parliamentary Group (MAPPG, 2015) reported that in the six-year period leading up to the publication of the report, the total sick days claimed in the US from stress, depression, and anxiety increased 24% while the number of days from serious mental illness doubled. Mindfulness offers a relatively inexpensive and effective approach to reducing such costs and the associated distress they signify. For example, in their meta-analysis of RCTs of workplace mindfulness programmes, Vonderlin et al. (2020) found evidence of small to large effect sizes for reducing stress, burnout, mental distress, and somatic complaints and improving (trait) mindfulness, wellbeing, compassion, and job satisfaction. It is worth noting that among the 53 studies, the most common employees studied were healthcare workers ($k$=19, 36%), followed by teachers, and industrial and financial sector employees.

The general population bears the burden of mental health challenges, with many sufferers remaining untreated when they opt to suffer beyond clinical surveillance. To ascertain the impact of mindfulness on the psychological health and wellbeing of such non-clinical, untreated populations, Querstret et al. (2020) reviewed 49 studies of mindfulness-based benefit collectives, not just individuals. Such collective mindfulness was defined by Weick & Sutcliffe (2001/2007) as a way to grow organizations through the "ongoing scrutiny of existing expectations, continuous refinement and differentiation of expectations based on newer experiences." This implies a kind of executive functioning with self-regulating features functioning at the collective level.

## RESEARCH

Research on the work-related applications of mindfulness investigates the effectiveness of mindfulness using a wide range of criteria, such as employee health and wellbeing; employee performance; leadership skills; work team functioning; and organizational cultures. Research methods include correlation studies that rely on measures of trait or dispositional mindfulness via tests like the Five Facets of Mindfulness Questionnaire (FFMQ); they also include Randomized Controlled Trials (RCT) where findings impute causality between mindfulness as a "treatment" and a range of effects. Although many of these RCT studies use passive and waitlist control conditions, more are using active control conditions to increase validity. Workplace mindfulness programmes are now commonplace, and the expectation for measurable outcomes has helped to increase the collecting and reporting of data. In their *Mindful Nation, UK* study, the Mindfulness All-Party Parliamentary Group (2015) identified work-related mindfulness as one of four significant and promising areas to develop mindfulness programming, alongside education, health care, and the criminal justice system. As they describe in the report: "This is the sector where there has been the most intense interest, widespread experimentation and enthusiastic media coverage of the subject of mindfulness" (p. 39).

### Employee Health and Wellbeing

One key motive for introducing mindfulness in the workplace is to support employee health and wellbeing. The health promotion potential of mindfulness offers both intrinsic benefits for workers and instrumental benefits for the business or organization in reducing absenteeism and benefit claims, work-related conflicts or interruptions, and burnout. This motive is borne out in research as well. In their meta-analysis, Mesmer-Magnus et al. (2017) found trait mindfulness was positively correlated with confidence, mental health, emotion regulation and negatively correlated with perceived life stress, negative emotions, anxiety, and depression. Such trait mindfulness, in turn, improves with state mindfulness, that is, through training and practice. Below, we consider a range of health-related effects in more detail, including stress reduction, improved mental health and wellbeing, and enhanced work-life balance.

#### *Stress Reduction*

Work-related stress is a significant source of chronic and persistent stress in the population. To explain the persistence of stress responses in the absence of identifiable stressors, Brosschot et al. (2018) proposed the Generalized Unsafety Theory of Stress (GUTS). This theory attempts to explain prolonged and generalized stress-related physiological activity, associated with improved job performance; relationships; and wellbeing. The authors also reviewed evidence suggesting that mindfulness affects all three aspects of attention regulation, i.e., stability, control, and efficiency, and their underlying neural networks (Sumantry & Stewart, 2021). Reb et al. (2013) identified two specific attention-related effects of mindfulness at work: Increased employee awareness and decreased employee absent-mindedness, which contributed to reduced emotional exhaustion and improved job satisfaction, psychological need satisfaction, and job performance.

### *Multitasking*

Levy et al. (2021) reported significant effects of an eight-week mindfulness programme on a range of operationalized multitasking behaviours, including reduced switching between competing tasks, fewer negative emotions, and more time spent on individual tasks in contrast to a relaxation or passive control group. Gorman and Green (2016) investigated if short-term mindfulness practices could also ameliorate the known negative effects of media multitasking on attention using two conditions – a breath-counting mindfulness practice and a Web browsing control – with two groups: Heavy media multitaskers (HMMs) and light media multitaskers (LMMs). The HMMs had poorer initial baseline attention rates than LMMs, suggesting that heavy media multitasking negatively impacts attention. They then introduced the experimental and control conditions – short but repetitive breath counting or mere Web browsing, respectively. They found that mindfulness-based breath-counting intervention improved attention measures for both groups, but disproportionately for HMM.

### *Interpersonal Relationships*

As Reb et al. (2020) argue, mindfulness' steady drift into the workplace marks a decisive shift from an orientation on the intrapersonal to the interpersonal effects of mindfulness. Eby et al. (2020) extrapolated findings from other contexts to propose a framework for considering the impact of mindfulness in organizations and at work. This review included evidence of the beneficial effects of mindfulness for partner relations, including higher levels of relationship satisfaction (e.g., Adair et al., 2018); improved relationship satisfaction levels following MBSR (e.g., Khaddouma et al., 2017); and reduced use of aggressive and negative strategies during conflicts, with more willingness to compromise among men (e.g., Harvey et al., 2019). Likewise, there was evidence of increased mindful parenting, reduced parenting stress, and improved relationships between parents and adolescents (Chaplin et al., 2021) and findings that adolescents exposed to mindful parenting exhibited more compassion and wellbeing (e.g., Moreira et al., 2018). Benefits of mindfulness in professional relations have been found in healthcare workers' relations with peers, patients, and patient families (Kulka et al., 2018); physician communications with patients (Beach et al., 2013); and counsellors' self-reported effectiveness and clients' perceived empathy (e.g., Fulton, 2016). Likewise, teachers' levels of trait mindfulness were found to correlate with their emotional support, communication, and perspective-taking with students (Braun et al., 2019; Jennings, 2015; Taylor et al., 2016), and students with teachers who undertook mindfulness training described an enhanced sense of relatedness to their teachers (Hwang et al., 2019).

There is also early evidence that mindfulness may enhance helping or prosocial behaviour at work. For example, Hafenbrack et al. (2020) used an RCT design to measure the impact of daily mindfulness on helping behaviours, finding that those in the mindfulness v. control group reported more helping behaviours over a five-day period. In two follow-up studies in India, they found those assigned to a breathing meditation condition were more financially generous than controls. Finally, they identified two mediators to explain these apparent positive effects of state mindfulness on prosocial behaviour: Empathy and perspective-taking. Therefore, in fostering empathy and perspective-taking, mindfulness indirectly affected prosocial helping behaviour among workers.

### *Conflict Management*

Kay and Skarlicki (2020) combined both a dispositional (correlation) and an experimental RCT study to consider the impact of mindfulness on constructive conflict management in the workplace. The first study affirmed their hypotheses that mindfulness is positively correlated with collaboration and inversely related to conflict avoidance – both key operationalized indicators of constructive conflict management. In the second RCT using an active control condition, the findings reaffirmed a positive causal effect on improved collaboration and reduced conflict avoidance with mindfulness training. Affect was stable throughout the study, which helped control for positive affect as a possible mediator, as was often believed. This study suggested that, rather than positive affect, it was enhanced collaboration and reduced conflict avoidance that explain the effectiveness of mindfulness in constructive conflict management. This is a noteworthy finding given some critiques of mindfulness in the popular and scholarly press, notably those by Ron Purser, suggesting that mindfulness increases conflict avoidance and passivity in organizational settings.

In a very important study, Thoroughgood et al. (2020) examined the relationship between trait mindfulness, perceptions of discrimination, paranoid cognition, and emotional exhaustion in transgender employees over a two-week period. They found that the higher the employees' levels of trait mindfulness, the lower their paranoid cognitions and emotional exhaustion the morning after reporting discrimination at work. This study is important for considering the ways in which mindfulness training can serve employees with a history of discrimination in the workplace to help them as they struggle to correct harms and support them in recovering from possible trauma. It should not be interpreted, of course, as a single strategy, for the very existence of discrimination is a systemic issue for the organization to address. At the same time, mindfulness may assist in reducing the prejudice or implicit biases of the general employee population. For example, early research suggests that mindfulness may reduce discrepancies between implicit biases and conscious beliefs or states, as in Remmers et al.'s (2018) finding that mindfulness training improved consistency between implicit and explicit moods in subjects with acute depression.

### *Decision-Making and Creativity*

Mindfulness affects decision-making in a number of ways, including through improved executive functioning and reduced cognitive biases. Executive functioning involves the coordination and coherence of goal-directed behaviour and decision-making through self-regulation. Cognitive biases refer to the now-established understanding that most of our decision-making is not deliberate and rational but driven by unconscious or non-conscious fast, automatic processing (Kahneman, 2011). Fabbro et al. (2017) suggested that mindfulness appears to shift cognition from habitual to more self-aware, conscious, and intentional decision-making associated with "a more coherent, healthy, and authentic sense of self" (p. 9). Karelaia and Reb (2015) tracked the positive effects of mindfulness in all four components of the decision process: Decision framing; information gathering and processing; coming to conclusion; and learning from feedback.

## Mindful Leaders

The impact of mindfulness on leaders is a key area of interest in the organizational applications of mindfulness. As Arendt et al. (2019) point out, one reason this area is of keen interest is that it bridges mindfulness as an intrapersonal to an interpersonal practice, wherein the impact on an individual shows evidence of impacting others, namely their "followers." Yet, it is also perceived by leaders themselves to improve their own performance and wellbeing. For example, following a ten-week mindfulness programme, 13 leaders from six organizations were interviewed 6–12 months later on the perceived benefits of mindfulness. They reported improvements in self-leadership capacities in mindful task management, self-care and self-reflection and in two leadership capacities: Relating to others and adapting to change (Rupprecht et al., 2019). Mindfulness has also been found to limit the negative impacts of emotional exhaustion on leaders. Walsh and Arnold (2018) found that higher levels of mindfulness in leaders mediated the negative affect and perspective-taking associated with abusive supervision and transformational leadership. Leaders higher in mindfulness were less likely to show as much increase in abusive supervision and as much decrease in transformational leadership arising from emotional exhaustion compared to those lower in mindfulness.

### *Communication and Emotional Stability*

Leaders' communication is a key mindfulness effect that impacts followers. Arendt et al. (2019), for example, found that leaders' self-reported dispositional mindfulness levels were associated with followers' satisfaction and entirely mediated by leaders' mindfulness in communication. Mindfulness in communication is characterized by awareness (i.e., paying attention); acceptance (i.e., having an open, non-judging attitude); and c) emotion regulation (i.e., displaying calm, non-impulsive, non-reactive manner). Mindful communication is reasoned to support follower satisfaction because it furthers their basic needs for relationships, autonomy, and competency as theorized by self-determination theory (SDT) (Deci & Ryan, 2000; Ryan & Deci, 2000). In a related study of transformational leadership, neuroticism, and mindfulness, Decuypere et al. (2018) found that neuroticism increased the impact of mindfulness on transformational leadership. Therefore, the researchers concluded that mindfulness had positive effects on followers' perceptions principally by lowering leaders' neuroticism and increasing their emotional stability.

### *Trust and Trustworthiness*

In a related vein, Stedham and Skaar (2019) reviewed studies to support their theory that mindfulness increases levels of trust and trustworthiness in leaders to improve leader-follower relations. Trust is a strategy whereby a person allows themselves to be vulnerable and accept uncertainty by following the leadership or direction of another. Using Mayer et al.'s (1995) model, the authors propose that mindfulness affects all three factors of trustworthiness: ability; integrity; and benevolence. Stedham and Skaar conclude:

> Mindful leaders will be effective because they are able to influence others' behavior because they are trusted. They are trusted because they engage in behaviors that increase their trustworthiness. Followers feel safe and are willing to be vulnerable in their relationship with their leader.

### *Humility & Employee Creativity*

Cheung et al. (2020) compared levels of mindfulness and creativity in employees in China, as well as the moderating effects of the perceived humility of their leaders. They found that more mindful employees were rated by supervisors as higher in creativity, but that this relationship was moderated by the degree of perceived humility of the supervisor. When a leader's humility was rated highly, the association between employee mindfulness and creativity increased, but when their humility was rated low, the association became nonsignificant. So, if we conclude that the supervisors who were perceived to be humbler *were* so, then this may have enabled them to recognize and acknowledge creativity in their followers more freely and accurately.

## Mindful Teams

There are increasing calls to develop mindfulness programmes for collectives and to investigate what it means for those collectives to function mindfully, say as teams or organizations. As Rupprecht et al. (2019) explain it:

> Just as one returns to present-moment awareness in the practice of individual mindfulness, so mindful teams will repeatedly return their awareness or attention to purpose, performance, processes, climate and problems. This may be mediated by processes such as changes in present moment experiencing and by the adoption of non-judgmental attitudes thus allowing members to become more sensitive to the dynamics of their teams and more capable of adapting team structures and processes.
>
> *(p. 33)*

### *Reducing Conflict and Social Undermining*

Yu and Zellmer-Bruhn (2018) offered evidence that team mindfulness can safeguard teams against negative interpersonal processes. Investigating 44 teams of 244 individuals in two incoming MBA classes, they found an inverse relationship between team-based trait mindfulness levels and reported task conflicts, relational conflicts, and perceived social undermining. Mindfulness levels were positively associated with reduced conflicts overall, with less likelihood that task conflicts would spill over to relational conflicts, and that relational conflicts would spill over to individual social undermining. They encouraged future research on how organizational and team performance affects team conflicts and, vice-versa, how both individual and team mindfulness impact performance.

### *Team Reciprocity and Exchanges*

In one such study investigating the impact of mindfulness on team performance, Hawkes and Neal (2019) reported that trait mindfulness was positively associated with increased perceived reciprocity in teams. Operationalized as team-member exchanges, such reciprocity increased with mindfulness, mediated by improved emotion regulation through reappraisal. So, while high levels of mindfulness were associated with increased reappraisal and exchanges, lower mindfulness was related to increased suppression and low exchanges. With this kind of evidence in mind, Rupprecht et al. (2020) recommended applying mindfulness more effectively beyond the individual to teams, departments, and whole organizations. They recommended integrating research alongside programme development, beginning with correlation and qualitative studies to ground new theories and progressing to more controlled RCT intervention studies. One area of inquiry they suggested was to compare and examine the relative impacts of coaching and mindfulness on teams, for example, or combinations of the two. Also, they suggested exploring possible mediators and moderators for each organizational level, including the impact of supervisory support, role clarity, clarity of team purpose and objectives, and organizational culture. Pertinent to our MBTL-TCF competency framework in Chapter 15, they recommended developing a competency framework that reflects what it means to understand and embody mindfulness in organizational contexts.

## Organizational Mindfulness/Mindful Organizing

Mindfulness can be introduced in organization-wide initiatives and targets. For example, Greiser and Martini (2018) report a range of programs that organizations or companies can use, including leadership training, meditation training, mindfulness micro-practices, and mindfulness coaching (p. 5). At the same time, new research suggests mindfulness may support higher-order community or social organizing associated with adapting to increased risk and climate change (Wamsler, 2018).

### *Collective Mindfulness in High-Reliability Organizations*

High-reliability organizations (HROs) refer to organizations that require high degrees of reliability because of the high-stakes risks associated with them, such as air-traffic control, hospital emergency intake or surgery, or nuclear power stations. These environments involve high-pressured, time-sensitive, complex, and dynamic error-free conditions. Research indicates that HROs benefit from mindful organizing that fosters the capacity to detect and correct errors and adapt to unexpected conditions (Weick & Sutcliff, 2001/2007). Weick et al. (1999) defined collective mindfulness in terms of five features that also characterized HROs: i) preoccupation with failure, i.e., fully discussing ways things can go wrong and analyzing early indicators; ii) reluctance to simplify interpretations, i.e., questioning the adequacy of existing approaches; iii) sensitivity to operations, i.e., developing and refreshing a shared understanding of operations; iv) commitment to resilience, i.e., analyzing and learning from critical incidents; and v) deference to expertise, i.e., deferring to local expertise v. formal authority in resolving emergent problems. This overlap between mindfulness effects and the features of high-functioning HROs provides a glimpse into how mindfulness might foster more open, collaborative, and self-critical organizational cultures.

Vogus et al. (2014) propose that mindful organizing involves two key mediating factors that give rise to these five HRO-aligned features: emotional ambivalence and prosocial motivation. Emotional ambivalence refers to the simultaneous experience of both positive and negative emotions, such as hope and doubt. This combination invites sufficient confidence, on the one hand, with enough worry or concern to be preoccupied with possible scenarios for failure. Prosocial motivation refers to the sense that one's personal actions are subordinate to the wellbeing of others and to a system and its constituents. Such other-orientation increases awareness of others – colleagues and stakeholders – and the impact of one's performance on potential harm to others. This was in marked contrast to pro-self motivation, which can lead to increased errors and lower reliability in organizations or work environments, as Ely and Meyerson's (2010) found in their study of oil rigs. Such mindful organizing changes can be made through a combination of leadership training, safety and team review policies, organization-wide training, and more informal organizational-wide communication systems.

### *Mindfulness in Organizational Culture and Change*

Interestingly, in the above Ely and Meyerson (2010) study, they found that when the two oil rig companies introduced changes to reduce errors and risks and enhance safety to better reflect HROs as mindful organizations, they experienced the unintended effect of freeing the largely male workforce of stereotypical "manly" behaviours, leading them to more readily admit mistakes, acknowledge limitations, and attend to others' feelings. This points to broader implications for mindfulness and mindful organizing on organizational cultural change beyond performance. The role of leadership and leader modelling and support can be crucial in mindful organizational change. For example, Baez (2020) reported on a study of Long Island school superintendents introduced to mindfulness via an organizational framework. The superintendents identified four areas they considered critical for mindfulness to impact their organization's culture: Developing personal mindfulness practices; engaging in ongoing professional development in mindfulness; providing opportunities for educators in their systems to receive mindful leadership professional development; and assessing the impact of mindfulness on student learning outcomes.

Mindful organizations are characterized by openness and knowledge sharing: They recognize that information accessible to individuals is necessarily incomplete, so sharing and open communication help to mitigate errors, manage the unknown, and promote learning (Mielke, 2020). In theorizing HROs as a case of mindful organizing, Weick et al. (1999) identified three organizational issues corrected by mindfulness: i) complacency, corrected by mindful intention, curiosity, and inquiry; ii) inattention, corrected through mindful focus, attention, and awareness; and iii) habituation, corrected by attuning to what is new and orienting on adaptive responses. Unchecked, these three tendencies make organizations susceptible to high rates of error and related problems, which appear to be corrected by mindful organizing. Notable, the first feature of mindful organizing and successful HROs – attentive to failure – provides a way to consider mindful organizing to address collective human challenges like global climate change. Human-generated climate change could be seen as rooted in these three problems with the corrective beginning with attention to the features of failure.

### *Mindfulness and Emotional Labour in the Workplace*

Emotional labour refers to the effortful regulation or management of emotions to support organizational objectives. Lyddy et al. (2021) extrapolated from earlier studies that found that employees with higher mindfulness were less likely to engage in surface acting, which involves the display of discrepant from actual emotions in workplace situations. They were also more likely to engage in deep acting, that is, changing emotions to align with their organization's desired emotions rather than merely suppressing them by surface acting. This was theorized as a positive effect of mindfulness in organizations. Not only did it involve greater authenticity and genuineness in communication, but, for surface actors, high levels of suppression and self-control led to fatigue through "self-control depletion." This depletion can impact task performance, turning constructive surface acting as citizenship performance, i.e., conforming to organizational expectations, into counterproductive performance when self-control is depleted (i.e., through outbursts or dysregulated emotions).

Yet, Lyddy et al. (2021) saw a potential cost or *dark side* to this seemingly bright picture of the benefits of mindfulness with respect to more authentic, deep acting. Recognizing that many organizations require forms of surface acting, they hypothesized that more mindful employees would experience greater rates of self-control depletion when required to surface act than those lower in mindfulness. Using six samples (N=180-409), they first confirmed the association between high levels of mindfulness and low levels of surface action; however, they also found much higher rates of self-control depletion when those higher in mindfulness were required to engage in surface acting. This suggests that when and if very mindful employees are forced to engage in surface acting, they may quickly deplete energy and become vulnerable to emotional reactivity; however, it implies as well that more mindful employees may be more motivated to establish conditions favourable for the communication of more authentic emotions as they have more at stake in having to surface act in the workplace.

## CRITICAL ISSUES AND CRITIQUES

The entry of MBTL within workplaces and organizations has generated considerable critique in popular and scholarly circles, perhaps more than in any other sector of secular-scientific mindfulness. Although much of this critique seems to focus on the worksite being for-profit corporations, in fact, many organizations employing mindfulness training are not-for-profit, public, or governmental. This assumption has led to ethical critiques, suggesting that mindfulness is complicit in capitalism and neo-liberal interests. Another slippage seems to be between the application of mindfulness within organizations and its development as a for-profit market product. Although these critiques may intersect with the concerns we raise below, we will not review the often overgeneralized and confused critiques made in the popular press. Instead, we restrict our discussion to critical issues raised or implied in scholarly sources.

### Individual or Organizational (i.e., Systemic) Responsibility

In research on mindfulness at work, there is a general lack of critique of the relative role of personal versus systemic organizational responsibilities. Take the very common topic of work-related stress and burnout (e.g., Querstrat et al., 2020; Surguladze et al., 2020; Vonderlin et al., 2020). These studies can seem to convey the message that the responsibility for stress management falls on individual employees, who are trained through mindfulness to self-regulate emotions and physiology in high-stress environments, rather than on organizations' policies leading to unfair workloads or compensation or on workplace cultures that tolerate bullying or discrimination, leadership shortcomings, or dysfunctional procedures or communications (Eby et al., 2019). If too much emphasis is placed on individual adaptation and too little on organizational adaptation, then the net effect of such programmes could be to diminish evidence of organizational dysfunction and the inclination to address it.

Within programmes specifically targeting outcomes for individual employees, without active organizational supports for the transfer of learning to the workplace, the impacts on work can be reduced or curtailed altogether. For example, in their review, Eby et al. (2019) point out that workloads, opportunities to use skills, recognitions, and organizational culture can all limit the transfer of skills from mindfulness training to the workplace. On the other hand, organizations can encourage employees to sustain mindfulness practices after training through such measures as providing dedicated spaces, opportunities and time to practice, posters with mindfulness tips, and refresher courses. If too much emphasis is placed on training and too little on the transfer of learning, such initiatives may benefit employees' personal lives but may have a limited impact on organizational outcomes.

## Ethics: People or Organizations as Ends

One key challenge as MBTL moves from religious, clinical, and educational environments to the workplace is how the mindfulness practitioners are viewed. All of these other contexts have some ethical framework to understand duties of care for trainees – be they students, patients, or clients – as persons who are treated as ends-in-themselves rather than the means to the ends of others. In workplace environments, however, this ethic is less clear; indeed, there is a tendency to view employees as subservient to the goals and needs of the organization or workplace rather than vice-versa, even if these interests intersect. As the term *human resources* even suggests, employees are viewed as resources or means-to-the-ends of others, namely of the organization and its stakeholders. Therefore, when discussions of the profitability and return-on-investment of mindfulness outweigh considerations of the intrinsic wellbeing of the people involved, the programmes can be seen as unethical. One way to address this concern is to frame discussions around how these interests intersect and, if they don't, how they might be reconciled. For example, mindfulness is associated with improved work-life balance. Although some of this is from enhanced attention on the present, some is from establishing limits and learning to say no to excessive work demands. Although this may seem like a negative for an organization, the health, wellbeing, and happiness of personnel is in everyone's interest.

## Mindfulness as Self-Determination

Although self-determination theory (SDT) is a popular theory in organizational psychology with respect to employee motivation and innovation, there are many challenges to maintaining intrinsic motivation, autonomy, and self-determination at work. Organizational practices like using salaries or pay as extrinsic motivators; micro-managing or fostering intrusive supervision practices; and a lack of a range of choices for employees are examples of such challenges. By promoting mindfulness at work, as Deci and Ryan (2000) suggest, organizations may increase employee expectations for greater basic need fulfillment at work. This may not be explicit but something that naturally arises as more employees engage in mindfulness and seek greater autonomy and wellbeing. As SDT theory suggests, one way out of this conundrum is to encourage values clarification, whereby employees are supported to negotiate and internalize workplace values and expectations in ways that align with their own intrinsic values and motivators. Another way is to ensure again that the organization is doing its part by integrating practices and policies more consistent with employee autonomy and self-determination (Ryan & Deci, 2017).

## Privacy: Is Mindfulness Personal, Spiritual, Clinical?

Although mindfulness teachers are trained to safeguard privacy and confidentiality for participants in programmes, in the workplace this becomes even more challenging. First, it is inappropriate to collect background health intake information as done in clinical settings. This is true of educational environments as well, in that both students and employees enjoy privacy protections against such intrusions. Intake might focus instead on reminding participants to consult with healthcare providers if they have any conditions that may be impacted by mindfulness. Also, teaching them explicitly to use self-regulatory tools like the Window of Tolerance (see Chapter 17) can help. Yet, even with such privacies protected, participants are still asked, if not required, to engage in ways that may make them feel more vulnerable than they are accustomed to experiencing at work. For example, they are encouraged to describe internal experiences in front of the class or in exchanges with participants. Although it is voluntary, it is nonetheless an expectation in most programmes. This may create tensions or discomfort for people who prefer stricter boundaries between their private and professional or work life. If a participant considers mindfulness to be a practice that is fundamentally personal, spiritual, or even clinical, then such discomforts may be aggravated more if they see it as an incursion into non-work-related aspects of life. That said, MBTL is founded on voluntary participation principles, including participating in programmes, reporting experiences, engaging in practices, and how much participants choose to engage.

## Research Design: Correlation v. Experimental v. Qualitative

Research in organizational mindfulness is dominated by correlation studies linking levels of dispositional (also referred to as "trait") mindfulness to a range of effects. Without control groups, such studies cannot infer causality. Furthermore, because these studies don't include interventions in the form of training or practice, the results offer limited data on designing and/or delivering mindfulness in the workplace. Instead, it just suggests whether or not it *may* be beneficial in generating this or another desired organizational outcome. Although the research is fairly robust that state mindfulness, via training and practice, increases trait or dispositional mindfulness, this cannot be presumed until tested. Also, properly designed experimental interventions with an active control (rather than a passive waitlist condition), offer more solid evidence of efficacy to legitimate more investments of time, energy, and reputation by the organization and its personnel. Finally, qualitative research is neglected as well, which offers the opportunity to explore the details of unique programs and specific participant experiences in a more nuanced, granular, and detailed manner.

## TRENDS: PROMISING AND CHALLENGING

To review promising and challenging trends in organizational mindfulness, we focus on understanding the complex relationship between mindfulness and other trends in organizational psychology and change.

### Mindfulness Respite Breaks and Intrinsic Motivation

Chong et al. (2020) conducted two studies to better understand ambiguous research on the benefits of respite activities at work on subsequent affective states and intrinsic motivation and engagement. They hypothesized that levels of trait mindfulness would mediate whether or not employees were able to disengage psychologically from work during respite activities. Such activities include walks or listening to music or interacting voluntarily with colleagues and coworkers. The researchers reasoned that, with lower levels of mindfulness, employees would experience intrusive rumination and worry about work during respite, thereby reducing its benefits. Indeed, they found that those with high levels of mindfulness did differentially experience more positive effects from respite activities. High degrees of trait mindfulness were correlated with positive affect, intrinsic motivation, and engagement in the afternoon following morning respite activities and negatively related to negative affect and work stress and emotional exhaustion.

The important trend here is that mindfulness is being situated as a mediator of other factors, such as respite activities, known to impact the quality of work, work relations, and organizations. It highlights the need to have mindfulness programming as part of a broad bundle of organizational strategies, such as providing or encouraging respite activities, to amplify the possible positive affect and intrinsic motivation fostered through mindfulness on its own. Furthermore, those with higher levels of mindfulness may cope better with more flexible working hours or conditions, including working from home, where they can choose when and how to disengage during non-work activities.

### Untangling Individual, Team, and Organizational Effects

Another trend is the focused effort in research and practice to untangle programmes that target individual employees from collective mindfulness for teams and organizations. As Rupprecht et al. (2019) suggested, this involves integrating research and programming on team-based and organizational mindfulness with the current individual orientation. To focus on individuals who voluntarily opt to learn mindfulness or on those with high trait mindfulness are insufficient to support the kinds of systemic changes and transformative effects sought from organization-wide mindfulness initiatives.

### Mindful Organizations, Mindful Communities, and Social Change

Efforts to develop mindfulness for collectives – teams and organizations – beyond a narrow individual orientation offer an intriguing case to consider what it might mean to cultivate more mindful communities. Communities are rather abstract concepts. Yet, a community emerges from the sum of its organizations, workplaces, *and* individuals. Accordingly, organizational mindfulness can serve as a stepping stone to community mindfulness if the relationship between the organization and the broader community is structured and recognized. Intriguingly, this connection could be reversed as well, whereby organizational workplaces are also understood more properly as communities or nested communities within broader communities. This, in turn, embeds a potential promise to shift how we view and engage in work and work relations, including the distribution of power and adaptation of democratic forms of governance within organizations. While too premature to forecast sunny horizons, these possibilities are part of the struggle of the discourse and programming around mindfulness in organizations and workplaces.

## REFERENCES

Adair, K., Boulton, A., & Algoe, S. (2018). The effect of mindfulness on relationship satisfaction via perceived responsiveness: Findings from a dyadic study of heterosexual romantic partners. *Mindfulness*, *9*, 597–609. https://doi.org/10.1007/s12671-017-0801-3.

Allen, T., & Kiburz, K. (2012). Trait mindfulness and work-family balance among working parents: The meditating effects of vitality and sleep quality. *Journal of Vocational Behavior*, *80*(2), 372–379. https://doi.org/10.1016/j.jvb.2011.09.002.

Allen, T., & Paddock, E. L. (2015). Work-family balance, conflict, and enrichment: A review of existing evidence, mechanisms and future directions. In J. Reb & P. Atkins (Eds.), *Mindfulness in organizations: Foundations, research, and applications* (pp. 213–238). Cambridge University Press.

Arendt, J., Verdorfer, A., & Kugler, K. (2019). Mindfulness and leadership: Communication as a behavioral correlate of leader mindfulness and its effect on follower satisfaction. *Frontiers of Psychology*, *10*, 667. https://doi.org/10.3389/fpsyg.2019.00667.

Baez, A. (2020). *Systems leaders' perceptions of mindfulness and its impact on effective leadership outcomes and sustainability organizational culture.* Dissertation for Russell Sage College, Esteves School of Education.

Bartlett, L., Martin, A., Neil, A., Memish, K., Otahal, P., Kilpatrick, M., & Sanderson, K. (2019). A systematic review and meta-analysis of workplace mindfulness training randomized controlled trials. *Journal of Occupational Health Psychology*, *24*(1), 108–126. https://doi.org/10.1037/ocp0000146.

Beach, M., Roter, D., Korthuis, T., Epstein, R., Sharp, V., Ratanawongsa, N., Cohn, J., Eggly, S., Sankar, A., Moore, R., & Saha, S. (2013). A multicenter study of physician mindfulness and health care quality. *The Annals of Family Medicine*, *11*, 421–428. https://doi.org/10.1370/afm.1507.

Braun, S., Roeser, R., Mashburn, A., & Skinner, E. (2019). Middle school teachers' mindfulness, occupational health and well-being, and the quality of teacher-student interactions. *Mindfulness*, *10*, 245–255. https://doi.org/10.1007/s12671-018-0968-2.

Brosschot, J., Verkui, B., & Thayer, J. (2018). Generalized unsafety theory of stress: Unsafe environments and conditions, and the default stress response. *International Journal of Environmental Research and Health*, *15*(3), 464. https://doi.org/10.3390/ijerph15030464

Brough, P., Timms, C., Chan, X., Hawkes, A., & Rasmussen, L. (2020) Work–life balance: Definitions, causes, and consequences. In T. Theorell (Ed.), *Handbook of socioeconomic determinants of occupational health* (pp. 473–487). https://doi.org/10.1007/978-3-030-31438-5_20.

Chaplin, T., Turpyn, C., Fischer, S., Martelli, A., Ross, C., Leichtweis, R., Miller, A., & Sinha, R. (2021). Parenting-focused mindfulness intervention reduces stress and improves parenting in highly stressed mothers of adolescents. *Mindfulness, 12*, 450–462. https://doi.org/10.1007/s12671-018-1026-9.

Cheung, S., Huang, E., Chang, S., & Wei, L. (2020). Does being mindful make people more creative at work? The role of creative process engagement and perceived leader humility. *Organizational Behavior and Human Decision Processes, 159*, 39–48. https://doi.org/10.1016/j.obhdp.2019.12.003.

Chong, S., Kim, Y., Lee, H., Johnson, R., & Lin, J. (2020). Mind your own break! The interactive effect of workday respite activities and mindfulness on employee outcomes via affective linkages. *Organizational Behavior and Human Decision Processes, 159*, 64–77. https://doi.org/10.1016/j.obhdp.2019.11.001.

Conklin, Q., Crosswell, A., Saron, C., & Epel, E. (2019). Meditation, stress processes, and telomere biology. *Current Opinion in Psychology, 28*, 92–101. https://doi.org/10.1016/j.copsyc.2018.11.009.

Deci, E., & Ryan, R. (2000). The 'what' and 'why' of goal pursuits: Human needs and the self-determination of behavior. *Psychological Inquiry, 11*, 227–268. https://doi.org/10.1207/S15327965PLI1104_01.

Decuypere, A., Audenaert, M., & Decramer, A. (2018). When mindfulness interacts with neuroticism to enhance transformational leadership: The role of psychological need satisfaction. *Frontiers in Psychology, 9*, 2588. https://doi.org/10.3389/fpsyg.2018.02588.

Djernis, D., Lerstrup, I., Poulsen, D., Stigsdotter, U., Dahlgaard, J., & O'Toole, M. (2019). A systematic review and meta-analysis of nature-based mindfulness: Effects of moving mindfulness training into an outdoor nature setting. *International Journal of Environmental Research and Public Health, 16*(17), 3202. https://doi.org/10.3390/ijerph16173202.

Eby, L., Allen, T., Conley, K., Williamson, R., Henderson, T., & Mancini, V. (2019). Mindfulness-based training interventions for employees: A qualitative review of the literature. *Human Resource Management Review, 29*, 156–178. https://doi.org/10.1016/j.hrmr.2017.03.004.

Eby, L., Robertson, M., & Facteau, D. (2020). Mindfulness and relationships: An organizational perspective. *Research in Personnel and Human Resources Management, 38*, 47–102. https://doi.org/10.1108/S0742-730120200000038004

Ely, R., & Meyerson, D. (2010). An organizational approach to undoing gender: The unlikely case of offshore oil platforms. *Research in Organizational Behavior, 30*, 3–34. https://doi.org/10.1016/j.riob.2010.09.002.

Fabbro, A., Crescentini, C., Matix, A., Clarici, A., & Fabbro, F. (2017). Effects of mindfulness meditation on conscious and non-conscious components of the mind. *Applied Science, 7*(4), 349. https://doi.org/10.3390/app7040349.

Fulton, C. (2016). Mindfulness, self-compassion, and counselor characteristics and session variables. *Journal of Mental Health Counseling, 38*(4), 360–374. https://doi.org/10.17744/mehc.38.4.06.

Garland, E., Farb, N., Goldin, P., & Fredrickson, B. (2015a). Mindfulness broadens awareness and builds eudaimonic meaning: A process model of mindful positive emotion regulation. *Psychological Inquiry, 26*(4), 293–314. https://doi.org/10.1080/1047840X.2015.1064294.

Garland, E., Farb, N., Goldin, P., & Fredrickson, B. (2015b). The mindfulness-to-meaning theory: Extension, applications, and challenges at the attention-appraisal-emotion interface. *Psychological Inquiry, 26*(4), 377–387. https://doi.org/10.1080/1047840X.2015.1092493.

Good, D., Lyddy, C., Glomb, T., Bono, J., Brown, K., Duffy, M., Baer, R., Brewer, J., & Lazar, S. (2016). Contemplating mindfulness at work: An integrative review. *Journal of Management, 42*(1), 114–142. https://doi.org/10.1177/0149206315617003.

Gorman, T. & Green, C. S. (2016). Short-term mindfulness intervention reduces the negative attentional effects associated with heavy media multitasking. *Scientific Reports, 6*, 24542. https://doi.org/10.1038/srep24542.

Greiser, C., & Martini, J. (2018). *Unleashing the power of mindfulness in corporations.* The Boston Consulting Group. https://image-src.bcg.com/Images/BCG-Unleashing-the-Power-of-Mindfulness-in-Corporations-Apr-2018_tcm30-190679.pdf.

Hafenbrack, A., Cameron, L., Spreitzer, G., Zhang, C., Noval, L., & Shaffakat, S. (2020). Helping people by being in the present: Mindfulness increases prosocial behavior. *Organizational Behavior and Human Decision Processes, 159*, 21–38. https://doi.org/10.1016/j.obhdp.2019.08.005.

Harvey, J., Crowley, J., & Woszidlo, A. (2019). Mindfulness, conflict strategy use, and relational satisfaction: A dyadic investigation. *Mindfulness, 10*, 749–758. https://doi.org/10.1007/s12671-018-1040-y.

Hawkes, A., & Neal, C. (2019). Mindfulness beyond wellbeing: Emotion regulation and team-member exchange within the workplace. *Australian Journal of Psychology, 72*, 20–30. https://doi.org/10.1111/ajpy.12255.

Heckenberg, R., Eddy, P., Kent, S., & Wright, B. (2018). Do workplace-based mindfulness meditation programs improve physiological indices of stress? A systematic review and meta-analysis. *Journal of Psychosomatic Research, 114*, 62–71. https://doi.org/10.1016/j.jpsychores.2018.09.010.

Hwang, Y., Goldstein, H., Medvedev, O., Singh, N., Noh, J., & Hand, K. (2019). Mindfulness-based intervention for educators: Effects of a school-based cluster randomized controlled study. *Mindfulness, 10*, 1417–1436. https://doi.org/10.1007/s12671-019-01147-1.

Jennings, P. (2015). Early childhood teachers' well-being, mindfulness, and self-compassion in relation to classroom quality and attitudes towards challenging students. *Mindfulness, 6*, 732–743. https://doi.org/10.1007/s12671-014-0312-4.

Kahneman, D. (2011). *Thinking, fast and slow.* Farrar, Straus and Giroux.

Kaplan, J., Bergman, A., Christopher, M., Bowen, S., & Hunsinger, M. (2017). Role of resilience in mindfulness training for first responders. *Mindfulness, 8*, 1373–1380. https://doi.org/10.1007/s12671-017-0713-2.

Karelaia, N., & Reb, J. (2015). Improving decision making through mindfulness. In J. Reb & P. Atkins (Eds.), *Mindfulness in organizations: Foundations, research, and applications* (pp. 163–189). University of Cambridge Press. https://doi.org/10.1017/CBO9781107587793.009.

Kay, A., & Skarlicki, P. (2020). Cultivating a conflict-positive workplace: How mindfulness facilitates constructive conflict management. *Organizational Behavior and Human Decision Processes, 159*, 8–20. https://doi.org/10.1016/j.obhdp.2020.02.005.

Khaddouma, A., Gordon, K., & Strand, E. (2017). Mindful mates: A pilot study of the relational effects of mindfulness-based stress reduction on participants and their partners. *Family Process, 56*, 636–651. https://doi.org/10.1111/famp.12226.

Kiburz, K., Allen, T., & French, K. (2017). Work-family conflict and mindfulness: Investigating the effectiveness of a brief training intervention. *Journal of Organizational Behavior, 38*(7), 1016–1037. https://doi.org/10.1002/job.2181.

Kulka, J., De Gagne, J., Mullen, C., & Robeano, K. (2018). Mindfulness-based stress reduction for newly graduated registered nurses. *Creative Nursing, 24*, 243–250. https://doi.org/10.1891/1078-4535.24.4.243.

Levy, D., Wobbroack, J., Kaszniak, A., & Ostergren, M. (2021). The effects of mindfulness meditation training on multitasking in a high-stress information environment. In *Proceedings of Graphics Interfaces (May 28–30, 2012)* (pp. 45–52). Toronto: Canadian Information Processing Society.

Lhl, A., Strunk, K., & Fiedler, M. (2020). Interpretations of mindfulness practices in organizations: A multi-level analysis of interpretations on an organizational, group, and individual level. *Organization*. Advance online publication. https://doi.org/10.1177/1350508420968195.

Lomas, T., Medina, J., Ivtzan, I., Rupprecht, S., & Elroa-Orosa, F. (2019). Mindfulness-based interventions in the workplace: An inclusive systematic review and meta-analysis of their impact on upon wellbeing. *Journal of Positive Psychology, 14*(5), 625–640. https://doi.org/10.1080/17439760.2018.1519588.

Lyddy, C., Good, D., Bolino, M., Thompson, P., & Stephens, J. (2021). The costs of mindfulness at work: The moderating role of mindfulness in surface acting, self-control depletion, and performance outcomes. *Journal of Applied Psychology*. Advance online publication. https://doi.org/10.1037/apl0000863.

MAAPG (Mindfulness All-Party Parliamentary Group). (2015). *Mindful nation, UK. Mindfulness Initiative*. https://www.themindfulnessinitiative.org/mindful-nation-report.

Mayer, R., David, J., & Schoorman, F. D. (1995). An integrative model of organizational trust. *Academy of Management Review, 20*(3), 709–734. https://doi.org/10.5465/amr.1995.9508080335.

Mesmer-Magnus, J., Manapragada, A., Viswesvaran, C., & Allen, J. (2017). Trait mindfulness at work: A meta-analysis of the personal and professional correlates of trait mindfulness. *Human Performance, 30*(2–3), 79–98. https://doi.org/10.1080/08959285.2017.1307842.

Michel, A., Bosch, C., & Rexroth, M. (2014). Mindfulness as a cognitive-emotional segmentation strategy: An intervention promoting work-life balance. *Journal of Occupational and Organizational Psychology, 87*(4), 733–754. https://doi.org/10.1111/joop.12072.

Mielke, F. (2020) *Steps towards a mindful organisation: Developing mindfulness to manage unexpected events.* Dissertation, University of Hamburg. Springer-Gabler.

Mindfulness Initiative. (2016). *Building the case for mindfulness in the workplace.* https://www.themindfulnessinitiative.org/Handlers/Download.ashx?IDMF=46ef10fd-4d64-41f9-91a6-163d52cd304c.

Moreira, H., Gouveia, M., & Canavarro, M. (2018). Is mindful parenting associated with adolescents' well-being in early and middle/late adolescence? The mediating role of adolescents'attachment representations, self-compassion and mindfulness. *Journal of Youth and Adolescence, 47*, 1771–1788. https://doi.org/10.1007/s10964-018-0808-7.

Querstret, D., Morison, L., Dickinson, S., Cropley, M., & John, M. (2020). Mindfulness-based stress reduction and mindfulness-based cognitive therapy for psychological health and wellbeing in non-clinical samples: A systematic review and meta-analysis. *International Journal of Stress Management, 27*(4), 394–411. https://doi.org/10.1037/str0000165.

Reb, J., Allen, T., & Vogus, T. (2020). Mindfulness arrives at work: Deepening our understanding of mindfulness in organization. *Organizational Behavior and Human Decision Processes, 159*, 1–7. https://doi.org/10.1016/j.obhdp.2020.04.001.

Reb, J., Narayana, J., & Ho, Z. (2013). Mindfulness at work: Antecedents and consequence of employee awareness and absent-mindedness. *Mindfulness, 6*, 111–122. https://doi.org/10.1007/s12671-013-0236-4.

Remmers, C., Zimmermann, J., Buxton, A., Unger, H., Koole, S., Knaevelsrud, C., & Michalak, J. (2018). Emotionally aligned: Preliminary results on the effects of a mindfulness-based intervention for depression on congruence between implicit and explicit mood. *Clinical Psychology and Psychotherapy, 25*(6), 818–826. https://doi.org/10.1002/cpp.2317.

Rupprecht, S., Falke, P., Kohls, N., Tamjidi, C., Wittmann, M., & Kersemaekers, W. (2019). Mindful leader development: How leaders experience the effects of mindfulness training on leader capabilities. *Frontiers of Psychology, 10*, 1081. https://doi.org/10.3389/fpsyg.2019.01081.

Rupprecht, S., Koole, W., Chaskalson, M., Tamdjidi, C., & West, M. (2019). Running too far ahead? Towards a broader understanding of mindfulness in organisations. *Current Opinion in Psychology, 28*, 32–36. https://doi.org/10.1016/j.copsyc.2018.10.007.

Ryan, R., & Deci, E. (2000). Self-determination theory and the facilitation of intrinsic motivation, social development, and well-being. *American Psychology, 55*, 68–78. https://doi.org/10.1037//0003-066x.55.1.68.

Ryan, R., & Deci, E. (2017). *Self-determination theory: Basic psychological needs in motivation, development, and wellness*. The Guilford Press.

Senge, P. (1990). *The fifth discipline: The art and practice of the learning organization*. Doubleday.

Stedham, Y., & Skaar, T. (2019). Mindfulness, trust, and leader effectiveness: A conceptual framework. *Frontiers of Psychology, 10*, 1588. https://doi.org/10.3389/fpsyg.2019.01588.

Suleiman-Martos, N., Gomez-Urquiza, J., Aguayo-Estermera, R., Canadas-De La Fuente, A., De La Fuente-Solana, E., & Albendin-Garcia, L. (2020). The effect of mindfulness training on burnout syndrome in nursing: A systematic review and meta-analysis. *JAN, 76*(5), 1124–1140. https://doi.org/10.1111/jan.14318.

Sumantry, D., & Stewart, K. (2021). Meditation, mindfulness, and attention: A meta-analysis. *Mindfulness, 12*, 1332–1349. https://doi.org/10.1007/s12671-021-01593-w.

Surguladze, S., Chikovani, G., Revazishvili, T., Dzadzamia, N., Razmadze, T., Iashvili, N., & Bergen-Cico, D. (2020). Mindfulness as a mediating factor between empathy and burnout in people of caring professions. *International Journal of Psychology and Psychoanalysis, 4*(1), 23. https://doi.org/10.23937/2572-4037.1510023.

Taylor, C., Harrison, J., Haimovitz, K., Oberle, E., Thomson, K., Schonert-Reichl, K., & Roeser, R. (2016). Examining ways that a mindfulness-based intervention reduces stress in public school teachers: A mixed-methods study. *Mindfulness, 7*, 115–129. https://doi.org/10.1007/s12671-015-0425-4.

Thimmapuram, J., Grim, R., Bell, T., Benenson, R., Lavallee, M., Modi, M., Noll, D., & Salter, R. (2019). Factors influencing work-life balance in physicians and advance practice clinicians and the effect of heartfulness meditation conference on burnout. *Global Advanced in Health and Meditation, 8*. https://doi.org/10.1177/2164956118821056.

Thoroughgood, C., Sawyer, K., & Webster, J. (2020). Finding calm in the storm: A daily investigation of how trait mindfulness buffers against paranoid cognition and emotional exhaustion following perceived discrimination at work. *Organizational Behavior and Human Decision Processes, 159*, 49–63. https://doi.org/10.1016/j.obhdp.2019.02.004.

Vogus, T., Rothman, N. Sutcliffe, K., & Weick, K. (2014). The affective foundations of high-reliability organizing. *Journal of Organizational Behavior, 35*, 592–596. https://doi.org/10.1002/job.1922.

Vonderlin, R., Biermann, M., Bohus, M., & Lyssenko, L. (2020). Mindfulness-based programs in the workplace: A meta-analysis of randomized controlled trials. *Mindfulness, 11*, 1579–1598. https://doi.org/10.1007/s12671-020-01328-3.

Walsh, M., & Arnold, K. (2018). Mindfulness as a buffer of leaders' self-rated behavioral responses to emotional exhaustion: A dual process model of self-regulation. *Frontiers of Psychology, 9*, 2498. https://doi.org/10.3389/fpsyg.2018.02498.

Wamsler, C. (2018). The role of mindfulness in adapting to risk and climate change. *Sustainability Science, 13*, 1121–1135. https://doi.org/10.1007/s11625-017-0524-3.

Weick, K., & Sutcliffe, K. (2001/2007). *Managing the unexpected: Resilient performance in an age of uncertainty*. Jossey-Bass.

Weick, K., Sutcliffe, K., & Obstfeld, D., (1999). Organizing for high reliability: Processes of collective mindfulness. In B. Staw & L. L. Cummings (Eds.), *Research in organizational behavior* (Vol. 21, pp. 81–123). JAI Press, Inc.

Yu, L., & Zellmer-Bruhn, M. (2018). Introducing team mindfulness and considering its safeguard role against conflict transformation and social undermining. *Academy of Management Journal, 61*(1), 324–347. https://doi.org/10.5465/amj.2016.0094.

# SECTION III

# Theories

## Why Mindfulness Works: Theories Informing MBTL

This section presents key theories informing research and practice in the field of secular-scientific mindfulness and MBTL. For scientific research, theories help organize and explain data. So, as data about mindfulness increases, it is critical to develop and evaluate theories to keep pace with new and emerging evidence. In MBTL practice, theories and theory-making help to guide how scientific research is applied and interpreted in practice. In this respect, MBTL is a form of *praxis*, that is, an evolving practice that is informed and shaped by emerging theories and theory-making.

In Chapter 9 we consider the biological theories of embodied cognition that have shifted our view of the nature of consciousness and cognition over the last half century. Theories like autopoiesis, enactivism, and the biology of cognition connect complex ecological and biological systems, including neurological and physiological, to the emergence of mind as a second-order biological system. This changing view of the nature of cognition has deeply impacted the study and practice of mindfulness. We consider as well key theories that grew out of this biological embodiment perspective that continue to inform MBTL praxis, notably self-determination theory (SDT); S-ART; and mindfulness-to-meaning theory (MMT); as well as the operationalization of mindfulness in MAAS. In Chapter 10, we focus on specific theories of cognition concerning cognitive bias, dual processing, and the operationalization of mindfulness in the FFMQ. Finally, in Chapter 11, we introduce three key Buddhist theories that continue to impact secular-scientific mindfulness and MBTL: The four foundations of mindfulness; the seven factors of awakening; and the three marks of existence (aka three characteristics).

DOI: 10.4324/9781003182467-12

# CHAPTER 9

# BIOLOGICAL THEORIES OF EMBODIED COGNITION AND MINDFULNESS

MBTL is not merely a practice or technique of teaching and learning but a significant revisioning of the nature of what it means to teach and to learn. Yet these practices are the visible tip of an iceberg rising above the ocean surface, supported by significant changes under the surface in our collective theories of mind, cognition, and human learning. The catalyst may well be the study of the brain and its relationship to learning and experience. As both mindfulness and learning became mapped onto, and understood within, human neurological systems, there arose a natural interest in mindfulness as a teaching and learning process. Yet, it was not only brain science that accounted for this radical shift, but the understanding of the embodied nature of the mind and experience, not only in the brain, but also in the physiological body and the environmental niche in which we navigate experience and living.

## BIOLOGICAL THEORIES OF COGNITION

In the late 20th century, systems theories of cognition prepared the ground for mindfulness to become a secular-scientific enterprise. Systems theories proposed nested relations between environments, human biology, cognition, culture, and social organizations. In the process, the mind became reinterpreted from being an abstract state of reason to an emergent property of living systems. In this reconceptualized view of cognition, the mind became understood as a domain of phenomenal experiences that functioned autonomously while structurally interconnected to underlying biological systems, without being reducible to them. In the face of this biological relational view of cognition, the question of biological autonomy and what constituted and conserved autonomy in living systems became critical.

Biological systems theories redefined identity from a unitary, reified, and taken-for-granted "self" to something co-constructed out of complex, distributed conditions and interactions, manifesting in human experience as perceptual and sensorimotor habits, socialized motivations, the sense of agency, and memory- and language-mediated historical narratives. In so doing, systems theories radically altered the meaning of "the self," "freedom," and, paradoxically, "meaning" itself within a biological perspective. Not only did this lead to questions of how to work with systemic structural forces to bring about change, but also how to cultivate or train the embodied mind directly as a self-regulating strategy to enhance wellbeing. What does it mean, for example, for a system to know itself, as human beings are able to do? Such an observer or observing mind might reasonably have a significant role to play within the self-regulatory systems of life or why would a phenomenological experiential order ever have arisen in the first place? Not only does this ability to know ourselves imply meta-cognitive observational powers, but also powers of meaning-making that can shape and reshape motivation, experience, and, ultimately, wellbeing.

### Constructivism

Constructivism was integral to the shift to a systems-oriented view of the human mind and experience, gaining sway as a theory of learning and cognition through the 20th century

DOI: 10.4324/9781003182467-13

as it supplanted objectivist views of cognition. In constructivism, experience was no longer considered to be a direct representation of the world; instead, experience was considered an emergent property of internal dynamics between cognitive structures and perception, including sensorimotor interactions and the interpretive filters we used to process them. First articulated in the structuralist cognitive psychology of Jean Piaget, constructivist theories were supported empirically by biological laboratory findings, such as Maturana's (1958) "What the Frog's Eye Tells the Frog's Brain" (Lettvin et al., 1959/1968). This study demonstrated that the frog's senses were generating information already highly abstracted from environmental signals: "That the eye speaks to the brain in a language already highly organized and interpreted, instead of transmitting some more or less accurate copy of the distribution of light on the receptors" (p. 1950). This finding suggested more operational closure to cognition than the earlier representational views had theorized.

## Embodied Cognition

Itself constructivist, the theory of embodied cognition reinterpreted the nature of the mind in the 20th century. According to this view, as an emergent yet non-reducible phenomenon arising from complex brain-body networks, the mind generated phenomenological experiences from underlying physiological processes. Strongly associated with cognitive science and cognitive psychology, embodied cognition came to view the human mind as an integrated manifestation of complex conscious, unconscious, and non-conscious processes that emerged out of evolutionary continua that we share with other species. Unlike Freudian psychoanalytic theory, the embodied mind theory did not define the mind as a mere symbolic order or abstract mediator of experience but rather as an emergent expression of the non-conscious physiologies that we don't directly experience as mental events.

In the process, what was once referred to pejoratively as a primordial "reptilian brain" became redeemed as markedly human and something to recover within experiential identity as much as love and reason were. These varied manifestations of embodied mind arising from autonomic, limbic, and higher cortical functioning that we shared with other living beings became both valued and required to integrate functionally as part of identity and wellbeing. Outcomes associated with mindfulness, for example, became attributed to these integrative processes, such as attention to experiential self-referencing based on viscero-somatic sensory momentary experience; or emotional regulation and self-care; or more cognitive dimensions of experience such as executive functioning, cognitive bias, and meaning-making. By parsing these embodied experiences out in mindfulness training, they become more accessible to awareness and recognizable as components of mind and identity.

The theory of embodied cognition informed embodied learning theory, whereby optimal learning shifted from abstract reasoning to the *realization* of embodied ways of knowing. Such embodied realization goes well beyond Whitehead's (1929) early 20th-century critique of education's focus on *inert* rather than *applied* knowledge as "the art of the utilisation of knowledge" (p. 4). As a theory of learning, *embodiment* considered how knowledge or learning alters the ability of the self to regulate or govern the body and, reciprocally, how the body alters the self, including what it means both to know and to *know thyself*. These reinterpretations of the nature of mind and body, of their inter-relationship, and of their role in wellbeing impacted how mindfulness became valued and used. Indeed, *wellbeing*, once represented and viewed as the progeny of genes, grace, God, karma, or enlightenment, became something amenable to our direct influence via mindfulness training, practices, and intention.

The enactivist theory of embodied cognition has roots in Maturana and Varela (1972) and Varela et al.'s (1974) early work on *autopoiesis* (lit. *self-creation*), a biological theory of cognition used to explain how living systems reproduce and conserve organization over time through self-regulation. Autopoiesis was a precursor to both family systems theory and enactivism and is closely aligned with cybernetics, which began as the study of communication and control in animals and machines (Weiner, 1948). In particular, autopoiesis is associated with second-order or the new cybernetics introduced by anthropologist Margaret Mead (1968) and physicist-philosopher Heinz von Foerster (1995). Second-order cybernetics investigated cognition as a recursive domain arising from biological (or machine) systems that produce observers looking back on themselves. Meanwhile, first-order cybernetics focused on the observed, and second-order cybernetics focused on the observer. Third-order cybernetics, in turn, focused on conditions in which multiple subjects look back on their own control and communication systems, both as observers and the observed, such as, social systems.

Enactivist theory builds on these earlier embodied models of mind to explain cognition as that which arises from dynamic sensorimotor interactions between an organism and its environment. As a constructivist theory, enactivism rejected cognitive realism and instead viewed cognition as emergent patterns arising from embodied sensorimotor processes based on structurally coupled organisms and their niches (DeJesus, 2014). "Enactivism instead emphasizes *emergent* cognitive structures that *self-organise* as a result of interactions between organism and environment" (Ward et al., 2017, italics original). The theory harkens back to Bateson's (1972/2000) *ecology of mind* that first introduced the idea that the individual human organism, human society, and ambient ecosystems were entangled in underlying biological systems that became *coupled* with human consciousness.

As key formulators of enactivist theory, Varela et al. (1991/2016) argued in *The Embodied Mind* that the enactivist view of cognition accepted that significant "sub-personal" processes of the mind or cognition lay outside conscious awareness; yet, unlike Freud's conception of the unconscious, cognitive science believed that these processes could never become conscious (p. 49). Yet, enactivism rejected more extreme views dismissing altogether the self and conscious experience as irrelevant to the study of cognition; instead, enactivism recognized the value of embodied phenomenological experience – the "personal level of consciousness" associated with the self – and its critical role in understanding the dynamics of the mind. "At this point, the tension between science and experience should be obvious and tangible. If cognition can proceed without the self, then why do we nonetheless have the experience of self? We cannot simply discuss this experience without explanation" (p. 51). As one of the authors, Thompson, later argued in the 2016 revised text, "Science departs from, and in the end must answer to, embodied experience and does not provide understanding on its own" (p. xxviii).

Mindfulness and enactivist theory co-emerged to form a mutually-reinforcing, symbiotic praxis. Rosch, another co-author of that original text, commented in her prefatory remarks to the 2016 edition that mindfulness was a form of first-person inquiry into the process of enactivist emergence and connectivism (Varela et al., 2016): "What Buddhist practices have to contribute…is that there is a different mode of knowing altogether in which the mind is neither absorbed nor separated but simply present and available" (p.

xl). In enactivism, cognition is an emergent global state irreducible to its underlying physiological bases, much like water emerging from $H_2O$ molecules. The underlying biological component systems giving rise to cognition function and coordinate using rule-based relations to generate observable effects on the functioning of the whole (i.e., organism). Through mindful enquiry into phenomena, it becomes possible to parse experience so as to observe coherent moments of emergence into consciousness. In this way, the "neurological approach" of enactivism was seen to be "compatible with the direct observations based on mindfulness/awareness meditation, thus making all more remarkable the fact that this tradition has continued to verify the parsing of experience into coherent moments of emergence" (p. 98).

## Self-Regulation

Self-regulatory processes are at the heart of all biological and embodied theories of cognition. Within biological systems, self-regulation is the key feedback process by which living systems maintain operational cohesion, integrity, and *autonomy* in the absence of extrinsic controls, over time and against entropy. Without such self-regulation, according to the second law of thermodynamics, a system would move towards increased disorder and chaos. An example of a self-regulated *involuntary* biological system is thermal homeostasis, for example, whereby our bodily temperature is maintained in a stable range over time despite varying external conditions. Other systems involve *voluntary* self-regulatory processes, such as emotion regulation, or partially *voluntary* processes like breathing.

### *Feedback*

Self-regulation refers broadly to feedback mechanisms in living systems that function to conserve life and to sustain wellbeing and adaptation within constantly changing environments and conditions. Biologically, self-regulation transpires through sensorimotor dynamics arising from the structural coupling between elements of the environment and the sensory systems of an organism. Some self-regulation is autonomic and non-conscious, such as thermal homeostasis or the pupils' response to changes in light intensity, while others involve some voluntary controls and awareness, as in the case of hunger and eating or moderating behaviours in response to emotion. Leduc-Cummings et al. (2017) define self-regulation as a psychological rather than biological process, focusing on goal attainment strategies: "Self-regulation consists of all manner of goal setting and goal pursuit, which can be accomplished through both effortful control of behavior and effortless, automatic, or habitual forms of goal-directed behavior" (p. 1).

Self-regulation is also a vital process for navigating groups or social environments, thereby impacting social, not just biological, adaptation and its critical role in wellbeing (Heatherton, 2011). Attention, emotions, thought, and behaviour are all moderated by self-regulatory processes, which appear to involve pre-frontal cortex neurological processes. Heatherton identifies four steps in self-regulation: a) awareness of states of mind, reactivity, and behaviour; b) awareness of the effects of our reactions and actions; c) detecting threats to assess and moderate them; and d) resolving conflicts between self-awareness and social expectations. Implicitly or explicitly, mindfulness impacts each of these components of self-regulation, thereby functioning to avoid social exclusion and to strengthen agency, autonomy, and wellbeing within social environments.

### *Self-Control*

As Textbox 9.1 suggests, mindfulness cultivates self-regulation through awareness rather than through control. The role of self-control in self-regulation is hotly debated. Gillebaart (2018) operationally defined self-control as all strategies used to realize pre-established goals through self-regulatory processes. Yet, this definition draws attention to one of the key problems with equating self-regulation with control: Pre-established conscious goals are not necessarily consistent with long-term biological or even felt wellbeing. Instead, Gillebaart's definition appears to equate self-regulation with willpower, which is inconsistent with new and emerging research.

## TEXTBOX 9.1 EXEMPLAR OR CASE:

### From Control to Self-Regulation in Mindfulness of Breathing

**Purpose:** This skills-focused practice includes a few purposes or potential benefits:

- In mindfulness of breathing, the breath is not controlled but observed as it naturally arises and changes. The purpose of this practice is to recognize and modulate control to foster the self-regulation of breathing using non-judgemental awareness.
- A second purpose is to assist those with overcontrol (e.g., OCD or eating disorders) or under-control (e.g., substance use disorders) disorders to become more mindful of control impulses in the mind.
- A third purpose is to support participants in *decentering* – that is, separating or distancing the self from experience.
- A fourth purpose is to train attention to an object of focus – in this case, the breath – to disrupt rumination and voluntarily direct attention with awareness.

**Context:** The breath is used because it is unique in offering degrees of volitional control and non-volitional functioning of a primary physiological function.

**Practice:** The following steps can help to guide this short skills-based practice.

1. Begin a mindfulness of breathing practice as usual, inviting attention to one location in the body to watch breathing (e.g., tip of the nostrils, back of the throat, chest, or lower abdomen.)
2. Intentionally take a deep breath in and then out, controlling your breath to encourage deeper intakes and exhalations. As you do so, notice the will behind this ability to control breath. Notice that "you" are appearing in this moment as the willpower or agent controlling the breath.
3. When you feel able, use the will to stop breathing momentarily. Notice how you have the capacity to prevent an automatic breath, but also how the body prevents you from stopping to breathe altogether.
4. When you feel comfortable, stop controlling the breath. Neither initiate the in-breath nor the exhalation. "You" are now standing back and witnessing this experience of breathing rather willing it or even influencing it. Trust that the body will breathe as it does and just be there, noticing. Allowing the breath to happen without making it do so.

**Inquiry:** These are possible queries for post-practice inquiry.

1. What did you notice in that practice? What came up?
2. What were the experiences of control and the giving up of control? How did they compare?
3. Why might we do this practice, say, at the beginning of a mindfulness of breathing sit?

Scholarly efforts to distinguish effortless self-regulation from effortful control from has brought into relief the question of whether or not self-regulation even involves the same neurological or cognitive processes as self-control. Given self-control tends to involve the exercise of will, it is associated with the conscious suppression and corresponding neural inhibition of impulses and temptations rather than the strengthening of the motivation side of self-regulation. In this way, Milyavskaya et al. (2015) emphasize the role of motivation rather than control in fulfilling a goal, demonstrating how what they call *want-to* motivation effortlessly reduces impulsive attraction to goal-disruptive temptations. They conclude that "*want-to* motivation improves self-regulation by reducing temptation rather than by increasing self-control" (p. 677). Later, Werner and Milyavskaya (2019) offered evidence of how effortless self-regulation is more adaptive for long-term goal attainment than the controlling and suppressive willpower and inhibition of effortful self-control.

Researchers investigated how mindfulness functions in top-down controlled self-regulation as compared to bottom-up automatic self-regulation (Chiesa et al., 2013; Vago & Silbersweig, 2012). Controlled self-regulation involved conscious cognitive or behavioural effort and the engagement of control/inhibitory systems involving increased prefrontal cortex (PFC) connectivity with the anterior cingulate cortex (ACC) and amygdala of the limbic system. In contrast, automatic bottom-up processes involved non-conscious effortless self-regulation in which physiological perturbations were modulated automatically in the face of stress and emotional reactivity, including strengthening and shifting the capacity to respond differently by reducing what Milyavskaya et al. (2015) call temptations. Werner and Milyavskaya (2019) argued that such automatic self-regulation improves through focusing on the intrinsic motivation for wellbeing, thereby using awareness to shift underlying autonomic tendencies, habits, and temptations that obstruct that general state-as-goal.

To conclude, biological systems approaches to embodied cognition drew attention to the complexity and emergence of the mind from distal and proximal components of the body and the environment that converge in our ordinary experience of the world. By attempting to ground the mind in the body, through the construct of the embodied mind, these theories can seem, paradoxically, remote and abstract in their emphasis on the non-conscious and semi-conscious parsed factors and elements that give rise to experience. The dominance of cognitive science in formulating these theories reinforced their abstract tone. As mindfulness was brought under their theoretical umbrella, many clinicians felt the emphasis on physiological and phenomenological complexity involving attentional and emotional self-regulation didn't adequately explain how mindfulness came to foster global effects on wellbeing. So, new theories emerged to explain the impact of mindfulness on wellbeing that focused on intrinsic motivation, autonomy, and meaning. It is to these theories that we now turn.

## SELF-DETERMINATION THEORY (SDT)

One such theory was Self-Determination Theory (SDT). Building on the biology of cognition and the primacy of organismic integration, Ryan and Deci (2017) conceived SDT to account for the relations between self-regulation and autonomy in the domain of human psychology and development. According to SDT, autonomy, competency and relationships constitute three natural motivations associated with wellbeing and flourishing. In this respect, SDT connects biological and psychological theories of motivation, self-regulation, and autonomy within a consistent developmental theory of human flourishing and wellbeing. Furthermore, they investigated mindfulness as a key practice that fosters and cultivates self-determination.

### Autonomy, the Self, and Authenticity

In SDT, Ryan and Deci (2017) present autonomy as the self-governance of an individual: "To the extent that action is regulated through the integrated (and integrating) self, it is said to be *autonomous*" (p. 52, italics original). Mapping it origins through philosophy and psychology, SDT proposed a set of primary requirements for autonomous self-regulation: first, that the self-as-process is a not an object or thing but "a set of integrative processes deeply rooted in nature," and, second, that autonomous functioning requires the ability to engage in self-endorsed (i.e., authentic) rather than alienating activities (i.e., inauthentic.) Autonomy arises from authenticity, as activities align with interests and integrated values such that one is wholeheartedly behind them, regardless of whether they originated internally or externally. Inauthenticity is associated with externally controlled or introjected values and actions that are not integrated or endorsed by the self. In this sense, autonomous functioning arises through internalizing the perceived locus of control (PLOC) guiding our actions as we develop. As they concluded, autonomy is contingent on specific forms of social support and environments:

> This reflects our position that autonomy, which we view as a holistic expression of "nature in context," will not result either from coercive forms of socialization or from transmitted practices or values that are inherently in conflict with basic psychological needs. Furthermore, when humans are autonomous, they are in touch with their true needs and are able to act in accord with them.
>
> *(Ryan et al., 1997, p. 716)*

Ryan and Deci (2017) stress that autonomy is not independence or individualism or separateness. SDT treats motivation complexly as derived from both external and internal sources, the issue being not so much the origins of a goal as whether or not it is aligned with self-endorsed values and integrated by the self as part of autonomous functioning. Also, autonomy is distinct from self-control, which implies introjected, extrinsically controlled motives or demands that inhibit and suppress rather than motivate. Finally, autonomy is not nonconscious action even if initiated or caused by nonconscious sources. "Instead, the issue of people's autonomy lies in the regulatory process through which the behaviors we engage in, even if originally non-consciously prompted, are governed" (p. 75).

## Mindfulness in Self-Regulation and Intrinsic Motivation

Ryan and Deci (2017) describe self-determination as self-governing behaviour, whereby "individual organisms are endowed with, and energized by, propensities to expand and elaborate themselves in the direction of organized complexity and integrated functioning" (p. 5). Self-regulation is the practice of self-determination, insofar as it navigates change and growth through autonomous agency to conserve wellbeing. "Clearly, it is in our 'natures'…to attain greater or lesser degrees of healthy psychological, social, and behavioral functioning and more or less to realize our human capacities and talents" (p. 3–4). Autonomy, competence, and relationships, therefore, are presented as the three intrinsic motives navigating self-determination in the direction of wellbeing, the most important being autonomy. Furthermore, SDT represents people as developing into and through adulthood on a spectrum of motivation that aligns with increasing levels of wellbeing, moving from amotivation through external and introjected motivation to identified and intrinsic motivation (Donald et al., 2020).

There is evidence supporting these links between mindfulness and self-regulation and intrinsic motivation. In their meta-analysis, Donald et al. (2020) found mindfulness predicted more autonomous motivation (i.e., intrinsic and integrated) and less controlled motivation (i.e., extrinsic or introjected) and amotivation. Ryan and Deci (2017) attribute this consistent finding of the positive effect of mindfulness on autonomous self-regulation to its self-regulatory processes as *a well-functioning 'self-compatibility' checker* that cultivates the "capacity for integrative awareness of one's sensibilities, values, and the consequence of possible actions" (p. 76). In their review of research on mindfulness, motivation, and SDT, Ryan et al. (2021) conclude that it is not that mindfulness directly impacts motivation or fosters autonomy so much as that it enables more autonomous functioning through its impact on self-regulation. Furthermore, they conclude that mindfulness has direct effects on wellbeing that are not merely through autonomous functioning, and some key theories to explain these direct effects are now considered.

# THEORIES OF MINDFULNESS AS SELF-AWARENESS

Self-awareness is identified as critical to all embodied cognitive theories of mindfulness, but is particularly salient in the S-ART theory of mindfulness and in the Mindful Attention Awareness Scale (MAAS), which embeds a theory of mindfulness-as-awareness within its operationalized scale.

## Self-Awareness in the S-ART Framework

Vago and Silbersweig (2012) proposed the S-ART theory of mindful self-processing as an "integrative theoretical framework and neurobiological model" involving three key interrelated self-processing activities: *Self-awareness*; *self-regulation*; and *self-transcendence*. The "self" in S-ART refers to three related but distinct neural systems: a) a non-conscious *enactive experiential self* (EES) arising from sensorimotor processing and structural coupling between the organism and the environment; b) a borderline conscious or unconscious *experiential phenomenological self* (EPS) with access to the EES so as to modulate, control, and/or amplify its primary experience; and c) a more explicit, evaluative *narrative self* (NS) in which experience is reconstructed within an autobiographical narrative, including filtering experiences through identifications with "me" and potentially slowing down experiential processing through rumination. In mindfulness, the EES and EPS systems appear to become strengthened and more integrated while the NS system becomes decoupled from the EPS and less activated (Farb et al., 2007). According to Vago and Silbersweig (2012), mindfulness reduces suffering by reducing such biased self-processing.

The question remains just how these three S-ART mindfulness-associated functions of awareness, regulation, and transcendence contribute to wellbeing. The theory proposes that self-awareness, self-regulation, and self-transcendence coinhere so as to correct processes that distort or bias perceptions, cognition, and emotions. Vago and Silbersweig (2012) theorized that mindfulness promoted wellbeing through its impact on the following six key cognitive processes involved in correcting cognitive biases: Intention and motivation; attention regulation; emotion regulation; extinction and reconsolidation; prosociality; and non-attachment and decentering.

### Mindful Attention Awareness Scale (MAAS)

Brown and Ryan (2003) operationalized mindfulness as awareness in the Mindful Attention Awareness Scale (MAAS). While validating the scale, they found that mindfulness positively correlated with psychological wellbeing; was associated with happiness, attentional sensitivity to present-moment sensory inputs, and self-regulation; and was negatively correlated with challenging states like neuroticism, anxiety, angry hostility, and depression. They identified *self-awareness* as the critical mechanism explaining the impact of mindfulness on self-regulation and wellbeing, evidenced by its impact on increasing the concordance between implicit (unconscious) and explicit (conscious) emotions. The MAAS provided an indicator for dispositional or trait mindfulness using 15 items to measure mindfulness as the ability to hold attention and awareness of the present moment.

The scale evaluates the frequency of the described experience, ranging from "almost always" to "almost never." Three examples of the 15 questions include the following (Brown & Ryan, n.d.):

- I could be experiencing some emotion and not be conscious of it until somewhat later.
- It seems I am 'running on automatic,' without much awareness of what I'm doing.
- I find myself preoccupied with the future or past.
- I snack without being aware that I'm eating.

These questions reflect how mindful awareness is being operationalized according to the MAAS model. As a self-report inventory, the questions reflect conditions that a person reports noticing in their own experience. Some questions suggest a lack of recognition of certain experiences, like an emotion. Many deal with the sense of being on automatic pilot, reflecting such mechanical analogies. Others deal with being separated from the present, and still others with being unaware of specific activities like eating.

## MINDFULNESS-TO-MEANING THEORY (MMT)

Ford and Shook (2019) reviewed mindfulness research to determine key underlying mechanisms that might explain the robust positive effect of mindfulness on improved mood and reduced distress and, accordingly, on wellbeing. They concluded that two independent mechanisms explained most of the positive effects of mindfulness on wellbeing: a) the reduction of perceived stress; and b) the reduction in cognitive biases. One key theory that emerged to explain this ability of mindfulness to reduce both perceived stress *and* negative cognitive biases was the Mindfulness-to-Meaning Theory (MMT) (Garland et al., 2015a).

## Eudaimonic Meaning

Garland et al. (2015a) proposed MMT as a scientific theory to explain the interface between attention, reappraisal, and emotion evident in empirical studies of mindfulness. The theory evolved out of an earlier, second-order cybernetic model of stress, mindfulness, and coping based on systems theory, cybernetics, and constructivism (Garland et al., 2015b). This earlier theory attempted to explain how mindfulness as present-centred attention enhanced stress-coping through reappraisal, that is, by fluidly adapting and reconstructing a practitioner's view of the self and world. MMT went beyond these earlier stress-coping theories to connect mindfulness to *eudaemonic meaning* through the dual mechanisms of *reappraisal* and *savouring*. "Eudaemonia" refers to the classical Aristotelian notion of wellbeing as a state of human flourishing, while "eudaemonic" refers to forms of meaning that enhance human flourishing or wellbeing. In MMT, reappraisal and savouring were posited as distal, downstream effects of mindfulness practices that gave rise to the positive emotions associated with eudaemonic wellbeing and meaning.

According to Garland et al. (2015a), MMT seeks to address "how mindfulness training fosters eudaemonic responses to stress that engender a sense of meaningfulness in life" (p. 295). MMT critics had argued that because mindfulness involves explicit training in non-judgmental and non-conceptual awareness, it precludes the conceptual- or language-mediated processes of cognitive reappraisal and meaning-making. Garland et al. (2015b) responded to this critique by clarifying that the theory did not equate mindfulness with reappraisal and savouring so much as to establish their connection, that is, to identify mindfulness as an upstream catalyst resulting in these downstream effects within a spiral or increasing-effects-over-time relationship. As Garland et al. (2015a) point out, although MMT is a secular-scientific theory, it is consistent with traditional mindfulness theories that describe mindfulness as effecting non-conceptual states of calm-abiding and mental stabilization (*samatha*) that can lead to special insight (*vipassana*) through conceptual inquiry. Indeed, the MMT notion that mindfulness is merely an initial catalyst in a broader chain of effects culminating in wellbeing resembles the Buddhist theory of mindfulness outlined in the seven factors of awakening (see Chapter 11) and the theory of interdependent origination.

## The MMT Developmental Sequence

Practising mindfulness as attentional modulation, a practitioner learns to redirect attention, usually towards sensations and direct perception and away from conceptual rumination. Garland and Frederickson (2019) describe the aftermath of this attentional training as de-automatization, which is an explicit objective in mindfulness training programmes like MBSR that target awareness of habitual "auto-pilot" reactive behavioural cycles. This attention control and de-automatization lead to decentering, that is, distancing the self from fusion and overidentification with experiences arising from excessive rumination and the

**Table 9.1** MMT's Model of Mindfulness and Its Downstream Effects

| *Component Process* | *Characteristics* |
|---|---|
| **attentional control** | redirecting attention with intention |
| **de-automatization** | shifting from habitual reactivity to intentional awareness |
| **decentering** | reducing fusion and identification within experience |
| **broadened awareness** | expanding attention and opening awareness to monitor and accept experience |
| **reappraisal** | inviting new perspectives that view experiences more positively or constructively |
| **positive affect or mood** | savouring life and deriving meaning through more positive affect |
| **savouring and meaning** | continuing to deepen the capacity for savouring and meaning |

storying of experience. Over time, decentering expands attention to include more subtle aspects of experience and, ultimately, opens awareness until it is possible to monitor and accept experience without attentional control. This state of broadened awareness invites cognitive reappraisal, which may extinguish biased, negative, or destructive interpretations and replace them with more adaptive perspectives that generate and sustain more positive affect or moods, such as joy or rapture. Part of this culminating process may involve the early recognition of negative cognitions or difficult emotional states, providing the opportunity for skilful attention and action as required. Ultimately, as outlined in Table 9.1, these stages in mindfulness processing culminate in enhanced meaning and savouring, which MMT uses to explain how mindfulness improves wellbeing.

Textbox 9.2 offers an exemplar from a post-practice inquiry session to illustrate an example of the MMT cycle of attention, de-automatization, decentering, broadening awareness, and reappraisal that occurs naturally in the context of mindfulness training.

## TEXTBOX 9.2 CASE/EXEMPLAR:

### Broadening Awareness through Mindful Inquiry

**Participant***:* For me, I always feel uncomfortable when we return to breathing. I panic and struggle to hold my attention and then eventually abandon it and just sit there with my attention on nothing.

**Facilitator***:* So did that happen in *this* practice? What did you notice just now?

**Participant***:* It always happens the same way. I am fine until you say to return from open awareness to the breath in the body. I feel this alarm as attention shifts to the breath, and an impulse to control it.

**Facilitator***:* …Please use the past tense. Specifically, what just happened…?

**Participant***:* I heard you say to shift to breathing, and when I did, I felt anxious.

**Facilitator***:* How did you know?

**Participant***:* I wanted to get away and felt that impulse to control the breath.

**Facilitator***:* Could you say more about that? Where was your attention when you first noticed the impulse to control it?

**Participant***:* I began inhaling, noticing inhaling, and then a strong need to control it.

**Facilitator***:* And then what happened? What about the exhalation?

**Participant**: Now that you mention it, I never noticed the exhalation. I was just focused on inhaling.

**Facilitator**: So, the attention shifted to inhaling where you noticed an impulse to control the breath, and then as it became an exhalation, the attention drifted or was interrupted or pulled away…

**Participant**: (With surprise)…Ya, that's right! Maybe I never exhaled!

**Facilitator**: So, inhaling – with its tension and effort – you noticed that, but not the release and relaxation experience of the outbreath? Why might it help to notice the outbreath as well?

**Participant**: Oh ya. That's true. It's like missing half the cycle; just noticing rising not falling tension. Not noticing if I'm even exhaling at all or merely holding my breath.

**Facilitator**: Lovely. Nice tracking with important insight. Thanks.

## Reappraisal

Garland et al. (2015a) describe mindfulness-based reappraisal in stress and emotion regulation as a two-prong process: first, the practitioner suspends the initial cognitive appraisal of the stressor, and, then, through decentering, they let go of its affective concomitants, eventually leading to the extinction of habitual conditioned responses. This results in a broadened scope of attention in which more positive perspectives and reevaluations of the stressor can be contemplated. Alternatively, such broadened attention can clarify negative aspects of a stressor so as to invite action for well-being. In this way, broadened attention ultimately leads to a positive reappraisal of the circumstance, if not the stressor, and thence leads to increased meaning. Garland and Frederickson (2019) described the ensuing state as "savouring that kindles momentary states of meta-awareness infused with positive affect, such as the self-transcendent positive emotions of awe, compassion, elevation, and love" (p. 186). Significantly, Tedeschi and Blevins (2015) linked this mindfulness-based reappraisal to their model of post-traumatic *growth*, in which even decidedly negative events and stressors are reappraised positively.

## Self-Transcendence

Garland and Frederickson (2019) described mindfulness-based reappraisal as unfolding on a gradient characterized by repeated and increasing self-transcendence over time, an expanding spiral with successive iterations of decentering, broadening, reappraisal, and savouring. With each iteration, moments of meta-awareness and positive emotions recur until a more stabilized state or condition of non-dual insight is attained. At the same time, reappraisal and the associated insight may evolve on a gradient from explicit reappraisals in programmes like MBCT aimed at decentering, such as "thoughts are not facts; they are transitory mental experiences" to positive reappraisal during extended practice, such as "the other side of suffering is growth" to more ontological reappraisal associated with deeply transformative realizations such the "self is not fixed and permanent as it can appear to be but rather empty and interdependent." The authors suggest that self-transcendence through deep states of mindfulness can produce a sense of ultimate meaningfulness. Testing the theory empirically, they found that robust increases in MMT mechanisms of positive emotions, savouring, meaning, and self-transcendent, non-dual states significantly reduce pain and the risk of opioid misuse, for example.

## Meaning and Savouring

In MMT, wellbeing is operationalized as *meaning* and *savouring*. The authors justify this by stating "that meaning-making lies at the heart of human cognition...[as] a fundamental feature of all living systems" (Garland et al., 2015b, p. 384). While perceptual biases and ambiguity challenge meaning-making processes, mindfulness enables more effective meaning-making in the face of ambiguity by extending awareness to elements of experience not previously recognized, thereby reducing avoidance and enhancing the capacity to take multiple perspectives. *Savouring* refers to a deepening state of positive affect associated with enhanced attention and self-transcendence, a kind of non-dual experience in which the object becomes more salient and the subject less so. In the process, the sensory-perceptual field becomes imbued with affective meaning. In this way, savouring is more than hedonistic pleasure; it is a state in which pleasure is experienced as eudaemonic wellbeing and flourishing, a non-dual awareness replete with positive affect and meaning.

## Empirical Support for MMT

MMT has a recent but growing body of empirical evidence to substantiate its claims about mindfulness, including the aforementioned study on chronic pain and opioid addiction (Garland & Frederickson, 2019). In a meta-analysis of the effect of mindfulness on meaning in life, Chu and Mak (2020) found evidence that mindfulness had a moderate effect on meaning in both correlation and RCT studies. They also found that this effect was mediated by decentering, authentic self-awareness, and attention to positive experience. Garland et al. (2017b) tested the theory using longitudinal data (N=107) to compare cognitive-behavioural therapy (CBT) and mindfulness-based stress reduction (MBSR) in the treatment of people with social anxiety disorder. They found that initial improvements in attention-control post-training (baseline) predicted increased decentering after three months, which in turn predicted increased broadened awareness by six months. Increases in broadened awareness predicted increases in the use of reappraisal by nine months, which culminated after 12 months' post-treatment in greater positive affect. Furthermore, MBSR resulted in significantly greater increases in both decentering and broadened awareness than CBT. Similarly, in a focused study of the relationship between mindfulness and positive reappraisal, Garland et al. (2017c) found that positive reappraisal increased significantly and robustly over the course of an eight-week mindfulness training in a process they liken to an upward spiral.

In an early study, Jacobs et al. (2011) found evident backing some of MMT's main premises. A group of 30 meditators were followed during an intensive three-month retreat and compared to a group of 30 meditators in a waitlist control condition. In addition to finding that intensive meditational practice differentially increased telomerase activity, a genetic biomarker associated with longevity, they found that increased telomerase activity was mediated by reduced neuroticism, increased perceived control, and increased purpose in life (aka meaning). Neuroticism and perceive control, in turn, were partially mediated by both purpose in life and mindfulness. The significance of the increase in a sense of purpose in life, an indicator of increased meaning through intensive mindfulness practice in retreats, suggested two possible implications according to the authors: a) the positive impacts of intensive mindfulness practice appear to be negotiated in part through attitudinal changes associated with an enhanced sense of meaning; and, b) despite participating in a silent retreat with a focus on *samatha* (largely non-conceptual meditative practice), effects on meaning were significant *even* compared to others who practised mindfulness during the same period but less intensively. This study and the MMT theory draw attention to the ways in which mindfulness appears to extend from an embodied practice to a sense of purpose.

## EMBODIED STRESS THEORY

While MMT emphasizes the downstream effects of mindfulness on meaning and the capacity to savour experience, embodied stress theory offers an alternative theory focused on the physiological and cognitive features of suffering associated with stress and how mindfulness can address it. In this respect, both theories are interested in the nature of the suffering that mindfulness corrects and the nature of the wellbeing it appears to foster. In embodied stress theory, stress is understood to be psychologically constructed through consciously labelling experience as stressful based on the unconscious automatic integration of data from the body, external environment, and prior experience. These data from the body and prior experience derive from both peripheral (e.g., musculoskeletal effects like posture or tense muscles) and central embodiment (memory and neuropathways) sources. Furthermore, stress is distinguished from emotions by distinctive patterns of physiological activity, rendering it is as much a response to emotions and emotional reactivity as a cause of them (Francis, 2018). Embodied stress theory is intended to replace simple stimulus-organism-response models of stress with a constructivist interpretation of stress as an emergent property of complex psychological and physiological processes that culminate in the label "stress" in conscious thought. Furthermore, as something that is constructed, experiences labelled as stressful can be deconstructed through awareness and are not determined by a simple linear stimulus-stressor so much as by complex reactions that include the final label.

Empirical support for embodied stress theory is fairly robust (e.g., Koury et al., 2015) but the mechanisms by which it works remain unclear. Garland et al. (2017a) attempted to answer this question of mechanisms by operationalizing chronic stress using the RDoC construct of sustained threat, which the NIMH (n.d.) defined as: "an aversive emotional state caused by prolonged (i.e., weeks to months) exposure to internal and/or external condition(s), state(s), or stimuli that are adaptive to escape or avoid." The authors mapped out the impact of mindfulness in regulating each of the ten components of behavioural dysregulation characterizing sustained threat, including: Conflict detection; anxious arousal; avoidance; attentional bias to threat; perseveration (rumination); anhedonia/decreased appetitive behaviour; decreased libido; helplessness behaviour; memory retrieval deficits; and punishment sensitivity. They then aligned the behavioural data with evidence of the biological effects of mindfulness on key underlying neurobiological systems associated with sustained threat, such as the hypothalamic-pituitary-adrenal axis and brain circuits associated with attention, limbic reactivity, habitual behaviour, and the default mode network. Finally, they applied these findings back to support the Mindfulness-to-Meaning Theory, concluding that mindfulness induces adaptive stress coping and self-referential plasticity in ways that enhance meaning and the capacity to savour life.

## SUMMARY TABLE WITH IMPLICATIONS

To assist readers in applying these embodied cognition theories to MBTL practice, we have prepared a summary table. The theories presented in the chapter and their key components are introduced or outlined in the first column of Table 9.2, followed by examples of implications for MBTL practice. These implications are not exhaustive but, rather, they invite readers to engage in an active process of reading research and theory more deeply to inform and apply in practice.

**Table 9.2** Summary of Embodiment Theories in MBTL and Their Applications

| *Theory/Concept* | *Implication(s) for MBTL (examples)* |
|---|---|
| **Constructivism** | |
| ***Learning is...*** | ***Can be applied in:*** |
| local/particular. | - post-practice inquiry: e.g., emphasis on specific v. general |
| active/reflective. | - inductive inquiry: e.g., moving from experience to ideas |
| built on prior knowledge. | - intake questions: e.g., recognizing and adjusting teaching based on participant experience<br>- investigative inquiry (v. didactic teaching): e.g., eliciting at outset |
| an emergent process. | - voluntary/invitational approach – safeguarding autonomy<br>- non-judgmental acceptance – fostering sense of safety |
| learner-mediated. | - inquiry-based v. transmission-based instruction |
| socially-negotiated. | - learning through group inquiry<br>- connecting individual experience to human experience |
| **Theory of Embodied Cognition** | |
| ***Learning involves...*** | ***Can be applied in:*** |
| embodied awareness. | - mindfulness of the body practices<br>- inquiry into voluntary/autonomic thresholds |
| linking neurobiology to phenomenology. | - phenomenological inquiry of experience precedes investigative inquiry of underlying brain-body mechanisms |
| evolutionarily distinct levels of processing. | - parse experience into body/feelings and emotions/thought/ behavioural or other phenomena<br>- in inquiry, attention to shared experiences with other species or human experience through time |
| body-mind interaction. | - noticing sequence and interactions between the parsed experiences of body/feelings and emotion/ thought / phenomena |
| multiple manifestations of a sense of self forming or expressing themselves in varying degrees of awareness and relation to the body. | - inquiry investigating the self as multiple with varying degrees of relationship to body - (e.g. S-ART – p.25 – EES / EPS / NS)<br>- decentering (v. fusion within experience) |
| self-regulation. | - inquiry into awareness and its aftermath (regulation v. control)<br>- tracking changes in the context of inquiry (via awareness) |
| **Self-Determination Theory** | |
| intrinsic locus of control | - non-authoritarian, learner-centred practices that conserve participants' sense of autonomy |
| intrinsically motivating | - following interest and curiosity; tracking change and effects of mindfulness to build motivation through direct experience<br>- organismic or natural intrinsic motivators derive from three motives or desires: autonomy, relationships, competence |
| internalization | - process whereby external values or goals are endorsed by the self to become intrinsic, rather than extrinsic, motivators |
| autonomy | - behaviour fully endorsed by the self, implying self-governance – awareness, self-regulation, and choice as means and wellbeing as end |
| authenticity | - the ability to recognize and express or manifest consistency between internal conditions and their external expression |

(*Continued*)

**Table 9.2** (Continued)

| *Theory/Concept* | *Implication(s) for MBTL (examples)* |
|---|---|
| self-regulation | - self-determination as an ecological condition depends on self-regulation (feedback systems and awareness) to manifest |
| **Mindfulness as Self-Awareness** | |
| ***Component elements include:*** | ***Defined or manifests as:*** |
| **S-ART Theory** | |
| self | - embodied, multiple iterations of self: EES, EPS, NS (see p. 25) |
| self-awareness | - broadening awareness<br>- acceptance/approach orientation<br>- intention and motivation<br>- attention regulation |
| self-regulation | - emotion regulation<br>- extinction and reconsolidation<br>- pro-sociality – empathic reactivity, emotion sharing, compassion |
| self-transcendence | - non-attachment and decentering |
| **MAAS** (Mindful Attention Awareness Scale) | |
| mindfulness | - ability to hold attention and awareness on the present moment |
| self-awareness | - ability to be attentive and aware of internal (psychological and physical) constructions, events, and processes – implicit and explicit<br>- implicit (unconscious) and explicit (conscious) affect more closely align with fewer discrepancies |
| psychological wellbeing | - its presence associated with happiness, attentional sensitivity to present-moment sensory inputs, and self-regulation<br>- its absence associated with negative states like neuroticism, anxiety, angry hostility, depression |
| **Mindfulness-to-Meaning Theory (MMT)** | |
| ***A key concept in this theory is/are:*** | ***Operationalized as:*** |
| eudaemonic wellbeing | - an orientation on wellbeing as flourishing (subjective and objective) |
| a developmental pathway of meaning (via mindfulness) | - attentional control to de-automatization to decentering to broadened awareness to reappraisal to enhanced mood (joy, etc.) to combined downstream effects on wellbeing via *meaning* and *savouring*. |
| reappraisal | - a two-stage process: i) *deconstructing* by letting go of original interpretation of a stressor and relinquishing its affective components via decentering; and ii) *reconstructing meaning* by reconsidering a stressor through a more positive light or perspective. |
| self-transcendence | - developmental cycles spiral in a self-transcending process. |
| the downstream effects of mindfulness on wellbeing: *meaning* and *savouring* | - mindfulness promotes wellbeing through its downstream effects on the capacity for meaning (reappraising experiences more positively) and savouring (engaging and enjoying life experiences more deeply.) |
| **Embodied Stress Theory** | |
| peripheral embodiment | - experiential phenomena associated with the viscero-somatic reflexes and systems. |

*(Continued)*

**Table 9.2** (Continued)

| *Theory/Concept* | *Implication(s) for MBTL (examples)* |
|---|---|
| central embodiment | - experiential phenomena associated with the CNS and brain, including cognitions. |
| acute stress | - a short-term adaptational response/reaction often an intense experience arising from a temporary and non-repeating stressor in the environment or person |
| chronic stress | - a longer-term mild or intense adaptational experience arising from a regular, repeated stressor in the environment or person |
| sustained threat | - an operationalized construct of chronic stress used by the NIMH to describe its manifestation in empirical, lived experience |
| ten links in the behavioural dysregulation chain arising from sustained threat | - conflict detection; anxious arousal; avoidance; attentional bias to threat; perseveration (rumination); anhedonia/decreased appetitive behaviour; decreased libido; helplessness behaviour; memory retrieval deficits; and punishment sensitivity |

## REFERENCES

Bateson, G. (1972/2000). *Steps to an ecology of mind: Collected essays in anthropology, psychiatry, evolution, and epistemology*. University of Chicago Press.

Brown, K., & Ryan, R. (2003). The benefits of being present: Mindfulness and its role in psychological well-being. *Journal of Personality and Social Psychology, 84*, 822–848.

Brown, K., & Ryan, R. (n.d.). *The mindful attention awareness scale (MAAS)*. https://ppc.sas.upenn.edu/sites/default/files/mindfulnessscale.pdf.

Chiesa, A., Serretti, A., & Jakobsen, J. (2013). Mindfulness: Top-down or bottom-up emotion regulation strategy? *Clinical Psychology Review, 33*, 82–96. https://doi.org/10.1016/j.cpr.2012.10.006.

Chu, S., & Mak, W. (2020). Mindfulness enhances meaning in life: A meta-analysis of correlational studies and randomized controlled trials. *Mindfulness, 11*, 177–193. https://doi.org/10.1007/s12671-019-01258-9.

DeJesus, P. (2014). Can the revolution be optimised? Oh yes it can! But, maybe not. Report on the one day symposium on "Varieties of Enactivism." *Connection Science, 26*(3), 293–296. http://dx.doi.org/10.1080/09540091.2014.925267.

Donald, J., Bradshaw, E., Ryan, R., Basarkod, G., Ciarrochi, J., Duineveld, J., Guo, J., & Sahdra, B. (2020). Mindfulness and its association with varied types of motivation: A systematic review of meta-analysis using self-determination theory. *Personality and Social Psychology Bulletin, 46*(7), 1121–1138. https://doi.org/10.1177/0146167219896136.

Farb, N., Segal, Z. V., Mayberg, H., Bean, J., McKeon, D., Fatima, Z., & Anderson, A. (2007). Attending to the present: Mindfulness meditation reveals distinct neural modes of self-reference. *Social Cognitive and Affective Neuroscience, 2*, 313–322. https://doi.org/10.1093/scan/nsm030.

Ford, C., & Shook, N. (2019). Negative cognitive bias and perceived stress: Independent mediators of the relation between mindfulness and emotional distress. *Mindfulness, 10*, 100–110. https://doi.org/10.1007/s12671-018-0955-7.

Francis, A. (2018). The embodied theory of stress: A constructionist perspective on the experience of stress. *Review of General Psychology, 22*(4), 398–405. https://doi.org/10.1037/gpr0000164.

Garland, E., Farb, N., Goldin, P., & Fredrickson, B. (2015a). Mindfulness broadens awareness and builds eudaimonic meaning: A process model of mindful positive emotion regulation. *Psychological Inquiry, 26*(4), 293–314. https://doi.org/10.1080/1047840X.2015.1064294.

Garland, E., Farb, N., Goldin, P., & Fredrickson, B. (2015b). The mindfulness-to-meaning theory: Extension, applications, and challenges at the attention-appraisal-emotion interface. *Psychological Inquiry, 26*(4), 377–387. https://doi.org/10.1080/1047840X.2015.1092493.

Garland, E., & Frederickson, B. (2019). Positive psychological states in the arc from mindfulness to self-transcendence: Extensions of the mindfulness-to-meaning theory and applications to addition and chronic pain treatment. *Current Opinion in Psychology, 28*, 184–191. https://doi.org/10.1016/j.copsyc.2019.01.004.

Garland, E., Hanley, A., Baker, A., & Howard, M. (2017a). Biobehavioral mechanism of mindfulness as a treatment for chronic stress: An RDoC perspective. *Chronic Stress, 1*, 1–14. https://doi.org/10.1177/2470547017711912.

Garland, E., Hanley, A. L., Goldin, P., & Gross, J. (2017b). Testing the mindfulness-to-meaning theory: Evidence for mindful positive emotion regulation from a reanalysis of longitudinal data. *PLoS One, 12*(12), e0187727. https://doi.org/10.1371/journal.pone.0187727.

Garland, E., Kiken, L., Faurot, K., Palsson, O., & Gaylord, S. (2017c). Upward spirals of mindfulness and reappraisal: Testing the mindfulness-to-meaning theory with autoregressive latent trajectory modeling. *Cognitive Therapy and Research, 41*, 381–392. https://doi.org/10.1007/s10608-016-9768-y.

Gillebaart, M. (2018). The 'operational' definition of self-control. *Frontiers in Psychology, 18*, https://doi.org/10.3389/fpsyg.2018.0123

Heatherton, T. (2011). Neuroscience of self and self-regulation. *Annual Review of Psychology, 62*, 363–390.

Jacobs, T., Epel, E., Lin, J., Blackburn, E., Wolkowitz, O., Bridwell, D., Zanesco, A., Aichele, S., Sahdra, B., MacLean, K., King, B., Shaver, P., Rosenberg, E., Ferrer, E., Wallace, A., & Saron, C. (2011). Intensive meditation training, immune cell telomerase activity, and psychological mediators. *Psychoneuroendocrinology, 36*(5), 644–681. https://doi.org/10.1016/j.psyneuen.2010.09.010.

Koury, B., Sharma, M., Rush, S., & Fournier, C. (2015). Mindfulness-based stress reduction for healthy individuals: A meta-analysis. *Journal of Psychosomatic Research, 78*(6), 519–528. https://doi.org/10.1016/j.jpsychores.2015.03.009.

Leduc-Cummings, I., Werner, K., & Milyavskaya, M. (2017). Self-regulation. In V. Zeigler-Hill & T. Shackelford (Eds.), *Encyclopedia of personality and individual differences.* https://doi.10.1007/978-3-319-28099-8_1179-1.

Lettvin, J. Y., Maturana, H. R., McCulloch, W. S., & Pitts, W. H. (1968). What the frog's eye tells the frog's brain. In W. Corning & M. Balaban (Eds.), *The mind: Biological approaches to its function* (pp. 233–258). Wiley. (Original Work Published 1959).

Maturana, H. (1958). *The fine structure of the optic nerve and tectum of anurans: An electron microscope study*. PhD Dissertation, Harvard University.

Maturana, H., & Varela, F. (1972). *Autopoeisis and cognition: The realization of the living*. D. Reidel Publishing Company.

Maturana, H., & Varela, F. (1987). *The tree of knowledge: The biological roots of human understanding*. Shambala.

Mead, M. (1968). The cybernetics of cybernetics. In H. von Foerster, J. White, L. Peterson, & J. Russell (Eds.), *Purposive systems* (pp. 1–11). Spartan Books.

Milyavskaya, M., Inzlicht, M., Hope, N., & Koestner, R. (2015). Saying "no" to temptation: Want-to motivation improves self-regulation by reducing temptation rather than by increasing self-control. *Journal of Personality and Social Psychology*, *109*(4), 677–693. https://doi.org/10.1037/pspp0000045.

NIMH (National Institute of Mental Health). (n.d.). *Construct: Sustained threat*. Accessed July 2021. https://www.nimh.nih.gov/research/research-funded-by-nimh/rdoc/constructs/sustained-threat.

Ryan, R. & Deci, E. (2017). *Self-determination theory: Basic psychological needs in motivation, development, and wellness*. The Guilford Press.

Ryan, R., Donald, J., & Bradshaw, E. (2021). Mindfulness and motivation: A process view using self-determination theory. *Current Directions in Psychological Science*, *30*(4), 300–306. https://doi.org/10.1177/09637214211009511.

Ryan, R., Kuhl, J., & Deci, E. (1997). Nature and autonomy: An organization view of social and neurobiological aspects of self-regulation in behavior and development. *Development and Psychopathology*, *9*, 701–728. https://doi.org/10.1017/S0954579497001405.

Tedeschi, R., & Blevins, C. (2015). From mindfulness to meaning: Implications for the theory of posttraumatic growth. *Psychological Inquiry*, *26*(4), 373–376. http://dx.doi.org/10.1080/1047840X.2015.1075354.

Vago, D., & Silbersweig, D. (2012). Self-awareness, self-regulation, and self-transcendences (S-ART): A framework for understanding the neurobiological mechanisms of mindfulness. *Frontiers of Human Neuroscience*, *25*, 296. https://doi.org/10.3389/fnhum.2012.00296.

Varela, F., Maturana, F., & Uribe, R. (1974). *Biosystems*, *5*(4), 187–196. https://doi.org/10.1016/0303-2647(74)90031-8.

Varela, F., Thompson, E., & Rosch, E. (2016). *The embodied mind: Cognitive science and human experience. Revised version*. MIT Press. (First Edition Published in 1991.)

von Foerster, H. (Ed.). (1995). *Cybernetics of cybernetics: Or, the control of control and the communication of communication* (2nd ed.). Future Systems.

Ward, D., Silverman, D., & Villalobos, M. (2017). Introduction: The varieties of enactivism. *Topoi: An International Review of Philosophy*, *36*, 365–375. https://doi.org/10.1007/s11245-017-9484-6.

Weiner, N. (1948). *Cybernetics, or control and communication in the animal and the machine*. Technology Press.

Werner, K., & Milyavskaya, M. (2019). Motivation and self-regulation: The role of want-to motivation in the processes of underlying self-regulation and self-control. *Social and Personality Psychology Compass, 13*(1), e12425. https://doi.org/10.1111/spc3.12425.

Whitehead, A. (1929). *The aims of education and other essays.* Macmillan.

# CHAPTER 10

# COGNITIVE PROCESSING THEORIES

The task of applying research to teaching and learning is eased by the fact that scientific evidence tends to be organized into theories, thereby allowing the translation of disparate data into meaningful bundles of relationships and reasoned inferences. Theories are neither mere ideas nor mere data but where data and ideas mix. As an example, in their review, Ford and Shook (2019) found two key factors independently accounted for unique variances in the mindfulness-reduced emotional distress relationship: Reductions in cognitive bias and reductions in stress. This led the researchers to conclude that cognitive bias and stress reduction together may explain how and why mindfulness promotes wellbeing. Therefore, in this chapter we consider two related cognitive processing theories of mindfulness: cognitive bias and dual processing theories. We conclude by introducing the operationalization of mindfulness as cognitive functions in the Five Facets of Mindfulness Questionnaire (FFMQ).

## MINDFULNESS AS COGNITIVE BIAS REDUCTION

Cognitive biases are distinctive ways that cognitive habits distort perception below the threshold of awareness. They are indicators of how cognitive processes can simplify the world automatically in a *thinking fast* or implicit mode of cognition (Kahneman, 2011; Ruth, 2020). Despite the seeming advantages of fast and efficient processing, these distortions from cognitive biases can result in unfavorable consequences, including depression, anxiety, addiction, and OCD. Cognitive bias theories recognize that cognitive errors or distorted cognitions can cause suffering, compromise wellbeing, and aggravate individual and social problems. Mindfulness, by regulating attention and expanding awareness, appears to correct some cognitive biases that give rise to habitual, automatic errors below the threshold of awareness. In this section, we consider five cognitive biases with implications for mindfulness: a) affective biases; b) attentional biases, including threat-avoidant and approach biases; c) interpretational biases; d) selective memory biases; and e) implicit association biases.

### Affective Biases

Affective biases distort other aspects of cognitive functioning, which leads some to subsume them under other domains of cognitive bias, such as attention, interpretation, or memory. In psychology, *affect* refers to underlying feeling tones that vary according to valence, arousal, and motivational intensity (Harmond-Jones et al., 2013). Like the Buddhist psychological perspective on feelings or feeling tones, affect can be characterized by one of three discrete valences (positive, negative, neutral) on a spectrum of intensity levels ranging from low to high arousal (Barrett, 2017; Batchelor, 2019). Barrett described affect in the unpleasant valence, for example, as varying in arousal on a spectrum from depressed and lethargic through miserable and displeased to upset and distressed. The positive valence was described as ranging from serene and calm to gratified and pleased to elated and thrilled. Barret did not describe the spectrum of neutral affect, the third valence, which is a persistent oversight across much of the scientific and practical writings on affect or feeling tones in both mindfulness and psychology. In MBSR and MBCT programmes, for

DOI: 10.4324/9781003182467-14

example, only pleasant and unpleasant experiences are explored and discussed, not neutral experiences. That said, inferring from Barrett's model, we might describe the neutral valence as varying across a spectrum of intensities and arousal levels from habituated and numb to dull and indifferent to bored and restless.

Affect-related cognitive biases are operationalized as non-conscious preferences for experiences with either a positive (positivity bias) or a negative (negativity bias) valence in contrast to neutral (Vago & Silbersweig, 2012). Such preferences show up in skewed attention, interpretations, and/or memories towards stimuli with a corresponding positive or negative valence. Positive affective biases refer to preferences for positive objects of attention, interpretations, or memories, whereas negative affective biases refer to preferences for negative objects.

In research, these biases are commonly operationally indicated by attention shifting more frequently towards positive or negative stimuli, in contrast to neutral. This relative frequency of shifting away from neutral is interpreted as evidence of an affect bias in that direction (note that neutral is defined as without bias, which is problematic). As Pool et al. (2016) concluded in their meta-analysis on attentional biases for positive stimuli, affect biases are rapid, involuntary, and occur during the early stages of attention processing but also in interpretive and memory processing. Affect bias research began with studies of negative attentional biases to *threat* associated with fear and later to more generalized negative affect biases found in people suffering from anxiety or depression (Koster et al., 2009). Yet, studies soon spread to investigate positive affect biases in healthy, non-clinical populations (see Sharot, 2011). Both negative and positive affect biases are associated with the amygdala; positive affect biases involve hormones associated with desire or comfort (e.g., dopamine or oxytocin) while negative affect biases implicate stimulant-like stress response hormones such as adrenaline or cortisol.

Working with affect biases in mindfulness begins with becoming aware of feeling tones as positive, negative, or neutral and their associated intensities in and across the full range of sensory experiences. Mindfulness practitioners learn to meet these feeling tones with curiosity and equanimity in order to move beyond preferences so as to reduce conditioned, habitual responses. This recognition of feeling tone through attentional training interrupts bias and automaticity leading *to de-automatization, a* critical step described in MMT by Garland et al. (2015). According to MMT, this ability of mindfulness to disrupt automatic habitual responses makes decentering possible, which distances the mind from prior, conditioned assumptions, identifications, and interpretations. The ensuing broadened awareness offers an enhanced recognition and experience of what is present and what is possible. Harmond-Jones et al. (2013) refer to this broadening of awareness through affective experience as the broadening of cognitive scope. Their study found that it was not the valence of affect but its motivational intensity that determined whether the cognitive scope was broadened or narrowed. Affect states with low motivational intensity, such as gratitude (pos) or sadness (neg) broadened cognitive scope, whereas affect states with high motivational intensity, such as desire (pos) or fear (neg) tended to narrow cognitive scope. This aligns well with mindfulness training insofar as it is not the content of experience and feeling tones that matter so much as how we react or respond to them. The object of mindfulness of feelings is to notice the feeling tone of experiences with equal interest without reacting or judging them, and thereby to widen attention, even in the midst of intense emotions. Such non-judgmental awareness can reduce high intensity feelings to lower intensity levels to enable the broadening of awareness. Textbox 10.1 offers an example of a specific technique to make train students in the recognition of feeling tones or affect in the body.

## TEXTBOX 10.1 EXEMPLAR OR CASE:

### Awareness of Feeling Tones in Bodily Sensations

**Purpose**: Exploring *feeling tones* through bodily sensations to investigate the following:

- What are feeling tones in the context of mindfulness, and why do they matter?
- What are component features of pleasant, unpleasant, and neutral (sensory) experiences?
- How do the feeling tones appear in sensory experiences, and how do they affect our reactions to them?
- What is equanimity, and what is its role in cultivating mindfulness of feelings?
- How does an attitude of curiosity affect feeling tones and foster equanimity, if at all?
- How do feeling tones, moods, and emotions relate? How do feeling tones become complex emotions?

**Context**: This bridging practice helps practitioners recognize pleasant/unpleasant/neutral feeling tones. The steps are designed to elicit positive, negative, and neutral feeling tones in order, but may vary.

**Practice**: This practice can be done in 10–15 minutes. Ask students to assume a relaxed-yet-alert posture to engage in this mindfulness-of-feelings practice, the intention begins to notice feelings.

1. Bringing together the first two fingers of the dominant hand (pointing and middle finger), bring the tips of the finger to the base of the ear on the same side of the body. Slowly draw the fingers down along the cheek towards the mouth, noting the sensations and if and when any discernible affect or feeling tone arises (pleasant, unpleasant, neutral). If and when one does, note what happens in your responses (body, mind, etc.). Continue to draw the fingers down along the lips, slowly and gently circling along the lips of the mouth. (pleasant)
2. Shifting now to bring the two fingers to the indentation where the two clavicles meet (called the suprasegmental notch). Slowly begin pressing in, gently, noticing if and when a feeling arises. (unpleasant)
3. Drawing the fingertips now along the side of the leg at the knee with the same instructions. (neutral)

**Inquiry**: After each step, review what feeling, if any, arose for participants (without a sense of right or wrong); how the experience changed with the feeling; and what reactions the feeling induced.

**Alternative**: This same feeling tone exploration can be done through a simple seeing meditation. Inviting participants to stand, invite them to slowly scan a room with sight noting where their eyes experience pleasure and wish to linger (pleasant); where they experience avoidance (unpleasant); and what they barely even notice (neutral). The point is not to analyse why so much as to notice the experiences associated with each feeling tone. This practice can end by inviting participants to scan the room and try to take in all that is seen with equal interest (i.e., equanimity).

### *Positive Affective Biases*

Pool et al. (2016) conducted a metanalysis of attentional affective biases among healthy, non-clinical populations and found a modest significant attentional bias for positive as opposed to neutral stimuli across the 243 studies with N=9120 healthy participants. The positivity bias was stronger in studies of earlier rather than later phases of attention, implying that this bias occurs rapidly and involuntarily. At the same time, such positive affective attentional biases are associated with higher and more stable life satisfaction. Cummins and Nistico (2002) identified three mediators to explain this connection between positive affect and life satisfaction: self-esteem, control, and optimism. Kral et al. (2018) compared an active control condition with short-term mindfulness practice (MBSR) and long-term practice (completing over 9000 h.). All mindfulness conditions reduced amygdala reactivity to positive pictures as compared to controls, suggesting that mindfulness may correct positive cognitive biases more readily than negative affect biases. Since mindfulness is also associated with enhanced life satisfaction and positive affect, it is reasonable to assume that it is not happening by increasing the positivity bias.

### *Negative Affective Biases*

Indeed, in the same Kral et al. (2018) study, no differences were detected for *negative* pictures except for long-term practitioners, and the reduction in amygdala reactivity to negative pictures varied in long-term practitioners proportionately to hours spent in retreat. This suggests more intensive practice may be required to moderate reactivity to negative as opposed to positive stimuli. Of course, mindfulness did appear to reduce amygdala reactivity overall, suggesting improved emotion regulation for all practice durations. Yet, the neural mechanism of control and regulation appeared to be quite different in the short- and long-term practitioners, with evidence of increased top-down control mechanisms in the short-term practitioners and more bottom-up automatic regulation patterns in long-term practitioners (Chiesa et al., 2013).

Negative affective biases refer to the involuntary preference for stimuli, thoughts, or memories associated with negative affect. Such biases in negative affect are associated with a range of pathologies, including anxiety disorders (Hallion & Ruscio, 2011; Okon-Singer, 2018) and fibromyalgia (Vago & Nakamura, 2011). Furthermore, negative affect biases in attention, interpretation, and memory associated with depression appear to be interconnected (Everaert & Koster, 2020; Nieto et al., 2020). Together, these negative affect biases suggest a kind of negative cognitive snowball effect that can intensify and exacerbate negative moods to manifest into full disorders. Even small doses of mindfulness have been found to modestly reduce negative affect (Schumer et al., 2018), with increasing effects with practice (Kral et al., 2018).

## **Attentional Biases**

Attentional biases operate at two points in attention processing: In the initial involuntary selection phase of noticing and/or in the final phase as attention disengages from the experience. Although there is strong evidence of a relationship between negative attention biases and mood and anxiety disorders (Everaert & Koster, 2020), the direction and degree of causality in the relationship between attentional bias and mood remain unclear: Do attentional biases in selecting negative information cause, contribute to, or maintain a mood disorder, or is it the other way around? Supporting the hypothesis that negative cognitive biases contribute to emotional vulnerabilities, Koster et al. (2009) suggest a preventative role for mindfulness. Mindfulness appears to lower levels of both negative cognitive biases *and* emotional distress (Vago & Silbersweig, 2012).

### *Threat Bias*

Threat bias is the most well-researched type of attentional bias. Believed to be of evolutionary significance in the early alerting of danger, this bias is common across populations but becomes exaggerated in clinical populations, particularly in those with anxiety disorders (Cisler & Koster, 2010). Attentional biases to threat manifest in three forms: a) facilitated attention towards the threat; b) delayed disengagement from the threat; and, c) attentional avoidance of the threat. Facilitated attention refers to the relative ease and speed with which attention is drawn to threatening information or stimuli, which is associated with anxiety, including increased attention to irrelevant threats (Cisler et al., 2009). Delayed disengagement from threat occurs when attention is captured by a threatening stimulus and unable to switch from that stimulus to another. Again, this pattern is strongly associated with anxiety, with some evidence in depression where negative attentional biases have been reported exclusively in the disengagement phase (Koster et al., 2009). Finally, the attentional avoidance of threat refers to a reverse tendency for attention to move away from threatening information to attend to opposite information or stimuli as an avoidance strategy. Research suggests that mindfulness can reduce all three types of attentional biases to threat, whether they involve hypervigilance (facilitation and delayed disengagement) or avoidance (Garland et al., 2017a).

### *Experiential Avoidance*

Experiential avoidance is associated with a range of symptoms in clinical presentations of anxiety and fear; furthermore, such avoidance is directly addressed in mindfulness. Experiential avoidance refers to a form of attention bias involving the tendency to move away from contact with distressing internal experiences and to control or avoid them. Such avoidance has been found to exacerbate distress and limit behaviour and appears to be maintained through negative and judgmental thoughts and failed attempts to suppress anxiety (Hayes-Skelton & Eustis, 2020). Mindfulness training emphasizes acceptance, non-judgment, and gently turning towards awareness of the experience of suffering (also known as exposure), rather than suppressing or avoiding adverse and distressing experiences. In MMT, Garland et al. (2017a) identify decentering via mindfulness as an explanatory mechanism, which "may facilitate metacognitive monitoring of present moment experiential avoidance of aversive cognitions, emotions, or behavioral urges" (p. 3). The authors point out that mindfulness programmes reduce avoidance and associated PTSD and depression symptoms, a finding of Vago and Nakamura (2011) identified as well in fibromyalgia patients in response to pain-related threats.

### *Conflict Monitoring and Detection*

Conflict monitoring and detection, an attentional bias that can become dysfunctional through hypervigilance in some psychiatric disorders like anxiety and depression, involves the processing of information to monitor conflicting goals and behaviors to detect when control needs to be exerted. Mindfulness appears to improve conflict monitoring and detection more than any other attentional bias (Garland et al., 2017a). This is believed to be linked to improved executive functioning associated with the acceptance of conflicting stimuli (often highlighted in inquiry in mindfulness) and the associated reduction in emotional and attentional reactivity arising from perturbation by the stressor.

## Interpretation Biases

Robust research has consistently linked negative cognitive interpretation biases to depression and anxiety, as Everaert et al. (2017) found in their meta-analysis of 87 studies, with an overall moderate effect size. This same study found that self-referencing seemed to be a key mechanism in this effect, whereby self-referent stimuli increased negative cognitive interpretation bias in people suffering from clinical depression or anxiety. These findings support earlier research linking increased cognitive interpretation bias to negative schemas and memory networks. The meta-analysis also found a general bias to interpreting negatively for *non*-self-referent stimuli, too. These findings appeared to hold across active depression or for remitted depressive periods. Yet, it was unclear if the increased negative cognitive interpretive bias reflected a vulnerability (cause) or scar (effect) of the prior depressive episode. Nevertheless, recent research has corroborated this strong relationship, demonstrating that the degree of negative cognitive interpretation bias is positively correlated with the severity of depression (Lee et al., 2016). In addition, depression and social anxiety are related to *both* cognitive interpretation bias and inflexible negative interpretations (Everaert et al., 2018). Interpretation biases were also found in common comorbidities of depression or anxiety, like eating disorders (Jones & Sharpe, 2017).

This consistent finding of the role of negative cognitive interpretation biases in depression and anxiety disorders informed the development of key cognitive therapeutic interventions like cognitive behaviour therapy (CBT) (Spinhoven et al., 2018); cognitive-bias modification (CBM) (Jones & Sharpe, 2017); and mindfulness-based cognitive therapy (MBCT) (Segal et al., 2019). Evidence suggests that mindfulness can directly reduce cognitive interpretational biases without explicitly relying on intervening cognitive-bias modification strategies (Ford & Shook, 2019; Mayer et al., 2019), in part through the teaching and learning of decentering, helping a meditator to move from identification and fusion with experiences, including negative interpretational biases, to a distanced, witnessing observational stance (Segal et al., 2019).

Aaron Beck (1963, 1967) developed the cognitive theory of depression that identified distorted thinking as a primary driver in mood disorders. Beck (1976) was also responsible for the genesis of cognitive therapy and cognitive behavioral therapy to treat depression and its associated interpretation biases. Nieto et al. (2020) conducted a recent meta-analysis of self-report data on cognitive interpretation biases in depression and arrived at ten predominant forms of interpretation bias commonly identified in depression, presented in Table 10.1. The authors reviewed 23 studies on catastrophizing biases and depression and 40 studies on (other) interpretation biases and depression. They found strong evidence for catastrophizing biases and moderate evidence for interpretation biases and depression, especially in female participants, when contrasted with healthy controls. They concluded that negative cognitive interpretation biases may be the antecedent of negative automatic thought (i.e., rumination); of negative beliefs (of oneself, the world, the future); and, hence, of depressive symptoms.

**Table 10.1** Cognitive Interpretation Biases from Beck's Model (derived from Nieto et al., 2020, p. 2)

| *Cognitive Biases* | *Definition* | *Example* |
|---|---|---|
| Catastrophizing or Fortune telling | Predicting exaggerated negative outcomes to events without evidence. | "This will never work." "This is going to end badly." |
| Personalization or Internal causal attribution | Viewing events narrowly from a personal perspective. Exaggerated guilt. | "She did it to spite me." "It's all my fault." |
| Dichotomous thinking | Thinking in binaries like all or nothing, good or bad. | "He said I was his second choice, so what's the point?" |
| Selective abstraction | Paying attention to negative features or outcomes and ignoring other information. | "Then, after praising me, he said I was too shy!" |
| Arbitrary inference | Drawing a negative inference without adequate bases. | "She said she was too busy. She must hate me." |
| Overgeneralization | Exaggerating and universalizing negative outcomes based on limited cases. | "I always fail, so what's the point of trying?" |
| Minimization/Discounting positives | Overlooking or minimizing the significance of positive cases or events. | "I won the medal but it was just a fluke." |
| Labelling | Fixing an identity on self or other based on just one incident or mistake. | "I yelled at my son. I'm a bad mother and he's a brat!" |
| Mindreading | Assuming the intentions of another person without evidence or knowledge. | "She asked me my marital status to embarrass me." |
| Emotional reasoning | Assuming negative thoughts, feelings, or emotions reflect reality. | "I'm unqualified or why else would I feel so insecure?" |

Mindfulness likely corrects interpretation biases for the most part implicitly and nonconsciously by training meditators to regulate attention towards sensation and away from rumination and self-referencing. Practitioners are instructed to directly perceive an object of attention free of narration, self-referencing, or identification. MBCT is an exception where CBT informs the programme to reinforce the identification and awareness of negative interpretation biases explicitly to prevent a depressive relapse. As Segal et al. (2019) demonstrate, both mindfulness and CBT together appear to reduce relapse and depressive symptoms through *decentering*. As indicated previously, these symptoms may be further reduced by cultivating equanimity (not immediately judging experience as good or bad) and by enhancing experiential rather than narrative self-referencing through attention to experience as sensations (Farb et al., 2007; Watkins, 2015).

## Memory Biases

The secular-scientific definition of mindfulness as present-centred awareness seems to suggest that all interpretive and analytical thought and memory can be obstacles to mindfulness, whether or not they are biased. Yet, there is also a seeming paradox that *biased* thoughts and memories are also *corrected* by mindfulness (Mayer et al., 2019). This paradox can begin to be resolved by acknowledging that this interpretation is overly simplistic given that certain common mindfulness practices include attending to thoughts and memories as they arise (see Textbox 12.3). We must also remember that in order to learn mindfulness one must make use of memory, discernment (evaluation or judgment) and cognition. Rather than encouraging the avoidance of, or resistance to, thoughts and memories, mindfulness fosters cognitive distancing between the observer and what is witnessed in experience, with less fusion and identification so as to cultivate a more *decentred* awareness. Added to this paradox is the fact that the traditional term for "mindfulness" in Pali, *sati*, means *remembrance*, suggesting a role for both the short-term working memory involved in encoding experiences and the longer-term prospective memory involved in moving intentions across time. Prospective memory has been linked to both episodic memory and executive functioning (Costa et al., 2018), both of which improve with mindfulness, as does working memory (Brown et al., 2016).

Drawing on "a cross-cultural cognitive science of mindfulness" that integrates traditional and secular-scientific theories of mindfulness, Davis and Thompson (2015) refer to mindfulness as a process of "bare sentience" involving the progressive discernment of increasingly subtle bodily sensations and emotions. Furthermore, they conclude: "The reason that resting on the level of bare sentience is said to be transformative is that often we are caught up in distortive interpretation and analysis" (p. 43). Distortive interpretation and analysis arise through thought and memory as elaborations layered onto bare sentience. Mindfulness is a corrective to distortions of thought and memory because of two factors, according to this cross-cultural cognitive science theory: a) increased alertness; and b) the attenuation of affective biases of attention and memory. Increased alertness enhances awareness of internal and external stimuli that might not otherwise be accessible. This broadening of awareness includes stimuli that attention might otherwise be biased against. Attenuating affective biases of attention and memory, on the other hand, reduce emotional fixations that narrow awareness to allow a wider field of experience while reducing emotional proliferations.

### *State-Dependent Memory*

Bower (1981) defined *state-dependent memory* in his associative network theory as "events learned in one psychic state can be remembered better when one is put back into the same state one was in during the original experience" (p. 130). This theory may explain in part why negative affect biases associated with depression and anxiety are also evident in memory biases (Everaert & Koster, 2020). The mood-congruity effect is an adapted incarnation of the state-dependent memory model that suggests that memories will be easier to retrieve if they were formed in the same emotional or affective state. Mazza et al. (2018) provided evidence of this effect in a study of chronic pain patients, who demonstrated superior recall of pain-related words than controls, despite otherwise showing indications of impaired memory processing in both encoding and retrieval. Indeed, these authors concluded that this negative memory bias could be sufficiently strong to be aggravating the chronic pain itself long after the immediate source of pain is eliminated.

Through its ability to alter mood states, mindfulness may function to engage memories of previous experiences of mindfulness rather than of pain or suffering, thereby supporting the snowballing effect of mindfulness rather than of negative moods. For example, Lindsay et al. (2018) provide evidence that mindfulness reduces negative affect through combining active acceptance with open monitoring, resulting in more positive emotions. State-dependent memory suggests that as our state of mind – i.e., affect, mood, and emotion – changes, it will skew memory towards times when we were in similar states of mind. Just as mindfulness makes moods more positive and thereby reduces negative memory biases for those suffering from depression, perhaps it also generates distinctive states in retreats that are associated with previous experiences of intensive practice, thereby skewing memory to recall other periods in retreat or during calm and insightful states of mind. Textbox 10.2 offers an example from one of the author's experiences during a retreat that, although anecdotal, does describe common experiences of intensive practice.

## TEXTBOX 10.2 EXEMPLAR OR CASE:

### When a Himalayan Leopard Crashed a Canadian Retreat

Some meditators report changes in the quality of memories they experience during intensive practice while on retreat. They describe distinctive shifts in the affective tones and contents of memories as they become more calm and their minds more absorbed. In some cases, these memories are very positive and meaningful yet somehow became forgotten or displaced. Alternatively, they may involve very ordinary but nearly forgotten mundane "moments" that were nonetheless emotionally significant. These surprising, sometimes intrusive memories seemed to alter participants' usual sense of themselves and their lives. This is quite different from trauma-related intrusive memories and dissociative amnesia associated with PTSD, insofar as the memories are *wanted* rather than *unwanted*, however mundane. Below is an example from one of the authors (SM):

Often in intensive retreats, I find that my experience is unexpectedly interrupted and flooded with memories from India, where I lived in a quasi-retreat in Tibetan monasteries for years. Sometimes these memories arrive more like virtual realities than film footage, providing an embodied simulated experience of being there, as if in a time machine. Alternatively, at other times, these memories arise like imagistic live snapshots of near-forgotten teachers, friends, or creatures encountered there. For example, in a retreat in Canada in 2018, during a group sitting meditation practice, a memory from 1998 erupted in my awareness as if appearing out of some liminal zone of consciousness. The memory was of an encounter with a leopard when I was alone one evening in a monastic courtyard where I was living in the Indian Himalayas. All of the nuns were gone to Dharamsala, and so I was alone with the leopard. We held one another's gaze, and then both reversed direction and fled! The incident was thrilling, reminiscent of adventure and of primordial wildness. In the ensuing days, the memory continued to resurface during practices.

(Recounted in more detail in Chapter 19).

### *Intrusive Memory and Dissociative Amnesia*

Textbox 10.2 is an example of a *wanted* involuntary intrusive memory; however, PTSD symptoms can include involuntary *unwanted* intrusive memories with traumatic contents that are vividly experienced as if reliving the event in the present. The intensity and involuntary nature of these intrusive memories are different from intrusive negative memories in anxiety, OCD, or depressive disorders or in healthy people (Brewin et al., 2010). Yet, the incidence of intrusive memories may be similar in PTSD and depression. For example, Payne et al. (2019) reviewed studies to find that people with depression faced the same rate of intrusive memories as those with PTSD (66%–76%) and both groups were far more likely to do so than healthy controls. Mindfulness is associated with both broadened awareness (Garland et al., 2017b) and with exposure through approach, both inferred to be correctives to intrusive memories. Likewise, Kubota and Nixon (2020) exposed students to a small dose of mindfulness following a traumatic film to manage post-trauma rumination in the coming week. The mindfulness did reduce the vividness of intrusions but not their frequency or distress; for those with high levels of trait mindfulness, however, lower post-trauma symptoms were reported.

Dissociative amnesia is a very different memory-related PTSD symptom. Unlike involuntary flashbacks, dissociate amnesia involves PTSD-related gaps in memory, often involving memories of traumatic experiences. Radulovic et al. (2018) reviewed a range of evidence on dissociative amnesia in PTSD to conclude that it was a bona fide condition. They attributed the condition to state-dependent memory. In the absence of the original conditions and state in which the memory was encoded, amnesia ensued. In contrast to verbally accessed memories, such situationally dependent memories are automatically, in some cases involuntarily, retrieved when in comparable situations (Brewin et al., 1996). Mindfulness has not been investigated in this condition, though its impact in correcting dissociated ego states suggests potential benefits (Smith & Hartelius, 2020). Others, like Britton (2019), theorize that because mindfulness affects PFC control networks and can induce high parasympathetic tones, both common in dissociative states, mindfulness-induced decentering could make some practitioners susceptible to dissociation if improperly practised. Still others, like Forner (2017), suggest that by correcting PFC dysfunctions associated with emotion regulation, cognitive flexibility, and fear responses, mindfulness is an ideal treatment for dissociation when properly used.

### *Self-Referencing Memory Biases*

Mindfulness appears to impact self-referencing and its memory-related biases. Self-referencing has been identified in two corresponding underlying neural networks, described respectively as the self in time (narrative focus, NF) and the self in the present (experiential focus, EF) (Farb et al., 2007). NF involves extended self-referencing that connects experiences across time to form a kind of remembered or storied self. NF self-referencing can involve over-identification with experiences, self-centred perspectives, and/or filtering experiences to conform to a limited narrated autobiographical storyline. On the other hand, EF self-referencing is momentary, involving experiences as they arise in the present, based more on sensed experience than memory. Farb et al. found distinctive neurobiological patterns associated with each type of self-identification. The NF, associated with the medial PFC, became significantly reduced through an eight-week mindfulness training programme, while the EF regions of the lateral PFC and viscersomatic areas increased. Furthermore, the strong coupling between the right insula (EF) and mPFC (NF) became uncoupled in trained participants by the completion of the programme. Likewise, in a study of the effects of psilocybin in conjunction with mindfulness in intensive retreats, Smigielski et al. (2019) found the same pattern of decoupling between these previously associated networks. Finally,

Nejad et al. (2013) reviewed studies of self-referencing in people suffering from major depression, finding neurobiological evidence of a connection between narrative self-referencing and rumination associated with the same cortical midline structures (mPFC).

The NF and EF are described as well in the *thinking fast and slow* dual-process theory of cognition, in which Kahneman (2011) describes two similar experiences of the self in time: the *remembering self* and the *experiencing self*. The *remembering self* arises from the slow, voluntary, and seemingly rational System 2 thinking and the *experiencing self* as part of the fast, implicit, and less voluntary System 1. Kahneman (2011) reported on how these differing memory and self-identification processing pathways influence or bias the experience of pain. He found that System 1 processed experiences in ways that generalized and distorted reality using two principles: a) *the peak-end rule*, in which experiences were evaluated based on peak and culminating experiences, and b) *duration neglect*, the tendency to disregard duration in evaluating the totality of an experience (e.g., of pain). These biases in peak-and-end and duration neglect are examples of a more widespread tendency to overgeneralize past experience based on limited information about the past.

People suffering from depression show this tendency to overgeneralize autobiographical memories. Williams et al. (2009) researched formerly depressed patients and found they overgeneralized memories in ways that impacted how they evaluated wellbeing and their quality of life. The researchers investigated the impact of an eight-week MBCT on this overgeneralization distortion and found that the treatment group showed significantly lower rates of generic memories than the controls. These self-referencing memory biases come from System 1 fast-thinking but impacted decision-making in the slow-thinking System 2. Mindfulness appears to bring unconscious, fast-thinking System 1 processes into more conscious System 2 awareness so as to de-automatize otherwise automatic, unconscious patterns of reacting and decision-making (Fabro et al., 2017). Overgeneralized memories will tend to distort and skew interpretations of experience to reinforce states or moods in the present. When particularized via mindfulness, such memories are more likely to offer insights regarding the impermanent and nuanced nature of experiences in the past with implications for the future.

## Implicit Cognition/Associational Biases

The dual-process systems are associated with unconscious implicit emotions and related associational biases (System 1) and conscious explicit emotions and decision-making impacted by both implicit and explicit emotions (System 2). Implicit biases produce automatic judgments and preferences that affect our behaviour and treatment of others, even when these evaluations contradict conscious and explicitly reasoned judgements. Greenwald et al. (1998) developed the implicit association test of Project Implicit (https://implicit.harvard.edu) to measure implicit associations by measuring differences in response times and accuracy when aligning evaluative words like "good" and "bad" or "pleasant" and "unpleasant" to pictures, images, or words about opposing classification, such as overweight/thin; women/men; Blacks/Whites, young/old, etc. Although there are uneven findings concerning how well implicit biases predict behaviour (Greenwald et al., 2009; Oswald et al., 2013), they have been shown to predict the following: hiring and medical biases against obese people (Agerström & Rooth, 2010; Sabin et al., 2012); suicide (Nock et al., 2010); marital separation or success (Lee et al., 2010); declining biases against homosexuality (Westgate et al., 2015); discrimination towards women in science careers (Reuben *et al*, 2014); and political preferences (Hawkins & Nosek, 2012).

Greenwald et al.'s (2015) meta-analyses concluded that even statistically small implicit biases are associated with significant social impacts from discrimination, both for individuals and for society. Greenwald's team documented examples such as differences in racial profiling by police in NYC or police willingness to use lethal force (Price & Payton, 2017). Given its theorized ability to expand awareness to include otherwise unconscious and more implicit emotions and reactions, mindfulness is being used to reduce implicit biases associated with oppression in education (Berila, 2016) and discrimination in clinical practice (Burgess et al., 2017) and social work (Wong & Vinsky, 2020), with evidence of reducing implicit age and race biases (Lueke & Gibson, 2015, 2016). In one study, for example, a mindfulness-based training session led to increased control in police responses to Black versus White targets, suggesting increased awareness of and internal readiness to encounter possible biases (Hunsinger et al., 2019).

Other research from Remmers et al. (2018) demonstrated that mindfulness led to higher levels of correspondence between implicit and explicit *negative* (but not positive) moods. Such increased alignment could suggest heightened awareness of the otherwise unconscious emotions of the implicit System 1. By making negative emotions more apparent or explicit, the slow-thinking System 2 remembering self is more in a position to down-regulate such negative emotions, moods, or associations and their possible behavioural impacts. In addition, Rosenstreich and Ruderman (2017) found evidence that mindfulness enhanced sensitivity to feelings at the fringe of consciousness associated with memory retrieval, thereby making practitioners more aware of such liminal feelings to signal that relevant information is available. This reinforces mindfulness' capacity to broaden awareness and increase information about unconscious feelings or emotions to inform conscious and deliberate decision-making. The term "unconscious" signifies that they are outside of functional awareness but nonetheless amenable to being known in awareness, as originally signified by Freud who coined the term.

## DUAL PROCESSING THEORIES

Dual-process theories represent a range of cognitive processes that appear to fall into two distinct yet interrelated cognitive processing systems. Indeed, the variation and scope of what is included in each system according to authors and contexts make it difficult to define the two systems in a way that captures the variation. One system is slower and more conscious and deliberate, involving thinking and decision-making (System 2); the other system is connected to autonomic functions and fast, habitual thinking often relegated to the unconscious (System 1). Some differentiate the latter from a third processing bundle representing autonomic, sensorimotor, neurobiological, and viscero-somatic processes not directly accessible to conscious awareness (System 3). These interconnected systems – two associated with conscious and one with non-conscious sources of experience and of the self – correspond with Vago and Silbersweig's (2012) conception of three iterations of what constitutes the autonomous self in their S-ART theory presented in the last chapter: the narrative self (NS) of System 2; the experiential phenomenological self (EPS) of System 1 associated with interpreting autonomic and environmental information into experiences; and the enactive experiential self (EES) of System 3, with direct structural coupling between the environment and organisms with the associated biological informational exchanges.

Overall, across varied manifestations, dual processing theories propose two general forms of cognitive processing associated with conscious awareness: A voluntary and conscious processing mode involving reasoning and language-mediated thought and a pre- or un-conscious mode (i.e., capable of being experienced or recognized but not) that involves more automatic or involuntary processes. These two systems interact together in relation to a third involving underlying non-conscious body-brain and sensorimotor processing systems that function outside of the scope of conscious awareness and are known only through inference, scientific inference in particular, rather than through direct experience.

## Dual-Process Theory: Thinking Fast/Thinking Slow

Kahneman and Tversky applied psychology to economic decision-making to arrive at this theory, for which Kahneman was awarded the Nobel Prize for Economics in 2002. They demonstrated that much of human decision-making is not rational and reasoned as self-interest but rather the result of habitual, fast-thinking presumptions that are often biased, in error, and against self-interest (System 1). This refuted key assumptions at the time in micro-economic theory like the assumption of the rational consumer. More importantly, it strongly pointed to the problems associated with relying on intuitive, automatic, and quick judgements that can obscure cognitive errors or biases.

## The IR/RR Dual-Process Model

Barsalou (2017) applied an adapted dual-process theory to traditional mindfulness and contemplative practices. He acknowledged concerns that dual-process theories unjustifiably reify System 1 and 2 processes, each of which involves highly diverse functions that cannot be simplified as originating within the same fixed system. Instead, he suggested that it is more accurate to think of System 1 as an *Involuntary Initial Response (IR)*, where the lion's share of experience is generated, and System 2 as an *Optional Regulatory Response (RR)* involving the voluntary regulation of IRs using a range of metacognitive and regulatory abilities and strategies. He mapped this dual-process model onto Buddhist or traditional views of the mind and how it might be corrected through mindfulness and related contemplative practices. He identified sources of mental distress associated with IRs, including problematic feeling tones associated with desire (pos.), aversion (neg.), or ignoring (neutral); negative or destructive emotions; illusory self-centredness; and distracted or wandering attention. There are a number of RR strategies used to down-regulate these problems, including inhibition or suppression, mindfulness, reappraisal, etc., but RR strategies can exacerbate the distress. According to Barsalou, mindfulness uses short-term and long-term strategies to transform these IR-linked problems into experiences more conducive to well-being, such as compassion, acceptance, joy, concentration or calm, and generosity, with the ultimate aim to turn these RR strategies into habitual, automatic IRs.

## Interacting Cognitive Subsystems (ICS) and Processing Mode Theories

To account for the role of rumination in depression and its adaptive or maladaptive outcomes, Teasdale and Barnard (1993) proposed the *Interacting Cognitive Subsystems (ICS) Theory* to describe two qualitatively distinct yet interacting cognitive subsystems interpreting meaning out of lower-level non-conscious codes relayed from sensory data. These two subsystems represent different levels of meaning, referred to, respectively, as *implicational* and *propositional* meaning. *Implicational meanings* are the meanings presented in consciousness that derive from direct sensory information. These are combined with the accrued patterns and themes developed across experience that shape the identity, concepts, and meanings ascribed to experience. Such meaning, sometimes referred to as "hot" knowledge (System 1), presents in consciousness as intuition or a gut sense that derives from direct perception or experience free of abstract conceptual elaboration. In contrast, *propositional meanings* derive from encoded explicit conceptual meanings that can be represented in language. This type of meaning can be described grammatically in a sentence and is sometimes referred to as "cold" knowledge (System 2).

Watkins (2008) proposed a parallel theory to ICS as part of control theory, the *Processing Mode Theory*, which shares an emphasis on two distinct systems, one concrete and the other abstract. Concrete processing associated with implicational meaning involves *How* questions, such as "How did I get these depression systems?" Abstract processing associated with propositional meaning involves *Why* questions, such as "Why did I get these depression systems?" Watkins and Baracaia (2002), for example, found that people recovering from depression faced impaired social problem-solving when induced to ruminate using an abstract mode of processing or *Why* prompt versus a concrete mode of processing or *How* prompt. Watkins (2015) conducted an analytical review demonstrating that the abstract ruminative processing of self-focused, everyday concerns reduced responsiveness to the environment and interpersonal concerns and increased the melancholia associated with depression.

Both ICS and processing mode theories hypothesize that there are two modes of experience, one more sensory, concrete, and experiential that draws on specific and particular information arising through direct perception and the other more abstract, conceptual, and language-based that forms generalizations across time and experiences to form inferences or ideas. Furthermore, these have been linked to specific neurobiological networks of self-focus in rumination described previously, the experiential-concrete associated with an experiential self and the conceptual-abstract with a narrative self. With mindfulness, these two networks decouple as activity decreases in the abstracting and generalizing narrative complex and increases in the more concrete, sensorial experiential system. These changes are hypothesized to explain the reduction in negative rumination and depression associated with mindfulness. In mindfulness practice, this points to the critical role of learning to shift from ruminative thinking to sensation (See Textbox 10.3).

## FIVE FACETS OF MINDFULNESS QUESTIONNAIRE (FFMQ)

In addition to MAAS (last chapter), another key operational theory or definition of mindfulness is the FFMQ. These operationalized scales embody theoretical constructs of the concept of mindfulness. Formed through a factor analysis of an item pool of five other mindfulness measurement tools, the FFMQ identified five factors that emerged as distinct yet valid components of cognitive skills in mindfulness. Whereas MAAS focuses on awareness of the present, the FFMQ focuses on five distinct cognitive abilities associated with mindfulness. In Park et al.'s (2013) review of ten scales across 79 studies, the MAAS was used the most but the FFMQ had the highest rating. Also, the *observing* questions have been found to be less accurate with non-meditators than with meditators. The five components are as follows:

- *Observing* involves attending to sensory information with varying focus, duration, and scope;
- *Describing* involves the ability to recognize, recall, and represent experience in language with varying accuracy and detail;
- *Acting with awareness* involves the ability to practise mindfulness while engaged in activities of varying complexity and demand;
- *Non-judging of inner experience* involves a state of interest in all experience free of over-identification and varying in degrees of acceptance, openness, decentering, and equanimity; and,
- *Non-reactivity to inner experience* involves the ability to respond more deliberately and with the intention to whatever experiences arise in the mind, varying in the degree of self-regulation of both emotion and behavioural responses to emotion.

In MBTL, the value of the FFMQ is not so much as a measurement tool as an operationalized set of observable features of mindfulness that can be explicitly taught or learned. In this respect, it tells teachers what component skills to look for in learners as they engage in mindfulness training. For example, the practice outlined in Textbox 10.3 below can be taught as a strategy to improve both observing and acting with awareness as a combined formal and informal practice. Such metacognitive reflection is part of what mindfulness and MBTL promote as autonomous self-regulation.

## TEXTBOX 10.3 EXEMPLAR OR CASE:

### Informal Mindfulness Practice: *Mindful Hands*

**Purpose**: This informal practice is an easy mindfulness anchor to the body so as to remember to practice mindfulness outside of formal practice.

- Anchors attention in the body to support informal mindfulness (*FFMQ: acting with awareness*).
- More trauma-sensitive than other anchors in that the breath is more introspective and can trigger anxiety v. anchoring on hands.
- Regulates attention away from rumination and towards bodily sensations (ICS/ Processing Mode Theory)

**Context**: The hands punch above their size in the sensorimotor cortex (e.g., sensory-motor cortical homunculi), making them an ideal anchor for attention. Also, they seem to be a more reliable anchor than the breath for use as a Window of Tolerance default practice during dysregulation.

**Practice**: Below are the key steps, which are intended to be practised continuously as an informal practice throughout the day.

1. **As soon as you wake up, gathering attention in the hands**, as if catching attention or awareness there, noticing them first as entire hands, then in more detail (fingertips, fingers, and thumbs, etc.). An option is to touch the tips of the second fingers to the thumbs to increase the stimulation.
2. **Holding and returning attention** to the hands throughout the day. As attention drifts, recollecting the hands and returning the mind there while carrying on with the day.
3. **Noticing** how the hands necessarily bring a non-judgmental, present-moment focus, noting as well what else can be experienced in this present-moment awareness of the hands and what is excluded.

**Inquiry**: Focusing inquiry on tracking the quality and duration of attention on the hands through the day. What happened when attention shifted away from the hands v. when the hands were remembered?

**Adaptations**: The most stimulating parts of the hand are the fingertips. Bringing and holding attention there, a practitioner will soon notice changes in sensations – often tingling and warmth. These experiences may be associated with increased vaso-dilation, which is why it was once used as a bio-feedback technique with migraine sufferers. This practice and investigation are interesting for noticing how bringing attention to the body is not neutral – it can actually alter physiological functions.

## CONCLUSION

This chapter presented key theories used to explain how mindfulness affects key cognitive functions. These included discussions of how mindfulness is construed to correct or affect cognitive biases; how mindfulness works with the theorized dual processing of cognition; and how mindfulness is operationalized in the FFMQ as observing, describing, acting, non-judging, and non-reacting. These are summarized in Table 10.2.

No one theory offers a comprehensive theory of mindfulness or MBTL. Instead, these theories together provide a nested series of theories used to organize evidence and inquiry into the explanatory mechanisms and effects of mindfulness on wellbeing. Each, in turn, offers clear implications for how it is best taught and learned (see Figure 10.1). Although the MMT integrates many levels, it falls short of accounting for the full significance of mindfulness and wellbeing for education, adaptation, and learning. A final integrative theory is needed to return to the embodied nature of mindfulness and its relevance to embodied wellbeing. This calls for a theory that might account for the evolutionary significance of mindfulness and MBTL as a process of lifelong learning and creative adaptation. This final step towards a more comprehensive, evolutionarily-significant scientific theory of MBTL to better accounts for its feedback loop to embodied biological systems is important to complete the journey of secular-scientific mindfulness as a consistent ecological systems theory of cognition. Yet, given that the evidentiary bases are not yet there, it is a work in progress to challenge us as we move forward.

**Table 10.2** Summary of Cognitive-Related Theories (presented in Chapter 10)

| *Theory/Concept* | *Implication/Example* |
|---|---|
| Mindfulness in... | |
| **Cognitive Bias Reduction** | |
| Affective Biases | Positivity biases<br>Negativity biases |
| Attentional Biases | Threat bias<br>Experiential avoidance<br>Conflict monitoring and detection |
| Interpretational Biases | Aaron Beck's ten types (see Table 10.1, p. 11) |
| Memory Biases | State dependent memory<br>Intrusive memory and dissociative amnesia |
| Self-Referencing Biases | Narrative self-referencing (system) v.<br>Experiential self-referencing (system) |
| Implicit Cognition/Associational Biases | |
| **Dual Processing Theories** | |
| Dual-Process Theory | Thinking Fast (System 1)<br>Thinking Slow (System 2) |
| IR/RR Dual Process Model | Initial Involuntary Response<br>Optional Regulatory Response |
| ICS/Processing Mode Theories | Concrete, sensed experience – *implicational meanings*<br>Abstract, language-mediated experience – *propositional* |
| **FFMQ (Five Facets of Mindfulness)** | |
| Observing | Noticing experiences and features of experience |
| Describing | Using language to recognize and represent experience |
| Acting with Awareness | Applying mindfulness in activities |
| Non-judging of Inner Experience | Accepting all experiences with equal interest and attention |
| Non-reactivity to Inner Experience | Refraining from reacting to experiences in habitual ways |

# REFERENCES

Agerström, J., & Rooth, D. (2010). The role of automatic obesity stereotypes in real hiring discrimination. *Journal of Applied Psychology*, *96*, 790–805. https://doi.org/10.1037/a0021594.

Barrett, L. (2017). *How emotions are made: The secret life of the brain*. Mariner Books / HarperCollins.

Barsalou, L. (2017). Understanding contemplative practices from the perspective of dual-process theories. In J. Kerremans & E. Papies (Eds.), *Mindfulness in social psychology* (pp. 30–49). Routledge.

Batchelor, M. (2019). Mindfulness theory: Feeling tones (*vedanas*) as a useful framework for research. *Current Opinion in Psychology*, *28*, 20–22. https://doi.org/10.1016/j.copsyc.2018.10.002.

Beck, A. (1963). Thinking and depression: I. Idiosyncratic content and cognitive distortions. *Archives of General Psychiatry*, *9*(4), 324–333.

Beck, A. (1967). *Depression: Clinical, experimental, and theoretical aspects.* University of Pennsylvania Press.
Beck, A. (1976). *Cognitive therapy and the emotional disorders.* Meridiam.
Berila, B. (2016). *Integrating mindfulness into anti-oppression pedagogy: Social justice in higher education.* Routledge.
Bower, G. (1981). Mood and memory. *American Psychologist, 36*(2), 129–148. https://doi.org/10.1037/0003-066X.36.2.129.
Brewin, C. Dalgleish, T., & Joseph, S. (1996). A dual representation theory of post-traumatic stress disorder. *Psychological Review, 103*(4), 67–685. https://doi.org/10.1037/0033-295x.103.4.670.
Brewin, C., Gregory, J., Lipton, M., & Burgess, N. (2010). Intrusive images in psychological disorders: Characteristics, neural mechanisms, and treatment implications. *Psychological Review, 117*(1), 210–232. https://doi.org/10.1037/a0018113.
Britton, W. (2019). Can mindfulness be too much of a good thing? The value of a middle way. *Current Opinion in Psychology, 28*, 159–165. https://doi.org/10.1016/j.copsyc.2018.12.011.
Brown, K., Goodman, R. Ryan, R., & Analayo, B. (2016). Mindfulness enhances episodic memory performance: Evidence from a multimethod investigation. *PLoS ONE, 11*(17), e0153309. https://doi.org/10.1371/journal.pone.0160280.
Burgess, D., Beach, M., & Saha, S. (2017). Mindfulness practice: A promising approach to reducing the effects of clinician implicit bias on patients. *Patient Education and Counselling, 100*(2), 372–376. https://doi.org/10.1016/j.pec.2016.09.005
Chiesa, A., Serretti, A., & Jakobsen, J. (2013). Mindfulness: Top-down or bottom-up emotion regulation strategy? *Clinical Psychology Review, 33*(1), 82–96. https://doi.org/10.1016/j.cpr.2012.10.006.
Cisler, J., Bacon, A., & Williams, N. (2009). Phenomenological characteristics of attentional biases towards threat: A critical review. *Cognitive Therapy Research, 33*, 221–234. https://doi.org/10.1007/s10608-007-9161-y.
Cisler, J., & Koster, E. (2010). Mechanisms of attentional biases towards threat in the anxiety disorders: An integrative review. *Clinical Psychology Review, 30*(2), 203–216. https://doi.org/10.1016/j.cpr.2009.11.003.
Costa, A., Caltagirone, C., & Carlesimo, G. (2018). Prospective memory functioning in individuals with Parkinson's disease: A systematic review. *The Clinical Neuropsychologist, 32*(5), 937–959. https://doi.org/10.1080/13854046.2017.1407457.
Cummins, R., & Nistico, H. (2002). Maintaining life satisfaction: The role of positive cognitive bias. *Journal of Happiness Studies, 3*, 37–69. https://doi.org/10.1080/13854046.2017.1407457.
Davis, J., & Thompson, E. (2015). Developing attention and decreasing affective bias. In K. Brown, D. Creswell, & R. Ryan (Eds.), *Handbook of mindfulness: Theory, research, and practice.* The Guilford Press.
Everaert, J., Bronstein, M., Cannon, T., & Joormann, J. (2018). Looking through tinted glasses: Depression and social anxiety are related to both interpretation biases and inflexible negative interpretations. *Clinical Psychological Science, 6*(4), 517–528. https://doi.org/10.1177/2167702617747968.
Everaert, J., & Koster, E. (2020). The interplay among attention, interpretation, and memory biases in depression: Revisiting the combined bias hypothesis. In T. Aue & H. Okon-Singer (Eds.), *Cognitive biases in health and psychiatric disorders: Neurophysiological foundations* (pp. 193–213). Elsevier/Academic Press. https://doi.org/10.1016/C2018-0-00401-6.
Everaert, J., Podina, I., & Koster, E. (2017). A comprehensive meta-analysis of interpretation biases in depression. *Clinical Psychology Review, 58*, 33–48. https://doi.org/10.1016/j.cpr.2017.09.005.
Fabro, A., Crescentini, C., Matiz, A., Clarici, A., & Fabro, F. (2017). Effects of mindfulness meditation on conscious and non-conscious components of the mind. *Applied Science, 7*(4), 349. https://doi.org/10.3390/app7040349.

Farb, N., Segal, Z., Mayberg, H., Bean, J., McKeon, D., Fatima, Z., & Anderson, A. (2007). Attending to the present: Mindfulness meditation reveals distinct neural modes of self-reference. *Social Cognitive and Affective Neuroscience*, *2*, 313–322. https://doi.org/10.1093/scan/nsm030.

Ford, C., & Shook, N. (2019). Negative cognitive bias and perceived stress: Independent mediators of the relation between mindfulness and emotional distress. *Mindfulness*, *10*, 100–110. https://doi.org/10.1007/s12671-018-0955-7.

Forner, C. (2017). *Dissociation, mindfulness, and creative meditations: Trauma-informed practices to facilitate growth*. Routledge.

Garland, E., Farb, N., Goldin, P., & Fredrickson, B. (2015). Mindfulness broadens awareness and builds eudaimonic meaning: A process model of mindful positive emotion regulation. *Psychological Inquiry*, *26*(4), 293–314. https://doi.org/10.1080/1047840X.2015.1064294.

Garland, E., Hanley, A., Baker, A., & Howard, M. (2017a). Biobehavioral mechanism of mindfulness as a treatment for chronic stress: An RDoC perspective. *Chronic Stress*, *1*, 1–14. https://doi.org/10.1177/2470547017711912.

Garland, E., Hanley, A. L., Goldin, P., & Gross, J. (2017b). Testing the mindfulness-to-meaning theory: Evidence for mindful positive emotion regulation from a reanalysis of longitudinal data. *PLoS One*, *12*(12), e0187727. https://doi.org/10.1371/journal.pone.0187727.

Greenwald, A., Banaji, M., & Nosek, B. (2015). Statistically small effects of the Implicit Association Test can have societally large effects. *Journal Personality and Social Psychology*, *108*, 553–561. https://doi.org/10.1037/pspa0000016.

Greenwald, A., McGhee, D., & Schwartz, J. (1998). Measuring individual differences in implicit cognition: The implicit association test. *Journal of Personality and Social Psychology*, *74*(6), 1464–1480.

Greenwald, A. G., Poehlman, T. A., Uhlmann, E. L., & Banaji, M. J. (2009). Understanding and using the implicit association test: III. Meta-analysis of predictive validity. *Journal of Personality and Social Psychology*, *97*, 17–41. https://doi.org/10.1037/a0015575.

Hallion, L., & Ruscio, A. (2011). A meta-analysis of the effect of cognitive bias modification on anxiety and depression. *Psychological Bulletin*, *137*(6), 940–958. https://doi.org/10.1037/a0024355.

Harmond-Jones, E., Gable, P., & Price, T., (2013). Does negative affect always narrow and positive affect always broaden the mind? Considering the influence of motivational intensity on cognitive scope. *Current Directions in Psychological Science*, *22*(4), 301–307. https://doi.org/10.1177/0963721413481353.

Hawkins, C., & Nosek, B. (2012). Motivated independence? Implicit party identity predicts political judgments among self-proclaimed independents. *Personality and Social Psychology Bulletin*, *38*, 1441–1455. https://doi.org/10.1177/0146167212452313.

Hayes-Skelton, S., & Eustic, E. (2020). Experiential avoidance. In J. Abramowitz & S. Blakey (Eds.), *Clinical handbook of fear and anxiety: Maintenance processes and treatment mechanisms* (pp. 115–131). American Psychological Association. https://doi.org/10.1037/0000150-007.

Hunsinger, M., Christopher, M., & Schmidt, A. (2019). Mindfulness training, implicit bias, and force response decision-making. *Mindfulness*, *10*, 2555–2566. https://doi.org/10.1007/s12671-019-01213-8.

Jones, E., & Sharpe, L. (2017). Cognitive bias modification: A review of meta-analyses. *Journal of Affective Disorders*, *223*, 175–183. https://doi.org/10.1016/j.jad.2017.07.034.

Kahneman, D. (2011). *Thinking, fast and slow*. Doubleday Canada.

Koster, E., Fox, E., & MacLeod, C. (2009). Introduction to the special section on cognitive bias modification in emotional disorders. *Journal of Abnormal Psychology*, *118*(1), 1–4.

Kral, T., Schuyler, B., Mumford, J., Rosenkranz, M., Lutz. A., & Davidson, R. (2018). Impact of short- and long-term mindfulness meditation training on amygdala reactivity to emotional stimuli. *NeuroImage*, *181*, 301–313. https://doi.org/10.1016/j.neuroimage.2018.07.013.

Kubota, R., & Nixon, R. (2020). The effect of mindfulness training on ruminating and intrusions after analogue trauma. *Australian Psychologist*, *55*(2), 108–120. https://doi.org/10.1111/ap.12410.

Lee, J., Mathews, A., Shergill, S., & Yiend, J. (2016). Magnitude of negative interpretation bias depends on severity of depression. *Behaviour Research and Therapy*, *83*, 26–34. https://doi.org/10.1016/j.brat.2016.05.007.

Lee, S., Rogge, R. D., Reis, H. T. (2010). Assessing the seeds of relationship decay: Using implicit evaluations to detect the early stages of disillusionment. *Psychological Science*, *21*, 857–864. http://doi.org/10.1177/0956797610371342.

Lindsay, E., Chin, B., Greco, C., Young, S., Brown, K., Wright, A., Smyth, J., Burkett, D., & Creswell, J. (2018). How mindfulness training promotes positive emotions: Dismantling acceptance training skills training in two randomized controlled trials. *Journal of Personality and Social Psychology*, *115*(6), 944–973. https://doi.org/10.1037/pspa0000134.

Lueke, A., & Gibson, B. (2015). Mindfulness meditation reduces implicit age and race bias: The role of reduced automaticity of responding. *Social Psychology and Personality Science*, *6*(3), 284–291. https://doi.org/10.1177/1948550614559651

Lueke, A., & Gibson, B. (2016). Brief mindfulness meditation reduces discrimination. *Psychology of Consciousness Theory*, *3*(1), 34–44. https://doi.org/10.107/cns0000081

Mayer, B., Polak, M., & Remmerswaal, D. (2019). Mindfulness, interpretation bias, and levels of anxiety and depression: Two mediation studies. *Mindfulness*, *10*, 55–65. https://doi.org/10.1007/s12671-018-0946-8.

Mazza, S., Frot, M., & Rey, A. (2018). A comprehensive literature review of chronic pain and memory. *Progress in Neuropsychopharmacology & Biological Psychiatry*, *87*, 183–192. https://doi.org/10.1016/j.pnpbp.2017.08.006.

Nejad, A., Fossati, P., & Lemogne, C. (2013). Self-referential processing, rumination, and cortical midline structures in major depression. *Frontiers in Human Neuroscience*, *7*, Article 666, 1–9. https://doi.org/10.3389/fnhum.2013.00666.

Nieto, I., Robles, E., & Vazquez, C. (2020). Self-reported cognitive biases in depression: A meta-analysis. *Clinical Psychology Review*, *82*, 101934. https://doi.org/10.1016/j.cpr.2020.101934.

Nock, M., Park, J., Finn, C., Deliberto, T., Dour, H., & Banaji, M. (2010). Measuring the suicidal mind: Implicit cognition predicts suicidal behavior. *Psychological Science*, *21*(4), 511–517. https://doi.org/10.1177/0956797610364762.

Okon-Singer, H. (2018). The role of attention bias to threat in anxiety: Mechanisms, modulators and open questions. *Current Opinion in Behavioral Sciences*, *19*, 26–30. https://doi.org/10.1016/j.cobeha.2017.09.008.

Oswald, F., Mitchell, G., Blanton, H., Jaccard, J., & Tetlock, P. (2013). Predicting ethnic and racial discrimination: A meta-analysis of IAT criterion studies. *Journal of Personality and Social Psychology*, *105*, 171–92. https://doi.org/10.1037/a0032734.

Park, T., Reilly-Spong, M., & Gross, C. (2013). Mindfulness: A systematic review of instruments to measure emergent patient-reported outcome (PRO). *Quality of Life Research*, *22*(10), 2639–2659. https://doi.org/10.1007/s11136-013-0395-8.

Payne, A., Kralj, A., Young, J., & Meiser-Stedman, R. (2019). The prevalence of intrusive memories in adult depression: A meta-analysis. *Journal of Affective Disorders*, *253*, 193–202. https://doi.org/10.1016/j.jad.2019.04.055.

Pool, E., Brosch, T., Delplanque, S., & Sander, D. (2016). Attentional bias for positive emotional stimuli: A meta-analytic investigation. *Psychological Bulletin*, *142*(1), 79–106.

Price, J., & Payton, E. (2017). Implicit racial bias and police use of lethal force: Justifiable homicide or potential discrimination? *Journal of African American Studies, 21*, 674–683. https://doi.org/10.1007/s12111-017-9383-3.

Radulovic, J., Lee, R., & Ortony, A. (2018). State-dependent memory: Neurobiological advance and prospects for translation to dissociate amnesia. *Frontiers in Behavioral Neuroscience, 12*, 259. https://doi.org/10.3389/fnbeh.2018.00259.

Remmers, C., Zimmermann, J., Buxton, A., Unger, H., Koole, S., Knaevelsrud, C., & Michalak, J. (2018). Emotionally aligned: Preliminary results on the effects of a mindfulness-based intervention for depression on congruence between implicit and explicit mood. *Clinical Psychology and Psychotherapy, 25*(6), 818–826. https://doi.org/10.1002/cpp.2317.

Reuben, E., Sanza, P., & Zingales, L. (2014). How stereotypes impair women's careers in science. *Proceedings of the National Academy of Sciences, 111*, 4403–4408. https://doi.org/10.1073/pnas.1314788111.

Rosenstreich, E., & Ruderman, L. (2017). Dual-process perspective on mindfulness, memory, and consciousness. *Mindfulness, 8*, 505–516. https://doi.org/10.1007/s12671-016-0627-4.

Ruth, M. (2020). Cognitive bias. In *Encyclopedia of health*. Salem Press.

Sabin, J., Marini, M., & Nosek, B. (2012). Implicit and explicit anti-fat bias among a large sample of medical doctors by BMI, race/ethnicity and gender. *PLoS ONE, 7*(11), e48448. https://doi.org/10.1371/journal.pone.0048448.

Schumer, M., Lindsay, E., & Creswell, J. (2018). Brief mindfulness training for negative affectivity: A systematic review and meta-analysis. *Journal of Consulting and Clinical Psychology, 86*(7), 569–583. https://doi.org/10.1037/ccp0000324.

Segal, Z., Anderson, A., Gulamani, T., Williams, L., Desormeau, P., Ferguson, A., Walsh, K., & Farb, N. (2019). Practice of therapy acquired regulatory skills and depressive relapse/recurrence prophylaxis following cognitive therapy or mindfulness based cognitive therapy. *Journal of Consulting and Clinical Psychology, 87*(2), 161–170. https://doi.org/10.0137/ccp0000351.

Sharot, T. (2011). *The optimism bias: A tour of the irrationally positive brain*. Knopf Canada.

Smigielski, L., Scheidegger, M., Kometer, M., & Vollenweider, F. (2019). Psilocybin-assisted mindfulness training modulates self-consciousness and brain default mode network connectivity with lasting effects. *NeuroImage, 196*(1), 207–215. https://doi.org/10.1016/j.neuroimage.2019.04.009.

Smith, G., & Hartelius, G. (2020). Resolution of dissociated ego states relieves flashback-related symptoms in combat-related PTSD: A brief mindfulness based intervention. *Military Psychology, 32*(2), 135–148. https://doi.org/10.1080/08995605.2019.1654292

Spinhoven, P., Klein, N., Kennis, M., Cramer, A., Siegle, G., Cuijpers, P., Ormel, J., Hollon, S., & Bocktine, C. (2018). The effects of cognitive-behavior therapy for depression or repetitive negative thinking: A meta-analysis. *Behaviour Research and Therapy, 106*, 71–85. https://doi.org/10.1016/j.brat.2018.04.002.

Teasdale, J., & Barnard, P. (1993). *Affect, cognition, and change*. Erlbaum.

Vago, D., & Nakamura, Y. (2011). Selective attentional bias towards pain-related threat in fibromyalgia: Preliminary effects of mindfulness meditation training. *Cognitive Therapy and Research, 35*(6). 581–594. https://doi.org/10.1007/s10608-011-9391-x.

Vago, D., & Silbersweig, D. (2012). Self-awareness, self-regulation, and self-transcendences (S-ART): A framework for understanding the neurobiological mechanisms of mindfulness. *Frontiers of Human Neuroscience, 25*. https://doi.org/10.3389/fnhum.2012.00296.

Watkins, E. (2008). Constructive and unconstructive repetitive thought. *Psychological Bulletin, 134*(2), 163–206. https://doi.org/10.1037/0033-2909.134.2.163.

Watkins, E. (2015). Mindfulness in the context of processing mode theory. In K. Brown, D. Creswell, & R. Ryan (Eds.), *Handbook of mindfulness: Theory, research, and practice* (pp. 90–111). The Guilford Press.

Watkins, E., & Baracaia, S. (2002). Rumination and social problem-solving in depression. *Behaviour Research and Therapy, 40*, 1179–1189. https://doi.org/10.1016/S0005-7967(01)00098-5.

Westgate, E., Riskind, R., & Nosek, B. (2015). Implicit preferences for straight people over lesbian women and gay men weakened from 2006 to 2013. *Collabra, 1*(1). https://doi.org/10.1525/collabra.18.

Williams, T. J., Segal, Z., & Soulsby, J. (2009). Mindfulness-based cognitive therapy reduces overgeneral autobiographical memory in formerly depressed patients. *Journal of Abnormal Psychology, 109*(1), 150–155. https://doi.org/10.1037/0021-843X.109.1.150.

Wong, Y., & Vinsky, J. (2020). Beyond implicit bias: Embodied cognition, mindfulness, and critical reflective practice in social work. *Australian Social Work, 74*(2), 186–197. https://doi.org/10.1080/0312407X.2020.1850816

# CHAPTER 11

# BUDDHIST THEORIES OF MINDFULNESS AND LEARNING

This chapter introduces Buddhist theories of mindfulness and learning that are particularly relevant to secular-scientific mindfulness. In using the term theory, we do not mean to argue in favour of Buddhist exceptionalism, that is, that Buddhism is a science of mind rather than a religion, a perspective critiqued well by Thompson (2020). Instead, we use the term theory to reflect their uses as predictive tools that derive from empirical sources, from evidence rather than a sacred text or mere belief, and from evidence in the form of observed and described experiences arising through introspective mindfulness practices. We focus on Buddhist theories of mindfulness explicitly, and how mindfulness contributes to learning, the end of which is represented in Buddhism as awakening. We selected three theories to focus on, which are common to all schools of Buddhism as they originate in early Buddhist texts and practices: The four foundations of mindfulness; the seven factors of awakening; and the three characteristics.

## FOUR FOUNDATIONS OF MINDFULNESS

The Four Foundations of Mindfulness constitute the core structure of the *Satipatthana-sutta*, one of the earliest texts written to represent the original oral teachings of the Buddha. Together, the four constitute a theory of how mindfulness and its core objects together provide a comprehensive path or education. As Analayo (2018) points out in his exegesis of the *Satipatthana-sutta*, mindfulness has three defining features: It is intentionally cultivated (learned); it co-exists with the use of concepts (so is both perceptually and conceptually mediated); and it involves proactive, but not retroactive, memory, that is, paying attention so as to recognize experiences as they arise in the future. In all four of the foundations, mindfulness is described as attending internally, externally, and both internally and externally, which Analayo interprets as combining introspective awareness of oneself; external attention on others; and/or both as awareness of oneself and others.

The four foundations of mindfulness refer to what we pay attention to and in what sequence in order to foster the kinds of insights that generate existential awakening and wellbeing. As Analayo (2018) suggests, mindfulness alone is insufficient without the wisdom that generates insight. The four foundations define the process by which the ground for such wisdom can ripen. The four foundations are mindfulness of the body; feelings; mind; and phenomena. Although often separated into discreet types and forms of practices, they can be cultivated sequentially within some integrated practices, such as *anapanasati* (mindfulness of breathing); open awareness; and body awareness (Analayo, 2018, 2019).

### Mindfulness of the Body

Mindfulness of the body is the first of the four foundations, this position signifying that it is also the foundation of the other three. The varied practices and methods used to attend to the body mindfully offer a way to anchor the mind in the present. This process and state of anchoring attention and awareness in the embodied, sensed present-moment goes to the

DOI: 10.4324/9781003182467-15

heart of mindfulness. In this respect, embodiment is not just an effect of mindfulness; it *is* mindfulness. There are two types of mindfulness practices associated with the body: mindfulness of breathing; mindfulness of the whole body; and mindfulness of parts of the body.

## *Mindfulness of the Whole Body*

Mindfulness of the whole body is accomplished through attending to the breath; bodily postures; and physical activities. In this way, mindfulness of the whole body provides an integrative form of mindfulness insofar as the breath, posture, and activities are constantly available for the mind to anchor in the present.

The first mindfulness of the body practice introduced in the Satipatthana Sutta is mindfulness of breathing. The meditator is directed to investigate or know the body while experiencing it in two steps - first attending to the breath and then knowing (or understanding) it. Furthermore, the attention is explicitly directed to inhaling and exhaling – as a short breath or a long breath. The meditor is then instructed to shift from this focus on the duration of the breath to the whole body breathing and then to calming the activities of the body. The sutta explicitly instructs the meditator to contemplate the body in the body internally, externally, and both internally and externally.

Mindfulness of posture, the third mindfulness of the whole body practice, does not require that we hold the body in controlled or special postures. As Analayo (2018) suggests, “Such embodied awareness does not need to interfere with other tasks and activities. Instead it can accompany them” (p. 13). As an embodied awareness of posture, it is not focused but open and diffuse, not lax but attentive and aware without being vigilant. Such an awareness requires training, for without training, the mind tends to either overly focus or ignore. Such an awareness doesn’t merely observe experience passively, it recognizes the whole-body posture as it arises. According to the *Satipatthana-sutta*, translated by Analayo:

> When walking, one knows: ‘I am walking;’ or when standing, one knows: ‘I am standing;’ or when sitting, one knows ‘I am sitting;’ or when lying down, one knows: ‘I am lying down;’ or, however the body is disposed, one knows it accordingly.
>
> *(p. 12)*

The third approach to cultivating mindfulness of the whole body is through mindfulness during activities and movement. This could be formal movement activities like yoga or informal activities associated with living. Again, this is described explicitly in the original text of the *Satipatthana-sutta*, translated by Analayo (2018), which draws attention to how mindfulness goes beyond merely observing activities to acting with *clear knowing*:

> When going forward and returning, one acts clearly knowing; when looking ahead and looking away, one acts clearly knowing; when flexing and extending [the limbs] one acts clearly knowing; when wearing the outer robe and [other] robes and [carrying] the bowl one acts clearly knowing; when eating, drinking, consuming food, and tasting, one acts clearly knowing; when defecating and urinating, one acts clearly knowing; when walking, standing, sitting, falling asleep, waking up, talking, and keeping silent, one acts clearly knowing.
>
> *(p. 15)*

## *Mindfulness of the Body in Parts*

In contrast to the anchoring practices of mindfulness on the whole body, specific formal practices orient on mindfulness of the body in parts. Analayo (2018) breaks these meditations down to meditations on anatomy, the elements, and death, all of which are classic mindfulness practice in traditional Buddhism that served multiple functions. In the first case, in addition to enhancing body awareness, meditation on the anatomical features of the body was done to reduce sensuality and attachment to the body for a largely celibate community of practitioners. There is an explicit intention reflected in this practice, in which the parts of the body are described as *impure* (see below), to cultivate a negative feeling tone with respect to the body and its features. So, whereas the body as a whole can present itself as attractive in consciousness, when broken down into constituent parts with a focus on secretions and functions, this apparent or illusory impression is interrupted. The intention in cultivating a negative feeling tone with respect to parts of the body was to foster renunciation of sensual attachments to the body, both internally (of self) and externally (of others).

In the original text of the *Satipatthana-sutta* with the instructions for mindfulness of the body in parts, we read:

> One examines this same body up from the soles of the feet and down from the top of the hair, enclosed by skin and full of many kinds of impurity: In this body there are head hairs, body hairs, nails, teeth, skin, flesh, sinews, bones, bone-marrow, kidneys, heart, liver, diaphragm, spleen, lungs, bowels, mesentery, contents of the stomach, faeces, bile, phlegm, pus, blood, sweat, fat tears, grease, spittle, snot, oil of the joints, and urine.
>
> *(Analayo, 2018, p. 47)*

Beyond the claim of "impurity," the foregoing description can sound quite clinical and anatomically accurate. This is consistent with the wisdom tradition in Buddhism that attempts to deconstruct into component parts all illusory appearances of the world as they present themselves habitually to consciousness. Seeing component parts is done to represent reality and truth beyond the projected wholeness or integration of permanent and fixed identities. Parsing into parts provides a way for a practitioner to distance, disengage, and disidentify with experience to cultivate the liberating insight of nirvana or emptiness (variously described in different Buddhist schools). It is worth noting how closely this corresponds to the process of parsing experience in MBSR or MBCT, which is done to enhance decentering, the mechanism known to account for much of these programmes' efficacy in the prevention of depressive relapse (Segal et al., 2019). Similarly, the division of mindfulness of the body into contemplations of wholes and parts reflects an important principle of classical mindfulness that continues in the secular-scientific variant: The juxtapositions of awareness of phenomena in ordinary experience and its truth on closer examination or analysis.

The adapted version of this practice, which corresponds more closely to the body scan, is the contemplation of the array of body parts that are available to experience within three categories: As skin, flesh, and bones. The skin provides the experience of the outer perimeter or limit of the body and is most available to awareness. Flesh is more internal but can be directly experienced in the mouth, for example. Even more internal are bones, which are subtler again in how they present in the experience. There are two key differences between the practice of mindfulness of the body as skin, flesh, bones and the practice of viewing the body as more complex anatomical parts. First, the sense of impurity or revulsion is minimized or removed in this practice and, second, it can be done entirely on the basis of what is experienced (i.e., the experiential body) rather than what is analyzed, inferred, conceptually known, or remembered about bodies (i.e., the objective body).

The second approach to contemplating the body in parts is to break it into manifestations of the four elements of earth, water, fire, and air. When done in the context of the body scan of skin, flesh, bones, the skin is used as the manifestation of fire given its sensitivities to temperature; the flesh is the manifestation of water, experienced concretely as saliva in the mouth or as blood pervading organs and muscles – perhaps as throbbing blood vessels or arteries. Bones are the manifestation of solidity, which is the earth element, and air is manifested in breath, digestion, or movement.

The final mindfulness of the body in parts practice is the meditation on death. Given the decomposition and dissolution of the corpse at death, this can be classified as a practice of the mindfulness of the body in parts. It is a key practice associated with meditating on the unpleasant features of the body in classical Buddhism to cultivate sensual renunciation and the motivation to practice. This practice often involved the literal meditation of a corpse in a charnel ground. Yet it also is undertaken to cultivate a sense of mortality or impermanence. For this purpose, Analayo (2018) suggests visualizing the body as a skeleton in conjunction with mindfulness of breathing. Mindfulness of mortality helps to clarify priorities and enhance the value of the present through recognizing its imminent loss and the unpredictability of when death will transpire.

Mindfulness of sensations (*vedana*) is a special case that is variously treated as mindfulness of body or as mindfulness of feeling, the second foundation. For example, attending to sense organs as they sense is an instance of mindfulness of the body. Also, sensation translates external phenomena as information recognizable in the mind or experience. Consequently, sensation becomes a process to observe to witness the communication between the body and of mind. So too are there close links between sensation and sensory experience and motor response systems as mindfulness of bodily activities, as in links between eating and taste, whereby the activity, sense organ, and sensation intertwine in the experience, culminating in digestive activity and the incorporation of the food into the body as nutriment. Although in Sanskrit *vedana* literally means both sensation and feeling, thereby suggesting that it is most closely related to mindfulness of feeling tones, Fleischman (2018) analyzes and interprets the term as *bodily sensations,* based on the Vipassana approach of S.N. Goenka.

## *Embodiment in Vajrayana Buddhism*

Although not commonly thought of as a mindfulness practice, deity yoga in Vajrayana can be viewed through such a lens. Embodiment is still critical in this theory and practice, which gradually developed over time from the four foundations to become more complex. Vajrayana theorizes three co-existing bodies embedded within our one body: the nirmanakaya (emanation body); the sambhogakaya (energy or bliss body); and the dharmakaya (truth body). Mindfulness of the emanation body involves attending to the body as it appears in the world, both objectively and experientially in ordinary consciousness as we move about the world. With the cultivation of an increasingly subtle consciousness or mind, often intentionally through deity yoga visualization practices, the energy or bliss body co-emerges with the emanation body. This bliss body can also be thought of as an imaginary or illusory body insofar as it is not restricted to features of the biological body but can include experienced or imagined forms based more on light, colour, and signs of various embodied expressions of mind. They are bliss or energy bodies because they are intended to cultivate energies or dispositions and to foster unworldly positive feelings associated with bliss. Likewise, subtler experiential bodily features are attended to, like the central and side channels, the chakras, and auras, etc. The third body is the truth body, which co-exists with the other two but without form, signifying the empty or non-inherent nature of all embodied experience. This is most closely akin to mindfulness itself, which is not tethered to an object but open and aware. In Dzogchen texts, for example, it is described as the primordial mind of clear knowing.

## Mindfulness of Feeling (Tones)

*Feeling tones* are equivalent to *affect* in the psychology or science of emotion. Both affect and feeling tones are described as imbuing experience with one of three valences (positive, negative, neutral) with varying intensity levels (low, medium, high) (Barrett, 2017). Although feeling tones are associated with sensory experiences, they can be identified in memories, images, thoughts, and even words (Analayo, 2018). They condition the mind to react to experiences in a habitual way and can spiral into reactive emotions. Suffering is considered to arise from such reactive afflictive emotions, so cultivating equanimity vis-à-vis mindfulness of feeling tones involves taking an equal interest and curious stance towards all experience, whether appearing initially as positive, negative, or neutral.

Given that sensation and feeling tones share the same term in Sanskrit, *vedana*, they are explicitly connected in the four foundations. This relationship is explained best by the Buddhist theory of the twelve links of dependent origination: As an external stimulus contacts a sense faculty, it is filtered and assigned one of three feeling tones – positive, negative, or neutral – in a range of levels of intensity (Batchelor, 2020). Over time, this feeling tone conditions our relationship with the stimulus and its source in the world. According to the theory of the twelve links, this habitual or conditioned response arises from desire and craving, which either reinforces attachment to what is present or to what is imagined or sought after as more desirable than what is present. This *conditioning* process is what gives rise to suffering, thereby implicating the second foundation – mindfulness of feeling tones – as a critical step to move beyond habitual cycles of suffering.

With mindfulness of feelings, as stimuli come into contact with sense faculties and sensory processes, the automaticity and certainty of the habitual evaluations of objects are interrupted. In turn, the subsequent chain of effects on desire, craving, attachment, and becoming are weakened. The habitual reactions (craving, aversion, ignorance) arising from such feeling tones (positive, negative, neutral) are reduced and replaced by equanimity, in which all sensory input gives rise to a kind of equal interest and attention. Such equanimity is not neutral but rather aware, attentive, and a source of unworldly positive regard, which we refer to as *appreciation* but is commonly translated as *joy* (Analayo, 2019; Roth, 2018). With such equanimity, the mind is freed of the downstream effects of suffering arising from compulsive conditioned reactivity. This explains why the state of wellbeing cultivated through mindfulness is referred to as *liberation* in Buddhism, as freedom from conditioning.

According to Buddhism, the conditioned reactivity of feeling tones associated with sensations are equally at play in relation to other people or living beings. Feeling tones ascribed to others leads to effects ranging from interpersonal preferences through to indifference to hatred through to racial and other forms of implicit biases (Gupta, 2020; Peacock & Batchelor, 2018). Interestingly, the path of compassion in Buddhism, referred to as the *Brahma Vihara* or four divine abodes, culminates in *equanimity*, through a progression from loving-kindness to compassion to sympathetic joy to equanimity. In this context, equanimity refers to a kind of equal regard or appreciation (feeling tone) for friends and intimates, strangers, and enemies. This goes to ethics as well in describing a state of open and equal regard for others that the Dalai Lama (personal communication) described as the ethic he follows as a teacher. Significantly, equanimity is also the final, seventh factor describing how mindfulness leads to awakening in the theory of the seven factors of awakening. In this respect, it is mindfulness of feeling tones and its role in the cultivation of equanimity that best describe the ends of training in both mindfulness and compassion.

Finally, feeling tones are differentiated according to worldly (*samisa*) and unworldly (*niramisa*) variations (Roth, 2018). Worldly feeling tones are defined as those arising in conjunction with sensory experience and desire, as outlined in the twelve links. Unworldly feeling tones, in contrast, are said to arise through mindfulness practice itself and not in dependence on sensory experiences. For example, in the *Anapanasati-sutta*, positive feeling tones such as joy, happiness, and gladdening are described as arising naturally through the practice of mindfulness of breathing (Analayo, 2019). Mindfulness of feeling tones is described as follows in the *Satipatthana-sutta* (Nanamoli & Bodhi, 1995):

> And how bhikkus, does a bhikkhu abide contemplating feelings as feelings? Here, when feeling a pleasant feeling, a bhikkhu understands: 'I feel a pleasant feeling;' when feeling a painful feeling, he understands: 'I feel a painful feeling;' when feeling a neither painful-nor pleasant feeling, he understands: 'I feel a neither painful nor pleasant feeling.' When feeling a worldly pleasant feeling, he understands: 'I feel a worldly pleasant feeling;' when feeling an unworldly pleasant feeling, he understands: 'I feel an unworldly pleasant feeling'...etc.
> *(149–150)*

## Mindfulness of Mind

The third foundation, *mindfulness of mind*, embeds a certain paradox: If all experience is mediated by mind, then is mindfulness of mind not mindfulness itself? Mindfulness of mind is fundamental to the praxis of Buddhism, as evidenced in the opening stanza of an early Buddhist text, *the Dhammapada*, "Mind is the source of all things; great mind; creative mind," or in the purported words of the Buddha on his awakening, "I have found you Oh Builder, you will build no more." As the Buddha here suggests, both the Builder and the process of building are rooted in the mind itself but are obscured in ordinary perception, which leads us to see things as existing more concretely, separately, and inherently than they actually are. Consequently, direct seeing into the constructed nature of experience in and by the mind is said to be *liberating.*

Mindfulness of mind points more narrowly to mind *states*, and often those involving emotions like lust, anger, or mental disturbanced like delusion, but also mental modes of representation, such as thoughts, and mental imagery, as its main objects. Its position as the third foundation signifies that the previous two foundations serve to scaffold the practitioner to recognize subtler objects of attention associated with the mind itself, given that mind and mind states do tend to be more challenging to notice without becoming overwhelmed or deluded than body sensations, sensory experience, and feeling tones. The *Satipatthana-sutta* presents this narrowed view of the third foundation as mindfulness of mind states (Analayo, 2018):

> One knows a mind with lust to be 'a mind with lust;' or one knows a mind without lust to be 'a mind without lust;' or one knows a mind with anger to be 'a mind with anger;' or one knows a mind without anger to be 'a mind without anger;' or one knows a mind with delusion to be 'a mind with delusion;' or one knows a mind without delusion to be 'a mind

> without delusion;' or one knows a contracted mind to be 'a contracted mind;' or one knows a distracted mind to be 'a distracted mind.'
>
> *(p. 127)*

The focus on lust, anger, and delusion illustrates the strong emphasis on being aware of defilements and afflictive emotions and of their absence. Notice, for instance, that it doesn't say "one knows a mind with joy" or "love" but merely a mind *without* lust, anger, delusion, and distraction. Furthermore, unlike secular-scientific praxis, it does not focus on the contents or modes of representation of the mind – e.g., thoughts, emotions, memories, or images. The modes aren't emphasized so much as mind states. Some might be inclined to refer to these identified states as moods or emotions, but that would be distorting. For example, states are closer to behaviour than are moods or emotions, as evidenced by the use of *lust* rather than sensual desire. Also, some explicit mind states are more cognitive or conceptual, such as delusion or distraction. This points to how mindfulness of mind in Buddhist praxis goes centrally to *knowing* (i.e., discerning) *the wholesome from the unwholesome,* using the conventional translation of the phrase. Furthermore, the wholesome is the mere absence of the unwholesome rather than an active state that involves some added qualities. Therefore, it implies that, when freed of unwholesome states, the mind is quite naturally wholesome and imbued with qualities like joy.

As Analayo (2018) points out in the previous passage, the contracted/distracted pairing most likely signifies that the problem is distraction and its absence a positive state: i.e., contraction. Contraction here signifies focus or holding attention. The text continues on to describe mindfulness of mind as expanding to include mindfulness of higher states of mind, described as follows:

> Or one knows a mind that has become great to be 'a mind that has become great;' or one knows a mind that has not become great to be 'a mind that has not become great;' or one knows a surpassable mind to be 'a surpassable mind;' or one knows an unsurpassable mind to be 'an unsurpassable mind;' or one knows a concentrated mind to be 'a concentrated mind;' or one knows a not concentrated mind to be 'a not concentrated mind;' or one knows a liberated mind to be a 'liberated mind;' or one knows a not liberated mind to be 'a not liberated mind.'
>
> *(p. 137)*

Such an awareness of the overall quality, or lack of quality, of the mind is critical given that mindfulness of mind (mind states, dispositions, modes) is at the gateway of action. Without awareness, reactive impulses would tend to carry these states into reactive behaviour or conduct.

## *How to Practise Mindfulness of Mind*

The meditation practices and techniques used to cultivate mindfulness of mind include both noticing and recognizing (i.e., "knowing") experiences of thoughts, emotions, mental imagery, and memories as they arise in the present moment. These are not attended to principally as contents but rather as patterns and qualities discerned across time and at increasing distance from self-identification (i.e., decentred). It is this meta-cognitive function of mindfulness, beyond mere observation, that generates its distinctive effects – what the text refers to as *knowing.* One doesn't just experience, one *knows* one is experiencing something, which implies a subtle level of naming or conceptual engagement. Also, the act of recognition is not entirely open as might be inferred of secular-scientific mindfulness.

The recognition is focused on knowing the wholesome from the unwholesome, with clear implications for the unwholesome to be supplanted by the wholesome. Still, this practice does not suggest how that is to be done, which suggests that, as in secular-scientific mindfulness, there is a theoretical assumption that it is possible to reduce and even eliminate the unwholesome through mere awareness and the natural intention to be free of suffering. Analayo (2018) also specifies opening the heart and the skillful use of labels as noteworthy examples of mindfulness of mind practices (see below).

**Opening the Heart**. This practice involves meditating on kindness and compassion. Although not technically mindfulness practices, they involve the awareness of the mind with respect to empathy and concern for self and others and altering the mind towards such ends. Mindfulness facilitates the continuous titration and adaptation of the practice in altering the quality of mind towards these ends.

**Skillfully Using Labels**. The accurate use of labels or naming the qualities of mind points to the integration of conceptual and perceptual systems in the mindfulness of mind. This is not ruminative nor discursive but points to what Analayo (2018) translates as *to know* in the above *Satipatthana-sutta* passages on the four foundations and Nanamoli and Bodhi (1995) translate as *to understand*. We prefer the use of the verb *to recognize* for this purpose. It suggests that an experience is not merely observed but also named or capable of being named or identified, much like *description*, the second of five functional operationalizations of mindfulness in the FFMQ. Yet, such recognition need not be mediated through language and conceptual thought per se. It is possible and often taught to recognize mind states through their texture, for example, which may be discerned directly as a quality of openness and flexibility, for example, or indirectly as an image of a textured object like the open and looped weaving of a basketball hoop net. As Analayo explains:

> A mind in which mindfulness is well established has a distinct flavour and texture, such as being open, receptive, flexible, alive, centred, clear, and calm. Familiarizing ourselves with how our mind actually feels when we are mindful helps us to recognize this condition even without any need for labelling.
>
> *(p. 143)*

**Open Awareness/Open Monitoring**. As a gatekeeper between mind states and reactive behaviour, mindfulness of the mind is used to continuously monitor the mind. This practice is the gold standard of mindfulness techniques. It depends on prior training and the ability to regulate attention through focused practices so as to hold attention on particular objects or domains like the breath, body, sensory information, and feelings, but it involves opening the mind ultimately to recognize whatever appears in the field of awareness in the present moment. In this respect, it does not involve focusing or contracting the mind, yet neither is it distracted or scattered. It is an integrated awareness that is nonetheless open to noticing whatever arises in the mind, naturally. As a monitoring practice, it helps to notice states and modes of mind that may be more elusive – such as subtle, liminal, or layered emotions or intentions.

**Impermanence**. As one of what is referred to as the three marks of existence (or three characteristics) discussed later in the chapter, *impermanence* is a key intended insight of mindfulness. Monitoring the mind over time through mindfulness of mind inevitably accentuates the fact that all things are impermanent. Eventually, all mental states, contents of mind or experience, and specific modes subside or change, whether they are thoughts, motions, memories, pain, or sensations. Seeing their temporal, transient nature enables decentering from some of the afflictive grip of mind states.

**Four Noble Truths**. Focused on insights into suffering or *dukkha,* another one of the three marks of existence, the four noble truths are a critical source of contemplative insight in Buddhism. The four truths are represented as suffering; suffering is caused; because it is caused, it can cease; therefore, there is a path to the cessation of suffering (through the eightfold-path, including Right Mindfulness). Although all four foundations offer insights into suffering, the monitoring of mindfulness of mind over time invites insights into realizing suffering as an effect not just as a state.

## Mental Distortions/Distorted Perceptions.

Another mindfulness of mind practice is to recognize and correct mental distortions and distorted perceptions. These are key objects for mindfulness of mind for a number of reasons. As cognitive biases and perceptual distortions or errors, they contribute to a false view of the world, including its existing more permanently, fixedly, or inherently than it does. Also, such distortions fuel afflictive emotions and suffering that develops on the bases of their erroneous or untrustworthy impressions. Afflictive emotions, in turn, are considered the principal obstacle to liberation according to Tibetan Buddhism, for example. Yet, the main cause is ignorance, which is corrected by removing such distortions.

### *Mindfulness of Mind in Vajrayana*

Although the four foundations are common to all schools of Buddhism, there is a distinctive praxis associated with mindfulness of mind in Vajrayana. In an exchange on the topic of *Satipatthana* with monks from the sutra schools of Buddhism in South and SE Asia, the Dalai Lama (2021) pointed out the centrality of mindfulness of mind in the practice of Tibetan Vajrayana:

> The four foundations of mindfulness is a very well-known teaching where the cultivation of mindfulness is applied to four specific objects: These are body, feelings, mind, and mental objects or mind objects...In the four foundations of mindfulness, what we see is a progressive movement through [these objects.] One is able to deepen one's ability to abide mindfully, beginning with the body, and so on. And in particular in relation to mindfulness of mind, the third object, then one will be able to gain mastery over one's states of mind as well.

The Dalai Lama (2021) then draws attention to distinctive features of the Vajrayana approach to mindfulness of mind that are not explicit in the sutra approach. One focal teaching is to distinguish mind states by their degree of coarseness or subtlety. As mindfulness of mind deepens, one is able to experience progressively more subtle aspects or levels of consciousness that enable one, in turn, to observe and recognize subtler objects of attention. Although mindfulness of mind begins with waking state consciousness in these practices, it progresses into meditating on dream states (dream yoga) and from there to meditate on deep sleep. Although these states are readily available to us every day, we are not usually able to observe and recognize the experiences during such states without extensive training and practice. The subtlest mind is referred to as *the pure luminosity of mind*, characterized by a state of luminous clear light, usually only available at death, but it can be accessed by deepening the mindfulness of mind practice. Once realized, mindfulness of mind becomes a direct precursor to the state of Buddhahood.

## Mindfulness of Phenomena

The Pali/Sanskrit term for the fourth foundation is mindfulness of *dharma/dhamma*. Although commonly translated as *phenomena*, it is often associated with *truth* when invoked as a source of refuge, for example. Yet, it is much more than an abstract truth; it is the implicit truth of the manifold things of the world, including that they depend on the minds that experience them. Nor is it referring merely to manifold things either, but rather to the truth of their conditioned *and* ultimate nature as they appear to an observer. Hence, notice in the previous translation of the Dalai Lama (2021) by Thubten Jinpa, *dhamma/dharma* was translated as *mental objects* or *mind objects*.

This seeming slippage between truth and things is apparent in how mindfulness of phenomena is often presented or interpreted both within Buddhism and in secular-scientific contexts alike. The confusion seems to stem from the fact that the source text for traditional mindfulness, the *Satipatthana-sutta*, explicitly identifies mindfulness of phenomena as the five hindrances and seven factors of awakening, alongside the five aggregates, six sense bases, and four noble truths: In other words, it is defined in reference to specific principles of Buddhist psychology. Yet all of these specifically referenced Buddhist theories about the mind constitute mindfulness of mind rather than of phenomena. So, why are they featured in the fourth foundation, mindfulness of phenomena, instead? Why aren't other examples of mental objects referenced that are not linked to principles of Buddhist psychology, such as any of the other billions of phenomenal things? Even Analayo (2018) opted to repeat this focus on mindfulness of phenomena as constituted by the two dominant teachings referenced: The five hindrances and seven factors of awakening.

We contend that the hindrances and awakening factors are more like prerequisite conditions that make the mindfulness of phenomena possible rather than principal objects of mindfulness of phenomena. So, for example, if any of the five hindrances (desire, aversion, sloth and torpor, restlessness and worry, or doubt) dominate the mind, mindfulness of phenomena is obstructed, much like dirt on a mirror obscures the image of whatever it reflects. Likewise, the seven factors of awakening present the step-wise conditions whereby mindfulness becomes an effective path or vehicle of learning, able to perceive the truth of phenomena, a topic that is taken up in the next section of this chapter.

Then what *are* the proper objects of contemplation in the practice of mindfulness of phenomena? They are all things and all topics of human interest and inquiry when properly investigated with a discerning, unhindered, and curious mind. Furthermore, such a mind understands any phenomenon to exist in dependence upon the mind perceiving it. The equanimity with which the object of inquiry is experienced and known provides a kind of parenthetic objectivity that recognizes any perceived object in the world as constructed by an observer. This opens up the theory of the four foundations of mindfulness to the entire human enterprise of the pursuit of learning and knowledge. So, the importance of this point cannot be overstated. Rather than a culturally- and historically-specific teaching about the mind, the mindfulness of dharma refers instead to the implications of mindfulness for the human capacity to inquire into all things. The focus of such inquiry, as Analayo (2018) points out with respect to the hindrances and seven awakening factors, is on conditionality.

In this way, the fourth foundation in the *Satipatthana-sutta* as the removal of hindrances and the cultivation of the seven awakening factors can be reconciled with this view of mindfulness of phenomena as mindfulness of all mental objects. Just as Analayo (2018) describes the mindfulness of the hindrances and seven awakening factors as a two-staged process, this same process can be applied to the broader practice of mindfulness of phenomena. First, the practitioner discerns having or not having hindrances or awakening factors, and then they explore the conditionality (i.e., causes and conditions) of whatever is present. This can be generalized as a two-stage process of checking in on the quality of the mind discerning the object, understanding the perception of the object as dependent on the quality of the mind perceiving it. This initial step of checking in on the mind is followed by an exploration of other features of the conditionality of the object, that is, of its causes and conditions, including its features and qualities.

There are precedents in the evolving praxis of Buddhism that support this interpretation. For example, the Thai monk and teacher Buddhadasa (1988) referred to his observation and study of nature as mindfulness of phenomena. Indeed, he defined the fourth foundation as mindfulness explicitly as the inquiry into nature, interpreted as: "i) nature itself; ii) the law of nature; iii) the duty that must be performed according to that law of nature; and, iv) the fruits or benefits that arise from the performance of that duty." Similarly, the Canadian-born lama, ordained and trained in Burma in the 1950s and later recognized by the 16th Karmapa as Ven. Namgyal Rinpoche (aka Ananda Bodhi) (1931–2003), spent much of the final two decades of his teaching and life promoting the study and inquiry of nature and the world as the proper practice of mindfulness. To do so, he encouraged and joined students to travel to nature reserves around the globe such as the Galapagos, the Grand canyon, and the African savannah; to scuba dive to investigate undersea life; and to explore rocks, minerals, and microscopic life, for example. It also involved the study and practice of the arts. His students and centres extended from the UK to Canada to Australia, New Zealand, Central America, Japan, and Europe (Wangmo, n.d.).

Textbox 11.1 offers an example of how the Dalai Lama echoed this view of mindfulness of phenomena in a dialogue with particle physicist Dr. Anton Zeilinger of the University of Innsbruck. Dr. Zeilinger spent an afternoon presenting the story of the sequence of experiments in physics to investigate the question of the nature of light. At heart was the paradox of whether light was a particle or a wave, supposedly two mutually exclusive conditions according to Newtonian physics but both with empirical evidence supporting their theories. That light could be both a particle and a wave depending on the observer gave birth to modern quantum mechanics. In response to this account, the Dalai Lama commented (something like): "This is consistent with our view in Buddhism: If you follow any phenomenon down to its fundamental nature, you will find this state or nature of its *lack of inherent existence*." Knowing that this process is associated with liberation in Buddhism, he posed the question reported in this case study.

## TEXTBOX 11.1 EXEMPLAR OR CASE:

### The Physics of Light as an Instance of Mindfulness of Phenomena

In the autumn of 1997, one of the authors (SM) joined a group of observers at HH the Dalai Lama's private residence in Dharamsala, India, for a week-long Mind and Life symposium. Five prominent physicists and three philosophers joined in a dialogue with HH the Dalai Lama on the topic of physics and Buddhism (Zajonc, 2004). During this exchange, Anton Zeilinger, Professor of Physics at the University of Innsbruck, presented key experiments investigating the nature of light as either a particle or a wave, paradoxically demonstrating that it was either, depending on the intention of the experiment/er. These results upset prior Newtonian assumptions about matter at the quantum level. Afterwards, the Dalai Lama queried Dr. Zeilinger: "So, how did these discoveries – this knowledge – affect you?" Zeilinger responded using the pronoun "we" to recount the implications for the scientific community. The Dalai Lama repeated his question again, with a similar response, until finally asking (something like): "Yes, but what about *you* - how did this knowledge affect *you*?"

"Oh!" said Professor Zeilinger, with appreciation and eagerness, "I see. Why it has made all the difference. Before this knowledge, I truly believed that I lived in a Newtonian universe that was predetermined and mechanistic, where the future was fixed, determined, and determinable. Now, I realize that the future is not fixed, that I am free. It has changed everything." There was joy in his voice.

The Dalai Lama reminded the scientists that this affirmed the Buddhist belief that sustained inquiry into the nature of *any* phenomenon, in this case of *light*, would ultimately lead an investigator to discover its conditionality, interdependence, and ultimate nature as empty, and that such a discovery was liberating. Less than a year later, Zeilinger completed the first successful teleportation experiment of a particle, which provided empirical proof of the theory of entanglement.

## THE SEVEN FACTORS OF AWAKENING

*Mindfulness* is merely the first of seven steps in mindfulness-based learning according to the seven factors of awakening, the main theory of mindfulness-based teaching and learning in Buddhism. In this sense, mindfulness on its own is insufficient to elicit transformative learning or *awakening* (the desired end of learning in Buddhism). The seven awakening factors, in order, are mindfulness, investigation, energy, joy, tranquility, concentration, and equanimity. Once established, *mindfulness* is catalyzed through questioning and curiosity to become *investigation*. Without such an investigative stance, mindfulness would be prone to become mere absorption, a kind of pleasure or savouring but without insight or wisdom. When *energy* – also translated as determination, perseverance, or effort – is added to the mix, it becomes stabilized as a combined state of mindfulness-investigation-energy that is sometimes described as *interest*.

These initial three factors are the only factors of the seven requiring intentional effort to cultivate. The other four are said to arise quite naturally, conditionally and in dependence upon the sustained state of interest generated by the first three. In this way, *interest* is a way to monitor and modulate the mind to sustain a learning or awakening pathway. With such interest, the remaining four factors arise in succession: Joy arises followed by tranquility, concentration, and equipoise/equanimity. Note that the emergence of joy would provide a condition to re-energize and sustain interest through intrinsic motivation (as unworldly positive emotion). This sevenfold chain would help to explain Csikszentmihalyi's (1990) findings of the intrinsically rewarding flow experience of highly creative people. It also aligns well with self-determination theory in explaining how mindfulness, what they call *interest-taking*, intrinsic motivation, and autonomy may connect.

Indeed, the fact that the term *interest* is used in relation to mindful inquiry in both the seven factors (in oral teachings at least) and in self-determination theory (SDT) requires some unpacking. Regrettably, research and scholarship on SDT have tended to describe *interest-taking* as a distinctive SDT contribution that is unrelated to Buddhist theories of mindfulness. For example, Rigby et al. (2014) explain the source of *interest-taking* as a construct as follows: "Whereas mindful awareness... emphasizes an open and receptive mode that is heavily influenced by Buddhist conceptions of mindfulness, interest-taking is drawn from early studies within SDT of self-regulation and growth that described 'relaxed interest' and reflectivity" (p. 217). In this way, the authors explicitly, albeit erroneously, represent *interest-taking* as a unique SDT contribution without precedents in Buddhist theories of mindfulness. This is partially attributable to textual representations of mindfulness, such as the *Satipatthana-sutta*, many of which are over two millennia old and never reference the language of *interest* explicitly in translations as part of the sevenfold awakening factor theory. Nor do they reference the fourth foundation of mindfulness as inquiry into nature and other phenomena, as outlined previously. Yet, these perspectives have circulated in contemporary Buddhist oral exegetical teachings for decades and perhaps longer.

The corresponding use of this critical term *interest* in both scientific SDT research and in Buddhist exegesis of the sevenfold factors enhances the validity of both theories. Indeed, Rigby et al. (2014) described interest-taking in parallel terms to the Buddhist theory of the seven awakening factors:

> Like mindful awareness, interest-taking is conceptualized as a relaxed attention that is open and receptive. But whereas, in mindfulness, one is actively aware of phenomena as they occur without actively choosing and exploring from said phenomena, in interest-taking, awareness is directed (i.e., actively focused) on specific phenomena that may be salient in the individual's experience. Interest-taking is thus a focused receptivity or detached curiosity and wonder about something that arises.
>
> *(pp. 218–219)*

Such interest-taking via curiosity suggests that concepts are deployed to guide or navigate the inquiry process. In this respect, what is being described is combining the perceptual capacity of mindfulness with a more conceptual process of investigation and curiosity. Worth noting then is that it suggests that a non-conceptual awareness arising from mindfulness can combine with a concept-mediated investigative process in learning. As Analayo (2018) suggests,

> Once established in this way, mindfulness [as 'an open receptivity and soft alertness to whatever is taking place'] can co-exist with the employment of concepts. In fact, the instructions in the *Satipatthana-sutta*, whose function is precisely to foster the establishing of mindfulness, clearly encourage the wise use of concepts...The forward thrust of *satipatthana* towards liberation does not require keeping the mind free from concepts. The main task is to cultivate a free mind even in the presence of concepts.
>
> *(p. 7)*

So, the seven awakening factors imply that concepts are integral to mindfulness-based learning, well beyond the seeming emphasis of mindfulness on non-conceptual experience. Dreyfus (1996) echoed this in citing the words of the Tibetan scholar, Sakya Pandita (1182–1251): "Sense consciousness is like the fool who sees. Conception is like a blind skillful speaker. Self-cognition is like [a person] with complete senses, who introduces one to the other" (p. 223). This process of "self-cognition" – the enriching of perceptual awareness with conceptual engagement – makes MBTL, as a seven awakening factor process, more complementary with existing, conceptually-oriented modern educational and therapeutic approaches.

As described in the previous section, the instructions on how to practise the seven awakening factors are presented in the fourth foundation of mindfulness of phenomena and describe a two-step process. The first step is to check in on the quality of the mind to ascertain the presence or absence of the factors. How do we discern these qualities? As a readily discernible state or condition of the mind, *interest* can be monitored as an indicator of the first three factors. The fourth factor, joy, is a non-sensory based pleasant feeling tone arising from the inquiry process itself, and brings with it more energy. Joy is followed by tranquility, with a calm and stabilizing quality, while concentration implies integration and cohesion rather than a narrowing of focus. Finally, equanimity or equipoise is again more than anything else a quality discernible through feeling tone, in this case the absence of positive, negative, or even neutral feeling tones pulling or pushing the mind towards or away from phenomena. Instead, it is an active state of equal interest, with a quality of what we like to call *appreciation* rather than neutrality.

The second step in the two-step process for mindfulness of the seven factors is to consider the conditionality of each of the factors, as modelled above, both their causes and their conditions. These two steps could be described as knowledge of their presence or absence in the mind (mindfulness) and knowledge of how to cultivate and development them (method). In the *Satipatthana-sutta*, these two steps in the mindfulness of the seven awakening factors are presented as examples of the fourth foundation of mindfulness of phenomena (Analayo, 2018):

> If the mindfulness awakening factor is present within, one knows: 'the mindfulness awakening factor is present within me;' or if the mindfulness awakening factor is not present within, one knows: 'the mindfulness awakening factor is not present within me;' and one knows how the unarisen mindfulness awakening factor arises, and one knows how the arisen mindfulness awakening factor is perfected by development.
>
> *(p. 171)*

## THREE MARKS OF EXISTENCE/ THREE CHARACTERISTICS

The three marks of existence, aka the three characteristics (of mind), is the core theory explaining the existential purpose of learning as *awakening* in Buddhism. The three characteristics are *anicca* (i.e., impermanence); *dukkha* (i.e.., suffering or struggle); and *anatta* (i.e., no-self), which together describe the three key features or conditions of all consciousness, mind, or experience. These three are what mindfulness and other Buddhist meditative and mind-training practices are intended to correct or address. Mindfulness is a corrective for the three marks or characteristics because it enables us to attend to, recognize, and track features of these characteristics that we might otherwise avoid, neglect, or miss. Of all else, it is the tendency to ignore these three features of mind that causes problems, while awareness is the antidote to ignorance through such means as mindfulness.

It is this tendency to deny and ignore the truth of suffering (struggle), impermanence (change), and no-self that entrap us within conditioned habits of suffering and distress. As a technique that enhances awareness and corrects ignorance – that is, the tendency to ignore – mindfulness is a key method or tool in this existential learning process. Therefore, perhaps it is not surprising to note that these three characteristics have re-emerged – albeit in translation – at the core of scientific theories about mindfulness. In doing so, the characteristics have not been borrowed so much as emerged as operationalized mechanisms to reaffirm their value through scientific inquiry. Like *dukkha*, secular-scientific constructs of *distress tolerance* and *approach/avoidance behaviour* have emerged as key explanatory mechanisms to explain the possible efficacy of mindfulness in mental health and wellbeing (e.g., Nila et al., 2016). Like *anicca*, the focus of post-practice inquiry in secular-scientific MBTL methods is in part on tracking experiences in practice to recognize that they change. This insight into change makes the mind more resilient in the face of unwanted, unpleasant experiences, including when they arise in relationships (e.g., Don & Algoe, 2020). Finally, like *anatta*, the practice of *decentering,* that is, the intentional distancing from a sense of absorption in experience or thought, has emerged in theory and research as a key mechanism explaining the cultivation of wellbeing and prevention of depressive relapse through mindfulness (e.g., Garland et al., 2015; Segal et al., 2019).

Although these three Buddhist theories of the four foundations of mindfulness, the seven factors of awakening, and the three characteristics provide a comprehensive way to understand how traditional, contemporary, and secular-scientific variations of mindfulness connect, they are in no way a comprehensive representation of Buddhism. Buddhist theories and practices are complex and shape it into a fulsome system of the science of mind and a meaningful religious path for millions of people.

## REFERENCES

Analayo, B. (2018). *Satipatthana meditation: A practice guide.* Windhorse Publications.

Analayo, B. (2019). *Mindfulness of breathing: A practice guide and translations.* Windhorse Publications.

Barrett, L. (2017). *How emotions are made: The secrete life of the brain.* Houghton Mifflin Harcourt.

Batchelor, M. (2020). *Vedanā* or feeling tone: A practical and contemporary meditative exploration. In J. Peacock and M. Batchelor (Eds.), *The definition, practice, and psychology of* vedanā: *Knowing how it feels*, (pp. 54–68). Routledge.

Buddhadasa, B. (1988). *Anapanasati: Mindfulness with breathing.* Dhamma Study & Practice. http://www.dhammatalks.net/.

Csikszentmihalyi, M. (1990). *Flow: The psychology of optimal experience.* HarperPerennial.

Dalai Lama, H. H. (2021). *Maha Satipatthana Sutta (YouTube). His holiness the 14th Dalai Lama of Tibet.* https://www.dalailama.com/videos/maha-satipatthana-sutta.

Don, B., & Algoe, S. (2020). Impermanence in relationships: Trait mindfulness attenuates the negative personal consequences of everyday dips in relationship satisfaction. *Journal of Social and Personal Relationships*, *37*(8–9), 2419–2437. https://doi.org/10.1177/0265407520921463.

Dreyfus, G. (1996). Can the fool lead the blind? Perception and the given in Dharmakirti's thought. *Journal of Indian Philosophy*, *24*(3), 209–229. http://www.jstor.org/stable/23448033.

Fleischman, P. (2018). *Vedana* and the wisdom of impermanence: We are participants in the experiment of the universe. *Contemporary Buddhism*, *19*(1), 102–112. https://doi.org/10.1080/14639947.2018.1443733.

Garland, E., Farb, N., Goldin, P., & Fredrickson, B. (2015). Mindfulness broadens awareness and builds eudaimonic meaning: A process model of mindful positive emotion regulation. *Psychological Inquiry*, *26*, 293–314. https://doi.org/10.1080/1047840X.2015.1064294.

Gupta, A. (2020). *Vedana* of bias: Latent likes and dislikes fuelling barriers to human connection. In J. Peacock & M. Batchelor (Eds.), *The definition, practice, and psychology of vedana: Knowing how it feels* (pp. 145–159). Routledge.

Nanamoli, B., & Bodhi, B. (1995). *The middle length discourse of the Buddha: A translation of the majjhima nikaya*. Wisdom.

Nila, K., Holt, D., Ditzen, B., & Aguilar-Raab, C. (2016). Mindfulness-based stress reduction (MBSR) enhances distress tolerance and resilience through changes in mindfulness. *Mental Health & Prevention*, *4*, 36–41. https://doi.org/10.1016/j.mhp.2016.01.001.

Peacock, J. & Batchelor, M. (2018). *Vedana*: What is in a 'feeling?' *Contemporary Buddhism*, *19*(1), 1–6. https://doi.org/10.1080/14639947.2018.1450966.

Rigby, S., Schultz, P., & Ryan, R. (2014). Mindfulness, interest-taking, and self-regulation: A self-determination theory perspective of the role of awareness on optimal functioning. In A. Ie, C. Ngnoumen, & E. Langer (Eds.), *The Wiley-Blackwell handbook of mindfulness* (pp. 216–233). Wiley Publishers.

Roth, J. (2018). Worldly and unworldly feelings, fabrication and letting go. *Contemporary Buddhism*, *19*(2), 398–416. https://doi.org/10.1080/14639947.2018.1576291.

Segal, Z., Gulamani, T., Williams, L., Desormeau, P. Ferguson, A., Walsh, K., Anderson, A., & Farb, N. (2019). Practice of therapy acquired regulatory skills and depressive relapse recurrence prophylaxis following cognitive therapy or mindfulness-based cognitive therapy. *Journal of Counselling and Clinical Psychology*, *87*(2), 161–179. https://doi.org/10.1037/ccp0000351.

Thompson, E. (2020). *Why I'm not a Buddhist*. Yale University Press.

Wangmo, K. C. (n.d.). *Venerable Namgyal Rinpoche (1931–2003)*. https://www.bodhipublishing.org/contents/en-ca/d34.html.

Zajonc, A. (Ed.). (2004). *The new physics and cosmology: Dialogues with the Dalai Lama*. Oxford University Press.

# SECTION IV

# Practices

## What We Teach: The What, Why, and How of MBTL

In this section, we consider how the theories and research presented in previous sections are applied in the praxis of MBTL. To do so, we review how research findings and theoretical principles are operationalized as concrete approaches to teaching and learning in MBTL. Although emphasizing the *what* of MBTL, as in what is taught, we also consider the *why* and the *how*. At its most general, the why of MBTL is given: Eudaemonic wellbeing or flourishing. Yet, to specify this very general goal of wellbeing, we offer a model in this section of the full scope of MBTL as three nested and interrelated orientations: as body-mind communication, social-emotional learning, and inquiry-based learning, the topics of each of the three chapters.

Chapter 12 considers the foundational role of MBTL in the teaching and learning of body-mind communication. This is the defining activity of MBTL and of all mindfulness programmes, without which a programme would not be mindfulness-based. Chapter 13 examines MBTL as social-emotional learning. Chapter 14 extends the scope to consider MBTL as a more integrative form of cognitive learning. The chapter focuses on how MBTL can be used as a comprehensive form of inquiry-based learning that links mindfulness inquiry, as pre-, in-, and post-practice inquiry, with investigative inquiry processes and, finally, with meta-inquiry processes turned on adaptive, anti-oppressive, and creative forms of inquiry. We summarize the topic with a nested visual model of these three proposed types of inquiry in MBTL. MBTL as body-mind communication; MBTL as social-emotional learning; and MBTL as inquiry-based learning (p. 261).

DOI: 10.4324/9781003182467-16

# CHAPTER 12

# MINDFULNESS AS BODY-MIND COMMUNICATION

When we *do* mindfulness, we engage in a unique form of awareness and introspective action, we might call communication, between the mind and the body. In this chapter, we address how mindfulness is used as a form of phenomenological inquiry to investigate aspects of experience that we commonly separate into body and mind. These are the sensations, feeling tones, thoughts, and other cognitions like images, language, and memory, and behaviours that coalesce as lived experience. These experiences are parsed and reflected on in MBTL in distinctive, intentional ways to enhance attention to the continuum of direct experience and our relationship to it. This feedback loop between the awareness of internal states and external conditions and our reactions to them constitutes a unique form of body-mind communication that can promote wellbeing. In this chapter, we consider four ways in which body-mind communication is practised in MBTL: Embodied (self-)awareness; self-regulation; executive functioning; and adaptation via stress/threat management.

## EMBODIED (SELF-)AWARENESS

As theories of mindfulness like S-ART (see Chapter 9) emphasize, the quality of experience cultivated in mindfulness can be represented as *embodied self-awareness*. As this construct suggests, embodied self-awareness involves three aspects: i) embodiment, deriving from interoceptive bodily and sensory experience; ii) the sense of self, as a deepening and examined experience, context, or process; and, iii) awareness itself, as both introspective perception *and* recognition (i.e., knowing) of experiences arising in the present and interconnecting across time.

### What Is It and Why Do We Cultivate It?

According to Dorje (2016, p. 11), the primary purpose of applied mindfulness is to enhance "introspective awareness and attention together with non-reactivity." This is part of the broader purposes of contemplative studies, which cultivate the metacognitive self-regulatory capacity of the mind-body through attentional training and regulation; emotion regulation; and conceptual processing. According to Dorje, these three cognitive processing systems modulate, and are modulated by, the autonomic nervous system and awareness, where body-mind communication transpires and impacts wellbeing.

#### *Embodiment*

Mindfulness practices begin with attention to physical sensations and movement, and this mindfulness of the body persists across practices over time. The body, the senses, and sensations provide a tangible location and reference point from which to train attention and awareness. These phenomena are more accessible and more intentional objects of attention than more conceptual or less concrete aspects of experience, like thoughts and emotions, in part because evidence of

DOI: 10.4324/9781003182467-17

attention lapses are more apparent. Intentional attention on the body and/or sensations necessarily connect awareness to the present moment and so serve as barometers for the ability of the mind to anchor in the here and now. Furthermore, bodily and sensory signals register with varying degrees of intensity, discrete or continuous, that we are naturally tuned to detect and monitor.

Anchoring attention to bodily and other sensations disrupts habitual tendencies of the mind and enhances executive control. This is not to suggest that non-sensory experiences like emotions and thoughts are not transpiring in the present as well; however, unlike the body or sensations, it is only with intentional metacognitive awareness that their connection to the present is recognized.

Training attention to the body and sensations enables the mind to recognize and modulate attention when it moves or becomes dull. This process disrupts habitual negative ruminative tendencies of the mind, which interrupts overly cognitive or abstract experiences of both the self and the world that contribute to difficult mind and mood states such as depression. This shift of attention to concrete sensation becomes a key factor in the ability of mindfulness to promote wellbeing. Attending to the present experience of the body and sensations from inside and out also provides the promise of more vivid experience. Such clarity and vividness may contribute to the capacity to savour described in the mindfulness-as-meaning theory.

### *The (Self)*

In mindfulness, we are concerned with the sense of the self-as-process and with the self as an object of attention. Mindfulness training *decenters* the sense of self in experience to reduce the tendency to personalize, to identify with, or to view the self as fixed. This is not to say that a sense of self is an obstacle; however, the problem is when we're too tightly bound to experience, projecting the sense of "me" or "mine" onto experiences so as to reinforce habitual tendencies and automatic behaviours. When these habitual tendencies involve negative or dysfunctional patterns, such self-identification becomes an obstacle to wellbeing. These patterns of self-identification limit us psychologically and behaviourally, potentially resulting in harm to self and others. Hence, the reason the (self) is in parentheses.

### *Awareness*

Mindfulness-based embodied (self-)awareness is a type of awareness that enhances mind-body communication and integration. So, what is awareness? In our view, one important distinction is to differentiate awareness from attention. Attention is the variable of awareness that is amenable to direction, training, and regulation. We don't regulate awareness directly so much as indirectly by expanding or broadening it through the regulation of attention. Awareness can be described as an introspective perception combining the *mere observation* (i.e., contemplation) and *recognition* (i.e., knowing) of experience arising in the present and interconnecting across time (Olendski, 2004). This ability to track experience across time is the basis for mindfulness-based inquiry and insight.

## How Do We Cultivate Embodied (Self)-Awareness?

How is mindfulness taught and learned to cultivate embodied (self-)awareness? Here we consider seven aspects of mindfulness training: attention; body awareness; sensory awareness; interoceptive awareness; parsing experience through inquiry; decentering; and visualization.

### *Attention Training*

Attention training is key to the process of enhancing mind-body communication through mindfulness. Mindfulness-based attention training involves learning to monitor and modulate attention to align with the intention of the meditator. This includes learning to orient, hold, and return attention, to shift attention, and to open attention (without focusing on any object in particular), as in the practice depicted in Textbox 12.1. This primacy of attention training is reflected in many of the key theories of mindfulness. For example, shifting attention from ruminative mental activities to more concrete sensorial experience is postulated by (dual) processing theory to explain the observed efficacy of mindfulness in reducing depressive relapse. Likewise, in the mindfulness-to-meaning theory (MMT), attention regulation is the most direct effect of mindfulness training, which in turn leads to a sequence of downstream effects that culminate in increased savouring and meaning, i.e., wellbeing.

Most attention training is conducted in relationship to the body as the object of mindful attention. Both mindfulness of the breath and sensations are instances of body awareness that can extend to include mindfulness of feeling (tones), mind, and phenomena. Most objects of body awareness practices are neutral in affect or feeling tone, which means they tend to be ignored. This makes them powerful objects to train to energize attention in the encounter with the neutral while calming the mind sufficiently to prevent moving away from the object in search of more entertaining stimuli. In this respect, interoceptive awareness, as the sense of signals originating within the body, goes to the root of what mindfulness appears to be doing i.e., mind-body communication

### *Body Awareness Practices*

In specialized interventions or bespoke programmes, training begins with practices to enhance attention to the body and body awareness. Common practices used to cultivate mindfulness of the body include mindful eating, body scans, yoga, or other mindful movement activities, or mindfulness of breathing with the attention to the breath in a particular place in the body. Subsequent practices usually emanate from initially attending to the sensations of breathing or return to it at the end of the practice. In this way, attention is continually grounded or anchored in the body. Likewise, informal practices used in the midst of daily activities often use bodily sensations as signals to remember to be mindful. From mindfulness of the hands or feet to the three-minute breathing practice (initially taught as a formal practice) used in MBCT, most informal practices involve shifting attention without judgement from rumination to sensations in the body as a strategy to open and extend awareness of the present.

## *Sensory Awareness Practices*

A related practice is to cultivate awareness of our experiences of the environment through attention to, and awareness of, sensations. The attention in such practices is not placed on the objects themselves so much as on the experiences of the objects and their qualities as we encounter them through the senses or the mind. Discrete senses are also often investigated and explored through formal and informal mindfulness practices. In MBSR, for example, the initial "raisin practice" follows a sequence of sensory experiences moving through each of the five senses and culminating in taste. There is a discrete "mindfulness of seeing" practice, and the hearing of sounds is a component of the opening awareness practice (outlined in Textbox 12.1). Touch is addressed through informal practices like washing the dishes or brushing teeth; in walking and movement practices; and during the beginning of formal meditations when attention is brought to points of contact between the back of the body and a chair, cushion, or surface one is lying on or, in the body scan, to the sensation of jewellery or clothing on the skin. Interoception, the perception of experiences from inside the body, is cultivated through practices like the mindfulness of breathing, body scan, and movement practices.

In formal education, sensory awareness offers a way to introduce and integrate mindfulness across the curriculum, thereby making all subjects avenues for embodied awareness. For example, in science, the capacity to engage in disciplined attention to the sensed world is critical to engaging in inductive inquiry, inductive reasoning, and discovery learning. The ensuing knowing is not merely abstract and conceptual but deeply embodied and realized (i.e., "real"). Most modern education trains students in deductive reasoning, at best, involving moving from theories and principles to noticing examples or instances in the world. Insofar as the theories and principles are given, deductive reasoning is a more reproductive, less critical or creative, form of learning and engagement with the world.

## *Interoceptive Awareness*

As Farb et al. (2015) suggest, interoceptive awareness appears to be at a key mechanism explaining the impact of contemplative practices like mindfulness on health. As a new and rapidly growing area of research interest, both the theories and empirical support for these processes are still in their infancy. Questions raised by interoception ask how does the body communicate what is happening given its "language" is electro-chemical, and how does the mind interpret what the body is experiencing? And what role does mindfulness play in this communication exchange? These researchers propose that a tension exists between top-down cognitive expectations (what they call *active inferences*) derived from prior experience and *perceptual inferences* arising from the bottom-up sensory signals of direct experience. They speculate that many contemporary maladies may be rooted in misconstruing body signals since the top-down abstract processing of active inferencing overrides the bottom-up direct perceptual inferencing of present moment sensory information. Mindfulness and other contemplative practices are postulated to lead to more accurate mind-body communication.

## *Parsing*

How might mindfulness help to improve how the mind reads the present via body and sensorial awareness? MBTL trains attention to discern increasingly intangible, subtle, and nuanced experiences of the body, feeling tones, thoughts, and emotions, and mental objects or phenomena more directly and less abstractly. We learn to parse each component of experience, increasing awareness of the compound, and constructed nature of both experience and of the self. This parsing is not arbitrary but reflective of the way perception constructs experience. By *deconstructing* experience, mindfulness reduces the power of oppressive thoughts, emotions, and the drivers of maladaptive behaviour patterns.

This emphasis on the parsing of experiences is evident in one of the earliest texts on mindfulness, the *Satipattana Sutta* (from 20 BCE or earlier):

> "Come, friends," the Buddha answered. "Dwell contemplating the body in the body, ardent, clearly comprehending, unified [e.g., focused], with concentrated one-pointed mind, in order to know the body as it really is. Dwell contemplating feeling in feelings…in order to know feelings as they really are. Dwell contemplating mind in mind…in order to know mind as it really is. Dwell contemplating dhamma in dhammas…in order to know dhammas as they really are."
>
> *(Gunaratana, 2018)*

In MBTL, most meditative and inquiry-based practices involve such parsing of experience into bodily sensations; feeling tones (pleasant, unpleasant and/or neutral); mind (i.e., thoughts, images, or emotion); and/or phenomena (the *dhamma* or truth about living beings and things). This parsing is exemplified in the *Opening Awareness* practice used in MBSR and MBCT described in Textbox 12.1, in which students train incrementally in mindfulness of breathing (in the body), bodily sensations, sounds, thoughts and emotions, and open awareness in sequence as a distinct practice.

## TEXTBOX 12.1 EXEMPLAR OR CASE:

### Opening Awareness

**Purpose**: The purpose is to scaffold practitioners into the experience of open and receptive awareness, as well as:

- Breathing awareness: Regulating attention; awareness of autonomic functioning; top-down processing
- Mindfulness of the body: Peripheral embodiment; regulating attention; distress tolerance (approaching)
- Mindfulness of sound: Extending or expanding awareness spatially; noticing feelings in sensations
- Mindfulness of thoughts/emotions: Decentering; awareness of rumination, images, and emotions
- Open awareness: Broadening awareness; opening to new experience; acceptance; bottom-up processing.

**Context**: The gold standard of mindfulness practices in MBSR and a key practice in MBCT, this practice is introduced incrementally (i.e., stepwise) over three weeks, culminating in Week 5 with the full practice.

**Practice**: The following six steps are equally distributed – approximately – across the 35-minute duration.

1. **Mindfulness of Breathing in the Body**: Bringing attention to breathing in a fixed place in the body e.g., nostrils, belly, etc.) and observing the breath rise and fall. Returning attention when it is pulled away.
2. **Mindfulness of the Body and Bodily Sensations**: Extending and foregrounding attention on the entire body as peripheral body awareness that is received and alternating with particular sensations in the body as they arise.
3. **Mindfulness of Sounds**: Foregrounding sounds, receptive to them, and with a focus on quality rather than identifying the source of sounds. This expands awareness from the body to the body in space and can be pleasant.
4. **Mindfulness of Thoughts and Emotions**: Turning attention to thoughts (images) and emotions as they arise, with a metaphor (e.g., clouds in the sky). Option to label emotions or types of thoughts.
5. **Opening Awareness**: Becoming aware of any and all experiences as they arise in each moment, without approaching or avoiding, merely noticing with openness, receptivity acceptance, interest, and curiosity.
6. **Returning to Breathing in the Body**: Returning to the same instructions in #1.

**Inquiry**: Allow time for enough people to describe experiences (horizontal inquiry) with only a few in more depth (vertical inquiry). Focus on the progression through the steps, transitions, or opening awareness.

### *Decentering*

Self-examination in mindfulness is a metacognitive activity oriented on noticing the subtle ways in which the self becomes habitually and rigidly identified with thoughts, associations, memories, or other experiences in a biased, distorted, or limiting way. Through the mere act of noticing *and* recognizing experience, mindfulness can interrupt the integrative storytelling with its associated self-referential, generalized narrative about the self over time. This narrative filter derives from a self-centred brain processing network associated with stereotypical perceptions and habitual responses that reinforce what Nejad et al. (2013) call the *ruminative brooding* of depression. In people recovering from depression or PTSD, this narrative self is reflected in a preponderance of generic rather than specific memories, which are believed to make them susceptible to relapse. Williams et al. (2000) found that this tendency was reduced with mindfulness (MBCT) training through the generation of more particular and specific memories, as the narrative self-referential neural network became disentangled from, and more integrated with an associated network grounding the sense of self in experience as it unfolds (Farb et al., 2007). Experiential self-referencing has a distinctive present-moment orientation based on the unique, particular conditions and immediacy of experience.

So, what does this imply about the mind-body communication cultivated through mindfulness? The shift in attention from ruminative brooding to immediate sensory experience helps retrains neural pathways and habits to de-emphasize the sense of self identified with negative, ruminative aspects of the mind to a more decentered sense of self based on myriad sensory, bodily, and other experiences. Such mindfulness-based *decentering*, "a central change strategy of Mindfulness-Based Cognitive Therapy, is a process of stepping outside of one's own mental events leading to an objective and non-judging stance towards the self" (Kessel et al., 2016). By cultivating this stance, mindfulness unveils the entangled nature of relations between the mind and body. A good example is in mindfulness of breathing practice in which practitioners attend to the momentary experiences of breathing. This begins from the initiation of the in-breath to its expansion to the transition to the out-breath to its expiration to the transition to the next in-breath, which can involve a momentary gap or stillness. Often, this practice involves attention to the sensations of breathing in one particular area of the body rather than following the breath as it cycles through the entire body.

What is interesting about the breath is that it is the only autonomic function accessible to conscious observation and voluntary control to this degree. When new meditators practise mindfulness of breathing, they may notice an impulse to control or change the breath. Skilled MBTL teachers often coach practitioners how to relinquish these control impulses (see Textbox 9.1 in Chapter 9). Bringing the mind to this witnessing or observational stance in relation to the body cultivates decentering and is used as a parallel process to generalize this stance to other experiences. Being mindful of breathing is about being with the body consciously, with intention and without judging or deliberately changing it. In this way, one may transcend the sense of self through the mind's observation of the body.

### *Visualization Practices*

Technically, visualization practices are meditative but not mindfulness practices because they rely on imagery rather than direct perception. These meditations reconstruct the embodied self and lived environment with alternative visualizations of embodied experience. These practices are developed in a sophisticated form in Tibetan Vajrayana practices, for example. In simpler forms, in MBSR for example, some versions of the curriculum include a visualization of the self as a mountain to instil the stability and grounding that mountains embody. The same can be done with a tree or water or other natural phenomena. These visualizations are thought to help to cultivate an awareness of the power of the imagination to construct qualities that may not otherwise manifest. Images or memories can arise in the mind during more intensive practice to convey an embodied presence of qualities they signify.

## SELF-REGULATION

Just as training in embodied self-awareness is considered an essential aspect of mindfulness, so too is self-regulation and self-efficacy – the degree to which we feel capable, confident, or able to cope with challenges by modulating our internal and external environments to sustain wellbeing. Self-regulation has been researched in many disciplines and contexts for a range of desired outcomes.

### **What Is Self-Regulation, and Why Do We Cultivate It?**

Self-regulation refers to both intentionally directed and automatic processes that are "initiated when routinized activity is impeded or when goal-directedness is otherwise made salient" (Karoly, 1993, p. 25). Early work in this area emphasized goal-oriented activities. More recently greater attention has been paid to affect regulation and self-management in the study of emotional intelligence. With mindfulness, we are concerned with learning to regulate attention, emotion, cognition, and behaviour, so as to enhance present-moment experience and the ability to manage difficult mind and mood states. Mindfulness involves the intentional self-monitoring of internal states and interpersonal and environmental interactions that may involve approach or avoidance reactions with associated affect and cognitions. Such self-monitoring is a significant aspect of many self-regulatory models (Karoly, 1993). When present, mindfulness enhances awareness of wellbeing. When distress is active, mindfulness-based awareness and self-regulation help to modulate these difficult emotional states more skilfully and reduce associated suffering.

Self-regulation in MBTL uses both top-down and bottom-up processes, which are particularly important for emotion regulation and dysregulation implicated in mental health and mental disorders (Guendelman et al., 2017). Self-regulation is a complex process involving interactive feedback loops between the various components of body and mind. For the purposes of discussion, a primary focus on emotion or affect regulation is presented here, which can be generalized to other targets of self-regulation, such as attention, cognition, and behaviour.

Guendelman et al. (2017) differentiate emotion regulation into an *explicit* (i.e., conscious and voluntary) top-down regulatory system and an *implicit* and *emotion-generating* (i.e., automatic) bottom-up regulatory system. Mindfulness increases attention to both systems, thereby enhancing communication between interoceptive bodily signals received externally and internally; emotions and their physical correlates; cognitions; and actions. As a vast source of information and a focus of attention in mindfulness, the body is intertwined with the brain and mind, as well as the environment and our relationship with others. In her book Th*e Extended Mind*, Annie Murphy Paul (2021) speaks to our tendency to ignore or dismiss this information, having become overly reliant on the brain at the expense of the body and what it has to offer, including how we and others are feeling emotionally and physically. This extended body-mind can let us know what is actually needed in any given moment if we learn to listen, and mindfulness is one way to enhance this ability. In addition, since the brain and mind interact with and in the body, it can affect how we think. As humans, we tend to focus on what is happening cognitively, from the neck up, so to speak, missing much else of what is going on in experience. The coordinated use of top-down and bottom-up self-regulatory processes exemplifies the distinctive way in which mind-body communication is taught and learned in MBTL.

In MBTL, separating attention, cognitive, body, emotion, and behaviour regulation is a contrivance given the interconnected nature of the body-brain-mind complex and the many ways in which these processes interact, loop back on one another, and form an integrated self-regulatory network; however, this parsing of experience serves as a way to make learning about them and overall self-regulation more recognizable and manageable. As suggested in MMT (see Chapter 9), this parsing process makes experience more salient and helps reduce tendencies to get immersed in habitual reactions, enabling us to step back to take a broader perspective and reappraise difficult or negative experiences. This, in turn, invites us to engage in meaning-making to foster alternate views and enhance the savouring of positive experience.

Regulating attention in mindfulness, whether for enhancing wellbeing or for coping with distress, begins by learning to direct attention and to monitor habits of mind (e.g., automatically turning away from distress or suffering or the habitual and seemingly automatic movement of attention). Commonly, we also learn to recognize what is the initial, most salient feature in our awareness of an experience by identifying where attention first lands or orients in the parsing process: The body, thoughts, or emotion. We learn about our personal patterns in the sequential unfolding of this processing, which are often otherwise habitual and automatic, involving aspects we don't notice or places in which we get stuck. In this way, in mindfulness we train attention to recognize and track experience (i.e., to see its contingent nature) and so widen awareness beyond a narrow and habitual focus as needed.

Emotion regulation involves monitoring and modulating emotions that interfere with social or executive functions. Dysregulated emotions can be *negative* (e.g., anger) or, less commonly, *positive* (e.g., excitement). Emotion regulation strategies can involve changing the situation causing the distressing emotion when possible (problem-solving); changing how we are attending to the emotion (e.g. through meta-cognition, monitoring, avoidance, or distraction); reappraising, reframing, or restructuring thinking; and/or working with emotional reactivity (e.g. labelling emotions, observing the breath or body, or exposure to reduce reactivity through saturating attention in the emotion or its cause) (Schuman-Olivier et al., 2020). Mindfulness is considered to be applied most effectively as a component of a broad emotion regulation strategy rather than as a specific strategy on its own (Peixoto & Gondim, 2020). That said, Brockman et al. (2017) found that of three approaches to emotion regulation – mindfulness, cognitive reappraisal, and emotion suppression – mindfulness was the most effective in regulating both positive and negative emotion, while cognitive suppression was the most ineffective. It is important to note this difference between mindfulness-based emotion regulation and suppression.

Cognitive regulation can be characterized as "the self-directed regulation of cognitions (thoughts, beliefs, affects) toward the achievement of goals" (Schunk & DiBenedetto, 2020). Cognitive regulation is studied in relation to the capacity to learn and regulate learning, often referred to as self-directed learning. It involves noticing, through mindfulness, a range of qualities of thinking such as bias or distortion; emotionally charged opinions; habitual thoughts harmful to self or others; authentic questions, interest, or curiosity; and the intrinsic motivation and tracking of learning towards a goal. Indeed, evidence suggests that cognitive regulation is a stronger predictor than behaviour regulation of middle school students' success in inquiry learning (aka self-directed learning) (Modrek et al., 2019) and their long-term academic achievement for periods over a one-year period as measured by standardized tests scores in maths and English (Modrek & Ramirez, 2021). In adults, mindfulness is associated with enhanced cognitive regulation through its impact on cognitive reappraisal (Garland et al., 2017b) and on intrinsic motivation and autonomy (Ryan et al., 2021).

Behavioural regulation refers to our ability to manage our actions in response to a stimulus, whether internal or external. This requires awareness, attention, and working memory. When thinking about wellbeing and mindful behaviour we utilize the same process as we do with attention and emotion regulation – reducing automaticity and decentering from reactive impulses and urges in order to increase skilful responding. The process of noticing and recognizing urges and impulses to act and the associated actions themselves replace automatic reactivity to provide more time for intentional choice in how we respond to various circumstances. By increasing the gap between a stimulus and our reaction, we learn to increase our behavioural and other options when possible, thereby increasing self-management.

## How Do We Practise Self-Regulation in MBTL?

In MBTL, attention regulation, emotion regulation, cognitive regulation, and behaviour regulation are taught discretely and sequentially, but also in an integrated manner. This first step requires enhancing meta-awareness, moving in and out of parsing experience, and then moving toward increased challenges to mindfulness in experience. Recognizing and returning the mind to objects of attention usually precedes working with difficult emotions, which in turn precedes the more challenging prospect of modulating cognitive issues (thoughts or motivators) or problematic behaviour.

### *Attention Regulation Practices*

Mindfulness focuses most directly on training the ability to deliberately direct attention to exercise choice in what is attended to in experience. This skill is highly associated with goal-directed activity, emotion regulation, and meta-cognitive skills, all essential to mindfulness and self-regulation. This kind of intentional attention is developed through a variety of formal practices. Using the body – interoception, proprioception, exteroception, senses, cognition, and emotion – practitioners learn to place attention, explore, and shift attention in systematic ways. They learn to both engage in focused attention and open awareness to a larger meditative field (receptive attention). The awareness of the automatic movement of mind into rumination, day-dreaming, or other aspects of experience is highlighted and the attention is directed back to the primary object of attention in the meditation.

### *Emotion Regulation Practices*

Emotion regulation practice begins by noticing a perturbation in experience. This initial awareness may show up as a thought, an emotional descriptor, a bodily sensation, or an impulse to act or an action. The awareness of perturbation is then named or labelled, where possible, using one word. This naming process makes them more salient and recognizable, thereby inviting a more subtle and granular attention to that emotion and the ability to discern it from other emotions that may be present. This naming and description process can reduce the power of the emotions by externalizing them and decreasing our immersion in them – what is referred to as *decentering*. Other aspects of emotion regulation involve attention to and investigation of associated thinking, bodily sensations, and behaviours. In addition, focussed attention on the physical correlates of emotion can provide direct experience of the arc of an affective state, disrupting unhelpful cognitive elaboration.

### *Cognitive Regulation Practices*

Cognitive regulation through mindfulness first involves recognizing many thoughts, images, and memories as involuntary cognitive events in which we tend to be embedded and immersed (e.g., rumination). This is done through parsing experience and tracking them over time, and thereby seeing how they arise and pass away, often of their own volition. In the process, we begin to recognize that attempts to control them, avoid them, or push them away only exacerbate their hold on us. Instead, in mindfulness we cultivate a more objective stance that enhances metacognitive awareness that assists us in perspective-taking and reappraisal in a way that is more consistent with wellbeing and learning.

### *Behavior Regulation Practices*

In mindfulness approaches to behaviour regulation, we begin with awareness of reactive habits that compromise our wellbeing. These habits often have a rapidity and automaticity that make them difficult to catch and control. With mindfulness, we often begin to regulate behaviour by reflecting on past experiences. We begin to track back and parse what occurred to help identify where we might intervene in the experiential cycle. This makes behavioural regulation both an awareness and investigative process. Once we come to know our signals and habitual patterns, we can begin to intervene and increase the gap between the stimulus and our automatic reaction in ways that invite greater choice and intention in responding.

### *An Example of Integrated, Mindfulness-Based Self-Regulation*

In most cases, mindfulness involves interacting processes of attention, emotion, cognitive, and behavioural regulation. Together, they disrupt the tendency to become stuck in a fixed narrative of experience associated with difficult states, rumination, and reactivity. An example of how this is done in one mindfulness practice is provided in Textbox 12.2 with the *Responsive Breathing Space* practice. This MBCT practice is designed to assist people in working with difficult emotions as a formal and informal practice to prevent depressive relapse (Segal et al., 2002, 2013). It involves sitting with the physical correlates of emotion and disrupting narrative self-referencing while enhancing bottom-up, experiential self-referencing. Attention is regulated by attending to what is present with curiosity, if that is available. Practitioners during this period of investigation of physical sensations attempt to bring a different relationship and attitude to challenging states, invoking where possible curiosity and acceptance. In this respect, the regulation and return of attention is done through interest and engagement, attitudes that also can effect a change in emotional valence (Farb et al., 2015).

The intention here is to reduce reactive and ineffective problem-solving, resistance, and/or immersion in fixed views of reality. Shifting attention to the sensations of breathing at the belly draws on both top-down (volitional) and bottom-up (viscerosomatic) attention. Finally, widening attention to the entire body is intended to bring appreciation to the broader scope of experience beyond the narrow view incited by difficult emotions. As predicted by the MMT, this *broadening of attention* enables the practitioner to engage in meta-cognitive *reappraisal* to identify deliberately what is required to address challenges using a top-down process: e.g., a different perspective, a reframing of attitude or behaviour, letting go, or simply letting things be as they are. At the same time, the bottom-up process of the non-conceptual engagement of mindfulness helps bring the body's visceral responses to attention and awareness to monitor, modulate, and re-regulate less voluntary reactivity. In this way, working with emotion involves attention and behavioural regulation that can ultimately develop self-efficacy within states that can be overwhelming.

## TEXTBOX 12.2 EXEMPLAR OR CASE:

### Responsive Breathing Space

**Purpose**: To teach practitioners to work with difficult states and challenging emotions by parsing the components of the experience, exploring the attendant emotional and physical correlates, tracking the experience, shifting attention to sensations of breathing and then widening attention to all bodily sensations.

- Attention regulation: Intentionally approaching difficulty versus avoidance: parsing; voluntary attentional control; cognitive flexibility, decentering
- Emotion regulation: Recognizing physical correlates of emotion, distress tolerance (approaching), identifying/tracking emotion and associated sensations, modulating affect
- Behavioral regulation: Interoceptive exposure leading to cognitive re-appraisal, emotion regulation and mindful responding

**Context**: An essential and formal MBCT practice to enhance turning toward difficult experiences in everyday life. It uses intentional interoceptive exposure and is practised repeatedly in class and informally outside of the sessions when challenging states arise.

**Practice**: The following steps are taught over approximately five minutes followed by inquiry.

1. **Invoking a Difficult Situation**: Bringing to mind a manageable worry or concern – observing what thoughts, emotions, and body sensations are present. Naming the emotions (e.g. sadness or anger is here).
2. **Bodily Sensations**: Attending to the physical correlates of emotion – exploring, breathing with sensations if needed or using encouraging cognitions (e.g., I can be with this; this is a moment of distress).
3. **Physical Sensations of Breathing**: Moving attention away from the somatic expression of emotion.
4. **Open Monitoring of Sensations**: Shifting attention to open and receptive attention to all bodily sensations.

**Inquiry**: Ask for descriptions of the experience (vertical inquiry). Focus on eliciting the progression through the steps, transitions to open awareness, and completion of the practice.

*Adapted from Segal et al. (2002, 2013)*

## EXECUTIVE FUNCTIONS

Executive Functions (EF) refer to "self-regulation to achieve goals" (Barkley, 2012, p. 60), so there is some overlap with self-regulation, discussed above. What distinguishes EF is its emphasis on goals and goal-direct behaviour, with wellbeing as the ultimate goal. The mind uses its capacities to navigate bodily and environmental sensory signals to discern suffering and wellbeing, thereby forming appropriate cognitive or motor responses. This cooperating mind-body communication has the potential to sustain wellbeing across changing circumstances, both for the person and for their nested communities, now and into imagined or unimaginable futures.

## What Are Executive Functions, and Why Do They Matter?

EF are a set of hypothesized neurocognitive skills that deploy reflective, top-down attentional controls to modulate emotion, thought, and action. These controls enable us to respond and adapt effectively to disruptive bottom-up challenges posed by stress, trauma, and adverse childhood experiences, for example (Zelazo, 2020). According to Barkley's (2012) evolutionary theory, EF are functional expressions of an extended phenotype linked to the prefrontal cortex (PFC) in humans that continues to emerge and express itself over time and across generations. Barkley concludes that human EF are intimately connected to self-determination, which is realized in the context of highly organized social and cultural contexts.

### *Top-Down/Bottom-Up Regulatory Processing*

Nakamura et al. (2021) found evidence for two distinctive, coordinated top-down and bottom-up EF regulatory processes associated with distinctive neural areas affected by mindfulness. During top-down deployment in attention control, the prefrontal cortex was found to *inhibit* amygdala activity, whereas during bottom-up processing of sensory stimuli from the external world, mindfulness *activated* the insulate and anterior cingulate cortex. Both of these EF systems improved with mindfulness – one top-down and associated with inhibiting emotional reactivity and the other with activating awareness and, presumably, the capacity to respond more skilfully to the world. Chiesa et al. (2013) found evidence of both these top-down and bottom-up affective regulation processes in mindfulness practitioners; however, whether the top-down or bottom-up approach dominated depended on the duration of training experiences. Using *f*MRI data, they found that novice meditators with less mindfulness experience deployed top-down inhibitory control EF strategies during mindfulness practice, whereas more experienced, long-term practitioners deployed more bottom-up EF strategies.

Difficulties in EF are viewed as transdiagnostic indicators of atypical neurocognitive development in children and of atypical neurocognitive functioning in adults, as in the aftermath of trauma and PTSD for example (Van der Kolk, 2014). EF disorders are characterized by impulsivity and disorganized behaviour; the inability to organize behaviour to achieve goals that directly affect wellbeing; and diminished self-efficacy and control. EF deficits are associated with disorders like ADHD (Barkley, 2012); substance use (Alizadehgoradel et al., 2019); and PTSD (Van der Kolk, 2014), and their improvement are linked to improved academic performance in those facing adverse childhood experiences (Zelano & Carlson, 2020). Meta-analyses and reviews of the impact of mindfulness on EF have indicated significant benefits both for adults (Im et al., 2021) and for children and youth (Mak et al., 2018), with implications for treating a range of other mental health or learning challenges.

## How Do We Teach EF in MBTL?

Zelano (2020) describes both top-down and bottom-up strategies to improve EF. Top-down strategies involve training EF skills explicitly and teaching reflective, meta-cognitive skills to promote training transfer into the future. Bottom-up approaches involve mitigating the disruptive effects of bottom-up influences like stress, trauma, emotions, and adversity. Mindfulness trains practitioners to develop both top-down and bottom-up EF strategies.

### *Delayed Gratification*

MBTL addresses EF both implicitly and explicitly. For example, MBTL *implicitly* augments EF by applying awareness to disrupt a range of problematic attentional habits that derail our capacity to focus and complete goals; on the other hand, MBTL *explicitly* teaches patience, ethics, and perseverance to set and to realize long-term goals or benefits associated with wellbeing. This role of mindfulness in long-term goal realization can be underestimated given the common representations of mindfulness as a present-centred awareness (Dreyfus, 2011). One way to reconcile this apparent paradox is to consider how delayed gratification plays out in mindfulness and EF. Delaying gratification in mindfulness involves teaching and learning how to turn attention towards unwanted experiences like suffering or perceived threat; how to correct approach/avoidance tendencies by tracking unwanted experiences as they unfold and change over time; how to tolerate distress; how to reflect on and, in some cases, inhibit responses to modulate emotional reactivity and judgment; and, in a related way, how to inhibit automaticity by interrupting or delaying conditioned patterns of responding. Mindfulness reduces internal and external stimulation that can limit introspective awareness, thereby providing the opportunity to experience alternative, more subtle forms of gratification. This is particularly salient during silent retreats.

We accomplish this delayed gratification and the reduction in stimulation in mindfulness first by encouraging practitioners to return to objects of attention that we often ignore or don't notice and experience as neutral in feeling tone, such as the body, breath, or background sounds. When the mind reacts to reduced stimulation, we encourage turning curiosity toward the experience of frustration, desire, boredom, agitation, or whatever arises. This curiosity itself can alter the negative experience into one of investigative inquiry.

### *Body-Mind Coordination Versus (Self)-Control*

The approach to EF in MBTL is not based on suppression through self-control i.e., on the mind *controlling* the body and its responses, including emotions. Instead, MBTL cultivates a distinctive approach to *coordinating* the mind-body by linking higher cortical (top-down volitional) reflective action to autonomic (bottom-up viscerosomatic) bodily actions and reactions. This difference between coordination and control was described by Milyavskya et al. (2015) and Werner and Milyavskaya (2019) as the effortless *want-to* of self-regulation rather than the effortful *have-to* of self-control. Likewise, Ryan and Deci (2000) differentiate *self-control*, as a set of strategies based on inhibition, suppression, and introjected forms of externalized control, from *self-determination*, as strategies involving self-regulation via intrinsically motivated executive functioning and awareness.

As further evidence of the distinctive approach to EF fostered through mindfulness, Boyd et al. (2018) examined brain imagery in PTSD patients exposed to mindfulness training. They found evidence of significantly enhanced functional connectivity between the prefrontal cortex and the amygdala through mindfulness. This improved functional connectivity was associated with correcting both PFC under-modulation (a lack of impulse control) and PFC over-modulation (over-control and dissociation), the implication being that mindfulness can enhance mind-body coordination both in experience and in a sustained way through neurological changes.

## ADAPTATION TO STRESS/TRAUMA/THREAT

As discussed in Chapter 5, both mindfulness and stress as constructs have been difficult to define consistently and are, therefore, difficult to operationalize and research. Stress, as a health construct has become more relevant when operationalized as trauma or *sustained threat.* That said, the power of the construct of stress is that it offers a way to describe a continuum of stressors of increasing intensity that pose increasing adaptive challenges to life, thereby directly impacting wellbeing. Stress management involves learning to adapt to perceived stressors – either by removing stressors from the environment or changing our behaviours or reactions to them.

Trauma is an extreme form of acute stress, which may or may not lead to persistent maladaptive responses associated with PTSD. On the other hand, chronic stressors – e.g., chronic trauma or adverse childhood experiences – is operationalized by the NIMH as *sustained threat*, pointing to the critical role of the perception of threat and the responses to it over time, including in the form of trauma. NIMH (n.d.) defined this operationalized construct of *sustained threat* as: "an aversive emotional state caused by prolonged (i.e., weeks to months) exposure to internal and/or external condition(s), state(s), or stimuli that are adaptive to escape or avoid." In this respect, stressors are understood as threats and prolonged exposure to sustained threat as a significant health and mental health challenge. Garland et al. (2017a) examined and demonstrated the impact of mindfulness on the full sequence of the sustained threat response using the NIMH operationalized model.

### What Does It Mean to Adapt to Stress/Trauma/Threat, and Why Does It Matter?

In the case of the aftermath of trauma experienced as PTSD, there are two dominant forms of neurocognitive responses to trauma and its subsequent re-triggering as flashbacks, what might be described as a loss of self-efficacy (e.g., agency) through sensory overload or as depersonalization through dissociation. Van der Kolk (2014) describes this through the case of an Ontario couple, Stan and Ute, who were caught in the midst of a horrific 87-vehicle pileup from dense fog conditions on a highway. Both developed PTSD in the aftermath of this trauma, but exhibited the effects in two very different neurocognitive responses. When triggered to remember the trauma, Stan demonstrated a dramatic overstimulated response in his *f*MRI, whereas Ute demonstrated a dramatic blanking out of all responses – a virtually blank canvas of neural activity. Stan described corresponding explosive flashbacks with signs of dramatic viscerosomatic arousal, while Ute experienced numbness with no physical or mental responses. Adapting well, in this sense, involves sustaining a full and functional brain-body-mind to respond appropriately and over time.

The tendency to treat the fight-flight-freeze responses to stress, trauma, and sustained threat in therapy by revisiting source memories to desensitize people is often ineffective, in part because people often cannot tolerate such exposure. As Van der Kolk (2014) suggests, "We must most of all help our patients to live fully and securely in the present. In order to do that, we need to help bring those brain structures that deserted them when they were overwhelmed by trauma back" (p. 73). This is why he recommends instead mindfulness, which offers top-down regulation through the medial PFC to monitor the body's sensations as well as the bottom-up regulation associated with recalibrating the autonomic nervous system through awareness of breath, touch, and movement. In this respect, mindfulness, other somatic therapies, and psychedelic-assisted psychotherapy (MDMA) show promise in supporting recovery from both the over-reactive hyperarousal and under-reactive dissociative responses to trauma, stress, and threat.

## How Adaptation to Stress/Trauma/Threat Is Taught and Learned in MBTL

Mindfulness works on at least three key contributing physiological features of sustained threat and trauma: Hyperactivity, diminished executive functioning, and avoidance. When a fight or flight response is triggered, it involves an activation of the sympathetic nervous system with concomitant heart rate increases, the release of stress hormones like cortisol or adrenal, and diminished alpha waves associated with wakeful rest. These are also associated with disturbed sleep. Cognitively, however, there is a reduction of *m*PFC activation associated with executive control and a decrease of associated beta waves and an increase in slow-wave delta activity in the prefrontal lobes. So, it would seem that sustained stress is characterized by an overactive bodily state and a decrease in cognitive functioning. Mindfulness training has been found to moderate these effects, including in altered brain wave patterns (e.g., Gau et al., 2016).

Related to this, because mindfulness programmes often attend to challenging mind and mood states, including those arising from trauma, many use a concept known as the Window of Tolerance to help practitioners self-assess their states in an ongoing way and adjust their practice accordingly (Siegel, 2012/2015; Ogden et al., 2006). This construct presents a model of regulation presupposing an optimal level of learning with a sufficient challenge but not so as to lead to the dysregulation of either hyper- or hypo-arousal wherein learning and self-management become suboptimal. Participants are presented with tools to manage these more extreme states such as opening their eyes, shifting attention to the hands or soles of the feet, getting up or walking, drinking a glass of water, or attending to each of the senses in a systematic manner.

Stress effects are also explicitly addressed in mindfulness, whereby we engage in intensive body awareness to recognize the experiences of the body and respond to them through the self-regulation of attention and the cultivation of calm through posture, body awareness and relaxation, and mindfulness of breathing. Although we don't explicitly teach people to change their breath or heart rate, these tend to happen naturally with focused practice. At the same time, there are a range of strategies to "wake up" the mind or attention as the body relaxes: paying attention, noticing more through curiosity and in-practice inquiry, and guidance that directs the mind to notice if it is moving into sleepy states or dream images and gently return to the object of mindfulness (if it is a focal practice). The body scan is a good example, which is done optimally in a lying posture without moving the body while observing it. This requires working with conditioned habits to fall into sleep in such circumstances. Indeed, it closely resembles a relaxation technique in which muscles in each location are flexed and relaxed, but unlike that relaxation practice, in the body scan, participants are supported not to fall into sleep.

Another important way mindfulness helps people to adapt to stress or trauma is to support them to sustain attention on whatever experience arises, including suffering or struggle. In contrast, one of the features of sustained threat and trauma is the avoidance of certain associated experiences or memories that can aggravate symptoms like anxiety and depression. For example, Garland et al. (2017a) applied MMT processes to demonstrate how mindful coping countered the spiral of sustained threat (i.e., chronic stress or trauma) outlined by the NIMH (n.d.) RDoC. They argued that mindfulness reduces attentional and emotional reactivity to a stressor by cultivating acceptance of the conflicting stimulus. In MBTL, as participants' practice deepens, it reduces arousal and anxiety by promoting decentering through parsing experience and disrupting self-centred perspectives. Metacognitive monitoring over time correct avoidance, while attentional broadening allows new data to counter attentional biases towards threat. In teaching practitioners to savour experience through attending to, being curious about, and parsing experiences, mindfulness helps them to recognize more subtle sensations, feeling tones, and positive emotions. Such savouring may offset the anhedonia (decreased appetitive behaviour) and decreased libido of sustained threat. Countering the helplessness, mindfulness promotes enhanced agency and the ability to respond to challenges by learning to extend the gap between stressors and automatic reactivity, a gap in which one can choose how to respond.

Such delays are explicitly taught in programmes like MBSR, for example, to extend the gap between stimulus and response by turning attention to the breath and/or body sensations, movement, and so on. This widening gap is intended to invite more deliberate, self-determined action in lieu of automatic, conditioned responses that may be maladaptive and contrary to wellbeing. At the same time, the delay does not involve an endless masochistic deferral of pleasure in search of some rational or imagined distant, elusive future. Instead, the delay in immediate gratification or habitual reactions is undertaken to pursue more adaptive coping strategies, as well as lasting and satisfying goals associated with wellbeing, specifically savouring and meaning as described in the Mindfulness-as-Meaning Theory (MMT) outlined in Chapter 9. According to MMT, the downstream effects of mindfulness involve the spiralling development of enhanced positive emotions and *savouring* through self-transcendence (Garland & Frederickson, 2019):

> [M]indfulness fosters self-transcendence by evoking upward spirals of decentering, attentional broadening, reappraisal, and savoring. Savoring is highlighted as a key, potential means of inducing absorptive experiences of oneness between subject and object, amplifying the salience of the object while imbuing the sensory-perceptual field with affective meaning.
>
> *(p. 184)*

In dissociative responses to trauma or threat, there is a general avoidance response that interferes with significant other areas of experience and functioning, including the sense of a coherent self or agency. In this condition, the slow reintroduction of sensory stimulation and body awareness with the steady increase in the intentional movement of attention can help participants to come back to re-associate over time and with it to improved agency and executive control. Not surprisingly, mindfulness has been shown to promote post-traumatic growth through this effect on sustained trauma or threat (Tedeschi & Blevins, 2015). As MMT suggests, mindfulness training involves downstream effects on positive reappraisal, which is often taught in programmes like MBSR and MBCT. This leads to positive emotions, savouring, and enhanced meaning, which effectively describes post-traumatic growth.

## CONCLUSION

As this chapter presents, mindfulness offers a unique form of teaching and learning to enhance interoceptive awareness and communicative interactions between the body and mind to enhance wellbeing. This unique objective can present challenges when integrated into mainstream curricula, which are biased in favour of the teaching of narrow intellectual and conceptual capacities and informational content. The difference in mindfulness to this other type of learning is evident to students and teachers, who are often conditioned to learn and teach through more isolated intellectual and reasoning faculties. They will recognize the difference and may even find fault with the subtleties and lower levels of stimulation involved in mindfulness. Therefore, it can be beneficial to contextualize these practices in discussions about the "hard-wiring" of the brain and the reconditioning of the body, mind, and autonomic nervous system through mindfulness. In this respect, MBTL is a form of "brain-based teaching and learning" in which scientific information about the brain informs teaching but also learning, and hence may be taught explicitly.

## REFERENCES

Alizadehgoradel, J., Imami, S., Nejati, V., & Fathabadi, J. (2019). Mindfulness-based substance abuse treatement (MBSAT) improves executive functions in adolescents with substance use disorders. *Neurology, Psychiatry and Brain Research*, *34*, 13–21. https://doi.org/10.1016/j.npbr.2019.08.002.

Barkley, R. (2012). *Executive functions: What they are, how they work, and why they evolved*. The Guilford Press.

Boyd, J., Lanius, R., & McKinnon, M. (2018). Mindfulness-based treatments for posttraumatic stress disorder: A review of the treatment literature and neurobiological evidence. *Journal of Psychiatry and Neuroscience*, *43*(1), 7–25. https://doi.org/10.1503.jpn.170021.

Brockman, R., Ciarrochi, J., Parker, P., & Kashdan, T. (2017). Emotion regulation strategies in daily life: Mindfulness, cognitive reappraisal and emotion suppression. *Cognitive Behaviour Therapy*, *46*(2), 91–113. https://doi.org/10.1080/16506073.2016.1218926.

Chiesa, A., Serretti, A., & Jakobsen, J. (2013). Mindfulness: Top-down or bottom-up emotion regulation strategy? *Clinical Psychology Review*, *33*, 82–96. http://dx.doi.org/10.1016/j.cpr.2012.10.006.

Dorje, D. (2016). Defining contemplative science: The metacognitive self-regulatory capacity of the mind, context of meditation practice and modes of existential awareness. *Frontiers in Psychology*, *17*. https://doi.org/10.3389/fpsyg.2016.01788.

Dreyfus, G. (2011). Is mindfulness present-centred and non-judgmental? A discussion of the cognitive dimensions of mindfulness. *Contemporary Buddhism*, *12*(1), 41–54. https://doi.org/10.1080/14639947.2011.564815.

Farb, N., Daubenmier, J., Price, C. , Gard, T., Kerr, C., Dunn, B., Klein, A., Paulus, M., & Wolf, E. (2015). Interoception, contemplative practice, and health. *Frontiers in Psychology*, *6*, 763. https://doi.org/10.3389/fpsyg.2015.00763.

Farb, N., Segal, Z., Mayberg, H., Bean, J., McKeon, D., Fatima, Z., & Anderson, A. (2007). Attending to the present: Mindfulness meditation reveals distinct neural modes of self-reference. *Social, Cognitive and Affective Neuroscience, 2*(4), 313–322. https://doi.org/10.1093/scan/nsm030.

Garland, E., & Frederickson, B. (2019). Positive psychological states in the arc from mindfulness to self-transcendence: Extensions of the mindfulness-to-meaning theory and applications to addition and chronic pain treatment. *Current Opinion in Psychology, 28*, 184–191. https://doi.org/10.1016/j.copsyc.2019.01.004.

Garland, E., Hanley, A., Baker, A., & Howard, M. (2017a). Biobehavioral mechanism of mindfulness as a treatment for chronic stress: An RDoC perspective. *Chronic Stress, 1*, 1–14. https://doi.org/10.1177/2470547017711912.

Garland, E., Hanley, A., Goldin, P., & Gross, J. (2017b). Testing the mindfulness-to-meaning theory: Evidence for mindful positive emotion regulation from a reanalysis of longitudinal data. *PLoS ONE*. Advance online publication. https://doi.org/10.1371/journal.pone.0187727.

Gau, J., Fan, J., Wu, B., Zhang, Z., Chang, C., Hung, Y., Fung, P., & Sik, H. (2016). Entrainment of chaotic activities in brain and heart during MBSR mindfulness training. *Neuroscience Letters, 616*(11), 218–223. https://doi.org/10.1016/j.neulet.2016.01.001.

Guendelman, S., Medeiros, S., & Rampes, H. (2017). Mindfulness and emotion regulation: Insights from neurobiological, psychological, and clinical studies. *Frontiers in Psychology, 8*(22), 1–23. https://doi.org/10.3389/fpsyg.2017.00220.

Gunaratana, B. (2018). The four foundations of mindfulness. *Lion's Roar: Buddhist Wisdom for Our Time*. https://www.lionsroar.com/living-with-awareness-an-excerpt-from-the-four-foundations-of-mindfulness-in-plain-english/.

Im, S., Stavas, J., Lee, J., Mir, Z., Hazlett-Stevens, H., & Caplovitz, G. (2021). Does mindfulness-based intervention improve cognitive function? A meta-analysis of controlled studies. *Clinical Psychology Review, 84*, 101972. https://doi.org/10.1016/j.cpr.2021.101972.

Karoly, P. (1993). Mechanisms of self-regulation: A systems view. *Annual Review of Psychology, 44*, 23–52.

Kessel, R., Gecht, J., Forkmann, T., Drueke, B., Gauggel, S., & Mainz, V. (2016). The relationship of decentering to health related concepts and cognitive and metacognitive processes in a student sample. *BMC Psychology, 4*(11), 1–10. https://doi.org/10.1186/s40359-016-0115-6.

Mak, C., Whittingham, K., Cunnington, R., & Boyd, R. (2018). Efficacy of mindfulness-based interventions for attention and executive function in children and adolescents: A systematic review. *Mindfulness, 9*, 59–78. https://doi.org/10.1007/s12671-017-0770-6.

Milyavskaya, M. Inzlicht, M., Hope, N., & Koestner, R. (2015). Saying "no" to temptation: Want-to motivation improves self-regulation by reducing temptation rather than by increasing self-control. *Journal of Personality and Social Psychology, 109*(4), 677–693. https://doi.org/10.1037/pspp0000045.

Modrek, A., Kuhn, D., Conway, A., & Arvidsson, T. (2019). Cognitive regulation, not behavior regulation, predicts learning. *Learning and Instruction, 60*, 237–244. https://doi.org/10.1016/j.learninstruc.2017.12.001.

Modrek, A., & Ramirez, G. (2021). Cognitive regulation outdoes behavior regulation in predicting state standardized test scores over time. *Metacognition and Learning, 16*, 113–134. https://doi.org/10.1007/s11409-020-09242-8.

Murphy Paul, A. (2021) *The extended mind: The power of thinking outside the brain*. Houghton Mifflin Harcourt.

Nakamura, H., Tawatsuji, Y., Fang, S., & Matsui, T. (2021). Explanation of emotion regulation mechanism of mindfulness using a brain function model. *Neural Networks, 138*, 198–214. https://doi.org/10.1016/j.neunet.2021.01.029.

Nejad, A., Fossati, P., & Lemogne, C. (2013). Self-referential processing, rumination, and cortical midline structures in major depression. *Frontiers in Human Neuroscience*, *7*, 1–9 (Article 666). https://doi.org/10.3389/fnhum.2013.00666.

NIMH (National Institute of Mental Health). (n.d.). *Construct: Sustained threat.* Accessed July 2021. https://www.nimh.nih.gov/research/research-funded-by-nimh/rdoc/constructs/sustained-threat.

Ogden, P., Minton, K., & Pain, C. (2006). *Trauma and the body: A sensorimotor approach to psychotherapy.* W. W. Norton & Co.

Olendski, A. (2004). The fourth foundation of mindfulness. *Insight Journal, Spring*, 13–17. https://www.buddhistinquiry.org/issue/spring-2004/.

Peixoto, L. S. A., & Gondim, S. M. G. (2020). Mindfulness and emotional regulation: A systematic literature review. *SMAD, Rev Eletrônica Saúde Mental Álcool Drog*, *16*(3), 88–104. https://dx.doi.org/10.11606/issn.1806-6976.smad.2020.168328.

Ryan, R., & Deci, E. (2000). Self-determination theory and the facilitation of intrinsic motivation, social development, and well-being. *American Psychologist*, *55*(4), 68–78.

Ryan, R., Donald, J., & Bradshaw, E. (2021). Mindfulness and motivation: A process view using self-determination theory. *Current Directions in Psychological Science*, *30*(4), 300–306. https://doi.org/10.1177/09637214211009511.

Schuman-Olivier, Z., Trombka, M., Lovas, D. A.,Brewer, J. A., Vago, D. R., Gawande, R., Dunne, J. P., Lazar, S. W., Loucks, E. B., & Fulwiler, C. (2020), Mindfulness and behavior change. *Harvard Review of Psychiatry*, *28*(6), 371–394. https://doi.org/10.1097/HRP.0000000000000277.

Schunk, D., & DiBenedetto, M. (2020). Cognitive regulation. In *Oxford research encyclopedias: Education.* https://doi.org/10.1093/acrefore/9780190264093.013.886.

Segal, Z., Williams, J., & Teasdale, J. (2002, 2013). *Mindfulness-based cognitive therapy for depression: A new approach to preventing relapse.* Guilford Press.

Siegel, D. (2012/2015). *The developing mind: How relationships and the brain interact to shape who we are.* Guilford.

Tedeschi, R., & Blevins, C. (2015). From mindfulness to meaning: Implications for a theory of posttraumatic growth. *Psychological Inquiry*, *26*(4), 373–376. https://doi.org/10.1080/1047840X.2015.1075354

Van der Kolk, B. (2014). *The body keeps the score: Mind, brain and body in the transformation of trauma.* Penguin.

Werner, K., & Milyavskaya, M. (2019). Motivation and self-regulation: The role of want-to motivation in the processes of underlying self-regulation and self-control. *Social and Personality Psychology Compass*, *13*(1), e12425. https://doi.org/10.1111/spc3.12425.

Williams, M., Teasdale, J., Segal, Z., & Soulsby, J. (2000). Mindfulness-based cognitive therapy reduces overgeneral autobiographical memory in formerly depressed patients. *Journal of Abnormal Psychology*, *109*(1), 150–155. https://doi.org/10.1037/0021-843X.109.1.150.

Zelazo, P. (2020). Executive function and psychopathology: A neurodevelopmental perspective. *Annual Review of Clinical Psychology*, *16*, 431–454. https://doi.org/10.1146/annurev-clinpsy-072319-024242.

Zelazo, P., & Carlson, S. (2020). The neurodevelopment of executive function skills: Implications for academic achievement gaps. *Psychology and Neuroscience*, *13*(3), 273–298. https://doi.apa.org/fulltext/2020-75726-003.html.

# CHAPTER 13

# MINDFULNESS AS SOCIAL-EMOTIONAL LEARNING

This chapter addresses how MBTL is applied in the context of social-emotional learning and the education of emotions. We focus on four salient features: The awareness of feeling tones (or affect); social-emotional learning; the cultivation of empathy, self-care, and compassion; and the reduction of implicit biases associated with systemic racism and discrimination. We focus on outcomes like *positive* affect to emphasize the role of mindfulness in wellbeing; however, mindfulness involves the mere observation and recognition of experience, regardless of whether it is experienced as negative, neutral, or positive. In this respect, practitioners are instructed not so much how to cultivate positive feeling tones or emotions directly but how to notice or approach all feeling tones and emotions mindfully, with acceptance. The downstream effect of this training is wellbeing, which is operationalized in part as increased positive affect or mood.

## FEELING TONES, EQUANIMITY, APPRECIATION

The terms *affect* and *feeling tones* can be used interchangeably, with the former more common in the psychology of emotion literature and the latter in Buddhist psychology. Working with affect or feeling tones and their relationship to emotions in MBTL are at the core of its project as a modern reinterpretation of a millennia-old practice to liberate human beings from suffering resulting from conditioned reactions and patterns. In Buddhism, *afflictive* or negative emotions are identified as a key obstacle to fulfilling human potential and wellbeing, primarily because of their role in perpetuating ignorance and habitual conditioned responses. The aim of mindfulness is not to generate positive affect *per se* so much as to practise the bare awareness of affect, however it appears as part of sensations, thoughts, emotions, and memories, etc. The end of such mindfulness, at least within the Buddhist theory of seven awakening factors, is *equanimity* or equipoise. This state of equanimity is not neutral but rather characterized by a non-worldly positive feeling tone we like to call *appreciation.*

### Feeling/Affective Tones

In MBTL, feeling or affect tones and emotions are interpreted through the intersecting lenses of scientific and Buddhist psychological theories. According to one scientific perspective on emotions, *affect* is a universal feature of human experience that colours all experience with a particular affective valence (positive, neutral, negative) and arousal level (low, medium, high) (Barrett, 2017). Grounded in new evidence, this theory refutes earlier claims by Darwin and others that emotions were universal expressions of human experience. Barrett argues instead that emotions are culturally conditioned and specified, though nonetheless built upon these universal affect valences and arousal levels. In this respect, it is affect that is universal, not emotions. Harmon-Jones and Harmon-Jones (2021) distinguish positive *affect* as the general and diffuse feeling of pleasantness at the opposite end of the continuum from negative affect. In contrast, positive *emotions* are specific and narrow constructs of discrete emotions like joy. Furthermore, they caution against confusing positive affect or emotions with approach behaviour, given that anger is associated with approach as well.

DOI: 10.4324/9781003182467-18

Similarly, in traditional Buddhist psychological theory, *feeling tones* are characterized by valence (positive, neutral, or negative) and intensity (light, habitual, intense) (Batchelor, 2019). Feeling tones are *not* innate to the objects and experiences themselves but precede the perception (identification, naming) of objects and experiences. Any mood arising from such feeling tones can distort perceptions (bias, skew) of the object but also contaminate the perception of proximal objects and experiences. Buddhist psychology views emotions as mental phenomena distinct from feeling tones. Consequently, the second of the Four Foundations of Mindfulness, mindfulness of feeling tones, is distinguished from mindfulness of emotions, which are considered to be part of the third, mindfulness of the mind. Although emotions may build on sensory experiences and associated feeling tones, they are mental phenomena related to thought and images that give rise to attachment or aversion (Olendski, 2004). At the same time, there are positive emotions, better described as unworldly feeling tones, associated with equanimity and awakening, notably joy (Analayo, 2019; Roth, 2018).

Unfortunately, both in standardized programmes and with many secular mindfulness teachers, there is a tendency to emphasize emotions at the expense of feeling tones. This tends to collapse the two experiences, such that affect-related feeling tones are interpreted as emotions and vice versa; however, the purpose of mindfulness of feeling tones is different. As mentioned, emotional regulation is associated with the traditional third Foundation of Mindfulness, the mindfulness of mind, in that in most cases, emotions are experienced as a package of conditioned thought-perception-reaction patterns, albeit from a seed of feeling tone. In contrast, feeling tones are affective associations that precede perception so as to mix with it and appear as if a feature of the object rather than of the mind perceiving it. They colour most, if not all, of our specific and particular sensory and related experiences, even in the absence of dysregulated emotions.

Therefore, to help practitioners disengage from habitual tendencies and autopilot-driven emotional reactivity, mindfulness of affect is a critical first step insofar as feeling-tones are often more accessible to awareness than the conditioned and sometimes torrential complexity of many emotions. The operational objective of such awareness of feeling tones is to cultivate *equanimity* – that is, a sense of equal interest and attention to what is perceived, regardless of the valence and intensity of feeling tones. In the scientific study of mindfulness, this quality of equanimity is, at least in part, operationally defined as *decentering*. There is evidence that such decentering is a key mechanism for the efficacy of mindfulness in some mental health challenges like depression (Segal et al., 2019). Decentering involves reducing the level of identification with, and immersion in, experiences. Likewise, in Buddhist practice, as Analayo (2019) describes mindfulness of breathing, equanimity arises in a comparable process of *letting go* of identification with what arises in the mind as *I* or *mine*. Such letting go is the outcome of stepping back, even from joy and happiness themselves, to calm mental activity (e.g., thought, imagination), to experience the mind itself, and to turn the ensuing gladdened and concentrated mind dispassionately on insight.

In MBTL, we explicitly train practitioners to cultivate mindfulness of feeling tones by observing them as they arise in everyday experiences and events – sensory experiences but also images, memories, and thoughts as mental "sensations" (see Textbox 10.1 for an example). This is done by discerning and parsing feeling tones from sensory experiences, emotions, and thoughts. This parsing is emphasized in post-practice and investigative inquiry. The feeling tone is discerned by both its valence (negative, neutral, positive) and degree of intensity or arousal (light, moderate, intense). In post-practice inquiry, the focus is on labeling the feeling tone and any emotions it gives rise to. Often, new practitioners can identify these feeling tones more easily than the emotions or bodily sensations associated with them.

Working with feeling tones can offer a teachable moment to explore how yielding to preferences is not the purpose of mindfulness. Indeed, we are trying to disrupt being controlled by our preferences and suffering related to avoiding unwanted experiences, pursuing wanted experiences, and ignoring neutral experiences. The path of equanimity is through cultivating awareness and interest-taking in *all* experience, whether wanted, unwanted, or unnoticed or to which we are indifferent. For mindfulness teachers as well, it is critical in their inquiry with participants to deconstruct what actually happened in a practice or exercise rather than reinforcing what a participant likes or dislikes, experiences as good or bad, or ignores or disregards as less relevant. It is worth emphasizing here that there may be unwanted negative experiences that require action in the world to reduce suffering, to ensure that participants are safe and able to protect themselves sufficiently from harm or unwholesomeness to actually practise mindfulness in the first place. Yet such challenges can only benefit from not avoiding but rather observing and recognizing the negative affect and associated negative emotions they give rise to. Acting to mitigate oppression can only benefit from the more dispassionate stance of equanimity, in clarifying conditions, intentions, and responses.

One way to teach how to navigate mindfulness of feeling tones is presented in Textbox 13.1. The pleasant/unpleasant events calendar is a common activity used in structured, standardized mindfulness-based programmes like MBSR and MBCT. We adapted it here to refocus attention on mindfulness of feeling tones, to include neutral feelings, and to make the objective of equanimity more explicit. Neutral feeling tones are critical for two reasons. First, most of what we intentionally attend to in mindfulness practices are neutral e.g., the breath, body, and many sensations. While the tendency is to be even compulsively attracted to positive affective experience and to avoid negative affect experience, the tendency with neutral affective experiences is to ignore them. Yet, intriguingly and importantly, when we bring mindfulness to a neutral object like the breath or body, for example, it is no longer neutral but takes on a non-sensory-based positive affect associated with mindfulness itself. This is described as well in Buddhist psychology to explain the nature of positive emotions that arise in the 16 stages of mindfulness of breathing – i.e., joy, happiness, and gladdening – and in the fourth of the seven factors of awakening – joy – that follows the practice of mindfulness, investigation, energy (combining in what might be called a process of *interest* or *interest-taking*) (Analayo, 2019). Yet, this same insight into the impact of mindfulness on neutral affect can be directly experienced by anyone by simply applying mindful attention and interest to neutral experiences as described in this activity: That is, playfully noticing what is neutral in any given moment and how it shifts from neutral to interesting with mindfulness as a form of unconditioned positive affect.

## TEXTBOX 13.1 EXEMPLAR OF MINDFULNESS OF FEELING TONES:

### Pleasant/Unpleasant/Neutral "Calendars"

**Purpose**: This practice adapts an established MBSR activity - the pleasant and unpleasant calendars. Instead, we propose three week-long journaling activities designed to pay attention to one feeling tone in succession (positive, negative, neutral).

**Table 13.1**

| *Day* | *Affect trigger (sensation)?* | *What did you first notice ("feel")?* | *Body* | *Emotions/Thoughts* | *Then what happened?* | *Reflection* |
|---|---|---|---|---|---|---|
| Mon | light on tree's leaves – seeming to hover above | eyes lingering and feeling light, peaceful, absorbed | energized | interested, thoughts about light | continued to walk and notice light | I should do this more |
| Tues | touching my own cheek | comfort and desire mix w/ sensations of touch | shoulder relaxing | "Mmmm." Thoughts of compassion. | carried on but more content | bring more self-care |

**Context**: This mindfulness of feeling tones activity is introduced early in students' mindfulness practices, prior to any explicit explorations of emotions, stress, etc.

**Practice**: Students first explore feeling tones through an introductory activity like that presented in Textbook 10.1. Then students are invited to focus on one feeling tone each week – beginning with the pleasant – and to document one experience a day in which they recognize that feeling tone arising or present. They are instructed to notice the sensation in which the experience arose, features of the feeling tone when it first arose, followed by what they noticed of associated experiences of the body, emotions, and thoughts, how did the act of noticing affect the experience, if at all, and what they noticed as they recorded the experience. This is then reviewed in inquiry sessions in the class or consult, where the focus is on reviewing the explicit parsed record of the experience rather than working from memory or interpretation. Intensity of the feeling can be discussed in inquiry as well. (NOTE: With neutral feelings, it is common for the feeling tone to shift to positive soon after noticing or paying attention to it, offering an opportunity to note, perhaps, such appreciation or interest as slightly different than regular positive affect.)

Table 13.1 is an example of part of an adapted **pleasant feeling tone calendar**.

## Equanimity (as Non-Judging Awareness)

The term *equanimity* (*upekkha/upeksha*) is a critical construct in traditional Buddhist psychology. Equanimity refers to a state in which one is no longer buffeted by conditioned fears (negative), desires (positive), and ignorance (neutral) but freed to witness experience more "objectively," from a more decentred, dispassionate perspective, and to respond in a manner that aligns more closely with intention. Equanimity is the seventh and final factor in the existential awakening that is the objective of mindfulness-based learning in this traditional perspective (Analayo, 2021). Equanimity is described, in a discourse attributed to the Buddha, in similar terms, as a natural objectivity comparable to the non-judgement emphasized in secular-scientific mindfulness (Fronsdal & U Pandita, 2005).

> [D]evelop meditation that is like the earth, for then agreeable and disagreeable sensory impressions will not take charge of your mind. Just as when people throw what is clean and unclean on the earth—feces, urine, saliva, pus, or blood—the earth is not horrified, humiliated, or disgusted by it; in the same way, agreeable and disagreeable sensory impressions will not take charge of your mind when you develop meditation like the earth.
>
> (Majjhima-nikaya *62)*

The seven factors of awakening (*Bodhi*), introduced in Chapter 11, form the traditional Buddhist theory that links mindfulness through investigation to the cultivation of equanimity. The theory suggests that when mindfulness (1st factor) is catalyzed through investigation (2nd) and energy or perseverance (3rd), it naturally gives rise to joy (4th), tranquility (5th), concentration (6th), and, finally, equanimity (7th). Therefore, there are explicit positive feeling tones and emotional states that accompany this kind of learning. As mentioned previously, the first three factors are referred to as *interest* or, in self-determination theory, *interest-taking*, which suggests a link between the intrinsic motivation of interest and its downstream effects in generating the open impartiality of *equanimity*.

In the context of self-determination theory, Deci et al. (2015) differentiate such interest-taking from mindfulness alone: "Whereas mindfulness involves being open and receptive to whatever is occurring in the present, *interest taking*...represents a form of inquiry that can lead to insight – for example, attending to an inner tension to learn more about it" (p. 124). The link between interest-taking, positive emotions, and prosocial attitudes and behaviours is suggested in a study by Weinstein (2009), in which participants who applied interest-taking responses to rejection, when compared to controls using suppression or expression, showed less inclination to displace negative feelings from the rejecting person to a neutral person and showed greater prosocial affect and less anger and feelings of rejection.

Desbordes et al. (2015) argue that many of the features of the scientific inquiry into mindfulness are actually better characterized as studies of "equanimity," which they define as "an even-minded mental state or dispositional tendency toward all experiences or objects, regardless of their origin or their affective valence (pleasant, unpleasant, or neutral)" (p. 4). These researchers align it with key attitudinal aspects of secular-scientific mindfulness as "acceptance, non-judgment, non-striving, and non-reactivity" (p. 9). They specify three ways in which equanimity is cultivated through MBTL: through the cultivation of an "observing attitude"; through emotional regulation strategies that calm or reduce reactivity; and through extending the time or gap between experience and response.

## Engaged Appreciation

Equanimity is not to be confused with indifference – in either theory or practice. Instead, it involves an engaged interest that is quite different from the indifference of neutral affect, for example. In traditional Buddhist teachings, this is described as an unworldly positive feeling that is described as joy, happiness, and gladdening in the 16 stages of mindfulness of breathing (Analayo, 2019). We opt to describe and name this feature of equanimity as *appreciation* based on the four general meanings of the term: i) gratitude and the recognition of something's good qualities; ii) an increase in its felt value; iii) a corresponding increase in interest and energy in the observer; and iv) a fuller and more engaged understanding. The description of equanimity, the outcome of the seven awakening factors, as a state of engaged appreciation points to how it differs from the mere objectivity of scientific inquiry.

In education, this engaged appreciative quality of mindfulness-based equanimity may seem to conflict with critical thinking, which is often interpreted as the identification of faults, problems, or limitations. In some cases, this may be true if critical thinking mistakenly cultivates a preoccupation with faults or limitations. Too often, critical thinking and critique mask unaddressed negative feeling tones and implicit emotions that can be unrecognized or unacknowledged in the pretense of objective scholarly inquiry. Instead, optimally, critical thinking engages in analysis beyond – or at least aware of the limitations of – felt negative, positive, or neutral feeling tones associated with a subject or object of inquiry. In scientific inquiry in particular, deepening the encounter with the object of inquiry through direct observation and engagement so as to cultivate interest-taking and equanimity need not, nor should not, optimally culminate in a disinterested stance. Instead, it should and often does lead to a deepening care for the welfare of what is being studied, despite the many disciplinary and scholarly conventions against directly expressing such caring. The current ecological and global climate change crises, however, have led to a nascent reassessment of such conventions. For example, Textbox 14.2 in the next chapter offers an exemplar from the documentary *My Octopus Teacher* of how mindful inquiry can culminate in appreciation and ultimately love for what is investigated. This quality of appreciation, in the words of the protagonist, naturally generalized to the entire, in this case wild, world.

In this way, engaged appreciative inquiry fits well within the mindfulness-as-meaning theory in supporting how attention regulation progresses through mindfulness to enhanced meaning and savouring. Engaged appreciative inquiry is fostered explicitly as well in MBTL through post-practice inquiry, where a skilled facilitator will persist in inquiring with a participant into details of their experiences and how they change (or don't change) over time. The resulting, more nuanced understanding of experience becomes a more intuitive, wider, and sustained expert gaze. So too, through investigative inquiry, participants may come to positively reappraise and appreciate the full depth and range of experiences related to a topic or object of study. It is not about cultivating "blue sky thinking," that is, identifying or recognizing only positive features of experiences, so much as to cultivate an engaged appreciation of the true complexity of experiences beyond the habitual narrow perception that they are simply wanted, unwanted, or irrelevant. As the appreciation and value of a particular experience increases, it can culminate over time in a generalized appreciation for life, for the world, or for a broader class of associated objects or relations.

## Mindfulness as Emotion Regulation

Increasingly mindfulness is being identified and recommended as a strategy for regulating emotions. Viewed principally as a behavioural problem, emotion dysregulation is seen as disruptive and threatening within social contexts; however, as described well in Buddhist theories of emotion, *afflictive* emotions create at least as much suffering for the person experiencing them, long before they manifest socially in behaviour. We can think of three possible pathways when emotions are triggered: *Suppression* (dissociative or expressive suppression); *reactive expression*; and *mindful investigation* (with or without cognitive reappraisal).

### *Suppression (Dissociative and Expressive Suppression)*

*Suppression* involves inhibitory responses that may eliminate both the expression and, in some cases, the experience of the emotion altogether. When emotional suppression eliminates the experience of the emotion altogether, it is often associated with dissociation, which can be associated with problems as diverse as identity loss (Boniolo, 2021) and addictions (Grajewski & Dragan, 2020) and is itself both a disorder and symptom of other disorders in DSM-5 (Dalenberg et al., 2022). As *expressive suppression* the emotion is experienced, at least partially, but the behavioural reactions are suppressed. In this form, suppression becomes a viable form of emotion regulation using a response-focused strategy. In her comparative review of research on expression suppression and cognitive reappraisal (form of experiencing) regulatory strategies, Cutuli (2014) found the people using suppression strategies displayed more memory impairment, lower self-esteem, were less happy and more depressed and avoidant with poorer life satisfaction, less autonomy, and fewer close relationships and support. Interestingly, she reports on a number of studies that indicate that this strategy is more associated with dysfunction and negative mental health in Western than Eastern cultures.

### *Reactive Expression*

The *reactive expression* of emotions involves an unfiltered manifestation of emotion in behaviour, be it in language, non-verbal communication, or conduct. The term "expression" should not be misinterpreted as communication; emotions and emotional states can be communicated and described without necessarily implying that a dysregulated state is present. This pattern of mere *reactive expression* is an unregulated response to emotions; however, it does not necessarily imply a dysregulated state but the heightened probability that such a state could arise.

### *Mindful Investigation (with or without Cognitive Reappraisal)*

The third pathway is a mindfulness-based strategy that we refer to as *mindful investigation*, that is, the mindful observation and investigation of emotions. In this condition, attention is diverted from reacting or suppressing to investigating the experience of the emotion itself and its associated thoughts and bodily sensations. This harkens back to the aforementioned study by Weinstein (2009) that compared strategies of suppression, expression, and what she called *interest-taking* in regulating emotions. In particular, she was tracking the relative impacts of these orientations on participants' incidental *rejection* emotions following being told that a peer had rejected them. Those in the interest-taking group (aka *mindful investigation*) were found to exhibit lower implicit aggression, less anger, more prosocial affect, and less internalization of rejection.

This strategy of mindful investigation is associated with cognitive reappraisal, an antecedent-focused regulatory strategy that Cutuli (2014) described as "the attempt to reinterpret an emotion-eliciting situation in a way that alters its meaning and changes its emotional impact" (p. 1). As cognitive reappraisal, Cutili found this strategy resulted in unaltered or improved behavioural memory with lower rates of depression and higher levels of life satisfaction, coping skills, autonomy, and optimism when compared to suppressors. In addition, the cognitive reappraisal condition resulted in interlocutors experiencing less stress with participants during communication. Yet, mindful investigation need not involve cognitive reappraisal explicitly; instead, it can merely holding attention on the emotional experience with curiosity, interest, and a decentred awareness until it dissipates, without really trying conceptually to reappraise the situation. In this case, the experience itself becomes a way to re-establish intention and equanimity and, on these bases, to assess how best to respond to a situation.

### *Mindfulness as an Experiential Strategy*

Mindfulness works on emotions through broadening awareness, metacognition, and reappraisal rather than through suppressing them. Although there is evidence that novice meditators do initially suppress emotions through top-down regulatory systems involving the medial prefrontal cortex (mPFC), with practice and experience, more expert meditators seem to show more bottom-up emotion regulation strategies through awareness and modulation of viscero-somatic experiences rather than through emotional control (Chiesa et al., 2013). We might ask at this juncture what the problem with emotions are from the perspective of MBTL. Emotions are a problem only insofar as they are part of automatic, habitual, and reactive patterns that reinforce and perpetuate suffering. To express an emotion is not at issue as a natural or intentional response to a particular set of conditions. Mindfulness is concerned with regulating wellbeing, so the issue is not the presence of emotion but rather how deeply the presence or expression of emotion disturbs such wellbeing and how quickly we recover from it.

## A Caveat: Expressing Emotions in MBTL

One of the purposes of mindfulness is the cultivation of positive feeling tones associated with wellbeing, whether as joy, happiness, gladdening, or satisfaction or as improved mood or savouring and meaning. Added to this is a recognition of the role of non-reactivity and equanimity in dealing with afflictive emotions that generate suffering. There is a paradox here, however, insofar as negative emotions don't only cause suffering, suffering itself can generate negative emotions. Therefore, suffering and mindfulness of suffering can generate strong emotional responses, ranging from sadness to crying through to rage. When the suffering seems to be socially aggravated through systems of oppression, for example, the sense of injustice can intensify these emotions and emotional responses.

Yet, there is a troubling tendency in mindfulness training contexts to avoid some topics or critical conversations that may incite negative emotions or communications, such as politics or critiques of abuse or systemic discrimination. This is a challenge both in traditional Buddhist and secular-scientific mindfulness contexts. Well-documented struggles in Europe and North America to deal with male Buddhist teachers, ordained and non-ordained, engaging in sexual improprieties and abuse of women students is a case in point (Langenberg, 2021). The challenge has been not only that such abuses continue to take place, but that the people who fall victim to these predatory teachers are sometimes unsupported by communities who seem unable to stand up to the offending teachers. Strictures against negative emotions and criticizing teachers are part of the problem. In secular-scientific mindfulness, the challenge is more about overpromising mindfulness as a panacea for all that ails us and a pernicious idealism that can tend to silence those with more negative experiences.

In MBTL, one effective way to counteract this tendency to suppress negative feeling tones or emotions is to encourage the reporting of negative experiences in post-practice inquiry by actively soliciting them – "So, did anyone experience challenges?" – and responding positively to reports of difficulty while merely acknowledging or tacitly thanking participants for reporting positive experiences. Less commonly practised is to invite conversations in which people share suffering in their lives and in ways that allow them to express emotions safely (Berila, 2016). By making the suffering of abuse or oppression the object of mindfulness, we constructively apply mindfulness and dispassion to navigate the edge of suffering while opening to their potential role in compassion and social justice.

Even more challenging yet important for MBTL teachers is to respond to unforeseen eruptions of intense emotion or criticisms from participants without succumbing to impulses to shut the conversation down. This "shutting down" can happen in many, often unintended, ways: For example, through displays of affection or solace during expressions of sadness and crying or, even more tricky, by asking them to check in with mindfulness when they voice disagreement, anger, or frustration over a concept, experience, or apparent injustice.

## SOCIAL EMOTIONAL LEARNING

A discussion of wellbeing and MBTL, as these relate to positive affect, necessitates a discussion of social and emotional learning (SEL). Positive affect is tied to social and emotional skills that are acquired throughout the life cycle, but these would seem particularly important to cultivate during the periods of rapid development of childhood and adolescence. Social and emotional learning as a competence to be developed in children and youth has been a focus within the preschool, elementary, and high school education system for over 20 years. The Collaborative for Social and Emotional Learning (CASEL, 2021a) was established in 1997 to ensure that this area of learning was founded upon a scientific evidence base. CASEL is also attentive to and concerned with effective practices and policies regarding the implementation of SEL throughout the United States (Weissberg et al., 2015).

### What Is Social Emotional Learning?

Mindfulness and SEL overlap in a variety of ways. Both are concerned with mental and emotional wellbeing, and teaching mindfulness within an SEL context provides an ethical and secular framework to support the practical and experiential learning associated with MBTL. Hence, it is no surprise that there have been a number of mindfulness programmes created that integrate SEL concepts. Some of these, such as the Stress Management and Resiliency Techniques (SMART) programme, are designed specifically for teachers to apply the concepts of mindfulness to themselves, while others, such as MindUP, provide a curriculum that integrates mindfulness and SEL for K-12 students. Still, other programmes may emphasize particular components of mindfulness such as kindness, awareness, self-regulation, executive functioning, or attention training. Regardless of their primary focus, mindfulness delivered within schools tends to be consistent with SEL concepts but may employ strategies that make it difficult to delineate mindfulness from SEL.

As an example, Flook et al. (2015) conducted a randomized controlled trial of a mindfulness programme focused on pre-kindergarten students that combined a number of activities including mindfulness, delayed gratification, and kindness exercises that showed a significant increase in typical SEL measures such as executive functioning, academic achievement, and prosocial behaviour. This is important to note because the tendency in the education system is to integrate mindfulness into existing school programmes rather than teach it as an independent curriculum or infuse it across the curriculum. The SEL curricula is the place in the school curricula in which mindfulness tends to be located, and there are pros and cons to this that will be discussed later.

Social and emotional development are now considered primary competencies for wellbeing and a fully functional life. As Weissberg et al. (2015) point out "Families, educators, and community members seek to raise and educate children who are knowledgeable, responsible, caring, and socially competent on their way to becoming positive family members and neighbors, contributing citizens, and productive workers" (p.4). Although these were previously the domain of families, communities, organizations, and other institutions, they are seen as the responsibility of educational institutions. SEL, therefore, has become integrated into the school system, and, hence, there is a focus on a structured implementation and the development of an evidence base for its use.

Although it is a rapidly expanding area of education and research, SEL has tended to be narrowly applied and researched in children and youth. Within the school system, SEL programmes are designed to enable students to develop skills, attitudes, and knowledge to apply throughout their lives. The basic framework for such programmes is derived from CASEL's (2021a) five foci for SEL: i) self-awareness (e.g. understanding one's emotions and knowing one's strengths and limitations); ii) self-management (e.g. stress coping, emotion regulation, behaviour regulation, and goal management); iii) social awareness (e.g. empathy and perspective taking); relationship skills (e.g. listening, communication, cooperation); and responsible decision-making (e.g. culturally normative and ethical constructive choices – personally and interpersonally). More directly, SEL programmes have been shown to increase students' connection to school and to enhance their academic achievement (Durlak et al., 2011).

Given such evidence and the fact that SEL is considered to contribute to a fully functioning life, why is it not given more attention in higher education or in adult learning? One possible explanation is that MBTL is filling this gap through its entry and uptake within so many modern institutions and contexts. This is evident in the orientation of many of the standardized mindfulness programmes. In MBSR, for example, emphasis is placed on social- and emotional-related outcomes associated with stress reduction, self-management, communication, and interpersonal relationships in MBSR. In MBCT, the emphasis is on social-emotional outcomes related to the management of challenging mind and mood states, emotion, and behaviour regulation. Finally, in MSC, the emphasis is on kindness and self-care.

## How Do We Cultivate Social-Emotional Learning?

One challenge in the design of SEL programmes is how to include all stakeholders from classrooms, schools, communities, and families in the design processes. Parents, teachers, school staff, and administrators need to model effective social-emotion skills and behaviour themselves, both inside and outside the classroom, so that the school and community act in sync with the students' lived experience of SEL. Also, different schools may use a variety of methods (discussion, games, other activities) and programmes to deliver SEL, which may not necessarily cover all domains. Programmes may place more focus on specific areas such as executive functioning, trauma-informed SEL, altruistic traits, emotion regulation, and so on (Jones et al., 2021). How SEL is taught and what is emphasized may depend on many variables, including but not limited to the population and diversity of the school and the specific needs of the school population and community. In addition, SEL skills take time to acquire and are most readily instilled through cross-curricular exposure rather than being left to the preferences and whims of individual teachers. MBTL can play a constructive role in supporting this infusion of SEL across the curriculum, given its potential as a method of inquiry into the content of specific subject areas.

The SAFE framework, a gold standard for teaching SEL, involves **S**equenced activities that are connected and build on one another sequentially. The learning is **A**ctive, that is, experiential and applied, and **F**ocused specifically on acquiring skills that are pertinent, both personally and socially. Finally, the SEL focus is **E**xplicit, making it clear that social and emotional learning is a valued part of student education (Durlak et al., 2011; Jones et al., 2021). The teaching and learning of mindfulness can work in parallel with SEL in this framework. Many of the aims and intentions overlap as do the domains of interest and their systematic and scaffolded implementation.

MindUp is an example of a programme that explicitly integrates mindfulness and SEL and provides extensive professional development for teachers. It emphasizes attention control, emotion and behavioural regulation, and perspectives – particularly openness. This programme relies extensively on the use of discussion, debriefing, and mindfulness meditation activities. Furthermore, MindUp has been supported by early research (Schonert-Reichl et al., 2015; Thierry et al., 2016) and is one of the programmes available in the CASEL programme guide (CASEL, 2021b). While most teachers are now required to teach SEL, when mindfulness is infused in programmes like MindUp, teachers may not be adequately supported or encouraged to develop a mindfulness practice of their own. This personal practice is considered critical in MBTL, where embodiment is one of the key teacher competencies (see Ch. 17). Another concern is the misuse of mindfulness as a means of social and behavioural control.

## EMPATHY AND COMPASSION

Like SEL, mindfulness and compassion programmes often include components to cultivate empathy and compassion. In teaching empathy, training can involve cognitive components associated with perspective-taking; a social component involving identifying and sharing experiences of emotions with others; and a meta-cognitive component involving the awareness that the emotion experienced derives from the experience(s) of another human being (Hoffman, 2008).

### What Are Empathy and Compassion?

Different forms of empathy that are taught differently. Empathic concern reflects the ability to know what a person needs (Goleman et al., 2017). Sympathy, often confused with empathy, is feeling emotions *for* someone else, such as feeling sad when encountering someone's grief. Compassion includes the ability to feel with another with the intention to respond in some way to reduce or alleviate their suffering. Empathy and compassion are aspects of social awareness, relationships, and prosocial behaviour, assisting children and adults to be good citizens and to develop healthy connections with themselves and others.

In addition, self-compassion is important in reducing depression, preventing its relapse, and enhancing self-care (Kuyken et al, 2010). Also, some research suggests that compassion for self and/or others even increases happiness (Saarinen et al., 2020).

Asset-based mindfulness research that focuses on positive outcomes and affect, including compassion, empathy, and wellbeing, has received less attention than deficit-based studies of outcomes associated with, say, depression relapse. In an example of a more balanced approach, Lomas et al. (2018) conducted a meta-analysis of mindfulness and the wellbeing of healthcare workers showing benefits from mindfulness for both *negative* and *positive* aspects of wellbeing. Although the studies have a number of limitations, the results are promising. This corroborates and further reinforces the compatibility between the combined cultivation of mindfulness, compassion, and wellbeing.

## How Do We Cultivate Empathy and Compassion?

The cultivation of empathy and compassion tends to be implicit in mindfulness-based programmes (MBPs). This is particularly true of clinical programmes oriented on conditions like depression, such as MBCT, where harsh views against the self may make it difficult for participants to feel empathy or compassion for themselves. Mindful Self-Compassion (MSC) programmes are quite explicit about the importance of learning self-compassion. According to Lopez et al. (2018), self-compassion training leads to different outcomes than compassion training (for others); furthermore, one form of compassion does not necessarily lead to the other. Compassion for self and for others, surprisingly, were constructs that did not prove to be significantly related. Instead, each form of compassion may require the use of different practices to develop. Neff (2003), one of the key developers of the MSC programme, identified three factors associated with self-compassion: i) self-kindness; ii) common humanity; and iii) mindfulness. MSC uses a variety of practices and didactic sessions to teach this approach to self-compassion, bringing attention to each of these variables in different ways.

Yet, all MBPs share common elements that contribute to fostering empathy and compassion for self and others, with stronger emphasis on self-compassion. These common elements include practising curiosity and non-judgment in formal meditation or bringing mindfulness to everyday interactions, experiences, and activities; identifying and labelling emotions to develop emotional literacy; practising mindful listening and speaking; and engaging in *metta* (friendliness) or kindness meditations for self and others to cultivate positive affect. MBSR uses an exercise in stressful communication to develop perspective-taking and affective empathy, while other programmes use meditations in which one imagines someone they know and considers all the ways in which they are similar to one another as a way to recognize common humanity. Another programme aimed at developing compassion from a basis of mindfulness is the Stanford-based Cultivating Compassion Training (CCT), where participants practise feeling loving-kindness and compassion for a beloved and move on to cultivate loving-kindness or compassion for an enemy or strangers. Another practice used in that programme is to imagine a person, symbol, or place that embodies compassion as a source of meditative inspiration or refuge. These are some of the ways compassion for others may be taught. Finally, many MBP use some form of home practice exercises that ask participants to deliberately engage in self-care activities.

For those in the helping or teaching professions, mindfulness fosters self-care as a value to help prevent burnout or compassion fatigue; however, it is important to remember that these professions, along with those in the corporate sector, are located within systems that may download stress onto the individual in ways that may divert attention from the need for systemic change. Thus, it is important to ensure that parallel initiatives are in place to embed mindfulness *and* compassion in organizational systems and not just in individual-oriented training (Rupprecht et al., 2019).

## PROSOCIALITY AND IMPLICIT BIAS REDUCTION

While empathy and compassion tend to focus on introspective qualities, the question remains how well these translate into more altruistic social behaviours and interpersonal relations as prosociality or implicit bias reduction.

### Prosocial Behaviour

Prosocial behaviour refers to behaviour oriented on helping others, including assisting, sharing, comforting, and cooperating. Mindfulness appears to promote prosocial behaviour and attitudes, even in the absence of explicit ethical training. For example, in their meta-analysis, Berry et al. (2020) first reviewed research linking mindfulness to prosocial mind sets or dispositions, including empathic attention; de-automatization; and dis-identification (or decentering). Then they analyzed 23 studies of mindfulness interventions without ethics components to measure the direct effect of mindfulness on prosociality. They found small to medium size effects sizes of mindfulness on overt acts of prosociality as compared to active and passive controls, as well as increased compassionate helping and reduced prejudice and retaliation. In another study, Poulin et al. (2021) found that whether or not mindfulness increased or decreased prosocial behaviour depended on whether a practitioner had an interdependent or independent self-construal, respectively.

In another interesting critique of mindfulness vis-à-vis apparent benefits to prosocial behaviour, Hafenbrack et al., 2021) examined the effect of mindfulness on guilt-driven inclinations to repair harms done to others. They found that mindfulness weakened the link between a transgression and reparative behaviour and that this relationship was mediated by reduced guilt. In other words, as mindfulness reduced the negative emotion of guilt, it also reduced the potentially prosocial behaviour associated with guilt: Repairing harms. Yet, participants who engaged in loving-kindness mediation showed significantly more prosocial reparations than those engaged in mindfulness-based focused breathing. This suggests that as mindfulness reduces negative emotions, it may reduce prosocial behaviours associated with negative emotions like guilt. This result suggests that offering complementary practices like loving-kindness may have the same positive effects on repairing harms without the meditation of guilt.

The current approach to teaching and learning mindfulness in many MBPs tends to be individualistic in orientation. There are, however, increasingly popular adaptations of the eight-week MBSR and MBCT programmes that explicitly identify prosocial outcomes and practices that are embedded within a mindfulness-oriented programme. Mindful Self Compassion (MSC) and the Cultivating Compassion Training (CCT) are two examples. In other mindfulness-focused programmes, inquiry processes often reinforce attitudes and behaviours associated with self-care, self-compassion, and reducing self-hatred or biases, which may well extend over time and experience as compassion for others.

## Implicit Bias

Implicit biases arise from unconscious, fast processing that may run counter to our consciously held values and intentions. Data from the Harvard-based Implicit Association Test (IAT) suggest that automatic feeling tones associated with general categories of people may lead to habitual stereotypical responses. These biases appear to form through upbringing and experience (e.g., media) and persist independently of our conscious reasoning and explicit views and values. Furthermore, negative implicit biases can exist for categories of people that include oneself. The test explores response times and error rates in test items associating paired categories of people (e.g., faces of people of European versus African descent) with good/bad words. Implicit biases are believed to explain, for example, the disproportionate killing of BIPOC people by police and hiring discrimination against minorities and marginalized groups even with affirmative hiring policies. So, a lot is at stake in this notion of implicit bias in social justice and social equity struggles.

Burgess et al. (2017), for example, outlined the promise of mindfulness as a method to reduce clinician implicit bias towards patients. They argued that while other interventions focus on declarative knowledge – that is, what is known about implicit bias – mindfulness training involves procedural knowledge – that is, learning *how* to reduce it or its impact. The actual processes that mindfulness uses to reduce implicit bias and its impacts include recognizing and sitting with negative emotions in awareness as they arise in viscero-somatic experiences alongside the biased habits of mind or impulses they generate. By parsing the experience of bodily sensations, feeling tones, emotions, thoughts, and possible imagery associated with negative of afflictive emotions, a space is created for more intentional responses. This points to a role for more visceral experience to work cooperatively with conscious intentions as a form of body-mind communication. As they conclude: "Mindfulness meditation, which trains the practitioner to focus on sensations in the body, provides a portal into the visceral experience of prejudice, and practices such as loving-kindness meditation can engender new automatic processes that lead to compassion and more effective communication" (p. 374).

In traditional Buddhism, there are other forms of meditation that are not mindfulness-based that are used to reduce bias and to foster prosocial behaviour. Many of these other meditations have found their way into mindfulness training because of their compatibility and complementarity with more narrowly defined mindfulness practices. Visualizations and analytical meditations are two key traditional types of non-mindfulness-based meditations used to counter hatred and antisocial attitudes and behaviours. The four "divine abodes" or "immeasurables" teach how to cultivate equanimity and remove afflictive emotions and negative feelings, attitudes, and behaviours towards our self and others. These four practices are loving-kindness, compassion, sympathetic joy, and equanimity, which are taught sequentially so as to build on the previous attribute. An exception, Klein (2014) places equanimity first in the sequence to support the positive regard for others. The contemplative practices of the four immeasurables combine mindfulness, visualization, and analytical meditation. It is worth pointing out that both the Buddha (Analayo, 2019) and the Dalai Lama (personal communication) claim mindfulness alone is insufficient to counter anger. The Dalai Lama, for example, teaches analytical meditation via mind training as the optimal way to counter anger.

## CONCLUSION

This chapter explored how too often the theories and practice of mindfulness focus on emotions but neglect the key building blocks of emotional regulation: awareness of feeling tones or affect. Mindfulness of feeling tones is one of the attentional tools that help people to identify biases that give rise to negative moods and associated emotions. Mindfulness functions to cultivate, among other things, more positive affect. According to the Mindfulness-as-Meaning Theory, the downstream effects of mindfulness include positive feeling tones and emotions that give rise to both meaning-making (via cognitive reappraisal) and savouring (via sensory pleasure and absorption). These effects on savouring and meaning are used to explain consistent findings that mindfulness improves wellbeing.

Meanwhile, as key institutions like K-12 education or criminal justice import mindfulness programmes as part of broader social-emotional learning agendas, it is important to disentangle mindfulness from other forms of social-emotional training, some of which may or may not be consistent with MBTL. Often these programmes embed motivations associated with social or behavioural control, for example, which is inconsistent with MBTL. Both ethically and empirically, mindfulness is associated with self-determination and autonomy, so to attempt to deliver programmes aimed at enhancing systems of control are antithetical, if not unethical. At the same time, it is natural to broaden the social and interpersonal applications of mindfulness to include social-emotional learning, compassion, and prosocial attitudes and behaviours, which are so critical to our personal and collective wellbeing. The place of explicit ethics in such training is still in debate, but part of that debate concerns whether or not ethical education needs to be explicit and, if so, to what ends. How does the focus on self-care extend to concern for others, for example, and what qualities and attitudes might secure more prosocial outcomes?

## REFERENCES


Analayo, B. (2021). Awakening or enlightenment? On the significance of *bodhi*. *Mindfulness*, *12*, 1653–1658. https://doi.org/10.1007/s12671-021-01628-2.

Analyayo, B. (2019). *Mindfulness of breathing: A practice guide and translations.* Windhorse Publications.

Barrett, L. (2017). *How emotions are made: The secret life of the brain.* Houghton Mifflin Harcourt.

Batchelor, M. (2019). Mindfulness theory: Feeling tones (*vedanas*) as a useful framework for research. *Current Opinion in Psychology*, *28*, 20–22. https://doi.org/10.1016/j.copsyc.2018.10.002.

Berila, B. (2016). *Integrating mindfulness into anti-oppression pedagogy: Social justice in higher education.* Routledge.

Berry, D., Hoerr, J., Cesko, S., Alayoubi, A., Carpio, K., Zirzow, H., Walters, W., Scram, G., Rodriguez, K., & Beaver, V. (2020). Does mindfulness training without explicit ethics-based instruction promote prosocial behaviors? A meta-analysis. *Personality and Social Psychology Bulletin*, *46*(8), 1247–1269. https://doi.org/10.1177/0146167219900418.

Boniolo, G. (2021). Demented patients and the quandaries of identity: Setting the problem, advancing a proposal. *History and Philosophy of the Life Sciences*, *43*, Art. 21. https://doi.org/10.1007/s40656-021-00365-y.

Burgess, D., Beach, M., & Saha, S. (2017). Mindfulness practice: A promising approach to reducing the effects of clinician implicit bias on patients. *Patient Education and Counselling*, *100*(2), 372–376. https://doi.org/10.1016/j.pec

Chiesa, A., Serretti, A., & Jakobsen, J. (2013). Mindfulness: Top-down or bottom-up emotion regulation strategy? *Clinical Psychology Review*, *33*, 82–96. http://dx.doi.org/10.1016/j.cpr.2012.10.006.

Collaborative for Academic, Social, and Emotional Learning (CASEL). (2021a). *What is SEL?* Retrieved August 24, 2021, from https://casel.org/what-is-sel.

Collaborative for Academic, Social, and Emotional Learning (CASEL). (2021b). *Program guide.* Retrieved September 4, 2021, from https://pg.casel.org/.

Cutuli, D. (2014). Cognitive reappraisal and expressive suppression strategies role in the emotion regulation: An overview on their modulatory effects and neural correlates. *Frontiers in Systems Neuroscience*, *8*, Art. 175. https://doi.org/10.3389/fnsys.2014.00175.

Dalenberg, C., Naish, B., & Abu-Rus, A. (2022). Dissociation, dissociative disorder, and their treatment. In R. Geffner, J. W. White, L. K. Hamberger, A. Rosenbaum, V. Vaughan-Eden, & V. I. Vieth (Eds.), *Handbook of interpersonal violence and abuse across the lifespan: A project of the National Partnership to End Interpersonal Violence Across the Lifespan (NPEIV)* (pp. 4383–4408). Springer Nature. https://doi.org/10.1007/978-3-319-89999-2_177.

Deci, E., Ryan, R., Schultz, P., & Niemiec, C. (2015). Being aware and functioning fully: Mindfulness and interest taking within self-determination theory. In K. Brown, D. Creswell, & R. Ryan (Eds.), *Handbook of mindfulness: Theory, research, and practice* (pp. 112–129). Guilford Press.

Desbordes, G., Gard, T., Hoge, E., Holzel, B., Kerr, C., Lazar, S., Olendzki, A., & Vago, D. (2015). Moving beyond mindfulness: Defining equanimity as an outcome measure in meditation and contemplative research. *Mindfulness*, *6*, 356–372. https://doi.org/10.1007/s12671-013-0269-8

Durlak. J., Weissberg, R., Dymnicki, A., Taylor, R., & Schellinger, K. (2011). The impact of enhancing students' social and emotional learning: A meta-analysis of scholl-based universal interventions. *Child Development*, *82*(1), 405–432. https://doi.org/10.1111/j.1467-8624.2010.01564.x

Flook, L., Goldberg, S. B., Pinger, L., & Davidson, R. J. (2015). Promoting prosocial behavior and self-regulatory skills in preschool children through a mindfulness-based kindness curriculum. *Developmental Psychology*, *51*(1), 44–51. https://doi.org/10.1037/a0038256.

Fronsdal, G., & Pandita, S., (2005). A perfect balance. *Tricycle: The Buddhist Review*, Winter. https://tricycle.org/magazine/perfect-balance/.

Goleman, D., McKee, A., & Waytz, A. (2017). *Empathy (HBR emotional intelligence series)*. Harvard Business Review Press. https://www.worldcat.org/title/empathy-hbr-emotional-intelligence-series/oclc/1015859642.

Grajewski, P., & Dragan, M. (2020). Adverse childhood experiences, dissociation, and anxious attachment style as risk factors of gaming disorder. *Addictive Behaviors Reports*, *11*, 100269. https://doi.org/10.1016/j.abrep.2020.100269.

Hafenbrack, A., LaPalme, M., & Solal, I. (2021). Mindfulness meditation reduces guild and prosocial reparation. *Journal of Personality and Social Psychology: Attitudes and Social Cognition.* Advance online publication. https://doi.org/10.1037/pspa0000298.

Harmon-Jones, E., & Harmon-Jones, C. (2021). On defining positive affect (PA): Considering attitudes toward emotions, measures of PA, and approach motivation. *Current Opinion in Behavioral Sciences*, *39*, 46–51. https://doi.org/10.1016/j.cobeha.2021.01.008.

Hoffman, M. L. (2008). Empathy and prosocial behavior. In M. Lewis, J. Haviland-Jones, & L. Barrett (Eds.), *Handbook of emotions* (3rd ed., pp. 440–455). The Guilford Press.

Jones, S. M., Brush, E. K., Ramirez, T., Xinyi Mao, Z., Marenus, M., Wettje, S., Finney, K., Raisch, N., Podoloff, N., Kahn, J., Barnes, S., Stickle, L., BrionMeisels, G., McIntyre, J., Cuartas, J., & Bailey, R. (2021). *Navigating SEL from the inside out looking inside & across 33 leading SEL programs: A practical resource for schools and OST providers.* The Harvard Graduate School of

Education. http://www.wallacefoundation.org/knowledge-center/Documents/Navigating-Social-and-Emotional-Learning-from-the-Inside-Out.pdf.

Klein, A. (2014). The four immeasurables: How to deepen equanimity, love, compassion, and joy. *Tricycle: The Buddhist Review*, Fall. https://tricycle.org/magazine/four-immeasurables/.

Kuyken, W., Watkins, E., Holden, E., White, K., Taylor, R. S., Byford, S., Evans, A., Radford, S., Teasdale, J. D., & Dalgleish, T. (2010). How does mindfulness-based cognitive therapy work? *Behaviour Research and Therapy*, *48*(11), 1105–1112. https://doi.org/10.1016/j.brat.2010.08.003.

Langenberg, A. (2021, February). The Buddha didn't teach consent: But can early Buddhism help us develop a better sexual ethics anyway? *Tricycle: The Buddhist Review*. https://tricycle.org/trikedaily/buddhist-sexual-ethics/.

Lomas, T., Medina, J. C., Ivtzan, I., Rupprecht, S., & Eroá-Orosa, F. (2018). A systematic review and meta-analysis of the impact of mindfulness-based interventions on the well-being of healthcare professionals. *Mindfulness*, *10*(7), 1193–1216. https://doi.org/10.1007/s12671-018-1062-5.

López, A., Sanderman, R., Ranchor, A. V., & Schroevers, M. J. (2018). Compassion for others and self- compassion: Levels, correlates, and relationship with psychological well- being. *Mindfulness*, *9*, 325–331. https://doi.org/10.1007/s12671-017-0777-z.

Neff, K. D. (2003). Self-compassion: An alternative conceptualization of a healthy attitude toward oneself. *Self and Identity*, *2*, 85–101. https://doi.org/10.1080/15298860309032.

Olendski, A. (2004). The fourth foundation of mindfulness. *Insight Journal, Spring*, 13–17. https://www.buddhistinquiry.org/issue/spring-2004/.

Poulin, M., Ministero, L., Gabriel, S., Morrison, C. D., & Naidu, E. (2021). Minding your own business? Mindfulness decreases prosocial behavior for those with independent self-construals. *PsyArXiv*. https://doi.org/10.31234/osf.io/xhyua.

Roth, J. (2018). Worldly and unworldly feelings, fabrication and letting go. *Contemporary Buddhism*, *19*(2), 398–416. https://doi.org/10.1080/14639947.2018.1576291

Rupprecht, S., Koole, W., Chaskalson, M., Tamdjidi, C., & West, M. (2019). Running too far ahead? Towards a broader understanding of mindfulness in organisations. *Current Opinion in Psychology*, *28*, 32–36. https://doi.org/10.1016/j.copsyc.2018.10.007.

Saarinen, A. L., Keltikangas-Järvinen, L., Pulkki-Råback, L., Cloninger, C. R., Elovainio, M., Lehtimäki, T., Raitakari, O., & Hintsanen, M. (2020). The relationship of dispositional compassion with well-being: A study with a 15-year prospective follow-up. *The Journal of Positive Psychology*, *15*(6), 806–820. https://doi.org/10.1080/17439760.2019.1663251.

Schonert-Reichl, K., Oberle, E., Lawlor, M., Abbott, D., Thomson, K., Oberlander, T., & Diamond, A. (2015). Enhancing cognitive and social-emotional development through a simple-to-administer mindfulness-based school program for elementary school children: A randomized controlled trial. *Developmental Psychology*, *51*(1), 52–66. https://doi.org/10.1037/a0038454.

Thierry, K. L., Bryant, H. L., Speegle Nobles, S., & Norris, K. S. (2016). Two-year impact of a mindfulness-based program on preschoolers' self-regulation and academic performance. *Early Education and Development*, *27*(6), 805–821. https://doi.org/10.1080/10409289.2016.1141616.

Weinstein, N. (2009). *Interest-taking and carry-over effects of incident rejection emotions*. A doctoral dissertation submitted to the University of Rochester.

Weissberg, R. P., Durlak, J. A., Domitrovich, C. E., & Gullotta, T. P. (Eds.). (2015). Social and emotional learning: Past, present, and future. In J. Durlak, C. Domitrovich, R. Weissberg, & T. Gullotta (Eds.), *Handbook of social and emotional learning: Research and practice* (pp. 3–19). The Guilford Press.

# CHAPTER 14

# MINDFULNESS AS INQUIRY-BASED LEARNING

The value of mindfulness as inquiry-based learning has been under-recognized, under-appreciated, and under-represented in secular-scientific mindfulness research and practice. This is regrettable as it is arguably the most important potential role for mindfulness in education. As inquiry-based learning, mindfulness becomes more than a technique. It is an integrated approach with implications across the curriculum rather than within a narrow social-emotional learning (SEL) agenda. In this way, MBTL shifts from being an *intervention* to address personal or social pathologies to becoming a distinctive way to investigate the world. As a systematic form of inductive experiential learning, MBTL fosters and trains free and open inquiry of the world around us. This is the world as it manifests in the felt present moment, beyond the constraints of inherited assumptions, practices, and theories. In this way, it goes to the heart of the evolutionary and adaptive value of learning and education.

## INQUIRY-BASED LEARNING

There are two distinctive forms of "inquiry" coming together in this chapter. In one case, inquiry refers to processes used to recognize, describe, and investigate mindfulness experiences, often directed towards insight. The use of the term inquiry can be found in many secular-scientific mindfulness programmes and teacher training materials. The other form of inquiry is inquiry-based teaching and learning found within the broader context of educational practice, often associated with science education. Hattie (2009) defined this broader use of the concept of inquiry, focused on K-12 education, as follows:

> Inquiry-based teaching is the art of developing challenging situations in which students are asked to observe and question phenomena; pose explanations of what they observe; devise and conduct experiments in which data are collected to support or contradict their theories; analyze data; draw conclusions from experimental data; design and build models; or any combination of these. Such learning situations are meant to be open-ended in that they do not aim to achieve a single "right" answer for a particular question being addressed, but rather involve students more in the process of observing, posing questions, engaging in experimentation or exploration, and learning to analyze and reason.
>
> *(p. 208–209)*

We bring these two forms of inquiry together to broaden the scope of MBTL practices and to represent more fully the contexts in which mindfulness is applied. The use of scientific procedural terms like data, experiments, and models in the description of inquiry-based learning may seem inconsistent with mindfulness; however, if understood more broadly, even these technical terms apply. To better appreciate inquiry in MBTL, we consider parallels and points of conflict in how mindful inquiry is or can be applied in two key educational contexts: First, in adult and professional education, where inquiry is understood as experiential learning (Kolb, 2015) and reflective practice (Schon, 1983) and, second, across educational contexts, including K-12

DOI: 10.4324/9781003182467-19

subject areas, where a distinctive view of the inquiry process or cycle is already in place (Pedaste et al., 2015).

## Experiential Learning

The theory of inquiry-based learning is entangled with experiential theories of learning, extending back to William James, John Dewey, Lewin, and, more recently, Kolb (2015) who proposed a distinctive model of experiential inquiry. Kolb's model suggests that *naive* or unexamined experience becomes knowledge through processes of reflection and abstract conceptualization. In this respect, Schon's (1983) theory of how practitioners learn through reflecting on experience or practice is a complementary and aligned notion to what is fostered in MBTL. Kolb's (1984) experiential learning cycle proposed a continuous cycle in which experience generates and refines knowledge. Derived from a definition of learning as "the process whereby knowledge is created through the transformation of experience" (Kolb & Kolb, 2013; p. 49), knowledge is considered to be the result of the grasping (experience/abstraction dialectic) and transforming (action/reflection dialectic) of experience. As depicted in Figure 14.1, concrete experience is the basis and catalyst for the other three steps in the cycle: Reflective observation, abstract conceptualization, and active experimentation. Although this cycle uses terms like "experimentation" associated with science, it is intended to portray a more universal pattern of human inquiry involving experiential learning.

As Kolb (2015) suggests, experiential learning does not necessarily follow a linear progression through the four components. Seemingly opposite functions can interact as binary pairs, such as concrete experience with abstract conceptualization or reflective observation with active experimentation. What distinguishes learning as experiential inquiry is the dynamic between reflection and the direct engagement with phenomena, that is, applying what is learned from direct experience to deepen and validate emerging conceptual knowledge and then returning to experience and reflection and so on. This implies specific

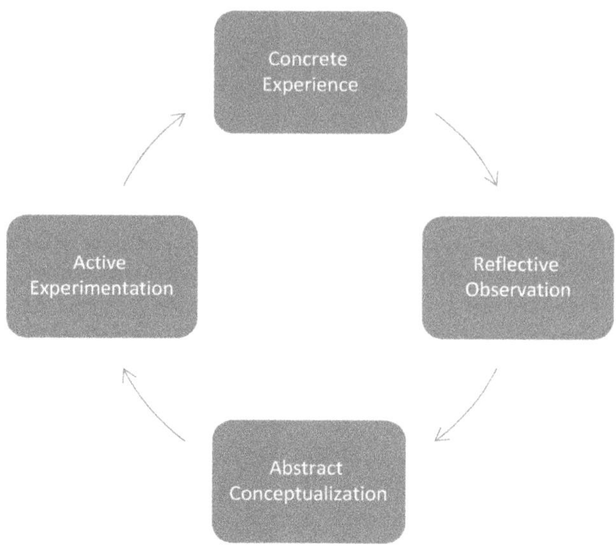


**Figure 14.1** The Experiential Learning Cycle (adapted and simplified from Kolb, 2015, p. 51)

skills in observing direct experience using bare attention (i.e., concrete experience or mindfulness); recognizing, describing, and reflecting on experience by conceptualizing (naming, labelling) without elaborating conceptually (i.e., reflective observation); analyzing and weaving experiences into integrative abstract principles, theories, and insights (i.e., abstract conceptualization or interpretation); and navigating and returning to experiences repeatedly to extend and validate emerging knowledge (i.e., active experimentation).

## MBTL as Experiential Learning

Mindfulness-based inquiry begins with the direct "facticity" of experience. This makes it both a unique form of experiential inquiry and at the same time compatible with empirical processes in science. Rather than ending with experience, mindfulness inquiry also starts there. It is, in this respect, a robust form of inductive inquiry. Experience is frontloaded in the learning cycle to ensure that the sensed facticity of the object of learning, or its approximation, precedes and informs subsequent conceptual elaboration. Unlike common forms of deductive experiential learning, such as practica or applied capstone projects, in which acquired principles and knowledge are applied in practice, mindfulness-based inquiry reasons through direct experience itself. Consistent with Kolb's (2015) model, the MBTL inquiry cycle returns again and again to experience for verification and knowledge development.

Indeed, Kolb (2015) now explicitly links his experiential inquiry learning model to mindfulness-based practices and processes, citing at length the Japanese Zen philosopher Kitaro Nishida (1990):

> To experience means to know facts just as they are; to know in accordance with fact by completely relinquishing one's own fabrications. What we usually refer to as experience is adulterated with some sort of thought, so by pure I am referring to the state of experience just as it is, without the least addition of deliberative discrimination. The moment of seeing a color or hearing a sound, for example, is prior not only to the thought that the colour or sound is the activity of an external object or that one is sensing it, but also to the judgement of what the color or sound might be.
>
> *(p. 3)*

As Nishida describes it, the facticity of knowledge is grounded in direct concrete experience – what he calls *pure* experience – freed from conceptual elaboration. Consequently, "knowing" is anchored in the immediate experiential encounter with what is to be known.

As closely aligned as experiential- and mindfulness-based inquiry may appear to be in theory, in practice they differ in critical ways. Within higher education, for example, the spectrum of what constitutes inquiry and experiential learning is quite narrowly defined. The American Association for Colleges and Universities (AAC&U) (2009a), for example, defines inquiry in higher education as follows: "Inquiry is a systematic process of exploring issues, objects or works through the collection and analysis of evidence that results in informed conclusions or judgments." On face value, this is consistent with mindfulness-based inquiry if and when "objects" are understood to include all phenomena and "evidence" is understood to include the direct experience of such an object of inquiry. Yet, conventional usage might not interpret either "objects" or "evidence" in this broad sense. Indeed, when "inquiry" is operationalized as assessment criteria in the associated AAC&U *Inquiry and Analysis VALUE Rubric*, "evidence" becomes defined narrowly as abstract conceptual processes or research-based (numeric or textual) information (i.e., topic selection, synthesizing perspective, research method or design, analysis, conclusions, and limitations and implications).

Experiential learning is also interpreted narrowly by the AAC&U so as to limit its broader interpretation as mindfulness-based inquiry. The AAC&U's (2009b) *Integrative and Applied Learning VALUE Rubric* defines *experiential learning* as "learning that takes place in a setting outside of the formal classroom, such as workplace, service learning site, internship site or another." This describes an approach to experiential learning in which abstract knowledge acquired in classrooms is deductively applied in the experiential contexts of field placements or practica. Entirely missing are approaches to experiential learning *within* classes, where experience is used directly in the initial knowledge creation and validation process. The capstone benchmark or criterion of "connections to experience," for example, is described as follows: "Meaningfully synthesizes connections among experiences outside of the formal classroom (including life experiences and academic experiences such as internships and travel abroad) to deepen understanding of fields of study and to broaden own points of view." Although such experiences could benefit from a mindfulness inquiry process, they tend to backload rather than frontload experiences, and there is no requirement in mindfulness that experiences be outside of the classroom.

The AACU definitions of inquiry-based and experiential learning reflect biases that conflict with mindfulness-based inquiry. First, they are biased in favour of conceptual versus experiential inquiry. Inquiry is described as beginning with a topic or question to initiate an abstract-conceptual rather than experientially-mediated process. The second bias is the deductive bias in how experiential learning is conducted. The reliance on backloading experiences in their description mirrors the deductive logic of much scientific empirical research, in which prior theories are used to generate hypotheses that are then tested. Yet, even in science, direct inductive reasoning from experience underpins key scientific theories like the theory of natural selection, which emerged from Darwin's direct observations of nature.

## MBTL as Inquiry-Based Learning

Inquiry processes are already integral to the teaching and learning of standardized mindfulness programs like MBSR and MBCT. Usually the term *inquiry* refers to a specific form of post-practice inquiry (Crane et al., 2015; Woods et al., 2019; Woods & Rockman, 2021). Yet, post-practice forms of inquiry are intended to reinforce in-practice inquiry through curiosity and recognition and may even be introduced during brief pre-practice forms of inquiry. Taken together, these are all forms of inquiry focused on the actual practice of mindfulness itself, what we might call *mindfulness as inquiry*.

As the Buddhist theory of the seven awakening factors reminds us, mindfulness is insufficient for deep or transformative learning. Investigative inquiry is needed to extend mindfulness to become a viable path of learning. Furthermore, such inquiry may well involve forms of conceptual inquiry or conceptual elaboration. Currently, this activity in MBIs tends to be referred to as didactic teaching (Crane et al., 2015), where, at best, concepts pulled from post-practice inquiry are developed as information. More commonly, teachers end up lecturing or downloading information, methods that have fallen into considerable disrepute in the past few decades (e.g., Lord & Orkwiszewski, 2006). Such teacher-centred practices conflict with the principles of MBTL, such as the respect for student autonomy and emphasis on inductive learning from experience. It is as if MBIs conserved the mindfulness components of their programs, including inquiry, in a cocoon that is dropped as soon the curriculum or session moves from formal mindfulness practices into discussing the themes and ostensible purposes or topic of the class (e.g., the stress response). For these reasons, we explicitly re-defined didactic teaching as *investigative inquiry*.

Finally, we propose the need for meta-inquiry into what and how we are learning, not just as teachers but as learners. In particular, such meta-awareness needs to be turned on colonial and oppressive imprints that may continue to infect or pervade what and how we teach and learn mindfulness. Although it may sound like a critical conceptual space, it is not only that. It is also opening to the awareness of other sentient beings, human and non-human, and viewing their interests as somehow equal to our own. In addition, this allows a creative impulse in MBTL that applies to ecological adaptation – the adaptation of learners but also of the methods we use in MBTL. We refer to this final, albeit rarer, form of inquiry as meta-learning or meta-inquiry. We now consider each of these three types of inquiry in sequence: Mindfulness itself as inquiry (pre-, in-, post-practice); investigative inquiry; and meta-inquiry.

## MINDFULNESS ITSELF *AS* INQUIRY

This form of inquiry is focused on inquiry during the practice of mindfulness. It is helpful to consider pre-practice, in-practice, and post-practice forms of inquiry, though the most formalized and challenging is post-practice inquiry.

### Pre-Practice Inquiring

Unlike other educational approaches that advocate stimulating students' "background knowledge," "schema," or interest in a topic of inquiry, mindfulness-based inquiry tends to move into experience without too much preparation or context setting. This minimalism reflects the need to reduce learners' conditioned expectations, interpretive filters, cognitive elaboration, and habitual impulses and perspectives from interfering with the direct engagement with what is being attended to. Yet, pre-practice inquiry can help in two ways. First, it can foster certain desirable attitudes like curiosity towards the object of mindfulness or the theme of that session. For example, before a mindfulness of breathing session, a teacher might start by musing or dialoguing about what it means to "breathe naturally" and how much control can or cannot be exercised over breathing. The second form of pre-practice inquiry involves introducing a particular skill that novices might then practice and reflect on in post-practice inquiry. Using the same example, it could be an exploration of how to relinquish control impulses to invite the observation of the natural breath (see Textbox 9.1 for an example of this).

### In-Practice Inquiring

MBTL teachers and facilitators foster in-practice inquiry in learners through the skillful use of guidance during mindfulness practices. They encourage participants to inquire directly, without conceptual elaborations, into experiences while the experiences are still unfolding. This direct inquiry in mindfulness involves both observing (noticing) and recognizing (knowing) experiences. In this respect, all mindfulness would involve some degree of in-practice inquiry with evidence of investigation, curiosity or energy, and interest; however, when attention is unregulated, dull, or unclear, then it is unlikely that there would be much evidence of in-practice inquiry. The interest and engagement accompanying in-practice inquiry enlivens energy, brightens the mind, and improves the capacity to hold the object quite naturally through interest. At the same time, in-practice inquiry *can* involve the explicit mediation of conceptual thought and questions. For example, Martine Batchelor (2008), a Buddhist teacher and author, uses a Korean Zen koan in the form of a question –– "What is this?" – when attending to experience during mindfulness. One of the authors (SM) has used part of a line from Psalm 46: "Be still and know that I am..." to awaken curiosity in open awareness practice.

Particular cues that may be used in guidance to support inquiry include reminding practitioners of the object of focus, if there is one, and the need to return to it with curiosity. Also, guidance can draw attention to finer details of experience to deepen or extend awareness. These details need not be specified, either; for example, when guiding the body scan practice, one of the authors (SM) often invites participants to "notice what is to be known here." Another feature of guidance that can support in-practice inquiry is the "attitudinal foundations." These are the set of attitudes considered to be supportive of mindfulness and the cultivation of mindfulness, such as a beginner's mind, patience, non-striving, non-judgment, acceptance, openness (to new experiences), loving-kindness, and curiosity. Woods and Rockman (2021) identify these attitudes in three general categories: presence, form, and process.

## Post-Practice Inquiring

Post-practice inquiry is a distinctive form of reflective inquiry involving the careful, scaffolded use of language, memory, and conceptual thought in the immediate aftermath of mindfulness experiences. Woods, Rockman, and Collins (2019) refer to such inquiry as a form of contemplative dialogue characterized by the following features:

> This interactive process uses a series of open-ended questions, observations, wonderings, and reflections. The objects of investigation are the actual noticing of experience (and one's relationship to it); its components, qualities, and temporal nature; and the integration of what is learned through this exploration into daily life. Through this process of honing the participant's skill of describing direct experience and reflecting on what has just occurred versus narrating (following a storyline), decreased identification with experience is cultivate.
> *(p. 125)*

The primary purposes of post-practice inquiry are to foster the capacity to describe introspective experience; to increase self-efficacy (agency or autonomy); and to learn to decentre (dis-identify) or distance from being immersed in experience. Although such dialogue can be conducted introspectively with oneself or with peers in small groups or dyads, the more common method is for a teacher to engage in 1:1 dialogue with a learner, often in a group setting so as to foster peer, not just individual, learning. The teacher invites learners to engage in a sequence of question:answer:reflection exchanges. These exchanges may move across three layers: First describing experiences that just occurred; then differentiating and/or to tracking those experiences in time; and then deriving principles or nascent insights from them. Through dialogue, teachers model key attitudes such as curiosity, investigation, non-judgment, and reflection in how they shift from direct experience into thinking about the experience.

The process entails using a sequence of three types of questions that move from more concrete to more abstract with both simple and complex responses. The first layer scaffolds learners from direct experience into language and memory by describing those experiences, using probes such as: "What did you notice?" or "What came up in this practice?" The ability to describe experience is the second of five operationalized indicators of mindfulness in the FFMQ (see the end of Chapter 10). By attending and returning attention to the description of direct sensorial experiences and away from interpretive elaborations, post-practice inquiry helps participants to recognize and differentiate direct experience and interpretation. The narrow attention to immediate experience reduces tendencies to substitute ideas, interpretations, and conclusions about experience for the experience itself. Also, it discourages participants from weaving meditative experience into stories about those experiences.

The second layer continues to compare or consider experiences unfolding across time through the use of probes like "How did this experience of the body differ from your usual experience of the body?" or merely "What happened then?" This brings the awareness slowly into time, first comparing the mindful condition against habitual experience, and then tracking experiences over time to realize their impermanence. In both cases, the shift into comparing experiences across time reflects an incremental degree of generalization or abstraction.

Finally, in the third and final layer, participants are invited to consider the purpose or principles of a practice, using probes such as "Why might we do this practice?" or "How might this be beneficial for wellbeing?" Although this resembles investigative inquiry in the use of concepts and reasoning, the focus is still narrowly placed on the recent experiences and generalizing from those experiences to applications in life. Now we turn to considering six key purposes and functions of post-practice inquiry.

### *Enhancing Awareness*

Post-practice inquiry enhances awareness of thoughts, emotions, sensations, impulses, or urges and behaviours by training participants to parse experiences into these categories to decrease their appearance as fixed, integrated realities that can overwhelm or intimidate our capacity to respond. By describing recent experiences still held in short-term memory, aspects of experience otherwise overlooked or ignored may come to the surface of awareness to be recognized and known. This may include encountering aversion (what we don't like) and attachment (what we do like) and to recognize how reactivity is tied up in these.

### *Increasing Sensorial Focus*

Post-practice inquiry invites participants to return attention and descriptions to direct sensorial experiences (treating the labelling of emotions and thoughts as sensorial), and away from discursive or elaborative thinking and interpretations. This reinforces attention regulation and the capacity to differentiate between rumination and direct perception. Navigating these differences in language enhances powers of recognition beyond mere observation, thereby supporting practitioners to remember such differences and retain such attention regulation practices over time.

### *Developing Observational Skills*

In addition, the backwash effect of post-practice inquiry increases observational skills by teaching how to attend to more details and features of experience. It provides a more detached place from which to witness, view, or review experience, thereby kick-starting the decentering process. This can lead to the development of meta-awareness or meta-cognition (awareness of awareness) abilities through deepening decentering and de-fusion allowing for the arising of insight and alternative perspectives on "reality."

### *Learning to Language Experience*

Capacities to observe and to describe experiences are distinct abilities in mindfulness, and evidence suggests that the capacity to describe may be the more important ability for wellbeing. For example, Mattes (2019) conducted metanalytical research on the FFMQ facets, concluding that the *describe* facet had the highest zero-order correlation with positive outcomes as compared to the other four; the *observe* facet, on the other hand, had the lowest. This suggests that training participants to develop a vocabulary in order to be able to describe what they just observed may be critical to cultivating positive outcomes from mindfulness. Furthermore, it is reasonable to suppose that this languaging of experience involves a distinctive neurocognitive process linking higher cortical functions with sensory and emotional processing regions of the brain, and that such descriptions broaden awareness by making more conscious what was only partially conscious through observation alone.

### *Enhancing Memory*

Also significant are the benefits of post-practice inquiry for memory retention of mindfulness experiences and associated skill development. The focus on recollecting features of immediate meditative experiences may remove potential interferences arising from moving too quickly back into autobiographical or narrative referencing of experiences. For example, Varma et al. (2018) found that autobiographical thought interfered with memory consolidation, whereas focusing on recall in a two-back task that reduced autobiographical thinking enhanced episodic memory consolidation. Furthermore, the movement from the recall of details of experience into progressive levels of abstraction across time, as in the second layer inquiry into change, or as principles and rationale via the third layer, may further help consolidate experiences as learning.

### *Enhancing Reflective Skills*

Post-practice inquiry deepens a practitioner's self-reflective skills and capacity to derive insights from meditative experiences. This is done in part through the use of simple (descriptive) and complex (extending, deepening, translating) reflections. An example is inquiring into how a person responded to challenges arising during a practice, focusing interest and attention on such difficulties and any unwanted experiences. Such inquiries can consolidate the link between the practice and dealing with difficult states in life – e.g., reactivity, depression, anxiety, or staying well. Such inquiry helps to normalize difficulty and enhance awareness of the universality of experience. Facing difficulties also increases the sense of options, agency, and choice. Likewise, in using language that is curious and non-judgmental, such post-practice inquiry reduces self-other evaluations and highlights attitudes of self-reflection, self-compassion, or self-care.

The layered nature of post-practice inquiry, depicted in the exemplar in Textbox 14.1, moves reflections from bare descriptions of experience into more abstract principles and knowledge. In the immediate first layer, the task of the teacher is to practice openness and awareness in listening to the experiences recounted by participants using a minimalist probe, such as "What did you notice?" So too, it involves responding without judgment in a way that affirms, clarifies, or deepens a participant's ability to observe and recognize experience, by inviting them to return to experience and away from narration or interpretation. The second layer is oriented on cultivating a reflective observer and the third layer is on developing inductively developed principles and generalizations from experience. Post-practice inquiry can be depicted as horizontal, that is, aimed at eliciting responses from many participants, or vertical, that is, inquiring in more depth. In both instances, the purpose is teaching the entire class or group, as the understanding is that the experience of one participant is instructive to many. Finally, as mentioned, teacher reflections or responses can be simple or complex. With experience, a teacher can let go of the three layers and respond more uniquely and directly to the experiences and insights of participants.

## TEXTBOX 14.1 POST-PRACTICE INQUIRY:

### Samples of Questions to Pose in Three Layers

**Layer 1 – Noticing or Recognizing Experience** (Can be a self-reflection or part of a dialogue between teacher and participant.)

- What came up? What did you notice?
- Can you name the emotion? Perhaps "anger" or "sadness" were present?
- What's present for you now?
- Isn't that interesting (bringing curiosity to experience)?

**Layer 2 – Comparing and Contrasting or Tracking**

The second layer highlights "noticing the noticing" and the creation of the observer as the one who witnesses experience and in the shift toward meta-awareness. It allows us to recognize that we are attending differently (salient attention) and also to develop the facility to track our attention and experience.

i) **Comparative Attention**: Intentional vs Habitual Attention
   - How is this different from your usual experience?
   - As the participant starts narrating, "so you noticed thinking" (or thoughts were present)
   - You're taking a step back and are witnessing your experience…

ii) **Tracking**
   - And then what happened? And then?

**Layer 3 – Integration**

The third layer makes the link between the practice, its integration into life, and staying well:

- How might this practice help us to stay well?...to work with stress?...to practise wellbeing?
- How might this be useful for dealing with anxiety/depressive states?
- What might be the relevance of this practice? Why might we do this practice?

## INVESTIGATIVE INQUIRY

Investigative inquiry both builds on and moves beyond mindfulness by "examining, scrutinizing, and investigating the information that has become available through the open receptivity of mindfulness" (Analayo, 2018, pp. 174–175). Most mindfulness programmes introduce mindfulness practices as part of a broader question or topic of investigation. In the case of MBSR or MBCT, for example, the topics of investigation are stress and depression, respectively. Although inquiry begins with mindfulness of the focal phenomenon itself, it is deepened through investigative inquiry with more conceptual, abstract, and intellectual reflections used to deepen insights and knowledge about the phenomenon. In this way, MBTL involves a robust inductive approach to inquiry that "frontloads experience." The integration of investigative inquiry in MBTL makes it consistent with inquiry-based experiential education across the curriculum. Investigative inquiry is promoted in MBTL through intentions and questions; inductive reasoning and reflection; and sustained focus.

### Intentions and Questioning

Investigative inquiry begins by working on focal themes, intentions, and outcomes for teaching and learning. In Chapter 16, we propose the S.T.O.P.(A) approach to specify component skills, themes, outcomes, practices (and specified activities). These help a teacher develop explicit awareness of the questions and intentions guiding a session or programme, which they can then share or extend to learners. In this way, learners arrive at personalized intentions and questions that support their own investigative inquiry of the topic at hand.

### Inductive Reasoning and Reflecting

With some degree of questioning and curiosity in place, participants are ready to exercise more autonomy as they engage in more abstract, analytical, conceptual, or text-based forms of inquiry. Furthermore, this investigation brings increased curiosity and interest in the form of energy back to the mindfulness process itself, which in turn informs later investigation. This is reflected in the cyclical experiential learning process depicted by Kolb. In this respect, as Analayo (2018) emphasizes, "mindfulness can coexist with the use of concepts; in fact the input provided through the wise use of concepts is of crucial importance for *satipatthana* meditation" (p. 23).

### Sustained Inquiring

In the context of mindfulness-based inquiry learning, investigation is sustained over time. Through such sustained contemplations, *mere* concepts develop into lived, realized, and embodied forms of knowledge. If we consider the seven awakening factors, for example, we see a movement from mindfulness to investigation becoming sustained through the third of the seven factors: *Energy* (or *perseverance*). The fourth factor, *joy*, arises naturally in response to the previous three factors – mindfulness, investigation, and energy – which together constitute interest. *Energy* is further reinforced through this fourth factor of positive emotion, translated as joy or even ecstasy, but connected as well to qualities of happiness and gladdening associated with mindfulness of breathing, for example (Analayo, 2019). This positive emotion is intrinsically rewarding and arises through mindfulness-based learning itself and its downstream effects on enhanced savouring and meaning (Garland et al., 2015).

In these ways, understanding mindfulness as inquiry-based learning enables further alignments between secular-scientific and Buddhist theories of mindfulness-based learning. As outlined in Chapter 11, once stabilized, joy deepens into *tranquility*, which broadens and integrates awareness as *concentration* and from there manifests in *equanimity*, the seventh and final factor. Equanimity is a state of openness and acceptance that enables valid, embodied insights to emerge through mindfulness-based investigative inquiry. In this respect, *investigation* begins the process by which mindfulness is nurtured to generate its downstream effects on *equanimity*. This is consistent with recent scientific scholarship arguing for the need to untangle mindfulness from broader effects that are more accurately associated with equanimity (Desbordes et al., 2015). Also worth noting is how the traditional theory of the seven factors of awakening aligns well with positive psychological theories, including *self-determination* (Sheldon & Ryan, 2011) and *flow* (Nakamura & Czikszentmihalyi, 2014).

## META-INQUIRY

The final form of inquiry may appear implicitly, if not explicitly, in MBTL. What we are calling *meta-inquiry* involves a process of looking back on the process of inquiry itself. This is more than just checking in on the mind state and the presence or absence of hindrances or awakening factors described in Chapter 11. Instead, it is entering a kind of transpersonal perspective that considers the biases implicit in mindfulness and inquiry themselves. We can examine the effects of such meta-inquiry in three areas: Adaptation, decolonization and anti-oppression, and creativity and insight.

### Adaptive Inquiring

Adaptation becomes a kind of meta-inquiry in itself. This kind of adaptive inquiry emerges quite naturally to discern how one adapts oneself and the world to new knowledge given the insights of the inquiry process. In this sense, we might say that mindfulness-based inquiry ends as it began, that is, in experience; however, this end is very different from where it began. As knowing through experience with the support of analysis, it is a form of knowing that is more complete, embodied, and integrated. It is not knowing intellectually or as information so much as through direct perception of what does or does not support wellbeing in oneself and others. It is part of the meta-inquiry process because in a sense this kind of inquiry involves reflecting on our experience not just as an individual but as a member of a community, as a member of a species, or as life.

## Decolonizing and Anti-Oppressive

In becoming aware of the conditionality of inquiry itself through meta-inquiry, we come to recognize layers of conditioning in our inquiry topics and approaches informed by a range of anthropocentric (species-centric), cultural, familial, or personal experiences, habits, and biases that may persist below the threshold of ordinary awareness. Mindful inquiry can broaden such awareness to enable us to see these biases up close and correct them. For example, we may come to notice that we avoid some studies or areas or potential interest because of conditioning – perhaps as a woman avoiding science, trades, or technology because of implicit biases or because of past traumas, such as being forced to dissect animals in a high school or university science classes.

Meta-inquiry invites a transpersonal critical lens as well to consider the histories of colonization and oppression not only of Indigenous and other colonized people but also of the Earth itself. These biases may be recognized as lingering and corrected by the intention to broaden, open, and eliminate the biases of the mind. This quite naturally leads to less self-centredness and offers a way to link mindfulness and meta-inquiry to the cultivation of compassion. To interrogate our questions and forms of inquiry for their impact on legacies of colonization and oppression shifts mindfulness-based investigation to an *interest* in social justice.

## Creativity and Insight

The connection between mindfulness and creativity was established early in the migration of mindfulness from traditional to modern secular contexts. More recently, a review found a weak but significant connection between the mindfulness and creativity (Lebuda et al., 2016). Other studies suggest mindfulness improves learning itself, as suggested by *meta-inquiry*. For example, in Ovington et al.'s (2018) study on insight, the researchers hypothesized that fixation with analysis in problem-solving would lead to a rut that might stymie insight and interfere with learning. They proposed that for insight, three conditions were required: "First, the solver must move from local to global processing. Second, they must persist with the problem and overcome frustration. Third, they need to break out of their mental rut" (p. 585). They then designed a study (N=1069) to measure the differential impacts of mindfulness, flow, and positive affect or feeling tones on insight. They found that mindfulness and flow both had a significant effect on insight, but that positive affect did not. Furthermore, in a second regression analysis, the components of flow were broken down to reveal that three key aspects of flow explained most of its effects: merging of action with awareness;

unambiguous feedback; and the transformation of time. Indeed, one factor, clear goals, had a negative relationship to insight, which suggests insight is an emergent rather than a planned outcome. This study provided an example of how research on mindfulness can be linked to other learning processes to optimize inquiry.

Creativity and flow remind us how dispositions known to foster learning and inquiry can be cultivated in conjunction with mindfulness in complementary ways. Interestingly, intrinsic motivation is thought to increase with all three factors – creativity, flow, and mindfulness – thereby suggesting that they may be mutually reinforcing. Furthermore, because inquiry-based learning often includes more project-, team-, or group-based learning, there can be an indirect effect of mindfulness on improved social skills linked to reduced team conflicts (Yu & Zellmer-Bruhn, 2018). As a new and emerging area of MBTL, there is a keen need for both research and practical models of inquiry-based learning that integrate mindfulness-based approaches.

## CONCLUSION

In this chapter, we introduced a spectrum of mindfulness-based inquiry techniques and approaches for use in MBTL. Figure 14.2 presents the three layers of inquiry we presented, in sequence, with implications for how MBTL is conducted and experienced as learners move from inquiry within the practice of mindfulness itself; to inquiry as an investigation of the broader topic or theme; and, finally, to meta-inquiry, which cultivates a critical, transpersonal, and reflective lens back on the inquiry process itself. Taken together, this spectrum of mindfulness-based inquiry suggests the value MBTL may have as a form of intrinsically rewarding lifelong learning.

Figure 14.3 represents and summarizes all three chapters of Section IV on the topic of what we teach in MBTL. The graphic depicts the nested nature of MBTL as body-mind communication, social-emotional learning, and inquiry-based learning. It reflects

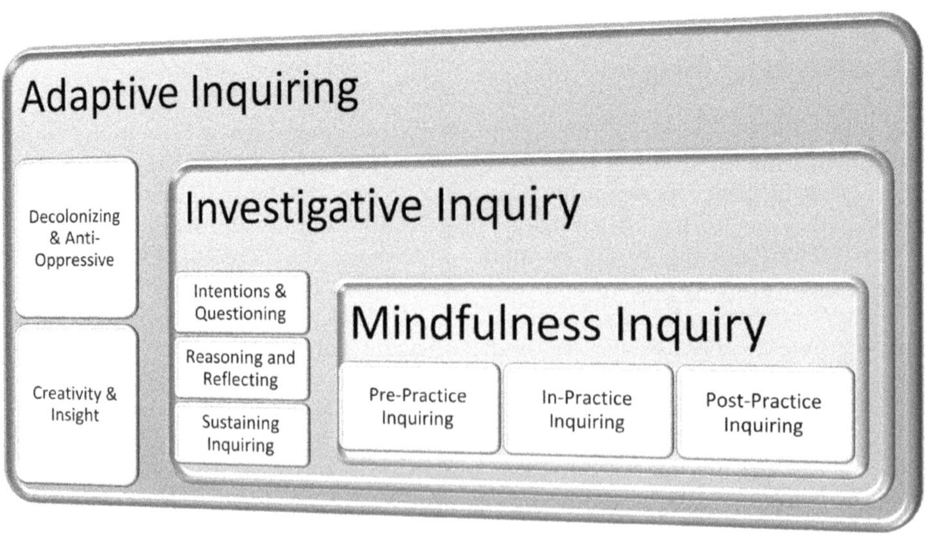


**Figure 14.2** The Mindfulness-Based Inquiry Spectrum

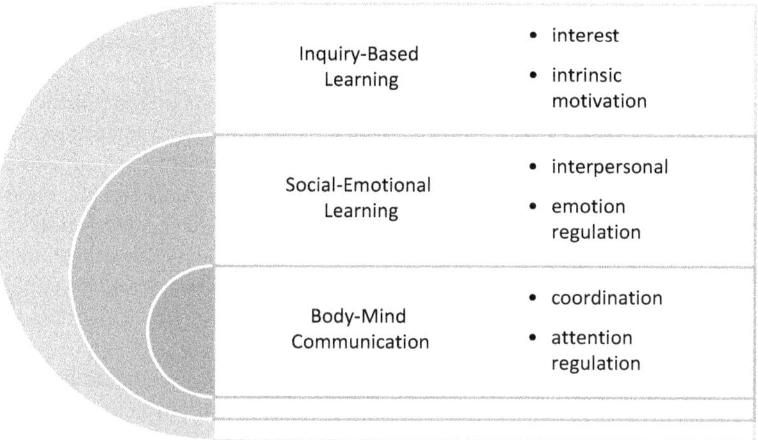


**Figure 14.3** An Integrative Model of MBTL

the potential integrative role of mindfulness itself across functional networks of the human brain and biology, progressing from the primordial relationship between physiology and cognition to the emotional and relational domain of the limbic system to the higher cortical functions of language, reasoning, and understanding. So too, with respect to the classical Buddhist theory of the four foundations, these three embedded orientations of MBTL reflect the movement from mindfulness of body to mindfulness of feeling and mind to mindfulness of phenomena. In this way, we can say that MBTL offers an integrative model of learning aimed at fostering sustained wellbeing.

Finally, we close the section with an exemplar in Textbox 14.2 to illustrate what such an integrated form of learning might appear like when embodied in a person and their learning journey. Although we are unsure if Craig Foster ever engaged in formal mindfulness practices or training, he nonetheless exemplifies and demonstrates trait mindfulness in his sustained inquiry and its impact on the other nested levels of SEL and body-mind communication.

## TEXTBOX 14.2 EXEMPLAR OF MINDFULNESS-BASED INQUIRY:

### My Octopus Teacher

*My Octopus Teacher,* the Netflix 2021 academy award winner for Best Documentary (Feature), chronicles the daily visits for a year of Craig Foster to a kelp forest near his home on the southern coast of South Africa. Without a wet suit or scuba tanks, he snorkelled and swam in the same location every day to visit, observe, and interact with an octopus. Although he isn't depicted on a cushion or referencing mindfulness, nonetheless he exemplifies informal mindfulness of the body (swimming) of feelings and sensations; and of phenomena (in this case, an octopus). His sustained attention on this creature for a year leads to insights, a deep appreciation and love, improved mental health and relationships, and, ultimately, what he describes as a transformed appreciation of wildlife and of the natural world.

The movie depicts interest-taking, for example, as Craig engages in daily mindful observations of the kelp forest followed by investigative inquiry (research) and energy (i.e., perseverance over a year). What he is doing can be called mindfulness as it includes a disciplined attention to his body and sensory experiences while swimming and snorkelling, including directing his attention to notice (mindfully) the octopus and to recognize or infer her intentions. He supports this mindfulness with active investigative inquiry, both by following his interest *in situ* and by engaging in research and studies when back at home. In sustaining these processes for almost a year, he provides the duration and conditions for insight.

In this way, Craig embodies equanimous appreciation as he navigates resisting the impulse to interfere while learning to understand and care for and about the octopus to the extent that such appreciation becomes, in his words, love. Ultimately, as the octopus' life draws to a close, Craig describes the broader effects of his sustained inquiry: Enhanced wellbeing, improved familial relations, and an expanded appreciation of the natural world. As he states: "It always starts with these little mysteries…all these mysteries you're trying to figure out." Such investigative inquiry is deepened with sustained observation and attention, he speculates, like observing a tree for a year to consider the many changes and living beings interacting with it: "I think that could have quite a large effect on your life" (Baker, 2020).

## REFERENCES

Analayo, B. (2018). *Satipatthana meditation: A practice guide.* Windhorse Publications.

Analayo, B. (2019). *Mindfulness of breathing: A practice guide and translations.* Windhorse Publications.

Association of American Colleges and Universities (AAC&U). (2009a). *Inquiry and analysis VALUE rubric.* https://www.aacu.org/value/rubrics/inquiry-analysis.

Association of American Colleges and Universities (AAC&U). (2009b). *Integrative and applied learning VALUE rubric.* https://www.aacu.org/value/rubrics/integrative-learning.

Baker, A. (2020). My Octopus Teacher became a viral sensation on Netflix. Its human star Craig Foster wants the film to inspire change. *Time Magazine*, November 2020. https://time.com/5909291/my-octopus-teacher-craig-foster-interview/.

Crane, R., Stanley, S., Rooney, M., Bartley, T., Cooper, L., & Mardula, J. (2015). Disciplined improvisation: Characteristics of inquiry in mindfulness-based teaching. *Mindfulness, 6*, 1104–1114. https://doi.org/10.1007/s12671-014-0361-8.

Desbordes, G., Gard, T., Hoge, E., Holzel, B., Kerr, C., Lazar, S., Olendaki, A., & Vago, D. (2015). Moving beyond mindfulness: Defining equanimity as an outcome measure in meditation and contemplative research. *Mindfulness, 6*, 356–372. https://doi.org/10.1007/s12671-013-0269-8.

Garland, E., Farb, N., Goldin, P., & Fredrickson, B. (2015). Mindfulness broadens awareness and builds eudaimonic meaning: A process model of mindful positive emotion regulation. *Psychological Inquiry, 26*, 293–314. https://doi.org/10.1080/1047840X.2015.1064294.

Hattie, J. (2009). *Visible learning: A synthesis of over 800 meta-analyses relating to achievement.* Routledge.

Kolb, D. (1984). *Experiential learning: Experience as the source of learning and development.* Prentice-Hall.

Kolb, D. (2015). *Experiential learning: Experience as the source of learning and development* (2nd ed.). Pearson.

Kolb, A., & Kolb, D. (2013). *The experiential educator: Principles and practices of experiential learning.* EBLS Press.

Lebuda, I., Zabelina, D., & Karwowski, M. (2016). Mind full of ideas: A meta-analysis of mindfulness-creativity link. *Personality and Individual Differences, 93*, 22–26. https://doi.org/10.1016/j.paid.2015.09.040.

Lord, T., & Orkwiszewski, T. (2006). Moving from didactic to inquiry-based instruction. *The American Biology Teacher, 68*(6), 342–345. https://doi.org/10.2307/4452009.

Mattes, J. (2019). Systematic review and meta-analysis of correlates of FFMQ mindfulness facets. *Frontiers of Psychology, 10*, 2684. https://doi.org/10.3389/fpsyg.2019.02684.

Nakamura, J. & Csikszentmihalyi, M. (2014). The concept of flow. In M. Csikszentmihalyi (Ed.), *Flow and the foundations of positive psychology: The collected work of Mihaly Csikszentmihalyi* (pp. 239–263). Springer. https://doi.org/10.1007/978-94-017-9088-8_16.

Nishida, K. (1990). *An inquiry into the good* (Trans. Maso Abe & Christopher Ives). Yale University Press (Originally Published in 1911).

Ovington, L., Saliba, A., & Goldring, J. (2018). Dispositions toward flow and mindfulness predict dispositional insight. *Mindfulness, 9*, 585–596. https://doi.org/10.1007/s12671-017-0800-4.

Pedaste, M. , Maeots, M., Siiman, L. de Jong, T., van Riesen, S., Kamp, E., Manoli, C., Zaharia, Z., & Tsourlidaki, E. (2015). Phases of inquiry-based learning: Definitions and the inquiry cycle. *Educational Research Review, 14*, 47–61. https://doi.org/10.1016/j.edurev.2015.02.003

Schon, D. (1983). *The reflective practitioner: How professionals think in action.* Basic Books.

Sheldon, K., & Ryan, R. (2011). Positive psychology and self-determination theory: A natural interface. In V. Chirkov, R. Ryan, & K. Sheldon (Eds.), *Human autonomy in cross-cultural context: Perspectives on the psychology of agency, freedom, and well-being* (pp. 33–44). Springer. https://doi.org/10.1007/978-90-481-9667-8_2.

Varma, S., Daselaar, S., Kessls, R., & Takashima, T. (2018). Promotion and suppression of autobiographical thinking differentially affect episodic memory consolidation. *PLoS ONE, 13*(8), e0201780. https://doi.org/10.1371/journal.pone.0201780.

Woods, S., & Rockman, P. (2021). *Mindfulness-based stress reduction: Protocol, practice, and teaching skills.* New Harbinger Press.

Woods, S., Rockman, P., & Collins, E. (2019). *Mindfulness-based cognitive therapy: Embodied presence and inquiry in practice.* Context Press.

Yu, L., & Zellmer-Bruhn, M. (2018). Introducing team mindfulness and considering its safeguard role against conflict transformation and social undermining. *Academy of Management Journal, 61*(1), 324–347. https://doi.org/10.5465/amj.2016.0094.

# SECTION V

# Methods – What We Do

## Competencies and Professional Practice in MBTL

This section introduces key innovations for the preparation of mindfulness specialists as teachers, curriculum designers, and other roles with direct contact with learners. Chapter 15 presents a validated competency framework that reflects the trans-professional competencies increasingly expected of MBTL specialists, straddling education, clinical care, and organizational awareness. The Mindfulness-Based Teaching and Learning – Competency Framework (MBTL-TCF) was designed and validated by an expert team of six leading MBTL specialists, trainers, researchers, and mentors. Chapter 16 introduces the topic of curriculum design in MBTL, a skill essential to respond to many of the new trends and expectations in the field. Finally, Chapter 17 moves into teaching itself and working with trauma, adverse effects, and the effects of colonization, racism, and gender discrimination in the MBTL classroom or context.

DOI: 10.4324/9781003182467-20

# CHAPTER 15

# TRANSPROFESSIONAL COMPETENCIES FOR MBTL SPECIALISTS

## The MBTL-TCF

Mindfulness-based teaching and learning (MBTL) refers to the growing body of knowledge and practices informing secular-scientific mindfulness studies. As a transprofessional practice, MBTL reflects an emerging field of practice in which a wide range of professions converge to integrate mindfulness into their professional practices. This includes people who don't traditionally self-identify as educators, such as clinicians or those who work in workplaces or organizations. So too, it includes educators who don't view themselves as clinicians, yet find themselves entrusted with learning educational skills and concepts to adapt clinical objectives into teaching and learning procedures. This chapter identifies what those MBTL transprofessional competencies look like through the lens of the Mindfulness-Based Teaching and Learning - Teacher Competency Framework (MBTL-TCF), which we developed and validated to support the continuous professional development of MBTL specialists.

## (TRANS)PROFESSIONAL COMPETENCIES

Competency frameworks are ubiquitous in most professions, including teaching and healthcare. Commonly advocated by agencies and professional associations to safeguard educational standards and systems of accountability, competency frameworks also empower professionals themselves to develop identities, values, and networks based on their common definitions. This function of competencies in the identity formation of professionals is one reason why competency frameworks are best initiated and designed from *within* the profession by members and only with input, rather than leadership, from external stakeholders like governments. Although competency frameworks are a necessary tool for the self-regulation of professions, they are also how professionals themselves learn to monitor and self-regulate their professional practice and ongoing education and development. In this respect, they are as much about professional autonomy as accountability.

Menter et al. (2010) identified four ways in which competency frameworks embed assumptions about teachers and their professional autonomy (i.e., intrinsic motivation) or external accountability (i.e., extrinsic controls). First, in the design process, the inclusion of professionals themselves in leadership roles safeguards professional autonomy. Second, the language and degree of specificity in the competencies denote a spectrum from open/interpretive to closed/prescriptive. Third, when translated into assessments, they can emphasize self-assessment, self-regulation, and self-monitoring or accountability and external monitoring. Finally, they embed assumptions about teachers' identities, representing teachers alternatively as self-directed reflective practitioners or as public servants requiring externally mandated and closely regulated monitoring and education.

MBTL specialists straddle clinical/education divides, whatever the specialist's personal investments may be. Clinicians, for example, are practising skills that are not commonly included in their initial professional training. For example, VanAalderen et al. (2014)

DOI: 10.4324/9781003182467-21

conducted a qualitative study of MBCT teachers and participants within a clinical context. All the participants suffered from recurrent depression and all of the trained MBCT teachers were clinicians (four psychologists, four occupational therapists, and one general practitioner). Results indicated that both the teachers and participants identified three common features of mindfulness training that differed from other therapeutic contexts: The teachers' *embodiment* of mindfulness through their personal practice; the *empowerment* of participants through emphasis on autonomy and self-determination; and the teachers' *non-reactivity* or equanimity (which one participant interpreted negatively as indifference). In addition, the participants alone identified a fourth feature – *peer support* – which they experienced through group activities and inquiry. This study reinforced how both facilitators and participants experienced MBCT differently from other clinical or therapeutic experiences.

So, competencies define professional identities with clear implications for practice. For example, as input to the 2012 and 2021 Scottish K-12 teacher competencies, Menter et al. (2010) identified four teacher identities that inform competencies implicitly if not explicitly: The *effective*, *reflective*, *enquiring*, and/or *transformative* teacher. The *effective teacher* orientation was associated with performance and accountability indicated by technical accomplishment and measurement (Menter et al., 2010). The *reflective teacher* orientation viewed teachers as active decision-makers engaged in *reflective practice* (Schon, 1983). The *enquiring teacher* reflected the teacher as researcher, engaged in evidence-based learning design with an active interest in sharing research within teacher communities. Finally, the *transformative teacher* orientation reflected emerging norms of anti-racist, socially just, and even activist teaching. These assumptions about teachers' identities and professional roles were implicit in competency frameworks.

For transprofessional practices like MBTL, teacher identities are more complex. While all members of the emerging community of practice are socialized within their primary professional identities, they find themselves encroaching on professions with different practice norms, skills, and evidence-based expectations. In this respect, the professional demands and training are more complex than for their first professions, and the competency framework becomes even more critical as a guide. So, clinicians starting to teach MBTL may feel very comfortable with an *effective* teacher aspirational identity, including in defining effectiveness as achieving health outcomes and possibly tolerating more accountability measures. Although arguably more comfortable with the *enquiring* teacher approach given the high demands for evidence-based practice in clinical care, these clinicians may find the *transformative* expectations anathema insofar as they may not see their role to correct social conditions or to address social justice concerns. On their side, professional educators may find themselves navigating unfamiliar health, wellbeing body-mind communication and evidence expectations.

## COMPETENCY-BASED EDUCATION

Today, most professions use competency-based frameworks to guide their initial and ongoing education and assessment. Mulder et al. (2009) defined *competence* as "a series of integrated capabilities consisting of clusters of knowledge, skills and attitudes necessarily conditional for task performance and problem solving and for being able to function effectively in a certain profession, organization, job, role and situation" (p. 757). *Competencies* refer to the discrete clusters of observable and situated elements of competence that can be disaggregated and arranged on a gradient for learning and assessment purposes. Competency-based education (CBE) refers to education organized around the teaching and learning of competencies to prepare graduates to become competent members of a specific community of practice (Lave & Wenger, 1991).

Associated with apprenticeship learning, CBE is one of the oldest forms of work-related education (Gallagher, 2014; Jones & Olswang, 2016). Recently, it has experienced a resurgence of interest as a way to foster practical skills as it shifts emphasis from disciplinary knowledge and time-spent-in-seats to the acquisition of agreed-upon competencies connected with real-world activities. As Klein-Collins (2013) suggests, this involves a shift from a teacher- to a learner-centred perspective involving an "intensive focus on what students know and can do rather than on what is taught" (p.4). In CBE, competencies are established through collaborative or consensus processes rather than at the whim of an instructor or teacher with incomplete knowledge of the contexts in which the competencies are to be applied. In professional education, this collaboration is formed by pooling expert practitioners to establish common core competencies based on their discernment, experience, norms, and research.

CBE derives from two interrelated theories of learning: Activity theory (Leont'ev, 1978; Vygotsky, 1986) and situated learning theory (Lave & Wenger, 1991). According to activity theory, any embodied social activity is mediated by a defined community using a common set of rules and an accepted division of labour. Together, these three constitute an embodied activity system, which manifests in three interconnected or nested layers of the activity: As embodiments of *culture* (activity level); as discrete, consciously enacted *tasks* (action level); and as automatic, semiconscious *skills* (operations level). To function within these embodied activities in the real world, professionals require some degree of competence within the three layers of the target activity: i.e., the culture, tasks, and component skills The culture is determined to a great extent by the community, by the *community of practice* as it is called in situated learning theory. The tasks, on the other hand, are focal teaching and learning sites in which both the culture and component skills are implicit and so can be learned or acquired implicitly through the performance of the tasks (Campbell et al., 2014).

Increasingly, professional education is expected to follow competency-based standards, including the use of competency frameworks and outcome-based designs. Although sometimes associated with conservative interests seeking accountability, they provide opportunities for exciting and important evidence-based innovations. An example is MBTL, where this rationalization process can hasten the inclusion of mindfulness as a respected aspect of professional activity. Grabovac and Burrell (2018) describe this in psychiatry, where the need for competency-based approaches and designs were required as part of a new strategic direction of the Association of Medical Faculties. This led to their framework for how to integrate mindfulness and MBTL in the preparation of psychiatrists in medical and ongoing professional education.

## PROFESSIONAL COMPETENCY FRAMEWORKS

Professional competency frameworks provide present the activities that support effective practice in a profession or field of endeavour. The development, structure, and use of competency frameworks share features across professions, as reflected in the common reliance on the Dreyfus and Dreyfus (1986) model, which continues to guide much professional education curriculum and assessment.

## The Dreyfus Scale of Professional Skills Acquisition

Mirroring their apprenticeship roots, competencies tend to follow a developmental sequence from novice to expert levels of professional performance. A generic apprenticeship scale was adopted by Dreyfus and Dreyfus (1986) to organize and represent professional competencies for technicians working for the US Air Force. The resulting Dreyfus model identified five *competency levels* (novice, advanced-beginner, competent, proficient, and expert) associated with four *mental functions* arranged by increasing challenge: Recollection; recognition, decision, and awareness. Since its development, it has expanded as a standard model for competency-based professional education.

There are three key critiques of Dreyfus' model that have led to calls for its revision or adaptation. One line of critique is that it mischaracterizes the novice learner as overly passive and rule-bound (Peña, 2010). Risjord (2016) pointed out that it failed to account for the "embodied coping" of novices nor for discrepancies between their propositional knowledge and practice (e.g., what they can actually do). Instead, he advocated an "ecological conception of agency," in which professional development was depicted as continuously developing as embodied engagement that is responsive and attuned to the encounter with a changing world. Other criticisms have focused on how the Dreyfus model misrepresents experts as holistic and intuitive thinkers and decision-makers, underestimating the role of reason in their decisions (Gobet & Chassy, 2009; Peña, 2010). Finally, Calder (2015) argued that the model misrepresented professional ethics, which she viewed as an embodied form of ethical conduct rather than a set of rational principles.

## Mindfulness Teaching Competency Framework

Both of the dominant mindfulness teacher competency frameworks – the MBI:TAC and the MBTL-TCF – were strongly influenced by the Dreyfus model. We will consider each of these competency frameworks in succession.

### *The MBI:TAC*

The earliest framework used to assess mindfulness teaching was the MBI:TAC, first released in 2012 as the Bangor, Exeter, & Oxford Mindfulness-Based Interventions Teaching Assessment Criteria (MBI:TAC) for assessing the competence and adherence of mindfulness-based class-based teaching. Developed in the UK for use in credit-based graduate programmes in higher education (Crane et al., 2012), the MBI:TAC since expanded across Europe and North America (Crane et al., 2013). As it expanded, it was frequently misinterpreted to be a teacher competency framework rather than as a set of teaching assessment criteria as the name implies. Although two of the key developers, Crane and Kukyen (2019), reiterated that it needed more research and development to serve as an assessment tool, they appear to fall short of ever recommending specific changes to the tool itself.

Applied as a *teacher* competency framework, there are two key limitations of the MBI:TAC. The first limitation is that it is explicitly intended for use with mindfulness-based *interventions* and hence preoccupied with intervention integrity (Crane et al., 2013). This orientation on control and accountability reflects the clinical bias of the MBI:TAC. Over time, as mindfulness expanded to an ever-widening range of contexts, expectations for control and the applicability of medicalized jargon like interventions and metaphors like doses lessened. MBTL reconceives mindfulness as a transprofessional teaching and learning enterprise across disciplines. This interdisciplinary and transprofessional approach to MBTL is accomplished by extracting the common practices and content elements from diverse contexts and by considering competencies across professions.

The second limitation of the MBI:TAC is that it was intended to serve as a set of assessment criteria for teaching within classes rather than as a *teacher* professional competency framework. Teacher profession competencies address the holistic lifelong professional development of MBTL teachers and specialists rather than the narrow band of skills associated with teaching. MBTL teachers are not restricted to teaching in classrooms but engage in a broad range of teacher professional activities that inform, but are not limited to, teaching, such as curriculum design and adaptation, research, personal mindfulness practices, networking, and professional learning. In contrast to the MBI:TAC, the MBTL-TCF identifies itself explicitly as a set of teacher competencies embedded in a framework of practice.

## *The MBTL-TCF*

To address the limitations of the MBI:TAC, we designed and validated the Mindfulness-Based Teaching and Learning - Teacher Competency Framework (MBTL-TCF). This framework expands on the earlier six competencies of the MBI:TAC by adding six more competencies to generate a holistic and robust teacher competency framework. We operationalized each of the 12 competency domains as component activities for task specification and sample performance indicators for assessing MBTL specialists in one of six distinctive levels. Therefore, the resulting MBTL-TCF has all four critical components to make it an effective tool in the design of MBTL specialist training: i) competency levels; ii) competency domains; iii) component activities; and iv) sample performance indicators.

**Competency Levels**. Competency frameworks present a developmental spectrum of benchmarks, bands, or levels of performance to represent how competencies develop over time as a learner progresses from novice to expert. We opted to use six terms that reflect the apprenticeship process of professional or, in this instance, transprofessional development: Novice, developing, supervised, competent, proficient, and expert. Table 15.1 illustrates the alignment and differences between the MBTL-TCF levels and those of Dreyfus and Dreyfus (1986) and the MBI:TAC (Crane et al., 2012). We opted to divide the single Dreyfus *novice* level into two distinctive levels to reflect better the time and training needed to reach the stage of practising under supervision: *Novice* and *developing*; however, unlike the MBI:TAC, we do not name or imply that this initial novice level involves *incompetence.* In our view, this would be inconsistent with the principles of apprenticeship- and competency-based education and design. If students are irredeemably *incompetent*, then it suggests a recruitment or admission problem rather than a performance problem. Not only does the label *incompetence* connote a negative *can't do* rather than *can-do* orientation, but it suggests failure and the incapacity to learn at the outset. Indeed, some descriptors went so far as to suggest that students so-assessed were dangerous, "leading to likely or actual negative therapeutic consequences" (p. 6), or, with respect to relational skills, that the prospective "[t]eacher has poor relational and interpersonal skills – they consistently 'miss the point' of what participants are communicating. Aspects of the interpersonal process are destructive" (p. 13). This kind of assessment could be very harmful to a learner well beyond their professional interest in MBTL specialist training.

**Table 15.1** Aligned Competency Levels

| *Dreyfus Model Competency Levels* | *MBI:TAC* | *MBTL-TCF* |
|---|---|---|
| Novice | Incompetent | Novice |
| | Beginner | Developing |
| Advanced Beginner | Advanced Beginner | Supervised |
| Competent | Competent | Competent |
| Proficient | Proficient | Proficient |
| Expert | Advanced | Expert |

### *Competency Domains*

A competency domain is a recognized activity domain that is deemed critical to the competent performance of a profession. Each domain reflects a cluster of component activities and skills that coalesce into competency in that particular aspect of the profession. Often, these competency domains are interrelated, such that they are not cultivated discretely and in succession but together in a progressive manner. The general consensus is that competencies should be defined to be both sufficiently open to reflect the holistic and diverse practices of a profession and sufficiently specified to make them amenable to teaching, learning, and assessment. The MBTL-TCF follows the common structure whereby a domain is specified by a set of what we call *component activities* that together define that competency domain. Table 15.2 demonstrates how the MBTL-TCF domains align with those of the MBI:TAC and the Dreyfus model's mental functions.

### *Component Activities*

We identified *component activities* as operationalized expressions of each competency domain. Although we initially turned to the MBI:TAC *key features* for this purpose (Crane et al., 2012), the expert reviewers felt these borrowed MBI:TAC features were too abstract, general, or unclear. To correct these problems, the MBTL-TCF specifies competency components as observable activities, such as "communicating authentically" rather than the MBI:TAC's more abstract terms "authenticity and potency." Another example is the MBTL-TCF's "recognizing distress and responding compassionately" in place of the MBI:TAC's "compassion and warmth." To reflect this, we shifted the grammatical form of the MBTL-TCF component activities to gerund phrases from the nouns used in the MBI:TAC.

### *Sample Performance Indicators*

Sample performance indicators provide clear criteria to assess competencies. Although the MBI:TAC is explicitly referred to as an assessment framework, the absence of observable indicators make this function challenging. In the MBTL-TCF, we sought to correct this by including clear *sample* performance indicators. The *sample* here reminds us that these are just examples and are not definitive, required, nor exhaustive. Table 15.3 presents

**Table 15.2** MBTL-TCF Competency Domains Aligned to MBI:TAC's and Dreyfus' Mental Functions

| *Dreyfus Model Mental Functions* | *MBI-TAC* | *MBTL-TCF* |
|---|---|---|
| **Recollection** (non-situational ⇨ situational) | Coverage, pacing, organization of session curriculum | Organizing |
| **Recognition** (decomposed ⇨ holistic) | Relational skills<br>Guiding mindfulness practices | Relational Skills<br>Guiding Mindfulness Practices |
| **Deciding** (analytical ⇨ intuitive) | Conveying course themes through interactive inquiry and didactive teaching | Conducting Post-Practice Inquiry<br>Conducting Investigative Inquiry<br>Differentiating Learners |
| | Holding the group learning environment | Enhancing Group & Ind. Learning<br>Designing Curriculum/ Interventions<br>Applying Scientific Literacy |
| **Awareness** (monitoring ⇨ absorbed) | Embodiment of mindfulness | Embodying Mindfulness<br>Reflecting on Practice<br>Practicing Ethically |

the entire MBTL-TCF with sample performance indicators by competency domain. Grammatically, we wrote the sample performance indicator using the third-person present tense to complete a sentence that begins with the common stem: "The MBTL specialist or professional…". Therefore, the indicator is framed around a verbal phrase, such as "actively recruits," rather than a noun phrase as used in competency domains and component activity. This convention highlights that it is something performed that is being observed, measured, or assessed.

## THE MBTL TEACHER COMPETENCY FRAMEWORK (MBTL-TCF)

We designed the trans-professional Mindfulness-Based Teaching and Learning – Teacher Competency Framework (MBTL-TCF) to serve the emerging field of MBTL across varied sectors and professions. As a transprofessional competency framework, it is designed to collate the values and practices of MBTL as a transprofessional specialization, which are determined by expert members and research and used by individual practitioners to guide their education and professional development. Although not itself a curriculum or assessment framework, the MBTL-TCF is intended to be used to design competency-based MBTL curriculum and assessment for training and continuing professional development (CPD) purposes. To ensure a breadth of professions and contexts were included, we invited a range of expert MBTL teachers and specialists from various professions to contribute to the design and validation of the framework, enhancing the flexibility of the MBTL-TCF for use across the full spectrum of MBTL communities of practice. Accordingly, the MBTL-TCF embeds a bold vision for the emerging transprofessional practice of MBTL while providing a practical map to guide MBTL professional education and development.

**Table 15.3** The MBTL Teacher Competency Framework (MBTL-TCF)

| *Competency Domain* | *Component Activities* | *Sample Performance Indicators* The MBTL specialist or professional… |
|---|---|---|
| **#1 Organizing** | 1. Recruiting with integrity and ethics<br>2. Conducting intake/induction, acknowledging differences with sensitivity<br>3. Preparing agendas<br>4. Preparing the site<br>5. Awareness of timing and pacing<br>6. Balancing curricular/intervention integrity with openness/responsivity | • Where applicable, actively recruits participants to enhance inclusion and equity in access to mindfulness.<br>• Accurately represents mindfulness, including by acknowledging limitations, risks, and benefits accurately.<br>• Engages in an intake process to identify learner needs and suitability and to manage expectations.<br>• Orients learners to obtain voluntary/informed consent.<br>• Prepares learning space to accommodate learner preferences and special needs.<br>• Attends to time in starting, pacing practices, and ending.<br>• Follows plan while responding to unplanned needs that arise. |
| **#2 Relating to Participants** | 1. Communicating authentically<br>2. Acknowledging challenges in society/current events affecting participants<br>3. Navigating acceptance/change continuum<br>4. Relating from a stance of curiosity and discovery<br>5. Adopting a learner-centred orientation<br>6. Respecting and inviting differences<br>7. Recognizing distress and responding compassionately<br>8. Managing adverse effects and risks<br>9. Establishing safety, trustworthiness, and transparency in classes or practices | • Engages in active listening.<br>• Discerns when acceptance or change is required/possible.<br>• Expresses acceptance and interest in learner's experience.<br>• Invites diverse views and adjusts language as needed to respond to culturally diverse communication styles.<br>• Invites participants to clarify meaning or experiences rather than making assumptions.<br>• Manages communication in small groups and offers suggestions for respectful communication regarding differences.<br>• Witnesses suffering of learner with empathy, understanding, compassion, and equanimity.<br>• Manages participant distress while balancing discernment and self-care with being present to all experiences |

| | | |
|---|---|---|
| **#3 Guiding Mindfulness Practices** | 1. Promoting present-centred attention and slowing down<br>2. Grounding guidance in one's own meditative experiences<br>3. Using invitational language and approaches to safeguard participant autonomy<br>4. Structuring and sequencing practice<br>5. Offering alternative practices to promote safety and self-care within participants windows of tolerance or capacity<br>6. Applying a range of attentional modalities, including focused attention, expanding awareness, and open monitoring<br>7. Encouraging equanimity<br>8. Fostering explicit awareness of body and senses; feeling tone (affective valence); mind (thoughts, emotions); and/or phenomena, depending on practice/need<br>9. Scaffolding guidance towards learner autonomy<br>10. Reinforcing evidence-based practices (such as decentering, distress tolerance, or shifting from rumination to sensation | • Practices while guiding (weaning off the use of scripts).<br>• Monitors & controls pacing, use of silence & language (e.g., simple, direct, "ing" verb tense), volume, tone.<br>• Uses invitational language and provides options.<br>• Limits metaphors and language that stimulate thought/images.<br>• Marks opening, closing, and transitions.<br>• Clearly teaches relevant techniques of a practice.<br>• Reminds to return gently to present or to widen attention.<br>• Directs, shifts, or widens learners' attention with curiosity and acceptance rather than suppression or exercise of will.<br>• Scaffolds learners between focal and open awareness.<br>• Reminds learners to accept what is present in introspective experience with discernment and without judgment.<br>• Reminds to recognize and shift from imagined to sensed body sensations (v. visualization).<br>• Fosters awareness of feeling tones (pleasant, unpleasant, neutral)<br>• Explicitly invites or suspends labelling of emotion or thought.<br>• Encourages equanimity towards all experiences, regardless of feeling tone.<br>• Reduces guidance commensurate with learner experience.<br>• Conveys key attitudes or mechanisms e.g., non-striving, openness, curiosity, decentering ("the" vs. "your" body etc.). |
| **#4 Conducting Post-Practice Inquiry** | 1. Demonstrating curiosity, interest-taking, and equanimity<br>2. Using horizontal (multiple responses) vs. vertical (in-depth) inquiry strategically<br>3. Transitioning from direct experience to conceptualizing to utility (e.g. the three layers)<br>4. Enhancing recognition and awareness of objects of attention using language<br>5. Noticing, tracking, integrating what is said in dialogue with participants | • Navigates dialogues with participants to encourage them to describe experience using subtler and increasing detail.<br>• Uses simple and complex reflections as needed.<br>• Redirects so as to recognize bodily sensations, feeling tone (affective valence), and decentered awareness in experience.<br>• Inquires into sequence of unfolding experience over time.<br>• Elicits learner experiential insights.<br>• Caps inquiry with queries on the purpose or utility of the practice. |

(*Continued*)

**Table 15.3** (Continued)

| *Competency Domain* | *Component Activities* | *Sample Performance Indicators*<br>The MBTL specialist or professional… |
|---|---|---|
| | 6. Modelling inductive process in language (moving from experience to concepts)<br>7. Maintaining focus on immediate experiences and redirecting away from storytelling or conceptual embellishment | • Gentle interruption and redirection if participants are getting lost in storytelling.<br>• Inquires to foster insight – showing v. telling; raising question v. answering; following v. leading. |
| **#5 Conducting Investigative Inquiry** | 1. Focusing inquiry on content specific to the exercise or topic of investigation<br>2. Drawing on learners' prior experience/knowledge<br>3. Demonstrating and conveying confidence and familiarity with contents<br>4. Connecting mindfulness practices to focal topic of investigation<br>5. Introducing and returning to key concepts and contents through analysis<br>6. Stimulating investigation, interest, insight<br>7. Relying on multi-modal teaching and learning<br>8. Assigning home practice to deepen practice, connections, and insights | • Introduces and presents a focal topic.<br>• Probes into learners' prior knowledge and/or experience.<br>• Weaves expertise/knowledge with that of participants.<br>• Balances presentation of contents, concepts, and/or research with inquiry-based and experiential activities.<br>• Fosters connections to mindfulness practice/insights.<br>• Clarifies, presents, and explores contents and key concepts.<br>• Raises questions, concerns, or information that stimulates interest and engagement.<br>• Progresses through topic with curiosity, openness, and beginner's mind.<br>• Uses a range of strategies, e.g., visual or graphic aids, partner or group work, or focal tasks or projects.<br>• Assigns and inquires into home practice. |
| **#6 Differentiating Learners** | 1. Acknowledging individual learners<br>2. Recognizing/addressing learners' contexts<br>3. Evaluating adverse effects and risks during intake and in teaching<br>4. Supporting learners to self-evaluate and regulate practices using such strategies as the "Window of Tolerance"<br>5. Adapting to a range of abilities and needs, trauma backgrounds, and safety | • Identifies needs through intake/ongoing assessment.<br>• Invites to identify personal pronouns.<br>• Remembers and uses correct pronunciation of participants' names, appropriate pronouns, etc.<br>• Recognizes/welcomes diverse backgrounds/experience.<br>• Sensitive to barriers to inclusion.<br>• Responds to controversial or critical conversations.<br>• Accommodates limited language or literacy levels. |

| | | |
|---|---|---|
| | 6. Using formative assessment to track learner development<br>7. Individualizing instruction as needed, including by offering alternative practices or activities if required<br>8. Adapting for diversity, culture, and language proficiency<br>9. Aspiring to effective teaching for all learners | • Checks for support or therapy received to process cumulative stress or trauma where applicable.<br>• Offers alternatives to serve a range of known or unknown abilities or capacities (e.g., different anchors for breath, eyes open/closed, options to move, external anchors).<br>• Is sensitive to possible triggers of emotional distress.<br>• Notices signs of emerging emotional or physical distress.<br>• Knows own limitations and when to refer or seek support.<br>• Remains non-defensive in responding to learners, using empathy, reflective listening, and apologies if needed.<br>• Reiterates applying self-compassion and respecting limits.<br>• Invites multiple sources of feedback to assess safety.<br>• Applies formative assessment methods to track learners needs, if they are being met, learning, development, etc.<br>• Accommodates practices for individual learners as required.<br>• Alters teaching, learning, or curriculum to accommodate specific cultures or interpretive frames. |
| **#7 Enhancing Relational Learning** | 1. Connecting participants to the universality of experiences, when applicable<br>2. Conveying the distinctive aspects of experiences, when applicable<br>3. Fostering individual and/or group autonomy in learning<br>4. Highlighting where applicable and possible relational or interpersonal concerns/impacts<br>5. Using invitational language with options to encourage voluntary participation, autonomous learning, and informed consent<br>6. Fostering a collaborative and accepting learning environment<br>7. Assessing, tracking, and responding to learner development<br>8. Modeling mindful interpersonal dynamics of collectives e.g., families, teams, organisations, and/or communities | • Establishes accepted group or interactive norms while arriving at situational norms via consensus agreement.<br>• Normalizes experiences as common and/or universal.<br>• Acknowledges/addresses unique issues/experiences.<br>• Responds to learners as individuals or as a group so as to conserve their sense of agency and self-determination.<br>• Relies on and encourages intrinsic motivation.<br>• Strategically navigates group forming-storming-norming-perfo rming-unforming sequences.<br>• Fosters an open and accepting learning environment.<br>• Interprets and clarifies "effectiveness" for specific profession, situation, and learners.<br>• Identifies clear indicators of effective group or individual learning to track over time (formative assessment).<br>• Analyzes what is noticed about group or individual learning and adjusts to sustain learning moving forward. |

(*Continued*)

**Table 15.3** (Continued)

| *Competency Domain* | *Component Activities* | *Sample Performance Indicators* The MBTL specialist or professional… |
|---|---|---|
| **#8 Designing Curriculum / Intervention** | 1. Engaging in constructive alignment (of outcomes, assessment, learning activities)<br>2. Identifying learning outcomes reflecting target knowledge, skill, and level<br>3. Preparing a range of assessment tools to offer evidence of learning (outcomes)<br>4. Sequencing themes, practices, topics of investigation using criteria (e.g., ease)<br>5. Applying evidence-based contents, principles, and practices in design<br>6. Rationalizing adaptations of established curricula and of the learning environment<br>7. Integrates culturally responsive features as needed to support learning | • Designs curriculum by aligning key outcomes (or inquiry questions) with assessment and learning activities.<br>• Arranges and integrates themes, practices, and investigations of curricular topic to fulfill curricular goal.<br>• Designs and/or plans curriculum using research and/or practice-based evidence.<br>• Adapts established curriculum judiciously, based on reasoned decision-making informed by evidence.<br>• Reflects systematically through delivery of curriculum to identify what works or doesn't or might be improved. |
| **#9 Applying Scientific Literacy** | 1. Engaging in continuous professional learning and research updates<br>2. Evaluating evidence from a full range of scientific and practice-based sources<br>3. Recognizing bias in research, including the backgrounds of participants/subjects, who is excluded, and how evidence is critically appraised in different contexts (e.g., education v. healthcare).<br>4. Applying research to rely as much as possible on evidence-based practices<br>5. Communicating scientifically-informed concepts and theories using lay language framed in accessible ways, especially in matters concerning risks and benefits.<br>6. Communicating potential risks and benefits of mindfulness accurately based on scientific evidence. | • Reads/critiques primary and applied mindfulness research.<br>• Adopts a critical and nuanced view of the evidence base, understanding that it is constantly evolving.<br>• Communicates critical and nuanced views of the evidence base to avoid overly idealistic or simplistic declarations of benefits.<br>• Applies scientific findings and practice-based evidence about mindfulness to teaching and learning (i.e., MBTL).<br>• In clinical settings and case formulations, applies specific psychological mechanisms of mindfulness to explain how specific mindfulness skills result in symptom reduction.<br>• Recognizes stages and developmental indicators in meditation and responds accordingly.<br>• Views MBTL through the lens of relevant scientific theories (e.g., sustained threat, dual processing, enactivism, neuroscience, self-determination, mindfulness-to-meaning). |

| | | |
|---|---|---|
| | 7. Acknowledging overlaps and distinctions between traditional (i.e., contemplative, Buddhist) and scientific approaches<br>8. Aspiring to enquiring teaching | • Compares traditional and secular-scientific perspectives on mindfulness.<br>• Engages in evaluation of own practices using feedback and evaluation systems and/or participates in formal research.<br>• Recognizes scientific findings as tentative and evolving.<br>• Code-switches as a "science translator" using clear, accessible lay language and concepts. |
| **#10 Embodying Mindfulness** | 1. Engaging in teaching and learning as a mindfulness practice<br>2. Conveying mindfulness both verbally and non-verbally<br>3. Cultivating mindful attitudes in and outside of teaching<br>4. Responding authentically to the situated & embodied present-moment of teaching<br>5. Applying personal mindfulness practice/insights<br>6. Embodying mindfulness in how the group or learning community interacts or relates | • Teaches from direct meditative and lived experience rather than from memory, abstractions, theories.<br>• Maintains a contemplative orientation while teaching.<br>• Conveys confidence with minimal self-consciousness.<br>• Aspires to *being present* rather than merely *performing*, valuing sincerity and spontaneity in teaching.<br>• Remains with difficulties in teaching, such as being criticized by a participant.<br>• Self-reveals by sharing personal stories selectively to enhance teaching and learning points.<br>• Sustains, and communicates insights from, a robust personal mindfulness practice, past and present. |
| **#11 Reflecting on Practice** | 1. Continuous self-assessing in the teaching and learning of mindfulness<br>2. Practicing mindful contemplation while teaching & learning (reflection-in-action)<br>3. Being receptive to feedback<br>4. Engaging in ongoing review/revising of teaching or clinical care<br>5. Self-reflecting on diversity, equity, and inclusion<br>6. Applying new research & learning in professional practice<br>7. Participating in ongoing learning & communities of practice<br>8. Aspiring to reflective teaching | • Solicits feedback from a mentor or peer.<br>• Engages in teaching as an informal mindfulness practice, combining introspection and compassionate attention.<br>• Cultivates humility in recognizing oneself as a learner, especially while teaching.<br>• Analyses what "works" or doesn't and experiments or alters teaching accordingly.<br>• Specifies anticipated clinical outcomes from the practice of mindfulness to inform and guide clinical practice.<br>• Reflects and works on comfort level with participant diversity (race, ability, gender, sexual orientation, etc.)<br>• Engages in ongoing personal mindfulness practice, continuing education, and professional communities of practice.<br>• Participates in annual, multi-day silent retreats.<br>• Participates actively in networks of professional mindfulness communities of learning and practice. |

(*Continued*)

**Table 15.3** (Continued)

| *Competency Domain* | *Component Activities* | *Sample Performance Indicators*<br>The MBTL specialist or professional… |
|---|---|---|
| **#12 Practicing Ethically** | 1. Developing professional/MBTL values of integrity, trust, respect, and social justice<br>2. Cultivating explicit qualities and attitudes associated with mindfulness<br>3. Practicing informed consent and voluntary participation.<br>4. Adopting a lens of diversity, equity, and inclusion *in* teaching but also *of* teaching and the broader field of mindfulness.<br>5. Monitoring/offsetting implicit biases in teaching and learning<br>6. Appreciating potential adverse effects and risks.<br>7. Representing the historical roots of mindfulness as a cross-cultural knowledge and practice and, where applicable, as the product of cultural appropriations.<br>8. Disentangling mindfulness from religion to enhance access and avoid proselytizing<br>9. Aspiring to transformative teaching | • Practises honesty and integrity, including in self-representation.<br>• Adheres to and respects normative certification and training expectations in the field of mindfulness teaching.<br>• Adheres to professional standards and codes of conduct.<br>• Accepts responsibilities as a mindfulness professional so as to convey trust, trustworthiness, and respect.<br>• Works intentionally to refine mindful attitudes such as openness, acceptance, beginner's mind, curiosity, etc.<br>• Considers teaching as a process of social justice.<br>• Acknowledges Indigenous lands, as applicable.<br>• Attends to implicit biases in or outside of teaching, aimed at reducing bias and fostering equanimity.<br>• Communicates potential risks and benefits.<br>• Identifies contributions from, or points of confluence with, traditional Buddhist mindfulness practice.<br>• Represents mindfulness, ultimately, as a human disposition and secular form of practice (with optional spiritual/religious uses.)<br>• Presents traditional (e.g., Buddhist) options as just one of many options for community, retreats, and practice.<br>• Cultivates an awareness or recognition of mindfulness as a socially, not just personally, transformative enterprise. |

## Purposes of the MBTL-TCF

Adapted from the Mindfulness-Based Intervention-Teaching Assessment Criteria (MBI:TAC) (Crane et al., 2012), this new MBTL-TCF revises and expands on that earlier version to address three key shortcomings or needs:

1. To extend mindfulness teacher competencies from a narrow MBI medicalized/ psychotherapeutic *teaching* focus to a broader MBTL transdisciplinary lifelong learning *teacher* perspective;
2. To reflect the widely-accepted conventions of competency-based education and design with implications for curriculum, assessment, and constructive alignment; and,
3. To represent and include evidence-based and content-validated MBTL competencies not covered in the MBI:TAC for a more robust and comprehensive teacher competency framework.

Together, these competencies support our broader intention to legitimate mindfulness as a viable specialization in professional education, where evidence-based, standardized competency frameworks are highly valued if not expected (Grabovac & Burrell, 2018).

More specifically, the MBTL-TCF is intended to support the design of the curriculum, training, and assessment of MBTL specialists as they navigate the field. This may be done in the context of formal training programmes or by individual practitioners engaging in self-directed professional growth. Competency domains are intended to inform the key topics or courses of MBTL training programs; the component activities are intended to inform the learning outcomes, activities, and assessed tasks; and performance indicators are intended to inform the assessment. This is illustrated in the final section of the next chapter. By providing a common validated competency framework, the MBTL-TCF supports the professionalization of MBTL with a pooled resource with input from across the field.

## The MBTL-TCF Design and Validation Processes

We designed and validated the MBTL-TCF over a 1.5-year period. These processes are described in relation to the construct, face, and content validation of the framework.

### *Construct Validity*

A construct is an operationalized indicator of a concept in the observable world. Construct validity indicates how closely the measurement criteria – e.g., the MBTL-TCF – aligns with the construct, i.e., MBTL teacher competency. We initiated the MBTL-TCF construct validation processes by first considering how to adapt the MBI:TAC for use in the MBTL graduate courses we were co-teaching at a Canadian university. In particular, we oriented on shifting from teaching to a wider teacher competency frame of reference and from mindfulness-based interventions to teaching and learning. Then, we used an earlier version of the MBTL-TCF framework to design the outcomes, learning activities and tasks, and assessments in the graduate courses, including self-assessments for students. Following the pilot, with input from students, we determined that the construct validity of the expanded competency domains of the MBTL-TCF were sufficient if not strong, including the need to add a 12th domain: practising ethically.

### *Face Validity*

Face validation refers to a more ad hoc form of content validation in which a scale or framework is piloted in the field to determine its recognizability and suitability for its intended purpose. As noted above, we piloted the initial MBTL-TCF in a graduate MBTL programme and found that the competency domains offered a robust and fulsome set of competencies; however, it seemed to lack suitable operationalization as component activities and performance indicators, which we had to develop through the course and teaching processes. Therefore, we recognized the need to revise by adding these features to a final framework.

### *Content Validity*

Content validation refers to the degree to which a scale or framework includes all aspects of a construct (definitional correspondence) and excludes any aspects unrelated to the construct (definitional distinctiveness) (Colquitt et al., 2019). For this purpose, we used a modified Delphi process (Janke et al., 2016) and gathered an expert panel together to engage in the final content validation of the MBTL-TCF. There were six members of the expert panel, all holding MBTL leadership and/or teacher training roles. Although this is a small number for a Delphi process, they were more actively involved in the actual redesign and final specification process to make the framework viable across professions. Three experts headed mindfulness teacher training programs in Canada or the USA. Two were psychiatrists, a community health physician, and an OT. Three were professors in higher education. One had expertise in K-12, adult, and higher education, including teacher education. All served as mentors of prospective mindfulness teachers and had experience in MBTL research and curriculum design. There were four experts who identify as women and two as men; one of the men was originally from SE Asia and the rest were White. An external consultant with expertise in BIPOC issues in MBTL offered a final review in the area of inclusivity and diversity.

The experts participated in specifying features of the framework, not just in its evaluation. They recommended altering some competency domain names. They confirmed the need to include a 12th competency on practicing ethically and to exclude one dealing with digital teaching environments. They collaborated on the wording of the final component activities and most performance indicators. This ensured that the nuance and granularity of the framework were suitable across the diverse professional contexts that the MBTL-TCF was intended to serve. These consultations and collaborations transpired over six weeks with three two-hour meetings and extensive written feedback and evaluations. Table 15.3 provides the results of this process in the final version of the MBTL-TCF. (See also MacPherson et al., 2022.)

# REFERENCES


Calder, G. (2015). Competence, ethical practices, and professional ethics teaching. *Ethics and Social Welfare, 9*(3), 297–311. https://doi.org/10.1080/17496535.2015.1031263.

Campbell, C., MacPherson, S., & Sawkins, T. (2014) Preparing students for education, work, and community: Activity theory in task-based curriculum design. *TESL Canada Journal, 31*, Special Issue 8, 68–92. https://doi.org/10.18806/tesl.v31i0.1187.

Colquitt, J., Sabey, T., Rodell, J. & Hill, E. (2019). Content validation guidelines: Evaluation criteria for definitional correspondence and definitional distinctiveness. *Journal of Applied Psychology, 104*(10), 1243–1265. https://doi.org/10.1027/apl0000406

Crane, R., Eames, C., Kuyken, W., Hastings, R., Williams, M., Bartley, T., Evans, A., Silverton, S., Soulsby, J., & Surawy, C. (2013). Development and validation of the mindfulness-based interventions - Teaching assessment criteria (MBI:TAC). *Assessment, 20*(6), 681–688. https://doi.org/10.1177/1073191113490790.

Crane, R., & Kuyken, W. (2019). The mindfulness-based interventions: Teaching assessment criteria (MBI:TAC): Reflections on implementation and development. *Current Opinion in Psychology, 28*, 6–10. https://doi.org/10.1016/j.copsyc.2018.10.004.

Crane, R., Soulsby, J., Kuyken, W., Williams, M., & Eames, C. (2012). The Bangor, Exeter & Oxford mindfulness-based interventions: teaching assessment criteria (MBI:TAC) for assessing the competence and adherence of mindfulness-based class-based teaching. http://www.bangor.ac.uk/mindfulness/documents/MBI:TACJune2012.pdf.

Dreyfus, H. L., & Dreyfus, S. E. (1986). *Mind over machine: The power of human intuition and expertise in the era of the computer.* Free Press.

Gallagher, C. (2014). Disrupting the game changer: Remembering the history of competency-based education. *The Magazine of Higher Learning, 46*(6), 16–23. https://doi.org/10.1080/00091383.2014.969177.

Gobet, F., & Chassy, P. (2009). Expertise and intuition: A tale of three theories. *Minds and Machines, 19*, 151–180. https://doi.org/10.1007/s11023-008-9131-5.

Grabovac, A., & Burrell, E. (2018). Standardizing training in mindfulness-based interventions in Canadian psychiatry postgraduate programs: A competency-based framework. *Academic Psychiatry, 42*, 248–254. https://doi.org/10.1007/s40596-017-0721-5.

Janke, K., Kelley, K., Sweet, B., & Kuba, S. (2016). A modified Delphi process to define competencies for assessment leads supporting a doctor of pharmacy program. *American Journal of Pharmaceutical Education, 80*(10), 167. https://doi.org/10.5688/ajpe8010167.

Jones, K. A., & Olswang, S. G. (2016). Building competence: A historical perspective of competency-based education. In K. Rassmussen, P. Northrup, & R. Colson (Eds.), *Handbook of research on competency-based education in university settings* (pp. 28–40). IGI Global.

Klein-Collins, R. (2013). *Sharpening our focus on learning: The rise of competency-based approaches to degree completion.* NILOA. Occasional Paper 20.

Lave, J., & Wenger, E. (1991). *Situated learning: Legitimate peripheral participation.* Cambridge University Press.

Leont'ev, A. (1978). *Activity, consciousness, and personality.* Prentice-Hall.

MacPherson, S., Grabovac, A., Collins, E., Heah, T., Rockman, P., & Winston, D. (2022). Transprofessional competencies across clinical, organisational, and educational professions: the case of mindfulness-based teaching and learning (MBTL). *Professional Development in Education.* https://doi.org/10.1080/19415257.2022.2143863

Menter, I., Hulme, M., Elliot, D., & Lewin, J. (With Baumfield, V., Britton, A., Carroll, M., Livingston, K., McCulloch, M., McQueen, I., Patrick, F., & Townsend, T.). (2010). *Education and lifelong learning: Literature review on teacher education in the 21st century.* Education Analytical Services, Scottish Government. https://dera.ioe.ac.uk/1255/1/0105011.pdf.

Mulder, M., Gulikers, J., Biemans, H., & Wesselink, R. (2009). The new competence concept in higher education: Error or enrichment? *Journal of European Industrial Training*, 33(8/9), 755–770.

Peña, A. (2010). The Dreyfus model of clinical problem-solving skills acquisition: A critical perspective. *Medical Education Online*, *15*, 4846. https://doi.org/10.3402/meo.v15i0.4846.

Risjord, M. (2016). The puzzle of evidence-based practice. In M. Lipscomb (Ed.), *Exploring evidence-based practice: Debates and challenges in nursing* (pp. 76–87). Routledge.

Schon, D. (1983). *The reflective practitioner: How professionals think in action*. Basic Books.

VanAalderen, J., Breukers, W., Reuzel, R., & Speckens, A. (2014). The role of the teacher in mindfulness-based approaches: A qualitative study. *Mindfulness*, *5*, 170–178. https://doi.org/10.1007/s12671-012-0162-x.

Vygotsky, L. (1986). *Thought and language*. MIT Press.

# CHAPTER 16

# CURRICULUM DESIGN FOR MBTL SPECIALISTS

This chapter remedies a missing link in the professional preparation of MBTL specialists. Mindfulness education has tended to be dominated by highly prescriptive and standardized curricula serving as *interventions* (MBIs) like MBSR and MBCT but also in the many K-12 programmes referenced in Chapter 7. Consequently, many leading mindfulness teacher training programmes have focused on preparing and certifying specialists to deliver one of these specific curricula. As a consequence, much attention has been given to *intervention integrity*, that is, fidelity in the delivery of a programme so as to adhere to the standarized framework, including practices, sequence, investigative inquiries, and homework (Crane & Hecht, 2018; Griffith et al., 2021). Very little is left up to a teacher in delivering these curricula beyond modest idiosyncracies in guiding and conducting post-practice inquiry. Investigative inquiry components, referred to as *didactic teaching*, tend to be delivered in a lecture mode that downloads narrowly prescribed contents as information, some of which may be out-of-date. The paradox is that recent evidence suggests that what is required instead is not so much intervention integrity as learner-specific programming. Galante et al. (2021) found that even credentialling mattered less than the ability to target specific student needs, the teaching and communication skills of teachers, and whether or not teachers had similar backgrounds to students – a teacher recruitment and representation issue.

This paradox or quandary is all the more challenging as mindfulness expands beyond clinically-oriented standardized MBIs to the wider transprofessional context of MBTL, which spans clinical, organizational, and educational contexts. As outlined in Section IV, for example, a fully integrative MBTL programme might simultaneously cultivate mind-body communication (e.g., self-regulation), social-emotional learning, and inquiry-based learning. Unlike MBIs, such outcomes could well be embedded in programmes whose explicit focus is not even on mindfulness but on disciplines or subject areas or, perhaps, for collectives, e.g., organizations or teams (Rupprecht et al., 2019).

## CURRICULUM DESIGN SKILLS FOR MBTL SPECIALISTS

In the emerging transprofessional landscape of MBTL, in which specialists are asked increasingly to address specific and diverse learner and community needs, this reliance on generic programmes delivered in formulaic ways seems antiquated. That said, it is difficult to overstate the value these standardized MBIs have had in establishing and supporting secular-scientific mindfulness. As Crane and Hecht (2018) argue, the promise of intervention *control* (which they euphemistically refer to as intervention *integrity*) is principally for mindfulness *research*. Yet, ethically, the needs of learners should, in balance, trump the needs of research. Specialists so trained may have knowledge of one curriculum but lack the flexibility and interpretive skills to apply principles and practices to new learners, designs, or adaptations. Therefore, what MBTL specialists require is not only skills in delivering *one* curriculum but the meta-awareness and skills to apply mindfulness practices, principles, and approaches in adapting or designing a wide range of curricula or programming for different needs. There are strong precedents in other teaching and learning environments for such skills. Many K-12 teachers work with required curricula, but these curricula tend to be only loosely defined and specified to allow interpretive space for teachers to address

DOI: 10.4324/9781003182467-22

particular learner needs in designing lessons. In higher education, the curriculum tends to be open for instructors to skillfully (one hopes) interpret how to meet required outcomes.

In contrast, clinicians are accustomed to engaging in prescribed, even ritualized, sequences of practices and behaviours associated with interventions and treatment protocols. So, they are accustomed to the idea, if not terminology, of *intervention integrity*. Indeed, the dominance of clinicians and clinical interests as secular-scientific mindfulness emerged and expanded may have contributed to this narrow approach of training specialists to teach a single curriculum. As MBTL becomes a transprofessional specialization, the educational and clinical streams are learning to support one another in professional cross-fertilization. Clinicians offer a keen sense of the value of standards and evidence-based practice, while educators contribute creative curricular design abilities and the teaching skills to interpret and apply them.

Below we outline seven fairly general curriculum design skill sets that are relevant to MBTL. These skills are covered under the MBTL-TCF competency #8 referred to as Designing Curriculum/Intervention. The design process is not merely putting ideas down on paper but implementing the curriculum in a highly reflective way to tweak it as a lived curriculum in practice and real time. Just as a teacher-trainee engages in critical self-reflection about teaching, they need to engage in an open critical reflection about their curricular designs. This enables them to refine and redesign appropriately without too much self-identification or resistance.

The model of design we are presenting is backwards or outcomes-based design, a design process that begins by imagining where the learners or learning ends. It is the dominant form of curriculum design used in higher and much K-12 education, in part to improve accountability; however, the reason it is particularly useful in MBTL is its efficacy in professional development. The overarching imagined outcome is the new teacher being able to function competently in the target occupation, activity, or community of practice. In this, curriculum design is associated with activity theory and task-based design (Campbell et al., 2014). Given that MBTL specialists often become transprofessional in skill and orientation, their target community of practice is both their specific profession and the MBTL transprofessional community. The six key steps we present here as essential for effective curriculum design are: Needs assessment; goal statement; evidence-based rationale; outcomes and alignment (using S.T.O.P.-A); curricular mapping; materials; and assessment. These are all necessary and sufficient for a well-designed MBTL curriculum.

## Needs Assessment

The first step to engage in curriculum design is to establish needs. These are not only learner needs but may include organizational, stakeholder, and community needs. Often this is done by expert analysis and determination, but it is preferable to do a more formal process if possible. That might include holding focus groups, surveys, or interviews with selected members of the above needs populations. Needs analysis also often includes environmental scans, which tend to be web-based these days, whereby current programming and programme structures are assessed to determine needs. This could be to avoid unnecessary duplication of services or to establish that there is a gap in services. Environmental scans can also help to document and understand existing conventions in programming. Minimally, the needs assessment process should establish a demand and rationale for the programme, insights concerning the target learners, insights concerning programme design, and a focal topic. This would be summarized in a few paragraphs at the beginning of the curricular document.

## Evidence-Based Rationale

Equipped with insights from the needs assessment, the next step is to establish the rationale for the programme and design. This twofold process involves first establishing the internal rationale for the programme within the context in which it is being delivered (e.g., community, institution, clinic, programme, class) and then engaging in a review of scientific literature on the topic. Such a review could involve as few as three or as many as 30 studies. Ideally, they would mix quantitative, qualitative, and conceptual studies that cover research or theory on the particular population receiving the mindfulness training, on the proposed focal topic of the curriculum (e.g., "stress"); and optimal programme design and delivery methods. This would then be summarized in a short rationale at the beginning of the curricular document after the needs assessment and could be as brief as one page in length.

## Goal Statement

The goal statement follows the rationale and clearly and concisely states the overarching purpose and focus of the curriculum *in a single statement* – which usually means a single sentence. Usually, it clarifies the intended audience (if there is one), the focal topic, the role of mindfulness, and any other critical information about the purpose. In the exemplar that follows, for example, the goal statement is: "The goal of this programme is to introduce and link mindfulness practices and Indigenous teachings to support participants to re-establish holistic health promotion strategies in their daily lives." (NOTE: This goal statement doesn't stipulate Indigenous learners as target learners because some of the community workers can be non-Indigenous.) It reflects backwards design insofar as it usually describes what learners will exit with, but it also should stipulate the overall topic and the methods (e.g., mindfulness). That said, the most common error in framing the goal statement is to be too detailed and specific.

## Outcomes and Alignment (Using S.T.O.P.-A)

This is the critical heart of the design process, reflected in the first two tables of the exemplar – Overview and Constructive Alignment. As one of the authors (SM) likes to say when she teaches curriculum design skills: "This section is the DNA of the curriculum, with each item part of the code. A skilled designer can read from this code the probable course of the entire lived curriculum." This section has two parts as per the exemplar "Mindfulness and Indigenous Teachings Pilot Curriculum" below: The S.T.O.P.-A and the constructive alignment table. Each of these is discussed below in more depth.

### *S.T.O.P.-A*

First, this section includes an overview of the S.T.O.P.-A steps in curriculum design: Skills, themes, outcomes, practices, and activities. In each category, the items selected are both exhaustive and inclusive; in other words, all items appear later in the map and none appear in the map that are not first identified here. Typically, because a curriculum would have more space, the initial needs assessment and rationale would occupy separate sections or pages with more depth than depicted in the exemplar, which was summarized for space considerations. The S.T.O.P.-A, on the other hand, appear as they might in a full curriculum, though their numbers may increase with longer curricula. Below we offer more specifications for each (remembering that this is something associated with a practice so only fully understood through the actual design process.)

**Skills**. In curriculum design, *skills* refer to the sub-skills of integrated practices that are explicitly taught and learned; it does not refer to skills that are acquired implicitly and embedded in integrated practices. Such skills may be learned but they are not usually intentionally taught. The items identified here are delimited as skills so as to be deliberately and explicitly taught and learned; however, they may be taught indirectly through intentional instructions during guidance or in inquiries. Often, explicit skills are overlooked in MBTL as teachers tend to focus on integrated practices like mindfulness of breathing. Yet, even in this practice, there is a range of skills that novice practitioners can benefit from learning more explicitly. For example, how to recognize and release impulses to control and direct the breath or how to use curiosity rather than willpower or judgement to redirect attention. Lastly, it is optimal to restrict the number of skills listed to two to three for every three-hour segment or so as such skills require time to learn and practice via some form of explicit teaching and assessment. Below in Table 16.1 we offer examples of skills associated with a range of mindfulness practices.

**Themes**. This category refers to the subtopics associated with the main topic of the curriculum. So, for example, with MBSR, the main topic is stress and the themes are the key ideas that appear as themes in various sessions. Here are a few examples of some of the main themes that might be explored under the main topic of stress in MBSR: The distress of stress is linked to habitual reactivity (autopilot triangle); when the body says no, awareness can bear it (embodiment); awareness increases the gap between stimulus and response; and/or moving from reacting to responding in stress (awareness triangle). An example of a theme from MBCT is *thoughts are not facts*, which

**Table 16.1** Sample Skills Common in Mindfulness Practices

| *Mindfulness Practice* | *Sample Associated Skills* |
|---|---|
| Mindfulness of Breathing | Relinquishing impulse to control the breath<br>Attention regulation through curiosity v. control |
| Mindfulness of Body | Using mindfulness of hands as an anchor attention when applying the window of tolerance<br>Identifying signs when the body is approaching its limit |
| Mindfulness of Feelings | Recognizing feeling tones (pos, neg, neutral) in a range of experiences e.g., in body sensations, sight, sound, etc.<br>Working with neutral experiences e.g., neutral experience calendar |
| Emotion Regulation | Identifying (labelling) emotions as the arise in direct experience<br>Parsing experiences into body, feeling tones, thought, emotion |
| Opening Awareness | Shifting attention by extending or broadening attention (including backgrounding what you leave and foregrounding as you add new layers e.g., breath + body + sound + thoughts/emotions = open awareness)<br>Releasing focal attention to notice whatever arises in the natural mind |

is the title of an entire session and relates to the main topic of depression relapse prevention. Usually, two themes at most would be used in every three-hour segment to provide sufficient focus and repetition to support learning. Also, if there are more, teachers stop paying attention to them. Unlike skills, they need not be explicit but can be implicit – though explicit components may help. Implicit approaches include drawing attention to related insights that happen to arise during inquiry, for example, and labelling them by the theme – even using its exact wording.

**Outcomes.** Learning outcomes are used extensively now in both higher education and K-12. These conventions derive largely from Bloom's taxonomy, which separated learning activities into three types: Cognitive, affective, and psychomotor. Yet, from the outset and ever since, the cognitive function has eclipsed the other two, leaving a very biased interpretation of learning as principally cognitive and associated with rational or conceptual contents (Bloom et al., 1956). Now, most higher education institutions don't even include the other two domains in materials for faculty to help them to prepare learning outcomes for classes. Also, as the scope and interpretation of valid knowledge and alternative ways of knowing expand, Bloom's taxonomy is proving increasingly inadequate for representing not just the *type* of knowledge but its *level*.

One key feature of Bloom's taxonomy is its hierarchical organization, scaffolding verbs as descriptors of types of learning activities into a hierarchy of increasing challenge. This hierarchy is then used to evaluate the appropriateness of learning outcomes or activity depending on the grade, year, or level of learners. So, for example, using the cognitive domain, represented below in Figure 16.1 (c/o Vanderbilt University Centre for Teaching, see Armstrong, 2010), activities of understanding (e.g., *recognize*) are considered less challenging and complex than those involving analyzing (e.g., *organize*). This is used to assess the level of a learning outcome and even to reject those deemed too easy for a higher-level grade or class. MBTL is an excellent case to consider the shortcomings of Bloom's model vis-à-vis the type of levelling of knowledge it represents.

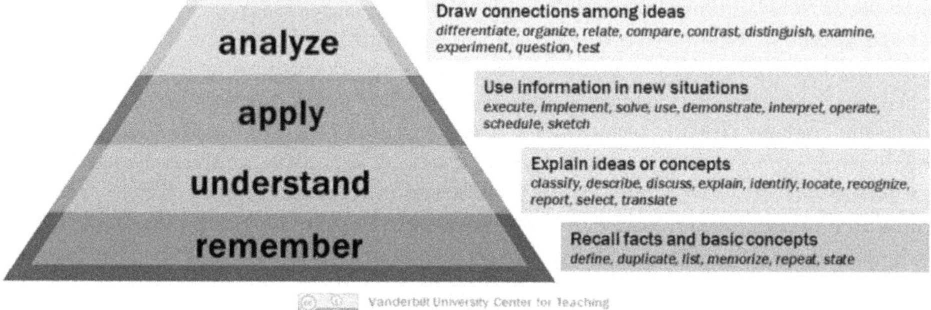


**Figure 16.1** Bloom's Taxonomy (Cognitive Domain) (Vanderbilt University Centre for Teaching)

In MBTL, mindfulness-related tasks associated with observing, recognizing, and describing are critical and backed by the validated operationalization of mindfulness in the FFMQ, for example, where observation and description are identified as the first two of the five factors. Yet, Bloom's model would locate mindfulness at a very low level of challenge and complexity and, hence, grade or level – probably as one of the bottom two functions labeled as 'remember' or 'understand.' Indeed, given that Bloom's model focuses almost entirely on conceptual knowledge in this scale, it does not even conceive mindfulness as a form of knowledge, that is, bringing awareness to less conscious aspects of present-moment experience.

Ethnography (often part of anthropology) offers a closely aligned precedent in higher education for MBTL's form of advanced knowing through awareness. The need for what is referred to as reflexivity in ethnography as a method of research and inquiry requires that those who practise it have the ability to observe, recognize, and describe their experience of a culture while still aware of the many biases that may interfere and distort their interpretations of those experiences. This skill is recognized as part of the mastery of this research method, even at the doctoral level.

So, while Bloom's taxonomy can be used, it should be applied critically, adaptively, and creatively to adequately reflect the needs of MBTL curricula as a distinctive way of knowing. Of all the components of S.T.O.P.-A, it is the learning outcomes that are most like the principle of DNA, especially when represented in a constructive alignment table (next section). In higher education and K-12, learning outcomes are usually represented as the only *required* component of a curriculum, because it is understood that the outcome is what matters to the learners, institution, and society but that teachers bring expertise in how to realize those outcomes for specific learners. There would usually be only one to three learning outcomes for a three-hour programme, for example. That rate may decrease for a longer programme. For example, the norm in higher education is for six to eight learning outcomes in a three-credit class (which reflects about 40 contact hours).

The learning outcome is a statement that completes a sentence when combined with a stem. A common stem to signify backwards or outcome-based design is something like: "By the end of this course/programme, students will be able to"…" This then requires that the learning outcomes statement starts with the verb to complete an infinitive, though it may look like the imperative (which it isn't). So, for example, a learning outcome for the initial session of MBSR might be: "Describe multiple sensory experiences arising from investigating eating a single raisin." A second learning outcome for this first session might be: "Apply the window of tolerance to self-regulate during mindfulness practices using such techniques as mindfulness of hands."

**Practices**. These refer to experiential learning activities involving formal or informal mindfulness practices aimed at cultivating mindfulness or improving awareness. Such practices are required for a programme to be labelled MBTL; however, they may include forms of practice that are not technically mindfulness-based, such as meditative, contemplative, or arts-based practices, including analytical meditations, visualizations or active imagination, arts-based (art, music, drama, dance), and the repetition of phrases (as mantra or prayer). What they share in common is the intention to improve and broaden the quality of attention, awareness, and recognition through experiential learning. Practices usually include some degree of post-practice inquiry, which is used to assess and support the development of observation and description skills about the introspective or sensory experiences. The ultimate aim is to improve

**Table 16.2** Sample MBTL Practices

| *Four Foundations* | *Mindfulness-Based* | *Other* |
|---|---|---|
| Mindfulness of the Body | Mindfulness of breathing<br>Mindful movement (e.g. yoga)<br>Body scan<br>Mindfulness of sensation | Deep or other controlled breathing<br>Active imagination in conjunction with the study of anatomy and physiology<br>Chanting, singing, dancing (linking sound to the body) |
| Mindfulness of Feeling (Tones) | Mindfulness of feeling tones in bodily sensations<br>Mindfulness of feeling tones in other sensory experience (e.g., seeing) | Pleasant/unpleasant/neutral event calendar<br>Recognizing and responding to implicit biases |
| Mindfulness of Mind | Mindfulness of thoughts and emotions<br>Opening awareness | Emotion regulation (as practice)<br>Analytical meditation |
| Mindfulness of Phenomena | Mindfulness of hindrances and seven awakening factors (i.e., mind/learning)<br>Mindfulness of plants, insects, animals, gemstones, rocks, soil, etc. | Interest-taking through investigation<br>Bird watching; forest bathing |

the capacity to recognize and learn through experience *and* to improve the quality of experience through such outcomes as enhanced positive emotion, meaning, and savouring. Table 16.2 offers some examples of mindfulness and non-mindfulness-related practices that might be included.

**Activities**. These refer to a limited set of particular learning activities associated with MBTL curricula and programmes. Their exhaustive inclusion in an MBTL curriculum ensures optimal inquiry and learning in lines with many of the evidence-based findings and theories introduced in this book. They appear as an add-on in the S.T.O.P.-A acronym only because they are given as a relative closed set of required elements rather than invented, created, and designed in the true sense. Their specific contents or directions may involve creativity and invention of course. Table 16.3 lists the eight core activities that might be expected to be included in an MBTL curriculum under normal circumstances along with a brief explanation of what they are or might include.

### *Constructive Alignment*

Biggs (1996) introduced constructive alignment to apply constructivist learning theory (see Chapter 9) and learning design principles together in practice in higher and professional education. Constructive alignment aligns explicit learning outcomes with proposed learning activities and assessments to design learning opportunities. This method of design fosters both curricular integration and better safeguards and assurances that the goal and outcomes of the curriculum will be met through learning. One key feature of constructive alignment is that all outcomes, activities, and assessments are exhaustively presented and

**Table 16.3** Core Activities in an MBTL Curriculum

| *Core Activity* | *Explanation* |
|---|---|
| orientation | Introducing students to what and why of mindfulness; to self-care principles like Window of Tolerance; to terms of conduct. |
| group development | Helping students to shift to more reliance on peer- v. teacher-centred expectations; non-authoritarian practices. |
| guiding practices | Guiding mindfulness (or other) practices in ways that foster autonomy, curiosity, openness, and attention. |
| post-practice inquiry | Engaging in explicit post-practice inquiry (see Ch. 14) by dialoging in sequence on noticing, tracking, deriving principles from experience. |
| investigative inquiry | Moving from direct experience into more focused investigative inquiries into the topic of the curriculum e.g., more conceptual, abstract forms. |
| skills & theme review | Explicitly reviewing or introducing a skill or theme through a discreet activity or practice. |
| home practice/ homework | Identifying and assigning home practice or homework that is then explicitly reviewed and reflected on in class. |
| feedback (assessment) | Using clear methods to track and assess students both with respect to mindfulness and to the topic of the curriculum. Revise accordingly. |

shown to align, and this alignment is then laid out in the curriculum mapping of sequence and scope. In Table 16.4 we presented a sample constructive alignment table using the two outcomes we used as examples from MBSR-Session 1. Note that the assessment can be informal via post-practice inquiry, homework, and home practice discussions.

## Curriculum Map

The curriculum map is intended to be a minimalist overview of the sequence, pacing, tasks, and alignment of the various S.T.O.P.-A components of the curriculum. It should unfold automatically and logically from the aforementioned stipulated features of the curriculum. The two salient features of a curriculum map are that it is: a) properly scoped and sequenced in moving from easy to more complex and demanding tasks, and b) demonstrates the alignment between outcomes, skills and themes, practices and activities, and assessment. Tables 16.5c and 16.5d illustrate how such a map might be represented. Note

**Table 16.4** Sample Constructive Alignment Table

| *Learning Outcome*<br>*By the end, students will be able to...* | *Learning Activity* | *Assessment* |
|---|---|---|
| Describe multiple sensory experiences arising from investigating something that is eaten, such as a single raisin. | Mindfulness of eating<br>Post-practice inquiry | Post-practice inquiry |
| Apply the window of tolerance to self-regulate during mindfulness practices using such techniques like mindfulness of hands. | Mindfulness of hands<br>Intro to window of tolerance<br>Body scan (class) | Post-practice inquiry<br>Home practice record |

that this is the probable document that a teacher would rely on in delivering a course or programme, though they may opt to prepare a more detailed lesson or class plans as well.

### Materials

This step involves pre-identifying the course materials and adapting or preparing those materials still needing to be developed. These would include organizational, learning, home practice, and record-keeping materials, including audio- or video-recordings required for home practice.

## 16.5 EXAMPLE OF A SHORT MBTL PILOT CURRICULA

**MBTL Student Three-hour Pilot**: Mindfulness and Indigenous Teachings Pilot Curriculum

This short curriculum was designed and delivered by Kelly and Martin (2022) as part of the MBTL programme at the University of the Fraser Valley. We include it to illustrate: a) the above design steps; and b) how this design approach can foster cultural or other types of adaptations.

Note that this cultural adaptation of mindfulness is similar to adaptations to integrate mindfulness in content areas in schools or higher education, where mindfulness is displaced as the central focus of the curriculum. Instead, mindfulness is represented as a means to address a broader range of needs and outcomes associated with specific learners, needs, or contexts. To reflect this perspective in their orientation materials for participants, Martin and Kelly (unpublished) cited Michael Yellow Bird: "I think of mindfulness as a springboard to get us back to who we really are and to our contemplative ceremonies and to our own forms of awareness and connection" (Dawson, 2021, para 6).

### Assessment(s)

This step, often overlooked in MBTL, need not be formal, as in a test, but instead provides a way that both (or either) facilitators and learners collect feedback about learning so as to inform learning moving forward through the revising or adapting of the lived curriculum.

**Table 16.5a** Constructive Alignment Table

| *Constructive Alignment Table* | | |
|---|---|---|
| *Learning Outcomes*<br>"Students will be able to…" | *Learning Activities* | *Assessment* |
| Integrate Indigenous teachings with mindfulness practices | 1. Smudging ceremony<br>2. Sensation of hands | Pre-assess using FFMQ<br>Inquiry |
| Apply aspects of the Medicine Wheel teachings | 1. Investigative inquiry of Medicine Wheel | Inquiry<br>Home practice |
| Use mindfulness skills to support individual health and wellness | 1. 5 min mindfulness breathing practice (w/ window of tolerance).<br>2. Mindfulness of walking practice<br>3. Sensing / sitting mindfulness | Inquiry |

**Table 16.5b** Preliminary Overview Table (Identifying S.T.O.P.-A)

| *Design Component* | *Overview* |
|---|---|
| *Needs Assessment | This three-hour programme, to be delivered in two 1.5-hr sessions, responds to the need for community health initiatives using alternative, complementary, and Indigenous approaches. The facilitators, Indigenous educators, collaborated with a local Indigenous health director and community in an urban reserve. |
| *Rationale | Yellow Bird (2013) saw mindfulness as a neuro-decolonizing practice with promise in healing intergenerational trauma for Indigenous people. Ragoonaden et al. (2021) suggested it could help to decolonize settler populations as well in the reconciliation process. Le and Gobert (2013) offer evidence of mindfulness as an effective youth suicide prevention programme with native populations. They conclude that close collaborations with Indigenous leaders and use of Indigenous methods improve feasibility of MBIs for this population. We modelled these recommendations by collaborating with the local First Nation to organize, design, and deliver a hybrid mindfulness/Indigenous healing programme. |
| Goal Statement | The goal of this programme is to introduce and link mindfulness practices and Indigenous teachings to support participants to re-establish holistic health promotion strategies in their daily lives. |
| **S**kills (special skills) | • Practising window of tolerance as self-regulating tool<br>• Using curiosity to pay attention<br>• Discerning presence or absence of balance in body, mind, spirit |
| **T**hemes | • Bridging Indigenous spiritual teaching with mindfulness<br>• Finding balance in body, mind, and spirit<br>• Knowing our own experience |
| **O**utcomes | Integrate Indigenous teachings with mindfulness practices<br>Apply aspects of the Medicine Wheel teachings<br>Use mindfulness skills to support individual health and wellness |
| **P**ractices | Mindfulness of hands, walking, breathing, sitting practice<br>Smudging ceremony; drum song |
| **(A)**ctivities | orientation, group development, guided practice, mindfulness inquiry, investigative inquiry, homework / home practice, feedback (assessment) |

*NOTE: Needs assessment and rationale sections are abbreviated for space considerations for this book.

## DESIGNING TRAINING FOR MBTL SPECIALISTS

The MBTL-TCF, outlined in the last chapter, is pivotal to designing effective training for aspiring MBTL teachers or specialists. We will focus on three explicit steps in particular: a) organizing competencies into courses and levels; b) applying competency-based component activities as learning tasks and outcomes; and c) specifying performance indicators as assessment. We will consider each of these in sequence.

### Arranging Competencies into Courses and Levels

As in all backwards design, the first step is to define what kind of skills and competencies you would expect MBTL graduates to have when they exit the programme. This

**Table 16.5c** Session 1 Curriculum Map

| *SESSION 1 (1.5 hrs)* | | | | | |
|---|---|---|---|---|---|
| *Time* | *Outcome* | *Theme / Skill* | *Practice / Activity* | *Materials* | *Assessment / Homework* |
| 20 min | Integrate Indigenous teachings with mindfulness practices | **Theme:** Bridging Indigenous spiritual teaching with mindfulness | Orientation | Orientation handout | FFMQ with debrief |
| 15 min | | **Skill:** Practising window of tolerance as self-regulating tool | Smudging ceremony | Smudging materials | As informal practices |
| 10 min | Use mindfulness skills to support individual health and wellness | **Skill:** Using curiosity to pay attention | Mindfulness of hands | Window of tolerance | |
| 20 min | | **Theme:** Knowing our own experience | Mindfulness of walking<br>Post-practice inquiry | | |
| 10 min | Apply aspects of the Medicine Wheel teachings | **Theme:** Finding balance in body, mind, and spirit | Medicine Wheel teachings | Handout | Locating self in Medicine Wheel |
| 15 min | Closing | **Theme:** Knowing our own experience | Sharing learning<br>Drum song | | |

can be thought of holistically as their ability to navigate a particular community of practice, which in the case of MBTL can be defined as transprofessional (across education and clinical care) and consistent with the secular-scientific mindfulness community. More helpful, however, is to consider what the component competencies of such membership in the MBTL community of practice includes. This herculean task was done in the design of the MBTL-TCF, which offers a comprehensive and robust representation of the full scope of competencies expected of an MBTL specialist across professions.

The next set of questions concerns how to distribute these competencies across the programme – assuming we are referring to an initial MBTL specialist training programme. We would want to include all of the competencies across all courses and repeat some that seem important to reinforce. Although all of the competencies would be developing and evident in performances across all courses potentially, their explicit identification indicates at what points in the curriculum they will be explicitly taught and assessed. The key here is to consider the scaffolded process by which students move from novice to competent practitioners through a sequence from less to more applied and integrated with the final target practice and performance being to teach or facilitate an MBTL class. Although this would be under supervision, it would culminate in the trainer and mentor determining that the student was prepared to deliver such classes independently. This final step would

**Table 16.5d** Session 2 Curriculum Map

| *SESSION 2 (1.5 hrs)* | | | | | |
|---|---|---|---|---|---|
| *Time* | *Outcome* | *Theme / Skill* | *Practice / Activity* | *Materials* | *Assessment / Homework* |
| 15 min | Apply aspects of the Medicine Wheel teachings | **Theme:** Finding balance in body, mind, and spirit<br>**Skill:** Discerning presence or absence of balance in body, mind, spirit | Home practice review | Medicine Wheel | Review reflections |
| 15 min | Integrate Indigenous teachings with mindfulness practices | | Smudging | | |
| 20 min<br>25 min | Use mindfulness skills to support individual health and wellness | **Themes:** (i) Bridging Indigenous spiritual teaching with mindfulness<br>(ii) Knowing our own experience<br>**Skills:** (i) Using curiosity to pay attention<br>(ii) Discerning presence or absence of balance in body, mind, spirit | Mindfulness of breathing<br>Mindfulness of surroundings (sitting practice) | | Choose a home practice |
| 15 min | Integrate Indigenous teachings with mindfulness practices | **Theme:** Bridging Indigenous spiritual teaching with mindfulness | Sharing learning<br>Drum song | Feedback forms | Feedback |

reflect shifting from a supervised to a competent level of performance in all competencies determined through assessment.

Table 16.6 offers a representation of a possible configuration of an MBTL teacher training programmes involving four courses. The targeted competency domains are arranged to progress from more cognitive and simple tasks to more complex, applied and integrated performative tasks. Four of the competency domains are repeated as they are more challenging to learn: #4 Conducting post-practice inquiry; #8 Designing curriculum/intervention; #9 Applying scientific literacy; and #10 Embodying mindfulness. These competencies will then be used to arrive at the learning outcomes (via their sets of component activities) and assessments (via performance indicators.) The development of the actual focus of the training moves from ideas (intro) to skills focus to discrete tasks and practices to integrated performance in MBTL teaching. This type of progression is consistent with activity theory and associated approaches to task-based design in professional and applied education, for example (Campbell et al., 2014).

**Table 16.6a** Distributing MBTL-TCF Competencies by Course and Level

| *Course #1 Intro* | *Course #2 Skills* | *Course #3 Practice* | *Course #4 Applied (e.g., practicum)* |
|---|---|---|---|
| #1 Organizing | #3 Guiding mindfulness practices | #4 Conducting post-practice inquiry | # 9 Applying scientific literacy |
| #2 Relating to participants | #4 Conducting post-practice inquiry | #8 Designing curriculum/ intervention | #8 Designing curriculum/ intervention |
| #9 Applying scientific literacy | #6 Differentiating learners | #5 Conducting investigative inquiry | #11 Reflecting on practice |
| #10 Embodying mindfulness | #7 Enhancing relational learning | #10 Embodying mindfulness | #12 Practising ethically |

**Table 16.6b** Identifying Key Learning Tasks and Outcomes - e.g. for Course #1 (from Table 16.6a)

| *Course 1 – Introduction* | | |
|---|---|---|
| *Competency Domain* | *Key Tasks (Based on MBTL-TCF Component Activities)* | *Learning Outcomes By the end, students will be able to…* |
| #1 Organizing<br>#2 Relating to participants | 1. In groups, lead a short mindfulness of sensation activity. | 1. Collaborate to design and lead a short mindfulness of sensation practice in groups reflecting research-based principles of attention-regulation. |
| #9 Applying scientific literacy | 2. Define mindfulness based on research, theoretical, and personal sources.<br>3. Prepare an annotated bibliography of 8–10 peer-reviewed research articles on mindfulness as it related to specific topic, profession, and context of interest. | 2. Define mindfulness and mindfulness practices, accounting for a variety of world-views.<br>3. Critique theories of mindfulness using research and analysis.<br>4. Critique research on the effectiveness of mindfulness practices, including possible negative aspects of the practices for certain populations.<br>5. Apply research to support evidence-based practice in particular professions. |
| #10 Embodying mindfulness | 4. Reflect on personal mindfulness practices in a monthly journal. | 6. Design a personal mindfulness inquiry programme. |

## Applying Competency-Based Component Activities as Learning Tasks and Outcomes

The next step is to develop key tasks with associated learning outcomes for the courses so as to reflect the component competencies. In MBTL, this involves using the MBTL-TCF to identify a task that incorporate most or all of the component activities. These tasks are the

**Table 16.6c** Identifying Performance Indicators by Level for Assessment

| *Competency* | *Novice* | *Developing* | *Supervised* | *Competent* | *Proficient* | *Expert* |
|---|---|---|---|---|---|---|
| **#3 Guiding mindfulness practices** | Clearly marks opening, transition, closing | Marks steps and transitions | Practices while guiding; Cues attention and attitudes | Fosters awareness of feeling tones. | Encourages equanimity regardless of feeling tone | Scaffolds well from focus to open awareness |
| **# 4 Conducting post-practice inquiry** | Inquires into sequence of unfolding experience over time | Uses simple reflections by listening/responding to specific contents | Redirects to bodily sensations, feeling, and decentred awareness | Inquires to foster insight - showing v. telling; following v. leading | Caps inquiry with adept queries on the purpose or utility of the practice | Effectively interrupts and redirects when participants get lost in storytelling |

**Table 16.6d** Exemplar of an Actual MBTL Rubric Used to Assess a Course #2 Teaching Task

| *Competency Domain* | Supervised *Level (2)* | Developing *Level (1)* | *Added Feedback* |
|---|---|---|---|
| **Organization** | Attends to time in starting, pacing practices, and ending. Follows plan while responding to unplanned needs that arise. | Uneven attention to time in starting, pacing practices, and ending. Follows plan but may struggle to address unplanned needs that arise. | **Strength:**<br>**Challenge:**<br>**Comment:** |
| **Relating to Participants** | Engages in active listening. Expresses acceptance and interest in learner's experience. Invites participants to clarify meaning or experiences rather than making assumptions. | Moves in and out of active listening. Some displays of acceptance and interest in learner's experience. May awkwardly attempt to clarify meaning or experiences in ways that suggest assumptions. | **Strength:**<br>**Challenge:**<br>**Comment:** |
| **Guiding Mindfulness Practice** | Practices while guiding; monitors/ controls pacing using invitational language. Marks transitions and introduces techniques. Fosters curiosity v. judgment. Returns attention to sensed v. thought/imagined experience and to feeling tones to cultivate equanimity and curiosity in practice. | Limited, but some, evidence of script-use. Timing and pacing worked. Use of "ing" verbs. Marks transitions and key steps in practice. Returns participants' attention to sensations and the present. | **Strength:**<br>**Challenge:**<br>**Comment:** |
| **Conducting Post-Practice Inquiry** | Encourages participants to describe experience in detail, using simple and complex reflections. Redirects to bodily sensations, feeling tone, and decentered awareness. Inquires into sequence of experiences over time and insights. | Invites and encourages participants to recount experience in language using simple reflections. Some evidence of listening and responding to distinct contents. | **Strength:**<br>**Challenge:**<br>**Comment:** |
| **Differentiating Learners** | Offers alternatives to serve a range of abilities or capacities. Remains non-defensive in responding to learners, using empathy, reflective listening, and apologies if needed. Reiterates applying self-compassion and respecting limits. | Invites identifying personal pronouns.<br>Remembers and uses correct pronunciation of participants' names, appropriate pronouns, etc.<br>Recognizes/welcomes diverse backgrounds/experience. | **Strength:**<br>**Challenge:**<br>**Comment:** |
| **Embodying Mindfulness** | Teaches as a contemplative practice, in the present with minimal self-consciousness. Communicates from a robust personal practice. | Moves in and out of contemplative presence and self-consciousness, which can even be uncomfortable or awkward. What is performed may be technically correct but still controlled. | **Strength:**<br>**Challenge:**<br>**Comment:** |

focus of explicit teaching, learning, and assessment in the course. The tasks are then used in design to arrive at target skills, themes, practices, and activities that might best model and support learners to perform the key tasks, thereby meeting the learning outcomes. In our example from Table 16.6a, there would be one to two tasks for every competency domain and one to three learning outcomes associated with each task. So, for example, in Table 16.6b, we offer an example of how this might be done for Course #1 – Introduction.

### Applying Competency-based Performance Indicators as Assessment

The final key additional step in using the MBTL-TCF in designing MBTL teacher training curricula and programmes is to develop assessment criteria aligned with the learning outcomes (as competency criteria) and tasks (i.e., learning activities). To do this, a designer needs to develop appropriate performance and performance level indicators. This requires that they identify those indicators that are less demanding from those that are more demanding to arrange appropriately in a developmental spectrum from novice through to expert. The performance indicators included in the MBTL-TCF are just examples, so it is fine to develop or use others based on analysis and application. For example, Table 16.6c illustrates a distribution of performance indicators across all six competency levels (from novice to expert) for two key competency domains: #3 (guiding) and #4 (inquiry). Note that there would usually be more indicators, as represented in Table 16.6d, which presents an actual rubric scale used in an initial practice facilitation for the equivalent of a Course #2 Skills (Table 16.6a).

## CONCLUSION

In this chapter, we outlined the key steps for designing MBTL curriculum, both for teaching mindfulness and for training MBTL specialists. MBTL specialists need curriculum design skills to apply new research to respond to a rapidly changing landscape of practice. Designing training using the MBTL-TCF offers a competency-based approach to design professional learning. Although we realize that the information load may sometimes have seemed like trees obscuring the forest, it was necessary to provide specialists and practitioners engaged in such practices adequate models and support.

## REFERENCES

Armstrong, P. (2010). *Bloom's taxonomy.* Vanderbilt University Centre for Teaching. https://cft.vanderbilt.edu/guides-sub-pages/blooms-taxonomy/.

Biggs, J. (1996). Enhancing teaching through constructive alignment. *Higher Education, 32*, 347–364. https://doi.org/10.1007/BF00138871.

Bloom, B., Engelhart, M., Furst, E., Hill, W., & Krathwohl, D. (1956). *Taxonomy of educational objectives: The classification of educational goals. Handbook I: Cognitive domain.* David McKay Company.

Campbell, C., MacPherson, S., & Sawkins, T. (2014) Preparing students for education, work, and community: Activity theory in task-based curriculum design. *TESL Canada Journal, 31*, Special Issue 8, 68–92. https://doi.org/10.18806/tesl.v31i0.1187.

Crane, R., & Hecht, F. (2018). Intervention integrity in mindfulness-based research. *Mindfulness, 9*, 1370–1380. https://doi.org/10.1007/s12671-018-0886-3.

Dawson, V. (2021). All our relations: Four Indigenous lessons on mindfulness. *Mindful: Healthy Mind, Healthy Life.* https://www.mindful.org/all-our-relations-four-indigenous-lessons-on-mindfulness/.

Galante, J., Friedrich, C., Dawson, A., Mondrego-Alarcon, M., Gebbing, P. L., Delgado-Suarez, I., Gupta, R., Dean, L., Dagleish, T., White, I., & Jones, P. (2021). Mindfulness-based programmes for mental health promotion in adults in non-clinical settings: A systematic review and meta-analysis of randomised controlled trials. *PLoS Medicine.* Advance online publication. https://doi.org/10.1371/journal.pmed.1003481.

Griffith, G., Crane, R., Baer, R., Fernandez, E., Giommi, F., Herbette, G., & Koerbel, L. (2021). Implementing the mindfulness-based interventions: Teaching assessment criteria (MBI:TAC) in mindfulness-based teacher training. *Global Advances in Health and Medicine, 10*, 1–6. https://doi.org/10.1177/2164956121998340.

Kelly, G., & Martin, F. (2022). Mindfulness and indigenous teachings pilot curriculum (Unpublished). Adapted with permission.

Le, T. & Gobert, J. (2013). Translating and implementing a mindfulness-based youth suicide prevention intervention in a Native American community. *Journal of Child and Family Studies, 24*, 12–23. https://doi.org/10.1007/s10826-013-9809-z.

Ragoonaden, K., Fraser, T., Hoffman, R., & Hebert, B. (2021). Mindfulness and Indigenous knowledge: Shared narratives about reconciliation and decolonization in teacher education. *The Journal of Contemplative Inquiry, 8*(1), 148–175.

Rupprecht, S., Koole, W., Chaskalson, M., Tamdjidi, C., & West, M. (2019). Running too far ahead? Towards a broader understanding of mindfulness in organisations. *Current Opinion in Psychology, 28*, 32–36. https://doi.org/10.1016/j.copsyc.2018.10.007.

Yellow Bird, M. (2013). Neurodecolonization: Applying mindfulness research to decolonizing social work. In M. Gray, J. Coates, M. Yellow Bird, & T. Hetherington (Eds.), *Decolonizing social work* (pp. 293–310). Routledge.

# CHAPTER 17

# TRAUMA-INFORMED PRACTICE IN MBTL

MBTL cuts across multiple disciplines and sectors, including healthcare, where it is being researched and used as a clinical modality for treating mental and medical disorders. These applications have only recently begun to address the issue of potential adverse effects arising from the practice of mindfulness in the clinical context. Such research is early and, therefore, evolving. A related issue, and of primary concern in this chapter, is the subject of trauma and what it means to deliver trauma-informed practice in MBTL. Examining the potential adverse effects that mindfulness practices may have for those who have experienced trauma, regardless of whether or not they have been diagnosed with or meet many of the criteria for Acute Stress Disorder (ASD) or Posttraumatic Stress Disorder (PTSD), is a complex issue given that mindfulness is also used as a treatment for trauma.

As a transprofessional practice, MBTL extends these concerns to non-clinical areas, to the varied contexts in which mindfulness is taught and learned. This is necessary given the high prevalence in the general population of both trauma and mental health challenges, which may or may not be identified or actively treated (e.g., Bethell et al., 2016; Tonmyr et al., 2020). Therefore, with respect to trauma and the potential adverse effects of mindfulness, distinctions between clinical and non-clinical populations blur. This chapter will consider trauma beyond the medical context, viewing it instead from the perspective of the impact of trauma on human functioning and resilience, given its capacity to cause distress, tax resources, and to interfere with the ability to cope. This is irrespective of its origins - whether it be incident-based, relational, developmental, medical or surgical, complex, intergenerational, vicarious, racial, from structural oppression and so on. Indeed, many behaviours and symptoms exhibited by a person who has experienced trauma are attempts at adaptation, regardless of whether or not the strategies actually work (US-SAMHSA, 2014).

It is worth noting that currently, research suggests that adverse effects are not particularly prevalent in secular-scientific mindfulness contexts. In their review of 83 studies with 6703 participants, for example, Farias et al. (2020) found an incidence rate of 8.3% reporting at least one meditation adverse effect (MAE) but only 3.7% when studies were limited to controlled experimental designs. Vieten et al. (2018) collected survey data from 1130 meditators from 66 countries on their mystical and extraordinary meditational experiences. They found that of the 18 identified "extraordinary experiences," the least common were "disturbing emotions" associated with fear and dread, though 32% had experienced it at some point. Most other experiences were perceived as very positive or constructive to their spiritual path. Also, some of the reported incidents of adverse experience come from intensive Buddhist retreats (Lindahl et al., 2017), which cannot be generalized to most MBTL contexts. These limitations notwithstanding, in this chapter, we will review the current literature on adverse effects and trauma, and discuss ways to mitigate and manage these should they arise.

## TRAUMA AND TRAUMA-INFORMED PRACTICE(S) IN MBTL

As mindfulness became transmitted within a secular-scientific framework, attention shifted from its ability to foster *awakening* to its ability to foster health and wellbeing, thereby altering its contexts, practitioners, and motivations. As a result, questions of adverse effects

DOI: 10.4324/9781003182467-23

have become salient in both research and teaching. Since mindfulness can be employed to support those with a trauma history or may trigger trauma reactions, trauma-informed practice is currently a prominent interest of the field, across its various social, therapeutic, and educational domains. In addition, the increasing incidence and/or reporting of trauma within the general population arising from adverse childhood experiences (ACEs) and forced human migrations, to name a few, make it an often invisible condition impacting many participants in non-clinical mindfulness programmes.

Trauma can be defined in various ways. When considered from an individual perspective, it may be diagnosed as Posttraumatic Stress Disorder (PTSD) via the DSM-V (2013). Alternatively, it may describe psychological vulnerabilities arising from acute incidents or the cumulative impacts of negative life events or experiences that do not meet the DSM criteria. The Research Domain Criteria (RDoC) of the US National Institute for Mental Health (NIMH) (n.d.) uses the rigorous and broader construct of *sustained threat* to investigate disorders from chronic exposure to trauma and stress, defined as:

> An aversive emotional state caused by prolonged (i.e., weeks to months) exposure to internal and/or external condition(s), state(s), or stimuli that are adaptive to escape or avoid. The exposure may be actual or anticipated; the changes in affect, cognition, physiology, and behavior caused by sustained threat persist in the absence of the threat, and can be differentiated from those changes evoked by acute threat.

Increasingly, clinical practice suggests trauma should be understood as "what happened to the person" rather than "what is wrong with the person" (Butler et al., 2011, p. 178). This less judgemental lens is used to consider a range of negative traumatic effects or disorders impacting wellbeing. This view led the U.S.-based Substance Abuse and Mental Health Services Administration (SAMHSA) (2014) to propose a specific definition of trauma to incorporate this same perspective or lens:

> Individual trauma results from an event, series of events, or set of circumstances that is experienced by an individual as physically or emotionally harmful or life threatening and that has lasting adverse effects on the individual's functioning and mental, physical, social, emotional, or spiritual well-being.
>
> *(p. 7)*

## Mindfulness and Trauma

As a common tool with evidence-based promise in the treatment of trauma (Hopwood & Schutte, 2017), mindfulness can be *strong medicine* with impacts well beyond the placebo effect. As with any strong medicine, there are known and unanticipated side-effects that need to be considered alongside the benefits. As in analogous pharmacological interventions, how mindfulness is delivered can impact whether or not such side-effects occur. These delivery variables include types of practice, dosage, teacher and peer support, and intensity levels. With the surging interest in trauma-informed practices in mindfulness (e.g., Burrows, 2018; Treleaven, 2018), related issues of meditation-related adverse events (MAE) and culturally inclusive practices tend to be subsumed under the broader category of trauma-informed practice (TIP) or trauma-informed care (TIC), depending on the context. The trouble is that often the slippage in terminology proceeds without explicitly being addressed. We, too, have chosen to use the term trauma-informed practice as an inclusive term to refer to these three broad categories, but will present the issues separately.

Therefore, we understand trauma-informed practice/care as applicable across sectors as a complex approach to trauma, MAEs, and decolonization in MBTL.

Trauma-informed practice or care also needs to be distinguished from trauma-specific services in which interventions are applied to treat trauma itself by therapists with specific skills (Butler et al., 2011). We focus instead on trauma-informed practice, in which trauma issues are not the direct focus of the multi- or trans-disciplinary mindfulness programs; at the same time, given the diverse participants, it is important to foster an environment that promotes safety and optimizes learning for all attendees. Thus, as per Gerber (2019), such an environment needs to embody safety, choice, dignity, self-efficacy, collaboration, connection, trust, the acceptance of the expression of emotions and predictable expectations, principles we have reworked into seven principles of trauma-informed practice in MBTL.

## Theorizing Trauma in MBTL

In an early conceptual study, Compson (2014) presented a rationale for trauma-informed practices in mindfulness. Drawing on a range of somatic therapeutic theories, she emphasized that trauma is a somatic phenomenon with a tendency for bodily systems and functions to go into hyper- or hypo-arousal in response to the triggering of traumatic memory. She suggested this somatic nature of trauma means traditional talk therapies have limited efficacy given their common focus on cognitive rather than somatic functions. Indeed, Mavranezouli et al.'s (2020) review did find somatic interventions like EMDR to be most efficacious in the treatment of trauma, but so too were cognitive behavioural therapy interventions, a special present-centred and behaviour-oriented form of talk therapy. Second, Compson concluded that because the prefrontal cortex (PFC) can play a decisive role in mindfulness-based self-regulation, people triggered and in a traumatic response may not share the same benefits if their PFC is disabled. Third, and for this very reason, she concluded that leaving participants with trauma histories to meditate on their own could put them at risk. Instead, she proposed that mindful interacting may be more important, whereby a facilitator, teacher, therapist, or peer empathically "listens" to mirror and support the person in returning to a more regulated state.

Another point Compton raised was to argue that authoritarian tendencies, more common in more traditional Buddhist mindfulness contexts, may exacerbate trauma responses in practitioners by reinforcing patterns of learned helplessness often at the root of trauma wounds. For instance, many of the dysfunctional effects of childhood adverse events are associated with sustained threats in which the child is helpless or impaired in their capacity to navigate the threat or to respond appropriately. Later, deference to strict rules and gruelling demands and schedules in intensive retreats, such as those found in some schools of Zen or S.N. Goenka, for example, can lead participants to override their inclination to adjust practices to avoid trauma-related dysregulation. This may be exacerbated by what Sparks (2011) described as a "suffocating compliance to authority" in some more traditional mindfulness contexts, which can keep the practitioner captive to past abuses of authority so as to perpetuate psychological challenges even with improved awareness through mindfulness (p. 39).

One common response to the re-experiencing of trauma is to dissociate: to cut-off from uncomfortable physical or mental experiences. The opposite of such dissociation is integration, whereby experiences are integrated into our understanding of ourselves and the world. Authoritarian cultures and practices in the teaching or learning of mindfulness can make trauma survivors susceptible to dissociation by leading them, in Treleaven (2018) words, "to override a survival strategy" (p. 137). Instead, trauma-informed practices start with safeguarding choice and protecting invitational, voluntary participation and choice throughout practices. To *leave people in choice,* Treleaven's first principle of trauma-informed MBTL, involves emphasizing choice and autonomy without "coddling trauma survivors" (p. 138). It is about turning towards the difficult and unwanted but only to the extent that one can bear without becoming dysregulated. This is the principle behind teaching and using the "window of tolerance," to be described later.

Finally, worth Garland et al.'s (2017) presented empirical evidence demonstrating the efficacy of mindfulness in the amelioration of all 10 elements of behavioral dysregulation in sustained threat using the RDoC criteria of the NIMH (n.d.). This included biological evidence implicating key brain circuits. They integrated this evidence, grounded in the operationalized RDoC criteria for *sustained threat* used to investigate chronic stress, adverse childhood experiences, and PTSD, in their proposed Mindfulness-to-Meaning Theory.

## Seven Principles of Trauma-Informed MBTL

Appreciating the value in practice of a sound set of trauma-informed principles for the practice of MBTL, we propose seven principles that draw on Compson's (2014), Treleaven's (2018), and Gerber's (2019) recommendations with those of the US-based SAMHSA (2014). SAMHSA engaged in a fairly rigorous process involving the triangulation of environmental scans and research, practical knowledge from trauma programs and specialists in the US, and the experiences of trauma survivors to arrive at six principles of trauma-informed practices for agencies and organizations: safety; trustworthiness and transparency; peer support; collaboration and mutuality; empowerment, voice, and choice; cultural, history, and gender issues. Specifying the implications specifically for MBTL, and triangulating them with Compton, Treleaven, and Gerber, we arrived at the following seven principles of trauma-informed practices in MBTL:

**Safety.** As emerging research and theories on the physiology of stress and sustained threat (Brosschot et al., 2018; Francis, 2018; Garland et al., 2017) suggest, the stress response may be a default survival setting, reinforced by the threat bias, that only turns off by being disinhibited by messaging or triggers of safety. The awareness of safety, in turn, can be bolstered through the broadening of awareness and positive emotions associated with mindfulness (or nature, in related studies). Applied to trauma-informed MBTL practice, this suggests the need for facilitators to *communicate and enact safety* - verbally, non-verbally, and contextually - to enable all participants to benefit from practices. This does not mean to overprotect but rather to encourage attention to challenges or difficulties within a context of confidence and safety, and as free as possible of fear, anguish, or terror, real or imagined. Finally, it extends to ensuring an environment in which emotions can be expressed in a safe and accepted way.

**Trust.** This principle refers to the need for MBTL facilitators to convey trustworthiness and transparency so as to engender confidence and trust in participants for the sake of learning. This translates into key practices such as soliciting *informed consent* where possible, even in smaller gestures such as asking a question of a participant who had not volunteered to speak. It involves *truth-telling,* that is, using painstaking accuracy and precision in describing and representing the benefits and risks of practices. Trust is enhanced as well by consistency, predictability, and providing information about the learning context. For example, if participants at a program orientation are told they have the choice to respond to questions or not, the teacher should not inadvertently coerce a participant into speaking when they have said they would rather not. This would include refraining from asking them a direct question or putting them in a breakout group if their objection extended to communicating with peers. Finally, it involves *avoiding cultural (mis)appropriation* by acknowledging the sources of practices or ideas.

**Autonomy.** The relationship between autonomy and mindfulness has solid empirical and theoretical support in self-determination theory (Ryan & Deci, 2017). This research suggests that mindfulness fosters autonomy, hence wellbeing, by promoting intrinsic motivation and self-regulation; yet, at the same time, as trauma-informed practice, mindfulness needs explicitly to safeguard and foster autonomy. This requirement distills down to the need for learners to be free to navigate mindfulness practices in relation to their own emerging experiences. This calls for conserving non-authoritarian, de-centered structures and practices that clearly situate controls in students or learners rather than teachers. It implies the need for a variety of invitational approaches, ranging from the use of invitational language to making participation voluntary. In post-practice inquiry, it is reflected in the disciplined practice of facilitators *eliciting* rather than *telling* in response to questions or issues. In formal education, it makes the grading of mindfulness practice problematic if and when the graded assessments reinforce extrinsic motivation. The "Window of Tolerance" introduced later in the chapter offers a very useful tool that embodies participant autonomy; students need to be encouraged to use and apply this self-regulatory tool during meditational practices. This aligns with what Gerber (2019) refers to as *self-efficacy*.

**Choice.** A closely related principle to autonomy is choice; indeed, the two combine to form what Treleaven (2018) refers to as the need to "leave people in choice" (p. 137). Yet, here choice refers to something distinct from learner autonomy. In trauma-informed practice, choice refers to a teacher or facilitator actively providing choices to reduce the pressures or impulses learners may perceive to conform to the dominant practice(s) or expectations in the face of contradictory personal experiences or resistances. Choice may extend to whether or not a learner participates at all, the decision to engage in self-care during a practice if it is experienced as too challenging, and other choices related to practices, duration, intensity, and posture.

**Collaboration.** Instituting strong peer, small group, and facilitator collaborations in MBTL further deepens this shift from teacher-centred to learner-centred and autonomous learning environments. The strong emphasis on relational learning helps participants to decenter from an intense sense of isolation, identification with certain experiences, and limiting beliefs. This is assisted by the teacher eliciting information about experiences and exercises from participants through dialogue and open-ended questions. Being able to communicate or describe their own experiences in dialogue with others can help create a change in perspective with respect to possible distorted perceptions or interpretations. When participants are experiencing similar things to others in the class or group but are reticent to speak about them, they may feel a sense of relief to hear others are experiencing similar things. It suggests to them that their experiences are normal and part of being human. Alternatively, when participants have different reactions to, or views about, similar experiences, these can lead to the understanding that reality is a construct rather than a fact. Note that this principle of collaboration embeds Gerber's (2019) principle of connection.

**Somatic Orientation.** Common practices in MBTL include teaching participants to observe and describe physical experiences; to locate and grounding themselves in the body; to learn somatic skills; to engage in mindfulness of movement; and to use a number of posture or other options to engage a practice. These all align well with the need to address non-cognitive somatic experiences in trauma-informed care. Also, introducing body awareness through the hands may be helpful and less threatening than more introspective practices like body scan or mindfulness of breathing as the predominance of the hands in both the motor and sensory cortex can make them more accessible to attention. Also, mindfulness of the hands, or feet, combine exteroceptive (sensing the external world) and interoceptive (sensing the internal world of the body) abilities. So too, alternating between movement and stationary practices like the body scan can be helpful, and, when the body scan is used, participants with trauma histories may benefit from posture options, being invited to keep eyes open but unfocused, more guidance during practice, and, after a period of time, alternative practice options altogether such as yoga, sensory bathing, or walking. Teaching learners to ground themselves using sensory experiences is another effective strategy when applying the Window of Tolerance, where learners can be taught to perceive and identify objects of each of the five senses (touch, smell, taste, sight, sound).

**Decolonization.** Trauma-responsive MBTL involves intentional strategies to remove lingering oppressive or colonizing attitudes or practices in mindfulness. Given that members of discriminated racial, ethnic, or gendered group experience higher rates of sustained threat and adverse childhood experiences, sometimes culminating in race- and gender-based traumas, it may be helpful to signal to learners clear intentions to decolonize mindfulness practices and learning environments. This may involve introducing culturally-appropriate practices, such as drumming or chanting for Indigenous learners. It may involve welcoming and normalizing critical conversations about oppressive histories or contemporary social issues. It may involve welcoming the expression of emotions arising from ongoing racist experiences. So too, it may extend to expanding who is invited to teach and learn in the first place and the examples of normative bodies used to illustrate topics. Also, just as mindfulness manifests as a neuro-somatic experience, it can become a conduit for either neuro-colonization or decolonization, depending on how it is taught (Yellow Bird, 2022, personal communication). This principle of *decolonization* also embeds Gerber's (2019) principle of treating all participants with *dignity*.

## Early Evidence of the Efficacy of Trauma-Informed MBTL

There is early evidence that trauma-informed mindfulness is effective with trauma survivors. For example, Aizik-Reebs et al. (2021) completed a RCT study of severely traumatized refugees using a specialized Mindfulness-Based Trauma Recovery for Refugees (MBTR-R) program. The treatment group experienced significant reductions in symptoms of PTSD, anxiety, depression, and multimorbidity compared to waitlist controls. So too, generic mindfulness programs like MBSR and MBCT may assist people with PTSD even without special trauma-related interventions given effective facilitation. In Boyd et al.'s (2018) review of studies using mindfulness with people with PTSD, they found low attrition rates with medium to high effects across studies. They theorized that these results offer early evidence that mindfulness improves brain connectivity, thereby supporting the

PFC to restore its capacity to modulate both hyper- and hypo-activity in the emotional centres as Compson (2014) predicted.

## MEDITATION-RELATED ADVERSE EFFECTS (MAE)

Often subsumed under trauma-informed practice, meditation-related adverse effects (MAE) constitute a different form of risk and evidence-base from trauma in MBTL. MAEs refer to unexpected adverse effects arising through the process of learning or practicing meditation, regardless of the trauma or mental health history of the person so affected. Operationalizing challenges have limited the construct validity of some of the studies. For example, Lindahl et al. (2017) claimed to be studying 59 people with "meditation-related challenges," yet their interview probes were as follows: "What kinds of experiences have you had as a result of meditation?" and "Have you had any significant experiences that were unexpected, challenging, or difficult?" (p. 9). Clearly, the generic use of the term "experiences" or "unexpected" or even "challenging" experiences do not suggest that these experiences are negative; it is crucial, therefore, that the definitions of such terms are clarified to participants if results are to be useful.

Another challenge in the Lindahl et al. (2017) study was that all 59 participants were (American) Buddhists, most of whom had experienced the so-called "challenges" during intensive retreats. Although those reporting they had *not* experienced challenges were excluded, the study included 11 teachers or *experts* who clearly had enough good experiences to persist in the practice. The findings were presented in a phenomenological table identifying experiences in seven categories: cognitive; perceptual; affective; somatic; conative; sense of self; and social, and included phenomena like "positive emotions" and "changes in self-other or self-world boundaries," both of which are clearly targeted in many practices. In contrast, Vieten et al. (2018) surveyed 1130 participants to identify 18 categories of phenomenological experiences, most of which were reported to be very positive, even mystical, with the least reported being fear and dread (by 32%). In this respect, unusual experiences should not be confused with MAEs.

What can be interpreted as distinguishing MAEs from most mystical experiences are distress to the participant and degrees of impairment or harm, both short- and long-term. In fact, the actual incidence of MAEs in regular practice contexts appears to be quite low. As mentioned in the opening of the chapter, Farias et al. (2020) reviewed 83 studies with 6703 participants and found an incidence rate of 8.3% of participants reporting at least one meditation adverse effect (MAE) but only 3.7% when the studies were limited to controlled experimental designs. Adverse experiences can include sleep impairment, anxiety, sense of loss of self or agency, depression, fear and dread, through to delusions or paranoia. Different mindfulness contexts can trigger different responses, including interpretive context with respect to how one understands them. For example, in Theravada Buddhist practices (see Grabovac, 2015) the identification of an anticipated insight stage characterized by fear and dread in Theravada Buddhist practices (see Grabovac, 2015) is absent in earlier Buddhist (Analayo, 2019) and later Mahayana texts on insight. Furthermore, in secular-scientific mindfulness contexts like MBTL, as Analayo outlines, there is no sense that fear and dread are expected or in any functional sense a feature of that training or practice. See Textbox 17.1 for more detail on this topic. Furthermore, the many recent additions of trauma-informed approaches to mindfulness in MBTL, such as the aforementioned seven principles, are introducing many preventative safeguards to prevent experiences of fear or dread.

## TEXTBOX 17.1 CASE STUDY:

### Precedents for Trauma-Informed Practice in Buddhism

The 2500-year history of mindfulness in Buddhism offers a contrastive case to managing trauma or meditative adverse effects. Two early accounts from the life of the Buddha offer some examples. The first is the account of Kisa Gotami, a distraught woman who lost her only child. Carrying around his corpse, she wandered from house to house asking for someone to revive the boy. When she approached the Buddha, he told her she must first collect mustard seeds from a household in which no one had died. Not finding any such household, she is said to have realized the pervasiveness of death: "Because I now see that my own sorrow is part of the sorrow of all people, and that the death of our loved ones is part of the pattern of life for everyone" (Rhys Davids & Norman, 1971, pp. 88-89).

When a group of monks committed suicide after contemplating the lack of beauty of the body (Analayo, 2014), the Buddha recommended *anapanasati sutta* or mindfulness of breathing as a practice to correct the imbalance that led to this mass suicides (Analayo, 2019b). In this respect, mindfulness was viewed as an antidote to mental instability (Analayo, 2019a).

With the emergence of Theravada Buddhism, difficult states began to be represented as intrinsic to the path of insight or *vipassana*. In the eight stages of insight, the fifth is described as "Knowledge of suffering: Dissolution, fear, misery, disgust, and desire for deliverance," which Grabovac (2015) suggests can involve intense psychological and even psychiatric symptoms that meet the criteria for depressive and psychotic disorders. Analayo (2019a) suggests, however, that this teaching is unique to the Theravada school and should not be interpreted as a description of all paths to or through special insight.

In later Mahayana schools, non-normative states, experiences, and dispositions became elevated as *crazy wisdom*. Accounts of iconoclastic and deviant, behaviour typified many of the biographies of the early yogis of these traditions. In Tibetan Buddhism, however, they do diagnose a distinctive pathology of meditation: *rLung* or negative winds (Deane, 2019): a disorder of the subtle body-mind believed to arise through stress or excessive or improper meditative practices (Rominger, 2013).

In a speculative paper based on her knowledge of brain science and mindfulness, Britton (2019) provided a model for thinking about MAEs given evidence of the otherwise positive outcomes of mindfulness and meditation. She suggested that like many positive phenomena, mindfulness may be "non-monotonic," following a U-curve whereby moderate exposure to practice provides benefits that diminish and reverse in excess doses. She pointed to theoretical challenges given current knowledge of mindfulness and its effects on the brain. For example, while mindfulness is known to enhance interoception with impacts on the insula, in excess, these insula changes could trigger a range of emotional effects like anxiety, panic, or depression. Similarly, although mindfulness has been found to improve emotion regulation, which is believed to be related to its effects on the PFC and its capacity to modulate the amygdala, if taken to excess such inhibition can lead to dissociation or emotional blunting. So, too, she points to potential problems with extremes or mistaken interpretations or practices of decentering, approach orientations, and even acceptance and reappraisal, all key mechanisms attributed to the efficacy of mindfulness. The question she poses is whether or not mindfulness can be too much of a good thing. She is, in short, proposing a middle-way in mindfulness, reminiscent of a central idea used to describe the Buddhist path: the way of moderation or the middle-way.

Given the seeming increased rate of MAEs in retreat contexts, it is worthwhile taking a moment to consider how to safeguard retreats to minimize the risks of adverse effects. The aforementioned seven principles of trauma-informed practice in MBTL would apply well to this context. Safeguards could include safety, trust, and transparency in making clear the risks and in establishing protocols to minimize risk. The environment is also important, such as providing a predictable schedule regarding practices, meals, start and stop times. Also important is autonomy and choice, including development of a more flat versus hierarchical or authoritarian culture in the retreat. This includes reducing the focus on teachers as authorities and on student-endorsed norms. Flexibility in practices are important, including alternating more interoceptive or introspective formal practices with less formal movement or contemplative practices such as observing nature while walking.

To reduce feelings of isolation and to help monitor student wellbeing, it can be helpful to provide daily opportunities for inquiry and debriefing experiences, both with a teacher and with peers. This helps to foster a sense of collaboration and connection among learners as well. It is best not to make such interactions mandatory; for example, even if required to be present in an inquiry session, retreatants should be given the option not to break silence to participate if they so wish. That said, it should be clear that such inquiry sessions are part of the practice and are not a form of breaking silence anymore than reporting to a teacher or asking questions in a teaching session might be. Finally, these precautions or efforts to secure safety for participants should not extend to surveillance or a sense that retreatants need to be monitored or supervised. This was reinforced in Vieten et al. (2019) findings that most positive experiences of meditators happened when they were meditating alone rather than in a group.

## DECOLONIZATION AND INTER-GENERATIONAL TRAUMA

Any meaningful agenda for equity and social justice needs to recognize the impact of histories of oppression and colonization on the bodies of diverse peoples, recognizing that these legacies are not only cultural but physiological and psychological. While this is most evident for Indigenous, Black, and certain peoples of colour, it extends to gender groups as well in the many ways in which social institutions and cultural practices have been organized around the premise of the white male heterosexual as normative. In many instances, and acutely for Indigenous peoples as Yellow Bird (2013) presents, the generational trauma of occupation and oppression created unequal conditions at the outset that continue in the ongoing legacies of inherited neural, somatic, psychological, familial, and social trauma. In this way, mindfulness is increasingly being recognized as a potential vehicle for neuro-decolonization in the project of recovery from race-based trauma. Yellow Bird defines neuro-decolonization as:

> *[N]eurodecolonization* [is] a conceptual framework which uses mindfulness research to facilitate an examination of ways in which the human brain is affected by the colonial situation and an exploration of mind-brain activities that change neural networks and

> enable individuals to overcome the myriad effects of trauma and oppression inherent in colonialism.
>
> *(p. 293)*

As promising and important as mindfulness may prove to rectify and help heal the conditions of oppression and colonization (see also Berilla, 2016, 2020), there is a certain irony, not lost to Yellow Bird (2013), that the ways in which mindfulness has been introduced and taught in North America and other modern contexts has tended to carry with it an unexamined colonizing agenda or set of practices. These include the closeness with which certain programs have been to Indigenous mindfulness practices, which are more familiar and accessible to these learners and come with less colonial baggage. Likewise, ideas about what an ideal meditator or mindfulness practitioner looks like - perhaps even inherited from Asia - someone sitting alone cross-legged in a cave, may not always match the collective practices that help some Indigenous learners find a sense of relationship and coordinated affiliation they may seek - as through drumming or talking circles, for example.

In this respect, for mindfulness to be a vehicle helping to free people from the oppressive legacies of colonization, it is important that aspects of the seven principles for trauma-informed MBTL be attenuated for the range of people suffering in the aftermath of social and cultural oppression. This includes opening to a spectrum of emotional contents and discussions about such legacies and not marginalizing people who voice distress arising from them as somehow given in the anger. Yellow Bird (2013), for example, recounts the story of an Indigenous woman at a retreat who participated in a conversation about the impact of the Chinese occupation of Tibet and pointed out that Indigenous people in the US also suffered from the occupation of their lands. Instead of a sympathetic or empathic response, someone said she seemed attached to her anger.

The first step in rendering MBTL as an anti-oppressive decolonizing program is to open to the full spectrum of forms of "oppression" or suffering that can arise. This awareness is used to foster awareness and, hence, wellbeing as human flourishing. Such eudaimonic wellbeing is not merely something physical or introspective but a fully functioning capacity for agency and self-determination able to manifest in the world. Yet, such an agenda begins with the body-mind, with recognizing the subtle limits and habits we perpetuate from sources known or unknown that undermine our capacity for wellbeing. To overcome something as pernicious and otherwise seemingly inaccessible as neuro-decolonization requires the adept practices of mindfulness to support such deprogramming, re-wiring, and establishment of more flexible and adaptive neuro-somatic practices and patterns (even habits).

## Race- and Gender-Based Trauma

Beyond the seven principles' we presented for trauma-informed practice in MBTL, the following added safeguards may help with race- or gender-based trauma in particular:

### *Safety and Trust*

In the case of survivors of intergenerational racism, creating an atmosphere of safety and trust in an MBTL context may be difficult to realize for them if the background identities of other students and the teacher are those of their oppressors. Therefore, there may be value in creating segregated cohorts with teachers from the same background to instill this sense of cultural safety. This reinforces the need to actively recruit MBTL specialists from more diverse and under-represented populations. It also involves using language and examples that are relevant to, and consistent with, the culture of the group. Finally, practices that invite dignity and respect, like acknowledging Indigenous territory, are essential.

### *Autonomy and Choice*

Being flexible in how participants choose to practice, including using unconventional approaches, positions, or formats like using the drum as part of breathing or body awareness practices, integrating certain practices into sweat lodge sessions in groups, allowing some artistic or expressive components during or following practices as mindfulness or inquiry. This would require some discernment on the part of the teacher to recognize what is diluting a practice from what is adapting it to accommodate cultural or gender-related needs. Also, sometimes a participant's need to affirm that they are working in an environment in which their autonomy and choices are respected may trump requirements to follow the regimen of a practice.

### *Collaboration*

Part of the challenge in generating a sense of collaboration and connection may be that a participant's trauma histories or more recent encounters with insensitive participants in a mindfulness class can undermine the efficacy of peer-learning through collaboration and connection. This can be addressed by recruiting and organizing cohorts of participants of the same background for a class or in sufficient numbers to form cohort groups within a more diverse class. Also, group interaction guidelines can be presented and discussed to foster more inclusive forms of collaboration.

### *Somatic Orientation*

Being flexible in approaches to mindfulness of the body and expanding our sense of what a somatic orientation looks like may be very helpful in providing ways for diverse learners with varied intergenerational trauma histories to learn to use this important re-regulation strategy. Dancing, for example, or drumming together may be as effective as yoga, as may be singing.

### *Decolonization*

This principle goes critically to the contents of what is taught and how it is framed. It begins with accepting, as a first principle or intention of any mindfulness program, the objective to decolonize mindfulness itself and, in turn, to decolonize and reduce the oppressive load on participants and their broader communities and society.

## TOOLS FOR WORKING WITH TRAUMA AND ADVERSE EFFECTS

Given that MBTL straddles clinical, education, and workplace contexts, mindfulness teachers need to know their individual limits regarding their competence and scope of practice when it comes to both determining who is suitable to participate in mindfulness programs and what teachers feel able to manage should adverse events arise. These issues are complex and further complicated by the fact that, depending on the teacher's profession, it may or may not be appropriate to collect private health information. Thus, the teacher may have limited knowledge about who is in the program, further reducing their ability to make informed decisions about who should or should not participate. Furthermore, we cannot predict with any certainty who may or may not experience adverse experiences. Also, as discussed, such adverse events are neither common nor often serious within the context of secular MBTL.

There are a number of available strategies that will go a long way to protecting both participants and teachers in the event that such problems arise, including soliciting informed consent from prospective participants; outlining what to expect and advising participants around what to do should they experience challenges they are unable to manage; and eliciting how they work with triggers or dysregulated states. In addition, participants should sign off on whether or not they have a history or condition that might make it difficult for them to benefit or in which mindfulness could put them at risk or even induce harm. For example, a person experiencing severe depression might face a further decrease in mood or, given limited cognitive-emotional functioning, might be unable to learn; engage in in-class sessions; or follow through with home practice. For this and other reasons, all participants in mindfulness programs need to understand that these programs are not a panacea, nor is mindfulness necessarily benign. As a mindfulness teacher, one needs at least a basic understanding of potential risks and knowledge of both benefits and possible pitfalls of MBTL. Lastly, a teacher needs to recognize challenges when they arise, to a minimum standard that allows for appropriate action or referral.

Many people come to learn mindfulness for a variety of reasons, not the least of which is for assistance with mental health problems that they may or may not acknowledge. Outside of a clinical context, and even within it, these issues may not be identified. In addition, there may be an anti-medical bias among participants and non-medical teachers functioning inside or outside of the education sector, whether that be post-secondary contexts, K-12, or in the workplace. The assumption is often made in these environments that MBTL is being provided to healthy populations, but insofar as one in five people have a mental health condition, this is clearly not the case (NIMH, 2020). Therefore it can be prudent for teachers to teach from a trauma-informed lens under the assumption that some participants will have experienced trauma or will suffer from mental health challenges.

Mindfulness can be considered to be both a skill and a way of being that encourages people to recognize, verbalize, and describe the components of experience - thoughts, emotions, body sensations and urges or actions. Any or all of these may be associated with negative mind and mood states. Thus, we can consider how to work with these components should the learner become dysregulated as a result of trauma, an MAE, or another reason. The common use of post-practice inquiry and other expressive practices in the more secular-scientific contexts of MBTL provide added safeguards for helping participants to recognize that they are in distress as a kind of early warning system.

For people with trauma histories or other mental health issues involving avoidance as a coping strategy, one can imagine that the MBTL skills of paying attention to whatever is present might be distressing or difficult to learn. While *exposure* or *turning toward* is part of mindfulness practice and a useful skill for increasing distress tolerance, decreasing reactivity, and developing the ability to decenter from an over-identification with experience, it is important to discern when such exposure is helpful and when it might be harmful or triggering. Hence, it is important for teachers to: a) know who is in the room (as much as is possible) and b) know how to assist participants to feel safe, manage triggers, and choose when to engage in a practice or not.

In conclusion, its important to consider possible external, interpersonal, and intrapersonal factors when teaching mindfulness to be responsive to trauma, potential adverse effects, and mental health concerns. External factors come from the environment, including how the room is set up, the logistics of the program (e.g, start and stop times, overview of the sessions), materials (handouts, readings), and communication mediums to be used outside of the sessions (secure email, text, phone), as well as broader socio-economic conditions and external supports. Interpersonal factors concern the impact of the teacher on participants, how the members of group or class communicate with each other (ensure clear group guidelines if working in a group), and how participants interact with the teacher. Finally, intrapersonal factors arise from the lived experience of the participant (trauma, mental health condition, current state of wellbeing, stressors, and risks), personality factors (ability to trust, self-regulate, communicate respectfully), and physical limitations.

## Teaching Self-Regulation: The Window of Tolerance

Integral to teaching mindfulness is giving due consideration to a participant's ability to regulate themselves should they experience an adverse event or reactivation or triggering of a traumatic memory or reaction. A common psycho-educational tool used in MBTL is referred to as the window of tolerance developed by Pat Ogden (2006) and Dan Siegel (1999). At the beginning of a mindfulness program, students are educated about the fight, flight, freeze, or fawn responses associated with the activation of the sympathetic nervous system when confronting perceived threats. This includes making it clear that mindfulness itself can trigger these responses for a variety of known and unknown reasons. Educating participants early on about how dysregulation may arise and how to manage it helps to normalize it; at the same time, such transparency can help to reduce stigma, denial, or avoidance behaviours associated with dysregulation while reinforcing many of the MBTL trauma-informed practice principles: safey, trust (including managing expectations), autonomy, choice, and somatic orientation.

Because the effects of trauma can reside in the brains and bodies of those affected, the Window of Tolerance is particularly useful for teaching participants how traumatic reactions can present themselves and how they might be managed. Those who *have* a history of trauma (whether extraordinary, life-threatening, cumulative, or ongoing) may experience these reactions in more extreme forms, particularly when activated. Any discussion of the Window of Tolerance needs to include presenting and brainstorming with participants suggestions for managing these reactions should they arise. This is particularly important when teaching online since participants will be in a space physically separate from other group members and the teacher.

There are many ways to expand the window of tolerance and/or to regulate if outside it. Indeed, mindfulness itself expands the window of tolerance through increasing distress tolerance, exposure to negative emotions or experiences, broadening awareness, and calming the nervous system. When dysregulation does arise, it may take a number of forms, including activating the nervous system; arousing emotions such as sadness, anger or, anxiety; and/or generating thoughts of incompetence, helplessness, inability to cope, dissociation, and urges to flee or lash out. In addition, equipping participants with safety behaviours to reduce or prevent dysregulated states arising is the first step towards working with them. Although it may seem a contrivance to tease apart dysregulated states into experiential component parts (body, feelings, thoughts and emotions, and inclinations to act) since we often experience these components simultaneously as an integrated complex; however, the act of parsing these experiences into components in this way is a critical mindfulness tool to work with such reactions.

In the MBSR program, for example, in Session 4 on Stress and Stress Reactivity, Woods and Rockman (2021) describe the use of a circle of awareness for working with and deconstructing difficult situations and challenging reactions. Participants identify a situation and identify it in the middle of the circle. Then, they label each quadrant as body sensations, emotions, thoughts, and behaviors/impulses to act. Then, participants record descriptors of the experience in each category in the sequence in which they presented themselves. For example, if someone lost their job (situation), they might record sadness, anger, and anxiety under emotions; crying and yelling as behaviors; tension in the throat, heart racing and pressure in the diaphragm as body sensations, and, "I'm not going to be able to cope. What am I going to do?" under thoughts. Then, the circles of awareness are assigned for home practice as a monitoring exercise to engage in during the week whenever distress arises, including describing the sequence in which they became aware of each by drawing an arrow between components and numbering them. Participants are then invited to discuss where and how they might bring mindfulness to disrupt these stress reactions. The object of this activity is to enhance awareness and the ability to describe experiences verbally and in writing and to develop skills to work with them (see Figure 17.2).

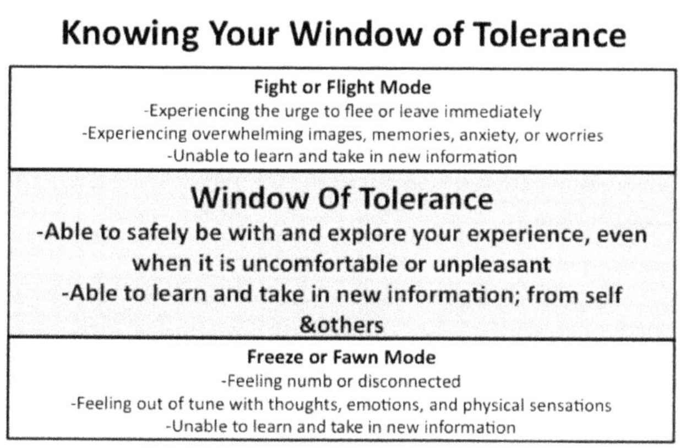


**Figure 17.1** The Window of Tolerance (adapted from Woods & Rockman, 2021)

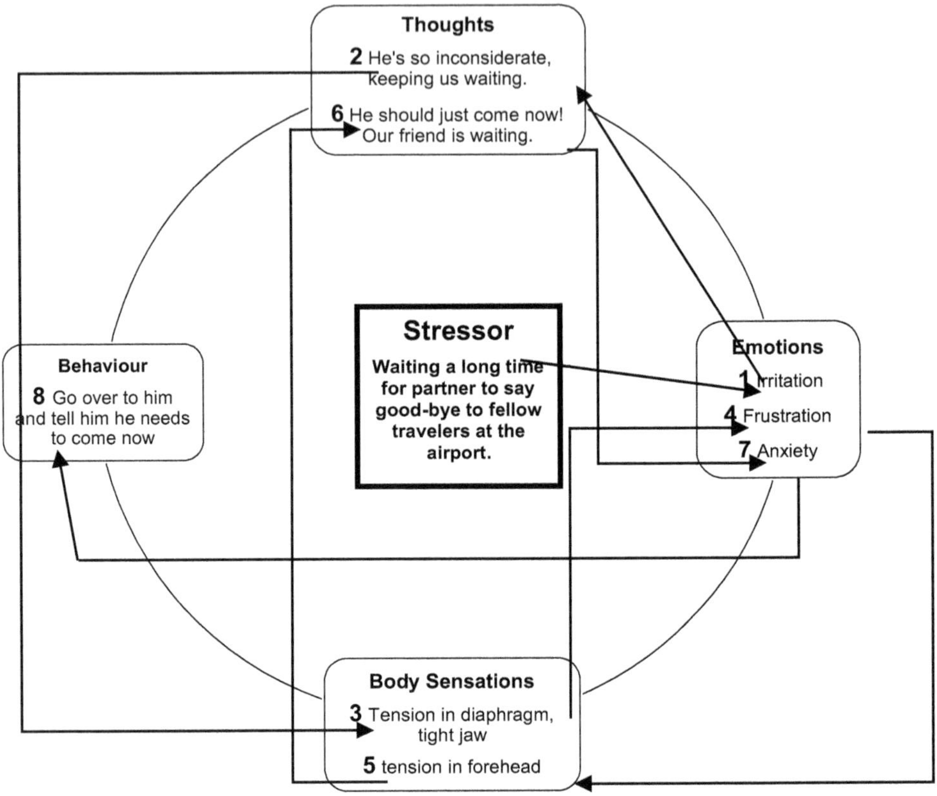


**Figure 17.2** Sample Completed Circle of Awareness Diagram from MBSR Session 4

## Managing Dysregulation

Within the context of MBTL, working with dysregulated states may be triggered by communication between participants and/or a participant and a teacher. Also, the teacher will need to recognize when they are themselves activated by a participant's reaction and take a moment to reflect on what is coming up for them and what they need to do next in the service of themselves and the participants. For teachers or participants who find themselves triggered or dysregulated, a critical first-step is helping themselves or participants to re-enter the window of tolerance, to stay with a challenging state if possible, and to take care of themselves as needed. Below are some specific strategies associated with dysregulation in specific areas of experience.

### *Emotion*

Dan Siegel is credited with first using the phrase "name it to tame it" to describe the effects of labelling emotions. Labelling emotions or *affect labelling* would appear to assist with emotion regulation (Torre & Lieberman, 2018)). This requires sufficient self-awareness to recognize what one is feeling in the first place and the capacity to describe or label it in language. Some specific suggestions for managing such emotion dysregulation through self-care are as follows:

- Name the emotions (single words - "*sadness* is here"); with younger children, sometimes the feeling equivalents in weather are sometimes used to relate the feelings to images - e..g, "I feel rainy" or "I feel sunny" or "I feel stormy."
- Explore and name the physical correlates of emotion by attending to them, including breathing with the sensations, if possible.
- If in a formal meditation practice, open the eyes and taking in the environment.
- Stand up, bring attention to sensing the hands or the feet on the floor, and/or walk around.
- Drink a glass of water or make a cup of tea.
- Name 5 things you notice in each sense - seen, heard, felt (physically), smelled, and tasted - then describe them in detail; then 4; then 3; then 2; then1.
- Splash cold water on the face or hold ice cubes in the hands.

### *Thoughts*

Thoughts generally come up as sentences or images. Mindfulness trains us to experience them as mental events or sensations of the mind, knowing that challenging thoughts are intertwined with emotions. A number of strategies for dealing with overwhelming thoughts:

- Developing the ability to recognize personal signatures that signal that unhelpful thoughts are present, such as recurring self-deprecating or harmful phrases, ideas, or images.
- Working to decenter from these thoughts or images by shifting attention to bodily sensations, the sensations of breathing, or the sensations of sound.
- Engaging in cognitive reappraisal or reframing by expanding or shifting how experiences are interpreted beyond harmful thoughts or narrow views.
- Naming the types of thoughts that are present, such as saying, "distressing thoughts are present," rather than remaining focused or absorbed on their contents.

### *Body*

Certain mindfulness practices (formal or informal) may trigger participants and lead them to states of hyper- or hypo-arousal in the body. Hyper-arousal may require slowing down (e.g., by taking slow, deep breaths), while hypo-arousal may necessitate activation (e.g., moving the body). Ways to work with a sense of being physically overwhelmed include the following strategies:

- Bringing attention to what is present and exploring the experience, if possible, with curiosity before making a decision to move or shift attention.
- Taking care of the body in whatever way is needed: e.g., exiting a practice altogether; getting up and walking around; taking conscious and connected breaths (no gap between the inbreath/outbreath) and prolonging the exhale in relation to the inhale.

- Wrap the body in a blanket and, if lying supine, cross the ankles and place the arms across the chest; consider stroking the upper arms when they are crossed or stroking or pressing gently into the heart area with the right hand.
- If a sensation is overwhelming consider titrating the practice by paying attention for a brief period and then moving attention elsewhere (e.g., to the hands), and then moving back in for a bit longer. Alternatively, explore the edges of the sensation and gradually move in more deeply.

### *Self-Compassion*

The attitude one brings to oneself during moments of dysregulation may also be important. For example, with respect to depression, Kuyken et al. (2010) found that self-compassion is an important variable for disentangling depression from its poor outcomes. Many people who suffer from mental health conditions or traumatic experiences may have a negative view of self that is contributing to their suffering. Teaching self-compassion can be helpful for self-soothing and increasing a sense of self-efficacy and agency during moments of trauma reactivation. These attitudes may initially need to be modelled by the teacher's own embodied practice, expressing attitudes of non-judgment, acceptance, and compassion for the participants' experiences. This does not mean a permissive stance towards behaviours but does mean a stance that reflects that all experiences are welcome. There are many self-compassion exercises and practice (e.g., Germer & Neff, 2019) that include engaging in soothing-self-touch when in distress (e.g., placing a hand on one's own face, chest, belly, or holding one's hands, possibly while saying to oneself, "This is a moment of distress; I can be with this." These practices are intended to help soften harsh self-judgment, increase distress tolerance, and encourage self-care.

### *Curiosity*

One may then be able to begin to turn toward, or approach challenging mind and mood states, reducing experiential avoidance. Using curiosity to examine such states helps people to remain within their window of tolerance or, at the very least, stay close enough to its limits to continue to explore those experiences until, through exposure, what is uncomfortable begins to decline in intensity and, in some cases, change. Such exposure enhances autonomy, and the ability to manage what was previously unmanageable.

## Phenomena or Problem?

An essential aspect of mindfulness is the observation of phenomena as they arise, persist and pass, and our relationship to them. Are we wanting more of them? Are we trying to get away from them? Are we having an emotional reaction to them? Do we view them as something to be fixed? Or are we able to simply witness them as events, bringing attitudes of curiosity and equanimity to their changing nature? These and other questions are critical to determining how teachers will need to address them. Unusual states, in and of themselves, do not necessarily need to be conceived as problematic if the person is not experiencing them as such, especially if they are not of long duration, intensity and frequency, and/or interfering with function or putting the person at risk.

Indeed, in Buddhist contexts, "unusual states" are to be expected and are often indicative of movement towards "awakening." At the same time, even if they are considered to be "signs" of progress, they are perceived as passing phenomena. Similarly, in MBTL, many of these benign or mystical experiences are neither to be pushed away nor gripped onto, but to be observed as just another form of sensation. It can be extremely useful for the teacher to normalize these occurrences for participants and to ask about them in the half-way check in of the program: "Have you had any unusual or challenging experiences during the course?"

Lastly, and importantly, addressing such occurrences during inquiry will enable the teacher to elicit how the participant is relating and reacting to these states. The teacher's attitude toward them as aspects of the practice of mindfulness that are to be expected and treated like any other experience - wanted, unwanted or neutral - will help shape the participant's response to them. In addition, such investigation of these experiences will help determine whether they need further addressing or not. The Vieten et al. (2018) study points to just how common these experiences are and of the possible benefits of addressing them explicitly to help participants learn to respond or interpret them in ways that deepen their practice and expand wellbeing.

## CONCLUSION

The practice of trauma-informed mindfulness enhances the professional ethics of the field and of individual teachers and learners. It is founded on the recognition that mindfulness may be very strong medicine and, therefore, needs to be practiced responsibly. The spectrum of challenges covered by trauma-informed mindfulness is broad and includes trauma but also needs to include meditative adverse effects (MAEs) and cultural colonization. This focus differentiates secular-scientific mindfulness in many ways from its predecessors, for whom many of these conditions or reactions were normalized or treated as part of the process of awakening. The seven principles recommended in this chapter are guideposts for those who would aspire to trauma-informed practice in MBTL - safety, trust, autonomy, choice, collaboration, somatic orientation, and decolonization.

There is a certain irony, pointed out by Analayo, that of all the robust range of meditative experiences of practitioners (e.g., Vieten et al., 2018), it would be the least frequent category of negative emotions (e.g., fear and dread) that would be the first to captivate the eye of secular-scientific mindfulness researchers and educators. This reflects the history and culture of secular-scientific mindfulness, emanating as it does from clinical and medical contexts, where considerations of risk and safety are critical. Yet, this focus potentially opens the door for broader research on the quality and nature of experiences in the trajectory of the life of a mindfulness practitioner and their relevance to the goal of mindfulness to foster eudaimonic wellbeing, that is, human flourishing. This implies both quantitative and, importantly, qualitative research that takes us inside experience more deeply.

## REFERENCES

Aizik-Reebs, A., Yuval, K., Yuval, H., Gebremariam, S., & Bernstein, A. (2021). Mindfulness-based trauma recovery for refugees (MBTR-R): Randomized waitlist-control evidence of efficacy and safety. *Clinical Psychological Science, 9*(6), 1164–1184. https://doi.org/10.1177/2167702621998641.

Analayo, B. (2014). The mass suicide of monks in discourse and Vinaya literature. *Journal of the Oxford Centre for Buddhist Studies, 7*, 11–55. https://www.buddhismuskunde.uni-hamburg.de/pdf/5-personen/analayo/mass-suicide.pdf.

Analayo, B. (2019a). The insight knowledge of fear and adverse effects of mindfulness practices. *Mindfulness, 10*, 2172–2185. https://doi.org/10.1007/s12671-019-01198-4.

Analayo, B. (2019b). *Mindfulness of breathing: A practice guide and translations.* Windhorse Publications.

Berilla, B. (2020). *Radiating feminism: Resilience practices to transform our inner and outer lives.* Routledge.

Berilla, B., Klein, M., & Robers, C. J. (2016). *Yoga, the body, and embodied social change.* Lexington Books.

Bethell, C., Gombojav, N., Solloway, M., & Wissow, L. (2016). Adverse childhood experiences, resilience and mindfulness-based approaches: Common denominator issues for children with emotional, mental, or behavioral problems. *Child and Adolescent Psychiatric Clinics of North America, 25*(2), 139–156. https://doi.org/10.1016/j.chc.2015.12.001.

Boyd, J., Lanius, R., & McKinnon, M. (2018). Mindfulness-based treatments for posttraumatic stress disorder: A review of the treatment literature and neurobiological evidence. *Journal of Psychiatry and Neuroscience, 43*(1), 7–25. https://doi.org/10.1503/jpn.170021.

Britton, W. (2019). Can mindfulness be too much of a good thing? The value of a middle way. *Current Opinion in Psychology, 28*, 159–165. https://doi.org/10.1016/j.copsyc.2018.12.011.

Brosschot, J., Verkuil, B., & Thayer, J. (2018). Generalized unsafety theory of stress: Unsafe environments and conditions, and the default stress response. *International Journal of Environmental Research and Public Health, 15*, 464. https://doi.org/10.3390/ijerph15030464.

Butler, L. D., Critelli, F. M., & Rinfrette, E. S. (2011). Trauma-informed care and mental health. *Directions in Psychiatry, 31*, 197–210.

Burrows, L. (2018). *Safeguarding mindfulness in schools and higher education: A holistic and inclusive approach.* Routledge.

Compson, J. (2014). Meditation, trauma, and suffering in silence: Raising questions about how meditation is taught and practiced in Western contexts in the light of a contemporary trauma resiliency model. *Contemporary Buddhism: An Interdisciplinary Journal.* Advance online publication. http://dx.doi.org/10.1080/14639947.2014.935264.

Deane, S. (2019). rLung, mind, and mental health: The notion of "wind" in Tibetan conceptions of mind and mental illness. *Journal of Religion and Health, 58*, 708–724. https://doi.org/10.1007/s10943-019-00775-0.

Farias, M., Maraldi, E., Wallenkampf, K., & Lucchetti, G. (2020). Adverse events in meditation practices and meditation-based therapies: A systematic review. *Acta Psychiatrica Scandinavica, 142*, 374–393. https://doi.org/10.1111/acps.13225.

Francis, A. (2018). The embodied theory of stress: A constructionist perspective on the experience of stress. *Review of General Psychology, 22*(4), 398–405. http://dx.doi.org/10.1037/gpr0000164.

Garland, E., Hanely, A., Baker, A., & Howard, M. (2017). Biobehavioral mechanisms of mindfulness as a treatment for chronic stress: An RDoC perspective. *Chronic Stress, 1*, 1–14. https://doi.org/10.1177/2470547017711912.

Gerber, M. (2019). *Trauma-informed healthcare approaches: A guide for primary care.* Springer. https://doi.org/10.1007/978-3-030-04342-1.

Germer, C., & Neff, K. (2019). *Teaching the mindful self-compassion program: A guide for professionals.* The Guilford Press.

Grabovac, A. (2015). The stages of insight: Clinical relevance for mindfulness-based interventions. *Mindfulness*, *6*, 589–600. https://doi.org/10.1007/s12671-014-0294-2.

Hopwood, T., & Schutte, N. (2017). A meta-analytic investigation of the impact of mindfulness-based interventions on post traumatic stress. *Clinical Psychology Review*, *57*, 12–20. https://doi.org/10.1016/j.cpr.2017.08.002.

Kuyken, W., Watkins, E., Holden, E., White, K., Taylor, R., Byford, S., Evans, A., Radford, S., Teasdale, J., & Dalgleish, T. (2010). How does mindfulness-based cognitive therapy work? *Behavioral Research and Therapy*, *48*(11), 1105–1112. https://doi.org/10.1186/s40359-020-00417-1.

Lindahl, J., Fisher, N., Cooper, D., Rosen, R., & Britton, W. (2017). The varieties of contemplative experiences: A mixed-method study of meditation-related challenges in Western Buddhists. *PLoS ONE*, *12*(5), e0176239. https://doi.org/10.1371/journal.pone.0176239.

Mavranezouli, I., Megnin-Viggars, O., Daly, C., Dias, S., Welton, N., Stockton, S., Bhutani, G., Grey, N., Leach, J., Greenberg, N., Katona, C., El-Leithy, S., & Pilling, S. (2020). Psychological treatments for post-traumatic stress disorder in adults: A network meta-analysis. *Psychological Medicine*, *50*(4), 542–555. https://doi.org/10.1017/S0033291720000070.

NIMH (National Institute of Mental Health - US). (2020). *Mental illness*. https://www.nimh.nih.gov/health/statistics/mental-illness.

NIMH (National Institute of Mental Health - US). (n.d.). *RDoC constructs: Sustained threat*. https://www.nimh.nih.gov/research/research-funded-by-nimh/rdoc/constructs/sustained-threat.

Rhys Davids, C., & Norman, K. (Trans.) (1971). *Poems of early Buddhist nuns (Therigatha)*. The Pali Text Society.

Rominger, A. (2013). *Illuminating rLung: The vital energy of Tibetan medicine*. SIT Graduate Institute/SIT Study Abroad. https://digitalcollections.sit.edu/cgi/viewcontent.cgi?article=2765&context=isp_collection#:~:text=The%20Tibetan%20approach%20to%20treatment,massage%2C%20moxibustion%2C%20and%20compression.

Ryan, R., & Deci, E. (2017). *Self-determination theory: Basic psychological needs in motivation, development, and wellness*. The Pali Text Society.

SAMHSA (Substance Abuse and Mental Health Service Association). (2014). *SAMHSA's concept of trauma and guidance for a trauma-informed approach*. HHS Publication No. (SMA) 14-4884. https://ncsacw.samhsa.gov/userfiles/files/SAMHSA_Trauma.pdf.

Sparks, F. (2011). Getting stuck in the present moment. *Psychotherapy Networker*, *35*(5), 38–39.

Tonmyr, L, LaCroix, J., & Herbert, M. (2020). The public health issue of ACEs in Canada. In G. Asmundson & T. Afifi (Eds.), *Adverse childhood experiences: Using evidence to advance research, practice, policy, and prevention* (pp. 185–207). Elsevier, Academic Press. https://doi.org/10.1016/B978-0-12-816065-7.00010-0.

Torre, J. B., & Lieberman M. D. (2018). Putting feelings into words: Affect labeling as implicit emotion regulation. *Emotion Review*, *10*(2), 116–124. https://doi.org/10.1177/1754073917742706.

Trevealen, D. (2018). *Trauma-sensitive mindfulness: Practices for safe and transformative healing*. W.W. Norton & Co.

US-SAMHSA (U.S. Substance Abuse and Mental Health Services Administration). (2014). A treatment improvement protocol: Trauma-informed care in behavioral health services. *Trauma-Informed Practice*, *57*. http://hdl.handle.net/10713/1550.

Vieten, C., Wahbeh, H., Cahn, B.R., MacLean, K., Estrada, M., Mills, P.., Murphy, M., Shapiro, S., Radin, D., Josipovic, Z., Presti, D., Sapiro, M., Bays, J., Russell, P., Vago, D., Travis, F., Walsh, R., & Delorme, A. (2018). Future directions in meditation research:

Recommendations for expanding the field of contemplative science. *PLOS One*, *13*(11), e0205740. https://doi.org/10.1371/journal.pone.0205740.
Woods, S., & Rockman, P. (2021). *Mindfulness-based stress reduction*. New Harbinger.
Yellow Bird, M. (2013). Chapter 15: Neurodecolonization: Applying mindfulness research to decolonizing social work. In J. Coates, T Hetherington, & M. Gray (Eds.), *Decolonizing social work* (p. 18). Routledge.

# SECTION VI

# Limits – What We Don't See

## The Postmodern Frontier of MBTL

This final section considers the limitations of current practices and perspectives in secular-scientific mindfulness given its embeddedness within modern cultural and scientific evidentiary norms. As we argued in Chapter 2, secular-scientific mindfulness – and MBTL – offer the paradoxical case of a traditional knowledge system that was modernized in ways that both reproduce and subvert modernity. In this way, secular-scientific mindfulness and MBTL are arguably more *post*modern than modern. The liminal nature of mindfulness across the conscious/unconscious boundaries of mind and experience make it uniquely positioned to defy the limits of modern institutions, professions, and practices that would contain and circumscribe its development. This section begins to explore these limits and what lies beyond them. Although it includes implicit critiques of secular-scientific mindfulness, these critiques are constructively offered to support the creative development of MBTL and mindfulness across the postmodern frontiers of the 21st century.

DOI: 10.4324/9781003182467-24

# CHAPTER 18

# THE LIMITS OF PROFESSIONALISM

## Navigating the Wilds of the (Post)Modern

The wilderness is a natural place: Uninhabited, untouched, unknown, and, in some cases, unexplored by human beings. In applying this metaphor to mind, we gesture towards aspects of human experience that are less conditioned, disciplined, and controlled or more spontaneous and, perhaps, neglected – more associated with the natural world than the cultural. It is likened by some philosophers to the experience of the infant prior to language and culture, as distant as that may be to imagine as we imbibe this highly rational text. In this chapter, we consider the modern origins of the wilding, or marginalization, of certain aspects of the mind and experience; the effects on the destruction of experience; and the implications of the movement of mindfulness from less controlled and unsurveilled environments to professional, institutional contexts. In taking up these topics, we move from the scientific and social scientific discourses that have dominated much of this text so far to discourses of the liberal arts and humanities.

## IN THE SHADOW OF THE ENLIGHTENMENT

What became popularized as postmodernism began with systematic critiques of modernism and its origins in the European Enlightenment, including the rather pernicious ways in which it normalized, circumscribed, and sanctioned a very narrow band of legitimate experience and cast what lay beyond that band as pathological (e.g., Foucault, 1961/1988). Bohme and Bohme (1996), for example, detailed how in the 1760s Kant helped to shape the European Enlightenment with the critical turn, in part, by vilifying and disparaging two popular German mystics in his writing: The so-called goat-mystic in his essay On Mental Illnesses and the popular prophetic mystic Swedenborg in his Dreams of a Spirit-seer. Despite acknowledging tacit respect for Swedenborg in private correspondence, Kant publicly claimed that all such expressions of human intuition, dreams, and prophetic visions were invalid sources of knowledge, claiming that those who claimed otherwise were merely mentally ill and unstable. As Bohme and Bohme described it:

> Whatever did not fall within the realm of reasonable speech, including speechlessness, became irrational: body, feelings, 'metaphysical needs,' needs for immediacy, life, and nature. When isolated, these spheres become 'crazy' – they take on ludicrous or chaotic traits. The reasonable person unlearns deportment with this Other and instead reacts to it with panic and dread.
>
> *(p. 437)*

So extreme was Kant's position as to suggest that anyone with visionary tendencies "simply be dismissed as candidates for the mental hospital." Tellingly, he directly equated his intolerance to prior practices of the Inquisition: "Although it was once deemed necessary to burn some of these [people], now it is enough that they be purged" (in Boehme & Boehme, p. 430). The ultimate effect of these purges was to banish to the wilds huge swathes of human experiences, cultural practices, and ways of knowing deemed Other to human

DOI: 10.4324/9781003182467-25

reason: Enthusiasm, dreams, sympathetic imagination (i.e., empathy), prophetic visions, and silence itself. As the authors concluded: "Reason withdrew into itself and thereby withdrew from the Other. Traffic over the fortified borders became difficult. The Other became foreign and incomprehensible" (p. 437).

Mindfulness and MBTL occupy an ambivalent role in these shadows of the European Enlightenment. On the one hand, they are opening a gateway in education to revisit, accept, and learn about this Other , to help make it less foreign and more rational and comprehensible. however, they are doing so within professional and institutional contexts still functioning in the aftermath of modernism and its controlling and pathologizing impulses toward what is not deemed normative. This creates challenges, for example, in fully including and recognizing Indigenous and other contemplative practices and ways of knowing. As mindfulness, MBTL, and their adoption within institutions and professions are going hand in hand with the science supporting them, they are greatly expanding the scope of access to such techniques and their benefits; yet, it would be disingenuous to suggest that this isn't significantly narrowing the scope of experiences and practices deemed desirable or legitimate outcomes of such practices – at least at this early juncture.

An example of this constraining effect of science in delegitimating the scope of valid experiences in contemplative practices can be seen in Lindahl et al. (2017). These researchers gathered interview data from Buddhist retreatants (N=60) posing one of two questions: "What kinds of experiences have you had as a result of meditation?" or "Have you had any experiences that were unexpected, challenging, or difficult?" Although the researchers reported collecting severity levels, these don't appear in the paper. Instead, they only present data on the frequencies of all experiences reported, leaving the impression that all of the experiences were "challenging" and somehow aversive, risky, or pathological. This study echoes well the enduring legacy of Kant's claims that experiences or imaginings beyond a narrow rationalism are instances of mental illness. Vieten et al. (2018) offered a contrastive study, which canvassed 1120 meditators from 66 countries to understand the frequency of their "mystical, transcendent, and/or extraordinary" experiences during meditation. These highly non-normative experiences were overwhelmingly positive. One example worth mentioning: "clairvoyance and telepathy" were reported by 56% of respondents, with 24% reporting they happened "many times" and 6% claiming "almost always". As Dorothy commented in the Wizard of Oz: "Toto, I've a feeling we're not in Kansas anymore!"

## AGAMBEN AND THE DESTRUCTION OF EXPERIENCE

In *Infancy & History: Essays on the Destruction of Experience* (1993), the Italian philosopher Giorgio Agamben questions modern assumptions of human exceptionalism: That our distinction as a species is our capacity for language denuded of the imagination (Mills, 2008). Instead, he suggests that it is the capacity for experience, for imagination, for the *voice* beyond mere *language* and closer instead to the experience of infants that offer promise for revitalizing ethics and community for the coming time. He documents the historical and cultural destruction of the possibility of pure experience in the modern era. He likens this state of *pure* experience to the prelingual experience of the infant, a state in which the constraints posed by abstract language and reason on experience are transcended: "One of the most urgent tasks for contemporary thought is, without doubt, to redefine the concept of the transcendental in terms of its relation with language" (p. 4).

Agamben writes in a time when philosophy was preoccupied with the impossibilities of transcendence in, from, or through language. As Walter Benjamin's Italian translator, Agamben was deeply affected by his notion of the *poverty of experience* that was deepening through the modern period. Attributing this impoverishment to the effects of World War I, Benjamin described the insidious and creeping state of collective trauma that infused European society and beyond, as its horrors and destruction became internalized and normalized. This process is depicted well, for example, in various memoirs of the war and its aftermath, such as Vera Brittain's (1933) *Testament of Youth* and Robert Graves' (1929) *Goodbye to All That*, where violence and loss transfer directly from battlefields to the psyches and lives of the authors. This collective trauma both contributed to and deepened with WWII, where Benjamin himself became a victim. A German-Jewish philosopher, he committed suicide while trying to escape Europe in 1940, after being threatened by Spanish border police of deportation back to France where the Gestapo had issued an arrest warrant for him. Benjamin, and later Agamben, argued that such collective trauma eroded the capacity to know experience beyond language, making it progressively more distant and difficult, culminating in the sceptical claims of philosophers of the impossibility of escape from language. And so Agamben (1993) begins *Infancy and History*:

> The question of experience can be approached nowadays only with an acknowledgement that it is no longer accessible to us...Indeed, his incapacity to have and communicate experiences is perhaps one of the few self-certainties to which he can lay claim...Today, ...we know that the destruction of experience no longer necessitates a catastrophe, and that humdrum daily life in any city will suffice. For modern man's average day contains virtually nothing that can still be translated into experience.
>
> *(p. 13)*

Critically, he also attributes the roots of the destruction of experience to the legacy of modern science: "In one sense, the expropriation of experience was implicit in the founding project of modern science...by displacing experience as far as possible outside the individual: on to instruments and numbers" (p. 17). The scientific requirement to verify experience through formal experimentation rendered experience as a (scientific) *method* and as a mere route to (abstract) knowledge. This devalued experience as an intrinsic and direct way of knowing, relegating it instead to a mere means to knowing. The pervasive nature of this destruction of experience, both cultural and epistemic, makes its retrieval and recognition challenging. For this, Agamben points to the *infant experience*, that developmental juncture at which the human subject emerges from pure experience into the world of language. "For the very fact that infancy exists as such – that is, ...experience as the transcendental limit of language – rules out language as being in itself totality and truth" (p. 51). Underlying this relationship between language and experience are their transcendental origins in infancy, where the commitment to truth is born:

> *The ineffable is, in reality, infancy.* Experience is the *mysterion* which every individual intuits from the fact of having an infancy. This mystery is not an oath of silence or mystical ineffability; on the contrary, it is the vow that commits the individual to speech and to truth. Just as infancy destines language to truth, so language constitutes truth as the destiny of experience.
>
> *(p. 51)*

In this respect, Agamben makes important connections between history, philosophy, and psychology to suggest that modern institutions, cultures, and educational systems and the discourses of science they rely on may not be entirely reliable spaces, or places, to cultivate experience as a viable source of truth. To some extent, this critique is readily available to ordinary experiences within these institutions, which we quite regularly navigate, accommodate, and adjust to by adhering to their norms and constraints. Yet, it also provides insights into how we might work within them more effectively to make them more hospitable to a wider scope of human experience by recognizing and providing more legitimate avenues to learn from and represent experience.

## BEYOND PROFESSIONAL ETHICS

One key source of professional and institutional constraints on experience comes from how ethics are framed and construed. Modern institutions and professions tend to function under secularized ethics that focus on standards of care associated with *inclusion*, *equity*, and *no harm*, rather than on behavioural norms associated with morality or virtues. Violations are sanctioned by institutions, via the threat of loss of employment, or by regulating professional bodies with the power to remove professional certification or the right to practice. At the same time, because professions are often publicly subsidized or funded, and because they are guided by evidence-based practices, they are open to a range of pressures to alter practices to accommodate changes driven by the expectations of clients, professional standards, societies, and cultures. For example, only a few decades ago in higher education, male professors having sex with female students was commonplace, so much so as to be a cliché, yet now it is relatively rare and subject to serious censure or dismissal. In contrast, repercussions for similar abuses in Buddhist contexts in North America have been minimal and largely ineffective to date.

Professional ethics do have notable idiosyncrasies, limitations, and shortcomings. For example, a common professional ethical standard is to respect "professional boundaries" between oneself, as a professional, and clients, patients, students, followers, or mentees. This can include limiting the degree of empathy or compassion for those under one's professional's care, thereby reducing the willingness to stand with, or act alongside, them as they navigate personal suffering or collective sources of oppression. Although these expectations of fixed boundaries are not necessarily followed, they remain part of the official guidelines of most professions. In marked contrast, in traditional Asian and Buddhist contexts, informed by such sources as Confucianism or Buddhism, teachers are often described as being like parents, albeit with differing responsibilities, in their commitments and relations to students. Zheng (2020) describes this in his depiction of the traditional Confucian view of teacher-student trust in Hong Kong v. US:

> Confucius and his students were on intimate terms, so they could care for each other not just in study but in daily life...They accompanied each other in even the most perilous situations. They experienced all the sorrow and happiness in life. The relationship between them was more like that of father and his sons than of a teacher and students.

Although likened to parent-child relations, such relationships involve bonds of culture rather than of nature, yet with similar broad limits. An example of this came to the attention of one of the authors (SM) when she posed a question to the Dalai Lama (personal communication, 1998) as part of her doctoral research on education. Diverting from answering the explicit question, he raised instead what he said was his preeminent concern with education: Compassion. He then criticized modern Western education for its practice of referring students to school counsellors (paraphrased from memory):

> I have heard that some teachers refer students with psychological or personal problems to a counsellor. Yet, this is a teacher's responsibility! A teacher teaches students, not just a subject. They don't just teach math; they teach students! They need to take responsibility for a student's wellbeing and not refer them elsewhere whenever there is a problem. This is what it means to practice as a teacher with compassion and to teach students what compassion is!

These conceptions of compassion in the teacher-student relationship offer a challenge to prevailing views of boundary-setting as the cornerstone of modern professional ethics. At the same time, this calls into question the identity position of a professional who teaches mindfulness, especially when they are tasked with supporting students to glimpse the origin of life and creativity that is the mind.

That said, evidence of the pitfalls of this traditional Asian view of teachers' deep and unbounded compassion and commitment to learners or clients suggests why modern professional ethics may still focus on boundaries and boundary-setting. For example, Vogd and Harth (2019) investigated the struggles of contemporary European students with Sogyal Rinpoche, a Tibetan lama from California who engaged in widespread sexual, physical, power, and financial abuses. The researchers documented students' discourse as they attempted to navigate discrepancies between the boundless trust they were called to feel as student practitioners with the growing evidence of the teacher's wrongdoing and abuse of power. Indeed, it was only when the Dalai Lama made a statement repudiating Sogyal Rinpoche as a "friend" in Ladakh in 2018, decades after the first allegations were made public, that Sogyal Rinpoche finally stepped down from his post and acknowledged his abuses. That it took such a powerful authority as the Dalai Lama to intervene to correct the problem, and to a very traditional Tibetan audience despite fairly well-publicized reports in the Western media, is a cautionary tale. When such boundless unconditional teacher-student bonds are encouraged and adopted by students or practitioners, they inevitably move beyond gratitude into love, adding to the complexity of subsequent betrayals. As an example, the researchers shared how one of their participants responded to the final public acknowledgement by Sogyal Rinpoche of his wrongdoings:

> Accordingly, in an interview that was conducted after the content of the open letter had been made public, Mr. Schneider described that he actually still wanted to love Sogyal—or to have loved him. However, the real tragedy with which he now had to deal was the fact that he was infinitely grateful to or loved somebody who had evidently severely disappointed the expectations of his students.
>
> *(para. 76)*

A very different line of critique of professional ethics came from Edward Said (1994) in his BBC lecture and book *Representations of the Intellectual*. Said's thesis was born of a concern that university professors were increasingly functioning as professionals governed by bureaucratic rules rather than as *public intellectuals*, which he saw as a far nobler and ethical role. As public intellectuals, they were obligated to speak truth to power and practise "*amateurism,* literally, an activity that is fueled by care and affection rather than by profit and selfish, narrow specialization" (p. 82). This was in marked contrast to what was expected of them as professionals, according to Said, which included a focus instead on specialization; certified expertise; power and authority; and intellectual conformity:

> By professionalism I mean thinking of your work as an intellectual as something you do for a living, between the hours of nine and five with one eye on the clock, and another cocked at what is considered to be proper, professional behavior – not rocking the boat, not

> straying outside the accepted paradigms or limits, making yourself marketable and above all presentable, hence uncontroversial and unpolitical and 'objective.'
>
> *(p. 74)*

This same critique could be levelled against professional mindfulness teachers for any range of reasons, including: i) considering themselves as experts rather than as compassionate explorers; ii) performing a job merely to earn a livelihood; and iii) orienting on reproducing a narrow set of outcomes rather than as change-agents transforming the culture towards what is more socially just. Yet, the ethical position Said represents, those of *amateurs* able to *speak truth to power*, requires that those in power are prepared to hear or respond adequately to whatever truth is being conveyed. If this fundamental relation is itself eroded, then the power accorded *the expert* may best be wielded instead within professional and institutional contexts. Likewise, for mindfulness teachers and MBTL specialists within the confines of modern bureaucratized institutions, the exigencies of compassion may make these places the most viable and effective environment to promote wellbeing with the most significant impacts.

## CONCLUSION

The purpose of this chapter has been to open up a critical space in which to consider the limitations, risks, and possibilities of the professionalization of mindfulness. We discussed how professions took on some aspects of modernity and modern institutions, including the sceptical view of experience; the diminished value accorded the direct experience of the untutored or unconditioned mind or its existence; and the ethics limiting relations between MBTL teachers and learners and the challenge of *expert* "professional" identities. Many of these professional constraints were less common in earlier, more traditional mindfulness contexts in which the perceived ends of mindfulness as *awakening* seemed to generate fewer restrictions on the means to achieve such a noble and significant, albeit idealized, end. The constraints associated with professionalism caution us to weigh what is to be gained by rapidly expanding the scope of access to mindfulness against the unanticipated erosion of its most powerful edges and possibilities.

In the next chapter we consider an example of what such ethics might look like through the experiences of one meditator during wilderness retreats over a 42-year period. Giving a meaningful voice to encounters with wildlife invites a challenge for both traditional and secular-scientific mindfulness alike to give voice paradoxically to an ethic of life that is both within, and outside of, language.

## REFERENCES

Agamben, G. (1993). *Infancy & history: Essays on the destruction of experience*. Verso.

Bohme, H., & Bohme, G. (1996). The battle of reason with the imagination. In J. Schmidt (Ed.), *What is enlightenment? Eighteenth-century answers to twentieth-century questions* (pp. 426–452). University of California Press.

Brittain, V. (1933). *Testament of youth: An autobiographical story of the years 1900–1925*. Victor Gallancz (UK) / Macmillan (US).

Foucault, M. (1961/1988). *Madness and civilization: A history of insanity in the age of reason*. Vintage.

Graves, R. (1929). *Good-bye to all that: An autobiography*. Penquin Classic.

Lindahl, J., Fisher, N., Cooper, D, Rosen, R., & Britton, W. (2017). The varieties of contemplative experience: A mixed-methods study of meditation-related challenges in western Buddhists. *PLoS ONE, 12*(5), e0176239. https://doi.org/10.1371/journal.pone.0176239.

Mills, C. (2008). *The philosophy of Agamben.* Routledge.

Said, E. (1994). *Representations of the intellectual.* Vintage.

Vieten, C., Wahbeh, H., Cahn, B.R., MacLean, K., Estrada, M., Mills, P., Murphy, M., Shapiro, S., Radin, D., Josipovic, Z., Presti, D., Sapiro, M., Bays, J., Russell, P., Vago, D., Travis, F., Walsh, R., & Delorme, A. (2018). Future directions in meditation research: Recommendations for expanding the field of contemplative science.. *PLOS One. 13*(11), e0205740. https://doi.org/10.1371/journal.pone.0205740.

Vogd, W., & Harth, J. (2019). A demonstration of contextural analysis, a methodology for reconstructing polycontextural configurations: Taking interviews on boundary violations in teacher-student relationships in Tibetan Buddhism as an example. *Forum: Qualitative Social Research, 20*(1), Art. 21. http://dx.doi.org/10.17169/fqs-20.1.3107.

Zheng, W. (2020). *A study of university teacher-student relationships from the perspective of trust: A socratic and confucian comparison.* PhD Thesis, Middlesex University.

# CHAPTER 19

# FROM SELF-AWARENESS TO ECOLOGICAL AWARENESS

## Mindful Encounters with Wildlife during Intensive Silent Retreats

Science has dominated the study of ecology for so long as to skew our view of nature, filtering knowledge and experience of the more-than-human (aka non-human) world through the biased lens of scientific *objectivity*. This bias continues today despite generations of scholars calling for an approach to better recognize the implicit impact of the human mind on ecological systems (Bateson, 2000; Evernden, 1992, 1993; Moran, 2017). This scientific bias is even more troubling in light of mounting evidence of the shortcomings of science as a motivator for environmental change. For example, in one study, a felt connectedness to nature was found to explain 69% of the variance in environmental behaviour as compared to science-based environmental knowledge, which explained only 2% (Otto & Pensini, 2017). This chapter chronicles the development of one of the author's (SM) *personalized ecology* (Gaston et al., 2018) and ecological awareness over a 42-year span as she learned through mindful encounters with wildlife during intensive silent retreats. By examining the intersecting experiences of mindfulness, nature, and silence, the chapter considers how ecological awareness might emerge from the ground of mindful self-awareness.

Beyond correcting biases in scientific ecology, linking mindfulness to ecology corrects two prominent critiques of secular-scientific mindfulness as well: a) its neglect of ethics; and b) its tendency to foster self-preoccupation (Hildebrandt, McCall, & Singer, 2017; Marx, 2015; Monteiro et al., 2014). The 17th Karmapa (2017), a Tibetan Buddhist teacher, echoed this concern during a public talk in Canada. Speaking in Tibetan, he code-switched the word *mindfulness* into English to reference the secular-scientific variant:

> *Mindfulness* has a lot to do with acquainting oneself with the profound connection that one shares with one's environment, deepening and promoting *that* awareness as well. So, it's very important for us to develop this more expansive understanding of what mindfulness is.
>
> *(Karmapa, 2017, 34:50–35.05 mins)*

## FROM SELF-AWARENESS TO ECOLOGICAL AWARENESS

Most existing research on mindfulness describes the awareness it cultivates as *self*-awareness. Although it may sound like a simple concept, *self*-awareness is paradoxical, suggesting that the self is both the agent and object of awareness. In this sense, it is helpful to unpack both terms: Self and awareness. In self-determination theory (SDT), Deci et al. (2015) identify *awareness* as key to autonomy, underpinning the self-regulation of behaviour and the intrinsic motivation propelling self-determination. They attribute such awareness to two factors: Mindfulness and interest-taking. In mindfulness studies, the *self* continues to be defined, redefined, and refined (e.g., Farb et al., 2007). These theories continue to inform mindfulness programmes, where participants are supported to shift from narrative to experiential self-referencing (Woods, Rockman, & Collins, 2019), by which the *self* we

DOI: 10.4324/9781003182467-26

construct through stories of the past and imagined futures are attenuated and eclipsed by the sense of self that is grounded in the changing continuum of experiences.

## Self-Awareness

Vago and Silbersweig (2012) contributed significantly to defining self-awareness with respect to mindfulness. As outlined in Chapter 9, they proposed a sequential flow of influence from self-awareness to self-regulation to self-transcendences (S-ART) as a neurobiological framework for understanding mindfulness. Together, these three iterations of self-awareness were described as developing awareness of "the conditions that cause (and remove) distortions and biases" (p. 1). Verhaeghen (2019) demonstrated how the development of S-ART from self-awareness to self-regulation to self-transcendence helped explain some of the beneficial psychological outcomes of mindfulness, and it is through its role in self-transcendence in particular that these benefits are believed to arise.

## Ecological Awareness

Vago and Silbersweig's conclusion of the link between mindfulness and self-transcendence was echoed in the work of Leary and Diedbels (2017), who described mindfulness as a hypo-egoic state that counteracts the deleterious effects of excessive self-reflection or self-preoccupation. By shifting to a present-focused, sensorial, more concrete, and less judgmental awareness, mindfulness was seen to provide a more objective and less distorted awareness or lens with which to experience the world. The authors provided evidence that mindfulness generates more accurate self-construals; more self-transcendent values, such as benevolence and universalism; less reactivity to negative or undesired events; reduced defensiveness; and enhanced relationships and connections with others and the natural world. In this way, this study provides a clear trajectory through mindfulness to self-awareness and, through the ensuing hypo-egoic state and transcendence, to ecological awareness. The relationship between mindfulness and ecological awareness appears to be reciprocal, as Lymeus et al. (2018) reported in their finding that natural settings can effortlessly restore depleted attention resources and foster open awareness.

## Connectedness to Nature

Ecological awareness may help to explain the relationship between mindfulness and *connectedness to nature* (Schutte & Malouff, 2018). For example, Unsworth et al. (2016) found that meditative experiences in nature produced significantly stronger self-nature connections than ordinary experiences in nature, building on Howell et al.'s (2011) earlier study linking mindfulness, nature connectedness, and wellbeing. Wang et al. (2019) found that mindfulness increased university students' belief in climate change, mediated by increases in connectedness with nature, suggesting a pathway from self-awareness to ecological awareness as cultivated through meditative experiences in nature, with implications for a possible link between ecological awareness and *global ecological citizenship* (MacPherson, 2005). Yet, ecological awareness and connection to nature shouldn't be thought of as additive but interactive effects. In support of this, Capaldi et al.'s (2014) meta-analysis found that happiness and nature connectedness were positively related, yet the most robust measures were from *inclusion of nature in self* rather than measures of nature relatedness and connectedness to nature. This reinforces the possibility that self-awareness may mature into ecological awareness through the realization of the interconnection between self and nature in identity itself.

### Compassion and Empathy

Compassion and empathy are related to both mindfulness and ecological awareness. Pfattheicher et al. (2016) found compassion for the suffering of humans to be connected to pro-environmental tendencies, while more abstract forms of empathy for the biosphere or nature writ large were correlated with a range of pro-environmental values or perspectives (Schultz, 2001, 2002; Tam, 2013; Tipsord, 2009). Jazaieri et al. (2013) found explicit compassion-based mindfulness training significantly increased compassion and empathy, increasing *compassion for others*, but with implications for *receiving compassion* and *self-compassion*, the three forms of compassion identified in human-to-human relations (Gilbert, 2010). In studies of compassion cultivation (Jinpa, 2015) and fears of compassion (Kirby et al., 2019), research continues to focus on compassion for *human* beings, including personal health and wellbeing, rather than on our relations with, and compassion for, more-than-human *wild* life.

In previous research, the author (SM) developed the concept of *petagogy* to describe the education of emotions associated with learning with a companion animal, a process that resulted in: Mutual social bonding and attachment; positive feelings and empathy; communicating to cooperate; and responding to suffering and death (MacPherson, 2011b). This current research extends this inquiry to mindful experiences with "wilder" members of the more-than-human community encountered during silent retreats. The questions driving this research are twofold: How does ecological awareness manifest in the experiences of a single practitioner over time? How might these experiences inform an educational agenda to promote ecological awareness through mindfulness?

## METHODOLOGY

Currently, mindfulness research is dominated by quantitative and mixed-method experimental or quasi-experimental studies using novice meditators as subjects exposed to non-intensive mindfulness practices taught in standardized or adapted eight-week programmes. What compromises the external and ecological validity of these studies is the absence of evidence of real-world naturalistic developmental pathways in the lives of individual practitioners over time. Furthermore, attention has been deflected to demonstrating a narrow spectrum of health and educational outcomes rather than investigating the nature of mindfulness experiences accompanying these changes. To correct these limited perspectives, more qualitative studies are needed of expert meditators and their developmental trajectories over time.

To this end, this study uses an autoethnographic approach to investigate the experiences of a long-term practitioner, the author (SM), over a 42-year period. The data focus on learning arising through mindful encounters with wildlife during intensive silent retreats.

Ellis and Bochner (2000) define autoethnography as "an autobiographical genre of writing that displays multiple layers of consciousness, connecting the personal to the cultural" (p. 739). This study considers the multiple layers of consciousness connecting the personal to the natural world, conditioned as they are by culture, through the lens of a single meditator. Consistent with a moderate autoethnographic approach (Wall, 2016), the documented experiences are analyzed as they relate to existing theories of ecology and as they might contribute to emerging theoretical principles of mindfulness and ecological awareness.

## Silent Retreats

Silent retreats continue to be common features of both contemporary and traditional mindfulness practices. They can be solitary or done in groups. They may vary in duration from one day to as long as three years or even decades and in intensity from as little as four hours a day to as much as 18 hours or even 24 hours per day. They include a range of practices and postures, often alternating between sitting and walking meditation with some resting or formal practice in a reclining posture. King, Conkin, Zanesco, and Saron (2019) argue that intensive residential retreats offer important research sites to bridge studies of novices in non-intensive mindfulness programmes with cross-sectional studies of expert meditators. Groen (2013, 2016) considers the role of the spiritual retreat centre as *place-based* education to counter the disenchantment and disconnection of the modern experience. Residential retreat centres are effective sites to investigate mindfulness and ecological awareness given: i) their remote wilderness or natural environment locale; ii) their respect for varying degrees of silence; and iii) their respect for wildlife, often with restrictions against harming or hunting them. These conditions, in turn, can deepen awareness of the natural world by reducing distractions and self-consciousness; increasing positive emotions and compassion; and decreasing mind wandering (Capaldi et al., 2014; Jazaieri et al., 2016). It is perhaps worth noting that one of the impacts of the Covid-19 pandemic was to move silent retreats, albeit temporarily, from these residential retreat sites into digitized, virtual worlds in which most participants remain at home and participate remotely.

## Procedures

**Timeframe/duration**. The time frame for this data covers 42 years, between 1977 and 2019, beginning when the subject, the author (SM), was 20 and culminating at 61. The duration of the silent retreats varied from three days to two weeks, many of which were solitary retreats though some were silent group retreats. The incidents are presented and organized chronologically, in part to represent a developmental trajectory, should that prove relevant and discernible.

**Sites – silent retreat centres**. The retreat centres are located in natural sites with limited local development, where wildlife is relatively protected and access to the property is limited or restricted. Most of the sites were actual retreat centres designed to support extended periods of contemplation, but if not, they were appropriately secluded.

**The mindfulness practices**. I interpret the term mindfulness in the broadest sense to include the full spectrum of practices commonly used in Buddhist and secular programmes. Therefore, the range of practices in this study all involved some degree of mindfulness practice – explicitly or implicitly. The first incident transpired during my first experience of formal meditation, on being introduced to Transcendental Meditation (TM) and not within a retreat setting; however, I included it because it indicates how directly meditative training can impact ecological awareness even without intensive or any practice history.

**Incident selection**. In selecting the ten incidents, I reviewed significant learning with more-than-human (aka non-human) beings, all of which transpired in the context of retreats. In every instance, I was experiencing elevated attention, interest, and reflective capacity arising from the practices. Some of the incidents were included in detailed and elaborate fieldnotes as part of other research while others were integral to less formal autobiographical reflections. Although not all retreats included learning encounters with more-than-human wildlife, most of the *solitary* retreats did involve such an encounter, which is why these are disproportionately represented in the data.

## Data Analysis

As a new area of inquiry, this study uses grounded theory to interpret the autoethnographic data (Wall, 2016) into themes and principles. The coding progressed through three iterations to identify nine key principles of ecology. These were identified and aligned to ensure that an inductive approach was applied consistently, moving from data to categories rather than forcing the data into pre-identified codes. Eight ecological principles were appropriately aligned arising from eight incidents, plus the combined first and final incidents (#1 and #10) which shared the category of *Learning to Co-Exist*, relating to the principle of co-existence.

To safeguard the inductive process, coding was conducted without reference to pre-existing theories until the end. During the final coding process, I aligned the findings to an emerging set of ecological principles for environmental education developed by the USDA forestry service (Barrett et al., 1997) and further refined by Mengak et al. (2009). I considered the alignment and, where applicable, recoded terms if and when they applied to any of the USDA's eight general ecological principles. I should add that I did not change the sequence or content to force a fit but rather included the framework as an added form of validation because they did correspond. The eight USDA principles are: Adaptation, behaviour, diversity, emergent properties, energy flows, growth and development, limits, and regulation. To this list I add a ninth key principle that is conspicuously missing: *Interdependence.* These key constructs of ecology were intended to serve as nodes to which diverse forms of research and evidence might relate, including first-person narratives, experiences, and perspectives. In this respect, the alignment between the autoethnographic data and this scientific ecological framework is consistent with the intended purpose of the model. The alignment corrects that serious gap in ecological science that Gaston et al. (2018) cautioned of: "[T]here has been little consideration of the converse need to understand the interactions between human observers and nature" (p. 916).

# RESULTS

The following ten incidents represent encounters with wildlife during intensive meditation periods in nature and documented in chronological order over 32 years.

## Learning to Co-Exist

This experience involved awakening to the presence of the more-than-human world and its (wild)life on hearing a *bird, singing* in April 1978 (age 19 or 20). The location was a private apartment in Nepean, ON (suburban Ottawa) where I was initiated in TM practice. This was the first meditation experience I had, and it arose as part of a private, hour-long training/initiation:

> Learning to meditate for the first time, I am left alone in the room to complete the session. As the practice ends, the sound of a bird, singing, erupts through a nearby open window. The clarity, its timbre and quality, its purity, both startles and soothes me. It is like hearing a bird sing for the first time and it comes with a mixture of awe and rapture, not just for the pleasure of the sound but for the sense of connection with another living being. There is an intimacy to it, conveyed only through sound for I don't even see the bird.

## Learning to Adapt

This experience arose by being in the more-than-human world and (wild)life community during a silent, solitary retreat and witnessing a *young fern frond, unfurling* in May 1985 (age 27). It was my first *solitary* retreat – for three days – in a retreat cabin on a mountainside on the north end of Galiano Island, BC. The practices were mostly informally being in and with nature but including formal mindfulness of breathing and compassion practices:

> After lunch, I take a sponge bath on the verandah of the cabin. As I finish, I realize I have to go to the bathroom. The outhouse is about 50 meters up a winding dirt path. I am still naked but confident no one is around to notice. The sun on my bare skin feels warm and soothing, and I soon feel exhilarated as I make my way up the dirt path. I weave my way through patches of shade and sunlight. Midway, I notice a young fern frond, unfurling and bend down for a closer look. Right then, the sun moves overhead and a band of warm light streams from the sky through the tree canopy to warm my body where I crouch. I remain captivated by the fern. The warmth makes me want to stay, as does the fern, now illuminated, its tiny nascent leaves uncurling to capture the sunlight. So absorbed am I by this small frond, unfurling, that I feel myself becoming planted yet photo-tropic, like the fern, in place yet pulled towards the sun, yearning and reaching for it. It is then I realize that it is 2:30 and the Earth just passed through a partial solar eclipse.

## Learning to Grow and Develop

This experience arose during a formal seven-day silent "Clearing Meditation" retreat in the autumn of 1986 (age 28) at Shawnigan Lake on Vancouver Island, BC. The group retreat was led by Namgyal Rinpoche, who developed the practice to open and expand our curiosity and awareness through investigation during mindfulness practice. We were instructed to investigate our strengths, weaknesses, and blocks to discover areas of potential growth. To help, we were advised to scan school subject areas or disciplines, trades, or other types of activities to consider how feeling tones about these areas had affected our interests in the world. We were instructed to identify the feeling tone of what arose rather than think about it, noting textures of the mind that might become actual images or memories. As I did the "blocks" practice, a hard-shell texture appeared followed by an image of a *praying mantis, eating*:

> As I repeat the prod – *blocks* – after some time the sensation of hardness emerges – a texture of hardness and resistance, like steel, concave and shaped yet smooth, like the shell of an insect. The image of a praying mantis suddenly pops into mind and startles me. I experience fear and then a memory: I am in grade three, and have joined a grade four science class as an initiative for gifted students. The class is host to a live praying mantis in a terrarium that a boy captured and brought to the teacher. One day, the teacher informs us – with vivid pleasure – that the boy has captured something else. A glass jar is circulated among us with a bright orange and black monarch butterfly inside. I love monarch butterflies and watch them for long periods of time in the garden at home. The teacher then says we're going to feed the butterfly to the praying mantis, and we are to watch. I am repulsed and refuse, as does another girl in class. It is not so much that I am squeamish as alarmed that we are killing the butterfly. The students line up and pass by the terrarium to view the spectacle. The other girl and I continue to refuse until she finally relents. I don't. Then, the teacher orders three boys in the class to force me physically to the terrarium to watch. I stand up and say that isn't necessary. As I approach the terrarium, I close my eyes to avoid witnessing the death of the butterfly. No one knows that I didn't look.
>
> In the retreat, as these memories flood unfold, intense emotions follow in rapid succession – moving from fear to anger to grief: anger for being excluded from science by such insensitivities and grief for blocking myself from the study of nature in response. I begin to cry as anger turns to disappointment and sadness. As the image of the praying mantis returns, I experience it differently. I am struck by the name – that it is "praying" rather than "preying." I notice this changes my view of the creature, making it seem calmer and more mindful, waiting and attuned to its surroundings, more teacher of patience and of the power of attention than predatory destroyer of all things beautiful and delicate. From this realization, I return to awareness of breathing, the body, sensations, and open awareness.
>
> *(see, too, MacPherson, 2000).*

## Learning Diversity

I first labelled this incident as *braving and fearing the wild* with a bit of tongue-in-cheek, involving as it did *mice, collecting,* and *buffalo, stampeding.* The winter of 1987 (age 28), I made the trip as a kind of pilgrimage or vision quest to prove, principally to myself, that I could be brave, rugged, and courageous and enjoy an adventurous life despite relative poverty (at the time). This solitary three-day wilderness retreat in the backcountry of Yellowstone National Park, USA (off-season) followed immediately by a formal seven-day retreat in Boise, Idaho. I camped along the Yellowstone River while engaged in a combination of mindfulness and nature study practices:

> After a two-hour hike down the canyon, I arrive on the shores of the Yellowstone River, where I hang up provisions with a rope in a tree and then set up camp. I eat dinner, clean dishes in the river, and sit on a log watching the sunset on the horizon before observing stars with my binoculars and star finder. Ursa Major is the most prominent constellation. My star guide says Ursa Major is Latin for the "Big Bear." I read it twice, not quite believing the coincidence as everyone had tried to scare me away with fearful tales and reported sightings of bears – Grizzly bears of course. Yet, now, I feel strangely protected by the presence of this big mythic version in the sky against any threats from imaginary versions lying

> closer to the ground. A pup-tent and down sleeping bag make cramped but cozy quarters. Zipping up as well as I can, I turn my attention to breathing to steady my nerves as I prepare to fall asleep. Flashlight ready, vigilant to every sound, near and afar, I finally slip into sleep. Then, I am jolted awake by something tugging at my hair. I scream. As I turn on the flashlight, confused, I see the backside of a tiny, furry black field mouse scurrying out with a strand of my hair. As the mouse runs away, I laugh. After that, I relax into place, practice, and retreat.
>
> A few days later, on returning to the main Park, the ranger offers a staff cabin for me at no cost. In the afternoon, I go for a walk on the plains, where a large herd of buffalo approach me at a distance on the horizon. Having heard that a tourist had been crushed to death in a stampede the previous month, I am wary but continue walking towards them. Soon they began running, stampeding, as a cloud of dust gathers around them. The distance between us narrows rapidly. I assess the chances of them reaching me and decide to turn around. Then I begin to run as fast as I can, away, all the way to the cabin. It doesn't feel brave at all – rather undignified and humbling in fact – but it feels right. As I arrive at the cabin, I find a tuft of buffalo fur on the doorstep awaiting me, seemingly put there by the wind.
>
> The next day, hitchhiking out of the park, a man in a pick-up truck offers me a ride. He tells me that he works in park maintenance and has done so for over 20 years. Large and muscular, he sports two large rifles in full view along the inside of the truck cabin, which frightens me. I ask if he's been down the canyon to the river. He says he hasn't, explaining it is too dangerous on account of the bears. I consider the irony but don't say anything.

## Learning to Behave

This experience involved learning to find new languages to affiliate with the more-than-human world and wildlife and communicating in primordial sounds with *eagle, responding.* This happened near the end of a seven-day solitary forest retreat on the north end of Galiano Island, BC, in March 1988 (age 29). Between sessions, I had walked a kilometre through back roads of the forest to bathe in a bog with a small pond in the middle. The main practice I was doing in that retreat was breathing meditation and compassion practices:

> The cabin has no running water, so as the retreat nears its end, I decide to bathe in a nearby bog with a pond. I had walked there several times already to watch its resident kingfisher. Local lore has it that ancient Indigenous shamanic ritual objects have been found there, preserved for millennia by the acids of the bog. As I approach the pond's edge, each footstep sank ever-deeper into the boggy, spongy ground, wet and relenting from water absorbed and retained by the Labrador tea. At the pond's edge, the water seems dark and opaque, with little visible life underneath. I strip off my clothing quickly to beat the bite of the frigid air and my teeth's inclination to chatter. I remind myself to be brave, that it will soon be over. Naked, standing there on the pond's edge, I scan the horizon before jumping into the dark murky waters. The cold is shocking, breathtaking. A primordial scream erupts out of nowhere, from inside of me. Surprised by the sound of my own voice, by its volume and force, I pull myself back up on the pond's edge and wrapped myself in a towel I've draped over a nearby shrub. Not having spoken or uttered a sound for a week, I am still reeling from the shock of the sound. Turning, I notice a bald eagle flying above and descending into bog area to rest on a nearby tree. The eagle watches me; I watch the eagle. He evidently heard me scream. It occurs to me then that my voice had seemed more eagle-like than human. We watch one another across air and water, held by some shared recognition or kinship with that primordial sound.

## Learning Energy Flows

This incident involved observing energy exchanges with wildlife in the more-than-human world via a *wasp, eating,* who assisted me to understand *interconnecting through eating and being eaten.* During the three-day silent (group) forest retreat on Galiano Island, BC, in August 1988 (age 30), we were led by a teacher, Cecile Kwiat, in mindfulness of breathing to cultivate *samatha* or calm-abiding:

> After a lunch of baked ham, we find hordes of late-summer wasps clamouring on our leftovers, cutting and lifting chunks of meat in their tentacles. (I hadn't even realized they were carnivores!) At that time of year, the wasps are listless and slow, unresponsive to gentle prods to move along, so we just watch them. Anyway, I had decided to welcome the many insects into my practice that week-end or I would spend the entire retreat contemplating irritation! So, when mosquitoes land on me, I imagine offering up my blood willingly rather than interrupting practice to brush them away or to don noxious repellants. The retreat is focused on the practice of *samatha,* so my resolution fits well with the training. Following our ham sandwich lunch, we congregate around the fire pit for a short talk on mindfulness of breathing practice. I meditate while Cecile speaks, the languid wasps still circulating among us. I concentrate on breathing, the topic of the talk. Breathing in. Breathing out. Gap. Open and calm. The ever-so slight disturbance of air. A creature hovers while I, unmoving, unafraid, breathe in. Breath out. Sensation on lower lip. Resisting impulse to swipe. Breathe in. Breathe out. Curiosity. The sensation of tender tentacles clasping, brushing, softness, pinch, a certain numbness, even pleasure.
>
> "Sweet nectar of the gods!" Cecile's words jolt my eyes open, "at least for the wasp. Sweet nectar." She is looking at me as she speaks, her index finger tracing a line from her lower lip to her chin, indicating what I only then realize: I am bleeding. "Oh," I say, more alarmed by the public acknowledgement of the intimacy than by what had occurred. Until that point, it is just sensation, but then I realize a wasp has taken a small nibble from my lower lip. "It's fine." I say, "he didn't sting or hurt me." Cecile hands me a tissue, and I wipe it away – the blood, that is.

## Learning Limits

This incident involved noticing the suffering of wild members of the more-than-human world, that is, *trees, crying,* and, in the process, learning to empathize through recognizing the shared experience of suffering. This five-day solitary forest retreat happened in the summer of 1992 or 1993 (age 34 or 35), on the north end of Galiano Island. The practices included mindfulness of breathing and Tibetan visualization practices.

> On the upper ridge of the retreat centre, above the cabin along a winding road, is a small concrete and gold-painted *stupa,* a monument with relics and dedicated to world peace. In 1984, I had joined a small group of Western meditators who gathered to build and bless the stupa with the Burmese monk and teacher, Sayadaw Utilla Wunta. Now, almost a decade later, I visit it each day in solitude, to meditate. Earlier that year, a logging company had clear-cut the forest adjacent to the retreat centre along a back road leading to the stupa. The denuded land looks like a war zone, and as I walk by, there is a sinking sense of loss and despair. By the third day of the retreat, as I meditate and walk around the stupa or weave among the adjacent arbutus and alder trees leaning over the ridge with a view of the Pacific Ocean beyond, I begin to hear eerie sounds. I look around, and realize they are coming from the trees. At first I think it must be the wind, but I notice that the creaks seem orchestrated or coordinated and sound like groans. The wind, furthermore, isn't

particularly strong. Initially, I am confused and uncertain what is making the sounds, and even after realizing it is the trees, I can't understand what is creating it. It isn't the rustling of leaves or an occasional swaying limb. It is as if the trees are being uprooted and moaning from the injury. I keep insisting to myself that it is the wind bending the trunks, that it is natural and I am projecting my own distress on the trees, but the strange sounds persist inexplicably. Every time I return, it intensifies and dominates my experience, sounding more and more like crying or wailing. I have the impression, not only that they are expressing distress, but that they are expressing this distress *to me*, as if the moaning only starts when I arrive. I try to witness the sensation of the sounds without judgement, including the interpretation that continues to impress itself on my mind: The trees are communicating suffering, to one another, to me. I feel responsible and sad, not so much personally but as a human being. The sounds never abate, and when I depart, I know I'll no longer return there to meditate. Something has darkened the land and its ability to promote peace, at least for the time being.

## Learning to Regulate

These incidents involved recurring encounters with mortality through contacts with *leopard, scorpions, and vultures, appearing*, while living at Dolma Ling nunnery and institute in the Kangra Valley in Indian, H.P. (MacPherson, 2011a). Transpiring in winter and spring of 1998, when I was 39–40, these mindful encounters taught me power and equanimity via fear and awe of the natural world. The practices included Vajrayana completion retreats and less formal silent and intensive practice periods focused on mindfulness of walking, breathing, and visualization practices.

All three of these incidents happened during one ten-month period, straddling 1997–1998 as I completed doctoral research. In the first incident, I find myself alone one evening at Dolma Ling, the nunnery and institute where I live at the time. It is Tibetan New Year, and the nuns are all in Dharamsala readying to mark the new year at the Dalai Lama's temple. I go out for a stroll around the nunnery, leaving my small guesthouse on the edge of the property. The nuns' quarters surround two sides of a courtyard, with the classrooms, meditation hall, kitchen, and dining hall framing the other side. As I approach, I expect to see one or another of the nuns there but am surprised to discover that not one of the 150 nuns, teachers, and staff remained. I realize I'm alone there. As I enter the courtyard, I see movement to my right and turn. Facing me is a leopard, who freezes when he sees me. He is near the classrooms and kitchen, while I am close to the front entrance. He is poised and ready, watching me yet not seeming inclined to move, forward or back. I realize he is as afraid of me as I of him. I watch him – excited yet aware of the danger. Adrenaline begins to rush through me, but I recollect myself enough to be with him in that moment: to behold him. A moment later, he turns and I turn and we each go in opposite directions. I return to my rooms, filled with a sense of awe, thrill, gratitude for the encounter.

The second incident occurs two months later in early May during a 10-day completion retreat for Yamantaka, "the conqueror of death" and an emanation of Manjusri, connected with wisdom and intelligence. During this retreat, I practice for long hours – about 18 hours a day – and end each session with a long period of mindfulness (meta-awareness). There is a small kitchen in my quarters, where I cook on-site. A few weeks earlier, I had encountered a large black scorpion there, about 4 inches in diameter, sitting on my kitchen counter under an open window. Then, I'd run outside to find a nun to remove it for me. I'd felt rather sheepish asking them to take the risk, but it scared me. Now, as I prepare food during the retreat, I reach for a pot next to the sink, where I again see a giant black scorpion on my counter under an open window. This time I realize there is a certain resemblance between Yamantaka, also black and fearsome, and the black scorpion. This recognition is followed by the clear recognition that it is my responsibility to remove the scorpion. I know I will not break silence and, anyway, there seems to be a purpose here, a purpose linked to the retreat. So, I pick up a flat-top pot and turn it upside-down over the scorpion. The pot's rim is flush with the counter, so I have time to collect myself to organize the next step. First, I slide a piece of thick cardboard under the pot, to elevate it ever-so slightly, and then I slide the flat pot-lid under the cardboard. I flip the pot upright, reassuring myself as I do so that the scorpion can't penetrate metal. Alert and filling at this point with adrenaline, I steady myself and start to walk with the covered pot firmly in both hands. I press down on the lid with each thumb just to ensure there is no escape hatch, as unlikely as that may be given the size of the creature. Then, I carry it outside, cross the narrow stream behind the house, and, on the other side of the stream, I put the pot down on the ground and, with a long stick, pushed it over so the lid falls off and the pot falls on its side. I don't see the scorpion escape. I leave the pot there to let him exit at his leisure. When I return later to retrieve the pot, the scorpion is gone.

The third incident happened a few weeks later. The Yamantaka retreat now over and no longer technically in retreat, I am still meditating quite intensively, daily, and only write fieldnotes to keep up with research. I spend most days alone, in silence, and every day at 5:00 pm, before my evening meal, I take a long walk through the rice paddies and bamboo groves behind the monastery. On this day, I am meditating and feeling rather melancholy as I will soon have to leave. Having walked for some time, I come to a copse of trees. Hearing screeching and rushing sounds, I look up to witness a dozen or more vultures swooping down into an adjacent ravine. They seem prehistoric, with a wing span well over six feet in length. There are so many that they create gusts of wind as they descend. I feel shock and fear, imagining they might mistake me for whatever fresh carrion draws them here. I walk around the copse to see what is attracting them. A water buffalo carcass lies splayed on the ground, already eviscerated by the vultures in these few minutes. Its internal organs are nearly consumed, while some birds lean in to grab intestines and rip them away from the body to avoid the frenzy. Others fight frantically for remnants on the bones. Within minutes, the water buffalo's skeleton is scraped and bared. Yet, the vultures' intensity seems to increase. As I watched, I am reminded of the relinquishing of death. All things come to an end. I turn and continue walking.

## Learning Emergent Knowledge

This seemingly simple incident – the most profound – involved a rare and mindful encounter with *white butterfly, landing*. In the process, I discovered the power of quantum encounters with nature through interacting with wildlife. I learned to appreciate and feel awe and humility in the face of such a significant challenge to my conditioned human way of knowing the world. The incident took place in July of 2002 (age 44) during a seven-day silent (semi-solitary) forest retreat at a Tibetan retreat centre on Saltspring Island, BC. The practices were designed to constitute what I viewed to be an *ecology retreat* that included mindfulness of breathing, nature meditations, and meditating on Green Tara.

> I undertook this self-organized retreat to prepare to lead a teachers' retreat the following month on *Satyagraha for the Earth* for the Gandhi Foundation and the University of Alberta. The director of the retreat centre asks only that I join them for a daily Green Tara puja before dinner. For my retreat, I decide to combine mindfulness practices – indoors and out – with occasional readings on ecology to prepare. On the first day, I begin to notice small white butterflies hovering around the low bushes surrounding the cabin. As I read and reflect, I consider them, how local governments sprayed nearby cities to kill their cousin,

> the gypsy moths' larvae. The spray would have impacted these butterflies' larvae as well. With enough spray over time, they might become extinct. I begin seeing them in time, and not just in space and geography. So, I invite these white butterflies to become an explicit mindfulness practice. I observe the light bouncing off their wings as they flutter through the air; I notice my own responses as they do so, shifting from negative feelings from worrying about the world to positive feelings of gratitude, appreciation, even joy. I considered their life cycle, too, and their transformation from pupae to caterpillar to butterfly – what that must be like for them moving from a stationary to a crawling to a flying creature, imagining joy in the experience of air.
>
> Meditating in this way, on the second last day of the retreat, I join the others to mediate in the small prayer hall before dinner. As the hour-long practice draws to a close, we rest for a few minutes in mindful silence. As we do, I raise my eyes upwards to where a few windows stand ajar where they meet the ceiling. Just then, a white butterfly flutters into the room through the open window. I see the butterfly enter the room and a kind of rapture fills me – the best descriptor I can come up with. I behold it as a beloved. This response continued to intensify as my eyes follow the butterfly's path through the room. Descending slowly, deliberately, across the room and over the heads of others, the butterfly approaches the area where I sit on the far-side of the room and finally, gently, comes to rest on my hand. As I observe the butterfly, gaze on it close up, an intense joy and love satiate me. Eventually, these emotions shift to gratitude and awe, aware of the great gift the white butterfly is offering to me in this moment.

### Learning to Co-Exist

This final incident, which weaves back to the same theme of the first, involves integrating and being integrated (and trusted) within the more-than-human world. With *rabbit (and deer), eating*, I am learning about being wild and becoming trustworthy. It transpired in June, 2019, at the age of 61, with recollections back to the autumn of 1986, when I was 28. This five-day silent mindfulness retreat in 2019 was one I was myself leading at Loon Lake Lodge in Maple Ridge, BC.

> Near the end of the retreat, I walk up a back path where I routinely do a moderately paced walking practice. I see a brown rabbit on the path eating some grass. I stop about three meters away, not wanting to disturb him. He stops eating and watches me, alert to potential danger. I focus on breathing and wait, watching the rabbit watching me. I relax into the moment, willing myself to wait as I continue watching my breath and the rabbit, and he returns to the grass, eating. Relaxed, he nibbles without watching me with quite as much vigilance. Nearly 33 years ago, on retreat at Shawnigan Lake, BC, while I sit meditating outdoors, a deer stands next to me eating grass.

## DISCUSSION

Intensive mindfulness retreats or semi-retreats foster ecological awareness in at least three ways: a) first, intensive mindfulness practice may foster self-transcendence; b) second, they are situated in close proximity to wildlife; and b) third, they involve contexts to practise "noble silence," that is, silencing not just the mouth but the mind to be more present to the world. These conditions make the kinds of mindful encounters reported here possible. Together, they also enhance the capacity to learn from such encounters with the natural and wild world in more meaningful ways. This type of learning goes well beyond learning *about* nature as might transpire in a scientific ecology classroom; indeed, they go beyond what it means even to learn *in* nature. Instead, they offer a way to learn *as* nature, made possible through silence and the distancing from an anthropocentric to a more open, empathic, and sensitive awareness of our profound interrelations with other species as life.

At the same time, this research offers implications for how we study and learning ecology. As Table 19.1 depicts, the ten incidents and their corresponding themes align quite closely with the key principles of scientific ecology identified by Mengak et al. (2009).

As Table 19.1 illustrates, the incidents and insights reported in this research, cultivated through direct contact with nature and non-human wildlife during mindfulness-based retreats, align well with key principles of scientific ecology. Although they derive from different contexts, epistemologies, and forms of knowledge, both scientific and mindfulness-based ecological knowing can contribute in important yet distinctive ways to our understanding of the natural world. The strength of the insights garnered through mindfulness and direct contact with wildlife is that this way of knowing fosters a felt connectedness, relationship, and identification with the natural world and environment so as to broaden self-awareness into enhanced ecological awareness.

This investigation of the experiences of a single meditator over the duration of a lifetime of experiences with wildlife during silent retreats points to the need for more qualitative studies of meditators' experiences during more intensive mindfulness practice. Instead, most mindfulness research is disproportionately focused on addressing whether mindfulness or related practices are efficacious in the treatment of conditions experienced by specific populations or as a general health-promotion strategy (see AMRA, 2010-2019; Brown

**Table 19.1** Alignment between Scientific and Experiential Ecology

| Ecological PrinciplesBarrett et al. (1997)Mengak et al. (2009) | # | *Incident Learning/Wildlife* | *Common themes or principles between experiential and scientific ecology* |
|---|---|---|---|
| Adaptation | 2 | Learning to adapt/fern frond | evolution; life history |
| Behaviour | 5 | Learning to behave/eagle response | inter-species communication |
| Diversity | 4 | Learning diversity/mice and buffalo | competition; survival |
| Emergent Properties | 9 | Learning emergent knowledge/white butterfly | complexity; emergence |
| Energy Flow | 6 | Learning energy flows/wasp | energy exchanges |
| Growth/Development | 3 | Learning to grow and develop/praying mantis (memory) | dynamic learning |
| Limits | 7 | Learning limits/crying trees | environmental stress; sustainability |
| Regulation | 8 | Learning to regulate/ leopards, scorpions, vultures | sensory-motor feedback loops; risk |
| Interdependence | 1, 10 | Learning to co-exist/bird song; rabbit eating | co-existence; cooperation |

et al., 2015). This causes a distorting focus on the efficacy of mindfulness as an intervention rather than as a site for specific forms of learning and values-formation. Qualitative research, like that presented here, on the longitudinal impact of intensive mindfulness practices in retreat conditions is scant, despite the fact that many eight-week interventions, like MBSR or MBCT, include and encourage retreats in their programs.

What little research that has been done on the impacts of intensive meditative practices during silent retreats offers surprising and interesting results. Jacobs et al.'s (2011) controlled study of meditators in a three-month intensive retreat found significant improvements in telomerase activity, decreased neuroticism; and increased sense of control and purpose in life as compared to waitlisted meditator-controls who were not engaged in the intensive practices. Likewise, Montero-Marin et al. (2016) found increased wellbeing, linked to non-attachment and cooperation, in meditators following a one-month intensive silent retreat as compared to non-intensive meditating controls. As discussed in Chapter 17, Lindahl et al. (2017) documented a range of challenging experiences associated with intensive retreats, but there was a troubling slippage in their analysis between *anomalous* experiences and *adverse effects*. Countering these findings, Vieten et al. (2018) surveyed 1120 meditators around the world, who together reported a broad range of "anomalous and extraordinary" experiences, most of which were positive and deemed mystical or transpersonal. Like us, they express the need for mindfulness research to venture more into this domain of qualitative experiences, which they describe as: "group and relational, transpersonal and mystical, and difficult aspects of meditation; anomalous or extraordinary phenomena related to meditation; and post-conventional stages of development associated with meditation" (p. 1). Without understanding the intrinsic motivators associated with such experiences, mindfulness research and the associated field of MBTL will be necessarily incomplete.

With respect to our relations with the non-human world, never has such a question warranted more serious consideration and reflection as we begin to recognize that our collective behaviour, practices, values, and cultures have imperilled the very existence of so many other species and of our common sources of life, wealth, and wellbeing. As powerful as the study of scientific ecology has been for raising awareness of the human impacts on global systems, it has proved wholly inadequate in fostering in human beings a sense of a shared welfare and belonging across species and with life on Earth. Mindfulness, as an experiential ecology process, offers a promising way to enflesh otherwise conceptual ecological principles, to render them lived and embodied ways of knowing cultivated through direct contact with wild things. This chapter considered an unconventional form of education – silent, mindful, in nature – to encourage readers, as learners or as teachers, to reconsider what education might be if we viewed ecological awareness as its necessary and fundamental outcome.

## REFERENCES

AMRA (American Mindfulness Research Association). (2010–2019). *Archived issues of mindfulness research monthly (vols. 1–10)*. https://goamra.org/publications/archives/.

Barrett, G., Peles, J., & Odum, E. P. (1997). Transcending processes and the levels-of organization concept. *Bioscience, 47*(8), 531–535.

Bateson, G. (2000). *Steps to an ecology of mind* (2nd ed.). University of Chicago Press.

Brown, K. W., Creswell, J. D., & Ryan, R. M. (Eds.). (2015). *Handbook of mindfulness: Theory, research, and practice*. The Guilford Press.

Capaldi, C., Dopko, R., & Zelenski, J. (2014). The relationship between nature connectedness and happiness: A meta-analysis. *Frontiers in Psychology*. Advance online publication. https://doi.org/10.3389/fpsyg.2014.00976.

Deci, E., Ryan, R, Schultz, P., & Niemiec, C. (2015). Being aware and functioning fully: Mindfulness and interest taking within self-determination theory. In K. Brown, J. Creswell, & R. Ryan (Eds.), *Handbook of mindfulness: Theory, research, and practice* (pp. 112–129). The Guilford Press.

Ellis, C., & Bochner, A. P. (2000). Autoethnography, personal narrative, reflexivity: Researcher as subject. In N. Denzin & Y Lincoln (Eds.), *Handbook of qualitative research* (pp. 733–768). Sage.

Evernden, N. (1992). *The social construction of nature.* John Hopkins University Press.

Evernden, N. (1993). *The natural alien: Humankind and environment* (2nd ed.). University of Toronto Press.

Farb, N., Segal, Z., Mayberg, H., Bean, J., McKeon, D., Fatima, Z., & Anderson, A. (2007). Attending to the present: Mindfulness meditation reveals distinct neural modes of self-reference. *Social, Cognitive, and Affective Neuroscience*, *4*(2), 313–322.

Gaston, K., Soga, M., Duffy, J., Garrett, J., Gaston, S., & Cox, D. (2018). Personalized ecology. *Trends in Ecology & Evolution*, *33*(12), 916–925. https://doi.org/10.1016/j.tree.2018.09.012.

Gilbert, P. (2010). *Compassion focused therapy: Distinctive features.* Routledge.

Groen, J. (2013). From malaise to re-enchantment: The spiritual retreat centre as a place of environmental adult education. *Journal for the Study of Spirituality*, *3*(1), 46–55. https://doi.org/10.1179/2044024313Z.0000000004.

Groen, J. (2016). Rediscover, reawaken, renew: The potential role of spiritual retreat centres in environmental adult education. *Canadian Journal for the Study of Adult Education*, *28*(1), 83–96. https://cjsae.library.dal.ca/index.php/cjsae/article/view/4798.

Hildebrandt, L., McCall, C., & Singer, T. (2017). Differential effects of attention-, compassion-, and socio-cognitively based mental practices on self-reports of mindfulness and compassion. *Mindfulness*, *8*, 1488–1512. https://doi.org/10.1007/s12671-017-0716-z

Howell, A., Dopko, R., Passmore, H., & Buro, K. (2011). Nature connectedness: Associations with well-being and mindfulness. *Personality and Individual Differences*, *51*, 166–171. https://doi.org/10.1016/j.paid.2011.03.037.

Jacobs, T., Epel, E., Lin, J., Blackburn, E., Wolowitz, O., Bridwell, D., Zanesco, A., Aichele, S., Sahdra, B., MacLean, K., King, B., Shaver, P., Rosenberg, E., Ferrer, E., Wallace, A., & Saron, C. (2011). Intensive meditation training, immune cell telomerase activity, and psychological mediators. *Psychoneuroendocrinology*, *36*(5), 664–681. https://doi.org/10.1016/j.psyneuen.2010.09.010.

Jazaieri, G., Jinpa, T., McGonigal, K., Rosenberg, E., Finkelstein, J., Simon-Thomas, E., Cullen, M. Doty, J., Gross, J., & Goldin, P. (2013). Enhancing compassion: A randomized controlled trial of a compassion cultivation training program. *Journal of Happiness Studies*, *14*, 1113–1126. https://doi.org/10.1007/s10902-012-9373-z.

Jazaieri, G., Lee, I., McGonigal, K., McGonigal, K., Jinpa, T., Doty, J., Gross, J., & Goldin, P. (2016). A wandering mind is a less caring mind: Daily experience sampling during compassion meditation training. *The Journal of Positive Psychology*, *11*(1), 37–50. https://doi.org/10.1080/17439760.2015.1025418.

Jinpa, T. (2015). *A fearless heart: How the courage to be compassionate can transform our lives.* Penguin.

Karmapa, H. H. XVII. (2017). Mindfulness and environmental responsibility. Video of talk at the University of Toronto. *The Karmapa.* https://kagyuoffice.org/video/mindfulness-and-environmental-responsibility/.

King, B., Conkin, Q., Zanesco, A., & Saron, C. (2019). Residential meditation retreats: Their role in contemplative practice and significance for psychological research. *Current Opinion in Psychology*, *28*, 238–244. https://doi.org/10.1016/j.copsyc.2019.12.021

Kirby, J., Day, J., & Sagar, V. (2019). The "flow" of compassion: A meta-analysis of the fears of compassion scale and psychological functioning. *Clinical Psychology Review*, *70*, 26–39. https://doi.org/10.1016/j.beth.2017.06.003.

Leary, M., & Diebels, K. (2017). The hypo-egoic impact of mindfulness on self, identity, and the processing of self-relevant information. In J. Karremans & E. Papies (Eds.), *Mindfulness in social psychology* (pp. 51–64). Routledge.

Lindahl, J., Fisher, N., Cooper, D., Rosen, R., & Britton, W. (2017). The varieties of contemplative experience: A mixed-methods study of meditation-related challenges in Western Buddhists. *PLoS ONE*, *12*(5), e0176239. https://doi.org/10.1371/journal.pone.0176239.

Lymeus, F., Lindberg, P., & Hartig, T. (2018). Building mindfulness bottom-up: Meditation in natural settings supports open monitoring and attention restoration. *Consciousness and Cognition*, *59*, 40–56. https://doi.org/10.1016/j.concog.2018.01.008.

MacPherson, S. (2000). Educating nature: On being squeamish in science. In B. Hockney, W. Lind, & J. Haskell (Eds.), *Unfolding bodymind: Exploring possibility through education* (pp. 204–215). Educational Renewal Inc.

MacPherson, S. (2005). Educating ecological citizens of "The Blue Planet." *Canadian Journal of Environmental Education*, *10*, 141–156.

MacPherson, S. (2011a). *Education and sustainability: Learning across the diaspora, indigenous, and minority divide*. Routledge.

MacPherson, S. (2011b). What Tashi taught me: "Petagogy" and the education of emotions. Special issue on animality and environmental education. *Canadian Journal of Environmental Education*, *16*, 76–92.

Marx, R. (2015). Accessibility versus integrity in secular mindfulness: A Buddhist commentary. *Mindfulness*, *6*, 1153–1160. https://doi.org/10.1007/s12671-014-0366-3.

Mengak, M., Rutledge, H., & McDonald, B. (2009). Ecological principles: A unifying theme in environmental education. *Journal of Extension*, *47*(5), 1–8.

Monteiro, L., Musten, R., & Compson, J. (2014). Traditional and contemporary mindfulness: Finding the middle path in the tangle of concerns. *Mindfulness*, *6*, 1–13. http://doi.org/10.1007/s12671-014-0301-7.

Montero-Marin, J., Puebla-Guedea, M., Herrera-Mercadal, P., Cebolla, A., Solar, J., Demarzo, M., Vazquez, C., Rodriquez-Boratxea, F., & Garcia-Campayo, J. (2016). Psychological effects of a 1-month meditation retreat on experienced meditators: The role of non-attachment. *Frontiers in Psychology*, *12*. https://doi.org/10.3389/fpsyg.2016.01935.

Moran, E. (2017). *People and nature: An introduction to human ecological relations* (2nd ed.). Wiley Blackwell.

Ogden, P., Minton, K., & Pain, C. (2006). Window of Tolerance: Capacity for modulating arousal. *Trauma and the body*, pp. 26–40.

Otto, S., & Pensini, P. (2017). Nature-based environmental education of children: Environmental knowledge and connectedness to nature, together, are related to ecological behaviour. *Global Environmental Change*, *47*, 88–94. https://doi.org/10.1016/j.gloenvcha.2017.09.009.

Pfattheicher, S., Sassenrath, C., & Schindler, S. (2016). Feelings for the suffering of others and the environment: Compassion fosters pro-environmental tendencies. *Environment and Behaviour*, *48*(7), 929–945. https://doi.org/10.1177/0013916515574549.

Schultz, P. (2001). The structure of environmental concern: Concern for self, other people, and the biosphere. *Journal of Environmental Psychology*, *21*, 327–339. https://doi.org/10.1006/jevp.2001.0227.

Schultz, P. (2002). New environmental theories: Empathizing with nature: The effects of perspective taking on concern for environmental issues. *Journal of Social Issues*, *56*, 391–406.

Schutte, N. S., & Malouff, J. M. (2018). Mindfulness and connectedness to nature: A meta-analytic investigation. *Personality and Individual Differences*, *127*, 10–14. https://doi.org/10.1016/j.paid.2018.01.034.

Siegel, D. (2001). *The developing mind: How relationships and the brain interact to shape who we are.* Guilford Press.

Tam, K. P. (2013). Dispositional empathy with nature. *Journal of Environmental Psychology, 35,* 92–104. https://doi.org/10.1016/j.jenvp.2013.05.004.

Tipsord, J. (2009). *The effects of mindfulness training and individual differences in mindfulness on social perception and empathy.* A dissertation presented to the Department of Psychology and the Graduate School of the University of Oregon for the degree of Ph.D.

Unsworth, S., Palicki, S. K., & Lustig, J. (2016). The impact of mindful meditation in nature on self-nature interconnectedness. *Mindfulness, 7,* 1052–1060. https://doi.org/10.1007/s12671-016-0542-8.

Vago, D., & Silbersweig, D. (2012). Self-awareness, self-regulation, and self-transcendences (S-ART): A framework for understanding the neurobiological mechanisms of mindfulness. *Frontiers of Human Neuroscience, 25,* 296. https://doi.org/10.3389/fnhum.2012.00296.

Verhaeghen, P. (2019). The mindfulness manifold: Exploring how self-preoccupation, self-compassion, and self-transcendence translate mindfulness into positive psychological outcomes. *Mindfulness, 10,* 131–145. https://doi.org/10.1007/s12671-018-0959-3

Vieten, C., Wahbeh, H., Cahn, B., MacLean, K., Estrada, M., Mills, P., Murphy, M., Shapiro, S., Radin, D., Josipovic, Z., Presti, D., Sapiro, M., Bays, J. C., Russell, P., Vago, D., Travis, F., Walsh, R., & Delorme, A. (2018). Future directions in meditation research: Recommendations for expanding the field of contemplative science. *PLoS ONE, 13*(11), e0205740. https://doi.org/10.1371/journal.pone.0205740.

Wall, S. (2016). Toward a moderate authoethnography. *International Journal of Qualitative Methodology, 15*(1). https://doi.org/10.1177/1609406916674966.

Wang, J., Geng, L., Schulz, P. W., & Zhou, K. (2019). Mindfulness increases the belief in climate change: The mediating role of connectedness with nature. *Environment and Behaviour, 51*(1), 3–23. https://doi.org/10.1177/0013916517738036.

Woods, S., Rockman, P., & Collins, E. (2019). *Mindfulness-based cognitive therapy: Embodied presence & inquiry in practice.* Guilford Press.

# INDEX

*Note*: Page numbers in *italics* indicate figures, and page numbers in **bold** indicate tables in the text.

For Product Safety Concerns and Information please contact our EU
representative GPSR@taylorandfrancis.com
Taylor & Francis Verlag GmbH, Kaufingerstraße 24, 80331 München, Germany

www.ingramcontent.com/pod-product-compliance
Ingram Content Group UK Ltd.
Pitfield, Milton Keynes, MK11 3LW, UK
UKHW022347190926
475702UK00015B/2154

* 9 7 8 1 0 3 2 0 1 8 9 2 8 *